CLIMBIN
THE MOUN

Saint Albert's Press & Edizioni Carmelitane

First edition 2010

Second edition 2014

CLIMBING THE MOUNTAIN

The Carmelite Journey

Second Edition

Edited by
Johan Bergström-Allen, T.O.C.

First published 2010 by Saint Albert's Press & Edizioni Carmelitane.
Second edition published 2014.

Saint Albert's Press
Whitefriars, 35 Tanners Street,
Faversham, Kent, ME13 7JN, United Kingdom
www.carmelite.org
ISBN-10: 0-904849-45-7
ISBN-13: 978-0-904849-45-5

Edizioni Carmelitane
Centro Internationale S. Alberto
Via Sforza Pallavicini, 10
00193 Roma, Italy
www.carmelites.info/edizioni
ISBN-13: 978-88-7288-113-2

Edited and designed by Johan Bergström-Allen, Carmelite Projects & Publications Office, York.

Typeset by Ing. Jakub Kubů, Prague, Czech Republic.
Production coordinated by Pavel Kindermann on behalf of Karmelitánské nakladatelství s.r.o., Kostelní Vydří 58, 380 01 Dačice, Czech Republic, www.kna.cz.
Printed by ERMAT Praha s.r.o., Czech Republic.

Quotations from Carmelite texts are taken with the relevant permissions. Bible passages are from the *New Revised Standard Version* © 1989 by the Division of Christian Education of the National Council of the Churches of Christ in the U.S.A.; used by permission; all rights reserved. Quotations from the English translation of the *Catechism of the Catholic Church* © 1994 Geoffrey Chapman, London / Libreria Editrice Vaticana, Rome. Every reasonable effort has been made to avoid copyright infringement of text and images; inadvertent errors will be corrected in any future editions.

Preface to the Second Edition
The first edition of *Climbing the Mountain* was very well received by the Carmelite Family internationally, not only by Lay Carmelites but also by Religious, vocations enquirers, and others inspired by the patrimony of Carmel. The first edition having sold out within the first two years of circulation, this second has been produced to meet continuing demand. The opportunity has been taken to make a handful of minor revisions and corrections to texts and images; many thanks to those who have pointed these out. The pagination has remained the same, allowing easy referencing to either edition. I would like to renew my thanks to all those who contributed to its production, and express my gratitude to those individuals, communities and provinces who have endorsed it so enthusiastically.

Johan Bergström-Allen
Carmelite Projects & Publications Office, York
January 2014

Contents

Foreword

*by the Prior Provincial of the British Province of Carmelites,
Fr. Wilfrid McGreal, O.Carm.*

The idea of 'journey' speaks powerfully to the human imagination. The notion of setting out on the road, perhaps getting diverted but steadily moving ever forwards towards an ultimate goal, somehow echoes our experience of travelling through life's journey on a quest for love and meaning. People of faith understand our journey as a pilgrimage through the ups and downs of life, and the longed-for destination to be God.

The first Carmelites were medieval pilgrims who had made the dangerous journey to the Holy Land. On Mount Carmel – recorded in Scripture as a holy place – they gathered as a praying community of hermits at the service of God's people. Here they pondered the Word of God in the Bible, including its many accounts of journeys: the people of Israel wandering in exile; the prophet Elijah sent on sacred missions; Mary heading with Joseph to Bethlehem; and Jesus travelling to Jerusalem, then on the road to Emmaus.

Mount Carmel depicted in ceramic by Adam Kossowski at Aylesford Priory.

When military conflicts in the Holy Land threatened the life of the hermits, it must have been with trepidation that the Carmelites left their spiritual home to make the journey back to their native lands in Europe where they founded new communities. Perhaps the voyage back to where they had set out from helped the Carmelites to appreciate that the spiritual path in fact entails a journey inwards, to the heart, where God dwells. The memory of Mount Carmel always remained for them a powerful symbol of the pilgrimage through life, and centuries later it inspired Saint John of the Cross to speak of ascending Carmel to encounter God at its summit.

When the hermits journeyed back from Carmel to Europe, one of the first communities they established was at Aylesford in the English county of Kent. In Old English the name 'Aylesford' means the crossing place over the river (ford) for all people (ayles), and it was then – as it remains now – a place of encounter between travellers. Nearby was the

Pilgrim's Way which linked London to Canterbury, and to the Continent beyond the shores.

It was at Aylesford that the hermits took a momentous decision which changed the route by which the Carmelites were travelling as a community. At the first general chapter (meeting) of the Order in 1247, the Carmelites took the momentous decision to join the mendicant movement of friars, whose vocation is to be in the midst of the people, fellow pilgrims and guides on the road. This was such a formative experience for the Order's future direction that Aylesford came to be nicknamed 'The Second Carmel'.

As with the first Mount Carmel, the Carmelites in Aylesford were to undergo exile from their homeland when the priory was seized by the Crown during the English Reformation of the 1530s. The Carmelite journey continued elsewhere and eventually, in 1949, the Carmelites were able to return to their ancient home.

The prior of the restored house, Fr. Malachy Lynch, wanted Aylesford to be 'a prayer in stone', and invited artists to beautify the shrine that developed to welcome thousands of pilgrims. The Polish artist Adam Kossowski was commissioned to decorate a chapel dedicated to the Saints of the Carmelite Order. Kossowski designed a truly beautiful space in ceramic, in which Carmelite saints – male and female – are depicted either side of Mount Carmel, dotted with hermits' cells. Above the mountain stands an antique Flemish statue of Our Lady of Mount Carmel presenting the scapular to Saint Simon Stock, and the infant Jesus to the world.

The Carmelite Saints Chapel at Aylesford Priory, England.

Whenever I pray in the Carmelite Saints Chapel I never fail to be struck by how far our Carmelite Family has journeyed, both geographically and spiritually, over the last 800 years. The faces of the men and women, religious and lay, who adorn the Chapel, are a reminder to me that we Carmelites today are treading a path by which God has led many ordinary men and women to extraordinary love and holiness. The journey of the Carmelite saints is complete on earth, but in their lives and writings they have left us signs and maps by which we too can come to the summit of the mountain that is Christ.

We need companionship and reliable direction on that pilgrim path, and it is thus with great pleasure that I commend to you this book which introduces the Carmelite way of life, and which can help inspire you – whatever your place in our great family of Carmel – to undertake the journey of initial and ongoing formation.

May Mary – patron, mother and sister of Carmelites – accompany us as together we 'climb the mountain' that is Jesus Christ.

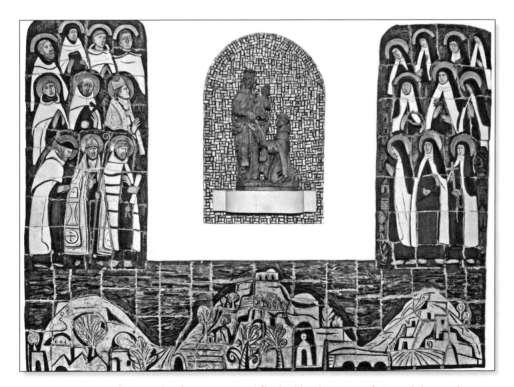

The Flemish statue of Our Lady of Mount Carmel flanked by the saints of Carmel depicted in ceramic by Adam Kossowski.

Introduction

by the Editor, Johan Bergström-Allen, T.O.C.

The origins and aims of this book

This book is an introduction to the spirituality and heritage of the Carmelites, an 800-year-old religious order of the Roman Catholic Church. It is offered as a resource for initial formation in the Carmelite tradition, primarily for lay people but also for religious, as well as serving as a general introduction for anyone interested in 'Carmel' and its riches.

The theme which recurs throughout this book is that of 'journey'. To equip us Christians for our journey through life, with and towards God, and to be properly orientated, we need formation. This book is offered as a map for the initial stage of the journey, as something of a *vademecum* (literally 'go with me') survey of Carmelite life.

This book is a result of the reform and renewal of the Third Order – the branch of Carmel for lay people who undertake the formal commitment of profession – that began in the British Province of Carmelites (of the Ancient Observance) in the late 1990s. At the National Gathering of Tertiaries (also known as Lay Carmelites) that took place in 2002 at Aylesford Priory, England, it was agreed that the Third Order needed renewal in the areas of formation, organisation and communication. This came to fruition in 2005 when *Assumpta*, the magazine for Lay Carmelites in Britain, printed the first of twenty modules that were to make up the Province's 'Initial Formation Programme'. The Programme gave an introduction to some of the main themes and persons of the Carmelite tradition, seeking not only to provide factual information but also to encourage a holistic living-out of the Carmelite contemplative charism of prayer, community and service. Over the next two years Lay Carmelites in Britain, and indeed beyond, reflected on the modules as individuals and as communities, a process which has borne much fruit.

Since 2005, Carmelites around the world – not only members of the Third Order but also friars and religious sisters as well – have requested that the Initial Formation Programme be published in book form. The Programme received a particularly warm reception at the 2006 International Lay Carmelite Congress held in Sassone near Rome. The book you are holding is essentially the Programme which appeared in *Assumpta*, but the opportunity has been taken by Saint Albert's Press (the publishing house of the British Province) to make some revisions.

First of all, Saint Albert's Press has sought to make the book as relevant as possible to a broad range of readers and vocations. The primary target audience remains Lay Carmel, but this book has much to offer religious of the Order, as well as general enquirers. It has been written with newcomers to Carmel in mind, assuming little prior knowledge about the Carmelite tradition. The revised Programme seeks to demonstrate the breadth of the Carmelite tradition in its rich and varied expressions; a broader geographic scope and cultural outlook are reflected in both text and artwork.

Additionally, since the final formation module was published in *Assumpta* in 2007, a number of significant developments have taken place within Carmel, such as a General Chapter of the Order, beatifications and canonisations, increasing collaboration with the Discalced (Teresian) Carmelites, and the availability of new publications and resources. Thus the material has been updated accordingly. Some sections have been added or developed to reflect comments received from students of the original Programme.

In terms of layout the advent of the Carmelite Institute of Britain and Ireland (CIBI) has been particularly influential on the revision of the Programme; the material is structured in a format more conducive to 'distance-learning' that will make it easier for use by individuals studying on their own, though it will still be ideal for guided reflection in groups.

Guidelines for the use of this book

Each chapter of the book considers a different aspect of Carmelite spirituality and history, though certain themes and personalities recur throughout, including: contemplation; prayer; community; service; the centrality of Christ, particularly in his humanity; our patrons Elijah and Mary; the saints of the Order; the grounding of our life in Scripture and the *Rule of Saint Albert*; and notions of *vacare Deo* (space for God) and *puritas cordis* (purity of heart).

Formation is partly about receiving good information. Since its early years Carmel has been a student order, and emphasised the value of learning. To keep on the 'Carmelite path' during our journey through life we need to know some facts about the Order, particularly its charism (that is, its God-given characteristics), its history, and its mission. Therefore some study is needed, and this book is designed to help in that process. Many people (perhaps remembering their schooldays) are put off by the notion of study, but this book offers information in a way that is hopefully accessible, engaging, enjoyable, and which draws out what you already know. Each chapter invites you to ponder your own experience and think about certain issues in Carmel and the Church today, but there are no exams to take or essays to write! You will find a blank page at the end of each chapter for you to jot down your own notes and reflections. Some of the chapters are longer than others, and you shouldn't feel that you have to read all the material in one sitting if you find it easier to break it into sections.

Each chapter is self-contained, presenting all the information you need to reflect on a particular topic; there is no need to have other books to hand, but if you are inclined to learn more about a subject you will find a list of recommended further resources at the end of each chapter. Don't be daunted by the length of any of the lists; you don't have to consult every book or website, but you might want to pick out one or two for your continued reflection.

More important than consulting all the recommended further resources is to become familiar with key documents of the Church and the Order, and whilst it's not essential that you have them to hand each time you open a chapter of this book it would certainly help your times of reflection and study.

The most fundamental resource is, of course, the Bible, the living word of God, and it should become second nature for a Carmelite to have a copy handy so that you can follow up Scripture references and perhaps engage in *Lectio Divina* meditation. The

Bible references in this book generally come from the *New Revised Standard Version* (*NRSV*).

In terms of Church documents, it would be useful to have, if you can, a copy of the 1992 *Catechism of the Catholic Church*, and the documents of the Second Vatican Council; these are readily available in print in a variety of popular and study editions, and also available online through a number of websites, including that of the Vatican (www.vatican.va). These websites – and the various official publishers to the Holy See around the world – also make available other modern Church documents, including papal encyclicals, which are occasionally referred to in the chapters of this book.

In terms of Carmelite resources that it would be useful to have at hand, the foundational text of the Order to which all Carmelites look for inspiration is the *Rule of Saint Albert*. A translation by Christopher O'Donnell, O.Carm., is printed after this introduction. The *Rule of Saint Albert* is interpreted and elaborated upon for contemporary Carmelite living by the *Constitutions* of the various branches of the Order. The *Constitutions of the Carmelite Order* compiled by the friars in 1995 are a particularly rich articulation of Carmelite spirituality; community libraries are more likely to have copies than individuals, but the text can be found via a number of Carmelite websites, including that of the British Province (www.carmelite.org). In 2003 a new set of *Constitutions* was issued for the Third Order, entitled *Living the Carmelite Way: The Rule for the Third Order of Carmel*. The friars' *Constitutions* and the *Rule for the Third Order of Carmel* (*RTOC* for short) are frequently referred to throughout this book. Reference is also made to the *Ratio* (rationale) documents on formation – *Ratio Institutionis Vitæ Carmelitanæ* (*RIVC* for short) – published for the Carmelite friars in 2000 and the nuns in 2007. At a local level it is helpful for Carmelites and enquirers to be aware of any key documents that might exist in their own province or region of the Order. Carmelite documents are available from a number of bookshops and distribution services around the world, including those listed at the back of this publication.

If you can, it is useful to supplement your study of the Carmelite tradition with reading the Order's various periodicals, journals and magazines such as *Assumpta*, *Carmel in the World*, *Mount Carmel*, *The Sword*, *The Vine* and *Carmelite Digest*. These help you to keep abreast of how the Carmelite way of life is expressed today.

As stated above, formation is partly about receiving information, but it is also much more than that. Formation is about integrating what we learn into the way we live. It is a holistic process that requires reflection and study, but also prayer and a practical living out of the Carmelite way of life, transferring knowledge from the head to love in the heart. Therefore, each chapter of this book concludes with ideas for reflection, discussion and action. These should not be treated as a check-list of things you have to do, but rather as a tool to help you integrate what you have learned with the way you live. In a sense this book provides you with the 'theory' of Carmelite spirituality in the abstract, but also encourages you to live it out in reality by suggesting some concrete actions you might take. Given the broad reading audience for this book, it is impossible to stipulate actions too precisely; each person and community reading this book will have to work out what is appropriate and relevant in a particular context. To paraphrase the closing words of the *Rule of Saint Albert*, this book provides you with some ideas and ideals, but if you feel able to do more your efforts will be rewarded.

It is important that any programme of formation in Carmel is not simply information about the Order presented in a vacuum, but is part of the Christian's ongoing exploration of the Church's doctrine, as well as participation in the sacraments, liturgy, prayer, and life of the local community and wider society. Carmelites need to immerse themselves in the broader life of the Order by engaging in prayer as recommended by the Carmelite tradition, through contributing to the apostolates of the Order, and through involvement (even if from a distance) in a Carmelite community.

Most members of the Carmelite Family belong to some form of community, such as a priory of friars, a monastery of enclosed nuns, a convent of apostolic sisters, a chapter of tertiaries, or a Carmelite Spirituality Group. This book is ideal for use by a community, either for the whole group or for those entering as new members. It is up to each community to determine how best to use the book. Some might like to read the text together at a group sitting, whilst others may find that more can be gained from individuals absorbing the book at their own pace and then coming together to discuss a chapter. If you are reflecting on the chapters as part of a group, it can be helpful if you establish some commonly-agreed ground-rules to ensure respectful discussion where different views can be heard and faith can be shared in a way that values honesty, respect and confidentiality. The book consists of 20 chapters; assuming that most groups might reflect on one chapter per month, the Programme could be completed within two years. However, there is so much material in each chapter that a group might want to reflect on it over more than one meeting. The important thing is not to impose an artificial timescale or to rush the process of study and reflection. When used for group formation it is recommended that after the discussion the community leader and/or formator undertake some form of evaluation asking: What in the chapter was helpful or challenging? How did members respond to the text, and how did it enable them to grow in their possible vocation as Carmelites?

Each chapter of the book is punctuated with invitations to stop and reflect, to pray or to read further; these are printed in blue, and you do not have to follow these instructions slavishly. Some of the questions for reflection are deliberately worded to provoke thought and discussion, playing 'devil's advocate' to get you to think through a particular question facing the Carmelite Family today. Often there are no right or wrong answers, and if you find that you have more questions at the end of a chapter than you had before reading it then that is probably a good indication that your mind and heart are well engaged in the formation process.

When questions arise, or the need for clarification on a particular issue, it can be helpful to seek the wisdom of experienced Carmelites. If you are not already a member of the Order, or are a 'distance member' outside of a community, then your formation might be aided by your making contact with Carmelites in your part of the world that can offer guidance and support. Information about the Carmelite Family worldwide can be found via the website of the Carmelite Curia, the Order's headquarters in Rome (www.ocarm.org).

This book seeks to present Carmelite spirituality and history in a way that is faithful to the authentic tradition and charism of Carmel in all its diversity. One of the reasons that the Order has survived for over 800 years is that in every age there has been healthy discussion and respectful debate about exactly what it means to be a Carmelite. There will no doubt be expressions and ideas about Carmel in this book that some people will question or would phrase differently. Rather than being a definitive statement about Carmelite life, this book is offered as a collection of reflections by particular Carmelites who hope to help others on their journey of discovery. No formation programme can cover every topic or say definitively all that can be said about Carmel. In the words of Bishop Ken Untener (often erroneously attributed to Archbishop Oscar Romero but very much in his spirit):

> No statement says all that could be said.
> No prayer fully expresses our faith.
> No confession brings perfection.
> No pastoral visit brings wholeness.
> No programme accomplishes the Church's mission.
> No set of goals and objectives includes everything.
> It may be incomplete, but it is a beginning, a step along the way,
> an opportunity for the Lord's grace to enter and do the rest ...

This book is humbly offered as a guide at the beginning of the journey, a step along the way. Suggestions for improvements to future editions would be welcomed.

Acknowledgments

Thanks are due in first place to those members and friends of the Carmelite Family – including laity and religious of both the Ancient and Discalced Observances – who so generously wrote original material for the Initial Formation Programme as it appeared in *Assumpta*, or who allowed the British Province to reprint existing texts, including: John Berry; Lourdes Crabtree; Veronica Errington; Jean Harrigan; Charmaine Jayasuriya; Rosemary Kinman; Antony Lester; Sylvia Lucas; Wilfrid McGreal; Philip McParland; Jennifer Moorcroft; Anne Pass; Joseph Patterson; John Welch; John Wilson; Patricia Wilson. It was a pleasure to collate and edit their materials, and thanks are likewise due to a number of proof-readers for their comments and corrections.

Special thanks are due to Father Brendan Grady, O.Carm., who as Provincial Delegate to the Third Order in Britain in the late 1990s was a great motivator in the renewal of Lay Carmel, and who as editor of *Assumpta* first printed the Initial Formation Programme. A debt of gratitude is likewise owed to recent Priors Provincial of the British Province – Fathers Antony Lester, O.Carm., and Wilfrid McGreal, O.Carm. – and their Councils for their support of Lay Carmel's renewal and their encouragement of this publication.

I am personally grateful to various friends and colleagues who have assisted the production and printing process, including: Father Kevin Alban, O.Carm., Maurzio Pietrangeli and the board of Edizioni Carmelitane (the Order's central publishing house in Rome); as well as our Carmelite brethren in the Czech Republic, especially Father Jan Fatka, O.Carm., and his colleagues Pavel Kindermann and Jakub Kubů, whose skill at typesetting has greatly enriched the publication.

Saint Albert's Press is grateful to the individuals, communities, galleries and churches which have allowed us to reproduce their artworks. Due to the large number of illustrations they are not individually credited, but amongst others we would like to thank the following for their collaboration and photography: The Board of the British Library, London; The Bridgeman Art Library, London; The Catholic Bishops' Conference of England & Wales (Mazur/catholicchurch.org.uk); Richard Copsey, O.Carm.; Edizioni Carmelitane; Gabrielle Fogarty, T.O.C.; Google Images; Rose Mary Lancellotti, T.O.C.; Antony Lester, O.Carm.; Lincoln College, Oxford; Kevin Melody, O.Carm. In certain cases it has not been possible to trace copyright holders for some images; inadvertent infringement of copyright will be corrected in any future editions of this book.

Conclusion

Formation is a journey on the road of transformation. If we give space to God (*vacare Deo*), God will open our eyes and hearts, remove our prejudices, dispel our ignorance and fear, spur us into service, and love others through us. The ultimate test of this book's success will be whether it helps people to deepen their appreciation of the Carmelite way of life, which is essentially nothing more and nothing less than the living out of the Good News of Jesus Christ, according to the Order's charism.

As we seek to live in allegiance to Jesus, may he, his mother Mary, the prophet Elijah, and the saints of Carmel in heaven and on earth accompany us on life's journey.

Solemnity of Our Lady of Mount Carmel, 16th July 2010

The Rule of Saint Albert

A Carmelite pattern of living

Sometime between 1206 and 1214, a community of Christian hermits living on Mount Carmel in the Holy Land asked the Latin Patriarch of Jerusalem, Albert Avogadro of Vercelli, for a letter setting out their 'way of life' (called a *formula vitae* in Latin). In 1247 Pope Innocent IV formally recognised this text as a *Rule* (*regula*) for the hermits, who were in the process of becoming mendicant friars. The text, now usually called the *Rule of Saint Albert*, is the first written expression of what it means to be a Carmelite, and is the basis of our family's spirituality to this day. It inspires both laity and religious of all sections of the Carmelite Family around the world.

The original document was written in Latin, and the English translation printed here is by Fr. Christopher O'Donnell, O.Carm. Alternative translations can be found on the website of the British Province of Carmelites (www.carmelite.org).

The numbering of the chapters – which was not part of Albert's original document – is that agreed by the General Councils of both the Ancient and Discalced Observances of the Carmelite Family in 1999. The numbers in brackets refer to the older chapter numbering previously used by different branches of the Carmelite Family, as found in older publications. The additions made to the text by Pope Innocent in 1247 are printed in italics.

1 [Prologue, i] Albert, called by the grace of God to be Patriarch of the Church of Jerusalem, greets his beloved sons in Christ, B. and the other hermits living in obedience to him near the spring on Mount Carmel: salvation in the Lord and the blessing of the Holy Spirit.

2 [Prologue, ii] Many times and in different ways the holy Fathers have laid down that everyone – whatever be their state in life or the religious life chosen by them – should live under the patronage of Jesus Christ and serve him zealously with a pure heart and a good conscience.

3 Now then you have come to me seeking a formula of life according to your proposed manner of life, which you are to observe in the future.

4 [I, iii] The first thing I lay down is that you shall have a prior, one of yourselves, chosen by the unanimous consent of all, or of the greater and more mature part. All the others shall promise him obedience fulfilling it by deeds, *as well as chastity and the renunciation of property.*

5 [II, iv] *You can take up places in solitary areas or in sites given to you, one suitable and convenient for your observance in the judgment of the prior and the brothers.*

6 [III, v] Moreover, taking account of the site you propose to occupy, all of you are to have separate cells; these are to be assigned by the prior himself with the agreement of the other brothers or the more mature of them.

7 [IV, vi] *You are, however, to eat in a common refectory what may have been given to you, listening together to a reading from holy Scripture, if this can conveniently be done.*

8 [V, vii] No brother is permitted to change the place assigned to him or exchange with another, unless with the permission of the prior at the time.

9 [VI] The prior's cell shall be near the entrance to the place so that he may first meet those who come to the place and everything afterwards may be done as he decides and arranges.

10 [VII, viii] All are to remain in their cells or near them, meditating day and night on the law of the Lord and being vigilant in prayers, unless otherwise lawfully occupied.

11 [VIII, ix] *Those who have learned to say the canonical hours with the clerics should do so according to the practice of the holy Fathers and the approved custom of the Church. Those who do not know the hours* are to say the Our Father twenty-five times for the night office, except for Sunday and solemn feasts when this number is doubled, so that the Our Father is said fifty times. It is to be said seven times for the morning Lauds and for the other Hours, except for Vespers when it must be said fifteen times.

12 [IX, x] *None of the brothers is to claim something as his own; everything is to be in common and is to be distributed to each one by the Prior – that is, the brother deputed by him to this office – having regard to the age and needs of each one.*

13 [xi] *You may have asses or mules according to your needs and some rearing of animals or poultry.*

14 [X, xii] An oratory is to be built as conveniently as possible in the midst of the cells; you are to gather daily in the morning for Mass, where this is convenient.

15 [XI, xiii] On Sundays, or other days if necessary, you shall discuss the preservation of order and the salvation of souls; at this time excesses and faults of the brothers, if such come to light, are to be corrected with boundless charity.

16 [XII, xiv] You are to fast every day except Sundays from the feast of the Exaltation of the Cross until Easter Sunday, unless illness or bodily weakness, or other just cause counsels a lifting of the fast, since necessity has no law.

17 [XIII, xv] *You are to abstain from meat, unless it is to be taken as a remedy for illness or bodily weakness. Since you must more frequently beg on journeys, in order not to burden your hosts you may eat food cooked with meat outside your own houses. At sea, however, meat may be eaten.*

18 [XIV, xvi] Since human life on earth is a trial and all who want to live devotedly in Christ suffer persecution; your enemy the devil prowls about like a roaring lion seeking whom he might devour. You must then with all diligence put on the armour of God so that you may be able to stand up to the ambushes of the enemy.

19 Your loins are to be girded with the belt of chastity; your breast is to be protected by holy thoughts, for the Scripture says, holy thoughts will save you. Put on the breastplate of justice, so that you may love the Lord your God from your whole heart, your whole soul and your whole strength, and your neighbour as yourselves. In all things take up the shield of faith, with which you will be able to extinguish all the darts of the evil one; without faith, indeed, it is impossible to please God. The helmet of salvation is to be placed on your head, so that you may hope for salvation from the one Saviour, who saves his people from their sins. The sword of the Spirit, which is the word of God, is to dwell abundantly in your mouths and hearts. So whatever you have to do is to be done in the word of the Lord.

20 [XV, xvii] You should do some work, so that the devil will always find you occupied and he may not through your idleness find some entrance to your souls. In this matter you have both the teaching and the example of Blessed Paul the Apostle; Christ spoke through his mouth; he has been set up and given by God as a preacher and teacher of the nations in faith and truth; in following him you cannot go wrong. In work and weariness, he said, we have been with you, working day and night so as not to be a burden to you; it was not as though we had no right, but we wished to give ourselves as a model for imitation. For when we were with you, we gave this precept: whoever is unwilling to work shall not eat. We have heard that there are restless people going around who do nothing. We condemn such people and implore them in the Lord Jesus Christ that working in silence they should earn their bread. This is a good and holy way: follow it.

21 [XVI, xviii] The apostle therefore recommends silence, when he tells us to work in it; the prophet too testifies that silence is the promotion of justice; and again, in silence and in hope will be your strength. Therefore we lay down that from the recitation of Compline you are to maintain silence until after Prime the following day. At other times, though silence is not to be so strictly observed, you are to be diligent in avoiding much talking, since Scripture states and experience likewise teaches, sin is not absent where there is much talking; also he who is careless in speech will experience evil, and the one who uses many words harms his soul. Again the Lord says in the gospel: an account will have to be given on the day of judgement for every vain word. Each of you is to weigh his words and have a proper restraint for his mouth, so that he may not stumble and fall through speech and his fall be irreparable and fatal. He is with the prophet to guard his

ways so that he does not offend through the tongue. Silence, which is the promotion of justice, is likewise to be diligently and carefully observed.

22 [XVII, xix] You, Brother B., and whoever is appointed prior after you, shall always keep in mind and practice what the Lord said in the Gospel: Whoever wishes to be greater among you shall be your servant, and whoever wishes to be first must be your slave.

23 [XVIII, xx] And you too, the other brothers are humbly to honour your prior, and rather than thinking about him, you are to look to Christ who set him as head over you; he said to the leaders of the Church, whoever hears you hears me, and whoever despises you despises me. Thus you will not be judged guilty on account of contempt but, on account of obedience you will merit the reward of eternal life.

24 [Epilogue, xxi] I have written these things briefly to you establishing a formula of your common life, according to which you are to conduct yourselves. If anyone does more the Lord himself when he comes again will repay him. You are, however, to use discretion, which is the moderator of virtue.

The journey begins...

CHAPTER 1

What is Formation?

Summary: This chapter considers the fundamental question of 'What is Formation?' We look first at our common origins and destiny as human beings created by God, and then consider more specifically the vocation of a Carmelite. Initial and ongoing formation is discussed in some depth, and thought of in terms of a journey through life.

Formation – a journey somewhere both new and familiar.

Get prepared: This first chapter is one of the shortest, but if you find it easier to read in sections rather than in one sitting that is fine. Whether you are studying this chapter on your own, or as part of a group, you might want to make some notes so have a pen and paper to hand; there's a blank page at the end of each chapter for you to record notes, ideas and reactions if you wish. Everything you need is contained within the chapter, which includes extracts from some key texts such as the Bible, the 1992 *Catechism of the Catholic Church*, the 1995 *Constitutions of the Carmelite Friars*, and the 2003 *Rule for the Third Order of Carmel*; you might like to have copies of these documents to hand for further reflection (details of where to find them are given in the list of resources at the end of the chapter). The *Rule of Saint Albert* is included at the front of this book. Carmelite life is rooted in prayer, so before reading the chapter you may like to call on the Holy Spirit to open your mind and your heart to God's presence and wisdom. Feel free to offer a spontaneous prayer, to use a text from a prayer book, or to use the text below:

> *Loving and merciful God,*
> *you guide your people through the journey of life.*
> *When Abraham and Sarah left their own land, you kept them safe.*
> *You led the children of Israel on dry land, parting the waters of the Red Sea.*
> *You guided the steps of Elijah and his fellow prophets.*
> *You brought Mary and Joseph safely to Bethlehem,*
> *and led the Magi to your Son Jesus by the light of a star.*
> *Bless us, your children, that our journey of formation in the Carmelite tradition*
> *may broaden our horizons, and bring us to the mountain that is Christ.*
> *Open our eyes to read the signs of the times, and open our hearts to your presence.*
> *Sustain us through prayer, through service, and through life in community.*
> *And when life's pilgrimage is over, welcome us to our heavenly home.*
> *We ask this through Christ our Lord. Amen.*

Mount Carmel in the early twenty-first century.

Formation: a journey of love

We are setting out on a journey of formation. What is formation, and why do we need it in order to grow as members of the Carmelite Order? Formation begins with a passionate desire: God's love for us, and our love for God.

In the 1992 *Catechism of the Catholic Church* we read that 'The desire for God is written in the human heart, because humanity is created by God and for God; and God never ceases to draw us to himself. Only in God will we find the truth and happiness we never stop searching for.' (*Catechism* §27). In the *Rule for the Third Order of Carmel* it is stated 'God wanted to make himself known' (*RTOC* §1). So formation begins with the truth that God exists, and wants to be in relationship with us.

God is the first mover in that relationship: 'If we love God, it is because God loved us first' wrote the Apostle John (*1 John* 4:19). In experiencing God's love we recognise and respond to this call: 'The Spirit urges us to be attentive, to listen to the voice of God, to welcome the Word, and to open ourselves to the divine transformation' (cf. *RTOC* §17)... And so our journey begins.

Stop and reflect: Have you personally felt that the desire for God is written in your heart? How have you understood formation up to now? You might like to jot down some ideas.

Through the action of the Holy Spirit, God the Father transforms us and conforms us to the image of his son Jesus Christ, guiding us to communion with himself and with each other. As individuals and as a community, we commit ourselves to this gradual journey of conversion, of turning back to God, of transformation, which is the root of formation and indeed of the whole Christian life.

Stop and think: Can you recall any passages in the Bible where the image of a journey is used? What journeys did Jesus himself undertake?

Ascending the Mountain

Mount Carmel in the Holy Land is where our Carmelite Family began sometime around the year 1200. The first Carmelites were, like us, pilgrims on a journey. Even once the hermits had begun to leave Mount Carmel from the 1230s onwards, Carmel remained a place within the heart. Carmelites – whether lay people, diocesan clergy or religious brothers and sisters of the Order – prepare themselves for the 'ascent of Mount Carmel'.

Mount Carmel is not only the physical place in the Holy Land where our religious family began; it has become a metaphor, an image of our journey with and towards God. The goal of our journey, the summit of the mountain, is Jesus Christ.

'I lift up my eyes to the hills – from where will my help come?
My help comes from the Lord, who made heaven and earth.'
(Psalm 121:1-2)
Hills and mountains – such as Croagh Patrick in Ireland – are often considered holy sites.

As we make our journey towards and up Mount Carmel – a journey of love – we learn to love, to be completely absorbed in God's love, and to allow this love of God to transform our very being. The core of our formation is to engage in a deep relationship with Christ. As the *Rule for the Third Order of Carmel* puts it:

> The ascent of the mountain implies in the first place following Jesus Christ with all one's being, serving him faithfully 'pure in heart and stout in conscience' (*Rule of Saint Albert*, Ch. 2). The spirit of Jesus should permeate our being to such a degree that we can repeat with St. Paul, 'it is no longer I who live, but it is Christ who lives in me' (*Galatians* 2:20). In this way all our actions take place with 'the Lord's word for accompaniment' (*Rule of Saint Albert*, Ch. 19). (*RTOC* §18).

The goal of our formation, therefore, is to let Christ live in us.

Companions on the journey

Jesus is not only the goal of our journey, the Master in whose footsteps we follow, but he is also our brother and companion along the way. As we journey, we meet Christ in prayer. Prayer is at the heart of the Carmelite *Rule of Saint Albert*, prayer which the Carmelite tradition describes as 'conversation with God'. Prayer, particularly *Lectio Divina* meditation on the Bible, allows the Word to penetrate our minds and hearts. We also meet Christ in liturgical prayer, especially the Eucharist and the Divine Office. We also meet Christ in one other, finding his companionship in our Carmelite communities. Therefore, the following of Christ – what Saint Albert calls 'a life in allegiance to Jesus' (*Rule* Ch. 2) – is the fundamental law marking out the path we have to follow on the way to an ever deeper experience of the love of God.

Jesus Christ – whose Transfiguration is depicted in ceramic by the artist Adam Kossowski at Aylesford Priory in England – is truly the focus of the Carmelite journey.

Did you know? The liturgy of the Church is a valuable and reliable source of Christian formation. The Latin phrase *Lex orandi, lex credendi* loosely translates as 'the law of prayer is the law of faith', and means that what the Church says in her prayers contributes to and reflects her doctrine and tradition.

We are not alone in our journey; not only are we supported by Christ, but we enjoy the company of his mother Mary, Our Lady, who encourages us along the way as a mother, as a sister, and as a teacher. Mary allowed herself to be transformed by the action of the Holy Spirit. She welcomed the Word of God into her heart and teaches us obedience (attentive listening) to the Spirit, which leads us to fulfil the will of the Father.

Mary's example inspires us to become 'God-Bearers' in all circumstances of life. As the *Rule for the Third Order of Carmel* puts it: 'We learn from her to welcome the Word, to be open to it and to embrace it fully. Mary, in whom the Word was made flesh, inspires us to be faithful to our mission.' (*RTOC* 34). The 2003 *Rule for the Third Order of Carmel* is a set of Constitutions setting out the vision for how Lay Carmelites should live. The 1995 *Constitutions* of the Carmelite friars also help us understand how Mary accompanies us on the journey of formation: 'Mary, overshadowed by the Spirit of God, is the

In this window by Richard Joseph King at the Carmelite friary in Faversham, England, we see Mary transformed by the Spirit, welcoming the Word.

Carmelites regard the Old Testament prophet Elijah as our spiritual forefather.

Virgin of a new heart, who gave a human face to the Word made flesh ... Mary followed Jesus, walking with the disciples, sharing their demanding and wearisome journey – a journey which required, above all, fraternal love and mutual service' (*Constitutions* §27).

We Carmelites also journey with Elijah, the Old Testament prophet, whom we read (in the Bible's *Books of the Kings*) burned with zeal for God (*1 Kings* 19:10).

The *Rule for the Third Order of Carmel* explains Elijah's role as companion on our journey to God: 'Together, with Elijah, we learn to feel the presence of the Lord which comes to humanity with strength and gentleness. He is the same yesterday, today and forever. Strengthened by this transforming and life-giving experience, Carmelites are able to face the realities of the world.' (*RTOC* §35). Some of Elijah's journeys were difficult and testing times, but his example and God's encouragement give us hope.

The Carmelite charism

As Carmelites we regard Mary and Elijah as our special role models, our patrons, and our friends on the journey towards Christ. They help us to be contemplatives, that is, people who seek to be open to God living within us. By reflecting on their lives we see how Elijah and Mary opened their hearts to God through prayer, through service of others, and through immersing themselves in the lives of their communities. These three elements of prayer, community and service are at the heart of the Carmelite 'charism', that is, the unique gift that God has given to the Carmelite Family so as to be of service to the Church and to the World.

Stop and review: The key elements of the Carmelite charism – prayer, community, and service – will be considered regularly throughout this formation programme, along with the three key persons from whom Carmelites take particular inspiration: Jesus, Mary, and Elijah. The theme of 'the journey' will also be a useful image for us to bear in mind.

John of the Cross sculpted by Michael Clark in the Great Courtyard at The Friars, Aylesford, England. John realised that the journey of transformation in Christ is an interior pilgrimage.

We journey too with all the saints of Carmel, from the origins of the Order in Palestine sometime around the year 1200, right up to modern times. We Carmelites therefore journey with the likes of St. John of the Cross, who became aware of Christ, the *living flame of love*.

Did you know? In his years of Carmelite formation, John of the Cross' love for and devotion to Mary would grow deeper and more intense. Very soon after his ordination to the priesthood in 1567, John came into contact with Teresa of Jesus (of Avila) and learned of her intention to extend the reform of Carmel to include friars as well as nuns. John informed Teresa that he was on the verge of leaving Carmel to join the Carthusians. Had he carried this out, he would have had to give up much that he deeply appreciated, not the least of which was Carmel's deep and pervasive Marian tradition. As Teresa testifies in the *Book of Foundations*, she urged John to reconsider, and 'pointed out the great good that would be accomplished if – in his desire to improve – were he to remain in his own order'. Happily for Carmel, John was open to Teresa's advice on his spiritual journey.

We Carmelites journey side by side with our fellow travellers, men and women in our community and the wider Carmelite Family, those who have received the same call, all on the journey to discover God's loving presence within themselves.

Formation results in transformation

Formation changes us; it removes our prejudices, opens our eyes and hearts to God, and converts every part of an individual's being:

- At a psychological level, conversion through formation frees us to hear the Word of God and respond to God's call more willingly, and so opens to us a Christian freedom.

- At a moral level, integrating gospel values into our lives through formation helps to strengthen our beliefs, and gives us a prophetic voice in society.

- At an emotional level, we can enter into relationships with one another through formation, not in order to be possessive or controlling, but so as to allow others their space to grow, and so as to create an environment of peace in which to mature. The environment is important in allowing the freedom to ask questions and explore answers. As emotional maturity develops we are able to give of ourselves, as Christ gives Himself to us.

- At an intellectual level we learn more about the history and spirituality of Carmel, and so the horizons of our mind are broadened, and our sense of belonging deepened as the Carmelite story becomes our own story. In seeking truth and understanding we are in fact seeking God.

- At a spiritual level, formation helps us open up to God's love so that God can increasingly work in and through us. Formation can transform the way we pray, and challenges our preconceptions about God.

- At a social level, we realise our responsibilities in developing our society and so commit more freely to the common good. Formation will impact not only on us, but convert and transform the way that we deal with others, and thus build up the Kingdom of God. Carmelite formation will help us appreciate Carmel as a family at local, national and international levels.

In other words, formation is holistic: it deals with the whole person, and every aspect of life. It bridges the false distinction between the 'spiritual' and 'non-spiritual', revealing that there is a spiritual dimension to every part of life.

A useful resource: In the year 2000, the Carmelite Order produced a document known as the *Ratio Institutionis Vitæ Carmelitanæ* (*RIVC* for short). It was published under the title *Carmelite Formation: A Journey of Transformation*. This document sets out the principles behind formation: what it is for and how it is conducted. Though it was written with friars in mind, much of it applies to other branches of the Carmelite Family. A copy should be found in every Carmelite community library, and it can be read on the internet via Carmelite websites such as www.carmelite.org.

Formation transforms Carmelites as individuals and also as communities.

Stop and think: How much do you think of formation as a 'mental exercise', for example learning new facts, dates and quotations from the Carmelite tradition? Is formation more about growing in relationships, and sharing experiences of Carmelite life? Or both?

Initial and ongoing formation

Initial formation in the Carmelite Order – whether as a friar or hermit, enclosed nun, active sister, or lay person – takes place between the time someone is received into the Order, and when they make final profession. Initial formation can be seen as taking the first formal steps on the journey in Carmel. During that time we acquire a deeper knowledge of ourselves and understand better what motivates our actions. Increasing our self-knowledge and self-acceptance is a crucial aspect of formation, through which we become aware of our limitations and of our potential. In this awareness, we can be free to respond to God's call.

Stop and think: Is formation a process of learning about 'external' things and other people, or learning more about yourself? Or both?

Formation continues after an individual has made their first profession, and is a lifelong process (no Carmelite is ever 'fully-formed' this side of the grave). Therefore we speak of 'ongoing formation'. Formation is not a diploma conducted in a limited time frame (though study can certainly be an important aspect), nor is it simply a means of obtaining membership within the Order. Formation – both initial and ongoing – is a journey of love, to love.

The formation process grows as we encounter Christ, answer his call, and follow him in the Carmelite way, allowing ourselves to be grasped and transformed by his love. Hence, formation is not another set of rules or a list of habits to acquire, but rather is about discernment and flexibility. We go where the Spirit leads.

Stop and ponder: We have spoken of formation as a journey. Do you think there is a clear map and compass for this journey, or is it a journey into the unknown? Who are reliable guides on the journey?

Each individual's journey is unique. We can share the experiences of our personal journey, but not impose on another person's journey. The Carmelite path to Jesus is a tried and tested route that many holy people have trod before us.

Formation helps us to attain a freedom which will allow us to go beyond ourselves, our own interests, our own ego, and our own personal needs, and thus open ourselves to the action of the Holy Spirit and grow in God's love. This freedom, which can be seen as *letting go and allowing God in* is to be encouraged in its growth.

Did you know? Formation of lay people is discussed in official documents of the Catholic Church following the Second Vatican Council, including *Apostolicam Actuositatem* (the Decree on the Apostolate of the Laity) promulgated by Pope Paul VI in 1965, and *Christifideles Laici* (the Post-Synodal Apostolic Exhortation on the Vocation and Mission of the Lay Faithful in the Church and in the World) published in 1988 by Pope John Paul II.

Authentically Carmelite formation

From its onset, formation for the Carmelite must be authentically Carmelite. That is, it must draw on the heritage of the Carmelite Family, focus on what is our 'family story', and not get diverted into following other spiritual traditions, valuable as they may be.

Formation in the Carmelite tradition is not separated from the usual growth in understanding that all Christians should have with regard to their faith. Those who embark on the Carmelite journey towards Christ should already have a basic grasp and practice of Christianity, and they should continue to ponder the mysteries of their faith. Formation will expose areas of our faith and understanding where we need to develop. Carmelite formation is essentially Christian formation from a Carmelite perspective.

Do not be afraid! If, during the course of this formation programme, you come across names, concepts, or anything that is unfamiliar to you or which you don't understand, don't be afraid to ask fellow Carmelites for help or guidance. If something does not make sense to you at first, it might be best to address the question immediately, or it might be preferable for you to set it aside for a while and come back to the issue later. If you find something you do not agree with that's okay; the purpose of this programme is to encourage your own reflection in the light of the Carmelite tradition.

Formation in the Carmelite tradition should only be undertaken seriously by those with a calling to Carmel. The Carmelite vocation and charism must be potentially present in each person who seeks to follow the Carmelite journey. In the process of formation an individual may identify with the Carmelite Order and continue to develop a deep sense of belonging while maintaining their essential identity. If, however, an individual does not identify with Carmel, then the process of formation may still have brought that person closer to God in their search by giving them a clearer understanding of themselves. In this context there is no 'right or wrong'; there are many paths to God, and many alternative paths to Carmel. A fundamental part of formation is that an individual is guided along *their own* path, the path along which God is calling them.

An image to think about: Some sculptors like Michelangelo say that they don't so much create a statue of someone but rather reveal or draw out the person's shape that is already within the block of stone or wood. Does this image apply to formation? Can you make someone a Carmelite, or rather do you enable them to discover the Carmelite vocation already alive within themselves?

During the formation process, we will develop new attitudes and values. These are to be integrated within our lives so that we can take responsibility for our actions and the choices that we make.

Formation in Carmel is a journey to the mountain that is Christ, depicted here in stained glass by George Walsh in the chapel of Avila Discalced Carmelite Friary, Dublin, Ireland.

The start of a lifelong journey

The journey of formation is a lifelong journey. Each day we take a new step. God renews his call day by day, and each day a new response is to be given. Sometimes we may stray from the path, but God is patient with us, and so we must be patient with ourselves, without becoming complacent. As we set out on the path to the mountain Jesus Christ, let us be confident that God will provide everything we need for our journey:

> You did not choose me; it was I who chose you;
> and I sent you to go out and to bear fruit, fruit that will last;
> And everything that you ask the Father in my name, he will give you.
> My command to you is to love one another.
>
> (*John* 15:16-17)

Conclusion: In this first chapter we have reflected on what formation is, using particularly the metaphor of a journey. We have seen that love is the motivation for setting out on this journey. Accompanying us on our pilgrimage are Elijah, Mary, the saints of Carmel, and our fellow members of the Carmelite Family. Embracing the Order's contemplative charism of prayer, community and service will allow us to be transformed by God's grace.

Why not conclude your session of reflection with a moment of simple prayer, such as the *Glory Be* (other suggestions for prayer are given in the list of ideas for reflection below).

In the second chapter we will look at how all people are called to holiness, and how formation in the Carmelite way of life can help us respond to that universal call.

Ideas for Reflection, Discussion and Action

- Take any paragraph above that has captured your attention and reflect on what it means to you, individually and/or as a community.

- Write down one point that struck you, and bring it to your next community formation meeting, or reflect on it at home in the coming days. Perhaps discuss it with friends.

- How would you summarise the chapter and its key points in one or two paragraphs? It might help you to write it down on the blank page following this chapter. You might want to write a summary of key points in the margins next to each paragraph, if that helps you remember them.

- How do you think the effects of formation can be judged? How do I know if formation is transforming my life?

- Look back on how God has formed you up to this point in your life.

- Consider how you came to Carmel. How did you discern the call?

- Reflect (perhaps using *Lectio Divina*) upon the Gospel passage of *John* 15:16-17.

- Read what is said about the formation of the laity in modern Church documents such as *Apostolicam Actuositatem* and *Christifideles Laici*.

- Look at any vision statements that might have been compiled in your province, or recent declarations from the Prior Provincial or his Delegate: how do they refer to formation? What part do you think formation has to play in the development of Carmel in your country?

- What keywords do you associate with the concept of 'Journey' (such as 'map', 'rest', 'getting lost', 'backpack', 'signpost' or 'companions')? How have these been evident in your own life?

- Consider how you could encourage another person to try the Carmelite journey.

- Applying the principle of *Lex orandi, lex credendi* (the Church believes as she prays), reflect on the liturgy of the Church in the days and weeks ahead, perhaps focussing especially on the opening prayer and preface of the Mass.

- Relationships are at the heart of the Carmelite dynamic: what aspects of your relationship with Jesus do you find most difficult and most rewarding?

- In the month ahead, try to spend just five or ten minutes each day in silent prayer, asking God to guide you on a journey of transformation.

- Reflect on these words from T. S. Eliot's play *The Rock*: 'Where is the life we have lost in living? Where is the wisdom we have lost in knowledge? Where is the knowledge we have lost in information?'

- We speak of the 'Carmelite Family'. How might you build up relationships with your brothers and sisters in Carmel?

- Pray for those who have particular responsibility for promoting initial and ongoing formation within the Carmelite Family.

- If Carmelite formation is 'holistic', what parts of your life might be affected by your life as a Carmelite? Are you open to change and to challenge?

The Blessed Virgin Mary accompanies us on the journey of formation. This icon of 'Our Lady of Hope', was written by the Carmelite nuns in Ravenna, Italy, as a focus of prayer during the 'Pilgrimage of Hope' to Rome of young people associated with the Carmelite Order in Europe, in July 2010.

Climbing the Mountain: The Carmelite Journey 37

Chapter 1 ■ What is Formation?

Recommended Further Resources

You might find some of the following books and articles helpful as extra reading for your own reflection, but remember to pace yourself and that formation is not simply a question of study. Most of the resources listed below will be available in Carmelite libraries and bookshops; find out what resources exist in your local area.

Johan Bergström-Allen, 'Go and bear fruit, fruit that will last', *Assumpta* magazine of the British Province of Carmelites, (November, 2004), pp. 2-10.

Catechism of the Catholic Church, (London: Geoffrey Chapman, 1992).

Joseph Chalmers, O.Carm., 'Carmel: a place and a journey into the third millennium', in *In Allegiance to Jesus Christ*, (Rome: Edizioni Carmelitane, 1999), pp. 7-14.

Constitutions of the Carmelite Order, (Rome: Carmelite Order, 1995). This text can be found in the library of every friar community, and can be purchased from Carmelite book services, such as Saint Albert's Press in Britain. The text can also be found online by visiting Carmelite websites such as the Curia (www.ocarm.org) and the British Province (www.carmelite.org).

Mark Davis, *Glimpses of the Carmelite Way*, (West Kirby, Wirral: Rockpool Publishing, 2007).

General Curia of the Carmelite Order, *Ratio Institutionis Vitæ Carmelitanæ – Carmelite Formation: A Journey of Transformation*, (Rome: General Curia of the Carmelite Order, 2000).

International Congress of Lay Carmelites, *Formation and Communication at the Service of the Community*, proceedings of the 2006 International Congress of Lay Carmelites, (Rome: Edizioni Carmelitane, 2007).

Irish Province of Carmelites, *Meeting God: Carmelite Reflections and Prayers*, (Dublin: The Columba Press, 2007).

Cheslyn Jones, Geoffrey Wainwright & Edward Yarnold, S. J., (eds.), *The Study of Spirituality*, (London: S.P.C.K., 1986).

Wilfrid McGreal, O.Carm., *At the Fountain of Elijah: the Carmelite Tradition* (London: Darton Longman and Todd, 1999).

Rule for the Third Order of Carmel, (Rome: Edizioni Carmelitane, 2003).

Vilma Seelaus, O.C.D., 'Transformation and Divine Union in the Carmelite Tradition', in Keith J. Egan, T.O.C., *Carmelite Prayer: A Tradition for the 21ˢᵗ Century*, (New York: Paulist Press, 2003), pp. 139-161.

Peter Slattery, O.Carm., 'Mount Carmel and the Rule of St. Albert', in *The Springs of Carmel: An Introduction to Carmelite Spirituality*, (New York: Alba House, 1991), pp. 1-21.

John Welch O.Carm., *The Carmelite Way: An Ancient Path for Today's Pilgrim*, (Leominster: Gracewing, 1996).

John Welch, O.Carm., *Seasons of the Heart: The Spiritual Dynamic of the Carmelite Life*, (Aylesford: Lay Carmel Central Office, 2001). Also available online via the website of the British Province of Carmelites: www.carmelite.org

Ask your Carmelite community leader, formator, or companion, if you have one, what forms of communication exist for the Order in your area. Carmelite magazines, journals and periodicals often have good articles that help initial and ongoing formation, such as *Assumpta* and *Mount Carmel* (in Britain), *The Vine* (in Australia), *Carmel in the World* (international) as well as *The Sword*, *Carmelite Digest* and *Carmel Clarion* (United States of America). Many provinces of both the Ancient and Discalced Observances of the Carmelite Family have good websites with useful resources for reflection.

Modules in formation and its methods are often included in Carmelite study-programmes such as the Carmelite Institute of Britain & Ireland (www.cibi.ie), the Carmelite Institute in Washington D.C. (www.carmeliteinstitute.org), the Carmelite Institute in Malta, and so on. Attending Carmelite retreats, study forums and days of recollection can also help your Carmelite formation.

If you don't already have a library of resources in your local Carmelite library, now is a good time to start gradually building up a collection. Advice on this is given in an article by Patrick Thomas McMahon, O.Carm., 'A Carmelite Library just for your Community', *Carmel in the World*, Volume XLV Number 1, 2006, pp. 47-65.

Notes and reflections on Chapter 1

CHAPTER 2

The Call to Holiness

Summary: In the first chapter we reflected on formation as a journey towards Christ. In this second chapter we will look at how all people are called to holiness, and how formation in the Carmelite way of life can help us respond to that universal call. At our baptism we received the call to holiness, and one way of responding to and nurturing this call is through the Carmelite vocation. Through grace we are called: to a loving service of each other; to be part of a community which radiates out to others in 'contemplative service'; to dwell in an interior cell, which is available to every person, not only religious. The interplay of God's initiative and our response is lived out by Carmelites in many ways, but is always part of the same vocation to holiness.

Baptism depicted in a Missal produced for the Carmelite friars in medieval London, now in the British Library.

Get prepared: As with the first chapter, you may want to check that you have useful resources to hand, including a pen, notebook, key texts, and so on. Since the chapter is about the fact that all people are called to holiness, why not begin with a prayer asking God to help you and others on this journey?

What is holiness?

What do you think holiness is? Who do you think is holy? The 2003 *Rule for the Third Order of Carmel* (*RTOC*) reminds us that God is holy and is the source of holiness: 'God never ceases to draw us to himself. Only in God will we find the truth and happiness we never stop searching for.' (§1)

God is holy. God is. As our spiritual father Elijah declared: 'The Lord of hosts lives, before whom I stand.' (*1 Kings* 18:15).

This action of God in drawing us to himself is the call, the first glimmer of light, the dawn of a knowing that sets the course of our journey. The thirsting soul is led to the water of life. It is a personal encounter, an invitation to total and eternal union. We awaken to God's presence in the depth of the heart, like St. John of the Cross:

> How gently and lovingly
> you wake in my heart,
> where in secret you dwell alone;
> and in your sweet breathing,
> filled with good and glory,
> how tenderly you swell my heart with love.
> (John of the Cross, *The Living Flame of Love*)

We are fully known and loved by God. Ponder the words of Psalm 139, verses 1-18:

> O Lord, you have searched me and known me … Such knowledge is too wonderful for me; it is so high that I cannot attain it … I praise you for I am fearfully and wonderfully made … My frame was not hidden from you, when I was being made in secret, intricately woven in the depths of the earth. Your eyes beheld my unformed substance …

God's presence is holiness, and only through God's free gift is God's love eternally revealed and experienced completely.

God's presence within us

This holiness – this presence of God within us – comes to perfection in us through a growing communion of love enlivened by God's Spirit. It is perfectly manifested in Jesus in whom God and humanity are perfectly united: 'In the beginning was the Word and the Word was with God and the Word was God.' (*John* 1:1)

Jesus is the Word who in his flesh and blood, his preaching and ministry, in his presence among us speaks the Father's love. This Word invites and leads all humanity to holiness. As we respond to this initiative of God in Christ, God's own holiness shines forth in its glory. As God becomes increasingly the centre of our longing and all our desires become focused in Christ, the Kingdom of God is more firmly established: the divine reigns in our hearts bringing to completion our own humanity. In Christ all is made whole. God's glory is made manifest in humanity fully alive.

Stop and recall: If you can remember your baptism, what led you to that moment? If you were baptised as a child perhaps, what inspired your parents or godparents to seek the sacrament on your behalf?

Baptism: a spring of holiness that waters the garden of Carmel

At baptism the call to holiness is a gift of grace freely offered and called forth from each unique individual human life. Co-operating with this grace leads to the fullness of love – being fully human – that Jesus offers to those who walk in his footsteps. We are called to life in communion through him, with him and in him. The glory and holiness of God will shine most fully when the Kingdom of God is made manifest at the resurrection of all.

'Carmel', the family of people who identify with the Carmelite Order and its charism, is described as a garden, orchard or vineyard. Each flower in the garden of Carmel has its own shape and destiny in plentiful profusion. Growing together through pondering the Scriptures, sharing in the Sacraments, and loving each other forms the greater picture of God's landscaped garden through relationship. Each person is essential to the Creator's joyful design:

> God calls each one to live in a mysterious relationship of communion with the Persons of the Most Holy Trinity. The Father searches out individuals, draws them to Himself and towards his Son; the Spirit urges them to be attentive, to listen to the voice of God, to welcome the Word and to open themselves to the divine transforming action. (*RTOC* §17).

Holiness starts with friendship with Christ

Jesus – perfectly uniting the divine and human – is the Carmelite's inspiration: the way, the truth and the life. His path is the sure way to holiness and his beatitudes (*Luke* 6:20-24) are signposts along the way. As we follow the light of Christ's example, his loving presence helps us face and overcome our weaknesses. The Spirit transforms and perfects us by using those very weaknesses to be the steps of love as we humbly seek his help. As Pope John Paul II said: 'Friendship with Christ is the start of holiness.'

Grace draws the human heart to yearn for God: 'As the deer yearns for the water so my soul longs after you.' (*Psalm* 42:1). This yearning gives us a restlessness that cannot be satisfied by false gods. Only the one who is God can truly satisfy this thirst.

Stop and ponder Scripture: Consider the prophet Elijah's witness to the prophets of the false god Baal and Elijah's own spiritual journey, especially *1 Kings* 17:1-19:21. How do we respond to the spiritual drought of our own times and the issues of life that face us?

Holiness leads us into solidarity with others

Grace activates a zealous charity, expressed through service of others with expansive generosity. A person growing in holiness recognises the hungers and thirsts in his or her own time and place. Such a person knows the love that alone can satisfy them. This love leads them into solidarity with others, so that St. Thérèse of Lisieux could declare 'I will be love in the heart of the Church'.

As members of Christ's body, hearing the Word and sharing the Bread, we are all drawn together into a loving community where God's will is the heart. The habit of holiness clothes each person with a mission to serve the other members of the one Body with heartfelt charity.

God calls everybody to holiness

God calls all people into relationship with him, regardless of their creed, their sex or sexuality, their age or ability, their colour or culture. Holiness is the vocation of every member of the Christian community, whether lay person or cleric. This idea of the 'universal call to holiness' is stressed by the Second Vatican Council. For example, Chapter 5 of *Lumen Gentium* (the 1964 'Dogmatic Constitution on the Church') states: 'The Lord Jesus, the divine Teacher and Model of all perfection, preached holiness of life to each and everyone of his disciples of every condition.' (§40) This echoes what we read at the beginning of the Carmelite *Rule of Saint Albert*: 'Many and varied are the ways in which our saintly forefathers laid down how everyone, whatever their station or the kind of religious observance they have chosen, should live a life of allegiance to Jesus Christ – how, pure in heart and stout in conscience, they must be unswerving in the service of the Master.' (Ch. 2).

From within the mystical body of Christ, the Church, different charisms or ways of responding to God's love spring forth. One of these is the Carmelite charism.

Go back and re-read: Remind yourself of what is said about the Carmelite charism in Chapter 1, namely that Carmelites are contemplatives who form praying communities at the service of all God's people.

The Carmelite charism is itself lived out in various different ways. Carmelite friars, hermits, enclosed nuns, apostolic sisters, and lay people are all responding to God's call to holiness in different ways, but share the Carmelite contemplative charism of prayer, community and service. As the *Ratio* formation document of the Carmelite friars recognised in the year 2000: 'All Carmelites participate in the one and only vocation to Carmel, in various and complementary ways, according to the call and the gifts of each individual.' (§22).

The Carmelite charism supports a life of holiness

The Carmelite charism waters the desert of contemporary times with contemplative service, inspired particularly by Christ himself, and by the examples of our patrons, Mary and Elijah. Their example, and our Carmelite contemplative tradition, invite us to be open to God's presence and friendship in a variety of ways.

A statue of the infant Christ on the lap of Our Lady of Mount Carmel at the National Shrine of St. Thérèse at Darien, Illinois, U.S.A.

Our relationship with God can be nourished if we immerse ourselves in the silence of a solitary and secret place where we can better hear the voice of the Beloved. Our charism calls us, like the first Carmelite hermits, to find the spirit of solitude, recollection and detachment necessary for the life of prayer.

The first Carmelites, our forebears, were Christian hermits living in the valley on Mount Carmel known as the *wadi 'ain es-siah*. They had probably been pilgrims en route to the holy city of Jerusalem, or perhaps crusading soldiers. Whatever their background, they heard the call to holiness, turning away from an exterior journey to follow an interior one, turning away from physical warfare to face the spiritual battle within their hearts. They knew that in the seclusion and solitude of Mount Carmel – a place regarded as holy since the time of Elijah – they could open their hearts to the Beloved's call to holiness.

This icon depicts Saint Albert of Jerusalem giving the Carmelite Way of Life (Rule) to Saint Brocard and the first hermits on Mount Carmel. It was written by Sister Petra Clare in 2007 to commemorate the 8th centenary of the Carmelite Way of Life and now hangs in the National Shrine of Saint Jude at the Carmelite friary in the Kent town of Faversham, England.

The hermits did not live alone however, but rather formed a community so that they could be more attentive to the call to holiness. Today the voice of the Beloved can also be heard through the sisters and brothers with whom we share our lives. Service of our communities, and of the wider Church and the World, also opens our minds, hands and hearts to the God who loves us.

Life in a restless world shows us our need for God. Our meditation of God in prayer sends us out from our 'cell' to meet God in his needy, restless world. There are many different ways in which we hear the call to holiness.

Stop and ponder: The *Rule of Saint Albert* (printed at the front of this book) speaks of each Carmelite having a separate cell (Ch. 6) in which the Carmelite is to stay, pondering the Law of the Lord day and night when not occupied in other duties (Ch. 10). How do you interpret these passages from the *Rule* according to your own life and situation? Where is your 'cell'? When do you leave it?

Entrance to the ruins of the medieval oratory on Mount Carmel.

Following the hermits' journey

Those who wear the Carmelite habit or scapular today follow in the footsteps of those early hermits who laid the foundations of Carmel's tradition of balancing solitude and community. Even when the hermits migrated to western Europe and gradually adopted the friars' mendicant way of life in the heart of society, solitude within the community remained an important concept. According to Saint Albert's vision of Carmelite life, it is in the solitude of the 'cell' that the Carmelite will spend most of his or her prayer time, and it is there that they will meditate on God's call to holiness:

> ... all of you are to have separate cells ... All are to remain in their cells or near them, meditating day and night on the law of the Lord and being vigilant in prayers, unless otherwise lawfully occupied. (Chs. 6 & 10).

So too today the Carmelite living in the world finds that cell within him or herself, in the busy daily routine. The cell is not so much a physical space as a space in the heart. This space is left open for God to enter. The Carmelite tradition refers to this open space for God as *vacare Deo*.

Discerning God's call in silence

An important aspect of leaving space for God to enter our hearts is not to fill our lives with noise but rather to cultivate silence. It was, after all, in silence that the prophet Elijah encountered God's presence on Mount Horeb (*1 Kings* 19:9-13).

But what of the busy parent or grandparent, the factory worker, the parish priest, or anyone occupied with work and the affairs of the world? Is it possible for them to live the Carmelite way of life? Indeed it is. Contemplative living does not mean that Carmelites should live in perpetual remoteness from others. The presence of God is in every face and place and moment. St Thérèse discovered that the noise of human distractions even in the chapel of Lisieux Carmel was the means to knowing the peace of God. Brother Lawrence of the Resurrection and Teresa of Jesus (of Avila) found God amongst the pots and pans.

Stop and reflect: Do you become more aware of God's presence in solitude or in community? How do we live the values of solitude and silence whilst also sharing God's love for the world?

Carmelites – whether lay or religious – are called to live the Word with their whole being, according to their own situation in the world. Their response is to attune themselves and others to the sound of God's silence wherever they are and whatever they are doing, since silence is not simply the absence of noise but an interior disposition. By uniting themselves to Christ Carmelites become more attuned to the will of God, the guiding power of love. As their cell is within them, the Carmelites' witness is to bring that peace of the Presence to others.

God calls us in different ways

God calls all people to holiness, but they are called in different ways with specific vocations. Most Carmelites today are immersed in the business of the world, and their calling is to transform the world in which they live according to the values of God's kingdom. As it says in the 2003 *Rule for the Third Order of Carmel*:

> All Carmelites are in the world in some way, but the vocation of lay people is precisely to transform the secular world. So Tertiaries, in as much as they are committed lay people, have this secular characteristic by which they are called to treat the things of the world correctly and to order them according to God's will. Their life, lived in the world in the midst of the people, is dedicated to the cares and tasks of the world, in the ordinary ups and downs of family and of society. Tertiaries are invited by God to contribute to the holiness of the world: they are to have the spirit of the gospel in their work and to be guided by Carmelite spirituality. It is their calling to illuminate and order the world's activities so that these may be carried out according to Christ's intention and be a source of praise to the glory of the creator. (§28).

In this way *all* Carmelites have a vocation to respond to in their daily lives. The Church is continuing to grow in its appreciation of this truth. The Second Vatican Council promoted the idea of the 'universal call to holiness' in the 1960s. In 1987, a Synod of Bishops was held to consider the lay members of Christ's faithful people, and their 'Vocation and Mission in the Church and in the World Twenty Years after the Second Vatican Council'. Following this gathering, Pope John Paul II wrote a letter entitled *Christifideles Laici* (Christ's Faithful Lay People), in which he reflected further on the laity's vocation and mission:

> The newness of the Christian life is the foundation and title for equality among all the baptized in Christ, for all the members of the People of God: "As members, they share a common dignity from their rebirth in Christ, they have the same filial grace and the same vocation to perfection. They possess in common one salvation, one hope and one undivided charity". Because of the one dignity flowing from Baptism, each member of the lay faithful, together with ordained ministers and men and women religious, shares a responsibility for the Church's mission. (§15)

This notion of equality, of collaboration between all Christ's faithful people, is becoming increasingly valued within Carmel, where each member of the 'Family' has a unique contribution to make as we help each other respond to God's call to holiness.

Hearing God's call in the routine of everyday living

If we respond to God's call, what can we expect life to be like? For most of us the journey to the mountain that is Jesus Christ will be one with a few high and low points, but mostly it will consist of slow and steady progress. Responding to God's call by following the Carmelite way of life will help us appreciate God's presence in the ordinary and the everyday. As formation deepens our appreciation of Carmel and attentiveness to God's call, we will grow in what our tradition calls 'the practice of the presence of God'. This 'practice' means developing an awareness of God's presence, and perceiving God's glory in even the most mundane situations.

God is present in all places and situations, and as Carmelites we strive to become aware of that presence. As we open ourselves to God's indwelling, as we make space for God in our lives, God grants us the gift of his friendship and makes us contemplatives, able to perceive his presence all around us and within us.

We are called to become aware of God's presence

This grace of God's presence which infuses every aspect of daily living, and our responsiveness to that grace, has been a constant theme in the Carmelite tradition. For example, it is referred to in an important medieval text called *The Ten Books on the Way of Life and Great Deeds of the Carmelites* (sometimes known as *The Book of the First Monks*) produced by the Catalonian Carmelite Felip Ribot:

> The goal of this life is twofold. One part we acquire by our own effort and the exercise of the virtues, assisted by divine grace. This is to offer God a pure and holy heart, free from all stain of sin... The other goal of this life is granted to us as the free gift of God, namely, to taste somewhat in the heart and to experience in the mind the power of the divine presence and the sweetness of heavenly glory, not only after death but already in this mortal life. (*The Ten Books*, Book 1, Ch. 2).

Stop and reread: This passage is one of the earliest statements about the Carmelite way of life. Do you find its words resonate with your own hopes and dreams?

Many years after Felip Ribot, in seventeenth-century Paris, a Discalced Carmelite friar called Brother Lawrence of the Resurrection also wrote about how the Lord was calling him to perceive the divine presence. Brother Lawrence's conversations and letters were collated together and published under the title *The Practice of the Presence of God*. As these extracts show, Lawrence's life was transformed by opening himself to God's presence and his responding generously to the call to holiness:

> I did not engage in a religious life but for the love of God, and I have endeavoured to act only for Him: whatever becomes of me, whether I be lost or saved, I will always continue to act purely for the love of God. I shall have this good at least, that till death I shall have done all that is in me to love Him.
>
> (*Second Conversation*)

> I make it my business only to persevere in His holy presence where I
> keep myself by a simple attention and a general fond regard to God,
> which I may call an actual presence of God; an habitual, silent, and
> secret conversation of the soul with God.
>
> (*Second Letter*)

Did you know? Brother Lawrence was a former footman and soldier who said that he broke everything. He developed his *Practice of the Presence of God* from his once observing a bare tree in winter and realising that God's love renewed its leaves in spring. This kindled in Lawrence a contemplative love that saw God's hand in everything and in everyone. On entering the Carmelite friary he was assigned to kitchen duties. He said that amid the general noise, clutter and shouting, he enjoyed 'as great a tranquillity as if I were upon my knees at the Blessed Sacrament'.

Other Carmelites have described the ways that God has called them into awareness of his presence. St. John of the Cross described it as the ascent of a mountain, where we encounter *nada*, nothing but God. St. Teresa of Jesus described it as a journey through an interior castle. St. Thérèse found God present in her life through the 'Little Way' of offering up the daily realities of life with childlike trust.

Our response to God's call is a journey that takes us through the suffering of the Cross to the glory of the Resurrection. We come to understand that even trauma, hardship and suffering, as well as joy and happiness, are part of our journey to holiness. As we grow in our Carmelite vocation, we come to realise with St. Paul that nothing 'in all creation will be able to separate us from the love of God in Christ Jesus our Lord' (*Romans* 8:38).

Something to be attentive to: The *Rule of Saint Albert* advises Carmelites that they should take the Apostle Paul as their particular teacher and model (Ch. 20). When you come across references to St. Paul in the formation programme, take particular note.

Helping others to hear the call to holiness

When we hear the call to holiness, and respond to God's presence, we are urged to help others hear the call of God and to perceive his reality around and within us. The call to holiness therefore gives us a mission to reach out to others. As it is put in the *Ratio* document on formation issued for the Carmelite friars in the year 2000:

> We journey within the Church, and with the Church we journey
> throughout the world. Like Elijah we journey side by side with the
> men and women of our time, trying to help them discover God's
> presence in themselves; for the image of God is present in every
> human being, and must be allowed to emerge in complete freedom,
> even when it is darkened by inner contradictions or by injustices
> perpetrated by others. (§2)

Sometimes the injustices in the world and the contradictions within ourselves seem to obscure God's presence and drown out the call to holiness. It is at such times that we have to listen out for – or even become ourselves – the voice 'crying out in the wilderness: "Prepare the way of the Lord, make his paths straight"' (*Isaiah* 40:3; *Mark* 1:3). As God's presence in our lives increases, the noise of the self must decrease, as John the Baptist witnessed: 'He must increase, but I must decrease' (*John* 3:30).

A sculpture of John the Baptist by Michael Clark in the Great Courtyard at Aylesford Priory in Kent, England.

Did you know? St. John the Baptist is a very important figure in Carmelite spirituality. Medieval Carmelites, taking their inspiration from Scripture, saw him as one of the desert prophets spiritually descended from Elijah. John points people to Christ, his kinsman, and is a model of complete self-surrender to God.

Allowing God to increase in us

Through the difficult process of decreasing our self-love and our self-centredness, our will is gradually drawn into communion with God's will. We learn to let go of the things we think will make us happy, and come to find happiness simply in embracing God's plans for us. We learn detachment, and through the purifying flame of God's love everything that would hinder our response to God's call is purged. Self-knowledge and self-acceptance is an essential part of this process. For our relationship with God to grow, humility is required so that we can accept and embrace our strengths and weaknesses.

The liturgical life of the Church can also help us to become more aware of God's presence and his call. The silent presence of God in the sacraments, particularly Reconciliation and the Eucharist, keeps us grounded, nourished, and in right relationship.

Nothing we can do can make God love us more; nothing we can do can make God love us less. We ponder that unchanging love through the challenges of confusion, aridity, ennui and darkness, as what is false and not of Christ is stripped away: 'Carmelites learn to appear before Christ empty-handed, by placing all their love in Christ Jesus, who becomes personally their holiness, their justice, their love and their crown' (*Rule for the Third Order of Carmel* §12).

God's call is an invitation, not a demand

God's call to us is never a shout, because God gives us the freedom to respond or not to his invitation. God invites us into a mature relationship with him: 'Mature relationships are never possessive; they give space to the other; they are committed and free, even to the point of giving one's self.' (*Ratio* §13). The call to holiness is a free initiative by God and it invites an unforced response from the person exercising their free will.

We may be afraid to set out on a journey towards God that we know will not always be easy, but we can be reassured by Christ's promise: 'Come to me, all you that are weary and are carrying heavy burdens, and I will give you rest. Take my yoke upon you, and learn from me; for I am gentle and humble in heart, and you will find rest for your souls. For my yoke is easy, and my burden is light.' (*Matthew* 11:28-30).

Did you know? When a member of the Third Order makes their profession, they are given a large brown scapular with the words "Receive the gentle yoke of Christ, and his burden which is light."

Responding to God's call to holiness: a member of the Third Order receiving his Profession Scapular.

Learning to listen

In order to hear the call of God, we have to cultivate the habit of listening sensitively to his Word. Since its earliest days on Mount Carmel, the Carmelite tradition has encouraged the pondering of God's Word in the Bible through the practice of *Lectio Divina* ('holy reading'). If we are to listen sensitively, our hearts have to be given over entirely to God, as Mary's heart. Mary is esteemed in the Carmelite tradition as embodying the principle of *puritas cordis*, or 'purity of heart'. Her heart was undivided, given over totally to God, and so she could treasure all God's words and 'ponder them in her heart' (*Luke* 2:19).

Did you know? The white mantle or cloak which Carmelite religious wear over their habit is said to symbolise Mary's purity of heart, and the Resurrection of Christ.

By pondering God's word, as our sister and mother Mary did, particularly through our meditation on the Scriptures, we will be better able to perceive those aspects of our life that specially need God's grace.

Mary, and the saints of Carmel, bear witness that God's call to holiness is an invitation to love and trust. We conclude this chapter with the confident words found written on a bookmark in the breviary of St. Teresa of Jesus of Avila:

> *Let nothing disturb you,*
> *let nothing frighten you,*
> *All things are passing;*
> *God never changes.*
> *Patience attains all that it strives for.*
> *The one who has God lacks nothing;*
> *God alone suffices.*

Conclusion: In this second chapter we have reflected on God's call to all people to enter into relationship with God. The Carmelite way of life - a deepening of our baptismal commitment to follow Christ - is one way of responding to that call, and has been lived out over the centuries by many different people in many different ways.

You might like to finish your time of reflection with *The Grace*:

> *The grace of Our Lord Jesus Christ,*
> *and the love of God,*
> *and the fellowship of the Holy Spirit,*
> *be with us all, evermore. Amen.*

In the next chapter we will consider what it means to live out this calling as a Carmelite, seeking to live - as Saint Albert puts it - 'in allegiance to Jesus Christ'.

Ideas for Reflection, Discussion and Action

- Take any paragraph above that has captured your attention and reflect on what it means to you, individually and/or as a community.

- Write down one point that struck you, and bring it to your next community formation meeting, or reflect on it at home in the coming days. Perhaps discuss it with friends.

- Ponder the experiences of those called by God to be holy in the Old and New Testament - what does their life story say to us?

- "You are God's holy people" – what might this mean in your life?

- Where and how do you find solitude with God?

- How would you summarise the chapter and its key points in one or two paragraphs?

- If you attend Carmelite community gatherings, how are they 'holy'?

- "All is grace". What gifts do you perceive in yourself and in others?

- How do you distinguish between 'holiness' and 'being religious'?

- Does your faith invite other people to listen out for God's call to holiness?

- Can you identify at all with the hermits of Mount Carmel? Does their way of life seem very remote to you, or do you share their inspiration and zeal for God?

Recommended Further Resources

You might find some of the following books and articles helpful as extra reading for your own reflection, but remember to pace yourself and that formation is not simply a question of study. Most of the resources listed below will be available in Carmelite libraries and bookshops; find out what resources exist in your local area.

The Constitutions of the Carmelite Order. (Rome: General Curia of the Carmelite Order, 1995). Also available online via www.carmelite.org and other Carmelite websites. The *Constitutions* set out how the Carmelite way of life is to be lived by Carmelites today. Although written by the friars for the friars, any member of the Carmelite Family can draw inspiration from this document.

General Curia of the Carmelite Order, *Ratio Institutionis Vitæ Carmelitanæ – Carmelite Formation: A Journey of Transformation*, (Rome: General Curia of the Carmelite Order, 2000), especially Section One entitled 'Called to follow Christ'.

Documents of Vatican II, especially *Lumen Gentium.*

Pope John Paul II, *Christifideles Laici*. Also available online via the Vatican website www.vatican.va.

Brother Lawrence of the Resurrection, *The Practice of the Presence of God*, translated by Salvatore Sciurba, O.C.D., (Washington, D.C.: ICS Publications, 1994).

John Welch, O.Carm., *The Carmelite Way: An Ancient Path for Today's Pilgrim*, (Leominster: Gracewing, 1996), especially the chapter on 'False selves'.

Remember what was recommended at the end of the first chapter? Ask your Carmelite community leader, formator, or companion, if you have one, what forms of communication – such as journals and websites – exist for the Order in your area. Attending Carmelite retreats, study forums, days of recollection, and so on, can also help your Carmelite formation and help you integrate what you have learned with how you live and love.

Notes and reflections on Chapter 2

Notes and reflections on Chapter 2

In Allegiance to Jesus Christ

Summary: In the first chapter we reflected on formation as a journey towards Christ, and in the second chapter we considered how the Carmelite way of life can help people with a vocation to Carmel respond to the call to holiness that God offers all people. This third chapter is concerned with a phrase from the Carmelite *Formula Vitae* ('Way of Life', the document which became *The Rule of Saint Albert*), that calls us to live 'in allegiance to Jesus Christ'. At the heart of this allegiance is a commitment to the three keystones of Carmelite life: prayer, community, and service. It is important to remember that our allegiance is to *Jesus*, and this leads us to reflect on how we know and serve him. Carmelites cling to the revelation of God through his incarnation and in Scripture. We aim to be followers of Jesus in the most complete sense.

Jesus Christ depicted in stained glass by Richard Joseph King at the Carmelite friary in Faversham, England.

Get prepared: As with previous chapters, you may want to check that you have to hand any practical tools and reference books. The chapter is about how we live in allegiance to Jesus Christ, so why not begin by praying in the words he taught us, the *Our Father*.

The heart of our Carmelite vocation

The call to live '*in obsequio Jesu Christi*', often translated as 'in allegiance to Jesus Christ', occurs early in the document we now call the *Rule of Saint Albert*:

> Albert, called by God's favour to be Patriarch of the Church of Jerusalem, bids health in the Lord and the blessing of the Holy Spirit to his beloved sons in Christ, B. and the other hermits living under obedience to him, who live near the spring on Mount Carmel.
>
> Many and varied are the ways in which our saintly forefathers laid down how everyone, whatever his station or the kind of religious observance he has chosen, should live a life of allegiance to Jesus Christ – how, pure in heart and stout in conscience, he must be unswerving in the service of the Master.

The notion of living *in allegiance to Jesus Christ* is the very heart of our vocation as Christians, and as Carmelites.

Stop and think: What do you understand by the term 'allegiance'?

One definition of allegiance is 'to be in a relation or obligation or subjection to a sovereignty or state'. The first members of the Carmelite Order in thirteenth-century Palestine would have understood allegiance in the terms of feudal society, as being vassals owing an obligation of fidelity to their lord, who in turn would provide for and protect his subjects. Other words for allegiance are 'obedience', 'faithful duty', 'devotion' and 'homage'. Saint Paul, whom Carmelites take as their particular teacher and model, calls us into 'obedience to Christ' (e.g. *2 Corinthians* 10:5).

The 1995 *Constitutions* of the Carmelite friars say that 'Carmelites live their life of allegiance to Christ through a commitment to seek the face of the living God (the contemplative dimension of life) through fraternity and through service (*diakonia*) in the midst of the people.' (§14). We will return later to the Carmelite charism of prayer, community and service.

Stop and reflect: Jesus asked his disciples: 'Who do you say that I am?' (*Matthew* 16:13-15). How would you respond if Jesus asked you this question?

Who is this Jesus to whom we give our allegiance?

The Carmelite way of life is entirely centred on Jesus Christ. Carmel is thus described as a 'Christocentric' spirituality. Even our devotion to the saints of Carmel is ultimately designed to help deepen our relationship with Jesus, our Master and our Brother.

In Carmelite formation great attention is given to nurturing a personal relationship with Jesus Christ, particularly as we encounter Christ in his humanity. What Carmelites say about Jesus Christ's humanity and divinity is not unique in the Christian tradition, but we speak that truth in a distinct way.

In the early Middle Ages Jesus was predominantly depicted in art and in poetry as a king and as a judge, the *Pantocrator*, which emphasised his divinity and cosmic power as the 'warrior' Christ. Later in the Middle Ages a shift occurred. Artists and poets began more frequently to depict Christ's humanity: the infant Jesus in the crib and the suffering Jesus on the Cross. Emphasising the humanity of Christ was a particular concern of the mendicant orders, such as the Carmelites and the Franciscans. They suggested that people meditate on Christ's human life, to imagine themselves to be present at moments such as the birth and the Passion, and thus draw very close to him emotionally. Carmelites reflected on specific episodes in the life of the saviour – his childhood, his ministry, his relationships, his death and resurrection – in order to meet the *real* Jesus in flesh and blood.

Despite the efforts of the friars to emphasise the importance of Jesus' humanity, when Saint Teresa of Jesus entered the Carmelite Order in Avila there was a tendency amongst some Christians to see the humanness of Christ as a stumbling block to appreciating his divine nature. They thought that meditating upon Jesus as a man diminished his identity as God. Teresa recognised that meditating upon Jesus as a man could actually draw her closer to him as God. She realised that whilst God the Father is 'above' us and distinct from us, in the person of his son Jesus, God has been revealed and become 'one like us', and that the Son leads to the Father, making us God's adopted children. Teresa told her sisters to meditate frequently upon Jesus as we encounter him in the Gospels. Since Jesus is 'the image of the invisible God' (*Colossians* 1:15), and the Gospels show God revealed in the humanity of Jesus, Teresa spoke of Jesus in very 'human' terms using images such as 'friend', 'gardener', 'leader', 'beloved', 'teacher', and so on. In Teresa's *Life* and *Interior Castle* she wrote that reflecting on the sacred humanity of Jesus is the surest step for initial and ongoing growth in prayer. Teresa called Jesus 'His Majesty', a friendly king beyond social conventions, and she had a great love for the humanity of Christ which she felt she could easily relate to.

Teresa of Jesus used paintings – such as this depiction of Christ with the Samaritan woman at the well (*John 4*), hanging in the Incarnation Monastery in Avila – to meditate upon Jesus.

All our Carmelite saints had a deep and enduring passion for Jesus Christ. Thérèse of Lisieux used the name of Jesus constantly in her writings as well as in her prayers. John of the Cross saw the whole Christian life as a love affair with Jesus, ending in union or spiritual marriage. All three of these Doctors of the Church spoke of Jesus in intimate terms such as friend, confidante, and lover.

> Each holy soul is like a garland adorned with flowers of virtues and gifts, and all of them together form a garland for the head of Christ, the Bridegroom.
>
> (John of the Cross, *The Spiritual Canticle*, 30.7)

For each of these Carmelite Doctors, allegiance to Jesus Christ was the whole meaning of their existence. Whatever life threw at them they tried never to waver in their devotion and complete dedication to him, knowing that Jesus had trodden the road of joy and suffering before them. As Teresa put it: 'Whoever lives in the presence of so good a friend … who went ahead of us to be the first to suffer, can endure all things. The Lord helps us, strengthens us, and never fails; he is a true friend.' (Teresa of Jesus, *The Book of Her Life*, 22.6).

Stop and think: What terms would you use to describe your relationship with Jesus? You might like to write them down and reflect on them in the coming months.

Carmel is enthralled by the Divine Humanity of Christ

The pursuit of getting to know the *real* Jesus, true God and true man, has influenced Carmelite spirituality over the centuries. Here is what a Carmelite friar, Fr. Patrick Thomas McMahon, has recently written about the Order's attitude to Christ:

> It cannot be sufficiently stressed that Carmelite spirituality is radically Christological and its Christology is focussed on the humanity of the Christ. That is to say that while for other Christians, the approach to God might be found in an emphasis on the Divinity of Christ, for the Carmelite, the visible sign that mediates the Invisible God is the raw humanity of Christ. We never lose sight of the flesh that the Word has become. Before we explore this idea, however, we need to understand that the Christ of Carmel is not the Jesus of history. This is not to say that the pursuit of the Jesus of History is not important to the Carmelite. To the contrary, because Carmel is focussed, to the point of being enraptured, on the humanity of Christ, whatever historical data about the man Jesus of Nazareth can be retrieved by competent scholars is an important contribution to our appreciation of Christ. Our interest, however, is not in obscure details of a life in first-century Syria-Palestine but in the Christ who embodies all that we aspire to as Christians and as Carmelites. We are not first-century Palestinian Jewish males, it is not the object of our spiritual life to become like first-century Palestinians, wearing what they wore or eating what they

ate. For all people of Christian faith, the Christ-Symbol, while never becoming other than the man in whom the Word became incarnate, transcends the historical particularities of Jesus of Nazareth. For us Carmelites, however, the Christ-Symbol never slips the bonds of humanity. The Christ to whom we are drawn is the naked Christ on the cross, the radically impoverished Christ who embodies the poverty of humanity. The Christ to whom we are drawn is the Christ who gave a perfect obedience to the Father, an obedience that manifested his salvific love for all humanity. The Christ to whom we are drawn is the chaste Christ, whose dedication to the kingdom freed him to have a love that had no desire to possess another but to liberate those whom he loved. It is the humanity of Christ that makes him the Symbol, the Sacrament of God. It is in his profound humanity that his Divinity, Divinity itself, is revealed. Carmel has always been enthralled by the divine humanity of Christ.

(Patrick Thomas McMahon, O.Carm., 'Passing on the Tradition')

Stop and think: When you reflect on the Gospel, does Christ come across to you as both human and divine, or more as one or the other?

_____

God made man

Jesus is the perfect union of the human and the divine: God made man. In Carmelite spirituality, Christ is very *real*, and the emphasis on his bodily presence on earth is expressed in many ways by our saints. They perceive him as an actual person we can have a relationship with, a person revealed in the Scriptures, in the Eucharist, and in fellow human beings. Perhaps because of the Order's roots in the Holy Land where Christ lived, the Carmelite approach to Jesus is very incarnational and emphasises his touch in our lives. Our tradition encourages us to identify with Christ as a real person who lived on earth and who leads us to the Father.

This mystery of the Incarnation is written about by Saint Paul:

> Let the same mind be in you that was in Christ Jesus, who, though he was in the form of God, did not regard equality with God as something to be exploited, but emptied himself, taking the form of a slave, being born in human likeness. And being found in human form, he humbled himself and became obedient to the point of death, even death on a cross. Therefore God also highly exalted him and gave him the name that is above every name, so that at the name of Jesus every knee should bend, in heaven and on earth and under the earth, and every tongue should confess that Jesus Christ is Lord, to the glory of God the Father. (*Philippians* 2:6-11).

At a time when some people said that meditating on the humanity of Christ was a hindrance to 'higher' forms of prayer, Teresa saw in Jesus a person who was both God and man, king and servant. For Teresa, meditating on Christ's humanity also meant putting-up with the limitations and weaknesses that we suffer as human beings, and learning to accept God's love for us just how we are.

The *Rule for the Third Order of Carmel* published in 2003 calls us to live in the same spirit as those saints of the Order who have gone before us:

> The Tertiaries' ascent [of Mount Carmel] begins with their act of faith which impels them to accept Jesus and the Easter event as the meaning of their existence. It also makes them want to look to him for guidance and have him, not themselves, as the centre of their lives. Rooted in this way in the love of the merciful God, Lay Carmelites prepare themselves for the ascent of Mount Carmel whose summit is Jesus Christ.' (§17).

Our personal and corporate ascent of Mount Carmel leads us to the summit, Jesus Christ. He alone must become the most important person in our existence.

The crucifixion of Christ depicted in ceramic by Adam Kossowski at the National Shrine of St. Jude in Faversham, England.

Knowing Christ in the Scriptures

We are called to follow the life and teaching of Jesus as recorded in the Bible, and with our brothers and sisters in Carmel to offer the world the Good News of sins forgiven and new life in Christ. This means that we need, as Carmelites, to take up the Word of God every day and ponder it. As Saint Jerome reminds us, 'ignorance of the Scriptures is ignorance of Christ'.

Did you know? Czech Carmelites have propagated meditation on Christ's childhood and kingship through the Infant of Prague statue since the 17th Century. This devotion has spread worldwide, helping people to reflect on Christ's humanity, innocence, gentleness, and heavenly reign.

The statue of the Infant Jesus in the Discalced Carmelite Church of Our Lady of Victories in Prague.

Jesus Christ carrying a Carmelite scapular, depicted in stained glass by Richard Joseph King at the Carmelite friary in Faversham, England.

Mary points us to Christ

In making Jesus central to all we are and do, we imitate Mary the mother of Jesus. She has been called the first disciple. She was open to the Holy Spirit, and obedient to the Father. Her *Fiat* (*Yes: let it be!*) brought Jesus into her womb and into the world. She nursed and nurtured him, followed his way of life, wept over him, and at the foot of the Cross offered him back to the Father. She rejoiced with the disciples in Christ's Resurrection, and with them received the Holy Spirit in a way that enabled the Good News to spread throughout the whole world. We too are called to be open to the Holy Spirit and to allow Christ to be born in us anew each day. Mary was totally focussed on Jesus, and we must be too; our devotion to her is false if it is not ultimately concentrating on her son. Though our Order is privileged to have Mary's name in its title, ours is a completely 'Christocentric' spirituality: everything is focussed on Christ. True Marian devotion leads us to Jesus. Can we obey the words of Mary, his mother and ours: 'Do whatever he tells you' (*John* 2:5)?

Chapter 3 ■ In Allegiance to Jesus Christ

Elijah inspires our allegiance to Christ
We are also called to imitate Elijah, our other great model in Carmel. He, too, was totally dedicated to God and obedient to him even when everyone else was against him. He was called to speak out in God's name against false prophets. He and Moses appeared with Jesus at the moment of the Transfiguration, showing that Christ is the fulfilment of the Law (symbolised by Moses) and the prophets (symbolised by Elijah). His zeal for God was prompted and balanced by his desire for real intimacy with him, as the story of Elijah's encounter with God in the 'sound of sheer silence' (*1 Kings* 19:12) teaches us. We are called to wait on God in silence and solitude, and to listen. We are also called to speak out with courage and conviction in Jesus' name against all that is false and evil in this world, as he did.

An African image of Our Lady of Mount Carmel at the National Shrine of St. Thérèse at Darien, Illinois, U.S.A.

An icon of the Transfiguration at Aylesford Priory in England, written by Solrunn Ness.

In order to live in allegiance to Jesus Christ, we don't need to be experts in Christology (the branch of theology focussed on Jesus). Jesus himself gives us every grace we need to follow him. Blessed John Soreth (1394-1471) was a medieval Prior General of the Carmelite Order who first formally incorporated nuns into Carmel, and laid the foundations for what developed as the Third Order. In his *Exhortation on the Carmelite Rule*, John gave this recommendation for how to live in allegiance to Jesus Christ:

> It is from Christ himself, that you will learn how to love him. Learn to love him tenderly, with all your heart; prudently, with all your soul; fervently, with all your strength. Love him tenderly, so that you will not be seduced away from him; prudently, so that you will not be open to deception; and fervently, so that downheartedness will not draw you away from God's love. May the wisdom of Christ seem sweet to you, so that you are not led away by the glory of the world and the pleasures of the flesh. May Christ, who is the Truth, enlighten you, so that you do not fall prey to the spirit of error and falsehood. May Christ, who is the Strength of God, fortify you when hardships wear you out.
>
> St. Basil says that we are bound to our benefactors by bonds of affection and duty. But what greater gift or favour could we receive than God himself? For, he continues, I experience the ineffable love of God – a love more easily felt than described. Since God has planted the seeds of goodness in us, we can be certain that he is awaiting their fruits.
>
> So let the love of Christ kindle your enthusiasm; let his knowledge be your teacher, and his constancy your strength. May your enthusiasm be fervent, balanced in judgment and invincible, and neither lukewarm nor lacking in discretion. Love the Lord your God with all the affection of which your heart is capable; love him with all the attentiveness and balance of judgment of your soul and reason; love him with such strength that you will not be afraid to die for love of him. May the Lord Jesus seem so sweet and tender to your affections that the sweet enticements of the world hold no attraction for you; may his sweetness conquer their sweetness.

In living in allegiance to Jesus Christ, it is Christ himself who is our greatest teacher and friend.

Supported by the Church in our journey
Additionally we have the sacraments of the Church – places where we encounter Christ – and the prayers of the whole Carmelite Family to support us on our journey towards the summit which is the Lord Jesus. We have the 'whole Christ'; as it says in Scripture, 'He is the head of the body which is the Church' (*Colossians* 1:18). Carmel exists in, and for, the Church, and our fidelity to and participation in both the local and universal Church is important. On her deathbed St. Teresa said: 'Thank God, I die a daughter of the Church'.

All Christians, and especially members of religious families such as ours, are invited to pray the Divine Office (Morning and Evening Prayer), the Prayer of the Church, joining with all those who pray this way, using the very same psalms that Jesus prayed.

On an individual level we Carmelites need to be obedient to the teaching of Jesus by reading, meditating on, and living out the Gospel. The Beatitudes (*Matthew* 5:3-12; *Luke* 6:17, 20-23) show us how to live in an attitude of humility and service. As we give time to *Lectio Divina* and spiritual reading, our knowledge and understanding grows. Knowledge must be nourished with time each day for personal prayer and meditation in silence. There in no specific Carmelite way to do this, and no single 'Carmelite method of prayer'. Rather, Carmelites encourage any form of prayer and meditation that is in harmony with our tradition.

In the Carmelite understanding, prayer is one of the components of a 'contemplative' life. Contemplation is pure gift from God, 'the inflowing of God' as John of the Cross called it in *The Dark Night of the Soul*. Meditation and prayer can predispose us to that gift, as can active service of others and the building up of community. Christ is the perfect model of the 'contemplative'; his life of prayer, service, and community-building shows that the distinction between a life of service and a life of prayer is a false one.

The crucifixion of Jesus, as sketched by John of the Cross, gave a revolutionary perspective on the self-giving of Christ, as seen by the Father.

Did you know? The language of the Carmelites is often bold. When John of the Cross describes the outcome of a contemplative life, he speaks of a transformation so profound that 'we become God'. For John, the attentive listening for God's presence and activity in one's life, and a willingness to be transformed by that love, results in divinisation. (cf. John Welch, *The Carmelite Way*, p. 160).

All is grace

St. Thérèse (whose religious name – 'Sister Thérèse of the Child Jesus and the Holy Face' – shows her devotion to Christ), knew that Jesus' love for her was a free gift that she did not have to earn by her own actions:

Your love has gone before me, it has grown within me, and now it is an abyss whose depths I cannot fathom … O my Jesus, perhaps it is an illusion, but it seems to me that you cannot fill a soul with more love than the love with which you have filled mine … here on earth, I cannot conceive a greater immensity of love than the one which it has pleased you to give me freely, without any merit on my part. (*Story of a Soul*).

Thérèse understood that Jesus himself had called her to a life of allegiance to him, and that this was a pure and unmerited gift from him to her and to all.

Albert's *Rule* and other Carmelite documents encourage our allegiance to Christ

We Carmelites – lay and religious – are called to give allegiance to Christ by our rule of life, the *Rule of Saint Albert* (printed at the front of this book). Our allegiance to Christ can be helped by regularly pondering Saint Albert's words (which are largely Scriptural), digesting them, and living them out in our everyday lives. Teresa of Jesus – whose reform of Carmel was inspired by her reading of the *Rule* – urged her sisters: 'Read the *Rule* every day and never let it slip from your heart'. Why did she do this? Because the *Rule* is centred on Christ, and full of references that point us always back to him.

As well as looking to the *Rule of Saint Albert*, Carmelites can learn much from pondering the modern official documents of the Order which are the collaborative fruit of much scholarship and practical experience of Carmelite life. For example, the 2003 *Rule for the Third Order of Carmel*, which is a set of constitutions elaborating on the *Rule of Saint Albert*, encourage us on the Carmelite journey:

> The ascent of the mountain implies in the first place following Jesus Christ with all one's being, serving him faithfully 'pure in heart and stout in conscience'. The spirit of Jesus should permeate the Carmelites' being to such a degree that they can repeat with St. Paul, 'it is no longer I who live, but it is Christ who lives in me' (*Galatians* 2:20). In this way all their actions take place with 'the Lord's word for accompaniment'. (§18)

Other official writings of the Order summarise very simply our calling to become part of the body of Christ, such as the guide to formation for the friars, published in 2000 under the title *Ratio Institutionis Vitae Carmelitanae* (*RIVC*):

> Carmelites feel drawn to the Lord Jesus Christ and invited to a deep, constant, personal and living relationship with him, to the point of taking on his spiritual features and personality.
>
> As they encounter Christ in prayer, in the Word, and in the Eucharist, as well as in their brothers and sisters and in the events of daily life, Carmelites are transformed and motivated to witness to Christ and to proclaim him throughout the world.

Thus 'the following of Christ is still and will always be for us the fundamental law, marking out the path we have to follow on the way to an ever deeper experience of the love of God.' The commitment to live a deep relationship with Christ and to conform to him is therefore the very core of our formation. (§6)

For centuries it was assumed that only those who lived the 'religious life', in whatever form, could give this wholehearted dedication to Jesus. Not so! The first followers of Jesus were ordinary men and women, invited by Christ to undertake a journey of discovery:

> The next day John [the Baptist] again was standing with two of his disciples, and as he watched Jesus walk by, he exclaimed, 'Look, here is the Lamb of God!' The two disciples heard him say this, and they followed Jesus. When Jesus turned and saw them following, he said to them, 'What are you looking for?' They said to him, 'Rabbi' (which translated means Teacher), 'where are you staying?' He said to them, 'Come and see.' They came and saw where he was staying, and they remained with him that day.
>
> (*John* 1:35-39)

The first disciples of Jesus were ordinary men and women. The first Carmelites were mostly lay people. As Carmelites of the twenty-first century we are called to live out our commitment to Jesus in the world. People from all walks of life, from all nations and cultures, every temperament and status, can give glory to God by simply being who they are, where they are, and living for Jesus Christ in the power of the Holy Spirit, and growing into the people they are called to be.

For those of us who are Lay Carmelites, work and family commitments may take up a considerable amount of our daily life. However, Brother Lawrence of the Resurrection, a simple yet deeply spiritual and wise man, said:

> To be with God it is not necessary to be always in church. We may make a chapel of our hearts whereto to escape from time to time, to talk with him, quietly, humbly and lovingly. Everyone is capable of such close communion with God, some more, some less; he knows what we can do.
>
> (*The Practice of the Presence of God*)

Christ has called us to make a journey

We are all on a journey. It began with the sense that human beings have of the transcendent in their lives, that awoke us to the One who is greater than we are. This revelation comes to us in time and space, in very human situations and encounters. As Christians we sense a call to holiness, coming especially through the revelation of Jesus Christ. This 'universal call to holiness' is indeed for everyone. We (or our parents on our behalf) took the first formal step in responding to this call through our baptism. Our journey has been sustained by our life in the community we call Church, and eventually we discerned the call to follow Jesus Christ in the Carmelite tradition. Jesus meets us where we are, and following his invitation we 'came and saw' (cf. *John* 1:35-39), and decided to accept his call. When we make final profession we Carmelites promise to follow this way for the rest of our lives, by the grace of God. As someone said 'A journey of a thousand miles begins with the first step' and so does our life in Carmel. Sometimes the road is rough and uneven and the going hard. Sometimes there are times of deep joy and contentment. Carmel is both desert and garden. Jesus spent time in both. The end of that journey is to be united to the Holy Trinity forever, in union with Mary and Elijah and all those who have travelled before us. Our destiny is to see God face to face:

> See what love the Father has given us, that we should be called children of God; and that is what we are ... Beloved, we are God's children now; what we will be has not yet been revealed. What we do know is this: when he is revealed, we will be like him, for we will see him as he is.
>
> (*1 John* 3:1-2)

Jesus our brother

Since we are children of God, we can truly relate to Jesus as our brother, 'the firstborn within a large family' (*Romans* 8:29). Jesus our brother offers us hope in saying 'I am the way, the truth and the life' (*John* 14:6). As we commit ourselves to him in love and confidence, he in turn promises to be with us always. He is 'ever interceding for us' (*Romans* 8:34) and will provide for all we need on our journey in Carmel. In turn, we, in obedience and faith, pledge our whole allegiance to him. We know, too, that there is a whole company of the faithful interceding for us in heaven, especially our Carmelite saints.

We finish this chapter with the words of the former Prior General of the Order, Fr. Joseph Chalmers, O.Carm., in his book *In Allegiance to Jesus Christ*:

> So what is this Carmelite way? First of all, as with every Christian spirituality, we are called to be followers of Christ. We keep our eyes fixed on him; he is our leader, our teacher, our brother, our saviour, our Lord. We seek to assimilate his message and to live the Gospel in daily life. The Carmelite way of doing this is to commit ourselves to search for the face of the Living God, which is the contemplative dimension of life, to fraternity, and to the service of other. (p. 15)

Conclusion: In this third chapter we have reflected on the Carmelite vocation to live *in allegiance to Jesus Christ*, and considered the ways in which we come to know and follow Christ, especially in his sacred humanity. We have reflected on the importance of the *Rule of Saint Albert* and other Carmelite documents as helpful sources for inspiration. We have seen how some of the saints of Carmel have lived in allegiance to Jesus Christ, and how we are called to live that same allegiance in the circumstances of our own lives, whatever part of the Carmelite Family we belong to.

You might like to conclude your time of reflection with a moment of silence, or perhaps with this simple prayer:

> *Holy Spirit, I want to live like Jesus – Guide me.*
> *Holy Spirit, I want to pray like Jesus – Teach me.*
> *Holy Spirit, I want to love like Jesus – Fill me.*

In the next chapter we will consider the Carmelite charism as understood in the history, mythology and symbolism of Carmel.

Ideas for Reflection, Discussion and Action

- Take any paragraph above that has captured your attention and reflect on what it means to you, individually and/or as a community. Perhaps discuss it with friends, or at your next community formation meeting. How would you summarise the chapter and its key points in one or two paragraphs?

- How do I live out allegiance to Jesus Christ in my everyday life?

- The Gospel accounts are God speaking to us here and now. Do I love and seek to live the Gospel of Jesus Christ, especially God's word to me each day in the Mass or Divine Office?

- Teresa of Avila said 'Prayer is nothing but an intimate conversation with someone we know loves us'. How do I pray? Do I speak simply and openly to Jesus? Am I afraid of intimacy with him? Do I share with him all my needs and desires? Do I believe that he hears and answers, even if it is not always what I want to hear?

- As we meditate on the passion, death and resurrection of Jesus Christ, let us give thanks for the gift of salvation, and make an offering of ourselves to him in a renewed way.

- St. Teresa loved to meditate on the humanity of Jesus, picking certain images from the Gospel, including the choosing of The Twelve, Jesus in the Garden of Gethsemane, his last words on the Cross, Christ on the road to Emmaus, and his ascension. What episode in Christ's life on earth speaks to you especially at this time? Reflect upon it.

- Using *Lectio Divina*, pray with one of the gospel accounts of the Transfiguration (*Matthew* 17:1-8; *Mark* 9:2-8; *Luke* 9:28-36).

- Jesus' command was for us to love God and to love our neighbour as ourselves. How do we show love for others? How do we nurture a proper love of ourselves that is not self-centred?

- Reflect on this quotation by Fr. John Welch: 'The language of the Carmelites is often bold. When John of the Cross describes the outcome of a contemplative life, he speaks of a transformation so profound that we become God.' (*The Carmelite Way*, p. 160).

In Allegiance to Jesus Christ | Chapter 3

Recommended Further Resources

Most of the resources listed below will be available in Carmelite libraries and bookshops; find out what resources exist in your local area. Extra reading for your own reflection is an important part of formation, but remember that formation is not simply a question of academic achievement.

Johan Bergström-Allen, 'Being Faithful to His Footsteps: Translating the Carmelite Rule for Life Today', *Assumpta* magazine of the British Province of Carmelites, April 2005, pp. 10-19. This article looks at the different ways in which the *Rule of Saint Albert* can be translated, setting the text in its original feudal context (as discussed at the beginning of this chapter). The article can also be found in the collection of reflections and articles on the British Province website: www.carmelite.org

Donald Buggert, O.Carm., 'The Christocentrism of the Carmelite Charism', in *Horizons: Carmelite Spiritual Directory Project*, 2, (Melbourne: Carmelite Communications, 1999) – available in larger Carmelite libraries.

Joseph Chalmers, O.Carm., *In Allegiance to Jesus Christ*, (Rome: Edizioni Carmelitane, 1999). This is an excellent collection of ten conferences on Carmelite life, given whilst Fr. Joseph was Prior General of the Order. It is also available via the website of the British Province of Carmelites: www.carmelite.org

Margaret Dorgan, D.C.M., 'Jesus Christ in Carmelite Prayer', in Keith J. Egan, (ed.), *Carmelite Prayer: A Tradition for the 21st Century*, (New York: Paulist Press, 2003), pp. 82-100.

Guy Gaucher, O.C.D., *The Spiritual Journey of St Thérèse of Lisieux*, (London: Darton, Longman and Todd, 1987).

Living the Carmelite Way: Rule for the Third Order of Carmelites, (Rome: Edizioni Carmelitane, 2003), especially paragraphs 19, 24-27.

Iain Matthew, O.C.D., *The Impact of God: Soundings from St. John of the Cross*, (London: Hodder and Stoughton, 1995). This is one of the most influential English publications about John of the Cross in recent years.

Mary McCormack, O.C.D., *Upon This Mountain: Prayer in the Carmelite Tradition*, (Oxford: Teresian Press, 2009). This is an excellent introduction to prayer in Carmel, emphasising that Carmelite Prayer is not so much a method as an attitude and relationship with Christ.

Patrick Thomas McMahon, O.Carm., 'Passing on the Tradition', in Fernando Millán Romeral (ed.), *In Labore Requies*, Institutum Carmelitanum Textus et Studia Historica Carmelitana Volumen 26, (Rome: Edizioni Carmelitane, 2007).

Vilma Seelaus, O.C.D., 'A Prophetic Journey: Walking in the Footsteps of Jesus the Mystic with Teresa and John', *Carmelite Digest*, Volume 25 Number 1, Spring 2010, pp. 27-46.

Vilma Seelaus, O.C.D., *Teresa, Feminism, and the Humanity of Christ*, available online via the website www.spiritualitytoday.org

Teresa of Avila, *The Book of Her Life*, especially Chapter 22, in *The Collected Works of St. Teresa of Avila*, translated by Kieran Kavanaugh, O.C.D., & Otilio Rodriguez, O.C.D., Volume 1, (Washington, D.C.: I.C.S. Publications, 1976).

John Welch, O.Carm., 'Desiring What God Desires: The Divinization of Our Humanity', in *The Carmelite Way: An Ancient Path for Today's Pilgrim*, (Leominster: Gracewing, 1996), pp. 160-170.

If these are not available in your local Carmelite community library, perhaps now is a good time to start building up a collection of resources.

Notes and reflections on Chapter 3

Notes and reflections on Chapter 3

Carmelite Spirituality and Charism

Summary: Thus far in our formation journey we have considered how the Carmelite way of life can help people to live in allegiance to Jesus Christ. This fourth chapter – based on a text by Fr. John Welch, O.Carm. – explores the essence of the Carmelite charism, that is, the particular gifts that God has given to the Order for the benefit of the Church and the World. Fr. John points out how the inherent restlessness of the human heart finds expression in the language and metaphors of Carmel. We see how the development of the Order – through its mythology as well as its history – has fed and nourished lives of prayer, community and service.

Continuing our journey to the mountain that is Christ.

Get prepared: When you begin, you might like to make notes, perhaps using the blank page at the end of the chapter. You might find it helpful to have a Bible to hand to look up Scripture references, and any other resources you've found useful so far. Prayer is the best way to begin your period of formation study and reflection; it needn't be complicated, as this prayer by Cardinal Newman shows:

O God, I ask not to see... I ask not to know... I ask simply to be used.

The Searching Heart

The Carmelite tradition begins in searching hearts. 'Where have you hidden, beloved?' writes the Carmelite poet and mystic, John of the Cross; 'You fled like the stag after wounding me' (*The Spiritual Canticle*, stanza 1). We fragile humans have an aching heart, a hunger, a desire which we seek to nourish and fulfil. Chasing after our desires in an effort to find happiness and peace, we live fragmented and dissipated lives. We are compulsive about our search, and we compulsively cling to what promises relief.

Our restlessness makes us dissatisfied with our lives. 'I wanted to live ... but I had no one to give me life' wrote the Carmelite reformer Teresa of Avila. For many people, the fire at the core of their lives has been poorly tended. We learn to speak with others' voices and see with others' eyes, to the neglect of our own voice and eyes. We often become puppets and functionaries, wasting away, victimized by over-domestication. John of the Cross complained about his ghostly existence, 'How do you endure O life, not living where you live?' (*Canticle*, 8). We have a vague idea that somehow God is the answer to our longing. At least we have been told so, and we want to believe. But who is this God? Where is this God?

The Carmelite tradition speaks to those who long to be apart, to separate from a smothering existence. The tradition offers the lure of wilderness, mountain retreat, vast expanses of desert. In solitude, in a place apart, we searchers hope to hear our heart's desires more clearly, to reassess life, to dream, to be nourished by hidden springs, to meet the One whom others speak of with great assurance. Those who are drawn by the Carmelite tradition are often pilgrims to places unknown, trusting the testimony of others who have taken the same ancient path.

Did you know? The Church speaks of each religious order or congregation having a 'charism', that is, a particular grace from God for building up God's kingdom. 'Whether extraordinary or simple and humble, charisms are graces of the Holy Spirit which directly or indirectly benefit the Church, ordered as they are to her building up, to the good of humanity and to the needs of the world.' (*Catechism of the Catholic Church*, 799).

The First Carmelites

The first group of people to be called Carmelites made such a journey to a place apart. When history first takes notice of them, they are a group of men living in a valley cut into the ridge of Mount Carmel in Palestine. Arriving just before the turn of the thirteenth century, they had clustered together in caves and huts to live an isolated existence. We do not know their names, nor what precipitated their coming to this remote place. The reasons for such a radical life were probably as numerous as the number of men. Usually such a radical shift in life is not the result of an unpressured decision. In their home countries they may have encountered deep disappointments, personal losses, estrangements of one kind or another. Their decision to come to this mountain may have been the result of years of dealing with slow-healing scars, or gnawing guilt, or the unquenchable desire for a saner life. Perhaps a deep faith drove them to live in a holy place where God might be met more simply. Some of the men may have come from other locales in Palestine which were now unsafe because of Crusader and Moslem warfare. For whatever reason, these westerners from European countries made a pilgrimage to the periphery of society and the Church. They became hermits, living where Jesus lived, knights in service of their liege Lord. They pledged to live in allegiance to Jesus Christ.

We may not know their personal reasons for coming into the *wadi* (valley) on Mount Carmel, but we do know the appeal of Mount Carmel itself. This mountain ridge was the scene of a great contest between prophets of a false god, Baal, and the prophet Elijah, champion of Israel's God, Yahweh. This contest provided an underlying theme for Carmelite spirituality: in which God will we place our trust? On this mountain, and in the confines of this *wadi*, the first Carmelites took their stand on behalf of the God of Elijah and Jesus.

Crusaders and Moslems fought around them for control of the Holy Land. Within the *wadi*, the men put on the armour of faith and opened their hearts and minds to an inner warfare. They opened themselves to the full force of their desires. They reflected on their lives. They ruminated on scripture, rehearsing its lines throughout the day. Silence pervaded the valley, as they kept guard against the demons, and listened for the approach of a merciful God.

This desert existence became a key theme in the Carmelite tradition. Carmelites continually described being led by the Spirit into a desert place. In the desert life is met on stark terms; one either succumbs, or finds hidden sources of new life. When lived in, and carefully tended, the desert became a garden, verdant with life.

Stop and reflect: What are the 'deserts' in your life? Can you see how some have been or are being transformed into 'fertile ground'?

Those who come to the Carmelite tradition are often people who have been thrown into the desert, who have had to face life on stark terms, who found nourishment and support where none was expected, who no longer fear being in an isolated, vulnerable place, and who, on the contrary, want to go deeper into the desert to find the One who awaits them. 'And then we will go on to the high caverns in the rock…' (*Canticle*, 37).

Life with Others

A hermit rarely lives entirely alone. As an early Church writer observed, 'If I live alone, whose feet do I wash? If I live alone, compared with whom am I the least?' Medieval hermits often lived with others in communities of solitude. The early Carmelites clustered together, much as the first Christian communities described in the *Acts of the Apostles*: 'They devoted themselves to the teaching of the apostles and to the communal life, to the breaking of the bread and to the prayers' (*Acts* 2:42). The first Carmelites lived in proximity to one another, and took responsibility for one another. When they asked Albert, the Latin Patriarch of Jerusalem, to draw up their way of life in a *Rule*, the relationships among themselves and with their leader, the prior, played an important part. They are reminded to celebrate the Eucharist together each day in an oratory located in the midst of the cells. They are told to gather regularly on a weekly basis to correct and encourage one another. They are to elect and reverence a prior, and he is to see to the needs of each, according to their individual situations. What they owned, they owned together. These independent hermits were encouraged, eventually, to pray together and take their meals together. The fraternity dimension of Carmel strengthened over the first decades of Carmel's existence.

Stop and think: When you think of 'Carmel', do you associate it primarily with solitude or with community?

This fresco of a Carmelite making profession on Mount Carmel is in the Carmine (Carmelite friary) in Florence. It was painted by a member of the community, Fra Filippo Lippi, c.1422. It is said to be the first depiction of a smile in Renaissance art.

The contemplative prayer of the Carmelites resulted in an ever-renewed appreciation for those with whom they lived and for those whom they served. The human tendency to over-estimate, or under-estimate, one's virtues and gifts is continually corrected through a prayer which undermines such judgments. True prayer continually dislocates the one who prays from a judgmental stance which perceives others as lower or higher, and inserts that person back into the circle of humanity as one equal with the rest. The one who prays begins to see others through God's eyes, and learns to appreciate and value what had previously gone unnoticed.

Teresa of Avila reminded us that Carmelite communities are meant to be communities of friends who are friends with Jesus Christ. Distinctions which create divisions or hierarchies, whether secular or religious, are to be vigorously shunned. Carmelite life undermines any claim to privilege other than the supreme privilege of being loved by God. Teresa challenged her sisters to strive for a high ideal: 'all must be friends, all must be loved, all must be held dear, all must be helped.' Philip Thibault, leader of a 17th-century reform of Carmel, offered as his motto: 'More unity, less perfection!'

Whether one lives in a religious community, or in a marriage, or in another lifestyle, the grand gesture is often not the most difficult. The magnanimous, admirable service of one's neighbours may not be the hardest task. The truly heroic actions often involve accepting and appreciating the small, daily inconveniences necessarily involved in life with others. The most difficult assaults on one's patience, time, energies, forbearance, do not usually come from strangers, but from loved ones, friends, colleagues with whom we share the struggles of daily existence.

The Carmelite nun from Normandy, St. Thérèse of Lisieux, gained many admirers when she identified a little way to God. One may or may not be able to do great things in the world's eyes; most of us live small, undramatic lives. But we can live those lives with love, a love which expresses the truly great drama of God's nearness and care for us. With loving eyes, our mundane existence opens to its depths revealing a dynamic, healing Presence in those lives. The 'allegiance to Jesus Christ', sworn by Carmelites, is lived out among the 'pots and pans' of everyday life.

St. Thérèse as a Carmelite novice in Lisieux Carmel in 1889.

The Prayer of the Carmelites

If Carmel has anything to say to a contemporary world, it is about prayer. All humanity is on a spiritual journey, acknowledged or not. The writings and structures which make up the history of Carmel were the result of attending to the Mystery met deeply within searching lives. Attentiveness to this Presence has been the continual goal of Carmelites. The first Carmelites carried the lines of Scripture in their minds and hearts and regularly rehearsed them, opening themselves to the One whom they met through their mystical reading. They eventually prayed this Scripture together as they took on the obligations of the Divine Office.

Chapter 4 ▪ Carmelite Spirituality and Charism

Stop and reflect: The *Rule of Saint Albert* (printed at the front of this book) encourages the praying of the Divine Office. Is this a form of prayer you are familiar with?

When this community moved to Europe and took its place among the mendicant Orders who were serving the poor and others in the emerging cities, the prayerful beginnings on Mount Carmel were never forgotten. Carmelites understood themselves to be a contemplative Order. Whenever they attempted to define themselves, or re-define themselves when reform was needed, they claimed contemplation as their primary activity and greatest priority.

Did you know? The 'mendicant' orders today include the Carmelites, Augustinians, Dominicans, and Franciscans. The name 'mendicant' means beggar (from the Latin *mendicare*, 'to beg'), because the friars ('brothers') took a vow of poverty and had to gather alms to support themselves, rather than earn an income from monastic lands as monks did. Some mendicant orders were suppressed in the Middle Ages, but the four 'great mendicant orders' listed above survived, as did groups such as the Servites and Trinitarians.

Statue of St. John of the Cross in the Spanish city of Salamanca.

Contemplation commits a person to complete confidence and trust in the love of God which is continually breaking into our lives. The contemplative stance is an openness to that love and the demands it makes on us to change our lives. To be a contemplative is to be a watch in the night for the approach of Mystery. And it is a readiness to be transformed in an engagement with that Mystery.

Carmelites offer no single method or approach to prayer. They learned that prayer was the Spirit's work in us. God speaks us into life, and continually addresses us in our lives, for greater life. Our effort, then, is one of listening. All our words are an attempt to speak the one Word which is God's.

Carmelite saints and writers are compelled to express their experience of prayer. Teresa of Avila described it as conversation with a friend, with one who loves us. Thérèse of Lisieux spoke of simply gazing at God. Lawrence of the Resurrection spoke of an habitual turning of his eyes to God. John of the Cross encouraged a silent attentiveness to where our heart is struggling and experiencing exhaustion. This 'dark night' is an experience of transforming love which first deeply unsettles.

The challenge for Carmelites and other Christians is to become regularly aware of this loving Presence, in good times and in bad. Teresa of Avila pictured her Friend alongside her, or inside her in one of the scenes from the Gospel, especially where He was alone and might welcome her approach. She also spoke of using a book, or flowers, or water to draw her into the presence of God, who is offering friendship, freedom, and greater life.

Elijah and Mary

Carmelites continually drew inspiration from the two great biblical figures of the prophet Elijah and Mary, the Mother of God. In the Bible, Elijah is the solitary figure who is not only true to God and defeats the prophets of the false god, Baal, but he is also the defender of the poor and disenfranchised. He stands with the dispossessed and against the oppressor. In the Order's mythical memory of Elijah, he is also the one who gathers other faithful servants of Yahweh into a community. He settles the community on Mount Carmel where they live a peaceful and just existence. In the Order's myth of its origins this prototypical Carmelite community eventually responds to the preaching of John the Baptist and the first disciples of Christ. The 'Carmelites' become Christian and, in time, form the Order of Carmelites.

A window in the parish church of Lourdes, France, depicts Elijah's 'vision' of Our Lady in the cloud that arose from the sea.

The Order remembers that Elijah foresaw the coming of Mary, the spotless virgin whose faithfulness would lead to the birth of the long-awaited Messiah. Carmelites remember Elijah and Mary as the first man and the first woman to take a vow of virginity. This 'purity of heart' meant they were free from the enslavement of idols, and fertile ground for the seed of the Spirit.

Did you know? The 'purity of heart' of Mary and the zeal of Elijah inspired the names of the two Carmelite provinces in North America: the New York Province of St. Elias (Elijah), and the Province of the Most Pure Heart of Mary (*Purisima Cordis Mariae*, often known as the PCM or Chicago Province).

The first chapel in the *wadi* on Mount Carmel was dedicated to Mary. The Carmelites became known as the Brothers of Our Lady of Mount Carmel. Mary is the contemplative who ponders in her heart. She is the disciple who follows her Son, the Wisdom of God. Her surrender to the working of God's Spirit in her life is captured in her *Magnificat*, a song of praise and thanksgiving for the mercy of God which raises the lowly of the earth. The scapular, a brown cloth worn over the shoulders, is a traditional Carmelite expression of devotion to Mary and, in imitation of her, our surrender to God's salvific plan.

The descent of the Holy Spirit upon Mary and the Apostles, depicted in ceramic by Adam Kossowski on the Rosary Way at Aylesford Carmelite Priory in Kent, England.

Serving God's People

Carmelites seek the face of the living God not only in prayer and fraternity, but also in service. The Carmelites' primary pledge is 'allegiance to Jesus Christ'. This allegiance, then, takes the form of continuing the mission of Christ to tell of the nearness of God's love and to celebrate the inestimable worth of every human being. Carmel has taken seriously the Gospel imperative: go to the ends of the earth and there proclaim the last are first. This mission has been expressed in innumerable pastoral situations though the centuries of Carmel's existence. Even on Mount Carmel men would occasionally leave the *wadi* to preach in adjacent areas. In Europe they were called to take their place with the mendicant communities who were ministering in various levels of society, teaching in universities, and crossing national boundaries in missionary efforts.

Did you know? All 'branches' of the Carmelite Family today exercise diverse ministries, including: teaching, health care, preaching, political campaigning, hospitality, study, drug-rehabilitation, prison chaplaincy, counselling, well-digging, youth work, liturgical life, publishing, schools, librarianship, child-care, administration, caretaking, hospital chaplaincy, university chaplaincy, manufacturing, ecumenical outreach, episcopacy, retreat direction… the list in endless!

No ministry has been judged incompatible with Carmel's charism. But any ministry is suspect if not anchored in a contemplative openness to that which God is bringing about. In particular, it is the contemplative dimension of Carmel which impels the community to pay special attention to the 'little ones' of the world, those left out of the world's attention and care. Contemplation leads one into an awareness of one's own poverty of spirit and the need to wait on God. From this self-knowledge it is possible to be in solidarity with and have concern for all who have to wait in hope for God's mercy and compassion. Contemplative prayer should be the deepest source of concern for the poor, the oppressed, and the marginalized of our world.

Did you know? Writing to the Carmelite friars on 8th September 2001, Pope John Paul II addressed the theme of their General Chapter, 'Carmel: the Journey continues'… 'The Journey continues' Yes, my brothers indeed it does in the world today. You are called to re-read your rich spiritual inheritance in the light of today's challenges so that 'the joys, the hopes, the sadnesses and the anguish of humanity today, of the poor and above all of those who suffer' are 'the joys and the hopes, the sadnesses and the anguish of Christ's disciples,' (*Gaudium et spes*, n. 1) and in a special way of every Carmelite.

The Mythical Land of Carmel

From the very beginning Carmelites had to live within tensions. They may have preferred to stay in their quiet, isolated valley, but it was impossible. They wound up in the middle of the mendicant movement in Europe, but describing their life as though they were still living in the valley. Nicholas the Frenchman, an early general of the Order, admonished them to abandon the noisy, dirty city streets where they were ministering, and retreat to the quiet beauty of pastoral settings for contemplative prayer. This admonition, too, was impossible to follow.

Carmelites began to understand themselves as inhabitants of two homelands. One homeland was where they lived in community and ministered among God's people. The other homeland became a metaphorical place where God pursued humanity in love. Carmelites lived on the border, and carried dual citizenship.

The initial threads of Carmel's story were woven from the memory of Mount Carmel itself and the biblical imagery which surrounded the mountain. In that late 14th-century foundational myth of Carmel, *The Ten Books on the Way of Life and Great Deeds of the Carmelites* (also known as *The Institution of the First Monks*), Carmel's story was no longer a story confined by historical conditions and a specific time. It was a mythic story, truer than a mere recitation of facts. It traced its outlines back to the source of all stories, a plot in God's mind. It was a story told, as it were, through God's eyes. And so the story of Carmel stretched back into pre-Christian history where the community witnessed the emergence of the one true God of Israel. Carmel's story also projects forward to a future time on the mountain when God's peace will reign, men and women will live justly, and all will gather at an eschatological banquet. Later Carmelites confirmed the essential truth of the vision: 'My beloved is the mountain,' wrote John of the Cross, 'the supper that refreshes, and deepens love' (*Canticle*, 14).

To 'enter Carmel' is not simply a matter of entering a building, joining a community, and taking on a ministry, whether of prayer or apostolic mission. It is that, certainly, but 'entering Carmel' is also entering a drama playing out deep within every human life. That drama of the human spirit encountered by God's Spirit is essentially inexpressible. Carmelites are explorers of an inner place of intimacy with God, a fine point of the human spirit where it is addressed by Mystery.

A powerful experience of God's love, known as the 'Transverberation' of St. Teresa, has been depicted in marble by the sculptor Bernini, at the Discalced Carmelite Church of Santa Maria della Vittoria in Rome.

Carmel honours that pristine, privileged relationship between creature and Creator. Carmelite mystics have used bridal imagery to capture the intimacy of this encounter. Some Carmelites told of visions and voices which they experienced as momentary forms of grace. Sometimes, even their bodies reverberated to the impact of God's love.

The Carmelite imagination describes a landscape whose topography has become a primordial wording of the soul's adventure. Carmel is a land of paradox, exposing the Carmelite to living within tension. It is a land of desert and garden, of heat and cold, of dark and light, of hunger and abundance. It is a place of God's absence which surprisingly reveals a compassionate presence. It is a place of suffering, a suffering which is healed by the same flame that hurts. It is a starless, trackless space in which the pilgrim is somehow led unerringly home. The pilgrim plunges more deeply into an empty vastness, and arrives at the heart of the world. The world, seemingly left far behind, becomes fully present and truly known for the first time. The 'cell' of the Carmelite becomes more and more spacious.

This tradition gives words and images to the hope that is constitutive of being human. 'The soul's centre is God' wrote John of the Cross. Carmelite saints and mystics experienced transformation in engagement with that Centre. They thought they were seeking God, but learned that the Centre had been approaching them all along. Humanity's story is not the story of our search for God, but of God's pursuit of us in love. Carmel's saints concluded that everything is a grace. The love they encountered deep within their searching lives invited them more deeply into their own life, gave them freedom from their idols, drew them into a divinizing union, and propelled them outward in service of their brothers and sisters.

Did you know? Over the centuries the Carmelite Order has drawn up *Constitutions* to help interpret the *Rule of Saint Albert* for contemporary circumstances. They offer not only practical guidelines for how the friars should live, but are an aid to reflecting on the very essence of the Carmelite way of life. The *Constitutions* contain wisdom applicable to every branch of the Carmelite Family.

The Constitutions

The 1995 *Constitutions* of the Carmelite Order are a rather remarkable testimony to 800 years of wrestling with identity, values, and world view. Battered by the winds of history, and at times in danger of extinction, this community has not only survived but now finds itself energized to live into the next phase of its story. Time has only deepened Carmel's ability to identify its core values and find an expression satisfying not only to Carmelites but perhaps to all who look to this tradition for help on life's journey.

Conclusion: In this fourth chapter we have reflected on Carmelite spirituality and the Order's charism with particular reference to some of Carmel's enduring themes and recurring images. We have seen how the Order's spirituality has been influenced by its historical development and geographical location. Prayer has been highlighted as central to the Carmelite project, as well as service of God's people, and the bringing together of solitaries into a community. 'Entering Carmel' is essentially entering a drama that is playing out deep within every human life, which is why Carmel's expression of its core values speaks so powerfully to many people outside the formal structures of the Order. All humanity is on a journey, and Carmel helps us to orientate our way.

You might like to conclude your time of reflection and study with a moment of prayer, perhaps in silence, or perhaps using these words:

> *Lord Jesus Christ, you call all of us to be a royal priesthood.*
> *Help all Carmelites to work – in whatever way is pleasing to you –*
> *to build up the Kingdom of Heaven. Amen.*

In the next chapter we will consider the special place that Mary, Our Lady, holds within the Carmelite Family.

Ideas for Reflection, Discussion and Action

- Reflect – either individually or as a community – on any passage in this chapter that has particularly sparked your imagination. Perhaps discuss it with friends, or at your next community formation meeting.

- The Carmelite tradition expresses Christian truths in an often unique way. What values, images, or language from the tradition draws your heart to Carmel?

- Can you perceive the Carmelite spirit in people who are not Carmelite in name?

- To tread the Carmelite road is a privilege and responsibility. Can you make a deeper commitment to playing your part in its story?

- Look again at the section 'Life with others'. What elements of the first Christian community and the first Carmelite community are relevant and practical to you today? If you are part of a Carmelite community, how does it compare with the description of the first Carmelite community on Mount Carmel?

- The Carmelite journey calls for the flourishing of the human person. How do we come to appreciate our worth in God's eyes? What support might we need – spiritual, psychological, social – on our journey of transformation?

- Use the internet to learn about the great diversity of Carmelite ministries lived out around the world. Useful sites include:

    - British Province of Carmelites: www.carmelite.org
    - General Curia of the Carmelite Order: www.ocarm.org
    - The OCarm-OCD web portal: www.ocarm-ocd.org
    - Irish Province of Carmelites: www.carmelites.ie
    - PCM Province of Carmelites: www.carmelnet.org
    - St. Elias Province of Carmelites: www.carmelites.com
    - Australia & Timor Lester Province of Carmelites: www.carmelites.org.au
    - International Carmelite Index: www.carmelites.info
    - General Curia of the Discalced Carmelite Order: www.discalcedcarmel.com

Recommended Further Resources

There are many books on the spirituality and charism of Carmel, and only a small selection is listed below. The list of resources, particularly those relating to the 1995 *Constitutions*, should be easily found in most good Carmelite libraries, and a number of them can also be found on the internet.

Joseph Chalmers, O.Carm., 'The fundamental elements of Carmelite spirituality', in *In Allegiance to Jesus Christ*, (Rome: Edizioni Carmelitane, 1999), pp. 15-23.

Joseph Chalmers, O.Carm., 'Silent Prayer', in *Mary the Contemplative*, (Rome: Edizioni Carmelitane, 2001), pp. 68-78.

Joseph Chalmers, 'A contemplative community in the midst of the people', in *In Allegiance to Jesus Christ*, (Rome: Edizioni Carmelitane, 1999).

The Constitutions of the Carmelite Order, (Rome: Curia of the Carmelite Order, 1995).

Journeying with Carmel: Extracts from the 1995 Carmelite Constitutions, (Middle Park, Victoria: Carmelite Communications, 1997).

Kevin Culligan & Regis Jordan, (eds.), *Carmel and Contemplation: Transforming Human Consciousness*, Carmelite Studies VIII, (Washington D.C.: I.C.S. Publications, 2000).

Janetze Hart, T.O.C., 'Carmel: from the Desert to the Garden', *Carmel in the World*, Volume XLVIII Number 2, 2009, pp. 85-89.

Bernard McGinn, 'The Role of the Carmelites in the History of Western Mysticism', in Kevin Culligan, O.C.D., & Regis Jordan, O.C.D., (eds.), *Carmel and Contemplation: Transforming Human Consciousness*, Carmelite Studies 8, (Washington, D.C.: I.C.S. Publications, 2000), pp. 25-50.

Wilfrid McGreal, O.Carm., *At the Fountain of Elijah: the Carmelite Tradition* (London: Darton, Longman and Todd, 1999).

Elizabeth Ruth Obbard, 'Land of Israel – Land of Carmel', in *Land of Carmel*, (Leominster: Gracewing, 1999), pp. 13-21.

Felip Ribot, O.Carm., *The Ten Books on the Way of Life and Great Deeds of the Carmelites (including The Book of the First Monks)*, translated by Richard Copsey, O.Carm., (Faversham: Saint Albert's Press, 2005).

Peter Slattery, O.Carm., *The Springs of Carmel: An Introduction to Carmelite Spirituality*, (New York: Alba House, 1991).

John Welch, O.Carm., 'The Flaming Arrow: An Early Plea to Return to the Desert', in *The Carmelite Way: An Ancient Path for Today's Pilgrim*, (Leominster: Gracewing, 1996), pp. 27-38.

John Welch, O.Carm., 'The Carmelite Tradition', in *Journeying with Carmel: Extracts from the 1995 Carmelite Constitutions*, (Middle Park, Victoria: Carmelite Communications, 1997), pp. 73-80. Available online at www.carmelite.org

Notes and reflections on Chapter 4

CHAPTER 5

Mary

Summary: The Blessed Virgin Mary, Our Lady, is considered one of the foundational figures of the Carmelite Family, and Mother and Sister of all Carmelites. In this chapter we will explore Mary's role in the history and development of the Order, her part in Scripture as the woman of prayer who leads us to Christ, and her place in the spiritual landscape of Carmel as 'Lady of the Place'.

Statue of Our Lady at the Carmelite Priory at Aylesford in England.

Get prepared: As no doubt you know by now, your reading might profit from you having reference texts to hand, such as the Bible, the *Rule of Saint Albert* (printed at the front of this book), the 2003 *Rule for the Third Order of Carmel*, the 1995 *Constitutions of the Carmelite Friars*, as well as materials to take notes with. You don't have to read the whole text of the chapter at once if you would find it easier to break it into sections. Why not begin your period of formation study and reflection with a prayer to Our Lady such as the *Hail Mary* or the *Memorare*.

Mary: Pointing us to Christ

The sacred humanity of Jesus, fully God and fully man, is the perfect model for all human beings. Most fully human when we most resemble Jesus, we are intended to reach the full maturity of sharing in the fullness of Christ (cf. *Ephesians* 4:13). A good way to respond to Jesus' invitation to share his life is to follow the example of his mother Mary, for she sought always to know and to do the will of God.

Stop and think: What role, if any, has Mary played in your faith journey thus far?

The *Rule for the Third Order of Carmel* (*RTOC*) tells us that 'Mary is a singular and eminent member of the Church' (§34). In giving birth to Jesus, Mary is unique, but as the 'woman of faith' she is for every Christian – and therefore every Carmelite – the model of perfect discipleship. Mary is blessed because she heard the word of God and kept it (cf. *Luke* 11:28), the supreme example of how to respond to God's grace and surrender to God's will.

How do Carmelites come to know Mary?

Carmelites look to Mary in the Bible – 'Miriam of Nazareth' – as the authentic guide of how to follow Christ. Our Carmelite tradition reminds us that Mary was the first teacher of Jesus, and the first follower, and she accompanies us on our journey towards our heavenly home. Papal documents since the Second Vatican Council have also helped us to appreciate the role of Mary in the life of Jesus, such as Paul VI's *Marialis Cultus* ('To Honour Mary', 1974), and John Paul II's *Redemptoris Mater* ('Mother of the Redeemer', 1987).

Did you know? Carmelites believe that authentic devotion to Mary should not detract from making Christ central in our lives. They therefore treat with caution any description of Mary that does not derive from the Scriptures or the ancient traditions of the Church. To be authentic, visions of Mary should simply call people back to the Gospel.

Stop and think: Mary is regarded as the Patron of the Carmelite Order. What do you understand by the notion of 'patronage'? How does this apply to Mary?

Mary: the 'Lady of the Place'

One of the special titles Carmelites give to Mary is the 'Lady of the Place'. This term takes us right back to the beginnings of our tradition. The first brothers gathered on Mount Carmel round a small chapel dedicated to Mary; in the spirit of medieval feudal society they devoted themselves to the service of their 'Lady' patroness, with the presence of Jesus Christ, their liege Lord, at the centre of their lives in the Eucharist. Ever since, Carmelites have dedicated themselves to Our Lady, and Jesus has been the focus of prayer and contemplation at the heart of every Carmelite community, whether in the religious life, in the various active congregations, or in gatherings of tertiaries.

Stop and reread: You might like at this point to remind yourself of the idea of living 'in allegiance to Jesus Christ' as we considered in Chapter 3.

'The Place' is a Hebrew way of referring to God. Mary points us to the place where God is. The title 'Lady of the Place' reminds us that her son, Emmanuel, is 'God with us', wherever we are: 'My word is very near you; it is already in your mouth and in your heart, so that you can put it into practice' (*Deuteronomy* 30:14).

Did you know? Although the Carmelite *Rule of Saint Albert* makes no explicit mention of Mary, we know from pilgrim accounts that there was a chapel on Carmel dedicated to Mary. The name of Mary in the title of the Order first appeared officially in the 1240s. Since medieval Carmelites claimed that the Order was founded in honour of Mary, commentators such as John Baconthorpe explained that she was not referred to in the *Rule* because she was herself the very embodiment of the *Rule*.

Stop and read from Scripture: Read the episode from the Elijah story in *1 Kings* 18:42-44.

_____

Mary: the 'little cloud'

In reading the account of the little cloud which Elijah saw rising from the sea (*1 Kings* 18:42-44), Carmelites have interpreted the coming of rain after prolonged drought as a foreshadowing of Mary. The most famous example of this is in Felip Ribot's medieval masterpiece *The Ten Books on the Way of Life and Great Deeds of the Carmelites* (sometimes known as *The Book of the First Monks*):

> When the servant of Elijah saw a modest cloud rising from the sea, God revealed to Elijah that a certain infant, that is, the blessed Mary, was symbolised by that cloud, and like that cloud, through her modest humility she would be born of sinful human nature, represented by the sea. This infant, already at her birth would be free from all stain of sin, just as that cloud was born from the bitter sea but without any bitterness.
>
> (Richard Copsey's translation of *The Ten Books*, p. 82).

This interpretation of the episode has become part of Carmelite tradition regarding Mary. As Elizabeth Ruth Obbard explains: 'Mary, as Christ-bearer, was the one carrying the water of life. She brings healing and refreshment to the parched earth, just as she is also the earth which receives the rain. There is in Mary that rhythm of giving and receiving, of fullness and emptiness, which makes her so truly woman. In pouring herself out she receives life anew.' (*Land of Carmel*, p. 84).

Elijah perceiving Mary in the cloud in a painting at Saint Albert's International Centre in Rome, one of the Order's leading institutes for research into Carmelite history and spirituality.

The Holy Spirit will overshadow you

Humanity's time of dryness – its separation from God – came to an end when the angel Gabriel announced to Mary that she would be overshadowed by the Holy Spirit (*Luke* 1:35). The bright cloud of God's presence, the 'shekinah', had surrounded the Ark of the Old Covenant. Now Mary, the Ark of the New Covenant, receives Jesus.

That great teacher and model for Carmelites, Saint Paul, reminds us that we too are temples of the Holy Spirit (*1 Corinthians* 6:19). In our baptism, the Holy Trinity – Father, Son and Holy Spirit – makes a dwelling within us (cf. *John* 14:23). In the Eucharist too, Jesus comes to dwell within us. Like Mary, Carmelites pray to be overshadowed by the Holy Spirit, so that we too may be, as it were, another incarnation of the Word in which Jesus continues to live out his mystery. Inspired by Mary, the Carmelite nun Blessed Elizabeth of the Trinity (1880-1906) realised that our vocation is to become a home in which God lives, as she wrote in her celebrated *Prayer to the Trinity*:

O my God, Trinity whom I adore; help me to forget myself entirely that I may be established in You as still and as peaceful as if my soul were already in eternity. May nothing trouble my peace or make me leave You, O my Unchanging One, but may each minute carry me further into the depths of Your mystery. Give peace to my soul; make it Your heaven, Your beloved dwelling and Your resting place. May I never leave You there alone but be wholly present, my faith wholly vigilant, wholly adoring, and wholly surrendered to Your creative Action.

Mary reveals to us our vocation of union with God, of which the Carmelite martyr Blessed Titus Brandsma said in 1936:

From all eternity God has chosen us, has loved us and has predestined us to live in intimate union with Him. God desires to live in us through grace. This union is sublime, like that of the divine maternity of Our Lady. Rightfully, we also can be called 'God bearers'. God sends the angel also to us to ask us continually to open our hearts to the light of the world in order to bear it like a lantern. We too must receive God in our hearts; we must carry God within our hearts, nourish him and allow him to grow in us in such a way that he will be born of us and live with us as God-with-us, Emmanuel.

(Quoted in *Lady of the Place*, p. 90).

We come to know Jesus through the pages of sacred Scripture, through the sacraments (especially the Eucharist), the teachings of the Church, the writings and example of the saints, through prayer, and through meeting with other Christians. The indwelling of the Holy Spirit opens up to us the treasures of all these things.

Just as Mary's first act after the incarnation of Jesus within her womb was to visit her cousin Elizabeth – which shows that prayerfulness leads to the service of others – so Carmelites are impelled, as they experience the presence of Christ within them, to share Jesus with others. The active apostolate expressed in different ways within the Carmelite Family is a direct result of our prayerful waiting upon, and continual receiving of, the Holy Spirit. We are to be his presence in the world. It is this realisation that inspired the words attributed to St. Teresa of Jesus (of Avila):

> Christ has no body now but yours.
> No hands, no feet on earth but yours.
> Yours are the eyes through which he looks
>   with compassion on this world.
> Christ has no body now on earth but yours.

Did you know? One of the oldest known images of Mary venerated by Carmelites is an icon in the basilica of the 'Carmine Maggiore' (Great Carmel) in the Italian city of Naples. Known as *La Bruna* ('the dark woman') it was probably painted in thirteenth-century Siena, though legend says it was painted by St. Luke and taken to Naples by the hermits fleeing Mount Carmel. Associated with miracles in the year 1500, the icon is still the focus of pilgrims' devotion to this day. This beautiful icon highlights the tenderness of Mary the mother.

La Bruna – probably the best known image of Our Lady within the Carmelite Family.

Pondering all these things

Scripture tells us that Mary was a contemplative woman who pondered in her heart the action of God in her life (*Luke* 1:29, 2:19, 2:51). Mary's whole life was like a form of *Lectio Divina*, meditating on God's Word. With Mary, Carmelites love to ponder the mysteries of Christ's life so that they can know him and imitate him. The sacred humanity of Jesus is our doorway to the divine. Mary shows us how to live in the presence of our brother and saviour Jesus Christ, and invites us to build up a personal relationship not only with her but primarily with him. St. Teresa said in her *Autobiography*: 'Whoever lives in the presence of so good a friend and excellent a leader as is Jesus Christ can endure all things… he is a true friend. And I see clearly that God desires that if we are going to please him and receive his great favours this must come about through the most sacred humanity of Christ, in whom he takes his delight.' (Ch. 22).

Woman of prayer

Meeting with her cousin Elizabeth, Mary sings her *Magnificat* (*Luke* 1:46-55), a text which is imbued with Scripture. With Mary, we learn how to listen to the Word of God, pondering God's wisdom in our hearts (cf. *Luke* 2:19; 2:51), as did all the great Carmelite spiritual writers.

Did you know? The *Magnificat* prayer takes its name from the first word of the Latin translation: 'to magnify' meaning 'to declare the greatness' of the Lord. In this prayer, Mary – a woman of the Hebrew scriptures – echoes the prayer of Hannah in *1 Samuel* 2:1-10.

Mary the Contemplative

Mary was a woman who built up community, but who also spent time in solitary prayer. The *Rule of Saint Albert* exhorts each of us Carmelites 'to stay in their own cell or nearby, pondering the Lord's law day and night and keeping watch at their prayers'. Blessed Jean Soreth, a medieval Prior General of the Order, wrote a *Commentary* or *Exhortation on the Carmelite Rule*, in which he speaks of the importance of the cell for a Carmelite: 'The cell is a holy land and a holy place, where God and his servant exchange their confidences as a friend with a friend. It is here, oftentimes, that

Two Carmelite devotees of Our Lady: John Soreth and Titus Brandsma, depicted by Adam Kossowski at Aylesford Priory.

the soul is caught up in union with God, as a bride is joined to her husband; it is here that heaven touches earth, and the divine is united with the human.'

As Carmelites living today, our cell is that 'inner room' in the heart which, as Elizabeth of the Trinity tells us, is one in which we can dwell at all times and encounter Jesus, whatever our outward preoccupations. Blessed Elizabeth wanted to be 'another Bethany', the home that Jesus loves, and the place where he could be at rest as once he was in the home of Mary, Martha and Lazarus.

A valuable aid to pondering on the life of Jesus throughout the day, within the inner cell of our hearts, is the rosary. This Marian prayer developed in the Dominican tradition. Though it is not required for Carmelites to pray it, many do so because it can aid their efforts to focus on Christ, and since the mysteries of the rosary are mostly episodes from Scripture they resonate with the Carmelites' love of the Bible. We can pray it as we work, as we walk to and from the shops, while waiting in a queue. In reciting the rosary we follow Jesus through the eyes of Mary, from his conception, through his public ministry, passion, and death, to his resurrection and triumph in heaven. By it, we can be reminded of the sanctity of our daily work and life as people of the Resurrection. As it says in the *Rule for the Third Order of Carmel*: 'Gathered by Mary, like the disciples, in the upper room, lay Carmelites come together to praise the Lord in the mysteries of his life and that of his mother: the devout practice of the Rosary can become an inexhaustible source of genuine spirituality which nourishes daily life.' (§41)

The Assumption and Coronation of Mary as Queen of Heaven, depicted in ceramic by Adam Kossowski on the Rosary Way at Aylesford Carmelite Priory in Kent.

Did you know? Carmelites have led the way in developing 'Mariology', the theological study of Mary. Medieval Carmelites in England – whose province was dedicated, as the British Province is now, to the Assumption of Mary – pioneered the belief in Mary's Immaculate Conception. It was also in England that the patronal feast of the Order, the solemnity of Our Lady of Mount Carmel (16th July) first developed.

One of the Order's great Mariologists in recent times, Fr. Christopher O'Donnell, O.Carm., writes: *We do not need more dogmas about Mary, or necessarily more prayers, celebrations or titles. We can never, however, sufficiently praise God for the wonders of his grace and love in the Mother of his Son. We can never thank her enough for her motherly care for us. We can never love her enough. As we think of her gentle presence, we are only beginning our future life in which with her we will eternally praise the Trinity.*

Mary: Queen and Beauty of Carmel

One of the ancient titles given to Mary by the Carmelite Order is 'Beauty of Carmel'. Mary is deemed to be beautiful because she has been filled with the grace of the Creator. Reading the biblical descriptions of Mount Carmel, Carmelites have interpreted the mountain's splendour as an allegory of Mary's holiness:

> The wilderness and the dry land shall be glad, the desert shall rejoice and blossom; like the crocus it shall blossom abundantly, and rejoice with joy and singing. The glory of Lebanon shall be given to it, the majesty of Carmel and Sharon. They shall see the glory of the Lord, the majesty of our God.
> (*Isaiah* 35:1-2).

Mary was one of the *anawim*, a poor person looking to God for deliverance. Yet in keeping with the feudal approach to Mary as patron and Lady of the Place, Carmelites have revered Mary as Queen, the Woman of the Apocalypse (*Revelation* 12:1) clothed in the sun with a crown of twelve stars on her head. Her crown is the sign of the triumph of God's grace in Mary, a glory awaiting all those baptised into the 'royal priesthood' who allow God's grace to triumph in them by overcoming the sinfulness human nature is prone to. We – like Mary – share in Christ's offices of prophet, priest and king (cf. *RTOC* 27), but Jesus reminds us that his kingdom is a kingship of service, not of this world.

Mary, Woman of the Apocalypse, depicted in glass by Richard Joseph King at the National Shrine of St. Jude at Faversham in England, cared for by the Carmelite friars.

Did you know? Many people have made links between the spirituality of Carmel, and the Marian apparitions at Fatima (where Mary is said to have appeared as Our Lady of Mount Carmel), and Lourdes (where the final vision of Mary took place on the Feast of Our Lady of Mount Carmel).

'On your right stands the Queen'

Jesus is our supreme advocate (*1 John* 2:1) whose self-sacrifice is the new covenant that has reconciled us with the Father. In approaching Jesus as advocate, Christians have always sought the prayers and intercessions of those saints who dwell on earth, and those who dwell in his presence in heaven. Honouring Mary and praying to her does not bypass our relationship with Christ, but acknowledges our relationship with her in the communion of saints. Just as Mary interceded with Jesus at the wedding feast in Cana (*John* 2:1-12), so she brings our needs to him today. We, too, are called by our Carmelite vocation to intercede for our brothers and sisters throughout life, in time and eternity.

Mary: Mother and Sister

Since the early Church Mary has been revered not only as Mother of God (*Theotokos*, the God-bearer), but by extension as mother of all humanity. The *Flos Carmeli* is an ancient Carmelite antiphon to Our Lady that invokes her as mother and incorporates other Marian titles:

Flos Carmeli	Flower of Carmel
Vitis florigera	Tall vine, blossom-laden
Splendor caeli	Splendour of heaven
Virgo puerpera	Child-bearing yet maiden
Singularis!	None equals thee!
Mater mitis	Mother so tender
Sed viri nescia	Whom no man didst know
Carmelitis	On Carmel's children
Da privilegia	Thy favour bestow.
Stella Maris!	Star of the sea!

St. Thérèse of Lisieux said that Mary was 'more mother than queen', at a time when Mary's regal power was often emphasised more than her maternal love. Mary does not leave us alone in our walk of faith, because she too has been a pilgrim on the journey to God. We are her sons and daughters, her brothers and sisters, given to her by Jesus as he hung upon the Cross, in the person of his beloved disciple John (*John* 19:25-27). With John, we accept Mary into our home.

The official title of the Carmelite Order is *The Brothers of the Blessed Virgin Mary of Mount Carmel*. This means that Mary is our sister, as well as our mother, and together we are children of God. To refer to Mary as our sister is not to 'reduce her to our level', but rather raises us to our proper dignity as God's beloved children.

Stop and ponder: How do you feel about referring to Mary as your sister?

The Symbolism of Mary in the Carmelite Tradition

Traditional depictions of Our Lady of Mount Carmel show Mary wearing the brown habit and white cloak of the Carmelite Order, since she is our patron, and the perfect model of how to be Carmelite. Our Lady of Mount Carmel is nearly always shown in artwork holding the infant Jesus, presenting Christ to the world and saying 'Do whatever he tells you' (*John 2:5*).

Depictions of Our Lady of Mount Carmel in different cultures (left-right): Gibraltar Catholic Cathedral; Japan; the Congo; Wentworthville in Sydney, Australia.

Images of Our Lady of Mount Carmel also usually show her holding a cloth known as the Brown Scapular. The scapular is part of a monastic habit, and is regarded as a symbol of Mary's love and protection towards the Carmelite Family, and the Family's service of Mary. Many depictions of Our Lady of Mount Carmel show her with her child presenting the scapular to St. Simon Stock.

Two depictions at Aylesford Priory of Mary presenting the Scapular to St. Simon Stock.

That humble piece of brown cloth, derived from the scapular worn by religious to protect their habit whilst at work, reminds us that our spiritual journey is lived out in all the humdrum, ordinary events of daily life and labour. Today the scapular is a symbol of belonging to the Carmelite Family. It is worn by Carmelite religious as part of their habit, and in a smaller version by members of the Carmelite Third Order. A miniature version of the Scapular is worn by members of the 'Brown Scapular Confraternity', who are affiliated to the Carmelite Family in a less formal way than religious and members of the Third Order.

The scapular is not an object of superstition; rather it reminds us of our divine work of co-operating with God in the building of God's kingdom and the salvation of souls. As the *Rule for the Third Order of Carmel* puts it: 'Lay Carmelites let themselves be accompanied by Mary in gradually taking on responsibility for co-operation in salvation and for the communication of grace given in the Church.' (§34).

Mary Most Pure

To receive Jesus, and to discern his will for us and his purposes for the world, we have to strive for a heart that is unfettered by distractions which detach us from God, a heart that worships not false idols but only the one true God. The Carmelite tradition often speaks of Mary's purity of heart using the Latin phrase *puritas cordis*. Carmelites

Lay Carmelites wearing the Profession Scapular of the Third Order.

see in Mary's purity of heart an imitation of the prophet Elijah who sought the face of the Living God, and who rejected the worship of anything or anyone other than God. In seeking purity of life and intention, Mary and Elijah are our radiant examples.

Mary's purity of heart meant that she cultivated what the Carmelite tradition terms *vacare Deo*, that is, 'space for God' or 'openness to God'. It was her trusting openness to God that allowed Mary confidently to advise others simply 'Do whatever he tells you' (*John* 2:5). This same God revealed to the Carmelite nun Saint Mary Magdalene de Pazzi what a great gift purity of heart is:

> This purity is such an intrinsic and immense thing that no human creature can perceive it and understand it fully, even though thanks to my grace and my pure generosity one may have some knowledge of it ... someone more and someone less, according to the disposition of each soul ... To acquire this purity the soul must purify all its thoughts, reflections, and all its feelings and desires, and direct them to me, its God and Creator; and that it let no thought creep into its heart and stain it.
> (*Selected Writings of Saint Mary Magdalen de Pazzi*, pp 242, 248).

Journey of faith

With Mary's cousin Elizabeth, in the mystery of the Visitation, we praise the faith that radiates from Mary: 'Blessed are you who believed that the Lord's word would come true (*Luke* 1:45). This is not always easy, for we are pilgrims who journey in both the light and the darkness of faith. God the Father did not reveal all of his will to Mary; she chose to obey without seeing the path ahead. At the Presentation in the Temple, Simeon warned Mary that a sword would pierce her heart. She had to trust herself to Joseph as they fled the persecution of Herod into Egypt. She did not understand when Jesus stayed behind in the Temple at Jerusalem. She who was all pure still endured the darkness of faith, and in pure faith she walked the way of the cross with her Son Jesus, and stood beneath his cross. We, too, are purified by the trials we meet in our daily life: 'Ascending the mountain implies a desert experience in which the living flame of God's love transforms and detaches the lay Carmelite from everything; even their image of God is purified and transformed. By putting on Christ, they begin to shine like his living image, being a new creation in him.' (*RTOC* §22).

Beneath the cross of Jesus stood Mary his mother

As our Mother, Mary accompanies us up the steep Mount of Carmel, which is both garden and desert. As one who stayed close to Christ during his suffering (*John* 19:24-27), so Mary stands in solidarity with us in the darkness of trials, reminding us that no sacrifice is wasted when offered in loving union with her son. Down through the ages, many of our Carmelite brothers and sisters have given their lives generously and lovingly, knowing themselves to be held in the loving arms of Mary, Queen of Martyrs: the martyrs of the Spanish Civil War, the Carmelite nuns of Compiègne, Titus Brandsma, Edith Stein, Isidore Bakanja, and countless others. We will learn more of these figures inspired by Mary as our Carmelite formation progresses.

Stop and reflect: Mary is often referred to as a 'foundational figure' within Carmelite spirituality. Think about the foundations of a building: they are unseen but keep the building rooted and secure. It is sometimes said that Carmelite devotion to Mary is like that; not always 'on display' but rather pervading all that we do at a very deep level. Is that your experience of Mary's place within Carmel?

Gathered in prayer with Mary the Mother of Jesus

At Pentecost, Mary was in the midst of the disciples, waiting in prayer for the outpouring of the Holy Spirit, and giving the first Christians – and hence Carmelites – an example of how they should form community. As she had given birth to Jesus in the stable at Bethlehem, so at Pentecost she was present at the birth of the new Body of Christ, the Church, which perpetuates the presence of Jesus down through the ages. She became the Mother of the Church. As Carmelites, what is true of Mary is true of us. Carmelites, by their prayer and self-giving love, become, like Mary, mothers of souls. This is true of cloistered Carmelite nuns, it is also true of our friars as they guide souls to holiness, and it is true of lay Carmelites as their lives of prayer are fruitful in active love for their neighbours. The example of Edith Stein (St. Teresa Benedicta of the Cross), is a poignant icon of this. She entered Carmel to pray for God's people, especially for her Jewish brothers and sisters. Before entering the gas chambers of Auschwitz, Edith stood out like the quiet centre in a whirlwind, praying though overwhelmed by sadness not for herself but for her people. She was, said an eyewitness, a Pietà without the Christ (cf. Joanne Mosley, *Edith Stein: Woman of Prayer*, pp. 54-55). Edith was truly a daughter and sister of Mary, of whom she wrote: 'Only a few words from the Virgin Mary have come down to us in the Gospels. But these few words are like heavy grains of pure gold. When they melt in the ardour of loving meditation, they more than suffice to bathe our entire lives in a luminous golden glow.'

We conclude with two reflections on Mary offered to the Carmelite Family in the twentieth century. Firstly, let us read the words addressed to the Carmelite Family by Pope Paul VI:

> May the most holy Virgin Mary confirm you in your Carmelite vocation. May she safeguard your love for the things of the Spirit. May she obtain for you the graces you need in your holy, laborious ascent towards the knowledge of the divine realm and the ineffable experiences of its dark nights and light-filled days. May she give you the desire for sanctity, the desire to bear eschatological witness to the kingdom of heaven. May she make you models for all the members of God's Church, and bind you to them in brotherhood. And may she one day lead you into that possession of Christ and his glory which, even now, is the goal towards which your whole life is directed.
> *(from the Allocutions of Pope Paul VI).*

Secondly, these are the words of the Carmelite friar and martyr Titus Brandsma, who said that 'Carmel is all Marian':

The devotion to Mary is one of the most delightful flowers in Carmel's garden. I should like to call it a sunflower. This flower rises high above the other flowers. Borne aloft on a tall stem, rich in green leaves, the flower is raised yet higher from among the green foliage. It is characteristic of this flower to turn itself towards the sun and moreover it is an image of the sun. It is a simple flower: it can grow in all gardens and it is an ornament to all. It is tall and firm and has deep roots like a tree... The flower itself represents the soul created after God's image in order to absorb the sunlight of God's bounty... Such a flower was Mary. Like her, so may we, flowers from her seed, raise our flower buds to the sun who infused Himself into her and will transmit to us also the beams of His light and warmth.

Conclusion: In this fifth chapter we have considered the special role of Mary within the Church and within Carmel in particular. She is Mother, Queen, Patron, Beauty of Carmel, Lady of the Place, and Sister. She is the perfect model of a praying woman, at the heart of the community, who serves those in need, and we can turn to her as an advocate and friend. We come to know her through the Carmelite tradition and specially through the Scriptures, and this knowledge leads us closer to her son Jesus Christ.

You might like to conclude your time of study and reflection with a prayer in honour of the Blessed Virgin Mary, perhaps one of the ancient Marian prayers of the Church, or with the following text:

> O God,
>   you have given us Mary as our Mother,
>   and through the Order of Carmel we learn to call her Sister.
> May we imitate her goodness, faith, and purity of heart,
>   and be ever joyful in the wonderful things you have done for us.
> May Mary watch over and protect us
>   on our pilgrim way to your holy mountain, Christ the Lord.
> We make our prayer through the same Christ, Our Lord and Brother. Amen.

We are now a quarter of the way through this programme of initial formation. In the next chapter we will consider the role of another foundational figure within Carmelite spirituality, the prophet Elijah.

Ideas for Reflection, Discussion and Action

- Reflect – either individually or as a community – on any passage in this chapter that has particularly sparked your imagination. Is there anything you have found challenging? Have you learned anything new?

- If you were to make your own *Magnificat* prayer to the Lord, what would you praise him for?

- John 'made room' for Mary in his home. If Mary is our mother too, what would we have to do to make our homes fitting places in which to welcome her?

- Read Felip Ribot's interpretation of Mary as the 'Little Cloud' in either the translation of the *Ten Books* by Richard Copsey (p. 82), or in Emanuele Boaga's *Lady of the Place* (pp. 50-51); details of these books are given in the list of resources below.

- How much is your image of Mary derived from the Scriptures? Is your image more dependent upon 'visionary' encounters with Mary?

- Do you find Our Lady easy to approach as 'Sister' as well as 'Mother' and 'Queen'?

- An ancient Carmelite adage is *Totus Marianus est Carmelus* – 'Carmel belongs totally to Mary'. How do you understand this phrase?

- Mary combined prayer with practical service of those around her. In your prayer, ask her to help you to reach out to those around you. How has Mary inspired social movements within the Church?

- Try to learn about one Carmelite saint's relationship with Mary by reading about him or her in *Lady of the Place*, referred to in the reading list below.

Recommended Further Resources

There are many publications on Carmel's relationship with Mary. Though there is much wisdom in older books, it is best to read materials published after the 1960s that reflect the teachings and insights of the Second Vatican Council. The list of resources below should be easily found in most good Carmelite libraries, and a number of them can also be found on the internet.

Emanuele Boaga, O.Carm., 'Carmel and the Immaculate Conception', *Carmel in the World*, Volume XLIII Number 2, 2004, pp. 85-90.

Emanuele Boaga, O.Carm., *The Lady of the Place: Mary in the History and in the Life of Carmel*, (Rome: Edizioni Carmelitane, 2001).

Donald W. Buggert, O.Carm., *et al*, (eds.), *Mother, Behold Your Son: Essays in Honor of Eamon R. Carroll, O.Carm.*, (Washington D.C.: The Carmelite Institute, 2001).

Edmondo Coccia, (ed.), *In Communion With Mary: Our Heritage and Prospects for the Future*, (Rome: Edizioni Carmelitane 2003).

Joseph Chalmers, O.Carm., *Mary the Contemplative*, (Rome: Edizioni Carmelitane, 2001).

Hugh Clarke, O.Carm., *Mary and the Brown Scapular*, (Faversham: Carmelite Charitable Trust, Second edition 2002).

Hugh Clarke, O.Carm., *Mary and the Rosary*, (Faversham: Saint Albert's Press, 2003).

Armando Maggi, *Maria Maddalena de'Pazzi: Selected Revelations*, Classics of Western Spirituality, (New Jersey: Paulist Press, 2000).

Elizabeth Ruth Obbard, 'Mary – Lady of the Place', in *Land of Carmel*, (Leominster: Gracewing, 1999), pp. 81-97.

Chris O'Donnell, O.Carm., *Loving Presence: Mary and Carmel*, available online via the website of the Carmelite Curia: www.ocarm.org

Felip Ribot, O.Carm., *The Ten Books on the Way of Life and Great Deeds of the Carmelites (including The Book of the First Monks)*, translated by Richard Copsey, O.Carm., (Faversham: Saint Albert's Press, 2005).

Peter Slattery, O.Carm., 'Mary and Carmel', in *The Springs of Carmel: An Introduction to Carmelite Spirituality*, (New York: Alba House, 1991), pp. 39-52.

Redemptus Maria Valabek, O.Carm., *Mary Mother of Carmel: Our Lady and the Saints of Carmel*, two volumes, (Rome: Edizione Carmelitane, 1987-88).

John F. Welch, O.Carm., (ed.), *Carmel and Mary: Theology and History of a Devotion*, (Washington D.C.: The Carmelite Institute, 2002).

Notes and reflections on Chapter 5

CHAPTER 6

Elijah

Summary: Having considered the place of the Blessed Virgin Mary within Carmel, we now turn to the Order's other foundational figure, the Old Testament prophet Elijah. Like Mary, Elijah is considered Patron of the Carmelite Order, and whereas she is Mother and Sister, Elijah is revered as 'Father of All Carmelites'. In this chapter we consider some of the reasons why this is so, and some of the implications for us as Carmelites today. Early Carmelites wove a mythology which spoke of Elijah as founding a 'brotherhood of prophets'; this mythology still speaks to us Carmelites today because Elijah's example has much to teach us about our own vocation as contemplatives and prophets.

Window of Elijah at the Carmelite-run National
Shrine of St. Thérèse at Darien, Illinois, U.S.A.

Get prepared: Before reading this chapter, have to hand any materials you might need, such as writing materials; you might like to summarise each section in your own words, or to write down your reactions and thoughts on the blank page at the end of the chapter. Perhaps access to the internet or reference books would help you to follow up points that interest you. Since Elijah is a biblical figure, it would be helpful to read this chapter with a copy of the Bible to hand; any translation will do, though the *New Revised Standard Version* is widely recommended. Why not begin with the following prayer inspired by Elijah's example:

> O LORD, *the God of Abraham, Isaac and Israel,*
> *you alone are God.*
> *Your servant Elijah lived in your presence,*
> *and acted on your Word.*
> *Help us to drink from the well of his wisdom.*
> *Shelter us in Cherith, and lead us to Carmel,*
> *luring our hearts away from all false gods.*
> *Open our eyes to the needs of those suffering.*
> *Open our mouths to speak comfort and justice.*
> *Open our hearts to your voice in the silence.*
> *Send angels to strengthen us.*
> *Send the rain of your grace to quench our thirst.*
> *Let us break bread with the starving*
> *and bring life to places of death and despair.*
> *Send us as prophets to herald your Gospel.*
> *Allow us to rise to you in paradise.*
> *Those who met your son Jesus saw in him*
> *the spirit of Elijah.*
> *May Elijah lead us to your son.*
> *We ask this in Jesus' name. Amen.*

A man like us?

'Elijah was a man just like us'; so says the letter of *James* (5:17). Anyone who reads the story of Elijah in the Old Testament's two *Books of the Kings* may find that rather hard to understand, given the dramatic events of his life.

Elijah was the great prophet in the Northern Kingdom of Israel in the ninth century before Christ, during the reign of King Ahab. Ahab, influenced by his wife Jezebel, had introduced into Israel the worship of a false God, Baal. This idolatry brought with it the suffering and repression of the common people. In fighting against the worship of Baal, and the unjust actions of the king, Elijah – on a mission from God – called a drought to befall the nation, called down fire, rebelled against the authorities, and stood in the presence of God himself. Yet Elijah was also a man who ran away from his mission, terrified of Queen Jezebel's retribution, who laid down wanting to die, and who hid in a cave. Elijah was, like us, capable of extremes. As we might say nowadays, Elijah lived life 'at the edge'.

So what is it about this great man of God that has drawn Carmelites to adopt him as one of our patrons? Why did the medieval friars feel able to enrol him as the first Carmelite? Was it significant that the first Carmelite hermits settled in the Wadi 'ain es-Siah, a valley on Mount Carmel watered by the Fountain or Well of Elijah?

Did you know? Elijah is sometimes referred to by his Latin name Elias, and his disciple Elisha is likewise sometimes referred to as Eliseus.

A patron alongside Mary, the 'Lady of the Place'

In the last chapter we read how the Carmelites had adopted Mary as Patron of their Order. When a group adopts a patron it is for a variety of reasons. In part, they want the protection of having that person 'on the board', someone who will give the group credibility and an identity. But we Carmelites wanted more than that when we chose to have Elijah as patron alongside Mary. We wanted to trace our origins way back to Old Testament times and to the great prophets of Israel. We are the only religious order in the Roman Catholic Church to claim such a strong relationship with a biblical figure who predates Christ himself, and the only group in the Western Church to keep his feast.

We have learned already that the Carmelite Order over the centuries has produced *Constitutions* that help its members to articulate its identity and mission in a particular time, and interpret the *Rule of Saint Albert* for the present age. The earliest surviving *Carmelite Constitutions* date from

Many traditional depictions of Elijah – such as this window at St. Edward's Church, Dringhouses, in the English city of York – show the prophet being fed by ravens during his time in the desert because God commanded them to do so (*1 Kings* 17:2-6).

An aerial photograph of Mount Carmel in modern times.

1281, and in that text our predecessors in Carmel traced a line from themselves back to Elijah and his follower Elisha. In the introduction to the 1281 *Constitutions*, known as the *Rubrica Prima*, the medieval Carmelites explained that they were simply carrying on the tradition of the 'brotherhood' or 'company of prophets' (mentioned in *2 Kings* 2) whose original leaders were Elijah and Elisha:

> Since some young brothers in the Order do not know how to reply truthfully to those who wish to know how and where our Order originated, we want to provide them with a written account of how to respond to such demands. We say that, on the evidence of trustworthy witnesses, that from the time of the prophets Elijah and Elisha, the holy fathers of both the Old and New Testaments have lived devotedly on Mount Carmel, true lovers of the solitude of that mountain for the contemplation of heavenly things. There, near the fountain of Saint Elijah, without any doubt, they lived praiseworthy lives, and their successors continuously thereafter.

Of course, historians tell us that it is extremely unlikely that there was a physical line of succession of men living on Mount Carmel from the time of Elijah down to the thirteenth-century. The *Rubrica Prima* and the Carmelite traditions that grew up about Elijah afterwards are myths. But myths are not to be dismissed lightly; they may not be factually true about the past, but they still contain important truths about the present. Why bother to construct such a mythical history in the first place?

Stop for a moment: Before reading on, why do you think the medieval Carmelites claimed to have descended directly from the prophet Elijah and the 'brotherhood of prophets'?

The Well of Elijah in the Wadi on Mount Carmel, photographed in 2008.

Telling our story

There are two main reasons why the first Carmelites developed a mythical history about descending from the prophet Elijah.

The first is that they wanted someone whose lifestyle and characteristics we could emulate. We wanted to be able to say to people "Elijah and Mary are authentic examples of what a true Carmelite is like."

The second reason for the medieval Carmelite friars constructing the myth of our Elijan heritage was that all the major religious orders in the medieval Church had a founder. Saints Francis, Benedict, Dominic and so on were real people who put their names to various orders, and to whose memory those orders could turn when they needed to discern their future direction, wondering whether they were being true to the founder's vision. We Carmelites had no such founder. We had also rejected the various religious *regulae* ('rules') that were around at the time in favour of a *formula vitae* ('way of life') written by Albert, the Latin Patriarch (Roman Catholic Bishop) of Jerusalem. Having no founder left us without a figurehead. "Who are these Carmelites?" people asked of us. So although they aren't mentioned in our *Rule of Saint Albert*, we Carmelites chose Elijah and Mary as our inspirations, referring to Mary as our Mother and Sister, and to Elijah as 'Father of All Carmelites'.

And that makes sense when you look at the geographical and historical context in which the Carmelite tradition developed. There was a long practice of men and women going off into the deserts of the Holy Land to seek God in solitude and silence. One of the first was St. Anthony who lived in the deserts of Egypt in the third century. Many followed him in a radical decision to forsake all and seek the face of the living God in solitary prayer. They are collectively known as the 'Desert Fathers and Mothers'. They had always regarded Elijah as their great exemplar, as the 'first monk', the template upon which they drew their own lives. Because Elijah was seen as the first monk it was only natural that he be chosen by the Carmelite hermits to be their patron, particularly since they themselves lived on Mount Carmel, the place where Elijah had carried out his great contest against the prophets of Baal.

It was Elijah's mythical role as 'founder' of the first community on Carmel that the medieval Prior Provincial of Catalonia, Felip Ribot, wrote about in his *Ten Books on the Way of Life and Great Deeds of the Carmelites* (often called *The Book of the First Monks*, after the first followers of Elijah).

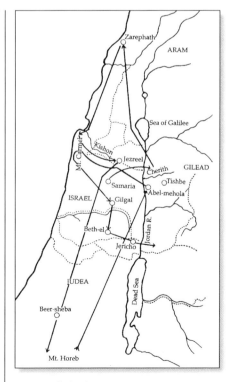

A map of Elijah's many journeys.

Contemplatives: standing in the presence of God

Of course, we are all called by our *Rule of Saint Albert* to live a life 'in allegiance to Jesus Christ'. But there are a variety of ways in which that can be done, just as there are a variety of temperaments. What unites all Carmelites, however different they may be in other ways, is that we are contemplatives by our very nature. Being contemplative is part of who we are. Contemplation is the unifying element at the heart of Carmel. Contemplation cannot be earned; rather, it is a gift of God to Carmelites and others who seek to be open to that gift, and given when and how God wills.

But what is contemplation? Contemplation is often spoken of synonymously with praying, but that is not the Carmelite understanding of the term. Contemplation is simply standing in the presence of God with an open heart. And that is exactly what Elijah did. Come hell or high water, he tried to make his heart always open to the presence of God. 'Standing in the presence of God' was Elijah's catchphrase. He would come up to the idolatrous King of Israel, Ahab, and say 'As the Lord lives, before whom I stand, there shall be neither dew nor rain these years, except according to my word' (*1 Kings* 17:1). We should note in this phrase that the first truth Elijah declares is that 'the Lord lives'. Elijah then puts himself in second place, in relation to God, 'before whom I stand'. As Carmelites our mission, inherited from Elijah, is to declare first the truth that 'God lives', and secondly, that we stand in God's presence, that is, we are in relationship with God.

Every action and thought of Elijah was done whilst standing in the presence of God. Elijah thus had a contemplative attitude, and encountered God when he prayed, when he engaged with his community, and when he served that community. According to the 1995 *Carmelite Constitutions*, Elijah represents for us Carmelites 'the solitary prophet who nurtured his thirst for the one and only God, and lived in his presence' (§26). All our Carmelite saints throughout the ages have attested to the fact that contemplation is the foundation and core of our spirituality. Arising from that contemplation comes our prayer, our building of community, and our service to the Church and the World.

The task that was before Elijah, and that is facing us as Carmelites today, is to cooperate with God in becoming contemplative. We can't achieve it by our own efforts, nor does God force contemplative grace on us; rather, it is a collaboration between us and God. In a spirit of *vacare Deo* (openness to God), we offer God a loving and pure heart (remember Mary's *purity of heart* discussed in the previous chapter), and our heart is filled with God's love as a pure gift. This two-way relationship is at the heart of the Carmelite way of life, as expressed beautifully and simply hundreds of years ago in *The Ten Books on the Way of Life and Great Deeds of the Carmelites* (better known as *The Book of the First Monks*):

> The goal of this life is twofold. One part we acquire by our own effort and the exercise of the virtues, assisted by divine grace. This is to offer God a pure and holy heart, free from all stain of sin ... The other goal of this life is granted to us as the free gift of God, namely, to taste somewhat in the heart and to experience in the mind the power of the divine presence and the sweetness of heavenly glory, not only after death but already in this mortal life.
>
> (translated by Richard Copsey, p. 9)

Did you know? In many cultures standing is a mark of respect. Elijah stood in the presence of the Lord, and his words remind us of the Eucharistic Prayer: 'we thank you for counting us worthy to stand in your presence and serve you.' In many Carmelite communities around the world it is common practice to stand during the Eucharistic Prayer. This is because before the reform of the liturgy around the time of the Second Vatican Council, the Carmelite Rite was not Tridentine but rather that of the Holy Sepulchre in Jerusalem, where standing (which is symbolic of Christ's Resurrection) is the tradition, as is common in the Eastern Rites.

What effect does contemplation have on us?

We have said that contemplation is simply standing in the presence of God with an open heart. It is not possible to spend your life standing in the presence of God with an open heart and not be filled with love. That love touches the world. It is that love which we are called to show in order to set the world on fire with God's love.

It is not possible to spend your life standing in the presence of God with an open heart and not be transformed, albeit gradually, from one degree of glory to another. It is that transformation that is called 'divinisation' – that process whereby women and men realise their roots in the divine nature because they have been made in the image of God, a God who became a man and who died for love of us. The journey of formation on which you are engaged is all about this transformation, this divinisation.

Elijah's experience of being in the presence of God transformed him, and made him full of ardent enthusiasm. Elijah's declaration 'With zeal I have been zealous for the Lord, the God of hosts' (*1 Kings* 19:10) is the motto we Carmelites have adopted. It is displayed in Latin on our crest alongside the hand and the fiery sword which indicate the passion of Elijah whose word 'burned like a torch' (*Ecclesiasticus* 48:1) for the one true God. Like Elijah, Carmelites carry 'the sword of the spirit, which is the Word of God' (*Rule of Saint Albert*, Ch. 19).

The Shield of the Order of Carmel

It is worth taking this opportunity to explore the symbolism of the Carmelite shield or crest. The Carmelite historian, Fr. Emanuele Boaga, O.Carm., tells us that the shield appeared for the first time at the end of the fifteenth century, on the cover of a book about the life of Saint Albert dated 1499. The symbol appears in the form of a *vexillum*, that is, a sign, standard or banner. With the passing of time this was modified until the present form of a heraldic shield was reached. There has never been an official explanation of the shield's symbolism, and therefore different interpretations of it have been given.

Elijah with his flaming sword, set against the Order's crest.

Stop and look at the crest over the page: What do you currently understand about the symbolism on the Carmelite shield?

At the centre is a stylised mountain whose peak points towards heaven; it has rounded sides and three gold six-pointed stars, one in the centre of the mountain, the others in the sky on either side of the mountain. With regard to colours, white and brown appear together and correspond to the colours of the Carmelite habit.

We can safely presume that the mountain is symbolic of Mount Carmel, where the Order originated. Thanks to the writings of the Carmelite saints, and the liturgy of the Order, the mountain has itself become a symbol of Christ.

The lower star is often interpreted as representing the Virgin Mary, Star of the Sea. The two higher stars flanking the mountain perhaps represent the prophets Elijah and Elisha. Seen in this way, the stars symbolise the Marian character of the Order and its Elijan origins.

A more recent interpretation is that the two upper stars represent Mary and Elijah, whilst the white star represents us – the Carmelites of today – ascending the mountain that is Christ. The fact that the stars are six-pointed perhaps is a reminder of the roots of Carmel (and indeed Christianity) in Judaism.

In the 16th century the shield began to appear bearing a crown above, from which the arm and sword of Elijah emerge, surrounded by a semicircle of a dozen stars. The stars are a typical depiction of Mary that recall the apparition of 'the woman clothed in the sun, with the moon under her feet and on her head a crown of twelve stars' (*Revelation* 12:1). The crown can likewise be seen as symbolising Mary's queenship, but could also be a symbol of the Kingdom of God with Jesus the sovereign Lord of Carmel. It is common also for the Order's motto – the words of Elijah from *1 Kings* 19:10 – to appear above or below the crest: *Zelo zelatus sum pro Domine Deo exercituum* ('I am full of zeal for the Lord God of Hosts').

A cross has sometimes been depicted on the summit of the mountain, and is often associated with reform movements within Carmel. Though this originated within the 'Ancient Observance' of the Carmelite Family, a cross on top of the mountain is now more commonly associated with the Discalced Reform. The Ancient Observance in Sicily places a Jerusalem cross above the mountain.

Elijah: example of prophecy and promoter of justice

Returning to the figure of Elijah, he bears witness to the fact that it is not possible to spend your life standing in the presence of God with an open heart and not be filled with a deep longing for justice, peace and love to abound in this world, because it is what God desires. This awareness is what made Elijah a prophet. Prophecy is not so much about foretelling the future but is rather about telling the truth of the present and speaking out that truth in the name of God. As it says in the *Creed*, God the Holy Spirit 'has spoken through the prophets'.

Elijah inspires Carmelites to be prophetic. That is why Carmel is dedicated to pursuing justice, building peace, and upholding the integrity of God's created world. Elijah is very much an inspiration to Carmel's apostolate, including the Order's presence at the United Nations as a Non-Governmental Organisation (NGO). We will return to the Carmelite vocation to work for justice, peace and the integrity of Creation in Chapter 17. Such work is not simply something we do, but is part of who we are as descendents of the prophet of Carmel.

Elijah's prophetic voice on behalf of God's people was heard not only on Mount Carmel, but in his condemnation of the king's possession of Naboth's vineyard (*1 Kings* 21). Urged on by his wife Jezebel, King Ahab plotted to have Naboth killed so that he could take possession of his subject's property. Elijah was charged by God with the mission of denouncing this injustice and calling the king to repentance.

Stop and ponder the Scriptures: Read the account of Naboth's vineyard in *1 Kings* 21. What can Carmelites learn from Elijah's prophetic stand against corruption?

Elijah: bridge between the Old and New Laws

According to the prophet Malachi, Elijah – who was taken up to paradise in a fiery chariot – would return to the Earth before the day of the Lord (*Malachi* 4:5-6). Because John the Baptist and Jesus spoke with the spirit of prophecy, many contemporaries thought they might be Elijah come back (see the descriptions of this in *Mark* 6:15, 8:28, 9:12; *Matthew* 16:14). Elijah is an Old Testament personality who figures very prominently in the New Testament, and he is a bridge between the two.

Did you know? Because Jesus associated his cousin John the Baptist with the prophet Elijah, and because John dwelt in the desert like Elijah, John the Baptist has a particularly important place in the Carmelite tradition. We know that some Carmelite statues of John the Baptist in medieval England depicted him wearing the Order's habit.

Elsewhere in the New Testament, Elijah is closely linked to Christ in the gospel accounts of the Transfiguration (*Matthew* 17:1-6; *Mark*; 9:1-8; *Luke* 9:28-36), when Jesus' divinity shone through his humanity, and he engaged in conversation with Elijah (representing the Prophets) and Moses (representing the Law). In this episode Jesus is seen as the fulfilment of the Law and the Prophets. In Jesus everything God wishes to say is spoken; in Jesus the new Law of God's Love find perfect expression. The Covenant of the Old Law finds its perfection in the New Covenant in Christ, brought about by his transforming life, death and resurrection.

Elijah: foreseer of Mary?

Carmelites have also associated Elijah with Mary. As we read in the last chapter, the 'cloud, small as a man's hand, rising from the sea' which Elijah's servant saw from the top of Carmel announced the end of the drought that Elijah had foretold to Ahab (*1 Kings* 18:41-46). Many have interpreted the cloud as a symbol of Mary, arising as pure water from the salty sea of sinful humanity, bringing rain (Jesus) so that the land and the people can live again. Carmelite legend says that Elijah was so moved by his 'vision' of Mary that he 'founded' the first hermit community on Mount Carmel in her honour. There is no historical evidence for this claim, but it shows how Carmelites have always given special honour to Mary and Elijah as patrons of the Order and as living embodiments of Carmel's values. Through such interpretations the medieval Carmelites sought to weave the Order into the history of salvation.

This sculpture at Aylesford Priory in England depicts Mary and Christ, Elijah and Elisha, Simon Stock and John the Baptist.

Elijah's 'vision' of Mary in the cloud arising from the sea, depicted in a woodcut from the *Speculum Carmelitanum* ('Mirror of Carmel') published in 1680.

Elijah: man of pure heart

We have already considered Mary's purity of heart (*puritas cordis*). We can also recognise in Elijah a man of pure heart. When confronting the prophets of Baal on Mount Carmel, Elijah asked the Israelites: 'How long will you go limping with two different opinions? If the Lord is God, follow him; but if Baal, then follow him.' (*1 Kings* 18:21). As Fr. John Welch, O.Carm., observes: 'A perennial theme in Carmel's spirituality is the need to decide which God to follow. Our tradition was born on Mount Carmel, the scene of the struggle between the followers of Yahweh and the followers of Baal. Elijah encouraged the people to be clear about their choice of the one, true God. The Carmelite community as well as individual Carmelites have had to continually wrestle with the forces of disintegration and fragmentation brought about by the pursuit of idols.'

Elijah: prophet of fire

One of the enduring symbols associated with Elijah is that of fire. He called down fire that set light to his sacrifice on Mount Carmel (*1 Kings* 18). Elijah's worship proved that the God of Israel is the one true God and that Ahab and the prophets of Baal had led the people astray, promoting false notions of who God is and what God is all about. Looking through the Bible we see that fire is a symbol of the presence of God: the burning bush which Moses was not allowed to approach without taking off his sandals (*Exodus* 3); Daniel's vision of God whose 'throne was a blaze of flames, its wheels were a burning fire' (*Daniel* 7:9); John the Baptist who told the people that the one coming after will baptise 'with the Holy Spirit and with fire' (*Luke* 3:16). Jesus himself said that 'I have come to bring fire to the earth, and how

Elijah's victory over the prophets of Baal, depicted in ceramic by Adam Kossowski at The Friars, Aylesford, England.

I wish it were blazing already!' (*Luke* 12:49). The Holy Spirit descended on the Apostles in what appeared to be 'tongues of fire' at Pentecost (*Acts* 2:3).

There is an ambivalence about fire. It is one of the most destructive forces on earth and yet it purifies, giving us light and heat. According to the 2003 *Rule for the Third Order of Carmel* (*RTOC*), 'every Lay Carmelite is like a spark of love thrown into the forest of life: they must be able to enflame anyone who approaches them' (§44). This fire gives light and heat and love, but it also burns away the dross. In *St Teresa: Her Life and Times*, G. C. Graham quotes a visitor to Avila speaking of the Carmelites there: 'Sir, in the eyes of the flesh they are mad; in those of faith, angels and ministers of fire in fantastic bodies, so that we, the weak, may see something of the flame which burns in them.'

Oh still small voice of calm

Although Elijah is a character associated with fire, with decisive action, and with zeal for God, he is also someone who realised that God is encountered in silence and stillness. On Horeb, the mountain of God (also known as Sinai where the Lord's presence was manifested in the burning bush), Elijah realised that God does not only reveal himself through dramatic earthquakes, fires, and winds, but primarily through 'the sound of sheer silence' (*1 Kings* 19:12). This episode has inspired Carmelites, and others, over the centuries, to seek God in silent prayer, and to find God in absence.

Stop and ponder the Scriptures: Read the passage from *1 Kings* 19 in which Elijah encounters the Lord in silence. What does this episode mean to you?

In his book on Elijah, *The Sound of Silence*, the former Prior General of the Order, Fr. Joseph Chalmers, O.Carm., offers the following reflection on the prophet's encounter with God in silence:

> The meeting between God and Elijah on Mount Horeb in 'the sound of a gentle breeze' or in 'the sound of sheer silence' or in 'the light murmuring sound' has been much used for prayer and meditation over the centuries. This experience must have been very difficult for the prophet Elijah because God came to meet him in a totally unexpected way. God did not come in the earthquake or in the fire or in the mighty wind, all the ways that God had used previously to announce the divine presence, but instead God came in silence.
>
> Through the gift of faith we can know something about God but God always goes beyond our human concepts. The contemplative way leads to the complete transformation of the human person whereby our human ways of seeing, loving and interacting with the world, which are always limited, become divine ways. This is naturally the work of God but we must do everything in our power to facilitate and accept this personal and structural transformation. We must learn gradually who is God. An intellectual knowledge of the fundamental truths of the faith is important. However, it is one thing to intellectually grasp what love means, and another thing to know love by experience. The

experience of God helps us to grasp theological concepts in a new way. Often God will surprise us and act completely outside our limited possibilities. Little by little we have to learn to see everything from another perspective. Everything may remain the same but may in fact appear totally different because we have a different way of seeing.

Prayer is in some way relating to God, and so every prayer is good, and every method of prayer that helps us to grow in our relationship with God can be helpful. Just as in a human relationship, so also in the relationship with God, it is very normal for it to become simpler with the passage of time. We become less and less surprised when God approaches us in a way that we are not used to. We learn to accept that we are always at the beginning of the spiritual journey and that God is always ahead of us.

All prayer, if it is authentic, must be open to contemplation in the sense that it must encourage the transformation of the human heart. The Christian tradition gives various suggestions regarding methods of prayer that have proved their worth over the centuries. After the liturgy, which is the prayer of the whole Body of Christ, head and members, comes *Lectio Divina*, the prayerful reading of the Word of God. Then we have many devotions approved by the Church. All these devotions or methods of prayer must be directed toward the contemplation of God and our own transformation.

(*Sound of Silence*, pp. 107-08)

Stop and reflect: Elijah's approach to life was grounded in reality, as was his relationship with God. When his pursuit by Jezebel and being the only faithful prophet left in Israel was too much for him, Elijah cried out to God that he wanted to die. He went to sleep (*1 Kings* 19:1-8), and in Elijah's utter desolation, God sent an angel with food. Are we this honest with God? Do we recognise the angels who come to help us?

Elijah in the Order today

Much work is being done to interpret the message that Elijah brings to our world in the 21st century. Since the Second Vatican Council called for religious communities to go back to their founding documents, and for Christians generally to return to the Scriptures, we are rediscovering the richness of our 'Elijan heritage'. In recent years scholars such as Jane Ackerman have produced excellent studies on Elijah in the Carmelite tradition (listed in the bibliography below). Other books have encouraged Carmelites to rediscover our Elijah heritage, such as Richard Copsey's translation of *The Ten Books* (*Book of the First Monks*) from Latin into English, and Joseph Chalmers' reflection on the Elijah narratives in *The Sound of Silence*.

Not everything Elijah is reported as doing in the Bible (such as the slaying of the prophets of Baal) makes comfortable reading today, but understood in the context of his times he can be upheld as a man for all times. An interesting recent development within Carmel is the way that devotion to him has encouraged interfaith encounter and dialogue, because Elijah is revered by the three monotheistic religions: Christianity,

Judaism and Islam. The 1995 *Constitutions of the Carmelite Order* take this fact as the starting-point for engaging in dialogue:

> In the Scriptures and in Carmelite tradition, the prophet Elijah is respected as the one who in various ways knew how to read the new signs of the presence of God and who was able, not least, to reconcile those who had become strangers or enemies. As Carmelites, heartened by this example and by our strong desire to put into practice our Lord's teachings of love and reconciliation, we shall take part in the ecumenical movement and in inter-religious dialogue, promoted by the Second Vatican Council. Through the former we shall promote relationships with the Orthodox and other Christians. Through the latter we shall promote dialogue at various levels with Jews and Muslims, with whom we share devotion to the prophet Elijah as a man of God. (§96)

Children of the one God, and inspired by Elijah: Carmelite laity and religious meeting with Muslims at the mosque in the English city of York.

Passing on Elijah's mantle

Elijah was not part of the priestly hierarchy, he spoke his mind, he was zealous for God, and he did not tolerate half-measures. He was a friend of God, a confidante of the almighty. Elijah is one of the keys to unlocking the Carmelite charism, and well worth studying and getting to know as a friend, not only in our initial formation but throughout our lives as Carmelites. He shows us all how to be contemplatives: people of prayer who are active in the midst of the world. He was solitary but not confined to any one spot, and drawn out of solitude to engage with God's people, such as the widow at Zarephath (*1 Kings* 17:7-16), Obadiah (*1 Kings* 18:1-6), and Elisha (*1 Kings* 19:19-21).

Elijah's relationship with Elisha is particularly important for Carmelites. We read in the *First Book of Kings* that God told Elijah 'You must anoint Elisha son of Shaphat, of Abel-Meholah, as prophet to succeed you' (*1 Kings* 19:16). Elijah made Elisha his successor symbolically by throwing his mantle or cloak over him (*1 Kings* 19:19-21). With

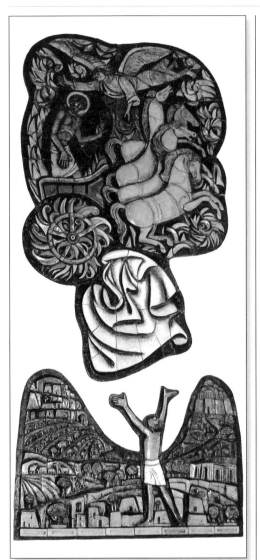

Elijah passing on his mantle to Elisha, depicted in ceramic by Adam Kossowski at The Friars, Aylesford, England.

this gesture Elijah transferred to Elisha his spirit, his gifts and his mission as a prophet. When Elijah finally ascended to paradise in a whirlwind accompanied by a fiery chariot (*2 Kings* 2:1-13) he again threw his mantle down to Elisha, confirming his prophetic vocation.

Did you know? Before the Carmelite cloak became plain white in the late 1200s (symbolising Mary's purity of heart and Christ's Resurrection), the cloak worn by the hermits on Mount Carmel used to be striped. Some medieval commentators interpreted the stripes as the different virtues of the hermits. Others said the stripes were burnt into the cloak when it fell from Elijah's fiery chariot!

Carmelites celebrate Elijah and Elisha with liturgical feasts on 20th July and 14th June respectively. Our tradition tells us that their gifts have been passed on through the 'company of prophets' who have inhabited Mount Carmel – physically and spiritually – through the generations. Living with Elijah as an inspiration for Carmel, we can be confident that there will always be someone who can pass on the Carmelite tradition to the next generation.

Stop and think: As a Carmelite you are part of an ongoing tradition, and you have a responsibility to pass that tradition on to others. How can you encourage someone to consider a vocation within Carmel?

Conclusion: In this sixth chapter we have considered the role of Elijah the prophet as an inspiration for Carmelites over the centuries. With Mary he is a model for living contemplatively, open to God's word and will in our lives. Elijah is regarded as 'Father of All Carmelites'; our appreciation of Elijah is based primarily on what we read about him in the Bible, and secondarily on the Order's own traditions.

You might like to conclude your time of study and reflection with a prayer, perhaps in silence, or pondering a passage from Scripture that relates to Elijah.

In the next chapter we will consider another man who can be considered foundational to our Carmelite Family, Saint Albert of Jerusalem, whose *way of life* is a touchstone for all of us in Carmel.

Ideas for Reflection, Discussion and Action

- Reflect – either individually or as a community – on any passage in this chapter that has stood out for you as significant. There's much more that could be said about Elijah, but space in this book is limited; is there anything in particular that you think should have been included but wasn't?

- How would you summarise the chapter and its key points in one or two paragraphs?

- Do you see any similarities between yourself and Elijah? What do you find attractive about him? What bothers you about his story?

- Is Elijah 'a man just like us'? Would you like to meet him?

- What 'false gods' do we recognise in our lives that weaken our resolve to stand in the presence of the living God?

- Why is the link between the Old and New Testaments so important for Christians, and especially for Carmelites?

- In what ways is it possible to live Elijah's radical lifestyle today?

- Find out what Jews and Muslims say about Elijah. Perhaps make contact with a local synagogue or mosque and ask if you can visit to learn more about that faith community.

- Identify someone you think might appreciate knowing more about Carmelite spirituality and invite them to a meeting of your community.

- Who are the prophets speaking God's truth in today's society? Do you see yourself as a son or daughter of the 'company of prophets'?

- The work of the Carmelite NGO and other groups within the Carmelite Family are inspired by Elijah's example. Consider finding out how you can get involved in their work.

- Mendelssohn's oratorio *Elijah* is often performed in different places; attending a performance or listening to a recording might be an entertaining way of enhancing your appreciation of the prophet.

Recommended Further Resources

A number of good resources relating to Elijah have become available in recent years, which you will find in most Carmelite libraries, or from Carmelite and other Christian bookshops.

Jane Ackerman, *Elijah: Prophet of Carmel*, (Washington D.C.: ICS Publications, 2003). This is an excellent study of the role that Elijah has played in the Carmelite Family over the centuries.

Emanuele Boaga, O.Carm., *Come pietre vive ... nel Carmelo*, (Rome: Institutum Carmelitanum, 1993). This is a very good introductory history of the Carmelite Order, but unfortunately is not available in English at present.

Joseph Chalmers, O.Carm., *The Sound of Silence: Listening to the Word of God with Elijah the Prophet*, (Faversham: Saint Albert's Press, 2007). In this beautifully illustrated book, the former Prior General of the Carmelite Order considers all the Bible passages that relate to Elijah and what we can learn from him today.

Kilian Healy, O.Carm., *Prophet of Fire*, Carmel in the World Paperbacks 5, (Rome: Edizioni Carmelitane, Reprinted 2004).

Eugene Kaboré, O.Carm., 'From Mount Carmel to Mount Horeb: a journey of transformation', in *In obsequio Jesu Christi: Praying and prophetic community in a changing world*, Proceedings of the 2007 General Chapter of the Carmelite Order, (Rome: Edizioni Carmelitane, 2007), pp. 25-35.

Fenella Matthew, 'Living in the Presence of God: Carmelites in the Footsteps of Elijah', *Mount Carmel: A Review of the Spiritual Life*, Volume 57 Number 4, October-December 2009, pp. 9-13.

Tony Mazurkiewicz, O.Carm., 'The Biblical Elijah: A Model for Spirituality', *Carmel in the World*, Volume XLVIII Number 2, 2009, pp. 90-106.

James McCaffrey, O.C.D., 'The Heritage of Elijah' in *The Carmelite Charism: Exploring the Biblical Roots*, (Dublin: Veritas Publications, 2004).

Wilfrid McGreal, O.Carm., *At the Fountain of Elijah: the Carmelite Tradition* (London: Darton Longman and Todd 1999), particularly chapters 3 and 9.

Craig Morrison, O.Carm., 'Elijah on Horeb', *Carmel in the World*, Volume XLIV Number 3, 2005, pp. 185-191.

Peter Slattery, O.Carm., 'Elijah' in *The Springs of Carmel*, (Homebush: St. Paul Publications, 1990).

Felip Ribot, O.Carm., *The Ten Books (The Institution of the First Monks)*, translated by Richard Copsey, O.Carm., (Faversham: Saint Albert's Press, 2005).

The website of the Carmelite NGO: www.carmelitengo.org

Notes and reflections on Chapter 6

The Rule of Saint Albert

Summary: After a consideration of the historical background to the *Rule of Saint Albert* and its origins, this chapter looks at the text's importance for all branches of the Carmelite Family. The *Rule* is indeed a 'key to Carmel', providing an endless source of inspiration for our way of life.

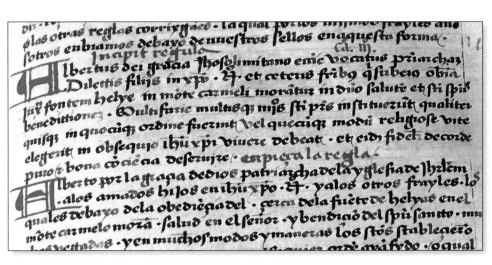

A medieval manuscript copy of the *Rule of Saint Albert* known as the Avila Codex.

Chapter 7 ▮ The Rule of Saint Albert

Get prepared: It would be helpful first to first read the *Rule of Saint Albert*; it's a short text and is printed at the front of this book. Before you delve into this chapter, get together whatever writing and reading materials you might need. Begin your time of reflection with a prayer; the one below was composed in 2007 as part of the 8th centenary celebrations of the Carmelite way of life.

> *Tender-hearted God,*
>> *through Saint Albert of Jerusalem you assembled the holy hermits of Mount Carmel*
>> *as a family of pilgrim people, seeking to live in allegiance to Jesus Christ.*
> *Like them, inspire us to imitate the first Christians of Jerusalem,*
>> *that we may build your kingdom, the heavenly Jerusalem.*
> *Like them, turn our hearts from conflict with others*
>> *to the spiritual fight against all that distracts us from you.*
> *Like them, help us to draw water from the spring of Elijah,*
>> *and to live deeply our baptismal calling.*
> *With Mary, we commit to standing alongside those who are suffering.*
> *Help us to find you alone in the cell of our hearts,*
>> *and lead us through solitude into community.*
> *Let our prayer inspire our service of others,*
>> *and our service show us our need for prayer.*
> *May our silent contemplation bear fruit,*
>> *and proclaim that God lives in whose presence we stand.*
> *Use our poverty, chastity, and obedience to be Good News for others.*
> *We thank you for our diversity, united by a common vision.*
> *We thank you for sustaining, reforming and transforming us over centuries,*
>> *for the benefit of the Church and the World.*
> *We thank you for the saints, those living and those gone before,*
>> *who have shown us an ancient path to the Mountain that is Christ.*
> *May all we do be done in your Word.*
> *This we ask, in Jesus' name. Amen.*

The panoramic view of Haifa seen from Mount Carmel today.

Seeking a way to live

The document we now call the *Rule of Saint Albert*, by which all Carmelites live, was first given to a group of Christian hermits gathered on Mount Carmel in the Holy Land. We don't know much about them, but they were probably European pilgrims to Jerusalem, or soldiers who had gone to fight in the Holy Land Crusades. Most likely the majority of them were laymen. They probably hadn't come to Carmel much before the year 1200, but by the first quarter of the 13th century they had already achieved some sense of community. Their community had grown to such an extent that they had developed a degree of organisation including a leader, and now they felt the time had come to codify and give some structure to already existing relationships. But it seems they didn't want to follow the existing regulations of other religious communities, such as the *Rule of Saint Benedict*; they wanted

A sculpture of Albert holding his *Rule* at Aylesford Carmelite Priory in the English county of Kent.

something new, and Albert acknowledged this in the opening words of his text, which took the form of a letter:

> Albert, called by the grace of God to be Patriarch of the Church of Jerusalem, greets his beloved sons in Christ, B. and the other hermits living in obedience to him near the spring on Mount Carmel: salvation in the Lord and the blessing of the Holy Spirit. Many times

and in different ways the holy Fathers have laid down that everyone – whatever be their state in life or the religious life chosen by them – should live under the patronage of Jesus Christ and serve him zealously with a pure heart and a good conscience. Now then you have come to me seeking a formula of life according to your proposed manner of life, which you are to observe in the future. (Chapters 1-3)

Saint Albert

Who was the author of this letter? His name was Albert Avogadro, and he came from the Italian town of Vercelli. He had been appointed by the Pope as the Latin Patriarch (Roman Catholic Bishop) of Jerusalem, and as such he was the ideal person for the hermits to approach in their search for a way of life. Because of the ongoing Crusader conflicts Albert was unable to reside in Jerusalem itself, so he lived in the port town of Acre or Akko, just a few miles north of the town of Haifa built on the slopes of Mount Carmel.

Before coming to the Holy Land Albert had been a bishop in Italy and was aware of the exciting developments emerging in the Church at that medieval period. A spiritual renewal was underway with people eager to follow Christ more closely, living in ways that aimed at mirroring the Gospels (hence the movement is called the 'Evangelical Awakening'). The hermits on Carmel were inspired by these same values, desiring deeply to share a life of penance (that is, turning continually back to God), serving Christ and living the values of the Gospel in a radical way. Albert was himself a member of a religious community, and had written guidelines for other Christian groups, so was well qualified to give the hermits advice.

In the technical sense of Canon Law (the regulations of the Church), the document that Albert gave to the hermits on Mount Carmel was not a *Rule* at that stage but a more informal text known as a *Way of Life* (*Formula Vitae* in Latin). Scholars are still debating how much of the *Way of Life* was written by Albert himself, and how much was proposed by the hermits, following the way they were already living. What historians have agreed on is that Albert was not the 'founder' of the Carmelite Order, in the way that St. Francis founded the Francisans or St. Dominic founded the Dominicans. Saint Albert helped the hermits to set out a vision of how they should live, but he was not so much founding a religious order as recognising a community of consecrated people that was already in existence. The vision of Carmel – now as then – comes from the community, not from one individual. To this day Albert is remembered affectionately and gratefully by the Carmelite Family not as founder but as the 'Law-giver' of Carmel, and he is celebrated liturgically on 17th September.

Did you know? Albert is not to be confused with another medieval saint of the same Christian name, Albert of Trapani (Sicily), a Carmelite friar famous for his preaching and miracles, who died in 1307. Nor is he to be confused with Saint Albert the Great (also known as Albertus Magnus or Albert of Cologne), a Dominican friar and bishop (d. 1280) whose great insights into philosophy and theology have earned him the status of a Doctor of the Church.

Stop and look at the picture below: It is a painting by Adam Kossowski that hangs in the Prior's Hall at Aylesford Carmelite Priory in the English county of Kent. It is full of symbolism. Albert is shown seated on the right, dressed as a bishop. He is handing the *Way of Life* document to 'Brother B.', whom Carmelites refer to by tradition as Saint Brocard. In the distance, on the left, is shown Mount Carmel, with the Carmelites' chapel that was dedicated to Our Lady, who herself watches the scene from heaven. Mary and the infant Jesus are surrounded by angels who hold a scroll bearing the words of the *Way of Life* in Latin.

Papal approval

Albert wrote – or at least approved – the Carmelite *formula vitae* at some point whilst he was Patriarch of Jerusalem, between 1206 and 1214. Sadly Albert was stabbed to death during a religious procession in 1214 by a disgruntled hospital administrator he had dismissed. This was problematic for the Carmelites because it meant that they were without a defender at the Fourth Lateran Council, a meeting of bishops held at Rome in 1215. The bishops were worried by the explosion in the number of religious communities and banned the approval of new orders. Happily the Carmelites were able to satisfy the Church that they predated the ban, and Albert's *Way of Life* was given temporary approval by Pope Gregory IX in 1229. In the subsequent years the continuing Crusader conflicts made it unsafe for the hermits to remain on Mount Carmel and they began returning to Western Europe, arriving in England in 1242. Faced with an entirely different social situation from what they had known in the Holy Land, the hermits gradually became

A painting in Naples depicts Innocent IV approving Albert's *Way of Life* as a religious *Rule*.

an order of mendicant (begging) brothers. In order to gain the Church's formal approval for this, they sent two brothers to Rome in 1247. Pope Innocent IV asked some Dominican cardinals to advise on how Albert's *Way of Life* document could be adapted into a more formal *Rule* for the newly constituted religious order. The Dominicans advised some minor revisions to the document, such as including the 'evangelical counsels' of poverty, chastity and obedience (Ch. 4) and specifying the Divine Office (Ch. 11). With these additions, Innocent IV approved the text, which came to be known as *The Rule of Saint Albert*.

It was the slight modifications made to the *Rule* in 1247 that enabled the hermits of Carmel to become part of the 'mendicant' movement in Europe. Until then they had technically been *hermits* living what is known as the *eremitical life*, living, working, and praying somewhat apart from the world. They were *solitaries* but gathered in *community* for prayer and mutual support. As the Carmelite hermits became *friars* (derived from 'frater', the Latin word for 'brother') they remained living in individual cells or dormitories but could live and work alongside the people in the growing towns. In some respects the friar's way of life is both *eremitical* and *monastic*, but unlike *monks* friars are not attached to one monastery, and they tend to live in towns rather than in secluded monasteries. Some medieval Carmelites obtained permission to be *anchorites*, living in more strict solitude 'anchored' to a particular cell.

Did you know? The Order is unable to give a precise date for its establishment, but decided to designate 2007 as a good time to celebrate the 8th centenary of the Carmelite *Way of Life*. This was marked in various ways around the world; Carmelites in Britain invited the current Latin Patriarch of Jerusalem to celebrate a special Mass with them.

The Rule: a key to Carmel

A structured religious rule – like structured prayer – needs to be inspirational and proportionate, not simply a set of imposed restrictions, since, as Albert's *Rule* itself states, 'necessity overrides every law' (Ch. 16). When we Carmelites read Albert's *Rule* we seek out the 'spirit', rather than the 'letter' of the law; it is a vision of Carmelite life, not a set of restrictions.

Even including the additions made to the text by Pope Innocent (often shown in editions in italics), Albert's *Way of Life* is a concise document, indeed the shortest of all religious rules. Yet it is rich in meaning and crucial for an understanding of Carmelite spirituality.

The two main branches of the Carmelite Family – the Carmelites (sometimes referred to as the Ancient Observance or O.Carm.) and Discalced Carmelites (sometimes referred to as the Teresian Observance or O.C.D.) – used to number the chapters of the *Rule* differently, until a system was agreed in 1999. The text that the whole Carmelite Family follows is Innocent IV's approved text of 1247, sometimes called the 'Primitive Rule' (to distinguish it from the text of the *Rule* after some mitigations and alterations were made to it in the 1400s).

What is at the heart of the Carmelite *Rule*? How can it speak to us today? What does it have to say to people at large?

Everything focuses on Jesus

The essence of the *Rule* is the desire to live a life of 'allegiance to Jesus Christ' (Ch. 2), serving him faithfully with a 'pure heart and a clear conscience', as we read in Chapter 3. These words that echo St. Paul in the Bible are crucial to an understanding of the Carmelite way. As the 1995 *Constitutions* of the Order state, 'Carmelites live their life of allegiance to Christ through a commitment to seek the face of the living God through community and through service in the midst of the people' (§14). The *Rule of Saint Albert* lays the foundations for the Carmelite charism of being *contemplatives who form praying communities at the service of all God's people.*

Spiritual battle

The notion of 'allegiance' to Christ – with its echoes of medieval feudal society – had a special meaning for the first Carmelites. To some degree they understood their allegiance as being like vassals loyal to a master. They were part of a struggle on behalf of Christ to free the Holy Land from the Saracens, though they gave up physical battle in favour of 'spiritual warfare', taking off the armour of war to wear instead God's armour (as set out in Chapter 18 of the *Rule*). We might say today that those early Carmelites realized that an armed struggle was not the way forward, as the Holy Land and the wider world would only be won for Christ if people fought for spiritual values. Jesus Christ claimed their total allegiance as they strove to work, in the land where he had lived, for the deepest living of the Gospel and all the values that Jesus represented. This is why in later chapters the *Rule* speaks of a spiritual struggle which needs the shield of faith and other strategies to outflank the forces of darkness (Chapter 19). The images and language are those of St. Paul and the sense of personal struggle by the early Carmelites echoes desert spirituality (referred to in the previous chapter on Elijah). In that warfare spiritual arms are needed. However, this struggle has moved from the warfare of the Crusaders fighting an external enemy, to the deeper struggle within ourselves; the vision of John's Gospel where the light will not be overcome by the dark (*John* 1:5) and truth is the source of freedom (*John* 8:32). Carmel is a garden and a desert; a space for growth and a place of struggle. Carmel was the scene for the great contest between Elijah and the priests of Baal where the one true God was vindicated (*1 Kings* 18), which has set a special seal on the place for all time.

Stop and reflect: Do you see your life as a spiritual struggle? If so, what 'spiritual armour' protects you?

The *Rule* and the Bible

Living in allegiance to Christ is the life of loving obedience that is the hallmark of all Christians. Christ on the Cross saves us through his loving obedience and our following of Christ is meant to reproduce that commitment of love. Faithfulness to Christ is enhanced for a Carmelite by a love of his Law – his Word in Holy Scripture. The *Rule* is shot through with Scriptural quotations and allusions, and has been called 'a masterpiece of *lectio divina*' because it is imbued with so many Bible references. Reflecting on the Word of God is central to the Carmelite project. Many commentators consider Chapter 10 of the *Rule* to be at the very heart of the Carmelite way of life: 'All are to remain in their cells or near them, meditating day and night on the law of the Lord and being vigilant in prayers, unless otherwise lawfully occupied.' The 'law of the Lord' refers to the Word of God: both the person of Jesus Christ, and the Scriptures. The hermits on Carmel knew the Law of God because they pondered Christ's life, they listened to his word through meditation, solitude, watchful prayer, the Divine Office, and coming together to reflect on the Scriptures.

Do you recall what we noted in previous chapters? Although the *Rule of Saint Albert* makes no explicit reference to our Order's patrons, Mary and Elijah, we know from accounts written by pilgrims to the Holy Land in the late 1100s that there were hermits living on Mount Carmel 'by the spring of Elijah' who by c.1220 (if not before) had built a chapel dedicated to Mary.

The ruins of the chapel on Mount Carmel.

The role of the Prior

According to Albert's *Rule*, the concrete living out of all this meditation is achieved by obeying the Prior. The community leader on Carmel at the time the formula was given is referred to by Albert simply as 'B' (Chapters 1 & 22), and tradition calls him Brother Brocard. In obeying the Prior, whom they elect, Carmelites see themselves as obeying one placed over them by Christ (Chapter 23). However, Albert made clear that the Prior is to exercise authority as Christ would have done, that is in a spirit of service: 'Whoever wants to be first among you let him be your servant' (Chapter 22). This vision of the leader of the community is very different from the Benedictine 'abbot' (which means 'father') who has complete authority within his monastery. The Prior, according to the Carmelite understanding, is not the 'father' of the community but rather the servant brother whose authority is given to him by the community. The relationship is not one of sons obeying a father but rather an attitude of faithfulness inspired by the common goal of following Christ.

Did you know? For many years the roles of Prior (the senior brother within a community), Prior Provincial (the senior brother within a province), and Prior General (the senior brother within the whole Order) were posts held for life. Today, duration of office is limited. Within the Third Order, the term 'Prior' has now generally been replaced by 'Leader' or 'Convenor'.

Life in community

The working out of the relationship between the Prior and the rest of the community is important in the *Rule*. It has implications for how we live together and how authority is

The ruins of what was perhaps the Prior's cell on Mount Carmel.

exercised within Carmelite communities, whether lay or religious. Albert's formula for living looks towards an interchange of ideas and aspirations within the community. The brothers are to meet weekly to discuss matters of importance, so that the common life and the well-being of each brother are considered (Chapter 15). The Prior then executes what has been decided by the community. Because his cell should be at the entrance of the community (Chapter 9), the Prior is also the one who welcomes visitors and ensures that hospitality and the needs of the community are not in conflict. Issues like where the brothers should make foundations are also part of the discernment of the whole community (Chapter 5), along with the allotting of separate cells for each brother (Chapter 6). However once decisions are made the Prior has the care of ensuring that any changes are made at his behest (Chapter 8). The picture that emerges is very much of a collaborative project where the Prior is entrusted with the oversight and enacting of the community's decision. To a degree he becomes the conscience or ongoing memory of the community, and he is as responsible and accountable to the brothers as they are to him. The Prior is therefore not there to exert power or to achieve a status, but is meant to be a person who serves the community. If the Prior really imitates Christ as the Servant of the Lord (Chapter 22), he becomes a symbol of the community's faithfulness to God through Jesus Christ (Chapter 23).

Not priests but priestly people

The whole structure of the Carmelite community and the relationships that exist inside it need to be always and ever more Christocentric, that is focussed and modelled on Christ, because Jesus and his way of living is at the heart of Carmel. Another 'community element' that is in the *Rule*, and sometimes neglected, is the fact that Albert makes no distinction between those who are ordained and the lay members of the community. Priesthood, except in so far as a priest is presumed for daily Eucharist when it is convenient (Chapter 14), is not taken into account, and Albert does not say that the Prior must be a priest. The only distinction made is between those brothers who can read and those who cannot (Chapter 11), with those who can praying the Canonical Hours (the Divine Office), thus taking part in the wider liturgical life of the Church.

Stop and ponder: Is it significant to you that the first Carmelite community probably consisted for the most part of lay people who had consecrated their lives to God, not clerics?

Solitaries in community

In any attempt to understand or live the *Rule* there can be conflict between its solitary aspect and the community dimension. The way we understand the *Rule* today can be culturally conditioned, or come through a particular focus that suits our own interpretation. It is often easier to emphasise the 'solitary' aspects of the *Rule* when we find it hard to live as a community and work through tensions towards a creative unity. Carmelites are called to be alone with God in their 'cell' (whatever form that may take), but also to live with other Carmelites. This way of life is crucial for friars, enclosed nuns, apostolic sisters, lay people, and for the communities of hermits who have been incorporated into the Order since the 1990s and who remind us of our eremitical origins.

Did you know? The Carmelite tradition emphasises the necessity of both communal prayer and prayer in private. Community prayer is vital but not a substitute for nourishing our personal relationship with Jesus, who said: 'whenever you pray, go into your room and shut the door and pray to your Father who is in secret; and your Father who is in secret will reward you' (*Matthew* 6:6). Prayer in the privacy of one's room or cell recalls the advice in the Psalms to ponder silently on your bed (*Psalms* 4:4), and the private prayer of Elisha in reviving a sick child (*2 Kings* 4:33).

Prayer at the heart of the *Rule*

Some commentators have taken Chapter 10 to be at the heart of the *Rule*: 'Each one of you is to stay in his own cell or nearby, pondering the Lord's Law day and night and keeping watch in prayer unless attending to some other duty.' This envisages an engagement of the mind and heart where a brother (or today a sister) is so absorbed by the Scriptures that God's word is in his or her heart and mind at all times. The solitude and silence that the *Rule* says should surround the Carmelite (Chapter 21) enables the focus to be on God and God's Word. However, even from the earliest days of the Carmelite project, the brothers left their solitude to preach and share their love of God's Word with God's people. In 1247 they opted for the mendicant life, which in principle meant mobility and association with the growing urban culture of Western Europe. Because the brothers committed to an active apostolate as well as to meditative life, their 'meditation' came to mean an ever deepening reflection on the Scriptures, so that they could help people at large by their insights and preaching. According to Albert, the Carmelite is also expected to be vigilant in prayer so that he (or today she) is ready to welcome the Lord when he comes again (Chapter 24). A consequence of this vigilance is a growing sensitivity and awareness that we must not allow our hearts to grow coarse or lessen the ardour of our love for our neighbour. Later chapters of the *Rule* – with their focus on spiritual warfare and commitment to fraternal living – give a more focused realization of the call to vigilant prayer.

Stop and reflect: Some would say, encouraged by the *Rule of Saint Albert* and the Carmelite tradition, that someone does not have the Carmelite spirit unless they spend some time each day, however brief, in pondering the Scriptures. Would you agree with this statement? How do you ponder the Bible in your own daily life?

Solitude and 'the cell'

The overall tenor of Chapter 10 of the *Rule* is to praise and value the solitude that enables prayer, but not in the sense of a flight from life or dislike of other people. Rather, solitude helps the Carmelite to gain the energy, focus and vitality to work with people, and above all to practice love as brothers and sisters in community at the service of others.

Given these considerations, modern commentators on the *Rule* have suggested that the heart of the Carmelite way of life is not just Chapter 10, but Chapters 10-15 which deal with the life of the community. The *Rule* does not just envisage isolated persons praying in their cells, but rather a fraternity which journeys in unity. Here we can feel inspiration from the second chapter of the *Acts of the Apostles* where Luke depicts the early Christians in Jerusalem. Chapters 10-15 take us from solitude to a celebration of praise, since the Psalms are to be prayed in common (Chapter 11). There is a sharing of goods (Chapter 12), an openness to poverty, and also a sharing of ideals and needs in regular meetings (Chapter 15). All this culminates in the celebration of daily Eucharist (Chapter 14). If anything is at the heart of the *Rule* it is the celebration of the Eucharist daily when convenient, and the fraternal communion that it achieves.

Did you know? The stipulation of Chapter 13 – 'You may have as many asses and mules as you need, and keep a certain amount of livestock or poultry' – may seen rather strange, until we realise that Innocent IV added this to Albert's text because animals were regarded as property, which the Carmelites did not want to accumulate because of their life of poverty. Mules could not breed, and therefore the community could not earn an income from rearing livestock as monks traditionally did. Another implication of Chapter 13 is that the brothers were not to have horses, which were speedy and powerful and used in war.

Growing together

The following of Jesus, the great project of the *Rule of Saint Albert*, is achieved by becoming a community of disciples who owe everything to Christ, but above all their allegiance. Discipleship in a community means that the Carmelite lives in Christ. It means that the *Rule* is not interested in an individualistic spirituality where everyone does their own thing. Rather, the *Rule* says we should grow towards God together, in the realization of an ecclesial communion. Reflecting on God's word and world in solitude energises and leads to community in Eucharist, and then to the living out of that love with one's brother or sister. Although the *Rule* calls for fasting (Chapter 16), the fraternity that grows from this prayer and celebration is not severe. The Carmelite way is not harshly ascetic nor is it overly enthusiastic or fantastical. Carmelites must do some sort of work (Chapter 20) and discipline is important (Chapter 15), but the *Rule* has no place for penalties. Albert envisages the brothers keeping the ideal of generosity vibrant through the interaction of community meetings and the role of the Prior as a servant brother. A freedom to serve emerges from this dynamic love and from the encounter with God that comes with pondering his Word in the heart.

Stop and think: Is your experience of Carmel that it is not a severe form of spirituality? A charismatic friar of the twentieth century, Fr. Elias Lynch, O.Carm., said that "Carmel is the least regimented Order." Would you agree with that assessment?

Jerusalem

An energy and symbol that is found in the Carmelite *Rule* is Jerusalem, the holy city whose Christian community is mentioned in Albert's opening words. The pilgrimage to Jerusalem was the original inspiration that brought the first Carmelites to the Holy Land. However, the central chapters of the *Rule* are obviously inspired by the vision of the Jerusalem community found in *Acts of the Apostles* (Chapters 2 and 4): a community of disciples who were fervent in prayer, sharing all in common, and bonded by the breaking of bread. The first Jerusalem community – a foretaste of the heavenly Jerusalem – was a gathering of prayerful people that attracted others by the quality of its being. We

Carmelites and our *Rule* are shaped and inspired by that ideal, an ideal that is constantly called into being in every generation, thanks to the Holy Spirit.

Do you recall? In the last chapter we read about the symbolism of the Carmelite crest or shield. Another symbol of our Order (and others) is the Jerusalem Cross.

This cross is important to Carmelites because it reminds us of our religious family's origins in the Holy Land. Its design – popular with Crusaders – uses fives crosses to represent the five wounds of Christ. Another interpretation is that the large cross symbolises Christ and the four smaller crosses are the gospel reaching the four corners of the earth, from where pilgrims come to Jerusalem.

Purity of heart (*puritas cordis*) and common sense

The final sentences of the *Rule* speak of common sense (that is the discernment of the community) and prudent discretion as important guides in all that we do (Chapter 24). The qualities that matter are a faithful commitment and a pure heart (Chapter 2) that listens to God and God's will. But the final lines also remind us that sometimes more will be asked of us by God, so we should be open to God disturbing what can sometimes be the tidiness of our lives; we are not in control.

Did you know? As well as being a holy site for Jews, Christians and Muslims, Mount Carmel is also an important place for the Bahá'í faith.

Returning to our roots

Carmelites have read and reflected upon the *Rule of Saint Albert* since it was first given to them on Mount Carmel. However, there has been a flourishing of interest in the *Rule* and academic study of it since the Second Vatican Council in the 1960s, which asked religious orders to return to their sources and rediscover their original inspiration. The *Rule* came to be re-appreciated as a text that Carmelites have to return to in study and prayer again and again. A debt of gratitude in facilitating this is owed to Carmelite scholars like Joachim Smet, Carlo Ciconetti, Kees Waaijman and John Welch; their insights have been beacon-like, guiding us all along the path up Carmel that leads to an ever closer relationship with Christ, under Mary's protection, and inspired by Elijah.

Vatican II's reminder that all people are called to holiness, and emphasis upon the vocation of the laity, has also reminded the Carmelite Family that the original *Way of Life* Albert wrote was meant for a group that in the main was lay not clerical. So today it is important to see the *Rule* speaking not just to 'religious' but to all those of different conditions who seek to follow the way that is Carmel.

To celebrate the 8th centenary of the Carmelite Way of Life, the British Province commissioned this icon by Sr. Petra Clare, which hangs in the National Shrine of St. Jude at Faversham in Kent. It is full of symbolism derived from the *Rule of Saint Albert*.

Another bonus that has emerged from studying the *Rule* with renewed vigour is a closer bonding between the two great branches of our family: the Carmelites (Ancient Observance/O.Carm.) and Discalced Carmelites (Teresian Observance/ O.C.D.). As all Carmelites have returned to our sources we can see how reforms in the Order have sought to recall the spirit of those first Carmelites who sought a way of life from Albert of Jerusalem. Thus, whilst Discalced Carmelites place a special emphasis upon the initiatives of Teresa of Jesus (of Avila) and John of the Cross as being a starting point for something new, they are also able to look with us to the 13th century for their origins, since the reformers, like us today, wanted to be faithful to their forebears.

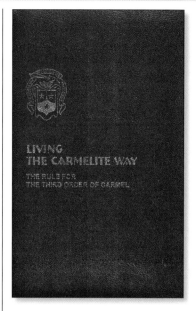

Living the Carmelite Way: The Rule for the Third Order of Carmel (2003)

The *Rule* of Saint Albert and the *Rules* for the Third Order

All Carmelites look to the *Rule of Saint Albert* for inspiration, so why is it that there is a separate document called the *Rule for the Third Order of Carmel* (*RTOC*), last issued in 2003? As we noted earlier, when the hermits from Mount Carmel became friars after 1247, Albert's *Way of Life* text became an official *Rule* for religious. Lay persons in Europe continued to be inspired by the Order's spirituality and followed the spirit of Albert's *Rule* in various different ways. In 1452 the Pope issued a Bull (letter) entitled *Cum Nulla* which gave official recognition to groups of women associated with the Order, and this laid the way for the gradual recognition of other lay groups such as confraternities (brotherhoods) linked to Carmel. In the 17th century the 'Third Order' as we recognise it today began to be formally organised. In the 1630s the Carmelite Prior General Fr. Theodore Straccio decided to organise groups of lay people who were inspired by Carmel's spirituality. It is now widely accepted that the foundational text of all Carmelites, religious and lay, is the *Rule of Saint Albert*, but Fr. Straccio decided to follow the model of the Franciscan Third Order and compose a separate *Rule* specifically for Carmelite tertiaries. In 1637 he produced a *Rule of Life for the Carmelite Third Order Secular*, which became extremely influential. This was revised many times over the ensuing centuries to reflect the changing spirit of the age.

In the 1990s various initiatives developed the notion of 'The Carmelite Family', with all the different expressions of the Carmelite charism – both religious and lay – being united by the *Rule of Saint Albert* as the common source of inspiration. Lay Carmelites recognised that they needed some legislation and guidelines that were specific to them, but increasingly felt that these should be in the form of *Constitutions* lived under the inspiration of the *Rule of Saint Albert*. In 2003 the Discalced Carmelite Secular Order (O.C.D.S.) made this move, saying that Secular Carmelites were to follow the *Rule of*

Saint Albert with distinct *Constitutions* interpreting the *Rule* for their way of life today. In the same year the Carmelite Third Order (T.O.C.) received a new *Rule for the Third Order of Carmel* (*RTOC* for short and published in book form with the heading *Living the Carmelite Way*). This new *Rule for the Third Order* combined legislation for the Third Order with a general vision for the Lay Carmelite vocation. Weaving together Scripture, the documents of Vatican II, subsequent papal writings and the insights of Carmel's saints, it was greeted as a rich spiritual text in its own right, providing a vision and material for reflection much as the 1995 *Constitutions* of the friars had done. Compared with the previous 1977 *Rule*, the 2003 text goes into much more detail about the universal call to holiness, the place of tertiaries within the Carmelite Family, contemplation, prayer, community building, and the apostolate of service. The Prior General at the time, Fr. Joseph Chalmers, O.Carm., prefaced the 2003 *Rule for the Third Order* with a letter saying that effectively the document could be taken as a set of *Constitutions*, since all Carmelites can legitimately look to the *Rule of Saint Albert* as their foundational text. It is likely that any future Third Order (T.O.C.) legislation will be submitted as a set of *Constitutions*, not a separate *Rule* in its own right.

Conclusion: In this seventh chapter we have been introduced to the person of Saint Albert of Jerusalem, and the first community of hermits living on Mount Carmel. We have seen that the *Way of Life* they sought to follow was based on the vision of the first Christian community living in Jerusalem, and it is a way of life we seek to follow today, whatever branch of the Carmelite Family we belong to. We have come to see that the *Rule of Saint Albert* is a key to understanding the contemplative spirituality of Carmel, which is rooted in the Scriptures, and which inspires us to form praying communities at the service of God's people.

To conclude your time of reflection and study, you might like to spend some time in prayer (some suggestions are given in the list of ideas for reflection).

In the next chapter we will consider the history of the Carmelite Family as it has developed from the first community on Mount Carmel up to the present day.

Ideas for Reflection, Discussion and Action

- Reflect on any passage in this chapter – or any passage from the *Rule of Saint Albert* – that has stood out as significant for you, either individually or as a community.

- Where is your cell? When do you leave it to gather with other Carmelites?

- The first Carmelites rejected physical warfare in favour of a spiritual battle. How can we follow that example and promote peace with our Muslim brothers and sisters, and others of different faiths?

- How can you deepen your commitment to the liturgical life of Carmel: the Eucharist, and the Psalms of Morning and Evening Prayer?

- Read about the development of the Third Order and its relationship to Albert's *Rule* in *Rule for the Third Order of Carmel*, paragraphs 6-10. Supplement this by reading the introduction to Patrick Thomas McMahon's book *A Pattern for Life: The Rule of Saint Albert and the Carmelite Family* (listed in the resources below).

- Given our spiritual and historical connection to Jerusalem, pray for the people of Christ's land so that conflict in the name of religion may end. Remember especially Albert's successor, the Latin Patriarch of Jerusalem, and the Carmelites living on Mount Carmel today.

- Re-read Chapter 21 of the *Rule*. Do you find it hard to guard your words or be silent?

- What does it mean for lay Carmelites to share everything in common? How could this be done?

- Could you invite others to 'ponder the Law of the Lord' through *Lectio Divina* meditation?

- Reflect on a passage from the *Rule of Saint Albert*, or a Bible passage quoted in the *Rule*, as a form of *Lectio Divina*.

- Does the Carmelite model of authority (the role of the prior and the shared responsibilities of the wider community) appeal to you?

Please turn over...

- An artistic exercise: When the Carmelite Family around the world celebrated 800 years of the Carmelite *Way of Life* in 2007, the students at Terenure College (a school run by the Order in Dublin) illustrated different passages from the *Rule*, producing the images below. If you were to pick a favourite passage from the *Rule*, how would you illustrate it?

Recommended Further Resources

There are various translations of the *Rule of Saint Albert* available, both in print and on the internet, and one is included at the front of this book. The *Rule of Saint Albert* is so fundamental to Carmelite spirituality that every library in the Order, whether religious or lay, ought to have a good selection of resources about it. Some of the following books are out of print, but others are more recent publications and so more widely available.

Johan Bergström-Allen, T.O.C., 'Looking Behind to See Ahead: Finding a Future from the Early Carmelites', *Assumpta* 46:4 (May 2003), pp. 13-27, and 'Being Faithful to His Footsteps: Translating the Carmelite Rule for Life Today', *Assumpta* 48:4 (April 2005), pp. 10-19. *Assumpta* is the Third Order magazine of the British Province of Carmelites.

Joseph Chalmers, O.Carm., 'Leadership and responsibility', in *In Allegiance to Jesus Christ*, (Rome: Edizioni Carmelitane, 1999), pp. 29-33.

Joseph Chalmers, O.Carm., 'Towards Contemplation', in *Mary the Contemplative*, (Rome: Edizioni Carmelitane, 2001), pp. 53-67.

Bede Edwards, O.C.D., *The Rule of Saint Albert*, Vinea Carmeli 1, (Aylesford & Kensington: Carmelite Press, 1973). This translation of the *Rule* is available online at: www.carmelite.org

Carlo Cicconetti, O.Carm., *The Rule of Carmel*, (Carmelite Spiritual Center, 1984).

Evaldo Xavier Gomes, O.Carm., *et al* (eds.), *The Carmelite Rule 1207-2007: Proceedings of the Lisieux Conference 4-7 July 2005*, (Rome: Edizioni Carmelitane, 2008).

Eltin Griffin, O.Carm., (ed.), *Ascending the Mountain: The Carmelite Rule Today*, (Dublin: The Columba Press, 2004).

The Irish Carmelites, *Meeting God: Carmelite Reflections and Prayers*, (Dublin: The Columba Press, 2007). This is a beautiful book of prayers, images and texts for meditation compiled to celebrate the 8th centenary of the Carmelite *Way of Life*.

Insun Joanne Lee, 'Carmelite Heritage Speaks Across the Cultures', *Carmel in the World*, Volume XLVIII Number 1, 2009, pp. 34-43.

James McCaffrey, O.C.D., 'The Carmelite Rule: A Gospel Approach', in *The Carmelite Charism: Exploring the Biblical Roots*, (Dublin: Veritas Publications, 2004), pp. 60-81.

Wilfrid McGreal, O.Carm., 'The First Hermits – A Way of Life', in *At the Fountain of Elijah: the Carmelite Tradition* (London: Darton Longman and Todd, 1999), pp 17-31.

Patrick Thomas McMahon, O.Carm., *A Pattern for Life: The Rule of Saint Albert and the Carmelite Laity*, Carmel in the World Paperbacks 14, (Rome: Edizioni Carmelitane, 2007). This is an excellent commentary on the *Rule*, chapter by chapter, which also discusses the debate about whether or not the *Rule of Saint Albert* is applicable to lay people as well as religious.

Fernando Millán Romeral, O.Carm., *The Community of the Rule as a Reconciled Community*, CD audio recording, (Dublin: Éist, 2009). This recording is of the Prior General who spoke about the *Rule of Saint Albert* at the 2009 lecture of the Carmelite Institute of Britain & Ireland (www.cibi.ie).

Peter Slattery, O.Carm., 'Elijah', in *The Springs of Carmel: An Introduction to Carmelite Spirituality*, (New York: Alba House, 1991), pp. 23-37.

Joachim Smet, O.Carm., 'The Carmelite Rule after 750 Years', *Carmelus*, 44, (Rome: Instituto Carmelitano, 1997), pp. 21-47. *Carmelus* is the academic journal of the Carmelite Order and is generally only found in scholarly libraries.

Superiors General of the Carmelite and Discalced Carmelite Orders, 'On citation of the Carmelite Rule in official documents', in John Malley, Camilo Maccise & Joseph Chalmers, *In Obsequio Jesu Christi: The Letters of the Superiors General O.Carm. and O.C.D 1992-2002*, (Rome: Edizioni OCD, 2003), pp. 127-39.

Kees Waaijman, O.Carm., *The Mystical Space of Carmel: A Commentary on the Carmelite Rule*, (Leuven: Peeters, 1999).

Notes and reflections on Chapter 7

CHAPTER 8

History of the Carmelite Family

Summary: The history of the Carmelite Family is our own story. We have before us a survey covering some 800 years. Beginning with a meditation on the meaning of history itself, key points in the development of Carmel are examined. The result is a very useful tool for study, reference and reflection. We all need to be attuned to the lessons of history – what has been worthy of humanity and what has been less so – and we can apply these lessons to the present and future.

The *Speculum Carmelitanum* – or 'Mirror of Carmel' – was written in the 17th century and is one of the classic histories of the Carmelite Family.

Get prepared: This chapter has so much material to cover that it is quite long, so you might want to divide it into two or three reading sessions. Before you begin gather together whatever writing and reading materials you might need; keeping notes of people and dates might help you build-up a timeline of Carmelite history. Why not begin your time of reflection with a prayer, perhaps with one of the ancient prayers of the Church such as the *Salve Regina* or *Come Holy Spirit*.

History: telling our story

This chapter attempts the impossible; to condense eight hundred years of Carmelite history into just a few pages. But first, let's think about what we mean by 'history'.

Individuals and groups use dates to mark out significant achievements, sorrows and hopes. Birthdays, anniversaries and memorials reconnect us with events that have shaped us. Some people record their history by keeping a diary, or storing precious or practical keepsakes such as a childhood painting, love letter, birth certificate, or a holiday photograph. These are all historical artefacts that help us tell our story. Compiling a family tree from records gives a family a sense of its 'roots'. So long as these 'souvenirs' don't make us live in the past, they can give us a wider sense of perspective of who we are.

The Carmelite Family is just the same. Over eight centuries the hermits, friars, nuns, sisters, and lay people within Carmel have passed on the Order's traditions and stories from one generation to the next, by word of mouth, in written texts, or through heirlooms and relics of the past. Carmelite history is the 'story' we tell of our collective journey towards God, of our journey with each other. It is a story with sadness and humour, low points and high points, but because it is an important story we must strive for the most accurate and objective version of it as possible.

This early modern wood-carving shows the 'Family Tree' of Carmel springing from the Fountain of Elijah.

Looking at history gives us a perspective not only on the past, but the present and future as well, prompting us to retain what is valuable in our tradition, or showing us where we must move on. By knowing our history we can make our own contribution to the Carmelite tradition with creative fidelity, and hand the legacy of Carmel on to others. History is about looking at time in the present moment of grace. Time has been made holy by God because Jesus himself came to live in a period of our history. By participating in our time, God became immersed in the symbolic values of sacred days and precious anniversaries. What unites us as a Carmelite Family –

those of us in the present, those in the past, and those yet to come – is the faith we share in Jesus who 'is the same yesterday, today, and forever' (*Hebrews* 13:8).

We are part of Carmel's history

The most important thing for a Carmelite is to live 'in allegiance to Jesus Christ' (*Rule of Saint Albert* chapter 2) in the ways recommended by our tradition. In order to do this, we must be informed not only about Christianity in general and the history of the Church, but also about that Carmelite tradition and our 'family history'. It is not necessary to be an expert in the Order's history to be a good Carmelite; Saint Thérèse of Lisieux met a Carmelite friar only once in passing and knew practically nothing of Carmel's historical development. However, she did immerse herself in the Order's spiritual traditions and the writings of its great saints. Like her, the more we appreciate Carmel's heritage, the better we can live its spirituality. There is a certain amount of misinformation about the Carmelite tradition that we need to avoid perpetuating if we are to live it authentically. As Carmelites in the twenty-first century we need to know something about our 'spiritual chronology' so that can have some perspective on where we have come from, but more importantly so that we can see where we are going in the future. We look at our family's past so that we can imitate its better moments, and so that we aren't condemned to repeat its mistakes.

Stop and think: If you were telling someone about the history of Carmel, in what historical period would you begin?

Carmel is an ongoing tradition. In 2006 Lay Carmelites held an international gathering in Rome (pictured above). In 2009 members of the Carmelite Third Order in Britain held their fifth national gathering of recent times (pictured below). Such gatherings reflect on Carmel's past, assess the present moment, and plan for the future.

The first Carmelites

The prehistory of the Carmelite Order (the context in which our family emerged) is the Judeo-Christian story. Our Order is one of many religious families which developed in the Christian Church in the so-called 'High Middle Ages', around the year 1200. The official name of our Order is the *Brothers of the Blessed Virgin Mary of Mount Carmel*, taking its name from the place where the first Carmelite hermits gathered. Carmel is not actually a single mountain but a small mountainous range in Palestine, overlooking the port of Acre (near Haifa) about three miles away. It is mentioned in the Bible's *Books of the Kings* as a place of beauty where the prophet Elijah contested the prophets of Baal and proclaimed the truth of the one God. Carmel is covered with little *wadis* (ravines),

One of the Order's ancient paintings depicting the hermits and their chapel on Mount Carmel.

and it was in one of these on Carmel's western slope, the Wadi 'ain es-Siah, that hermits were seen by pilgrims who were visiting the Holy Land in the late twelfth century. From the days of the early Church the Holy Land had been home to such solitaries. It is likely that these hermits (who were probably mostly laymen) were from Europe, perhaps crusaders and pilgrims who had settled in the land where Jesus had lived.

Sometime between 1206 and 1214 the hermits asked the Latin Patriarch of Jerusalem, Albert of Avogadro, to write for them a *Way of Life* (as we read in the previous chapter). In 1226 the Pope in Rome gave limited recognition to the hermits' *Way of Life*, and three years later gave the group special privileges and protections. Albert's *Way of Life* tells us a little about how the first Carmelites were supposed to live. The opening paragraph informs us that the hermits were gathered near a well; this 'Fountain of Elijah' is still on Carmel, as are archaeological remains of the first community's cells and chapel.

A sculpture of Samson and the lion discovered in the archaeological dig at Coventry Whitefriars.

Did you know? Archaeology is an important discipline in understanding Carmelite history, giving us many insights into the past. A full survey of the Order's house in the English city of Coventry, published in 2005, detailed remnants of stained glass, choir-stalls, tiles, pottery, and sculpture. Important archaeological surveys have been carried out on Carmelite sites in various places including Scotland, Germany, and Mount Carmel itself.

Migration and expansion of the Order

Today the importance of Elijah to the Carmelite Family spurs us to form bridges between cultures and other faiths that revere him, especially between Christians, Jews and Muslims. Sadly, in the Middle Ages the fighting between the children of Abraham around Mount Carmel became so bad that the hermits had to abandon their cells and return to the West. It is possible that the hermits on Carmel spread their way of life to other parts of the Holy Land, but because of the continuing Crusader wars the hermits eventually left the region from about 1238 onwards. They left the physical Mount Carmel behind, but carried its spirit and values with them, and the image of 'the mountain' reaching to heaven has been important in Carmelite spirituality ever since.

The hermits first sailed to Cyprus, then Sicily, and some went on to southern France. They arrived in England in 1242, forming hermitages that year in Hulne (Northumberland) and Aylesford (Kent). Eventually England would become the largest Carmelite province before the Reformation, and from here the Order spread to Scotland, Wales and Ireland. The Carmelites also expanded to what is now Holland, Belgium, Germany, Poland, the Czech Republic, Portugal and Spain.

Did you know? Our knowledge of the medieval Carmelites in England, Scotland and Wales has been promoted through the *Carmel in Britain* series of scholarly books produced since the 1990s.

The ruins of the Carmelite house at Hulne, Northumberland.

The 1247 General Chapter in Aylesford

In 1247 the dispersed Carmelites gathered at Aylesford hermitage in England for their first general chapter. They had found that hermit-life in Western Europe was very different from that they had known in Palestine, and change was needed. They could have decided to become monks, living in fixed monasteries with estates to farm. Instead, the Carmelites were inspired by the 'Evangelical Awakening' sweeping through and reinvigorating the Church. A few years earlier Saints Francis and Dominic had founded communities of men who went into the towns to preach to the people and minister to their needs. These men were known as *mendicants*, or beggars, because they relied on the townspeople for their upkeep rather than on income from monastic estates. Instead of being called monks, they were known as *friars*, from the Latin word for 'brothers'. The Carmelites decided to develop into such a mendicant fraternity, and sent two of their number from Aylesford to Rome to request the necessary permission. This was granted on 1st October 1247 in a Papal letter called *Quae honorem*, in which Pope Innocent IV published a modified version of Albert's *Way of Life* as an official religious *Rule*. *Quae honorem* allowed the Carmelites to set up communities in towns as well as in solitary places, which meant that they could beg for alms and attract new vocations more easily. The Carmelites were largely successful in both aspects, and the Order quickly spread in Britain and Europe as a whole, gradually being recognised as a mendicant fraternity.

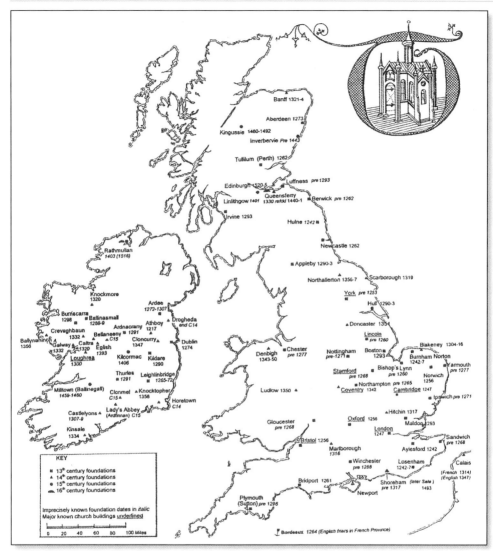

A map (made by Charmian and Paul Woodfield) of the Carmelite houses in Britain and Ireland before the Reformation.

Did you know? The Carmelite Order was expelled from its priory at Aylesford at the Reformation, but always sought to return there because of its importance in the development of Carmel. Sometimes nicknamed 'the Second Carmel', it was reacquired by the Order in 1949.

What did medieval Carmelites do?

We don't know a tremendous amount about what medieval friars actually did every day. What we know comes from legal records, liturgical manuscripts, the *Constitutions* of the Order and the *Acts of the General Chapters* written at various intervals throughout the Middle Ages. Albert's *Rule* specified that the Carmelites should 'ponder the law of the Lord day and night when not engaged in other lawful activity' (Chapter 10), and prayerful meditation was certainly the most important aspect of a friar's contemplative life.

However, to keep a community running it would also have been necessary for friars to maintain their houses, and going out into the service of others proved to be another source of contemplation. Carmelite friars have adapted themselves in every time and place to meet the needs of local people, and have provided necessary apostolates by reading the signs of the times. The main ministries included preaching and administering the sacraments. The friars' main source of income would have come from donations given by the public (especially rich benefactors) or the crown. In return, some Carmelite houses provided not only prayers for their benefactors, but also schooling, health care, and manuscript copying. Some Carmelites were diplomats and advisors at royal courts.

Did you know? A Carmelite Missal used in London c.1395 is one of the treasures of the British Library. It contains some of the finest illuminations surviving from medieval England, such as the one to the right, which shows the dedication of a church with Carmelites singing from a sheet of music.

An image from the so-called 'Reconstructed Carmelite Missal'. British Library, Ms. Additional 29704-5 folio 68v (detail).

Internal aggravations

Not all Carmelites were happy with the new mendicant way of life in the West. Some brothers who remembered the life on Mount Carmel felt that the Order should return to its desert roots; they were not opposed to an active apostolate as such, but felt that the Order was not qualified or experienced enough to engage in such ministry. In a famous letter called *The Flaming Arrow*, Nicholas the Frenchman, a prior general in the 1270s, proposed that the Order should return to its eremitical foundations, though it seems his letter (which has been the subject of much debate) fell on deaf ears and may even have been lost (or perhaps not even truly composed) until the early 1400s.

Stop and think: How can Carmelites today be inspired by the Order's eremitic roots?

Aggravation with other orders and Carmel under threat

Criticism of the Carmelites came from outside the Order as well as from within. People are often suspicious of newcomers, and the Whitefriars (as the Carmelites were known because of the white cloaks they had adopted in the 1280s) were no exception. Whilst some towns welcomed the new friars with open arms, sometimes they met with great hostility from bishops, monks, and other mendicant orders who were angry that the Carmelites were taking donations away from them. Some people argued that there were too many new religious movements springing up, and at the Second Council of Lyons in 1274 the Church made an important declaration: religious orders founded after 1215 were to be suppressed, and those founded before that date (such as the Carmelites and Augustinians) were allowed to continue only if they could prove their usefulness to the Church.

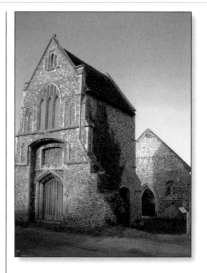

Did you know? The Carmelites built a hermitage in Burnham Norton on the north Norfolk coast in England sometime before 1247. Its surviving gatehouse is one of the most complete artefacts of medieval Carmelite life in Britain. Pilgrimages sometimes come here and to other ancient Carmelite sites in Britain such as Hulne, Coventry, Doncaster and South Queensferry (near Edinburgh, the capital of Scotland).

Carmel: a student order

The Second Council of Lyons forced the Carmelites to look seriously at their history and mission. The Carmelites eventually managed to convince the Pope that they should be allowed to continue, but in order to be 'useful' to the Church the brethren decided they had to be better educated, and better formed for ministry. Every house of the Order developed as a place of study, and the Order began sending its brightest young men to Europe's universities such as Paris, Bologna, Oxford and Cambridge. Until then, the Dominicans and Franciscans had been the major student orders, but now Carmel joined their ranks.

Stop and think: For the bulk of its history Carmel has been a student order. What significance should study have in Carmelite life today, for Carmelite laity and religious?

Carmelite-related sites in Britain at (top-bottom) Burnham Norton; Doncaster; South Queensferry.

Chapter 8 ∎ History of the Carmelite Family

Thomas Netter of Walden on the wall of the Old Library in the Carmelite house at Krakow, Poland.

Although all friars received some education in order to pray the Divine Office, and those who were ordained received training for ministry, only a small minority (probably no more than 1%) attended university. However, some of those who did became the best known scholars of their day. The English friars were particularly noteworthy for the scholars they produced in the Middle Ages, including the theologians John Baconthorpe (d. c.1348) and Thomas Netter of Walden (d. 1430). Other important Carmelite scholars from across Europe include Gerard of Bologna (1240-1317), Guido Terrini (d. 1342) and Michael Aiguani (d. 1400). Carmelites wrote on all manner of subjects: philosophy, the Bible, medicine, astronomy, music, grammar, physics, theology and poetry. One interesting aspect of medieval Carmelite scholarship is how many friars were engaged in combating heresy (such as Lollardy), and how many were well versed in the Holy Scriptures. This was seen in some of Carmel's great saints of the age: Angelus, Peter Thomas (c.1305-66), Andrew Corsini (d. 1374), Nuno Alvares Pereira (1360-1431), Aloysius Rabatà (d. 1490), Jane Scopelli (1428-91), Albert of Trapani (d. 1307), Angelus Augustine Mazzinghi (c.1386-1438), and Bartholomew Fanti (d. 1495). We shall learn about them in Chapter 18.

We know that the Carmelite sense of history and identity must have come under scrutiny because of a text called the *Rubrica Prima*. As we read in Chapter 6, the *Rubrica Prima* prefaced the Order's earliest surviving *Constitutions* (set of regulations), issued at a general chapter held in London in 1281. The *Rubrica Prima* is the earliest surviving document which attempts to write the story of the Carmelite 'journey'. It is also the first document in which the Order refers to the Carmelites as imitators of the prophets Elijah and Elisha:

> *Since some young brothers in the Order do not know how to reply truthfully to those who wish to know how and where our Order originated, we want to provide them with a written account of how to respond to such demands. We say that, on the evidence of trustworthy witnesses, that from the time of the prophets Elijah and Elisha, the holy fathers of both the old and new testaments have lived devotedly on Mount Carmel, true lovers of the solitude of that mountain for the contemplation of heavenly things. There, near the fountain of St. Elijah, without any doubt, they lived praiseworthy lives, and their successors continuously thereafter.*

Elijah's contest on Mount Carmel depicted in a woodcut in the *Speculum Carmelitanum* (1680).

Carmel's Elijan heritage

Given the link between Carmel, Elijah and Elisha in the Bible's *Books of the Kings*, it is likely that those prophets featured in the Order's tradition before 1281, but the *Rubrica Prima* is the first known written example. Linking the Order's origins to Elijah was significant because it meant that the friars could claim to be the oldest religious order within the Church, founded well before the 1215 cut-off date for mendicant orders, and even predating Christ! This meant that they had more seniority than their 'rival' religious

A page from one of the first printed copies of Felip Ribot's *The Ten Books*, one of the most significant Carmelite texts of the Middle Ages after the *Rule of Saint Albert*.

orders. The Carmelites and Augustinians were finally approved by Pope Boniface VIII in 1298. For centuries now the Carmelite Order has been classed in Canon Law as a 'clerical religious institute of pontifical right', with the power to govern its own affairs, exempted by the Pope from the governance of bishops in internal matters for the better good of the Order and its apostolate (c.f. *Code of Canon Law* §591).

The Carmelites' claims to antiquity were mocked by other religious orders until a debate and ruling at Cambridge University in 1374 confirmed the Carmelites' assertion that they were founded by Elijah. Shortly after these claims were reinforced in a very important document of the medieval Order, the *Ten Books on the Way of Life and Great Deeds of the Carmelites* (better known as *The Book of the First Monks*) compiled by Felip Ribot, the Carmelite Prior Provincial of Catalonia. Ribot describes the Carmelite life as seeking union with God in love through withdrawing from the world's attachments so as to have a pure heart like Elijah.

Today the Order accepts that the link with Elijah cannot be proved historically. However, we still regard Elijah as one of the key inspirations in our Order's spirituality, and he is celebrated in our calendar on 20th July as Saint Elijah, Prophet and Founder of the Carmelite ideal.

The difference between myth and history

Of course there is no historical evidence that the Carmelites were indeed founded by Elijah. However, the fact that this claim took such hold within the Order shows the power of myth. Whereas historiography ought to depend on provable facts, myths are not provable or literally true. Nevertheless, myths contain 'truths' about how a group regards itself. Therefore, while the Order's medieval claim to descend from Elijah is not literally true, it shows the Order's desire to imitate his zeal for God.

Well into the twentieth century, some Carmelites believed that the Order really did descend from Elijah. However, as the century developed the Order encouraged its scholars to look objectively at the historical evidence. This was encouraged in the 1960s by the Second Vatican Council which urged religious orders to go back to their roots and to give an honest account of their development. In so doing, Carmelites were able to discover what is distinctive about our Order, and also to see from the wider context of medieval contemporaries that our forebears shared much with other orders. Since the twentieth century Carmelite history has been promoted by Carmelite Institutes (in Rome, Washington D.C., Holland, the Philippines, Malta, Britain and Ireland, and elsewhere) through the Order's academic journal *Carmelus*, by scholarly research and seminars, and through similar initiatives in the Discalced Carmelite Order.

Fr. Bartolomé Maria Xiberta, O.Carm.

Did you know? Fr. Bartolomé Maria Xiberta, O.Carm. (1897-1967), was one of the Order's greatest recent scholars, not only in revising attitudes to Carmelite history, but also as a leading theologian of the Second Vatican Council, particularly on the sacrament of reconciliation. Fr. Bartolomé was also renowned for his personal holiness, and his cause for beatification is being considered. He is proof that scholarship and pastoral care should go hand-in-hand.

Mary in Carmel's history

Another area where the Carmelite Order has been active in distinguishing myth from history since the twentieth century is in its relationship to Mary, the Mother of God.

As we read in Chapter 5, since the Middle Ages the Order has claimed to have a special relationship with the Blessed Virgin. Medieval friars claimed that the Order had been founded in honour of Mary, and that she was their 'sister' and 'patron'. Certainly the Order built a chapel on Carmel dedicated to Mary, the 'Lady of the Place', and her name − although it is not mentioned in the *Rule* − occurred in the Order's title from an early date. Carmelites in the medieval universities strongly promoted the doctrine of Mary's Immaculate Conception, and regarded her as the pure-hearted Virgin, totally obedient to God's will in her life.

However, perhaps the best known link between Mary and Carmel − the Brown Scapular devotion − is an example of where history and myth have become blurred. Legend claims that in the 1250s, an English Prior General of the Order called Simon Stock received a vision of Mary in which she gave him the Carmelite scapular as a sign of her special protection. However, whilst we know that there was a Prior General called Simon (who was venerated as a saint within the Order from an early date), the story of the scapular did not emerge until the fifteenth century, that is, two centuries after his death. Similar stories existed in other religious orders at the time. By the sixteenth century,

Our Lady and the infant Christ surrounded by Carmelite friars, depicted in a Carmelite manuscript in Lincoln College, Oxford, Ms. Lat 106 folio 3r.

Simon Stock was known as 'Simon the Englishman' and probably died around 1265 in Bordeaux, France (where there was an English colony). In 1951 some of the relics of Saint Simon were brought from Bordeaux to the new shrine at Aylesford Carmelite Priory in the English county of Kent, and placed in this reliquary designed by Adam Kossowski.

the claims and superstitions surrounding the vision story had become so exaggerated that the Vatican ordered the Carmelites to restrain how they promoted the devotion. Today, Carmelite historians tell us that the Scapular vision story is a myth which cannot be proved literally true, but we can still take 'truths' from the story: the truth that Mary loves and protects us, and the truth that when we wear her scapular (a miniature form of the Carmelite habit) we clothe ourselves in the values that Carmel stands for.

In the Middle Ages the Order was sometimes ridiculed for its more outlandish claims, which undermined its more important message of living 'in allegiance to Jesus Christ'. This will still happen to us if we cling to myths as historical facts. Whilst not losing our heritage and the beauty of our family's stories, we need to move beyond fabricated history since 'the truth will free you' (*John 8:32*).

Stop and think: What is the role of myths in cultural and religious traditions?

Carmelite liturgical life

Mary featured strongly in the liturgy of the Order too. In 1312 an *Ordinal* (a text setting out the feasts of the Order) compiled by the Carmelite Sibert de Beka was approved, which was used across the Order until 1580. Rather than using the liturgical texts common in Europe (such as the Roman or Sarum rites), the Carmelites followed that of the Holy Sepulchre, recalling the Order's origins in the Holy Land, and again making us a cultural bridge between East and West. Marian feasts, and feasts celebrating figures from the Holy Land, played a prominent role in the Carmelite *Ordinal*. Mary also featured strongly in the writings of Carmelite theologians such as John of Hildesheim and Bernard Oller.

The emergence of Lay Carmel

As mentioned earlier, the majority of the hermits on Mount Carmel were probably unordained men. When the Order was officially recognised as such these men became 'religious' in the eyes of Canon Law, and as the Order developed its official status it became increasing clericalised. This did not mean, however, that 'Lay Carmel' died out. On the contrary, as the Order grew it attracted increasing numbers of women and men who were drawn to its life of prayer and service, lived in the community. Some of these lay people were employed by the friars as servants and helpers. Some lived as 'oblates' or lay-brothers and lay-sisters, attached to a particular convent of friars. Others were given affiliation to the Order through 'letters of confraternity', which meant that in return for living the Carmelite way and supporting the Order materially a lay person was entitled to dress as a Carmelite and be buried within the Carmelite cemetery. Some entire parishes or guilds associated themselves in one way or another with a particular friary, and some of these had specific *Rules of Life*. Some of these lay Carmelites lived as 'anchorites', that is, solitaries restricted to living within one building on the grounds of the friary. The earliest known Carmelite anchorite was the lay-brother Franco Lippi who died in 1291.

Did you know? Some modern-day Carmelite confraternities – such as the one in Rome pictured below – still wear versions of the Order's habit and cloak.

Members of a Carmelite Scapular Confraternity at the Order's church of Santa Maria in Traspontina, Rome.

Women in Carmel

Given the Order's special relationship with Mary, it is natural that its spirituality should have attracted women as well as men. One of the earliest known women associated with the Carmelites is Blessed Joan of Toulouse, who died in that French city in 1286. She was another anchorite, who apparently instructed the male novices. A woman of the same name is known to have lived as an anchorite outside the friary gates in Norwich, England, in 1382. There were many such Carmelite women in medieval England, but there were no nuns in the country before the Reformation.

The ruined archway to the Carmelite anchorite's cell still stands in Norwich.

A panel from a 15th-century painting by Tommaso de Vigilia that depicts women being admitted to the Order.

Sometimes these women wore a special headdress and cloak, and were known as *mantellate* (from the Latin for 'cloak'). Sometimes they were known as *pinzocchere*, *beatae* or *conversae*, who consecrated themselves to God through the three vows sworn by the friars (poverty, chastity and obedience).

Indeed, there were many different names for these groups of Carmelite women, and several are referred to in Pope Nicholas V's Bull *Cum Nulla*. Issued in 1452, this papal document gave the first official recognition to women within the Order, although they had already been active in Carmel for centuries, and paved the way for new lay groups to develop.

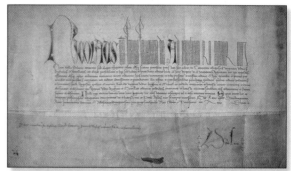

The papal bull *Cum Nulla*.

The emergence of the nuns

Nuns, in the legal sense of Canon Law, did not emerge in Carmel until the fifteenth century, when Blessed John Soreth (c.1395-1471), a reforming Prior General of the Order, saw the potential role women could play in reviving the Carmelite ideal across Europe. It was he who ensured the passing of *Cum Nulla* and in the same year he incorporated a group of 'beguines' (consecrated women) in the Lowlands into the Order. A community of women in Florence also began around this time, and the movement spread across Italy and the Netherlands. It was in the Low Countries that John met the recently widowed Duchess of Brittany, Francoise d'Amboise (1427-85). He persuaded Francoise to use her political and financial power to back the new movement of Carmelite women, and in 1468 Blessed Francoise received the Carmelite habit herself. Thanks to the work of John and Francoise, the Carmelite nuns became well established, and it is testimony to their work, as well as that of Teresa of Jesus, that today the nuns are the best known expression of Carmelite life around the world.

Blesseds John Soreth and Francoise d'Amboise depicted in an icon by Sr. Petra Clare at the National Shrine of St. Jude in Faversham, England.

The reforming instinct of the Order

The nuns came about because of John Soreth's desire to reform the Carmelite Order. Practically all religious orders (and the Church in general) have periodically experienced the need for reform to bring them back to the reasons why they began in the first place; otherwise they would die out. Just as individuals need to stop now and again to assess their lifestyles and values, so religious orders, as they have become institutionalised and part of the establishment, have tried to turn from easy living and power back to the simplicity of the Carmelite *Rule*. In 1432 Pope Eugene IV had 'mitigated' (relaxed) the Carmelite *Rule* in certain aspects, allowing friars to wander between cells and to eat meat. Some said that this freed the brethren from unnecessary and cumbersome restrictions, whilst others felt that the Carmelite way of life was becoming lax. The general lapse in Church discipline was typified by the 'Great Papal Schism' (1378-1417) when there was one pope in Avignon and a rival pope in Rome. Carmel was divided between the two popes, and many felt that the Order had a role in calling the Church back to its simple core vocation of 'living in allegiance to Jesus Christ'.

Sometimes in Carmelite history inspired and inspiring individuals have grouped together to make reforms which others resisted. The first large-scale reform movement in Carmel took place in northern Italy, where like-minded Carmelites joined together to form what became known as the 'Congregation of Mantua'. This grouping of communities was a largely autonomous body within the Order, and they returned to the way of life before Eugene IV's mitigation. They emphasised various ascetic aspects of the *Rule* such as silence and poverty, but also community life. The best known figure from this reform period is Blessed Baptist Spagnoli of Mantua (1447-1516), one of Carmel's greatest Priors General and also a poet. Another important reform of the Order later emerged from the town of Albi in France.

Did you know? Blessed Baptist is the only Carmelite referred to by William Shakespeare ('the good old Mantuan' in *Love's Labour's Lost*, Act IV, Scene II).

Stop and think: Do you reckon there are aspects of Carmelite life in need of renewal and reform today? How would you discern this? Why might people resist your suggestions?

Blessed Baptist of Mantua.

Reformation and Renaissance

John Soreth and his supporters spread reform across the Order at a time when Protestant ideas were gaining momentum across Europe. As well as seeing parts of the Order decline, the late Middle Ages saw great periods of growth and creativity with Carmelites returning to the values of meditation, poverty, and loving service. There was a flowering of Marian devotion, as well as outpourings of literature and liturgy. Across Europe Carmelites gained a reputation as great patrons of the arts. In England writers such as Richard Maidstone, Richard Lavenham, and Richard Misyn were writing theological treatises and poems in English as well as in Latin. In Italy, the friars at the 'Carmine' (Carmelite Priory) in Florence were commissioning artists like Masolino, Masaccio, and Fra Filippo Lippi (himself a Carmelite) to produce some of the masterpiece frescos of western art. Some Carmelites also immersed themselves in 'humanism', the new realm of learning, and in England John Hothby (d. 1487) wrote on the art of music.

A fresco in the celebrated Brancacci Chapel in the Florence *Carmine* (Carmelite friary) depicts the myth of the Apostle Peter preaching to a crowd of pilgrims in Jerusalem that included hermits from Mount Carmel.

Stop and think: Why do you think Carmelites over the centuries have been interested in the arts, sciences, and creative projects?

Did you know? One of the most ancient churches in the care of the Carmelite Order is that of San Martino ai Monti (St. Martin on the Hill) in Rome. This basilica was built on the site of a *titulus* or house church, in which members of the early Christian community in Rome worshipped. The Carmelite Order has had care of the Church since the thirteenth century, and at various times the house has served as the Order's General Curia (international headquarters). The present-day Curia adjoins San Martino. Various churches have been built over the site, but the crypt preserves buildings from ancient Rome. It is the burial place of several Priors General of the Order, including Nicholas Audet (1481-1562), a reforming Prior General during the turbulent years of the mid-16th century.

Left: the facade of San Martino ai Monti. Right: the grave cover of Nicholas Audet.

Reform in Spain

Perhaps Carmel is best known today because of the reforms it underwent in sixteenth-century Spain. In this country, divided by social distinctions and wars with the Moors, communities of Carmelite women had been established after *Cum Nulla*. It was one of these communities in Aragon, a house of *beatae* or *beguines* known as The Incarnation, that housed Teresa de Ahumada y Cepeda, better known by her religious name Teresa of Jesus (1515-72).

Teresa had left her bourgeois household in the town of Ávila to join the Incarnation as a Carmelite sister in 1535. The Incarnation was not a monastery in the modern sense, but a community of over a hundred women with varying degrees of commitment to a life of prayer. Teresa lived in and out of this community for some twenty years before she felt called to make a deeper commitment to God.

From the late 1550s onwards Teresa was inspired by a number of mystical experiences (and the themes of purity of heart, withdrawal, and union with God that she read in *The Ten Books*) to form a new community, known as the Convent of Saint Joseph (another patron of the Carmelite Order). She wanted this community to be small enough that all the sisters could know and love each other as friends, and dedicate themselves to a life of prayer and service. The community's dedication to prayer and silence would be supported by enclosure, that is, limited contact with the outside world but praying intently for its needs. Despite much opposition Teresa's hope was achieved. She became prioress of the new community in 1563, and set about restoring the observation of Albert's *Rule* as adapted by Pope Innocent IV in 1247, which she called the 'Primitive Rule'. Teresa's hope was that her reform of Carmel would contribute to the wider renewal of the Catholic Church, which was challenged at the time by the Protestant Reformation.

Statue of St. Teresa of Jesus outside the Incarnation Monastery in the Spanish city of Ávila.

Teresa's first foundation, the Monastery of St. Joseph in Ávila.

To promote her reforms, and inform her sisters about developing a prayerful relationship with God, Teresa began writing books that have become classics of our Carmelite tradition, including *The Way of Perfection* (c.1565) and *The Interior Castle* (1577). Although her movement became known as the 'Teresian reform', and her followers as 'Discalced' (shoeless) Carmelites, Teresa's actions were conducted within the framework of the Carmelite Order and with the blessing of the Prior General John Baptist Rossi who came from Rome to visit and encourage her. He urged Teresa to found as many monasteries as she had hairs on her head, and she took him at his word, travelling across Spain making dozens of foundations in the ensuing years.

In order to support her communities, Teresa looked for Carmelite friars who would be able to

This window from St. Teresa's Church (the Discalced Carmelite friars' church) in Ávila depicts the saint teaching her brethren about the *Rule of Saint Albert*.

celebrate the sacraments with them. One young man, Juan de Yepes (1542-91), joined the growing band of Discalced Carmelites. We know him better as Brother John of the Cross. Again, John was a friar of the Carmelite Order, working within the Discalced Reform, and following the 'Primitive Rule'.

John of the Cross depicted in mosaic at Whitefriar Street Carmelite Church in Dublin.

Did you know? The term *discalced* means 'shoeless'. As a sign of poverty Discalced Carmelites wore sandals rather than shoes with leather uppers. There were a number of discalced movements in various religious orders in the sixteenth century, such as the Discalced Franciscans.

Different readings of history

The next stage in Carmel's history is a somewhat painful one to look back on because the division it provoked in the Carmelite Family is with us to some extent to this day.

As we have seen Carmel has a long tradition of reform movements, all working as part of the Order to bring about renewal from within. The Discalced reform began in this way, but soon the movement caused division amongst the friars and sisters which wasn't helped by the outside intervention of Church and Civil authorities. Attaching themselves to Teresa's reform movement and using the protection of the Spanish court, a number of friars from the province of Andalusia rebelled against the Prior General and the heavy-handed Carmelite superiors in Spain. Each side of the debate held visitations (inspection tours of the provinces) and chapters (meetings) that the other declared invalid. The Papacy, the King of Spain, and other religious orders (notably the recently-formed Jesuits) became embroiled in the debate. The Carmelite friars of the Discalced movement were led by the charismatic Jerome Gracián (1545-1614). Teresa was deeply saddened by the divisions growing within Carmel.

During Teresa's later life (and after her death), disputes continued within the Carmelite Order about the way in which the Discalced Reform should be governed. An upshot of this dispute in 1577 was the removal of Brother John of the Cross from his house near the Incarnation monastery. He was placed in prison (commonly found in Carmelite houses at that time for the detention of wayward friars!), where he remained until his escape in August 1578. During this time, he wrote a number of poems including most of *The Spiritual Canticle* and *The Dark Night*.

A sad division

Despite Teresa's desire for unity within the Order (she was friends with both Gracián and the Prior General), the political strains were too much and the Discalced movement asked for independence from the Carmelite Order. Within a decade and a half of the death of John Baptist Rossi in 1578 there were effectively two autonomous branches of the Carmelite Family in Spain, each recognised as independent by the Papacy: the Carmelites ('O.Carm.', sometimes called the 'Ancient Observance' to distinguish them from the Discalced), and the Discalced Carmelites ('O.C.D.'). Eventually the Discalced Reform itself split between its Spanish and Italian congregations.

It is said that history is written by the victors, but in the case of the split in our family it is hard to see whether anyone won! Both sides of 'the divide' have traditionally interpreted the Spanish reform differently, and this has sometimes led to painful distrust on both sides, although there have been many examples of close collaboration between the two branches of the Order since the very first days of their formal division. In the Ancient Observance Teresa is regarded as one of the great saints of Carmel, and as our sister. In the Discalced Carmelite Order it is traditional to refer to Teresa as 'La Madre' ('our holy mother'), and until relatively recently many Discalced Carmelites regarded her

Discalced Carmelite artwork in the Early Modern period adapted existing iconography to highlight Teresa's importance.

as not only the founder of the Teresian Reform, but indeed the founder of 'the true Carmel'. However, this is changing, and as James McCaffrey, O.C.D., observes in his book *The Carmelite Charism*, Teresa and John did not found a new Order but rather reformed a three hundred year-old tradition that traces its roots back (at least spiritually) to Elijah and Mary, and the first Carmelites in the Holy Land.

Did you know? In some Discalced Carmelite paintings in the Early Modern period, Teresa was depicted in ways that previously the Virgin Mary had been shown in Carmelite art, to stress the idea of Teresa as foundational to the reform. Whereas tradition said that Our Lady had given the Carmelite Scapular to Simon Stock, new devotional pictures emerged in this time showing the Scapular being entrusted to Teresa and John.

The result of the protagonists' unwillingness to listen to the other parts of the Carmelite Family – a fault on both sides – has been that traditionally many Discalced Carmelites have tended not to know very much about the three hundred years of Carmelite spirituality and history before Teresa, and tend to read Carmelite history through the eyes of Teresa and John. On the other hand, some Carmelites (O.Carms.) have been slow in appreciating all there is to learn from the great saints of the Discalced tradition, not only Teresa and John but also later saints such as Lawrence of the Resurrection, Elizabeth of the Trinity, and Edith Stein. There has also been a mutual suspicion that Discalced Carmelites are more given over to prayer and asceticism whilst Carmelites of the Ancient Observance are more given over to the active apostolate. Today most accept that these are false distinctions and caricatures based on prejudice.

Dialogue heals division

Thanks to the call of the Second Vatican Council for religious orders to return to their roots, both branches of the Carmelite Family have been united in their renewed appreciation of the *Rule of Saint Albert* as the text that unifies all Carmelites, and equally committed to the honest reappraisal of Carmelite history. Since the 1970s regular talks have taken place across the Carmelite Family at every level. Of particular note are the discussions between the Prior General (O.Carm.) and the Prepositus General (O.C.D.), and the letters they have issued together since 1992 (printed in the collection *In obsequio Jesu Christi*). Also beneficial have been the Carmelite Forums and Institutes established in various parts of the world, and other joint projects and formation programmes. We also share a common liturgical calendar (with slight variations). It has become clear that we must collaborate and recognise each others' gifts, and that what divides the traditions is tiny in proportion to what we share.

What do you think? It is sometimes said today that any major initiative which the Carmelite Family cannot undertake as a joint project is probably not worth bothering with. Would you agree?

Did you know? Statues around the interior of St. Peter's Basilica in Rome depict the 'founders' of religious orders. Both Elijah and Teresa are included.

The Carmelite Family has tended to follow the pattern of most divided communities, as seen in places like the north of Ireland and the different denominations of the Church: first the different sides argue and the tension becomes so great that the community splits; then there is a period of not talking to each other when ignorance feeds prejudices; then we wake up to the scandal of division and our hearts are touched to begin polite communication, before we get down to debating our differences in a frank but mature and respectful fashion; finally, either unity is achieved, or we learn to celebrate the different gifts that each group brings to being Carmelite.

Some people would like to see the two branches of the Carmelite Family formally reunited, whilst others believe that something distinctive would be lost from either Order; they say that just as a rainbow is one entity consisting of many colours, so being united doesn't mean that we all have to be the same. Today most people recognise that there is only one Carmelite charism but that it is lived distinctively in two orders (and indeed in several other independent congregations that have developed in recent centuries, such as the Carmelites of Mary Immaculate, largely based in India). In terms of terminology, some speak of the one 'Carmelite Order' consisting of two or more branches; others speak of 'The Carmelite Order' and 'The Discalced Carmelite Order' as two separate orders but sharing a common heritage.

Statues of Elijah and Teresa among the founders of religious orders in Saint Peter's.

Perhaps a more useful term, and one that has found widespread acceptance, is that of 'The Carmelite Family'. The notion of Carmel as a family was particularly developed from the 1980s onwards by the then Prior General of the Order, John Malley, O.Carm. This term is defined as follows in the 1995 *Constitutions* of the Carmelite friars:

The many and various embodiments of the Carmelite charism are for us a source of joy; they confirm the rich and creative fruitfulness of our charism, lived under the inspiration of the Holy Spirit – a fruitfulness to be welcomed with gratitude and discernment. All individuals and groups, whether institutional or not, which draw their inspiration from the *Rule of Saint Albert*, from its tradition and from the values expressed in Carmelite spirituality, constitute the Carmelite Family within the Church today. This Family includes ourselves and our brothers of the Teresian Reform; the women religious of both branches; affiliated religious congregations; the Third Orders Secular; secular institutes; individuals affiliated with the Order through the sacred scapular; and those who by whatever title or bond are affiliated with the Order; those movements which, though juridically not part of the Order, seek inspiration and support from its spirituality; and any man or woman who is drawn to the values of Carmel. (§28)

Stop and think: Do you like the idea of Carmel being a 'family'? What challenges does that idea present us with today?

A modern painting of 'The Carmelite Family' from El Salvador.

The Dissolution of the monasteries

Let us return to our historical overview, and look in more depth at the Carmelite Family in Britain and Ireland at the time of the Reformation. This is another sad period for the Carmelite Family as a whole.

Following the split between Henry VIII and the Roman Church, religious life in Tudor England, Wales and Ireland came under threat. In those countries, and in Scotland, Carmelites were forced to surrender their houses as part of the 'Dissolution of the monasteries', and friars either had to sign-up to the 'new religion' of Protestant Christianity or live in exile. By 1540 no friars remained resident in the Order's houses, and great Carmelite shrines such as that of Our Lady of Doncaster were destroyed. Some friars readily embraced Protestantism; perhaps the best known of them, John Bale, had been one of the Order's leading historians until his conversion and appointment as a Protestant bishop. Much of what we know about medieval Carmelite life comes from his notebooks, now preserved in the British Library in London and the Bodleian Library in Oxford. The last known Carmelite friar in England, George Rayner, was imprisoned in York castle in the early 1600s.

An impression by the artist Geoffrey Hall of Aylesford Priory at the time of its suppression in 1538.

Carmelites and the Counter-Reformation

In areas of Europe where Carmel had not been wiped out, Carmelites did what they could to strength the Catholic faith. At the Council of Trent in 1545, Carmelites were prominent speakers on the theological matters of Scripture, tradition, justification, grace, Episcopal authority, and the sacraments.

During the sixteenth and seventeenth centuries several English Catholic men in exile entered the Carmelite novitiate on the Continent, and attempted to re-establish Carmelite life in Britain in secret; none of these missions was successful in the long term. The 'English Mission' began in 1688 and there are references to it up to 1731 with Englishmen travelling to the Continent to join the Order certainly up to 1762. Also on the Continent, various exiled Catholic English women formed communities of Carmelite nuns. The Carmelite Order in Ireland never died out entirely, but lived under persecution. At this time communities of Carmelites from Europe began their first missions to Latin America, and brought Carmel to the 'new world'. Eventually, Carmelite missions would spread to every continent.

The 'Igreja do Carmo' in Olinda is the oldest Carmelite church in Brazil, built in 1580 by friars from Portugal. Olinda, in the state of Pernambuco, is one of the best-preserved colonial cities in Brazil and because of its cultural importance in South America has been nominated a World Heritage Site by UNESCO.

The Reform of Touraine

In this atmosphere of mission and re-establishment of the Catholic and Carmelite way of life, the need for reform was continual. Reform was promoted in the seventeenth century by a developing Curia administration in Rome, and by a movement known as the *Reform of Touraine*. Touraine was one of the provinces of the Order in France, and houses of friars in this province – partly inspired by the Discalced reform of the previous century – experienced a renewal in their religious observance. Led largely by two friars called Peter Behourt (1564-1633) and Philip Thibault (1572-1638), and supported by the Discalced Carmelite nun Blessed Marie of the Incarnation (1566-1618), this movement called for proper observance of the Carmelite way of life. The reform attracted a young blind man who took the religious name John of Saint-Samson (1571-1636), and during his life he was noted for his musical skills and great spiritual insights which still influence Carmelite spirituality today.

Carmelite mysticism in the seventeenth century

Two contemporaries of John of Saint-Samson must be mentioned at this point: Mary Magdalene de'Pazzi (1566-1607) a Carmelite nun in Florence, and Lawrence of the Resurrection (1611-91) a Discalced Carmelite brother in Paris. Mary Magdelene underwent a number of mystical experiences that were written down by her sisters, whilst Lawrence is best known for his collected letters and maxims, published as *The Practice of the Presence of God*. Marian mysticism also flourished in the Order at this time, with the likes of Brother Michael of Saint-Augustine, and the tertiary Maria Petyt. These figures and others are testimony to Carmel's great spiritual flourishing in the seventeenth century. During this period the Third Order and Carmelite confraternities continued to develop across Europe and the Americas, as did the Order's devotions to Jesus and his mother.

Do you remember? As we read in Chapter 3, Carmelites have promoted meditation on Christ's childhood and kingship through the *Infant of Prague* statue since the 17th Century.

A statue of John of Saint-Samson at Whitefriars Carmelite community, York, England.

A copy of the Infant of Prague statue by Krechler at the Carmelite shrine in Faversham, England.

The development of the Third Order

The seventeenth century has been called the 'Golden Age' of the Carmelite Third Order because it was in this period that it became organised for the first time. As you may recall, in the Middle Ages there was no formal 'Third Order' as such within Carmel; instead most communities of Carmelite friars had lay people associated with them who shared something of their spirit and way of life, sometimes in a structured way, but there was no organised system for lay membership of the Order across Carmel as a whole.

In the 1600s the Reform of Touraine was such a successful and inspiring movement that many lay people were once again attracted to the Carmelite way of life. In the 1630s the Carmelite Prior General Fr. Theodore Straccio (sometimes written Strazio or Stratius) decided to organise groups of lay people who were inspired by Carmel's spirituality. As we read in the previous chapter, Fr. Straccio followed the model of the Franciscan Third Order and composed a separate *Rule* specifically for Carmelite tertiaries. His 1637 *Rule of Life for the Carmelite Third Order Secular* became extremely influential. In 1678 a later Carmelite Prior General, Emilio Giacomelli (sometimes spelt Jacomelli), produced a revised *Rule of Life* for the Third Order. A year later a set of *Statutes* to interpret the *Third Order Rule* was compiled by the Procurator (legal expert) of the Order, Ferdinand Tartaglia. This *Rule/Statutes* was adopted by the Discalced Secular Order (which did not exist in the early years of St. Teresa's reform). The first known English translation of the 1678/9 *Rule/Statutes* appeared in Ireland about 1845, and another *Rule* – that of John Baptist Bettini – became popular in Italy, Germany and Holland after its publication in 1849. Different *Third Order Rules* by different people appeared in different languages in different provinces in the nineteenth century, suggesting that in fact there were different Third Orders. The latest legislation of the Third Order (T.O.C.), issued in 2003, still speaks of Third Orders in the plural, recognising the diversity of Lay Carmelite life to this day.

Carmelites in France: two types of Revolution

Since the days of the Reform of Touraine, and the spread of the Discalced Reform, France had become an increasingly important centre of Carmelite activity. Sadly the

Street names sometimes bear witness to a present or former Carmelite community, such as Rue des Carmes (Carmelite Street) in Paris, and Whitefriars Street in London.

flourishing of Carmel in France was halted by the Revolution of 1789. The Catholic Church was regarded by the revolutionaries as an agent of oppression, and in particular they targeted its religious. In 1794, sixteen Carmelite nuns from Compiègne and their lay collaborators were guillotined in Paris the day after the feast of Our Lady of Mount Carmel; a month later Carmelite friar Blessed Jacques Retouret died following his imprisonment for defending religious freedom.

As well as in France, the Church was oppressed in Italy, Germany, Russia, Spain and Poland, with the Carmelite Order almost dying out in the nineteenth century. However, the blood of the martyrs of Compiègne (beatified in 1906 and made famous by an opera by Poulenc) was fruitful one hundred years later in the Carmel of Lisieux, which witnessed a very different kind of revolution.

In 1897 a Discalced Carmelite nun – Sister Thérèse of the Child Jesus – died aged 24 having lived a seemingly unremarkable life, and leaving behind the material for a spiritual autobiography known as *The Story of a Soul*. We need say little about her here, since the insights of the 'Little Flower' have brought joy to millions around the world, who have revered her since 1997 as a Carmelite Doctor of the Church (along with Teresa and John). Thérèse bore testimony to a very different revolution from that of the 1790s. She rejected the Jansenist heresies of her day which over-emphasised humanity's sinfulness, and started a spiritual revolution: the *Little Way of Spiritual Childhood*.

In 1900 the situation of the Order in France and beyond was looking up with the restoration of old provinces and missions into new territories.

In the twentieth century the Carmelite way of life also began to inspire the establishment of religious communities in Churches other than the Roman Catholic, with a number of Anglican/Episcopalian Carmels being founded in Europe and America.

From Ireland to the rest of the world

The Irish Province of Carmelites had been founded from the English Province in the 1270s. Despite years of oppression against Catholics, the Carmelite Order flourished anew in Ireland around the end of the seventeenth century.

Did you know? The Carmelites of Whitefriar Street have been present in the city of Dublin since 1274. Their church houses a beautiful medieval statue of Our Lady of Dublin, and the relics of Saint Valentine. A very well respected social outreach programme is operated from Whitefriar Street Carmelite Community Centre.

Left: Whitefriar Street Carmelite Church. Right: Our Lady of Dublin.

In the nineteenth century the Irish Carmelite friars undertook a number of missions, including to Australia. The first Carmelites in Australia were actually two Lay Carmelites, James Dempsey and John Butler, who arrived in Sydney having been transported for their alleged involvement in the Irish Rebellion of 1798. The first friar to set foot on Australian soil was in 1824, but it wasn't until 1881 that the mission began in earnest. The Australian mission became an autonomous Province in 1948, and in 2001 incorporated Timor Leste (East Timor).

Lay Carmelites leading a religious procession in Timor Leste.

The Irish Province also founded the St. Elias Province in New York in 1889, and in 1946 Irish Carmelites began a mission in Zimbabwe.

It is thanks to the Irish Province that the Carmelite presence in Britain was firmly re-established. Between 1864 and 1879 a joint attempt was made by the Irish and Lower German Provinces of the Order with a foundation in Merthyr Tydvil, Wales. Father Martin Bruton was a part of this project and died there in 1875. Between 1901 and 1907 the Dutch Province had a foundation in Pudsey, Yorkshire. Simultaneous with these efforts, the Discalced Carmelite friars made their first firm foundation in the London suburb of Kensington in 1862. In 1878 the first monastery of Discalced Carmelite nuns in Britain was founded in the London suburb of Notting Hill.

The first Chapter of the Third Order in the United States was founded in New Jersey in 1870. It is known there were many Chapters in the Philippines in 1881. There was a revival in Lay Carmel in Italy, Sicily, Malta, Spain and Brazil where a Third Order

Congress was held in 1922. In Ireland, Carmelite tertiaries such as Frank Duff were instrumental in starting initiatives such as *The Legion of Mary*.

In 1926 two Irish Carmelites of the Ancient Observance came to take charge of the parishes of Faversham and Sittingbourne in the English county of Kent, before moving on to establish a house in Wales in 1935. Faversham and Sittingbourne were conveniently located near to the Order's ancient priory at Aylesford, known as *The Friars* since it had passed into private hands at the Reformation. In 1949 the Carmelites were able to buy back The Friars, and the priory where the Order had resolved to become a mendicant movement quickly developed as a pilgrimage and retreat centre.

A pottery developed at The Friars, and in 1954 the Carmelites established a publishing house at Aylesford, Saint Albert's Press. The first prior of the restored house at Aylesford was the charismatic Father Malachy Lynch.

The Lynch brothers (left-right): Malachy, Elias, Kilian.

Malachy's brother Kilian became Prior General of the Order, and another brother, Elias, became the Prior of Faversham. In 1955 Elias established a shrine at Faversham dedicated to Saint Jude the Apostle.

Left: The friars returning to Aylesford in 1949. Right: the shrine at Aylesford in 2007.

The statue of St. Jude at his shrine served by the Carmelite friars at Faversham.

In 1980 the Carmelite friars took charge of English Martyrs parish in Walworth, South London. It is a very vibrant and ethnically-diverse inner-city parish.

By 1952 the Carmelite presence in Britain had grown sufficiently for the formation of a General Commisariate (a step on the road to being an autonomous province). On 12th September 1969 the ancient province of England and Wales again became a reality under the title of *The Assumption of the Blessed Virgin Mary*. Since 1999 the title of the province has been that of the British Province, since the presence of friars and lay Carmelites was re-established in Scotland.

In 2010 the British Province of Carmelites had six friar communities with a variety of apostolates.

The growth of the Carmelite Family in Britain and beyond

Along with the development of communities of nuns and friars of both the Ancient and Discalced Observances, Carmel witnessed the growth of the Third Order in the twentieth century, with some thirty Lay Carmelite (T.O.C.) communities being established across Britain, as well as communities of the Discalced Secular Order (O.C.D.S.). In the twentieth century England also nurtured other branches of the Carmelite Family. The community of apostolic sisters that developed into the Corpus Christi Carmelites was established in Leicester in 1908, being affiliated to Carmel in 1927. In 1949 a lay Carmelite association for single and widowed women, known as *The Leaven*, was established at Aylesford Priory, formally affiliating to the Order as a Secular Institute in 1965. Also present in the Order today, in Britain and Ireland and beyond, are Carmelite solitaries and lay associations linked to Carmel such as the Donum Dei Missionary Family (affiliated to the Carmelite Order in 1987) and movements such as *La Famiglia* ('The Family') in Italy.

Lay Carmel in Britain began to experience something of a revival at the start of the Third Millennium. New forms of Lay Carmelite community known as Carmelite Spirituality Groups began to develop in Britain, based on the model of Third Order Chapters but open to people of different Christian denominations and a variety of Carmelite vocations. Similar movements have developed in Ireland, The Netherlands, and elsewhere. In 2005 the British Province of Carmelites was the first to appoint a lay person as Provincial Delegate to the Third Order.

The Twentieth-Century: martyrs, reformers, and new directions

More Christians were martyred in the twentieth century than any other, and the Carmelite Family was not exempt from this painful yet fruitful experience. Of particular note are: lay Carmelite Isidore Bakanja (martyred in the Congo in 1909 for wearing the Brown Scapular); Carmelite martyrs of the Spanish civil war of the 1930s, including the

An icon depicting Titus Brandsma and Edith Stein, written in 2008 by Sr. Petra Clare for the Shrine of St. Jude at Faversham.

religious and laity of Baetica, Catalonia, Guadalajara and Segorbe-Castelló; and Titus Brandsma, Hilary Januszewski and Edith Stein (Teresa Benedicta of the Cross), who were martyred during the Second World War. The latter was declared one of the six patron saints of Europe in 1999.

A joy for Carmel has been the great number of our family whose holiness has been recognised (as 'blesseds' or 'saints') within the last hundred years, including: Edith Stein, Elizabeth of the Trinity, Francis Palau y Quer, Mary of Jesus Crucified (the 'Little Arab'), Teresa 'de los Andes', George Preca, Maria Crocifissa Curcio, Nuno Alvares Pereira and Angelo Paoli. We shall learn more about them and their witness to Christ in future chapters, as well as others whose cause for canonisation is in progress. They inspire us to respond to the call to holiness.

The twentieth century also saw great reforms in the Church such as the Second Vatican Council in the 1960s, and the revision of important texts such as the *Catechism* and the *Code of Canon Law*. Such changes allowed new expressions of the one Carmelite charism to develop, such as the *Donum Dei Missionary Family*, the *Carmelite Missionaries of St. Thérèse of Lisieux*, and the *Carmelites of Mary Immaculate* founded in India by Blessed Kuriakos Elias Chavara (1805-71). In the last ten years a number of Carmelite hermitages have also opened, for women and for men, in North America; these mark an interesting return to the primitive origins of the Order.

The promotion of Carmelite spirituality in the 1990s

The Holy Spirit was specially active in the Order in the last decade of the twentieth century, inspiring a rediscovery and redefinition of the Carmelite charism for the present age. At the General Chapter of the Order in 1995 a Scotsman, Fr. Joseph Chalmers, was elected Prior General; he set about encouraging Carmelites to rediscover their contemplative vocation, finding God's presence in prayer, community-living, and apostolic service. At the 1995 General Chapter the friars agreed a new set of *Constitutions* which expressed in a radical way how the Order perceived itself. This was supplemented, in the Great

Fr. Emanuele Boaga, O.Carm. (second right), one of the Order's best-known historians, shows fellow friars a manuscript kept in the Carmelite archives in Rome, during a conference in 2004.

Jubilee Year of 2000, by a new *Ratio* document which set out how Carmelite formation should be developed. At the beginning of the twenty-first century, the Order established its presence as an N.G.O. (non-governmental organisation) at the United Nations, thus taking a leading role in the promotion of justice and peace on the world stage. In such ways Carmel continues its historic role of being at the heart of the Church, and a voice for common sense and the truths of the Gospel.

The Third Order has matched these developments by establishing an international secretariat in Rome, and in 2003 a revised *Rule for the Third Order of Carmel* (*RTOC*) was promulgated. In 2006 a major international gathering of the Third Order looked at how Lay Carmel can develop in the future, and in various parts of the world new groups (especially youth groups) are finding inspiration from the Carmelite way of life. Carmel is very much alive!

The future is in God's hands

Looking back is important to help us tread the road ahead. This history is necessarily selective and anyone seriously interested in their Carmelite 'family history' is encouraged to read further.

Carmelites have been around in one form or another for over eight hundred years. In every age we have seen that Carmelites have had the same preoccupations: a life centred on Christ, devotion to his mother, Elijah's desire to sweep away false gods, an attentiveness to the Bible, the need to build communities, the urge to be of service. Whereas most religious congregations die out after a century or two having fulfilled their purpose, God seems to renew the Carmelite Family in every age, since we still have the task of building up his Kingdom. We all share this gift and responsibility, and we must pass it on to the next generation.

Conclusion: In this eighth chapter we have seen a broad sweep of Carmel's history. As with any family story, it has periods of great joy and excitement, as well as times of pain. It is possible to trace God's hand through every moment.

Perhaps you could conclude your time of study and reflection with a brief moment of prayer, in whatever way you wish.

In the next chapter we will consider an idea that has preoccupied Carmelites in every period of the Order's history, that of living in God's presence.

Ideas for Reflection, Discussion and Action

- Reflect on any passage in this chapter that has stood out as significant for you, either individually or – if you have been reflecting with others – as a community.

- Write down one point that struck you, and bring it to your next community formation meeting, or reflect on it at home in the coming days. Perhaps discuss it with friends. How would you summarise the chapter and its key points in one or two paragraphs?

- What period of Carmelite history most attracts you and why?

- Does Carmel's history resonate with you as *your* story?

- Find out if there are any Carmelite artefacts (buildings, manuscripts, archaeology, etc.) near you.

- Do you think that the Carmelites and Discalced Carmelites should 'reunite'? If possible, make contact with another branch of the Carmelite Family and meet with them as brothers and sisters.

- Read an official document of the Discalced Carmelite Order. Do you detect any difference of tone or emphasis from the documents of the Ancient Observance?

- Pray for scholars engaged in researching the truth of our Order's history.

- Pick a 'Carmelite theme' (such as 'the Eucharist', 'Mary', or 'prayer') and find out how it has developed over the centuries.

- How do you think the 'Carmelite story' is best told: writings, saints' lives, paintings, music, architecture, or word of mouth?

- Do you know much about the history of your own Province? Where might you find out about this?

- If you are a member of a Carmelite community, do you know the history of the community? Does your community keep an archive you could consult?

- What aspects of Carmelite spirituality must we retain in the future? In what areas must we 'move on'?

Recommended Further Resources

History books tend to be quite specialised, and there are not many general histories of the Order readily available in English. However, some of the following will no doubt be of interest to anyone attracted to Carmel.

Frances Andrews, *The Other Friars: Carmelite, Augustinian, Sack and Pied Friars in the Middle Ages*, (Woodbridge, Suffolk: The Boydell Press, 2006). This is an excellent overview of the Order in the Middle Ages.

Johan Bergström-Allen, T.O.C., 'The Whitefriars Return to Carmel', in Elizabeth Herbert-McAvoy & Mari Hughes-Edwards, (eds.), *Anchorites, Wombs and Tombs: Intersections of Gender and Enclosure*, (Cardiff: University of Wales Press, 2005).

Johan Bergström-Allen, T.O.C., & Richard Copsey, O.Carm., (eds.), *Thomas Netter of Walden: Carmelite, Diplomat and Theologian (c.1372-1430)*, Carmel in Britain 4, (Faversham: Saint Albert's Press, 2009).

Richard Copsey, O.Carm., *Carmel in Britain 3: The Hermits from Mount Carmel*, (Faversham: Saint Albert's Press, 2004).

Keith J. Egan, T.O.C., 'The Spirituality of the Carmelites', in Jill Raitt, (ed.), *Christian Spirituality: High Middle Ages and Reformation*, (London: Routledge & Kegan Paul, 1987), pp. 50-62.

Valerie Edden, 'The Mantle of Elijah: Carmelite Spirituality in England in the Fourteenth Century', in Marion Glasscoe, (ed.), *The Medieval Mystical Tradition, England, Ireland and Wales, Exeter Symposium VI*, (Cambridge: D. S. Brewer, 1999).

Patrick Fitzgerald-Lombard, O.Carm., (ed.), *Carmel in Britain, Volumes I & II*, (Rome: Institutum Carmelitanum, 1992).

Elizabeth Ruth Obbard, 'The Advent of the Nuns', in *Land of Carmel*, (Leominster: Gracewing, 1999), pp. 99-113.

Christopher O'Donnell, O.Carm., 'Carmelite spirituality in the nineteenth century', *Carmel in the World*, Volume XLVII Number 2, 2008, pp. 87-101.

Felip Ribot, O.Carm., *The Ten Books on the Way of Life and Great Deeds of the Carmelites (including The Book of the First Monks)*, translated by Richard Copsey, O.Carm., (Faversham: Saint Albert's Press, 2005).

Otilio Rodriguez, O.C.D., *A History of the Teresian Carmel*, (1979).

Joachim Smet, O.Carm., *The Carmelites*, (Rome: Institutum Carmelitarum, revised edition 1988). This is widely regarded as the most comprehensive history of the Order available at present, and is printed across several volumes.

Joachim Smet, O.Carm., *Cloistered Carmel: A Brief History of the Carmelite Nuns*, (Rome: Institutum Carmelitarum, 1986).

Joachim Smet, O.Carm., 'Some Notes on the Touraine Reform', *Carmel in the World*, Volume XLVIII Number 2, 2009, pp. 118-144.

John Welch, O.Carm., '*The Institution of the First Monks*: Carmel's Foundational Story', in *The Carmelite Way: An Ancient Path for Today's Pilgrim*, (Leominster: Gracewing, 1996), pp. 49-62.

John Welch, O.Carm., 'To Renew a Tradition: The Reforms of Carmel', in Kevin Culligan, O.C.D., & Regis Jordan, O.C.D., (eds.), *Carmel and Contemplation: Transforming Human Consciousness*, Carmelite Studies 8, (Washington, D.C.: I.C.S. Publications, 2000), pp. 3-23.

Walter Whitman, T.O.C, & Johan Bergström-Allen, T.O.C., 'Carmelites at the shrine of Our Lady of Doncaster', *Assumpta*, Volume 48 Numbers 7/8, 2005, pp. 21-25.

Charmian Woodfield, *The Church of Our Lady of Mount Carmel and some conventual buildings at the Whitefriars, Coventry*, BAR British Series 389, (Oxford: Archaeopress, 2005).

As a supplement to your initial formation, you might be interested in some formalised study of the Carmelite tradition. There are various study institutes in different parts of the globe offering courses in Carmelite history and spirituality at different levels. Distance-learning programmes in Carmelite Studies are offered to anyone in the world by the Carmelite Institute of Britain & Ireland (CIBI). For details please visit the CIBI website: www.cibi.ie. Other institutes and study centres are located in Washington, D.C., Malta, Australia, Holland, the Philippines and elsewhere.

Notes and reflections on Chapter 8

Notes and reflections on Chapter 8

CHAPTER 9

Living in God's Presence

Summary: One of the enduring themes of the Carmelite tradition over the centuries has been the notion of living in the presence of God, being consciously and subconsciously aware of the reality that God is all around us and within us, and that as Christians we can help others to experience God's presence. This chapter examines the many facets of this truth which is at the heart of our Christian vocation: we are all called to live in God's presence. We find God present in our brothers and sisters, and similarly we are a sign of God's presence to them. By looking at Elijah, Mary and other Carmelite models, we can learn a great deal about how to build on the habit of spending time with God. The process requires us to learn to look, and above all to listen, for signs of God's presence, and to be generous and consistent in giving time to God. This chapter will present this popular theme of Carmelite spirituality with reference to some of the main texts, personalities and ideas of our Family's tradition, and encourage you to consider for yourself how God's presence might be a feature of your life.

This window by George Walsh in the chapel of Avila Discalced Carmelite Friary in Dublin shows Mary in front of Mount Carmel surrounded by God's presence in the person of Christ and the Holy Spirit.

Get prepared: There is much to ponder prayerfully in this chapter, so you might want to reflect on it over a number of sessions rather than reading it all at once. You might like to have pen and paper to hand to write notes or highlight passages that are significant for you. Before you begin reading, recall that you are already in God's presence by spending some time in prayer, and offering yourself to God with an open mind and an open heart:

> *Heavenly Father,*
> *Many people in the world today are looking for meaning in life*
>   *and an awareness of your presence.*
> *Use me as a witness to bring others to faith in you,*
>   *by the way I love and serve them.*
> *In Jesus' name. Amen.*

Standing in the Presence of God

In a sense the 800 year-old Carmelite tradition is inspired by a simple yet profound statement of fact proclaimed by our spiritual forefather, the prophet Elijah, almost 3,000 years ago: 'Elijah said… the Lord the God of Israel lives, before whom I stand' (*1 Kings* 17:1).

Elijah proclaimed that God exists, God lives, God is present. This is the first truth. The second truth is that Elijah stood before the presence of God, in relationship with God. For those of us who are Carmelites the purpose of our existence is to declare this truth about our relationship with an ever-present God: 'God lives, in whose presence we stand.'

Some 3,000 years after Elijah, the very idea of 'living in God's presence' is still awesome. No doubt we all question, in our darker moments, whether it is possible to live with an awareness of God's presence in the 21st century. Many people deny the presence of God, much of society is concerned with the false gods of materialism and consumerism, and it often seems that God's presence is only called upon 'in emergencies'.

The 1995 *Constitutions of the Carmelite Friars* observes: 'The practice of the presence of God, which is a Carmelite tradition, has become increasingly difficult in these modern times. We must therefore make special efforts to help one another to seek God through prayer that is intimately linked with ordinary life. In the same way Carmelites are called to a deeper experience of those forms of prayer which are most in harmony with our own particular spirituality. We are encouraged to seek new forms of prayer in line with our charism.' (§77).

Carmelites are called – like our father Elijah – to bear witness to the truth that God exists, and is present in all times and places whether we perceive him or not (throughout this chapter we will refer to God in the masculine form, though God's presence has also been expressed in Scripture and in the Carmelite tradition in feminine and maternal forms).

According to the former Prior General of the Carmelite Order, John Malley, O.Carm., speaking in 2006, 'the presence of God has been and should still remain the first and most fundamental value of our Carmelite spirituality and tradition' ('Fundamental values of Carmelite Spirituality', p. 21). The goal of the Carmelite journey is to become ever more aware of God's presence, and to help others to appreciate that reality. We seek to know and love God, and to make God known and loved. Carmel's great mission today is to share with people an experience of God in prayer. We realise our vocation as evangelists, who bear witness with Elijah and Moses that God is the great 'I AM' (*Exodus* 3:14).

Stop and reflect: Have you ever taken part in a prayer meeting where someone has said 'Let's ask for God to be present' or 'Let's put ourselves in the presence of God'? What do they mean by this? Does it reflect the reality of the situation?

The universal call to holiness

As we read in the second chapter on 'The Call to Holiness', all human beings – not just Carmelites or Christians – are invited to journey towards holiness, and to live with God's presence and all that that implies. We read in the documents of the Church (especially Vatican II's *Lumen Gentium*, promulgated by Pope Paul VI in 1964) that everyone is called to experience the reality of God's life-giving presence: 'The Lord Jesus ... preached holiness of life to each and every one of His disciples, *regardless of their situation*' (§40).

The *Rule* (or *Way of Life*) of Saint Albert, written for the first hermits on Mount Carmel around 1206-14, reiterates the fact that: '*everyone*, whatever their station or the kind of religious observance they have chosen, should live a life in allegiance to Jesus Christ' (Chapter 2).

To enjoy God's presence is a gift freely offered by God, not something we achieve on our own. Those of us who believe in God know by faith that God is present all the time; what we have to try and do as his beloved children is to become increasingly conscious of and comfortable with that fact.

Seeking to live within the reality of God's presence has an impact on our life. People in search of holiness allow the process of 'divinisation' to take place; that is, we participate in the life of God so that we see as God sees, love as God loves, and so that we grow more and more into the image of God in which we were made (*Genesis* 1:26). As St. Paul wrote to the Corinthians: 'we all, with unveiled faces, beholding the glory of the Lord, are being changed into his likeness' (*2 Corinthians* 3:17-18).

God is both Other and Familiar; removed from us yet very close to us. That is the mystery of Christ's Incarnation: God made man, the unknown being revealed. In seeking out the presence of God we should not presume to be God, but we know that our destiny is to be united with God (*Ephesians* 1:10). By seeking God with a pure heart (*puritas cordis*) and a spirit of humility, God raises us to intimate knowledge of God's own self. Our God is a God who wants to communicate with us, who wants to nourish a relationship with us. God never forces his presence upon us, but continually invites us to discover his presence in a variety of ways.

This painting of Our Lady of Mount Carmel by Roswitha Bitterlich-Brink (1954) hangs in Saint Albert's International Centre in Rome (CISA). It depicts Mary holding Christ, who himself holds open a book containing various seals, representing the papal bulls granting privileges to the Order.

Did you know? The Vatican II document *Lumen Gentium* was promulgated by Pope Paul VI in 1964. Ten years later his document *Marialis Cultus* (§8) declared that certain Marian feasts which had originally been celebrated by particular religious families such as ours were of universal significance for the Church, including that of Our Lady of Mount Carmel on 16th July.

God is present in our brothers and sisters

Seeking to live with God's presence is not simply a matter of doing 'holy things'. God is present in all aspects of our lives, not simply the 'religious' or 'pious' parts of it. There should be no divide between 'the spiritual life' and 'the rest of life', since it is all lived in the presence of God. The Prior General of the Carmelite Order in the 1960s, Fr. Kilian Lynch, O.Carm., wrote 'if the spiritual life is to be relevant today, it must be a dimension of real life. The earthly path is the one to heaven and one must find God in the works of his hands, especially in persons.' (Lynch, *The Practice of the Presence of God*, p. 3). In the person of Jesus, God's presence on earth became known to humanity in a new way, which is why Carmelites focus so much upon the sacred humanity of Christ. In becoming human, Jesus showed us what God is like, present among us.

The implications of seeing that all life is lived in God's presence is that people who live with this awareness are not only 'spiritual' but also practical, recognising the needs of others and responding according to their means. God is present in our neighbours, whom Jesus asks us to love as we love ourselves (*Mark* 12:30-31).

When we love our sisters and brothers as ourselves, God's kingdom is manifested, because we acknowledge God's presence in them, and we become the visible presence of God for other people. God is present in our service, both in us when we serve and also in those we serve, especially in the poor and outcast whom Jesus empathised with so closely: 'whatever you do to the least of these who are members of my family, you do it to me' (*Matthew* 25:40). St. Gregory the Great said 'God is love and love is never idle', and since the Spirit of God dwells within us we are moved to action, and to love. This is why the active service of others can be a contemplative experience, because it exposes us to the presence and love of God.

Did you know? The Corpus Christi Carmelite sisters have communities present in England, the Caribbean, the United States of America, and in the African state of Liberia. Following the Liberian civil wars in the 1990s, the sisters have ministered in schools and clinics. As well as manifesting God's loving presence through their service, the sisters say that they find God's presence revealed to them in the poor. This is the experience of other women's congregations affiliated to the Ancient Observance of the Order, including the Carmelite Sisters for the Aged and Infirm (New York), the Carmelite Sisters of Our Lady (Philippines), the Congregation of Our Lady of Mount Carmel (Louisiana), the Handmaids of Our Lady of Mount Carmel (Zimbabwe), the Carmelite Sisters of Mother Candelaria (Venezuela), the Carmelite Sisters of the Sacred Heart of Jesus (Spain), the Daughters of Carmel (Indonesia), the Carmelite Sisters of Grace (Italy), and others.

The Corpus Christi Carmelite Sisters in Greenville, Liberia.

We are signs of God's presence

Manifesting God's love is so necessary in the present world. Natural disasters (earthquakes, hurricanes, tsunamis and so on) make people ask: 'Where is God?'. It is up to people of faith to show that God is present in the world, present in those who are suffering, and present through our loving service of those who suffer. God uses us to reach out to others, to stand in solidarity with those who are suffering, and become God's hands of healing today. We become living testimonies of God's love.

If the Church fails to do this, Christians become a stumbling block, a barrier to people's ability to live with God's presence. If our 'allegiance to Jesus Christ' (as Saint Albert puts it in the Carmelite *Way of Life* document) becomes embroiled in struggles for power or money, even Carmel itself would be denying the reality of God's liberating presence. That is why Carmel has reformed and adapted itself in every age. Living with God's presence comforts and disturbs, challenges and changes us.

Stop and think: Do you know of any Carmelite mission where service amongst the poor manifests the presence of God? Do you find the notion of God's presence reassuring, or disturbing? Do you think of God's presence as loving, judging, consoling or condemning?

Natural disasters – such as the tsunami that struck Banda Aceh in 2004 – can make some people question God's presence, simultaneously spurring people of faith to make God's love manifest to those in doubt. Carmelites around the world were able to respond quickly to the disaster by sending aid via our brethren in Indonesia.

The early Carmelites sought God's presence

The first hermits on Mount Carmel settled there around the year 1200 because they wanted to dedicate themselves entirely to dwelling within God's presence. They lived in private cells for pondering God's presence in solitude, but also gathered together at set times, since God is also present in a community: 'For where two or three are gathered in my name, I am there among them' (*Matthew* 18:20).

Stop and ponder: In your experience, is God's presence felt more keenly when you are alone or with other people?

When people gather in community God sends his Holy Spirit to be present with them. The Spirit has a transforming effect upon us and draws us into the presence of God. The

For peoples of the Abrahamic faiths – Judaism, Christianity and Islam – Jerusalem has always been an important symbol and promise of God's presence among his people.

life of the early Church (as described in the Bible's *Acts of the Apostles*) has always inspired Carmelite communities. At Pentecost God sent the Holy Spirit upon the followers of Jesus. With the coming of the Spirit, the Apostles and Our Lady were filled with the divine presence in a new way. Carmelites – and indeed most Christian communities – seek God's presence in communities faithful to the vision of life shared by the early Church in Jerusalem.

Elijah: standing in God's presence

Some places seem to be touched by God's presence in a particular way. In the thirteenth century Mount Carmel was – as it remains – a place associated with the presence of God. The Carmelite hermits must have recalled that the prophet of Carmel, Elijah, had sought to live always in the presence of the Lord God, and that it was on that mountain range that Elijah had proclaimed the reality of the Lord in the face of the prophets of Baal. The Bible's *First Book of the Kings* tells us in Chapter 18 that Elijah proved the truth of the presence of the one true God by calling down fire from heaven to consume the altar he had prepared. On Mount Carmel, the truth of God's presence was demonstrated in a very powerful, dramatic, even flamboyant, way.

After proving the presence of God to the people of Israel, Queen Jezebel (who had imported the worship of false gods into Israel) had soldiers pursue Elijah, wanting to kill him. Elijah fled for his life, feeling dejected. He fled to Mount Horeb, usually identified as being the same place as Mount Sinai, where God's presence had been revealed to Moses in the burning bush (*Exodus* 3). On Mount Horeb Elijah experienced dramatic events such as earthquake, wind and fire, but didn't discern God's presence in these things. Instead, Elijah perceived God's presence in 'a sound of sheer silence' (*1 Kings* 19:12).

The exact location of Mount Horeb/Sinai is not known, though Christians have traditionally regarded it as being in the Sinai peninsula of Egypt, where Saint Catherine's Monastery was built in the 6th century.

Stop and read: Look in the Bible and compare how God's presence was experienced by Elijah on Mount Carmel (*1 Kings* 18) and on Mount Horeb (*1 Kings* 19). Compare also Elijah's experience of God's presence on Horeb/Sinai with that of Moses (*Exodus* 3 & 19). Have you experienced God's presence more in action and marvellous events, or in stillness and emptiness?

From Elijah Carmelites learn to be people of the desert who seek the presence of God with zeal and an undivided heart. Elijah was the solitary prophet who lived so entirely with the presence of God aflame within him that he dedicated his life to the service of the poor and oppressed. As a prophet, Elijah proclaimed the reality of God's presence; that is our mission too. Inspired by Elijah's rejection of idolatry we bear witness that God's presence is not found in the 'false gods' of power or wealth or possessions. Elijah was so open to God's presence that he allowed himself to be led to places he did not wish to go, but he knew God was leading him.

Mary: absorbed by God's presence

The other Biblical figure who inspired the hermits on Carmel how to live within God's presence was Mary the mother of Jesus. Mary, our mother and sister, is the faithful disciple who allowed herself to be moulded by the Holy Spirit so that she was able to journey with her son. Mary lived with God's presence in a special way, both before and after the incarnation of her son Jesus. Like Elijah she asked questions and expressed doubts, but she rested and trusted entirely in God's presence. She was open, and listened to God. Even when she could not make out the road ahead she journeyed in faith, drawing closer to God one step at a time. Mary is the model of how silent prayer leads us into the presence of God: '*Mary kept all these things and pondered on them in her heart*' (*Luke* 2:19).

Both Elijah and Mary have been taken up into heaven body and soul; Elijah in the fiery chariot, and Mary at the Assumption. They therefore live entirely in God's presence forever. To live in God's presence is our destiny too, and the desire that God has for every single human being.

Our Lady depicted 'in the Carmelite Tradition' by the artist Frances Biggs in a stained-glass window in the chapel of Terenure College, Dublin.

Jesus: God's presence among us

It was Mary's willingness to cooperate with God's will that allowed us to see Jesus – the 'revelation of the Father' – the perfect expression of God's presence. Christ is the image of the invisible God (*Colossians* 1:15) and that is why Carmel is completely Christo-centric (Christ-centred) in its message.

The Old and New Testaments give witness to God's abiding presence (see for example *Ephesians* 1:2 & 4:10; *Acts* 17:28). The history of Christianity (and the Jewish tradition from which it rose) is the story of God's presence with his people, from the revelations of YHWH in the Old Testament (the burning bush, the pillar of fire in the desert, and so on) to God's perfect revealing in the person of Jesus of Nazareth.

Out of respect for the presence of God on Mount Horeb, Elijah wrapped his face in the cloak which has such symbolism for Carmelites.

In Psalm 139 the Psalmist (who frequently describes seeking the presence of God) finds that God's overwhelming presence cannot be escaped. He may on this occasion have wanted to flee from God because we read in the Old Testament that the presence of God was often too awesome for the human mind and heart to comprehend. It was rare to behold God's face, and following the 'sound of sheer silence' on Horeb Elijah 'wrapped his face in his mantle' (*1 Kings* 19:13) out of respect for God's presence. In the person of Jesus, however, God's presence is revealed in a radical way; through *Emmanuel* ('God is with us') the divine is present among us in human form.

It is this Jesus – the perfect presence of God among us – that Carmelites strive to live in allegiance to. Like Jesus, we try to live a life that is fully in accord with what is human, and at the same time fully in accord with the divine.

God's presence in the Liturgy

In the *Way of Life* Saint Albert approved for the Carmelite hermits, the celebration of the Eucharist was a daily duty for them whenever possible, which was unusual in the Middle Ages. Albert knew that frequent contact with our Lord's presence in the sacrament cannot fail to have a profound influence on us – both our lives of prayer and our active striving for God's kingdom on earth – because in the Mass we 'taste and see that the Lord is good' (*Psalm* 34:8). Albert instructed that the chapel on Carmel was to be built 'among the cells' (Chapter 14). This indicates the importance of all being able to attend and suggests that it is prayer – the Divine Office and the Eucharist above all – that unifies all members of the Carmelite Family and all members of the Church wherever we may be.

Carmel draws us to God's presence

Carmelites are committed to a life of prayer as the best way of growing more aware of God's presence. Carmelite spirituality can sometimes seem complicated, but it is really very simple. At its best Carmelite spirituality simply invites us to live within God's presence, to sit at the feet of Jesus, to look at him and to listen to him. In our tradition the prayers or attitudes that help us to do this have been given various names: the prayer of recollection, the prayer of simplicity, the practice of the presence of God, the prayer of silence, the attitude of loving attentiveness, 'Vacare Deo' (space for God), and prayer of the heart. Ultimately these terms all point to the same thing: living in God's presence.

In Carmel's imagery the search for God's presence is not so much an outward pilgrimage as an interior journey of 'climbing the mountain within'. Blessed Elizabeth of the Trinity spoke of finding God in the 'cell within the heart', and Saint Teresa of Jesus (of Avila) spoke of God as dwelling within the *interior castle* of her soul. She said 'We need no wings to go in search of him but have only to find a place where we can be alone and look upon him present within us.' (*The Way of Perfection*, Ch. 28).

John of the Cross wrote: 'The Word, the Son of God, together with the Father and the Holy Spirit, is hidden by His essence and presence in the innermost being of the soul … Be joyful and gladdened in your interior recollection with Him, because you have Him so close to you. Desire Him there. Adore Him there.' (*Spiritual Canticle* B, 1, 6 and 8). Pope John Paul II, who did his doctoral studies on the Carmelite friar John of the Cross, recommended John as a guide to those seeking the presence of God: 'He [John] knew how to introduce people to familiar conversation with God by teaching them to discover His presence and His love in all circumstances, whether favorable or unfavorable, in moments of fervour and in periods of apparent abandonment alike.' (*Master in the Faith: Apostolic Letter of John Paul II on the Occasion of the IV Centenary of the Death of St. John of the Cross*).

John of the Cross depicted in Whitefriar Street Carmelite Church, Dublin.

Learning to relate

In order to appreciate living with God's presence we must learn to *know* God, and to know God as *someone* not *something*. We have been in God's presence from the moment of our first being, but our awareness of that only grows slowly. God wants to reveal himself to us, but he does not want to overwhelm us with his presence, nor are we aware of his presence in the way we are aware of our friends and neighbours. But God in fact wants to be our closest friend and neighbour. God does not force his presence on us, but invites us to come to know him - to 'come and see' as Jesus said (*John* 1:39) – whenever we are ready to make that journey, whenever we are ready to commit to that relationship.

The ways we relate to those around us are the ways we first learn how to connect to God. Just as we build-up a friendship with someone through conversation, 'Carmelites live a life of intense prayer, focused on a personal dialogue with the Lord, the true friend of humanity' (2003 *Rule for the Third Order of Carmel* §36). Looking at our human relationships is often the best way for starting a deeper relationship with God. In the early stages there are the first, rather hesitant, formal greetings and meetings, then the talking and learning more about the 'friend'; this will gradually, hopefully, relax into a relationship where there is such intimacy that no words are necessary.

Elizabeth of the Trinity in March 1903.

Teresa of Jesus tells us that getting to know God in prayer is a matter of nurturing a relationship: 'Prayer … is nothing more than an intimate and frequent dialogue of friendship with the one whom we know loves us.' (*Life*, Ch. 8.5). John of the Cross saw our relationship with God as a bond between the lover and the beloved, whilst Thérèse of Lisieux regarded her relationship with God as that of a child with a loving father. Thérèse also came to learn and appreciate what Christ said, that 'the Kingdom of Heaven is within you'. Blessed Elizabeth of the Trinity described herself as a home for the 'indwelling of the Trinity'. She wrote 'It seems to me that I have found my heaven on earth since heaven is God and God is in my soul.' She had a strong awareness that God's presence was within her, not something external.

Letting God be God

If God is calling us into an intimate relationship with him then he desires a relationship between the *real* person that I am and the *real* God that he is. That means that we

God the Father depicted in stained glass by Richard Joseph King at the Shrine of St. Jude served by the Carmelite Friars at Faversham, Kent, England.

have to get to know the *reality* of God, and move beyond the images and preconceptions we have about him (or her!). It can be hard to let go of the ideas and language we may have used to discuss God since our childhood. In a world where fanatics and fundamentalists commit acts of terror 'in the name of God' we Carmelites must remind all believers to *let God be God*. We cannot impose upon God's presence our own agendas and prejudices.

Living with the presence of God 'our parent'

It is right for us to be awed by the presence of God and to approach him with reverence, but it is also appropriate not to be afraid of closeness with God. Jesus showed us this when he invited us to address the Father in the intimate way he did; 'Abba', which is an Aramaic word preserved in the Greek text of Mark's Gospel (14:36), means 'Daddy'. Jesus' presence among us was to remind us that we are loved by God as a parent loves (or ought to love) a child. As our model and teacher Saint Paul put it:

> For all who are led by the Spirit of God are children of God. For you did not receive a spirit of slavery to fall back into fear, but you have received a spirit of adoption. When we cry, 'Abba! Father!', it is that very Spirit bearing witness with our spirit that we are children of God. (*Romans* 8:14-16).

Through prayer we grow as the children of God and realise our place in God's family. If we have not known the love of parents, or been hurt in our relationships, we may be fearful of trusting God and believing that his love is unconditional. But the death and resurrection of Jesus show us that there is nothing God will not do for love of us: 'God is faithful' (*1 Corinthians* 1:9).

The heart yearns for God's presence

The deepest longing of the human heart is to be loved *as we really are*, and to know the company of God who called us into being and into love. As John Welch, O.Carm., has said 'the Carmelite tradition begins in searching hearts'. As the Psalmist put it:

> O God, you are my God, for you I long;
> for you my soul is thirsting.
> My body pines for you like a dry weary land without water.
> So I gaze on you in the sanctuary,
> to see your strength and your glory. (*Psalm* 62:2-9)

This thirst for God's presence is the root of our Order's spirituality. Carmelites share the restlessness of Carmel's saints to experience the presence of God, but they teach us that our desire is nothing compared to God's desire for us.

Trusting in love

It is not only that we desire to know God's presence, but more importantly God desires our presence with him. There are no barriers to this. Although we may not feel worthy God accepts us as we are, and we must be prepared to accept his acceptance of us. We must also acknowledge that God loves people we may disapprove of. There are times when we think we know better than God; that God couldn't *really* love *me*, or that God couldn't *really* love *them*. But he does! Do we fear to expose to our creator the reality of who we are? Do we adopt a pose before God, just as we do before other people? If others have disapproved of us because of our being who we *really* are, are we willing – consciously or unconsciously – to see ourselves as acceptable in the eyes of God?

It can be difficult to immerse ourselves completely in the loving presence of God because perhaps we may feel unworthy of the relationship God is calling us to. Relationships are the most significant factor in anyone's life, and it is hard to relate to God if we haven't first learnt how to relate to those around us. We need to let God help us overcome our hurts and obstacles in order to live more fully in God's presence. Growth in friendship with God is a lifetime's journey. God will lead us gradually, gently, to an uncovering of ourselves and an acceptance of our weaknesses and failings, and an increasing reliance on him. This calls for conversion on a *daily* basis, a journey taken *day by day*; letting go and allowing ourselves to be changed. Our conversion – our growth – does not usually happen in an instant and last forever, but rather it is a process that takes time. Brother Lawrence – whom we shall read about soon – said, 'You don't become a saint in a day!'. Divinisation is gradual. God is patient (*2 Peter* 3:9).

As Carmelites we are asked to live with God's presence *today*. We should not worry about the 'thieves of the past' or the 'thieves of the future' because they rob us of enjoying being in God's presence *today*. We must accept with thanks *today* and live with God's presence in the grace of *now*. Living with God's presence is today's reality; we can't put it off till tomorrow. As Jesus reminds us in the 'waiting' parables, if we read *the signs of the times* we'll recognise that the Kingdom of Heaven is not far off.

Questions for your own personal development: If regular prayer leads to a deepened relationship with God, do I always find time for the Lord or just 'fit him in'? Do I need to prioritise?

God's presence is revealed in signs around us

God is present in all times and circumstances, whether we perceive it or not. Signs and situations can point out to us God's presence, such as the beauty of nature, the friendship of a loved one, or in rare cases some miraculous event. As Gerard Manley Hopkins wrote, 'The world is charged with the grandeur of God'.

Stop and think: Cardinal Danielou said 'Nature sings the glory of God; the machine sings the glory of man.' Do you agree? Is the modern ear attuned only to the machine?

The Dominican St. Thomas Aquinas argued that the beauty of the natural world is one of the proofs of God's existence.

Since God is present in the world he has created, we must be committed to protecting his world as good stewards. This is why Carmelites are committed to upholding justice, peace, and the integrity of Creation (as we shall consider in Chapter 17). God's presence is most clearly revealed in his greatest achievement of Creation: humanity. As St. Irenaeus of Lyons said 'The glory of God is men and women fully alive'. Therefore, it is legitimate to seek God's presence in the things and relationships that give us life. God's presence can clearly be manifested in good things that bring us joy, such as happy occasions, loving relationships, hobbies, creativity, honest work, a new-born baby, and beauty in the natural world. However, good as these things are, we must be careful not to regard them as gods themselves. It's sometimes said that faith has declined in the economically developed world when the benefits of society (such as good housing, healthcare and education) have made us feel so secure that we feel we no longer need the God who gave them to us. People in need, the poor, often perceive the presence of

Humanity is made in God's image. Adam and Eve carved by the West Door of York Minster, England.

God more than those in comfort: the Living God was felt closest to the people of Israel in the desert of exile, not in the Promised Land. The developments of modern science are marvellous, but have they given humanity a sense of self-importance, usurping the place of God in directing human life? Instead of aiming for eternal happiness with God, we settle for gratification in the present moment. But even the 'miracles' of the modern world leave us feeling unsatisfied; as Gerard Philips wrote 'Never has man had such a surfeit of good things, and never has he hungered as he does today.' Some people try to fill this hunger for the divine with pseudo-spirituality, such as horoscopes or New-Age rituals. The prophet spoke truly: 'The time is surely coming, says the Lord God, when I will send a famine on the land; not a famine of bread, or a thirst for water, but of hearing the words of the Lord' (*Amos* 8:11). The challenge to Carmel is to offer people who are searching for God an authentic and challenging spiritual experience.

Stop and ponder: What gives you life? Do you appreciate God's presence in what makes you feel fulfilled?

Seeking God's presence in contemplation

We know that God's presence is sometimes clear to see, but at other times the signs are lacking. In the noise and haste of the world we need to seek out beauty, tranquillity, and love to reconnect us with the source of those things. At various times our great models in Carmel – Elijah, Mary, and Jesus – withdrew from the bustle of the world in order to be still so that they could be more aware of God's presence in contemplation.

Contemplation is being open to God's presence and friendship in a heightened way. It is not something that we can achieve by ourselves; it is God's gift, and we must simply be open to it. There is a distinction between *contemplation* and an acquired *contemplative attitude*. There are certain things which can help us be better disposed to God's gift of contemplation, and the Carmelite tradition emphasises among them the importance of silence and solitude in the development of a habitual attitude. The Carmelite *Rule* stresses the need for silence and solitude so that the Word of God may 'abound in our mouths and hearts' (Chapter 19). The chapter on silence in the *Rule* (21) is one of the longest, and as this excerpt shows Albert links the practice of silence to the teachings of the Scriptures:

> The Apostle [Paul] would have us keep silence, for in silence he tells us to work [*2 Thessalonians* 3:12]. As the Prophet [Isaiah] also makes known to us: Silence is the way to foster holiness [*Isaiah* 32:15-17].

Does silence lead to prayer or to contemplation? Not necessarily. We can be silent without praying, and we can pray without being silent. But as Carmelites we appreciate that 'Silence is the way to foster holiness' (*Rule* 21) and that God reveals his presence in silence. We need to be vigilant to 'hear' God despite the noise and confusion around us. Silence can involve the absence of speech but it *always* involves the act of *listening*. Silence is much more than the absence of noise, and it is not a luxury reserved for monks, hermits and nuns. Rather, it is a *necessity* for all of us, as vital as the air we breathe. The world is full of noise, and without some silence in the day we are drowned in a tidal-wave of words and tossed about by blasting stereos. But silence is more importantly an attitude of the mind and heart; a refusal to let anything distract us from the God who is at the centre of our being. Some people dislike silence precisely because it opens their hearts to the presence of one who may challenge and comfort them. People often fill their lives with noise, activity, food, drink or drugs because they cannot face the empty stillness at the centre of their lives which can ultimately only be filled by God. As Saint Augustine said: 'Our hearts are restless Lord, until they rest in you.'

Mother Teresa of Calcutta knew the importance of this silence: 'We need to find God and he cannot be found in noise and restlessness. God is the friend of silence. We need silence to be able to touch souls. The essential thing is not what *we* say, but what God says *through* us.'

Ponder for a moment: What part does silence play in my life? Do I work in silence? What are the chief obstacles to silence in my life? Do I suffer from 'sensory overload'? What choices do I have to make in order to accomplish my day's work in a quieter, more stress-free way?

'Being' in God's presence is enough

Listening prayer is primarily done not with the ears but with the heart. The more we open ourselves to God in silence, the more we will hear and discern in our hearts. We may not be conscious of any sounds or words, but God will be speaking to us at our deepest level. St. John of the Cross tells us that private revelations of God's presence in visions and miracles can happen but that they are for 'spiritual beginners' and not to be relied upon. A more sure form of prayer can be to empty our minds of all thoughts and images (as much as is ever possible) and simply to *be* in God's presence; to *rest* in God's presence; to let *God* envelop us, speak to us and listen to us at a level deeper than our words, thoughts, and senses can comprehend. By praying in this way we come to live more and more deeply in the presence of God, and thus come to be transformed by him. Saint Augustine said 'God is nearer to me than I am to myself'. Like John the Baptist, by being in God's presence we will decrease so that Christ can grow (*John* 3:30) and our very lives will announce the reign of the Lamb of God.

John the Baptist depicted in ceramic by Adam Kossowski at The Friars, Aylesford, England.

The presence of God revealed in the Scriptures

As we know, Carmelites seek to live *in allegiance to Jesus Christ* (*Rule of Saint Albert* Chapter 2). Jesus, the Lamb of God, gives us the perfect example of how to live in the divine presence; always relating to God as Father and seeking to live out his will. We cannot know about Jesus, and the way he showed us how to live in God's presence, unless we commit ourselves to reading the Bible, the Living Word of God. As Saint Jerome said, 'Ignorance of Scripture is ignorance of Christ.' Carmelites must frequently, daily,

Our Carmelite tradition stresses that God's presence must be sought regularly in the Scriptures.

encounter Christ's presence in the Holy Scriptures.

In reading the Gospels we encounter Jesus seeking the presence of God his father. Sometimes Jesus prayed alone, sometimes with others. His prayer was a time of reflective discernment on the Father's will for him. Prayer was not always an easy experience for Jesus. For example, after his baptism Jesus was drawn into the wilderness to pray in preparation for his ministry; in this prayer Jesus experienced temptation. Think also of the agony Jesus knew when he prayed in the Garden of Gethsemane as his human will came face to face with the divine will. Prayer is not always an easy experience for us either, because being in the presence of God can challenge our own desires and hopes. It is sometimes said that prayer doesn't change God's mind; prayer changes us.

Nevertheless, Jesus clearly taught that we should pray, and gave several parables and other teaching on how we should do so, including the 'Our Father'. In the midst of his busy public life Jesus felt the need to pray, the need to spend time alone with his Father. We should pray as an expression of our status as God's creatures and God's children, completely dependent on him. To ask God for blessings is an expression of our human poverty and dependence on his goodness and generosity. To pray for guidance and strength is an expression of our desire to do his will in spite of our human frailty.

Above all we pray – we become aware of the presence of God – because we are inspired to by the Holy Spirit. The Holy Spirit dwells within all of us, desiring to communicate with the Father in the love of the Trinity. We can choose whether or not to follow that urgent longing within us to pray. If we love God, we will want to be with him, and prayer brings us closer. Once we have tasted prayer we will know that it is an experience of the presence of God who makes his home with us – an experience that cannot be achieved in any other way.

Stop and think: What role does prayer have in your life? What form(s) does your prayer take?

God the Holy Spirit, depicted as a dove, above St. Joseph's Monastery in Avila, founded by St. Teresa.

Feeling a lack of God's presence: the Dark Night

Prayer can be a wonderful occasion for experiencing the presence of God and when we take it seriously for the first time we often 'feel' the presence of God close to us. But once we have become used to prayer we question its value and even doubt the presence of God, judging our prayer by how it leaves us 'feeling'. The Welsh poet R. S. Thomas expressed his doubts and hopes beautifully:

> Prayers like gravel flung at the sky's window,
> hoping to attract the loved one's attention.
> But without visible plaits to let down for the believer to climb up,
> to what purpose open that far casement?
> I would have refrained long since
> but that peering once through my locked fingers
> I thought that I detected the movement of a curtain.

The Carmelite tradition teaches us that there are times when – even if we are praying – we do not perceive the presence of God. This is often called 'The Dark Night'. It has probably been experienced by all of Carmel's saints, and is a natural (even inevitable) part of the spiritual journey. During this period of dryness, even our prayer-time and our relationships can leave us cold. During the 'Dark Night' we feel that God has withdrawn his presence from us, and we may feel unloved. This is not the case, and it is important not to judge our prayer-life on how it makes us *feel*. What is actually happening in this time is that God is transforming us at a level beyond our senses and feelings so that we can live in his presence in a new and deeper way. In the 'Dark Night' God strips us (temporarily or permanently) of all the pleasures we derive from the 'attachments' and 'securities' that we cling to in place of him – such as rituals and feelings in prayer – and makes us rely entirely on him. The Dark Night 'declutters' our faith. It is 'dark' because God is in fact so near to us in the process that if we could perceive his presence we would be 'blinded' and overwhelmed by his brilliance. Because the 'Dark Night' deprives us of our *feeling* of God's presence (hence the term 'Dark Night of Sense'), the temptation is either to give up on prayer, or to redouble our efforts; neither response will help. All we can do is to trust, continue our journey of faith allowing God to work within us, and know that God is present and loving us regardless of whether we feel it or not.

Stop and reflect: Do I 'feel' God's presence in prayer? Should I?

The 'dark night' is in fact a time when God's brilliance draws ever closer.

The simplicity of prayer for Brother Lawrence and Saint Thérèse

Brother Lawrence of the Resurrection (1611-91) was born Nicolas Herman and became a Discalced Carmelite friar in seventeenth-century Paris. He is now revered as one of the Carmelite Family's greatest experts on prayer.

In the priory, among his everyday tasks as a cook and cobbler Lawrence enjoyed a continual sense of God's love. Lawrence maintained a regular correspondence and received many people seeking his advice, realising that since Jesus became human and 'dwelt among us' (*John* 1:14) he too had to be where the people are, with and for those needing help. After Lawrence's death his letters, conversations and spiritual maxims were published, and this book, *The Practice of the Presence of God*, is a classic of Carmelite wisdom and an international bestseller among both Catholics and Protestants (it was highly prized by the great Methodist John Wesley). It's a short book, and well worth reading.

Brother Lawrence realised that prayer can become more complicated than it actually needs to be, and we don't need to use a lot of words. Jesus said 'When you pray, don't gabble' (*Matthew* 6:7). Perhaps this teaching inspired Lawrence to understand how God had stripped him of the clutter in his prayer life: 'I gave up all devotions and prayers that were not required and I devote myself exclusively to remaining always in his holy presence. I keep myself in his presence by simple attentiveness and a general loving awareness of God' (*Letter 2*). Lawrence appreciated that prayer is, quite simply, a process of turning our hearts to God in acknowledgment of his presence. This might be for a prolonged period, or just a few seconds, and gradually helps us acquire the habitual attitude of being aware that we are always in God's presence.

A similar insight of how to 'Practice the Presence of God' was given by Brother Lawrence's compatriot, Saint Thérèse of Lisieux (d. 1897). She wrote: 'For me, prayer is an aspiration of the heart, it is a simple glance directed to heaven, it is a cry of gratitude and love in the midst of trial as well as joy, which expands my soul and unites me to Jesus.' This *prayer of aspiration* has long been favoured by Carmelites as a way to take up Saint Paul's injunction to 'Pray without ceasing' (*1 Thessalonians* 5:17) and continually acknowledge God's presence in our hearts. It is a way of keeping vigil with God, of 'keeping watch in prayer' as Saint Albert states in Chapter 10 of our *Rule*. The word *aspiration* means 'the action of breathing' as well as 'the action of desiring'. The *prayer of aspiration* reflects both these meanings: with every breath we take we are in the presence of God who breathed life into the world, the God whom we desire.

Brother Lawrence perceived God's presence in the world of nature around him. The sight of a leafless tree in mid-winter led him to reflect on the divine power that would transform it in the spring.

St. Thérèse at recreation in Lisieux Carmel.

Pray as you can, not as you can't

Lawrence of the Resurrection and Thérèse of Lisieux encourage us to pray as we can, pray as we are, and pray where we are. We have feelings and emotions and we tend to rely on these as guides to how 'successful' our prayer is, but Lawrence and Thérèse knew that it was God who was working in them when they prayed, whether they felt it or not. We are influenced by the 'instant coffee' syndrome: from modern technology we demand instant results, immediate communication, and rapid transport. We run the danger of applying this to our prayer-life, expecting trouble-free and instantly-effective ways of relating to God. If this doesn't happen, we want to bring in an expert to trace the fault, or we just give-up! But God's ways are not our ways, neither are his thoughts our thoughts. Prayer is God's country that we gradually explore. We must put ourselves into his care and allow him to arrange things for us. Prayer is always possible, no matter what we feel like, because God is actually the one reaching out to us before we ever reach out to him. Sometimes offering our emptiness and dryness is enough.

All prayer is a gift from God and a unique experience for each one of us, within the guidance and wisdom of the Church. Whilst we may need to persist in certain types of prayer that we find difficult at first, on the other hand we shouldn't force ourselves to pray in a way that is not suitable for us at that particular time. Nor should we expect others to pray like us.

At various times in our lives we pray in different ways, and just as our relationships grow so does our prayer-life. When we were children we learnt to relate to God in vocal prayers such as the *Our Father*, *Hail Mary*, and so on. These simple and beautiful prayers remain with us for life. They can be used at times of great joy, or can be a great consolation in sickness or in the turmoil of a family crisis. We may also need to find new ways of expressing our relationship with God, and not be restricted by one familiar form of prayer.

Am I too busy to live with God's presence?

Our lives are so busy, whether we are engaged in priestly ministry, coping with a demanding family or a stressful job, being a carer, or suffering the pain of illness or bereavement twenty-four hours a day. How can I fit prayer in to my busy life? How can I live aware of God's presence?

First of all we must acknowledge that God's presence is a constant reality and a gift whether we are at prayer or in the business of life, what Teresa of Jesus called 'finding God amid the pots and pans'. God doesn't ask us to stop living our lives in order to enjoy his presence. All the aspects of life can reveal God's presence to us, since there is no human experience God himself has not gone through, even suffering and death. However, there are times when if we are to respond to God's desire to be with us, we will have to cooperate with him and actively look for ways to make space for God in our schedules. This may mean reassessing our priorities and realising that God comes first.

'Vacare Deo': space for God

Making space for God in our timetables, in our homes, and in our hearts is known in the Carmelite tradition by the Latin phrase *Vacare Deo* (translated as 'freedom for God', 'emptiness for God', or 'space for God'). Abandoning ourselves to the will of God and being free for him (as Mary was) is closely linked to that other important Carmelite notion of *Puritas Cordis* (an undivided 'purity of heart' given over to God alone). *Vacare Deo* means making regular time to be aware of God's presence, even if only for a short while. If we are too busy to live in the presence of God we are too busy to be living life to the full. We *have* to find time for prayer and this requires some self-discipline. This is where a community (be it a family, chapter, spirituality group, friary, parish, or whatever) can help us, with its rhythms of regular prayer.

Ways of making 'space for God'

As we grow in our relationship with God we try to find ways of nurturing our love (like we would in any healthy relationship). What matters is not what techniques or approaches we try but rather whether we are cultivating our relationship with the ever-present God. There is no single 'Carmelite method of prayer'; rather, Carmelites encourage people to pray in whatever way(s) help them to grow in relationship with God.

Did you know? Some older *Manuals* of the Carmelite Third Order specified set prayers to be conducted each day, such as half an hour of silent meditation and a mystery of the rosary. Today the choice of prayer is left to the individual, but some set time for meditation is still highly recommended.

As our prayer-life grows, some people find retreats, quiet days, and periods of recollection helpful in developing their relationship with God. Some Carmelites establish a small corner of a room as a meditation space. Making a literal 'space' in our lives through time spent away on retreat or by setting-up a meditation area can help us focus on the 'practice of the presence of God'; we just have to remember that God cannot be confined to one space or one form of meditation. Our *Rule of Saint Albert* encourages Carmelites to stay in our cells

A simple arrangement of icon, candle and Bible can help focus our prayer.

and to meditate there day and night on the law of the Lord. Christ himself said: 'whenever you pray, go into your room and shut the door and pray to your Father who is in secret; and your Father who is in secret will reward you' (*Matthew* 6:6). For some of us the cell will be a literal space within our home, such as a bedroom where we can pray in secret. For others it may be a beauty spot in nature. Ultimately, it is a space within the heart.

Another form of vocal prayer that many people find helps them focus on the presence of God is the rosary. Carmelites are not required to pray the rosary but for those who find it helpful it can be encouraged as a great means of meditating on Christ's life in the company of Mary, reflecting on episodes from Scripture.

Some people find that they can develop *Vacare Deo* in their lives – and thus be more open to the presence of God – through 'Centering Prayer'. Centering Prayer is a resting in the Lord, relaxing the mind and listening to God in the silence of our hearts. In Centering Prayer it is more important to have the right *intention* than to worry about paying *attention*, because the aim is to be open to God, to be available to the Divine, to give everything to the God who is within us. Centering Prayer is not new; its roots have existed since the earliest days of the Church, and it is practiced by many Carmelites today. Among the Carmelites who have written on Centering Prayer, perhaps the best known is the former Prior General of the Order, Fr. Joseph Chalmers, O.Carm.

Another Carmelite writer who has given many people insights into methods of prayer that help us be aware of God's presence is Ernest E. Larkin, O.Carm. (d. 2006). His particular interest was Christian meditation using some of the techniques of Eastern religions. In a reflection on 'Carmelite Spirituality Today', Fr. Larkin wrote:

> We Carmelites are serious about our vocation of prayer. We would walk with God through life; we would stand before Him like our father Elias [a.k.a. Elijah]; we would see the world suffused with the divine, bathed in his Precious Blood. But how shall we become aware of God's presence? How can we develop a realization that Christ is all about us?
>
> The answer is disarmingly simple. It is again to practice charity. The charity of Christ opens our heart to others, but at the same time it opens our heart to the Divine Presence. A down-to-earth charity will purify: it will drive out pettiness and sinfulness, and we will see Christ revealed in our neighbour and in our own life ... We attain union with God when our wills are attuned to His, when we are keeping the commandments and loving our neighbours. We are present to God and God is present to us, in other words, in charity. 'He who keeps his commandments abides in God, and God in him,' says the Apostle of Charity (*1 John* 3:27). 'And everyone who loves is born of God, and knows God ... for God is love' (*1 John* 4:7-8). This is why we say we meet God in the concrete daily actions of our Christian lives ... If we are trying to do God's will, trying to love God and our neighbour, trying to pray according to our rule of life, we are building up a deep sense of God's presence in our world.

Finding God's presence in *Lectio Divina* and the Liturgy

An ancient method of prayer (in the tradition of the Carmelites and other orders) that has been revived in recent times is *Lectio Divina* which is Latin for 'holy reading'. This method of praying with the Bible and other spiritual texts was practiced by monks and friars for many centuries but fell into disuse towards the end of the Middle Ages. It is a particularly good way of consciously being in God's presence because it encourages the sharing of silence and insights into the Scriptures, where – as we've seen before – God's presence is revealed.

Another way of living in the presence of God through the Living Word of the Bible is to reflect upon the Psalms, especially through the liturgy of the Divine Office. At the time Saint Albert wrote the Carmelite *Rule*, few people could read and books were scarce. Those who could say the Divine Office (the 'canonical hours' which the *Rule* refers to in Chapter 11) would probably have learnt the Psalms by heart. How privileged we are to have the Psalms translated and readily available to us. Saying the Morning and Evening Prayers of the Office is no longer the preserve of priests and religious; lay-people can and do participate in this wonderful 'Prayer of the Church', which unites not only all Carmelites but all Catholic Christians. Although the Office is usually a community prayer, when we say it alone we can meditate on the Psalms or other Scripture readings, pausing as we wish. The Psalms are possibly 2,400 years-old, and throughout the centuries people have found in them the words to express many emotions: joy, sorrow, thanksgiving, fear, repentance, and praise. Praying the Office enriches our appreciation of God's presence in all the situations and experiences of life. The Eucharist is another form of liturgy in which we encounter God's 'true presence', and we will reflect further on this in Chapter 13.

Making God's presence known and loved

When we adore Christ's presence in the Eucharist, we are challenged to be his body in the world. When we encounter the Father's word in the Scriptures, we are called to

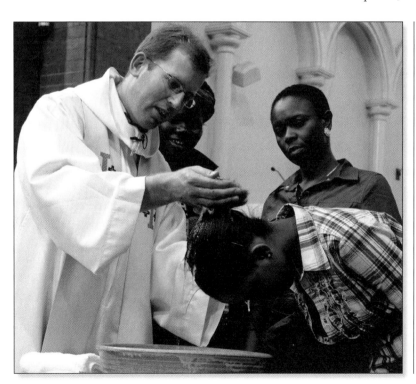

Carmel: a deepening of our baptismal vocation to proclaim God's presence.

preach his good news to all people. When the Holy Spirit stirs us to contemplation of God's presence, we are sent out in mission to be his presence for those thirsting for him today. Baptism has made us part of the mystical body of Christ, and therefore part of God's presence in the world. Engaging with the Carmelite tradition is a deepening of our baptismal commitment. Carmel is a gift to us and to the world for all those seeking to live with God's presence.

Contemplating God's presence in the ongoing Carmelite tradition

The Carmelite tradition invites us to make an ongoing journey of transformation. The official documents of the Carmelite Family can be thought of as useful maps that give us directions on this journey. In the year 2000 the Curia of the Carmelite Order (O.Carm.) published a guide for forming friars in the Carmelite tradition, entitled the *Ratio Institutionis Vitæ Carmelitanæ*, known simply as the *Ratio* for short. In 2007 the Curia likewise published a *Ratio* for the Carmelite nuns of the Ancient Observance. Both documents offer wise guidance to the wider Carmelite Family, and both contain the same statement about contemplating God's presence. This chapter concludes with that statement; you might feel inspired to read more from the *Ratio* documents as authentic guides in your own Carmelite formation.

> Contemplation is the inner journey of Carmelites, arising out of the free initiative of God, who touches and transforms us, leading us towards unity in love with him, raising us up so that we may enjoy his gratuitous love and live in his loving presence. It is a transforming experience of the overpowering love of God. This love empties us of our limited and imperfect human ways of thinking, loving, and behaving, transforming them into divine ways and enables us to taste in our hearts and experience in our souls the power of the divine presence and the sweetness of heavenly glory, not only after death, but during this mortal life. (*Friars' Ratio* §23 & *Nuns' Ratio* §9).

Conclusion: In this ninth chapter we have considered different aspects of what it means to live with God's presence, and what Carmelites have said about this over the centuries. What has stood out for you? What has been difficult to understand? How might you live more fully in the presence of God?

Consider ending your time of reflection and study by acknowledging God's presence in prayer.

In the next chapter we will consider the ways that God speaks to Carmelites and to all his people today.

Ideas for Reflection, Discussion and Action

- If any passage in this chapter has stood out as significant for you, either individually or as a community, reflect on why that is and what God might be saying to you through it.

- In prayer there can be a fear that God will ask me to change my life and I might be happy as I am; what is my level of trust in God?

- If you haven't already prayed using *Lectio Divina*, why not give it a try now? A good passage to reflect on might be: 'If you search for him honestly and sincerely you will find him ... for the Lord your God is a merciful God and will not desert you.' (*Deuteronomy* 4:29-31).

- We perceive God's presence through faith. Ask for that gift to be given to those who do not believe in God's presence.

- Buy or borrow a copy of Brother Lawrence's *Practice of the Presence of God* to read.

- Imagine a typical Carmelite or other Christian group meeting: Where might God's presence be perceived in such a meeting, in terms of people, places and things?

- Do you agree that being in God's presence can be thought of in terms of a human relationship?

- Have you experienced something of the 'Dark Night'?

- Read the *Ratio* documents of the Carmelite friars and nuns; notice how often the presence of God is referred to.

- Carmelites have always valued silence as a tool for immersing themselves in God's presence. Why do you think that is? Do you perceive God's presence more in stillness or activity, in solitude or in community?

- Go back to Chapters 5 and 6 and perhaps make some notes about how God's presence was experienced in the life of Mary or Elijah.

Recommended Further Resources

A number of Carmelite books on prayer discuss the 'practice of the presence of God', as of course does Brother Lawrence's classic of that title. Many of the resources listed below are widely available in Carmelite libraries, Christian bookshops, and online book ordering services.

Joseph Chalmers, O.Carm., 'Hearing the Word', in *Mary the Contemplative*, (Rome: Edizioni Carmelitane, 2001), pp. 35-52.

Curia of the Carmelite Order, *Ratio Institutionis Vitæ Carmelitanæ*, (Rome: Friars' edition 2000, Nuns' edition 2007). These texts are available in print, and online via www.carmelite.org.

Michel De Vertueil, *Meditating on the Mysteries: The Rosary as Biblical Prayer*, (Dublin: Veritas Publications, 1998).

Eltin Griffin, O.Carm., (ed.), *Hidden Riches: The Eucharist in the Carmelite Tradition*, (Dublin: The Columba Press, 2005).

James W. Kinn, *The Practice of Contemplation According to John of the Cross*, (Washington, D.C.: I.C.S. Publications, 2009).

Ernest Larkin, O.Carm., *Contemplative Prayer for Today: Christian Meditation* (Singapore: Medio Media, 2007).

Ernest Larkin, O.Carm., 'Carmelite Spirituality Today', published in *Ascent* and available online at www.carmelnet.org

Brother Lawrence of the Resurrection, O.C.D., *The Practice of the Presence of God*, Critical edition by Conrad De Meester, O.D.C., (Washington D.C.: ICS Publications, 1994).

Lumen Gentium: Dogmatic Constitution on the Church, 1964, in Walter M. Abbott, (ed.), *The Documents of Vatican II*, (The America Press, 1966). Available online at: www.vatican.va

Kilian Lynch, O.Carm., *The Practice of the Presence of God*, (Faversham: The Carmelite Press, 1974). Available online via the spirituality reflections on www.carmelite.org

John Malley, O.Carm., 'Fundamental values of Carmelite Spirituality', in *Formation and Communication at the Service of the Community*, Proceedings of the 2006 International Congress of Lay Carmelites, (Rome: Edizioni Carmelitane, 2007), pp. 19-34.

Fenella Matthew, 'Living in the Presence of God: Carmelites in the Footsteps of Elijah', *Mount Carmel: A Review of the Spiritual Life*, Volume 57 Number 4, October-December 2009, pp. 9-13.

Patrick Thomas McMahon, O.Carm., 'Nine Themes in Carmelite Spirituality', published in multiple parts in 2009 in *Assumpta* and *Carmel in the World* magazines, and available online at www.carmelite.org

Elizabeth Smith & Joseph Chalmers, O.Carm., *A Deeper Love: An Introduction to Centering Prayer*, (Tunbridge Wells: Burns & Oates, 1999).

Falco Thuis, O.Carm., *In Wonder at the Mystery of God. Contemplation: The Life Stream of Carmel*, (Rome: General Council, 1983).

John Welch, O.Carm., 'The Carmelite Tradition', in *Journeying with Carmel: Extracts from the 1995 Carmelite Constitutions*, (Middle Park, Victoria: Carmelite Communications, 1997), pp. 73-80. Available online at www.carmelite.org

John Welch, O.Carm., 'Prayer and the Self: Issues in Human Development', in *The Carmelite Way: An Ancient Path for Today's Pilgrim*, (Leominster: Gracewing, 1996), pp. 81-101.

John Welch, O.Carm., *Seasons of the Heart*, (Aylesford: Lay Carmel Central Office, 2001). Available online at www.carmelite.org

Notes and reflections on Chapter 9

Notes and reflections on Chapter 9

CHAPTER 10

God Speaks

Summary: God is accessible to us, revealed both through history and in the immediacy of a one-to-one relationship. Many of the now-familiar Carmelite themes are present in this chapter, but seen afresh from the perspective of God communicating his love to us. The chapter also considers the role of feelings in prayer.

A carving of God the Father above the entrance to the Church of the Annunciation which houses the tomb of Saint Teresa in the Spanish town of Alba de Tormes.

Get prepared: You know the advice by now! Have to hand the writing implements and reference books that you might find helpful, and any other resources you normally use when spending time in study, reflection and prayer. Since this chapter is about how God speaks to us, why not begin with a brief period of *Lectio Divina* meditation using the following Bible text:

> Long ago God spoke to our ancestors in many and various ways by the prophets, but in these last days he has spoken to us by a Son, whom he appointed heir of all things, through whom he also created the worlds. He is the reflection of God's glory and the exact imprint of God's very being, and he sustains all things by his powerful word.
>
> (*Hebrews* 1:1-3)

God is not only present but active

We read in the previous chapter how Carmelites are called to bear witness to the reality of God's existence, God's presence in our world. In this chapter we will see that God is not only present but actually *speaks*. The mission of Carmel is to know God and to make God known; we can do this if we listen for God speaking today, and help others to know his voice by our lives of prayer, community, and service.

Throughout human history God has addressed his beloved people and made his will for them known. As a contemporary Carmelite has observed:

> God is accessible. He is not some vague distant shadow out in the unknown. God has come and told us about himself. Just as friends and lovers share secrets, God has shared his secret with us: the secret that he is love and that we are called to share it.
>
> (Eugene McCaffrey, O.C.D., *Patterns of Prayer*, p. 23)

The heart of the Christian message, and therefore the heart of Carmel, is that God lives and God loves.

God speaks love - a revelation

God's voice calls us; God gives us a *vocation*. When God communicates, it is to tell us how much we are loved, just as we are, far more than we love ourselves. Carmelites have always heard this message spoken strongly in the Bible's *Song of Songs*, where the poet realises 'I am my Beloved's, and his desire is for me' (*Songs* 7:10). God speaks this message to all, not just to 'holy people'.

Theologians call God's speaking about God's self to us *Revelation*. God speaks or reveals him/herself to us in a number of ways. The first expression of God's power was verbal, when 'God said "Let there be light": and there was light' (*Genesis* 1:3). The Bible opens with the creative word of God, and continues as a statement of God's speech throughout human history.

Did you know? One of the Church's most important documents in our time is *Dei Verbum* ('Word of God'), the *Dogmatic Constitution on Divine Revelation* compiled at the

Second Vatican Council. This document has profoundly influenced modern Carmelite understanding of how 'God speaks'. The decree quotes Teresa of Jesus: 'prayer should accompany the reading of Sacred Scripture, so that God and people may walk together; for "we speak to Him when we pray; we hear Him when we read the divine sayings"' (§25).

God speaks through the prophets

The phrase 'word of the Lord' occurs over two hundred times in the Old Testament, especially in the activities of the prophets. God spoke his laws and commandments through the prophets and angels. The spiritual father of the Carmelite way of life, the prophet Elijah, heard God speak and was charged with communicating God's message (as we read in *1 Kings* 17). Elijah was so enflamed by the voice of God that the prophet's own words 'burned like a torch' (*Ecclesiasticus* 48:1). Prophecy means speaking in the name of God; not so much predicting the future but telling the truth of how things are in the present. We must be attentive to God speaking through the prophets of today, and as Carmelites we share Elijah's prophetic mission to speak of God and God's love for the world.

Stop and think: Do you think of yourself as a missionary charged with speaking God's word?

The renowned Carmelite friary at Boxmeer in The Netherlands contains many windows depicting the saints of Carmel. This depiction of Elijah shows him carrying a flaming sword, a symbol of his prophetic role to speak in God's name.

God spoke to Mary

As well as looking to Elijah, Carmelites regard Mary as a model of someone transformed by the word of God. Mary is our sister, the great disciple, and above all the woman of faith who 'heard the word of God and obeyed it' (cf. *Luke* 11:28). She could do this because she had purity of heart (*puritas cordis*). As the friars' 1995 *Constitutions* state:

Mary, overshadowed by the Spirit of God, is the Virgin of a new heart, who gave a human face to the Word made flesh. Mary is the virgin of wise and contemplative listening who kept and pondered in her heart [*Luke* 2:19] the events and words of the Lord. (§27).

Mary co-operated with the Word of God and gave God space to work in her life. Mary was a contemplative. That does not mean that she spent all her time on her knees, but rather Mary's openness to God speaking transformed her and the lives of those around her. It is this aspect of Mary that inspires Carmelite devotion to her, as described by the Discalced friar Aloysius Deeney:

> The particular aspect of the Blessed Virgin Mary that must be present in any person called to Carmel is that of an inclination to 'meditate in the heart', the phrase that Saint Luke's Gospel uses twice to describe Mary's attitude vis-à-vis her Son. Yes, all the other aspects of Marian life and devotion can be present: devotion to the scapular, the rosary, and other things. They are, however, secondary to this aspect of Marian devotion. Mary is our model of prayer and meditation. This interest in learning to meditate or inclination to meditation is a fundamental characteristic of any Carmelite. It is perhaps the most basic.
>
> (*Welcome to the Secular Order of Discalced Carmelites*, p. 11)

Jesus: the perfect Word of God

Thanks to Mary's openness, God spoke his word in a new way with the coming of Jesus of Nazareth. As the author of *Hebrews* says in the opening words of his letter: 'Long ago God spoke to our ancestors in many and various ways by the prophets, but in these last days he has spoken to us by a Son' (*Hebrews* 1:1-2). At the baptism of this 'beloved son', the voice of God the Father was heard (*Matthew* 3:17;

Mary was open to God's word. This is often depicted in art by her holding the Scriptures, as in this sculpture at Whitefriar Street Carmelite Centre in Dublin, created in 2005 by Simon Robinson.

The Transfiguration of Christ depicted in mosaic by Father Marko Ivan Rupnik on the facade of the Rosary Basilica in Lourdes, France. The Transfiguration is one of the Rosary's *Mysteries of Light*, first devised in the twentieth century by Maltese priest and Carmelite tertiary Saint George Preca.

Mark 1:11). The Father spoke again when Elijah and Moses appeared with Jesus at the Transfiguration: 'This is my Son, my Chosen; listen to him!' (*Luke* 9:35). God the Father speaks through Jesus.

The Gospel refers to Jesus as the Word of God made flesh (*John* 1:14). Through the speech, deeds and character of his son, God the Father has revealed to humanity his nature and will. Jesus is the perfect revelation of God. That is why Carmelites seek to live, as Saint Albert says in our *Rule*, 'in allegiance to Jesus Christ' (Chapter 2).

Jesus learned to know his Father's will and his love by spending time in the dialogue of prayer. Prayer enabled Jesus to become the authentic voice of God. In the *Our Father*, Jesus tells us we should speak to God intimately, as we would to a parent.

Actions speak louder than words

God speaks not only in words but through actions. In his ministry Jesus spoke of how much God desires us, not only by his words but also by his deeds, especially his death and resurrection. It was the humanity of Jesus that allowed him to speak to us of his divinity.

The Church describes Jesus as the complete and perfect revelation of God. There is nothing necessary for our salvation which Jesus has not taught us by his words and actions. Therefore Carmelites need look no further than Jesus – as he is revealed to us in the Gospels – for how we should live holy lives. We derive guidance from Elijah, Mary, and the Carmelite tradition, but these always point us back to Jesus. As Carmelites we reject any so-called 'revelations' that distract us from the Living God.

Did you know? The Hebrew term *dabar* means both 'word' and 'event'. It implies communication and action. When God speaks, he acts in a powerful way.

_____

God speaks in the Scriptures

As well as referring to Christ, the phrase 'Word of God' is also applied to the Bible, especially the Gospel or 'Good News' of Jesus. If we are to know Jesus, we have to read the Bible, the word of God, which 'is living and active, sharper than any two-edged sword' (*Hebrews* 4:12). The Word of God is so sharp it cuts away all the barriers we put up against God, and lays bare everything false that needs healing.

Written by human beings inspired by God, the Bible gives witness to God's powerful presence manifest in the history of his people. It speaks to us today as it spoke to our ancestors, which is why Carmelites are practitioners of *Lectio Divina*, an ancient method of meditating through the Scriptures on God and God's action in our lives.

Saint Albert makes it clear in our *Rule* (printed at the front of this book) that Carmelites should ponder the Law of the Lord day and night (Chapter 10). The 'Law of the Lord' refers both to Christ and to the Bible. Everything we Carmelites do must be touched by Christ and by the Word which God has spoken to us in Scripture: 'The sword of the spirit, the word of God, must abound in your mouths and hearts. Let all you do have the Lord's word for accompaniment' (Chapter 19).

Stop and reflect: Would you say that every aspect of your life is accompanied by God's word? What does that mean, and how can it come about?

Reflecting on how Carmelites can live the *Rule of Saint Albert* today, the 1995 *Constitutions of the Carmelite Order* states:

> Hearing, praying and living the Word in silence and in solitude, and in community, especially in the form of *Lectio Divina*, the Carmelites are led day by day to know and experience the mystery of Jesus Christ. Inspired by the Spirit and rooted in Christ Jesus, abiding in him by day and by night, Carmelites allow every choice and every action to be guided by his Word. (§20)

Lectio Divina is normally thought of as praying with the Bible, but rather than being a strict method of prayer it is a way of reading our own lives in the light of God's word, and so a *Lectio Divina* approach can be taken with whatever we are reading. Some people find that reading the newspaper can be a form of *Lectio Divina* as they ponder the happenings in the world, trying to see things as God does.

Closely connected with *Lectio Divina* is spiritual reading. It is important for Carmelites to be open to God speaking through classic spiritual texts, as well as through contemporary writers and the ongoing publication of documents by the Church at local and international levels. Carmelites ought to be open to the Church's long tradition of saintly writings, as well as being prepared to reflect on what today's Christians are writing and saying. As the Discalced Carmelite friar Aloysius Deeney writes:

There is an academic aspect to the formation of a Carmelite. There is an intellectual basis to the spirituality and identity of one who is called to the Order. And, as with each friar and each nun, each Secular [Lay Carmelite] represents the Order. A Carmelite who does not have the interest in studying or deepening the roots of his/her identity through prayer and study loses their identity and can no longer represent the Order. Nor does that person speak for the Order. Many times, when listening to a Carmelite speak, it becomes obvious when hearing what is said that they have not gone beyond what they heard in formation years before. This intellectual basis is the beginning of an attitude that is open to study. It leads to a deeper interest in Scripture, theology, and the documents of the Church. The tradition of spiritual reading, *Lectio Divina*, and time for study are the intellectual backbone of the

The writings of Carmel's saints, the documents of the Church, the Scriptures, and contemporary theology are important sources of ongoing intellectual and spiritual formation for all Carmelites.

spiritual life. Good formation depends on good information ... It is not a question of "being an intellectual" in order to be a Carmelite. It is a question of being intelligent in the pursuit of the truth about God, about oneself, about prayer, about the Order, and about the Church.

(*Welcome to the Secular Order of Discalced Carmelites*, p. 14)

God speaks to us and through us

We encounter God's word not only in Bible meditation but also in the Liturgy of the Church, notably the Eucharist and the Divine Office. Albert's *Rule* emphasises that God speaks to us in the liturgies and prayers of the Church, and so liturgical prayer is an essential aspect of a Carmelite's daily life, whether a lay person, friar, enclosed nun, hermit, or apostolic sister.

Another important form of prayer is meditation, sometimes known as *mental prayer*. It may involve our 'speaking' to God through words spoken aloud or in the silence of our hearts, or it might simply involve listening and being silent in the presence of God. Some people like to meditate by writing poetry or keeping a spiritual journal. Others use icons or the beauty of nature to focus their prayer; for others still such objects would be a distraction. It has long been Carmelite practice to recommend a set period of time each day for meditation, often half an hour for lay people and as much as an hour or two hours for religious (the reason for the difference being the supposed variation in the demands on a person with family or work commitments). In the present age the Order is wary of setting prescriptive amounts of time for meditation, as each person does what they can within the limits of their circumstances and the bounds of common sense. However, it is still recommended that every Carmelite, whatever their form of lifestyle, set aside some time each day for meditation. Thirty minutes a day is manageable for most people, either in one sitting or divided across two or more sessions at different points of the day.

Carmel encourages various ways of praying as a means of hearing God speak, and despite its 'mystical' reputation the Carmelite tradition is not complicated when it comes to prayer. Whatever form our prayer takes – *Lectio Divina*, the Liturgy, mental prayer, the rosary, spiritual reading, or silent meditation – the key is to allow God to speak to us, as well as us speaking to him. Saint Teresa said that prayer is a dialogue between friends.

Did you know? *The Catechism of the Catholic Church* (§2697-2720) defines three types of prayer: vocal prayer, meditation, and contemplative prayer. Do you know the difference?

Regular meditation and Bible-reading help us to be open to God's gift of contemplation, given where and when God wishes. By promoting within us a spirit of *vacare Deo* (space for God), such prayer opens us up to a deeper relationship with the Lord. This relationship is so wonderful it compels us to share the Good News of God's word with other people. That is why Carmelites are called to be prophets and preachers, telling the world by our speech and by our actions of the love that God has for every single human being. As we have read before, God entrusts us with the mission to go out and be – as Teresa of Jesus reputedly said – the hands of Jesus for others.

Did you know? The largest community of the Carmelite friars (O.Carm.) in Ireland is Gort Muire (the Irish for *Mary's Field*) in the Dublin suburb of Ballinteer. In the community chapel the Gospel-book (shown right) is permanently displayed near the tabernacle as a sign of God's presence in both the Scriptures and the Eucharist.

The chapel of Gort Muire Carmelite Community in Dublin, with its beautiful painting by Sean Keating of Mary and the Christ child above Mount Carmel, flanked by angels, Simon Stock, and the prophet Elijah.

God speaks in our communities

When we hear God speak his word to us, we communicate it to others and share it in communities. Carmelites are solitaries who are called to form communities. Living alongside other Carmelites prompts us to speak God's word of love, and to hear God's word of love from other people. Members of our communities can be the means by which God speaks to us. It is in communities that we recognise our strengths, and also our failings, when our sisters and brothers speak the truth to us in love (*Ephesians* 4:15). The joys and tensions of life in a community – be it a family, a workplace, a convent of friars, a monastery of nuns, or a chapter of Lay Carmelites – can be an opportunity for God to speak to us, if we are open to the collective wisdom of the group. Spiritual direction from an experienced guide can also be a useful means for Carmelites to be attentive to what God is saying in their lives.

Stop and think: Can you recall an incident where someone has said something to you – a word of comfort or confrontation – that you perceived at the time or later on to be a word from God?

Carmelites – even enclosed nuns or hermits – live their vocation in communities that are in touch with the people around them. It is in this social context that the friars try to share the word of God:

> This way of being 'in the midst of the people' is a sign and a prophetic witness of new relationships of fraternity and friendship among men and women everywhere ... It is also an expression of 'the choice to share in the lives of "the little ones" of history, so that we may speak a word of hope and of salvation from their midst – more by our life than by our words'.
>
> (1995 *Constitutions of the Carmelite Order* §24)

Lay members of the Carmelite Order also live out their vocation 'in the midst of the people', and can speak God's words of love to those around them:

> All Carmelites are in the world in some way, but the vocation of lay people is precisely to transform the secular world. So Tertiaries, in as much as they are committed lay people, have this secular characteristic by which they are called to treat the things of the world correctly and to order them according to God's will. Their life, lived in the world in the midst of the people, is dedicated to the cares and tasks of the world, in the ordinary ups and downs of family and of society. Tertiaries are invited by God to contribute to the holiness of the world: they are to have the spirit of the gospel in their work and to be guided by Carmelite spirituality. It is their calling to illuminate and order the world's activities so that these may be carried out according to Christ's intention and be a source of praise to the glory of the creator.
>
> (2003 *Rule for the Third Order of Carmel* §28).

By forming contemplative communities in the midst of the people, we Carmelites become witnesses of the God who speaks to us.

In the midst of the people: Carmelite friars and laity in Britain marching for Climate Justice in 2009.

God speaks for a purpose
The Word of God is never empty, as the prophet Isaiah – speaking in the Lord's name – reminds us:

For as the rain and the snow come down from heaven, and do not return there until they have watered the earth, making it bring forth and sprout, giving seed to the sower and bread to the eater, so shall my word be that goes out from my mouth; it shall not return to me empty, but it shall accomplish that which I purpose, and succeed in the thing for which I sent it. (55:10-11)

When God speaks he calls us to love those around us through active service. Hearing God's word makes us prepared to serve his people, and leads us to be concerned for our neighbour and for the problems of the Church. Our service may take many different forms.

In this way, being open to God speaking makes us concerned with issues that concern him; not only matters of faith, but also of politics, society, justice, and peace. As it is stated in the *Ratio* document compiled in the year 2000 to guide friars in their formation, Carmelites 'must create a climate of silence and of conversion capable of opening hearts, eyes and minds, so that, enlightened by the Word of God, we may learn to read the signs of the times, listen to others, and be attentive to what is happening in the world and in the environment in which we live' (*Ratio Institutionis Vitae Carmelitanae* §45).

Stop and think: How do you feel about the prospect of being God's prophetic voice in today's Church and Society?

Discerning God speaking: a Carmelite necessity

The Carmelite tradition is well aware that many voices compete for our attention, and so we have to use *discernment* to figure out when God is truly speaking to us and what he is asking of us. Sometimes we think we hear God speaking when actually it is other desires and distractions. Therefore, Carmel recommends a four-stage process of engaging with the voice of God: (1) Listening; (2) Discerning; (3) Obeying; (4) Acting.

First we must open our hearts to hear the Word of God, so that we can say like Samuel 'Speak, Lord, your servant is listening' (*1 Samuel* 3). We must then discern what is of God and what is not; this means reflecting on what it is we think God is asking of us, not only as individuals but as a community. Having discerned God's Word we must accept it as the will of God, for which we need a spirit of obedience. Finally, we act upon it.

God speaks to initiate a relationship

God speaks about himself because he wants to enter into a deep relationship with us. That is the reason why Jesus – the perfect 'Word' spoken by God – came among us. When we hear the Word of God, we are transformed so that we become more like him and be united with him:

> Carmelites are called to live in the presence of the living and true God, who in Christ has come to live among us. They look for every possibility and occasion to reach divine intimacy. Letting themselves be guided by the action of the Holy Spirit, Carmelites are open to a transformation of mind and heart, of their vision and their actions.
> (2003 *Rule for the Third Order of Carmel* §32)

Did you know? Liberata Ferrarons y Vivés (1803-42) was a Carmelite Tertiary in Olot (Catalonia, Spain) who was especially open to the active Word of God. Known as 'The Little Worker' because of the vibrant faith she witnessed to her factory colleagues, her prayer-life deepened profoundly in the Carmelite Third Order. Her cause for beatification took a step forward in 2009 when Pope Benedict XVI authorised the Vatican's Congregation for the Causes of Saints to publish a declaration of her heroic virtue, bestowing on her the title 'Venerable'.

Venerable Liberata Ferrarons y Vivés.

God speaks to transform us

As Elijah discovered on Mount Horeb, God can communicate his presence to us in periods of silence and emptiness. Hearing God speak in 'the sound of sheer silence', our hearts are touched and our lives transformed. The former Prior General of the Order, Joseph Chalmers, O.Carm., explains the role that God's Word has in the process of transforming us:

> Union with God involves us in total transformation of our being. God alone can bring this about. We begin the journey of transformation when we hear God's call to take the relationship with God seriously and begin to do something about it...
>
> The closer we allow God to come to us, the more clearly do we see ourselves. This can be very painful, but it is in fact a healing process...
>
> We have a wonderful facility for blocking out what we do not want to hear. How often have we read the Gospel and heard it proclaimed, but have we really grasped what God is saying to us? ...
>
> The Word of God is addressed to us in many different ways each day. God gradually reveals to us what we are, if we are open to hearing the Word, and often the revelation will come in moments of darkness and through those areas of our lives which we would rather not look at.
>
> (Joseph Chalmers, O.Carm., *Mary the Contemplative*)

When we listen to God speaking our lives are transformed, because we begin to live as he wants us to. Ultimately this makes us freer and happier than if we follow our own desires and limited vision. God's journey is more exciting than our own. As we begin to see as God sees and love as God loves our lives are transformed, and so are the lives of those around us. In an imperfect world, we become like John the Baptist, proclaiming in the desert 'Prepare the way of the Lord!' (*Mark* 1:3).

Prayer: opening our hearts to God speaking

When we desire to hear God's word we can trust that God will reveal himself to us. We have God's word on it: 'When you search for me, you will find me; if you seek me with all your heart, I will let you find me' (*Jeremiah* 29:13-14). God is always wanting to communicate with us, but he never forces his word upon us. To hear God speak we have to cooperate with his desire. We do this by cultivating the right environment and making time for prayer. Sometimes we worry about the way that we pray, but Carmelites appreciate that what matters is not so much how *we* pray, but rather what *God* does within us when we pray.

> Carmelites offer no single method or approach to prayer. They learned that prayer was the Spirit's work in us. God speaks to us in life, and continually addresses us in our lives, for greater life. Our effort, then, is one of listening. All our words are an attempt to speak the one Word that is God.
> (John Welch, O.Carm., *The Carmelite Way*)

For us Carmelites, listening in prayer is as important as speaking. We focus on the Word, rather than many words. Jesus himself said 'When you pray, don't gabble' (*Matthew* 6:7).

There is much useful information about prayer to be found in the recent documents of the Carmelite Family, including the 1995 *Constitutions* of the Carmelite friars (O.Carm.), the 2003 *Rule for the Third Order of Carmel* (T.O.C.), and the 2003 *Constitutions of the Secular Order of the Teresian Carmel* (O.C.D.S.).

Stop and broaden your reading: Why not read what is said about prayer in one of the recent official publications of the Carmelite Family, such as those listed above?

Prayer is God's language

Prayer is God's language, and it can seem strange to us. Saint Edith Stein (Teresa Benedicta of the Cross) felt that when God speaks he does not communicate with words and images that we recognise, but rather he communicates the reality of who he is. God is always close to us, indeed closer to us than we are to ourselves. In prayer we let go of everything and realise that God is in the centre. We cannot bring about an experience of God's speech through our own efforts and images of God:

> Listening to God does not depend on you or the effort you make. It depends entirely on God, on God's freely made decision to come into dialogue with you and to allow you to listen to the voice of God. Thus you need to prepare yourself by asking God to send his Spirit, since without the Spirit of God it is impossible to discover the meaning of the Word.
> (Carlos Mester, O.Carm., *Meditating Day and Night*)

God wants to give us the gift of his voice, but we will only hear it if we listen with an open heart.

God speaks to our hearts

Saint Augustine's phrase *Cor ad cor loquitur* ('heart speaks to heart') helps us understand that prayer is the key to hearing God speak; not to our ears, but to our hearts. Saint Teresa of Jesus said that God 'speaks clearly to the heart when we beg him from our heart' (*Way of Perfection*, Chapter 26). Prayer is a meeting of hearts; we talk to someone who is listening, and listen to someone who is talking. Praying well means listening to God, to others, and to our inner selves where God lives.

God speaks in whispers and parables

We know that God's self-revealing is gradual, and he does not overpower us with his awesome presence. God often speaks with a whisper, as Elijah perceived in the 'sound of sheer silence' on Mount Horeb (*1 Kings* 19:12). Jesus sometimes spoke in parables; he knew that he had to speak his Father's message in a way everyone could understand. Carmelite saints, such as Thérèse of Lisieux, have often heard God's voice as a simple whisper, not a complicated shout:

> When God speaks to his child who is selflessly seeking him, he speaks quietly and intimately. The closer the child comes to God, the simpler does he or she become, and quieter and closer the voice.
> (John Nelson, *Living the Little Way of Love with Thérèse of Lisieux*)

Listening to God speak is easier in silence

To hear God's gentle voice the Carmelite tradition recommends silence and solitude. Silent prayer quietens the noise within us so that we can hear what God has to say. It was in the silence of the void that God spoke to create the world. Sometimes we have to pause in our busy lives so as to give space for God to speak. The Carmelite tradition calls this attitude of openness to God *Vacare Deo*. This means being empty so that God can fill us with his word:

> To be attentive to God we must be completely self-forgetful, intent only on listening to the one who speaks to us. Contemplation means receiving; and we cannot receive unless we are empty, prepared to accept whatever God wishes to say and do with us.
> (Elizabeth Ruth Obbard,
> *The Living Flame of Love of John of the Cross*)

When we are silent we stop talking and entrust ourselves to the unlimited and gratuitous love of the true God, without clinging on to any other means of security.

Did you know? Thousands of people come to Carmelite & Discalced Carmelite retreat centres around the world. Many come wishing to hear the Word of God preached, and also to listen to God in peaceful silence. Do you know of such a retreat house near you?

Carmelite retreat centres around the world include (top-bottom, left-right): Aylesford (England); Darien (U.S.A.); Springiersbach (Germany); Kostelní Vydří (Czech Republic).

Silence: an environment for contemplation

Remaining in the presence of God in silence can help dispose us to receive God's gift of contemplation, which is the heart of the Carmelite charism. Contemplation is a journey of transformation that conforms all dimensions of our lives to the will of God, or as the friars' *Ratio* describes it, 'contemplation is understood as an attitude and a life style' (§38). Again, we cannot 'achieve' contemplation by our own efforts – it is a gift given by God – but silence helps contemplation come about because 'silence is of course not just a lack of words. It is a way of communicating. Indeed, silence is God's way of communicating *par excellence*' (Joseph Chalmers, O.Carm.). As the late Cardinal Basil Hume put it:

> Silence is a presence of God. It is in this silence that we shall hear a voice deep within us speaking to our noble selves, calling us to high ideals and generous instincts. Silence is the voice of God, sometimes no louder than a whisper, but speaking to us unmistakably if we learn

to listen to God. That silence, the presence of God, will bring peace to our divided and troubled hearts.

The 1992 *Catechism of the Catholic Church* says something similar:

> Contemplative prayer is silence, the 'symbol of the world to come' or 'silent love'. Words in this kind of prayer are not speeches; they are like kindling that feeds the fire of love. In this silence unbearable to the outer man, the Father speaks to us his incarnate Word, who suffered, died and rose; in this silence the spirit of adoption enables us to share in the prayer of Jesus. (§2717)

As Carmelites we all need to find the time to be silent, to reflect and listen to the voice of God that speaks deep within us. The great Carmelite John of the Cross says that silence is vital if we are to know Jesus: 'The Father spoke one Word, which was his Son, and he speaks it in an eternal silence, and in silence it must be heard by the soul.' (*Words of Light and of Love*, 99).

Did you know? St. Joseph heard God speak through the message of an angel in a dream (*Matthew* 2:13). Joseph is invoked by Carmelites as a special patron and *principal protector of our Order*, because as 'Mary's Order' we look to Joseph – like his wife did – to provide for us. Teresa of Jesus had great devotion to Saint Joseph.

A man attentive to God's word: Saint Joseph depicted at Aylesford Priory in England (left) and Gort Muire Carmelite Centre in Dublin, Ireland.

God speaks in the desert

The image of the desert is very important to Carmelites, because its dryness and solitude allow men and women seeking holiness to focus entirely on God's voice without the distractions and false idols we so often live with:

> None of us is perfect and all we can do is our best in the circumstances. However, it is very important to be faithful to our vocation, which will lead us into the desert where we have to let go of all our supports in order to hear the voice of God, who speaks in our hearts.
>
> (Joseph Chalmers, O.Carm., 'Sharing Experience with God')

It was in the desert that God spoke to Moses, to Elijah, and to Jesus. It was in a fertile valley between the desert and the sea that the Carmelite tradition began, as the *Ratio* document reminds us:

> The first Carmelites, in tune with the spirituality of their time (the 12th - 13th centuries), attempted to live out their ascetic commitment by withdrawing into solitude. Their desert was more than a physical reality; it was a place of the heart. It was the context in which could be lived the commitment to focus one's being on God alone. They had chosen to follow Jesus Christ, who denied himself and emptied himself to the point of dying naked on the cross. People of pure faith, they awaited the gift of new and eternal life, fruit of the Lord's resurrection. The desert, a place of solitude and aridity, blooms and becomes the place where the experience of God's liberating presence builds fraternity and inspires us to service. In the footsteps of the first Carmelite hermits, we too journey through the desert, which develops our contemplative dimension. This requires self-abandonment to a gradual process of emptying and stripping ourselves, so that we may be clothed in Christ and filled with God. This process begins when we entrust ourselves to God, in whatever way he chooses to approach us. For we do not enter the desert by our own will: it is the Holy Spirit who calls us and draws us into the desert; it is the Spirit who sustains us in our spiritual combat, clothes us in God's armour, and fills us with his gifts and with the divine presence, until we are entirely transformed by God and reflect something of God's infinite beauty.
>
> (*Ratio* §27)

It is in the starkness and asceticism of the desert that we overcome our demons to hear the voice of God. The desert can thus become a fertile and necessary place to travel in our journey of transformation, as stated in the 2003 *Rule for the Third Order of Carmel* (*RTOC*):

> Ascending the mountain implies a desert experience in which the living flame of God's love transforms and detaches the lay Carmelite

from everything; even their image of God is purified and transformed ... Carmelites learn from the prophet Elijah to leave everything to go into the desert in order to be purified, made ready for their meeting with the Lord and to welcome his word ... The desert experience which was so determining in the life of the Prophet, becomes an obligatory phase for lay Carmelites who are called to be purified in the desert of life in order to meet the Lord authentically. Lay Carmelites must travel along this road, in the desert of interior mortification. This is so that they may listen to the Lord who speaks to their heart in new and surprising ways of the world, and also in signs which are sometimes hard to interpret, or in the silent and barely perceptible voice of the Spirit. They come back enthused after this encounter and realise that they are to be tireless in giving life to the setting in which they are called to work. Inspired by this encounter, they can proclaim it as the only answer to the ever present temptation to deny God or to be proudly self-sufficient. Sustained by the Spirit, Tertiaries do not let themselves be disappointed by apparent failure, by meagre results, by indifference or by the success of those who live contrary to the gospel. (§22, 35, 48)

The desert – literal or metaphorical – is a place where God speaks to the heart.

When God seems not to speak

There are times when even committed Christians feel that God no longer speaks to them, and they may doubt his very existence. The prayers and rituals which used to mean so much gradually lose their attractiveness, and the spiritual life seems to be without value. As we read in the previous chapter, the Carmelite tradition calls this experience the 'Dark Night', and it recognises it as a natural stage in a deepening relationship with God. Although the person of faith feels abandoned by God, in reality he or she is being stripped of any attachments so that the reliance on God in faith is total. In fact God is speaking to them at a level deeper than they can comprehend, and much deeper than any 'religious' observances can communicate.

God speaks in any situation of life

God speaks in the ordinary situations of our lives – in our pain as well as our joy, in our weakness as well as in our strength – because Jesus himself knew these experiences. It is untrue that God only speaks to us when we feel worthy of it, or when we think he is happy with us. God speaks in times of sin and distress as much as in times of goodness and love. God spoke to Adam after the Fall when he asked his wayward child 'Where are you?' (*Genesis* 3:9). God spoke to Moses when the leader of the Israelites was most disappointed with his own people (*Exodus* 34). God spoke to Elijah on Horeb when the prophet was at his lowest (*1 Kings* 19). It is especially when we feel depressed, sinful, or unworthy of love that God speaks words of comfort, hope, and compassion.

A word about 'affective' and 'negative' prayer

Emotional feelings in prayer – either despondency or joy – can be helpful in developing our relationship with God, but they can also be deceptive if we judge the effectiveness of our prayer by how it makes us 'feel'. To understand this we need to appreciate the difference between two approaches towards the Christian's relationship with God, often known as 'affective' and 'negative' forms of prayer. The goal of both types of prayer is *contemplation*, which is sometimes described as 'resting in God', 'union with God', or the journey towards 'living in the presence of the living God'.

Affective prayer or *affective piety* is a form of mental prayer or active devotion that uses emotions and the senses in a positive way to lift-up the person's heart to God. It was particularly encouraged by the early mendicant orders, such as the Franciscans, as a way for people to focus on God through their feelings and ideas. One of the most popular forms of affective meditation was to consider the Passion and Crucifixion of Jesus: to visualise the scene in one's mind, to focus on his pain and suffering, and thus be moved to pity, remorse, repentance, and love for Christ. Affective forms of piety could include meditating upon a passage from the Bible or a saint's life, venerating icons, chanting, praying the rosary, and any thought or action that leads to the heart rising towards God. In the early Carmelite Order there was plenty of this type of prayer, sometimes known as the *via positiva* ('positive way') or *cataphatic spirituality*. For example, medieval and renaissance Carmelites encouraged regular devotions before statues of the saints, developed shrines for pilgrims, and propagated devotion to Our Lady through the Brown Scapular, all of which were designed to encourage affective popular piety. Bible meditations which lead us to feel compassion for the suffering of Jesus, awe at the beauty of Creation, and joyful praise for God's glory can stir us to reach out to God in tears of repentance or in cries of love and affection. Carmelite experts on prayer, such as Teresa of Jesus and John of the Cross, wrote poems and prayers full of emotion. However, they also knew that the value of prayer should not be judged by how it makes us feel. They also realised through their experience of the 'Dark Night' that God loves us whether we feel it or not.

In apparent contrast to affective piety is *negative piety*. It is sometimes known as the *via negativa* or 'negative way' because it seeks to draw the soul close to God by rejecting all thoughts, images, and actions, relying solely on God to dwell within the heart in silence and stillness. It draws on *negative* or *apophatic theology* which attempts to describe God by negation, that is, to speak of God only in terms of what may not be said about God, because God is ineffable (he/she can never be fully defined by words or images). *Negative piety* is often associated with 'detachment' and linked to so-called *mysticism* because it focuses on the soul's experience of God as something beyond the realms of ordinary perception and unmediated by the structures of traditional organised religion. The 'founding-father' of negative theology was Pseudo-Dionysius or Pseudo-Denys, an anonymous theologian and philosopher of the fifth century. His influence came to flourish in medieval books on the spiritual journey such as *The Cloud of Unknowing* and later in Saint John of the Cross' *Dark Night of the Soul*. John wrote about coming to a state of union with God by following the path of 'nada' (nothing).

Stop and reflect: Looking back at your life, can you see periods when you have favoured either 'positive' or 'negative' prayer?

The huge impact of Saints John of the Cross and Teresa of Jesus on Carmelite spirituality meant that increasingly Carmel came to be seen in the wider Church as a *spirituality of negation*, despite the Carmelite Family's continuing support for devotions and popular piety. In the late 1500s after the Discalced reform split from the 'Ancient Observance' of the Carmelite Order there also emerged a stereotyping of the Ancient Observance (O.Carm.) as affective in its spirituality, and the Discalced Carmelite Order (O.C.D.) as negative. This caricature was neither true nor constructive for either branch of the family.

In the modern Church affective and negative forms of prayer and piety are not regarded so much in the binary terms of the Middle Ages. It is probably true to say that negative prayer is still held-up as more 'advanced' or more 'mature' than affective prayer and popular piety, but the two can be closely linked, both can be practised by the same person, and Saint Teresa observed that affective prayer can dispose a person to God's gift of contemplation. The Church recognises that different people are led to God by different ways, and that the deepening of prayer is not achieved solely by human effort but by the grace of God.

The important thing to remember in our life of prayer is that God speaks, and we must listen.

We don't have to be 'super-saints' to hear God speaking or to converse with God in return. Our desire for God comes from God himself; from the God who speaks one word to us in Jesus… Love.

Conclusion: In this tenth chapter we have considered the many ways that God speaks to us and through us. The word God speaks is love, spoken most eloquently in the life of Jesus Christ. God speaks to us in Scripture, in silence, in the desert. We hear God speaking through prayer (in its various forms), through the voices in our communities, and through our experiences of service. When we hear God's word in the heart we are compelled to speak that word to others. Whether our response to God in prayer is either active or passive, God's speech goes beyond words to the depths of our hearts.

Perhaps conclude your time of reflection and study with a prayer; rather than speaking aloud, why not spend a few moments in silence so you can hear God speaking to your heart more clearly?

We are now half way through this programme of initial formation in Carmelite spirituality. How have you found the journey thus far? Who and what have helped you follow the Carmelite path to this point?

In the next chapter we will consider in greater depth the practice of *Lectio Divina* and Carmel's attentiveness to God speaking through the words of Scripture.

Ideas for Reflection, Discussion and Action

- God speaks, and perhaps you have heard his call in your heart whilst reading this chapter. Have any passages stood out in a particular way for you or – if you are following this formation course with a community – for those around you? If describing the chapter to others, how would you summarise its key points?

- Who are the prophets of today, speaking the word of God?

- How would you speak to a stranger about God?

- Do Carmelites speak more with words or with actions?

- How does God speak to non-Christians?

- How much of your faith-life depends on 'revelations' beyond Jesus? Are 'vision-revelations' more important to you than the Gospels?

- Do you see yourself as a contemplative?

- Scrabble is perhaps the ultimate word game! If you could pick your own letters, what words would you form that mean 'Carmel' to you? Perhaps jot some key words down now.

- How do I pray? Am I open to Jesus? Am I growing in intimacy with him?

- In my relationship with God, how tight a rein do I keep on my emotions? Does 'affective' or 'negative' piety describe my prayer life?

- Spend some time today in silence, allowing God to speak to you on your journey of transformation.

- Can you see how God speaks in and through your local Carmelite community?

- World leaders sometimes act in a certain way because they claim that God has 'spoken' to them. How might we discern this?

- In a *Lectio Divina* meditation, reflect on one of the occasions in the Bible when God speaks: *Exodus* 20:1-17; *Deuteronomy* 1:6-8; *Matthew* 5:1-12; *Matthew* 10:16-20.

- Read the chapter on 'Hearing the Word' in the book *Mary the Contemplative* by the former Prior General, Joseph Chalmers.

Recommended Further Resources

The idea of God speaking is fundamental to Christian belief, so there are many resources you could read to develop your understanding of this topic. Below are listed a few Carmelite and other books that you will find in most of the Order's libraries and bookshops.

Ruth Burrows, O.C.D., *Essence of Prayer*, (London: Burns & Oates, 2006).

Carlo Carretto, *The Desert in the City*, (HarperCollins, 1981).

Catholic Bishops' Conference of England & Wales, *The Gift of Scripture*, (London: Catholic Truth Society, 2005).

Joseph Chalmers, O.Carm., 'Hearing the Word', in *Mary the Contemplative*, (Rome: Edizioni Carmelitane, 2001), pp. 35-52.

Joseph Chalmers, O.Carm., 'Sharing Experience with God', in Alexander Vella & Günter Benker, (eds.), *Carmelite Formation*, (Rome: General Curia of the Carmelite Order, 2002).

Matthew Connors, 'The Most Perfect of Prayers: The Lord's Prayer, its depth and roots', *Carmelite Digest*, Volume 24 Number 4, Winter 2009, pp. 66-79.

Dei Verbum: Dogmatic Constitution on Divine Revelation, 1965, in Walter M. Abbott, (ed.), *The Documents of Vatican II*, (The America Press, 1966). Available online at: www.vatican.va

Aloysius Deeney, O.C.D., *Welcome to the Secular Order of Discalced Carmelites*, (Washington, D.C.: I.C.S. Publications, 2009).

Keith J. Egan, T.O.C., *Carmelite Prayer: A Tradition for the 21ˢᵗ Century*, (New York: Paulist Press, 2003).

John Fitzgerald, *Backwards into the Future: Meditations on the Letter to the Hebrews*, (Faversham: Saint Albert's Press, 2005).

Joel Giallanza, C.S.C., 'On Faith and Prayer: The Contribution of St. Teresa of Jesus and St. John of the Cross to *The Catechism of the Catholic Church*', *Carmelite Digest*, Volume 25 Number 1, Spring 2010, pp. 47-55.

Penny Hickey, O.C.D.S., *Drink of the Stream: Prayers of Carmelites*, (San Francisco: Ignatius Press, 2002).

Journeying with Carmel: Extracts from the 1995 Carmelite Constitutions, (Melbourne: Carmelite Communications, 1997).

Ernest Larkin, O.Carm., 'Aspiratory Prayer in the Carmelite Tradition', *Carmel in the World*, Volume XLVII Number 2, 2008, pp. 142-55.

Ernest Larkin, O.Carm., 'The Carmelite Tradition and Centering Prayer/Christian Meditation', in Keith J. Egan, T.O.C., *Carmelite Prayer: A Tradition for the 21ˢᵗ Century*, (New York: Paulist Press, 2003), pp. 202-222.

Eugene McCaffrey, O.C.D., *Patterns of Prayer*, (New Jersey: Paulist Press, 2003).

James McCaffrey, O.C.D., *Captive Flames: A Biblical Reading of the Carmelite Saints*, (Dublin: Veritas, 2005).

Alister E. McGrath, 'The Idea of Revelation' in *Christian Theology: An Introduction*, (Oxford: Blackwell, Second Edition 1997), pp. 181-187.

Thomas Merton, O.S.C.O., *Contemplative Prayer*, (London: Darton, Longman and Todd, 2005).

John Nelson, *Living the Little Way of Love with Thérèse of Lisieux*, (London: New City, 1999).

John Welch, O.Carm., 'Visions and Voices: Extraordinary Religious Experiences', in *The Carmelite Way: An Ancient Path for Today's Pilgrim*, (Leominster: Gracewing, 1996), pp. 122-140.

Notes and Reflections on Chapter 10

CHAPTER 11

Lectio Divina & Carmel's Attentiveness to the Bible

Summary: This chapter reminds us of the central importance of the Scriptures in the Jewish and Christian traditions, and then goes on to review the essentials of *Lectio Divina* meditation on the Bible. Whilst there is great flexibility in approaches to *Lectio Divina*, the basic dynamic is: reading or listening to the text; meditation, through which one seeks to understand and ponder the meaning; prayer, inspired by the fruits of meditation; leading to making space for God, so that God can give us the gift of contemplation. This chapter explores how *Lectio* has developed as an attitude of the heart rather than a strict methodology, how this attitude was present in a perfect way in Elijah and Mary, and how it enables our relationship with Jesus to grow.

Carmelites: Proclaimers and Hearers of God's Word.

Get prepared: Having a Bible to hand ought to be second nature for Carmelites, and it would certainly be advisable whilst studying this chapter. Any translation will do; the *New Revised Standard Version* (NRSV) is widely acclaimed and available in a variety of study and popular editions (make sure you get an edition with the 'Catholic' books included, sometimes known as the Apocrypha). Get together any materials you might need to take notes or highlight points in the chapter. Begin your time of reflection with a prayer, perhaps inspired by Scripture; why not simply read the Gospel text of the day and spend some time in silent reflection.

Holy Words

Reading the Scriptures has long been a key practice for Christians and the custom has its roots in Judaism. Devout Jews are expected to know Holy Scripture (especially the first five books of the Bible known as the *Pentateuch* or *Torah*), to study it, and to take it into their hearts. This is summarised in the *Shema* (in Hebrew שְׁמַע יִשְׂרָאֵל), a fervent declaration of the Oneness of God, based on *Deuteronomy* 6:4-9:

שְׁמַע יִשְׂרָאֵל יְהוָה אֱלֹהֵינוּ יְהוָה אֶחָד ...

> Hear, O Israel: The LORD is our God, the LORD alone. You shall love the LORD your God with all your heart, and with all your soul, and with all your might. Keep these words that I am commanding you today in your heart. Recite them to your children and talk about them

Jewish men carry the scrolls of the Torah during morning prayers at the Western Wall in Jerusalem.

Climbing the Mountain: The Carmelite Journey 255

when you are at home and when you are away, when you lie down and when you rise. Bind them as a sign on your hand, fix them as an emblem on your forehead, and write them on the doorposts of your house and on your gates.

The *Shema* reminds us that the reality of God's presence (as we discussed in Chapter 9) must be written within our very hearts, and God's Word should be with us whatever we are doing. Bearing the Word of God within the heart comes about through the process of *interiorisation*, that is, not only listening to the Scriptures but also allowing them to transform us. Once upon a time every Jewish male was expected to write out a copy of the Torah because copying helps the memorisation process. You can read more about Judaism's approach to the Scriptures from books listed in the bibliography at the end of the chapter (especially *The Spirituality of Judaism* and *Like the Deer that Yearns*).

Attending to the Scriptures

In the early days of the Christian community, the Jewish practice of everybody reading and reciting the Scriptures continued among the followers of 'The Way' (as Christianity was first known). It was not until much later that Bible reading was reserved to clergy and religious. The Desert Fathers and Mothers of early Christianity were also avid readers of Scripture. They would memorise parts of the Bible in order to meditate on them and to allow the Word of God inscribed within their minds and hearts to form them and help them turn gradually into saints by the grace of God.

Most probably the hermits on Mount Carmel around the year 1200 learned passages of the Bible off by heart, especially the Psalms. They would not have read these passages in silence but most likely proclaimed them aloud, filling the valleys with the sound of God's Word.

The hermits on Carmel were following the tradition of the hermits of the desert who had first begun to gather in monasteries from the fourth century onwards. Monasteries (and eventually friaries and nunneries) developed across Europe, and in time these communities reached such a size that there could be hundreds of religious located in one building. Order was kept among so many people by establishing timetables. In Western Christendom everything formal was written in Latin and the timetable was called the *Horarium*. The

The Bible is not meant to sit on the book shelf!

Horarium set the schedule for the various chores that needed doing around the place, as well as meals and constitutionals, in order to preserve time for the most important aspect at the heart of religious life, the Liturgy, especially the Mass and the Divine Office. Additionally, there was often a special place reserved within the Horarium for something called *Lectio Divina*.

Did you know? The expression *Lectio Divina* was first used by Origen (c.185-254), a Father of the Church. He affirmed that to read the Bible profitably it is necessary to do so with attention, constancy, and prayer.

What is *Lectio Divina*?

Lectio Divina is simply the Latin term for reading of a 'holy', 'spiritual' or 'divine' nature. It is both a practice and a process, and there are many ways of doing *Lectio*, but it essentially consists of reading Sacred Scripture or another religious text meditatively. This ideally leads to prayer, to active service, to closer bonds with the community we belong to, and thus ultimately to God's gift of himself, known as contemplation.

Every religious community in the Middle Ages practiced *Lectio Divina* in one way or another, though perhaps not always under that title. Religious regulations, including the *Rule of Saint Benedict* and our own Carmelite *Rule of Saint Albert*, said that the monk, friar or nun should give time over to holy reading, either on their own or in a group. Pioneers among Bible meditation were the Benedictine, Cistercian and Carthusian Orders.

Like Carmelites, Carthusians blend solitude with community life.

Did you know? There are a number of similarities between the spiritualities of the Carmelite and Carthusian Orders. Both emphasise the role of silence in prayer and work, both regard the solitude of the cell as essential, and both stress attentiveness to Scripture. The major difference is that Carmelite spirituality places more emphasis upon the role of the community in bringing solitaries together on a daily basis, whereas the Carthusian vocation is to spend more time in solitude, coming together normally just once a week.

As the practice of *Lectio Divina* developed, some people attempted to set down guidelines so that others would be confirmed in good practice. The most famous 'method' of *Lectio* was set out in the 1100s by a Carthusian monk called Guigo de Castro (also known as Guigues du Chastel or Guigo II), in his book *Scala Claustralium* ('The Monk's Ladder'). Guigo believed that the 'ladder' of *Lectio* consisted of four rungs or stages.

The traditional 'method' of Lectio

Guigo said the first stage was *Lectio* (reading). This meant listening to (not necessarily reading) a passage from the Bible or another spiritual text several times. The second stage Guigo identified was *Meditatio* (meditation). This meant reflecting upon the passage and its meaning. The third stage is *Oratio* (prayer) inspired by the passage which turns us to God. Guigo said that the final stage of *Lectio* – in fact the reason we do it at all – is *Contemplatio* (contemplation); this is a stage that we cannot bring about by ourselves – rather we have to wait for that grace from God, and silence is often recommended as an aid to this.

Don't get bogged down by the Latin terms, or the idea of *Lectio* as a 'method'. *Lectio* is really very simple: we read the Scriptures, we reflect upon them, this leads us to prayer, and waiting on God in silence. Finally, this opens our hearts in a spirit of *vacare Deo* and disposes us to God's gift of contemplation.

Meditation and contemplation

Guigo's breakdown of the stages of *Lectio* is not accepted by everybody today, and many practitioners of *Lectio* would add the importance of *Collatio* (sharing the insights of others in a group) and *Actio* or *Operatio* (allowing *Lectio* to lead you into concrete action and service of others). However, Guigo does point out to us that *Lectio*'s purpose is to lead us to the point of contemplation, that is, an openness to God and God's action in our lives. Meditating on the Bible in the spirit of *Lectio* disposes us to seek union with God in contemplation. Previous chapters have already pointed out the difference between meditation and contemplation. This is how it is described in a modern book about *Lectio*:

> *Meditation* refers to a reading process in which words and events are prayerfully pondered and reflected on with the object of drawing from them some personal meaning or moral. It is basically an activity of the intellect and reason, aided by grace. *Contemplation* is variously described as a 'resting' in God, or a 'loving gaze' upon him, or a 'knowing beyond knowing'. All attempts at verbalizing the experience necessarily fail to express the reality, for the simple reason that contemplation transcends the thinking and reasoning of meditation.
>
> (Thelma Hall, *Too Deep for Words*, p. 9).

We Carmelites – like all humanity – are called by God to become contemplatives. Therefore *Lectio* is not an end in itself; we practice *Lectio* in order to be united face to face with the living God. There are other means of becoming contemplative, but the Carmelite tradition over the centuries has constantly recommended *Lectio* and the pondering of the Bible as a particular element of our charism.

Did you know? Carlos Mesters, O.Carm. (1931-) is one of the Carmelite Family's greatest exponents of *Lectio Divina*. Dutch by birth, he has lived mostly in Brazil, praying with the Bible amid the Christian Base Communities. Fr. Carlos says that the Church has much to learn from the way the poor read the Scriptures, and he recommends group

Chapter 11 ■ Lectio Divina & Carmel's Attentiveness to the Bible

Carlos Mesters preaching on the Word of God at Aylesford Priory in 2006.

Lectio as well as individual *Lectio* so that we can hear God speaking to us not only through the Bible but also through the insights and experiences of one another.

Stop and think: Can you recall any occasion when you were inspired to undertake a particular action because of your pondering of Scripture?

Lectio: an attitude, not a method

Lectio Divina can be practiced on your own or as part of a group. It can be done in complete silence, or with group discussion. It can be done for a few minutes, or for over an hour. It can be done with a single line of Scripture, or with a longer passage. Some religious orders tend to emphasise one particular method over another. There are many guidelines for how *Lectio* might be done, and among the Carmelites who have written on the practice are Carlos Mesters, Joseph Chalmers, and Bruno Secondin (see the resources listed at the end of this chapter). But it is very easy to become embroiled in technique, and that is not the point of *Lectio* at all. What method you choose is not as important as developing a regular habit of encountering God in the Bible and in other spiritual writings such as those of the Carmelite saints. This might mean setting aside half an hour each day to pray with a Gospel passage, or it might mean reflecting on a line from the readings at Mass. This pondering of the Word can happen as a designated activity, or be something that we ruminate upon as we go about our other routines and tasks.

Although *Lectio* involves reading or listening, it is naturally inclined towards simplicity and silence. As we read in the last chapter, Carmelites are aware that listening to God is more important than speaking to him. Through *Lectio* our hearts penetrate the words and discover the Word; or rather, the Word penetrates our hearts. Therefore most *Lectio* sessions – however long or short they are – consist mostly of silence in which we open our hearts and make 'space for God' (*vacare*

Bruno Secondin, O.Carm., has encouraged Carmelites to return to their roots in pondering Scripture and the *Rule of Saint Albert*.

Deo). Some have likened the dynamic to a meeting of the Society of Friends (Quakers) in which people remain silent, speaking only when they feel truly moved by the Holy Spirit. Many practitioners would recommend sitting in complete silence for the last 5 or 10 minutes of any *Lectio* session, setting aside the text itself and simply resting in the presence of God. In the silence we can try to clear the mind (as much as is ever humanly possible), perhaps selecting a 'sacred word' from the text to voice silently in the heart when we become distracted, a word that symbolises our desire to give the time and space to God (our *intention* rather than just our *attention*).

The contemplative gaze

Ultimately, *Lectio* becomes an attitude rather than a method. The gift of contemplation from God gradually allows us to read everything – not only the Bible but also our own lives and the world around us – with the eyes of God, and to love with the heart of God. Developing a *Lectio*-type awareness means that we can pick up a newspaper and read it with a contemplative gaze.

The idea behind *Lectio* is the same now as it was for the monks who followed Guigo's guidelines, and it is really very simple and beautiful. The Bible is a collection of holy texts written by human hands but inspired by God so that he could communicate with his people. God still wishes to communicate to us through Holy Scripture which is 'alive and active' (*Hebrews* 4:12), and which guides, rebukes, comforts and teaches us. As we ponder the Bible – whether in *Lectio* or in any other form of Biblical prayer – we gradually come to see how our lives can be read within the light of God's Word, and discern how God is speaking to us today through the ancient Scriptures.

Lectio: in the spirit of the *Rule of Saint Albert*

When the bell indicated the time for *Lectio Divina* in a medieval monastery, the religious would stop whatever they were doing and go to their cells or gather together to read. They might do that for between 2 and 3 hours a day, as well as listening to holy texts in the Liturgy and over meals in the refectory.

A Carmelite friar engaged in spiritual reading.

Medieval Carmelites followed timetables too, and the additions to the *Rule of Saint Albert* made by Pope Innocent IV in 1247 speak of observing the canonical 'Hours' of the Divine Office throughout the day and night. The first task of a religious in the Middle Ages was to learn the Psalms of the Office by heart so that they could always live with the Scriptures within themselves; their hearts became living books containing God's Word. The Divine Office and *Lectio* are part of the same process: listening regularly to the Holy Word and using it as a way of discovering the one God who dwells deep within us.

Lectio Divina is not unique to our Carmelite Order, but it is profoundly in the spirit of Carmel because the *Rule of Saint Albert* (printed at the front of this book) says that the Carmelite is to 'stay in his (or her) own cell or nearby, pondering the Lord's law day and night and keeping watch at prayers unless attending to some other duty' (Chapter 10). The *Rule of Saint Albert*, that all Carmelites share as a foundational document, specifies little about a Carmelite's daily routine, except that pondering the Lord's law – that is the person of Christ and the Scriptures – is to be the Carmelite's constant activity. In this regard, our *Rule* echoes the Psalmist:

> Happy are those who have not walked in the counsel of the ungodly,
> and have not stood in the path of sinners,
> and have not sat on the seat of the pestilential;
> but whose desire is the Law of the Lord,
> and who will meditate on his Law day and night.
> They shall be like the tree planted by streams of waters,
> which shall give its fruit at the right time;
> its leaf shall not fall off,
> and whatever they do shall prosper.
>   (*Psalm* 1:1-3, translated by Nicholas King, S.J.)

In the vision of life approved by Albert, rooted in the Scriptures, Carmelite life is to become a constant *Lectio Divina*, since he says everything we do 'should have the Lord's word for accompaniment' (Chapter 19). Albert demonstrated this in the very structure of the *Rule* itself; many passages are extracts from the Bible or allusions to it woven together.

Albert also recommended that Carmelites should find particular inspiration in a Biblical figure who himself contributed to the canon of Scripture, Saint Paul: 'You have both the teaching and the example of Saint Paul the Apostle, into whose mouth Christ put his own words. God made him preacher and teacher of faith and truth to the nations: with him as your teacher you cannot go astray.' (*Rule*, Chapter 20).

Rather than setting strict prescriptions for how we should spend our time, Albert reminded Carmelites that seeking God is not so much about following strict timetables but rather about a general desire to be in the presence of the living God day and night, and that a wonderful way to do this is to immerse yourself in the Word of God.

Stop and think: How do you ponder the Lord's law day and night? What does it mean for you, given your particular life circumstances?

Did you know? A hallmark of the pontificate of Benedict XVI is his call for Christians to return to a prayerful study of the Scriptures. On 16th September 2005 the Holy Father said: 'I would like in particular to recall and recommend the ancient tradition of *Lectio Divina*: the diligent reading of Sacred Scripture accompanied by prayer brings about that intimate dialogue in which the person reading hears God who is speaking, and in praying, responds to him with trusting openness of heart. If it is effectively promoted, this practice will bring to the Church – I am convinced of it – a new spiritual springtime.'

Pope Benedict receiving a presentation copy of the Bible.

God is revealed through Holy Scripture

Carmelites seek to be contemplatives. To grow in friendship with God we spend our time reflecting on the Scriptures, nurturing brotherhood and sisterhood with our fellow Carmelites, and growing in love with the rest of the world. The fuel to sustain this sort of life comes from Christ himself, as we encounter him in prayer, in other people, in the

Eucharist, and in the Scriptures. The Church reminds us of this in the Second Vatican Council document *Dei Verbum*:

> The Church has always venerated the divine Scriptures just as she venerates the body of the Lord, since, especially in the sacred liturgy, she unceasingly receives and offers to the faithful the bread of life from the table both of God's word and of Christ's body. (§21)

Dei Verbum, the Dogmatic Constitution on Divine Revelation, was promulgated by Pope Paul VI in 1965. It is the Church's declaration on how God reveals himself to his people, and as one of the great documents produced by a recent Council of the Church it should be studied by all members of the Carmelite Family to deepen our appreciation of the faith. In *Dei Verbum* the Church teaches us that the Scriptures are just as much part of the bread of life as is the body of Christ in the Eucharist. As we will read in Chapter 13,

'One does not live by bread alone, but by every word that comes from the mouth of God' (*Matthew* 4:4).

The Gospel book carried in procession at Aylesford Carmelite Priory in England.

the Eucharist or Mass feeds us from both hands: on one hand the reading of Scripture, and on the other hand the body and blood of Our Lord. When we read the Scriptures at home, in addition to what we hear in Mass, *Lectio Divina* becomes a continuation of that feeding from God.

A phrase often used in conjunction with *Lectio Divina* is 'rumination on the Scriptures'. Rumination means literally 'to chew over'. Some of the early exponents of *Lectio Divina* likened it to a cow chewing grass; the cow ruminates on the grass, extracting as much goodness as possible. The cow then swallows, regurgitates the grass, ruminates further, and then swallows to another stomach. The whole process is slow and gentle, extracting goodness over a considerable period of time, and producing – like the cow producing milk – nourishment not only for ourselves but also for the benefit of others. Likewise when we ruminate on the Scriptures, gradually, ponderingly, repeatedly, the Word of God gives us food for the journey, and allows us to nourish others on the same pilgrimage through life.

Did you know? In the Catholic and Orthodox liturgies it is traditional for bishops to bless the people with the Book of the Gospel after it has been proclaimed.

Contemplation is for anyone and everyone

We've seen that *Lectio* was preserved within the monastic tradition, and one might be inclined to say 'Well if *Lectio Divina* was developed by monks and friars then reading the Bible only applies to religious professionals'. Sadly this is what some Church leaders believed for a long time, particularly during the Reformation when bishops often decided that ordinary people could not be 'trusted' to read the Bible without supervision from trained clerics. For this reason *Lectio Divina* declined as a practice for many centuries, except in a few monasteries, and reading the Scriptures was wrongly seen as something uniquely 'Protestant'. In place of reading the Scriptures, devotions such as the rosary developed, the recitation of the *Hail Mary* 150 times corresponding to the 150 Psalms. However, the Second Vatican Council in the 1960s brought about a new appreciation of the importance of the Bible for everybody. We are still encouraged to read the Bible with others as well as on our own so that we can share and 'test' our experience and insights with other people, but the Church now actively encourages all Christians to read the Bible for themselves. Just as the Eucharist is for us all, so the Scriptures are for us all. *Dei Verbum* (§25) states that the Church 'earnestly and especially urges all the Christian faithful … to learn by frequent reading of the divine Scriptures the 'excellent knowledge of Jesus Christ' (*Philippians* 3:8).' And that is why we read the Bible and practice *Lectio* – to arrive at *an excellent knowledge of Jesus Christ* – because in the Christian understanding all the Scriptures, both Old and New Testaments, are about Jesus, to whom we Carmelites give our allegiance.

Did you know? In the Middle Ages Carmelite scholars helped develop the Church's understanding of the 'four senses' of Scripture. Bible texts can be read in: (1) the *literal* sense, in which the text is taken at face value; (2) the *allegorical* sense, which interprets certain passages to produce statements of doctrine from the Christian perspective; (3) the *tropological* or *moral* sense, which interprets passages to produce ethical guidelines for Christian conduct; (4) the *anagogical* or *eschatological* sense, which interprets passages in the light of hope, looking towards the future fulfilment of the divine promises in the New Jerusalem.

What did Jesus think about the Scriptures?

We Carmelites – like all Christians – are called to a life of allegiance to Christ (*Rule of Saint Albert*, Chapter 2). That being the case, we should consider what Jesus himself thought about the Scriptures.

There is only one Gospel – one Good News of Jesus Christ – and it is recorded in four accounts: *Matthew, Mark, Luke* and *John*. The first three Gospel accounts are known as the Synoptic Gospels, from Greek words meaning 'seen together'; the Synoptic Gospels give 'eye-witness' style accounts of Jesus' life, showing a high degree of similarity in terms of content and point of view. According to the Synoptic accounts, Jesus' public ministry began with his baptism by his cousin John. Jesus then left straightaway to go into the desert where he was tempted. In the desert the only words Jesus used when responding to the devil's taunts were quotations from Scripture (*Luke* 4:1-13). When Jesus started preaching it was in the synagogues, where the practice was to read a passage from the Scriptures and comment on it, just as we have our homilies today. According to Luke (4:16-21) Jesus unrolled the scroll of Isaiah and having read the text (sometimes dubbed the *Lucan manifesto*) proclaimed that 'Today this scripture has been fulfilled

Many ancient depictions of Christ show him holding a book representing his teaching of the Word of God, such as this medieval mosaic in the Cathedral at Cefalù, Sicily.

in your hearing.' Jesus showed the scribes how they had misunderstood Scripture by explaining the true meaning to them (*Matthew* 22:29-33). At his Transfiguration (*Mark* 9:2-4) Jesus was not alone; he was flanked by Moses and Elijah who represented the Law and the Prophets recorded in Scripture. Jesus' parables and teachings were littered with references to Scripture.

The account of the Gospel given by John the Evangelist likewise highlights the importance of Scripture to Jesus. John's account was written after the Synoptic Gospels and offers more theological reflection. *John* demonstrates that Jesus' actions had scriptural echoes, and often his actions are described as taking place 'so the Scriptures would be fulfilled'. The Crucifixion is a prime example. John describes the casting of lots for Jesus' clothing (19:23-24), the drinking of sour wine (19:28), and the piercing with a spear (19:32-37) all in terms of how through them Jesus was the fulfilment of the Scriptures. In John's account of the Crucifixion Jesus declares 'It is finished!' as he dies, meaning that the revelation of God's love for us has been completed: there is no more to say, as John of the Cross explained (*Sayings of Light and Love* §100). After his Resurrection, Jesus continued to explain the Scriptures to two disciples on the road to Emmaus (*Luke* 24:13-35), causing their 'hearts to burn' within them.

In summary, Jesus knew the Scriptures, and is himself Scripture living and breathing. He is indeed the Word of God made flesh (*John* 1:14). Jesus is the Word that God the Father speaks to reveal his love for all of us. If we are to become like Jesus, then we too need to be familiar with the same things that Jesus found so important – and one of them was the Scriptures. Jesus was the perfection of *Lectio Divina*.

The Old and the New Testaments

All four gospel accounts start with a reference back to the Old Testament: *Matthew* with a genealogy putting Jesus firmly in the line of kings; *Mark* with a quotation from *Isaiah*; *Luke* with the story of Zechariah performing his duties in the Temple; and *John* with a passage which goes right back to Creation and *Genesis*. Christianity has no difficulty in reading the New and Old Testaments together.

This partly explains why Carmelites have no difficulty in tracing our own spiritual roots right back to Elijah and Elisha. The Carmelite Family has an important role in reminding the Church of the enduring relevance of the Old Testament.

Elijah and Mary: models of Lectio

The prophet Elijah, Father of all Carmelites, was a man who listened to God's Word, and acted upon it. He learned to read the experiences of his life in the light of God's loving presence. He pondered God's will for him and for the people of Israel, and thus can be seen as a model of *Lectio Divina*.

The Blessed Virgin Mary, Mother and Sister of Carmelites, is another classic example of someone whose whole life became a *Lectio Divina*. She knew the Scriptures and thought about them. When she proclaimed her *Magnificat* (*Luke* 1:46-55) Mary's own voice was full of God's Word, her hymn of praise being wall-to-wall Scriptural quotations. This was not simply an accident; Mary had interiorised the Bible to such an extent – that is, she had read, absorbed, and lived according to the Torah so much – that she spoke in Scriptural terms. This came about through the Holy Spirit, since Jesus promised that 'the Counsellor, the Holy Spirit, whom the Father will send in my name, will teach you all things and will remind you of everything I have said to you' (*John* 14:26). Mary was reminded by the Holy Spirit of all the great promises of God and burst forth in a song of joy.

Mary was the epitome of *Lectio Divina* because whenever the word and will of God was made known to her she 'treasured up all these things and pondered them in her heart' (*Luke* 2:19, 51). Our Lady shows us that *Lectio* isn't confined to when we read the Bible for five minutes or an hour, but rather it is a process that carries on throughout our daily lives. Mary probably knew the words and actions of Jesus more intimately than anyone else, and thought deeply about them. That is why Mary is the perfect example of one who 'hears the word of God and obeys it' (*Luke* 11:28).

Stop and think: A Carmelite once described Mary as 'an icon of *Lectio Divina*'. What does that phrase mean to you?

This sculpture in the Spanish town of Avila depicts the Annunciation. Mary is shown listening, and touching God's Word which Gabriel holds in a book. On the page are inscribed the words of Mary's Fiat, 'Let it be with me according to your word.'

The Bible in the early Carmelite tradition

As we read in previous chapters, the Carmelite Family has always regarded Elijah and Mary with reverence as people who proclaimed and pondered the word of God. They are therefore models of *Lectio Divina*, not simply as a method of prayer but as a way of life. Perhaps it is because of our Order's devotion to these figures from the Old and the New Testaments that we Carmelites have always had a particular attentiveness to the Bible, studying it, reflecting upon it, and preaching it.

As we learned in Chapter 8 on Carmelite history, the Carmelite Order first began to send friars to universities in the Middle Ages. Here it would have been standard for Whitefriars to learn not only about the Bible, but also what famous commentators had written about it. A number of Whitefriars became Bible commentators themselves, and although ours was never the biggest order in fifteenth-century England there were more Carmelite doctors of Sacred Scripture at Oxford and Cambridge than any other group of religious. Many treatises and sermons about the Bible were written by pre-Reformation Carmelites. Most of these were in Latin, but some were in the mother tongue. A medieval Carmelite from Aylesford, Richard Maidstone, wrote a version of the seven *Penitential Psalms* in English verse as a way of teaching people their meaning in Latin:

For love of God, who bought us dear,
To whom we ought to make our cry
Because of sins committed here
In youth and age, so many, aye;
The seven psalms are often sought
To purge us of our faults committed,
And into English they've been brought
So sin in man may be repented.

(Preface to Richard Maidstone's *Penitential Psalms*,
translated from Middle English by Johan Bergström-Allen)

One of the most famous medieval Carmelite texts, *The Ten Books on the Way of Life and Great Deeds of the Carmelites* (better known as *The Book of the First Monks*), places great emphasis on the Bible's importance within our Order. The compiler, a Catalonian friar called Felip Ribot, wrote that in the early days of the Order the brothers gathered in the chapel on Mount Carmel, 'commending themselves to the Virgin in the seven canonical hours each day, pouring forth fervent prayers, petitions, and praises to the Virgin and her Son. There also they assembled for humble discussion about the word of God' (Book 6, Chapter 5).

We know that some medieval Carmelites promoted Bible-reading among the laity, which was not common in those days. A pious woman in medieval East Anglia, Margery Kempe, records that a local Carmelite, Alan of Lynn (c.1348-1432) discussed the Bible with her on many occasions (*Book of Margery Kempe*, Book 1, Chapters 69 & 70).

Stop and think: Do you know of any Carmelite individuals or projects that promote the study of or prayer with Scripture?

Study of the Scriptures is encouraged for all Carmelites, religious and lay; many Bible study resources are now widely available.

Carmel's promotion of the Bible today

The Carmelite Order today continues to promote reflection on Holy Scripture as a marvellous way of encountering Jesus; indeed, it is one of the foremost apostolates we can offer the Church and the World, whether as lay people or as religious.

Mention has already been made of Carlos Mesters, O.Carm., and his promotion of *Lectio Divina* among the poorest of the poor, sharing with them the liberating message of God's love to all of us as revealed in the Gospel. Fr. Carlos has written extensively about his experience of *Lectio Divina* and it is largely thanks to him that this important tradition has been rediscovered in the Carmelite Family since the Second Vatican Council.

At an academic level, Carmelites have been in the forefront of Biblical scholarship in modern times. Roland E. Murphy, O.Carm. (1917-2002), was a renowned scholar and co-editor of the *New Jerome Biblical Commentary*. Craig Morrison, O.Carm., has taught at one of the Church's leading centres for Bible research, the Biblicum (Pontifical Biblical Institute) in Rome. The former Prior General, Joseph Chalmers, O.Carm., has written and translated books on *Lectio Divina*. Among the Discalced Carmelites James McCaffrey, O.C.D., has traced the links between the Bible, the *Rule of Saint Albert*, and the writings of Carmel's saints. Today, all Carmelite friars must study and reflect upon the Bible as part of their formation, which includes learning an ancient biblical language such as Hebrew or Greek. Lay Carmelites too are expected to immerse themselves in Scripture as part of their formation; the 2003 *Rule for the Third Order of Carmel* states that 'Great importance is to be given to a prayerful listening to God's word: *Lectio Divina* involves and transforms the believer's entire existence' (§39).

In the Eucharist we receive the bread of life from the table both of God's word and of Christ's body; Carmelite preachers help to 'break open' the Scriptures.

As well as encouraging Bible study, Carmelites help others to ponder God's word in the prayerful, prayer filled, attentive reading of Scripture. Twice a month Carmelites in Rome, lay and religious, gather in the ancient Carmelite church of Santa Maria in Traspontina for *Lectio Divina*. These are attended by a wide variety of people from across the city, including senior Vatican officials. Before he became Pope Benedict XVI, Cardinal Joseph Ratzinger attended the Carmelite *Lectio* sessions, and his pontificate has been marked by his frequent calls for the growth of *Lectio Divina* within the Church.

Lectio Divina has become a way of life central in most Carmelite communities. These communities approach *Lectio* in a variety of different ways. In some houses of the Dutch Province, for example, the same passage of Scripture will be read at community celebrations for a month, allowing for plenty of rumination. In some Carmelite houses in Italy, Scripture is reading during some meal times, as Chapter 7 of the *Rule of Saint Albert* recommends. Lay Carmelites are also experiencing and sharing the fruits of *Lectio Divina*; not only has *Lectio* become a standard feature of many Lay Carmelite meetings, but it has also proved an effective means of introducing new people to Carmel because it emphasises important aspects of our spirituality: openness to God, silence, attentiveness to the Scriptures, private and public prayer. Since attentiveness to Scripture is common to all Christian traditions, *Lectio* can also be promoted by Carmelites as a way of overcoming denominational differences, as Carmelite Spirituality Groups have discovered in Britain and Ireland, and beyond.

Knowledge of and immersion in the Word of God is truly characteristic of a community that authentically reflects the Carmelite tradition. Patrick Thomas McMahon, O.Carm., makes the following observation:

Members of the Carmelite Family in Britain gathered around the Word of God.

The Carmelite today must be a person who is impregnated with the Word of God. This is perhaps why Carmel has never much been given to devotional prayer. The sort of devotions that characterized some other orders, especially those from the 18th and 19th centuries never took hold in Carmel. The prayer life of Carmel has always been simple: the Mass, the Liturgy of the Hours, and meditation on the sacred text of Scripture.

(*Nine Themes in Carmelite Spirituality*)

Stop and think: How do we choose a text for *Lectio*? Some people pick passages for meditation at random, seeing at what page the Bible opens; this method allows plenty of opportunity for the Spirit to breathe, but sometimes the passage is not obviously meaningful. Others choose a favourite passage, but the risk in this is that we only meditate on texts that make us feel comfortable; to avoid this most people choose the day's readings in the Church's *Lectionary* cycle. Others go through a book of the Bible bit by bit. Some communities pick a passage that seems appropriate to the theme of their meeting or the needs of the time. What method do you think is best?

Did you know? Saint Thérèse of Lisieux had a particular love of Scripture, knowing the gospel accounts practically by heart. To mark the visit of her relics to England and Wales in 2009, the British Province of Carmelites published a collection of articles about how Thérèse lived and loved the Bible, in a book entitled *The Gospel Sustains Me*.

THE GOSPEL
SUSTAINS ME

The word of God in the life and love of Saint Thérèse of Lisieux

Carmelite Saints and Scripture

A long litany of how our Carmelite Saints have read the Bible would not be very useful in an introduction to the topic, but the following summary is informative:

Lectio Divina, the practice of the prayerful listening to the Word of Scripture, leads to an ever more intimate communication with Christ and an ever more radical conversion in one's own life. Today this practice has returned to being a daily form of nourishment in our communities. There are many echoes of this too in the spiritual tradition of Carmel. For example John of the Cross advises: 'Leave behind all the other things which you still have and limit yourself to only one which contains in itself all the rest: that is sanctified solitude accompanied by prayer and holy divine reading. Persevere in this by forgetting all other things.' Mary Magdalen de Pazzi compares the Word to Jacob's ladder which enables us to climb to the Father's 'womb'; Thérèse of Lisieux writing to Father Roulland communicates her experience of being a disciple of the Word in this way: 'I close the book of the wise that breaks my head into little pieces and turns my heart dry and I take the Scriptures in hand. Then everything becomes clear to me; a simple word unlocks infinite horizons for my soul and perfection suddenly seems so easy.'

(Growing As Brothers,
Carmelite Spiritual Directory Project 10 § 2.1.1)

The hard part: the Word transforms us

Lectio sounds pretty attractive, doesn't it? Well, there is a hard part. Not only do the Scriptures tell us the truth about God, but they also tell us the truth about ourselves, and that can be uncomfortable. As you read the Scriptures you find examples not only of holiness but also of all sorts of nastiness: from the pettiness of the disciples arguing about who would be the greatest (*Luke* 9:46) to David arranging the death of Uriah so that he could marry his wife Bathsheba (*2 Samuel* 11). As we read these sad stories we find so much that actually applies to us. We can be just as self-centred, as unfaithful and capable of sin as the people we read about. We are not inherently evil, but we often choose the selfish and easy way over the will of God. By reading the Scriptures we are brought face to face with the holiness of God and our own deep need of redemption. But that is liberating because the truth is we can open our hearts to receive the mercy of Christ. *Lectio Divina* is a transforming experience, provided we are honest and prepared to change. It is for this reason that the 2003 *Rule for the Third Order of Carmel* emphasises the role of *Lectio Divina*, the Divine Office, and the Sacraments so that Carmelites may 'regularly receive forgiveness for their sins and the grace to continue the journey' (§37). *Lectio* develops in us the 'purity of heart' (*puritas cordis*) and 'space for God' (*vacare Deo*) which are so central to the Carmelite way of life.

Lectio waters the desert into a garden

When we looked at Elijah in Chapter 6, the image of fire was prevalent. The image which might serve us best when considering *Lectio Divina* is water. Reading the Scriptures is like watering the garden. Without water plants grow brittle and eventually die; it is the same with us. We are called to bear fruit that will last (*John* 15:16), and fruit cannot grow without plenty of water. Like fire, water is a constant image throughout the Scriptures: the Garden of Eden was between the four mighty rivers (*Genesis* 2:10); when the Israelites crossed the desert God provided water from the rock (*Exodus* 17:1-7) later interpreted as Christ (*1 Corinthians* 10:4); Ezekiel had a vision of the river coming from the Temple (*Ezekiel* 47:1-6); Jesus talked about life-giving water (*John* 4:14); and Paul said that 'Christ loved the Church and gave himself up for her to make her holy, cleansing her by the washing with water through the word' (*Ephesians* 5:26). And, if you want to extend the metaphor, at Cana Jesus turned water into wine at the behest of his mother. Jesus can transform the water of our lives into the new wine of God's kingdom, and wine brings joy (*Psalm* 104:15).

Lectio Divina in the community and in private

Part of the responsibility of the Church is to show us how to develop a relationship with Christ. One of the principal ways in which she does this is through the Liturgy, that is, the public prayers and rites of the Church, primarily the Divine Office and the Eucharist. In the Eucharist or Mass, Scripture is a principal ingredient; we are nourished by both the breaking of the bread and the breaking-open of the Word. The text of Morning and Evening Prayer is pretty much all Scripture; the other offices are the same (only in the Office of Readings is a text taken from outside Scripture, such as the writings of a saint). Likewise the Rosary (although not formally part of the Liturgy) is a meditation on Scripture; most of the 'mysteries' are Biblical events, and reciting the *Hail Mary* 150 times (for the original 15 mysteries) corresponded to the 150 Psalms. Through these forms

of worship the Church teaches us that one of the principal means of fostering a relationship with Jesus is through reciting and interiorising the Scriptures. Saint Jerome (c.340-c.420), the most famous biblical scholar in Christian history, said that 'Ignorance of Scripture is ignorance of Christ' (*Commentary of Isaiah*, Nn. 1.2: CCL 73, 1-3). Thérèse of Lisieux appreciated the truth of this statement, and carried a small book of Gospel extracts next to her heart. Blessed Elizabeth of the Trinity was deeply influenced by the letters of St. Paul, which led her to the excellent knowledge of Jesus Christ.

Did you know? Carmelite missionaries have been taking the Word of God to the people of Latin America for hundreds of years. The pastoral care of a whole region of Peru known as Sicuani is entrusted to the Carmelite Family. Since the North American Province of the Pure Heart of Mary (PCM) arrived in 1949, seven houses of friars have been established as well as communities of sisters. In 1958 the Holy See created Sicuani an Apostolic Prelature; this is similar to a diocese but entirely administered by the Order, and the Carmelite friar in charge of the Prelature is usually ordained a bishop. The Carmelite Family in Sicuani – including lay people – minister to a population of some 300,000 people in 29 parishes and about 800 chapels spread across a vast and mountainous area of Latin America. Evangelizing in this region requires the use of hundreds of catechists, who spread the Word of God in communities with low literacy levels and low incomes.

Scenes from Sicuani where the Carmelite Family shares God's Word with his people.

Saint George
Preca, T.O.C.

Did you know? The *Mysteries of Light* which Pope John Paul II added to the Rosary in 2002 were first proposed by a Third Order Carmelite. Saint George Preca (1880-1962) was a priest in Malta, and a Carmelite Tertiary. He formulated the *Mysteries of Light* in 1957 as a way of meditating on the Good News of Jesus' life and ministry.

Our relationship with Christ is formed within the community of the Church, but we also have a personal relationship with him. *Lectio Divina* is a wonderful way of developing that relationship, either communally or individually. The Liturgy, our worship of God, our relationships with other people are all part of one massive *Lectio Divina!*

Given that we encounter Christ in the liturgies of the Church, why does the Carmelite tradition emphasise individual *Lectio* in private as well as *Lectio* in the community? It could be said that someone who listens to the Word through the Liturgy in a prayerful manner has already done enough *Lectio* for one day. That might be true. However, there are two main reasons why private *Lectio* is also important. The first is that private reading exposes us to more passages from the Bible than are possible from the snatches we hear in communal reading. We therefore appreciate the Bible in a wider context, and are more able to link our public worship of God to our private relationship with God. The second reason is that Jesus wants to develop a direct personal friendship with us. There are things that Jesus wants to say to us personally in the heart – and one of the surest ways for that to happen is through our private meditation on the Scriptures.

Lectio is not about studying the Scriptures at an intellectual level, although Bible study is well worthwhile and may richly deepen our appreciation of *Lectio*. Rather, *Lectio* is an aid to fostering 'the conversation with the one whom we know loves us' (as Teresa of

'Carmelites strive to create opportunities for proclaiming Christ, offering again that ever new message that he is the Lord of life, and of history, that he is a sure point of reference for all' *Rule for the Third Order of Carmel* §47.

Jesus defined prayer). *Lectio* at home on a daily basis enables us regularly to be challenged, comforted and inspired at a personal level. *Lectio* is the most wonderful experience and can very often lead to an emotional outpouring of some sort – whether that is repentance at the recognition of some deep-rooted sinful attitude or sheer joy. Tears are not uncommon with *Lectio* because it opens our hearts to the healing presence of God, and tears can sometimes be more easily shed in private. In the last chapter we considered *affective* and *negative* forms of prayer; *Lectio Divina* can blend both approaches. In the early stages of *Lectio* meditating on the passage before us can lead us to respond emotionally, perhaps imagining ourselves in the Biblical scene. In the later stages of *Lectio* we might set the text aside and simply rest in God's presence without particular thoughts or feelings.

Stop and think: As well as pondering God's word, how do you proclaim it? How do you evangelise?

What more can be said about Lectio?

Lots! In an introductory chapter there is no time to cover more technical matters or specific methods of *Lectio*. The resources listed below discuss *Lectio* in further depth. You could consult all the suggested resources, or you could read this chapter again, but if you do not put on the habit of reading the Scriptures regularly, all the books in the world will never enable you to understand what *Lectio* is truly about, namely a deeper relationship with – a fuller allegiance to – the Lord Jesus Christ. So, pick up your Bible, open it and read it. And read it. And read it. Ruminate upon the Word of God, ponder it in relation to your life. Then you will begin to glimpse the height and the depth of the love of God which passes all understanding (*Ephesians* 3:18-19).

Conclusion: In this eleventh chapter we have seen how Lectio Divina is more an attitude and way of life rather than a strict method of prayer. We have considered how its various stages can benefit individuals and communities, and we have seen how the Bible has always been placed at the heart of the Carmelite tradition, from the Rule of Saint Albert down to the rediscovery of Lectio Divina in the twentieth century. We have seen how an attitude of 'holy reading' was embodied in the lives of Elijah, Mary, Christ, and the saints of Carmel, who came to read the world around them with a contemplative gaze. Lectio Divina is most truly Carmelite, and no process of formation in our tradition is complete that leaves a lay person or religious ignorant of the different theories and practices of Lectio.

Perhaps conclude your time of study and reflection with a moment of prayer. Actually doing Lectio Divina would be wonderful; you might like simply to pray using a phrase from Scripture that has caught your attention, and ruminate on it in the days ahead.

In the next chapter we will reflect on other aspects of Carmelite living that might be termed Carmel's attitudes.

Ideas for Reflection, Discussion and Action

- Reflect on any passage in this chapter – or any passage from Scripture – that has stood out as significant for you, either individually or as a community.

- Has your appreciation of Scripture deepened or been affected in any other way since you came to Carmel?

- How much time do I devote to *Lectio* on my own or with a group? How can I arrange my life to fit in a stretch of time devoted to reading Scripture?

- Do you agree with Pope Benedict XVI that *Lectio* could bring about a new springtime in the Church? How might this be manifested?

- Am I really willing to allow the process of *Lectio* to transform me?

- Do some parts of the Bible excite or move me more than others?

- Do I read about the life of Jesus so that I can learn about him? How much of my spiritual reading is from the Bible, and how much is from other sources?

- In what ways do you take Saint Paul as your model and teacher?

- How do you think that *Lectio* might support you in your work, in your family life, and in your service of others?

- What is the link between Scripture and a spirit of service?

- Do you know anyone that you could introduce to the practice of *Lectio Divina*?

- How important is it to know something about the Bible's textual history and biblical culture in order to engage in *Lectio*?

- Pray for Carmel's work of evangelization in Sicuani, in your own country, and in other parts of the world.

- Now that you are over half way through this series of reflections on Carmel's rich spiritual heritage, why not look back over a chapter you have already read and revisit some of your ideas and reactions?

Recommended Further Resources

There are hundreds, indeed thousands, of books and other resources on the Bible, and more titles on *Lectio Divina* are appearing in bookshops all the time. Any good resource which helps deepen your appreciation of Scripture is worth spending time with, and you might find some study aids useful such as a Biblical commentary or concordance. Realistically, it might be best to start with reading more about how Carmelites have approached the Word of God over the centuries, and some of the following titles would be helpful to you. Best of all is actually reading the Word of God itself and pondering it alone and with others.

Raymond E. Brown, Joseph A. Fitzmyer, Roland E. Murphy, O.Carm., *The New Jerome Biblical Commentary*, (London: Geoffrey Chapman, 1989).

Carmelite Curia's online *Introduction to Lectio*: www.ocarm.org

The Catholic Biblical Association of Great Britain: www.cbagb.org.uk

Joseph Chalmers, O.Carm., 'The Goal of the Christian Life', in *Mary the Contemplative*, (Rome: Edizioni Carmelitane, 2001), pp. 19-34.

Joseph Chalmers, O.Carm., *The Sound of Silence: Listening to the Word of God with Elijah the Prophet*, (Faversham: Saint Albert's Press, 2007).

Keith J. Egan & Craig E. Morrison, (eds.), *Master of the Sacred Page: Essays and Articles in Honor of Roland E. Murphy*, (Washington D.C.: The Carmelite Institute, 1997).

John FitzGerald, O.Carm., *Backwards into the Future: Meditations on the Letter to the Hebrews*, (Faversham: Saint Albert's Press, 2005).

Patrick Fitzgerald-Lombard, O.Carm., *Gospel Reading* website: www.gospelreading.org.uk

Thelma Hall, r.c., *Too Deep for Words: Rediscovering Lectio Divina*, (New York: Paulist Press, 1988).

Nicholas King, S.J., *The Psalms: A new, cutting-edge translation*, (Stowmarket: Kevin Mayhew, 2008).

Romero de Lima Gouvêa, O.Carm., *Lectio Divina*, available on the Contemporary Authors page of the Carmelite Spirituality section of www.carmelite.org

Mariano Magrassi, *Praying the Bible: An Introduction to Lectio Divina*, (The Liturgical Press, 1998).

Edward Malatesta, S.J. (ed.), *The Spirituality of Judaism*, (Anthony Clark, 1977), especially Chapter 6.

Mario Masini, *Lectio Divina: An Ancient Prayer That Is Ever New*, (Alba House, 1998). Reviewed by Michael Cox, O.Carm., in *Assumpta*, (Vol. 46 No. 12/Vol. 47 No. 1).

Patrick Thomas McMahon, O.Carm., *Nine Themes in Carmelite Spirituality*, printed in 2009 in *Carmel in the World* and *Assumpta* magazines, and available online at www.carmelite.org

Carlos Mesters, O.Carm., *Meditating Day and Night on the Law of the Lord*. This is printed at the back of John FitzGerald's, *Backwards into the Future*, (listed above), and also on the Contemporary Authors page of the Carmelite Spirituality section of www.carmelite.org

Carlos Mesters, O.Carm., *Defenseless Flower: A New Reading of the Bible*, (Orbis Books, 1989).

Carlos Mesters, O.Carm., in *Reading Scripture for Living the Christian Life*, A *Doctrine and Life* special, (Dublin: Dominican Publications, 2009).

Craig Morrison, O.Carm., 'Rooted in the Bible', *Carmel in the World* (2005), Vol. XLV, N. 1-2.

Roland E. Murphy, O.Carm., *Experiencing our Biblical Heritage*, (Peabody, Massachusetts: Hendrickson Publishers, 2001).

Roland E. Murphy, O.Carm., 'The Spirituality of the Psalms', in Keith J. Egan, T.O.C., *Carmelite Prayer: A Tradition for the 21st Century*, (New York: Paulist Press, 2003), pp. 24-37.

Salvatore Panimolle, (ed.), *Like the Deer that Yearns*, (St. Paul Publications, 1987).

Wilfrid Stinissen, O.Carm., *Nourished by the Word* (Redemptorist Publications, 1999).

Patricia Tomkins, T.O.C., *Feasting on God's Word*, available online on the Contemporary Authors page of the Carmelite Spirituality section of www.carmelite.org

Notes and Reflections on Chapter 11

Notes and Reflections on Chapter 11

CHAPTER 12

Clothed with Carmel's Attitudes

Summary: As individuals, and as a human family, the imagery of clothing and being clothed has formed us. In this chapter the imagery of clothing will serve as a way of reflecting on what 'attitudes' Carmelites might be expected to 'put on'. We will meditate on the idea of clothing ourselves in spiritual armour, the symbolism of the Order's brown scapular and white cloak, and the role of clothing in the stories of Elijah and Elisha, and other figures important in the Carmelite tradition.

Mary is often depicted in Carmelite art
wrapping her mantle around members of the
Order as a sign of protection and belonging.

Get prepared: This chapter is about 'attitudes', and a good attitude to adopt as regards formation or immersion in the Carmelite tradition is to approach it with proper care and preparation. Think about what resources might be helpful to you in taking notes, or in preparing notes for others. It's good to precede your study with a time of prayer and reflection, and here is a possible suggestion for individuals or groups. On pieces of paper write down words which to you are admirable 'attitudes', such as *kindness*, *humility*, *honesty*, etc. Place the pieces of paper in a bowl and draw out one word at a time. Reflect for a moment on what you understand by each word, and pray for an increase of that attitude in your own life and the life of your community.

Metaphors

The beautiful hymn *Come down O love divine* expresses the hope of one who longs, by God's grace, to show love to the world and be clothed in humility: 'Let holy charity my outward vesture be, and lowliness become my inner clothing.' We often describe spiritual attitudes through the metaphor of clothes, and in this chapter we shall use the idea of clothing to see what it means to 'put on' the attitudes one would expect of a Carmelite.

Externally we can sometimes be identified as Carmelites by our outward clothing. Friars, nuns, sisters and hermits wear a religious habit. Members of the Third and Secular Orders wear a reduced version of that habit in the form of Reception or Profession Scapulars, at least on certain occasions. Millions of people worldwide wear the miniature Carmelite Brown Scapular, either the cloth form or medal substitute. But more important than this 'outward show', we should be recognised as members of the Carmelite Family by putting on an attitude – an 'inner clothing' – of love.

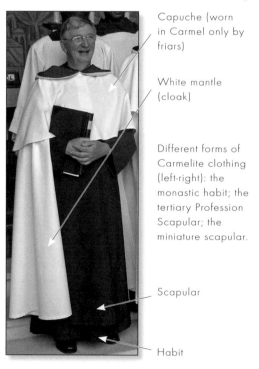

Capuche (worn in Carmel only by friars)

White mantle (cloak)

Different forms of Carmelite clothing (left-right): the monastic habit; the tertiary Profession Scapular; the miniature scapular.

Scapular

Habit

What do we mean by Carmel's attitudes?

One dictionary defines an *attitude* as: 'A relatively stable and enduring predisposition to behave or react in a characteristic way'. An attitude is a state of mind, a disposition, a way of thinking and living that is normal for us. Attitudes can be good: maybe we have a positive attitude to Carmelite formation! Attitudes can be less good: we might talk of people who are difficult to relate to as having an 'attitude problem'.

As Carmelites we need to adopt Carmel's attitudes. We ought to live in a manner that is in keeping with the Carmelite way of life, making the Order's tradition our own way of being. When we put on the Scapular it isn't just for show; it is a sign that we have committed ourselves to developing a Carmelite disposition, a state of mind and heart, and a way of living that it true to the charism and spirit of the Order. This is what our Carmelite journey of formation is about.

What is Carmel's charism? We can summarise it simply:

> *Carmelites seek the face of the living God in contemplation, forming praying communities at the service of God's people.*

The Carmelite charism – the 'attitude' of the Order – hopes to take up Jesus' great commandment and invitation in the Gospel: *Love God, and love your neighbour as yourself* (*Mark* 12:29-31). Love is the most important Christian value and therefore the most fundamental 'Carmelite attitude'.

The first encyclical of Pope Benedict XVI, *Deus Caritas Est* (*God is Love*, 2005), reminded us that 'love' can mean many things, but it is also a very simple thing. To give and to receive love means living in the presence of God and other people with open hearts and open hands. For the Carmelite, God's love isn't only manifested at formal prayer times but also in our service of others and in our community relationships. The important thing is to nurture a spirit of openness to God (*vacare Deo*) and to others.

Stop and think: What do you understand by the word 'love'?

_____

Carmel's contribution to the Church

The twentieth-century Cistercian monk and writer Thomas Merton said that all Christians owe a debt to Carmel. We Carmelites are proud of our distinctive heritage and considerable contribution to the Church, but we must never think that ours is the only way worth following, or that *Carmel's attitudes* are essentially anything other than Christian attitudes. Carmelite spirituality is distinctive but many of its key points are also emphasised in one way or another by other religious orders and Christian traditions. An image that is sometimes used of religious orders is that of a series of houses: all the houses are built using the same basic materials, but in each the materials are arranged slightly differently; it is not that one house is inherently better than another, rather the important thing is for us to find the house where we feel most at home. As we come to know more about Carmel and make its charism our own, there can be a tendency to devalue the contribution of other movements, and to overstate our own importance. Titus Brandsma, who was an expert on Carmel's history and spirituality, invented a term for unhealthy bias towards the Order: *Carmelism*!

Chapter 12 ▪ Clothed with Carmel's Attitudes

Stop and think: Can you recall times in your own faith journey when you have had an unhealthy bias towards a particular form of spirituality?

The task facing Carmelites is to find a balance between a deep love and appreciation for our own spiritual heritage as members of the Order on the one hand, and on the other a respectful acknowledgment of the value of different traditions. So how might we distinguish a 'Carmelite attitude' from a 'Dominican attitude' or a 'Jesuit attitude'? Kilian Healy, Prior General of the Order between 1959 and 1971, described the distinction like this:

> All orders use the same essential means to conduct their members to perfection, but they apply them differently, depending upon the particular work for which the Order was instituted. Every Order, for instance, recognizes prayer as a normal, ordinary means to grow in charity. But because each Order has a special aim, it gives more or less emphasis to the various exercises of prayer. For the Jesuit, prayer, both oral and mental, is necessary, but precisely for the inspiration and perfection of action to which it is ordered. Whereas for the Carmelite the various exercises of prayer are means *par excellence* to attain the contemplative spirit which is not ordered a means to the active life. The Jesuit seeks the glory of God and his own perfection as well as that of his neighbour through the active apostolate. The Carmelite seeks the same end especially through zeal for prayer or the contemplative life. It is zeal for prayer fostered by silence, solitude, self-abnegation and a tender devotion to Mary as Mother and Patroness of the contemplative life that helps to give Carmel its distinctive nature. To

In this thirteenth-century icon from one of the Order's ancient churches in Cyprus (now in the Museo Macarios I in Nicosia) Carmelites are shown wrapped in the mantle of Mary.

this contemplative ideal the Order has joined the active apostolate, but in such a way that the contemplative spirit predominates and ever remains the principle part, governing and limiting the active apostolate which may vary from age to age depending upon the needs of the Church.

Methods of Prayer (Reprinted 2005), p. xiii.

For Carmelites, contemplation – openness and friendship with God – is at the very heart of our way of life, and it shapes how we live, how we 'arrange our house'. We seek to know and love God, and to make God known and loved. We do this through our prayer, our building of community, and through our active service of others.

The image of clothing

Contact with others through community and service is an essential component of a contemplative life. Indeed, it is often personal contact with a Carmelite that marks the first step in a relationship with the Order. Many people are first drawn to the charism of the Carmelite Family by the example of those who live a life inspired by Carmel, each in their unique way, often in spite of obvious weaknesses. Such witnesses draw the interest of others and, once drawn, they ask to learn more about the Carmelite way, its history, and spirituality.

Stop and reflect: How did you come to Carmel? What role did others play in your journey?

The Carmelite habit and scapular may attract people's attention, but unless those people encounter a loving Carmelite beneath the outer layers no one will be drawn to Carmel. You can't judge a book by its cover, but an 'inner clothing' of love shines through the outer layers. Christians don't simply exhibit love through what we wear physically. We are called to witness to Carmel's attitudes through our everyday living. As Pope Paul VI said, people are attracted to the Church by witnesses not teachers; people who draw others to Jesus because of their integrity and authenticity.

We are Carmelites because God called us, and we responded to that *vocation*. The first verse of the hymn *Come down O love divine* reminds us that we need God the Holy Spirit to come, seek and kindle within us the desire to live holy lives and it is the Spirit who gives us the power to do so. True holiness is God's gift, and everybody is called to embrace it. We know that we can love God because God loved us first (cf. *1 John* 4:10).

Stop and reflect: What role do you think the Holy Spirit has had in calling you to Carmel?

Uniforms do not mean uniformity

In secular society and in religious life there are many examples of clothing which display an allegiance, status, or profession. People who are otherwise perhaps very different become united when they put on a shared uniform. Nurses, policemen, soldiers, religious – to name but a few – wear uniforms that tell us something about what they do, and by

'When the day of Pentecost had come, they were all together in one place ... Divided tongues, as of fire, appeared among them ... All of them were filled with the Holy Spirit.' (Acts 2:1-4). The Holy Spirit calls us to make the Carmelite habit more than mere outward show.

assumption, what they are like. All nurses are caring, all policemen are law-abiding, all soldiers are disciplined, and all religious are holy. Or are they?

Unless the inner person is in agreement with the outer persona then the image projected through a uniform is false. This is also true of us Carmelites. When we wear the Brown Scapular – the 'uniform' of the Carmelite Family if you like – we must remember that Carmelite life is not about how we dress but about the attitudes that we project.

If someone dresses in a uniform that commands respect, but the person wearing it behaves in a way that is inappropriate, we say that he or she has no integrity, or is hypocritical. In the Gospel, Jesus had plenty to say about such people, particularly those who wore the uniforms of religion but whose hearts were far from God. Conversely, when people live in a way that truly reflects the dignity they project by their outer clothing or actions, we admire them.

Sometimes we 'put on different clothes' and live a number of lives because we are not comfortable with who we are. Sometimes we dress-down; perhaps we are ashamed of something, afraid of ourselves or other people, or unwilling to accept that we are loved by God. Sometimes we dress-up; perhaps we have a high opinion of ourselves and even think that we are God. Either way, we put on masks, and wrap ourselves in layers to stop God, and other people, getting to know the *real* person inside.

Reflect privately: How do you 'dress up' or 'dress down' in your view of yourself?

Dress to impress

The Carmelite saints – particularly Teresa of Jesus and John of the Cross – tell us that the first task facing a person embarking on the spiritual journey is to strip away the masks, to lose our attachments to 'false gods', in order to face the reality about ourselves and feel comfortable in our own skin. This is not an easy process, but people who are true to who they really are inside are said to have *congruence*. There's something attractive, isn't there, about those people who are 'fully alive', who are comfortable with themselves warts and all? They put others at their ease, and allow others to be themselves too.

Stop and reflect: Would you consider yourself to be self-aware? How have you hidden behind masks? What have you done to let those masks drop? What have been the consequences?

Teresa of Jesus spoke of the need for self-knowledge, not so that we feel bad about ourselves nor become self-obsessed, but so that we accept ourselves as deeply and recklessly loved by God. Through self-knowledge we gradually come to recognise those parts of our lives that need God's healing touch. Teresa said that true humility means knowing the reality about ourselves, not a grovelling self-abasement that is actually a perverted form of pride. The word 'humility' comes from *humus* the Greek word for the ground. We still speak about people who are 'grounded', who face the realities of life head on. The confidence to do this comes about through being loved. Saint Paul talks about being *rooted and grounded in love* (*Ephesians* 3:17). Elsewhere Saint Paul tells us about the attitudes we should exhibit to others:

Mosaic of St. Paul at the Vatican.

> Love must be sincere. Hate what is evil, cling to what is good. Be devoted to one another in love. Honour one another above yourselves. Be joyful in hope, patient in affliction, and faithful in prayer. Share with God's people who are in need. Practise hospitality.
>
> (*Romans* 12:9-13)

In his *Way of Life* letter to the hermits on Mount Carmel, Saint Albert said that Carmelites should take Saint Paul as our particular model and teacher. In our Carmelite communities do we heed Paul's call to love? Do we live the attitudes he holds out to us?

Stop and ponder God's word: In his *Letter to the Corinthians*, Saint Paul encourages Christians to 'strive for the greater gifts' and shows us 'a still more excellent way' (12:31). Read the Apostle's famous passage on love in *1 Corinthians* 13 and consider how it can help us form a Carmelite attitude to life.

Jesus - not clothing - covers our shame

The account of the Fall in *Genesis* would suggest that pride – putting ourselves in the place of God – is humanity's first sin. When Adam and Eve disobeyed God, it was because they sought to have God's knowledge and power. Banished from the Garden of Eden, they realised their nakedness and put on clothes because they were ashamed of themselves. In the Old Testament we read of clothing as a sign of holiness (such as Joseph's coat), and of clothes being torn in repentance. When Jesus came among humanity as 'the Word made flesh' he reminded us that the human form is holy because it is made in the image of God. At the Transfiguration the clothes of Jesus 'became dazzling white' (*Matthew* 17:2) to represent his divinity. People who touched the hem of Jesus' clothes were healed (*Luke* 8:44). At his crucifixion Jesus was stripped of his clothing which was divided between the soldiers (*John* 19:23). Jesus' empty grave clothes bore testimony to his resurrection (*John* 20:6). These and other examples in the Bible show us that states of dress and undress can be powerful metaphors of how we relate to God and to others.

Stop and think: What other Bible episodes can you recall in which clothing is significant or symbolic?

Putting on Christ

Carmelites look to Jesus, before all other people, as the supreme model of how to live. We see in our Lord and Saviour Jesus Christ, in his humanity, the perfect person whose 'attitude' is love. Teresa of Jesus called her fellow Carmelites to live the Gospel, reading and rereading the accounts of Jesus' life and being with him at each step of his journey among us. (By the way, it's good to accept the readings of the day in the Mass and Divine Office as God's word for *today* and spend time encountering Jesus in them).

The Scriptures tells us that Jesus 'went about doing good and healing all who were oppressed by the devil, for God was with him' (*Acts* 10:38), and that sums up all the virtues and attitudes that we are called to follow. At the heart of the Scriptures, at the heart of the life of Jesus, and therefore at the heart of our own lives, is what theologians call the *kerygma*. The word *kerygma* is related to the Greek verb κηρύσσω which means 'proclamation', 'announcement' or 'preaching'. The *kerygma* is the basic essence of the Christian message. Through his ministry and preaching Jesus proclaimed the Good News of God's love for us – particularly the poor, the blind, and the captive – and announced the Kingdom of Heaven.

Stop, read and pray: The *kerygma* – the fundamental message of Jesus' life and preaching – is expressed in a number of New Testament passages. Why not use some of the following for *Lectio Divina* meditation: *Mark* 10:45; *Luke* 4:16-19; *John* 3:16; *Acts* 10:38; *Romans* 10:13-17.

By the way he lived and by what he preached, Jesus revealed the Father to humanity and showed us how to live the life of true believers. Jesus asked the Father to send the Holy Spirit to guide, direct and fill us with the same power, if we but avail ourselves of it. Life in Carmel, whether as a religious or as a lay person, is meant to help us live as Jesus wishes, to help us proclaim the *kerygma*. We know from the previous chapter that we will come to know Jesus' life and will for us better if we have daily contact with him through the Scriptures and *Lectio Divina*.

The habit: a sign of good habits?

Just as in the Bible, clothing has a symbolic value in religious families such as Carmel. When a Carmelite religious is first clothed in the brown habit, or a tertiary receives the scapular, it signifies to the world the candidate's allegiance to Jesus and membership of a religious family. Putting on a habit or a reduced version of it denotes a radical lifestyle decision. It is a deepening of the commitment made previously at baptism. Following an ancient custom from the early Church, newly baptised Christians put on a white garment which signifies a new life in Jesus Christ. We've read in previous chapters that the Carmelite white cloak – which gave the brothers their nickname of *Whitefriars* – recalls this baptismal clothing, and the robes of the Resurrection.

The best known item of Carmelite clothing is the Brown Scapular. Most of the ancient religious orders wear a scapular of some sort over the shoulders (the name comes from the Latin for 'shoulder'). It was originally an apron that protected the habit during manual labour. The scapular therefore came to be symbolic of working for the Lord, and of service to others.

A Carmelite sister in the Order's brown habit and white cloak.

Did you know? Carmel is recognised not only by the Order's habit, but also through 'monastic produce'. *Tripel Karmeliet* is a popular Belgian Beer made from a recipe used in 1679 by the friars of Dendermonde in East Flanders.

The logo of *Tripel Karmeliet* bearing a form of the Carmelite crest can be found across Belgium.

Faith not fashion

In the Carmelite Third Order (Secular) the scapular is sometimes called the 'little habit of Our Lady'. Once an enquirer has studied Carmel for at least some months, discerned that they might have a vocation, and been accepted into our family by a local community, the scapular is placed upon him or her in the *Rite of Reception*.

Receiving the Scapular during the Third Order's *Rite of Reception*.

After at least two years of initial formation, a member of the Third Order (sometimes called a 'Tertiary', 'Lay Carmelite' or 'Secular Carmelite') can apply to make First Profession. If the request is accepted by the community, then in the *Rite of Profession* the Lay Carmelite makes a solemn promise to live as a Carmelite, embracing the 'Evangelical Counsels' according to his or her state in life. The promise is made, by the help of God's grace, for the rest of our lives, and it is an undertaking to be clothed with Carmel's attitudes inside as well as out. The placing of the scapular upon a candidate for the Third Order symbolises a deeper undertaking to live 'in allegiance to Jesus Christ', through the Carmelite way of life. It should only be done by those who understand the serious commitment involved. The 2003 *Rule for the Third Order of Carmel* (*RTOC*) makes the following statement about profession:

> The fundamental bond between the Tertiary and Carmel is profession. This commitment is made explicit in some form of promise, or otherwise in keeping with our ancient custom, by the profession of vows of obedience and chastity according to the obligations of one's state. In this way, the Tertiary is consecrated more deeply to God and is able to offer more intensive worship. By means of profession, the Tertiaries seek to strengthen their baptismal promises to love God more than anything else and to renounce Satan and all temptation. The uniqueness of this profession is to be found in the means that are chosen to reach full conformity with Christ. Indeed, Carmelites learn to appear before Christ empty-handed, by placing all their love in Christ Jesus, who becomes personally their holiness, their justice, their love and their crown. Jesus' message – to love God with all one's being and one's neighbour as one's self – demands from the Tertiary a constant affirmation of the primacy of God, the categorical refusal to serve two masters and the pre-eminence of love for others which fights against all forms of egoism and self-centredness. The spirit of the evangelical counsels, common to all Christians, becomes for the Tertiaries a plan for life which touches the areas of power, of sensuality and of material goods. The vows are an ever greater demand not to serve false idols, but to attain that freedom of loving God and neighbour which is above all forms of egoism. Holiness lies in the fulfilment of this double command to love. (§12-13)

The scapular: sign of a deeper reality

Seen in this light, we come to understand the scapular as a sacramental, that is, a material object which should point to a deeper spiritual reality. The scapular is a sign of our willingness to adopt the 'habit' – the habitual attitude – of seeking God's presence (as discussed in Chapter 9). It symbolises belonging to a large religious family, Carmel, and various forms of scapular are worn or carried by all those who formally profess to belong to Carmel. The scapular is worn by the Prior General, to whom Carmelite religious and laity promise obedience, and by all the other professed members of the Carmelite Family. The scapular signifies our inclusion in all the blessings and benefits worked for by others who wear the scapular. We share in the graces of the Carmelite Order, and are also asked to contribute to its work and prayer.

Millions of people around the world wear the Brown Scapular, either as professed members of the Carmelite Order (friars, hermits, nuns, sisters, and tertiaries), or as members of *Scapular Confraternities*. Confraternities ('brotherhoods') exist all around the world – some have thousands of members – and extend a connection with the Carmelite Family to people who do not feel called to make a deeper commitment within the Order by receiving formation and making formal profession. The Brown Scapular Confraternity is ideal for people who have devotion to Our Lady of Mount Carmel, but who are not called to live out the Carmelite charism as fully as through profession.

Lay people being enrolled in the Brown Scapular Confraternity.

The choristers in this Carmelite choir in Rome show their link to the Order by wearing the miniature scapular.

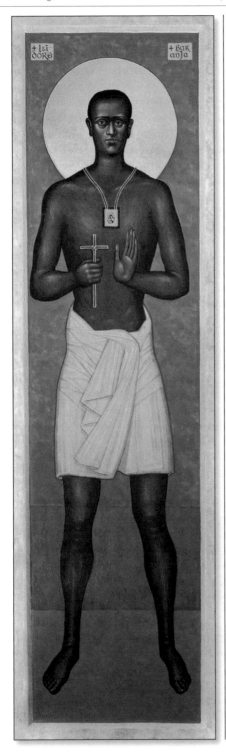

An icon of Isidore Bakanja by Sister Petra Clare at the National Shrine of St. Jude in Faversham, England.

Did you know? Blessed Isidore Bakanja (1887-1909) is known in his native Congo region as the *martyr of the Brown Scapular*. He was beaten and left to die for refusing to remove his Carmelite scapular and for promoting Christianity among his fellow workers. He was beatified in 1994.

Mary: wrapped in God's grace

For centuries people have been identified as 'belonging' to a person or a community by what they wear. As Carmelites, we belong to a family where Mary, Our Lady, is mother, sister and patron, and we wear her 'uniform'. In Carmelite art she is often portrayed as wrapping the white mantle or cloak of the Order around all her brothers and sisters, religious and lay.

Carmelites turn to Mary as a model of how we should dress ourselves in Carmel's attitudes. Mary was, from the moment of her conception, free from original sin, and in the Carmelite tradition she is often called *Most Pure Virgin*. Mary grew up 'full of God's favour' (*Luke* 1:28). She was someone who prayed, who lived a simple and holy life, and who was open to God's word.

This life of intimacy with God gave Mary an 'attitude' of holiness. By making space within her heart for God (*vacare Deo*), she developed a

Carmelite religious gathered under the mantle of Mary in the *Speculum Carmelitanum* (1680).

disposition to live and express the love of God with those around her. Mary thus cared for others: first Elizabeth her cousin; then Jesus and Joseph in their home in Nazareth; after the death of her Son she cared for the disciples, especially John the Beloved Disciple, and she allowed herself to be cared for as well. Mary now spends eternity loving and drawing us all to Jesus.

Mary also knew incredible sorrow, as most of us will do at some point in life. Again, Our Lady is an example to us of living with an attitude of trust. Mary lived through her suffering, grieving yet accepting, and this is a powerful witness to the unfailing care of God.

The development of the Brown Scapular

As well as being a sign of belonging to the Order, and of service, the Brown Scapular is traditionally symbolic of Carmelites' relationship with Mary. The popularity of the scapular is inextricably linked to a legend that Our Lady appeared to Saint Simon Stock and blessed his scapular.

As the eminent Carmelite historian Richard Copsey, O.Carm., has pointed out, the legend of the 'Scapular Vision' is a blending of different stories with little historical basis. Simon Stock the Englishman really existed; he was an early prior general of the Carmelites, and after his death and burial in the French city of Bordeaux he attained a reputation for holiness. Long after his death accounts emerged of another holy man called Simon who apparently received a vision of the Virgin Mary giving him a scapular as a pledge of protection. Such accounts were common in various religious orders in medieval Europe. At some point the 'visionary' Simon and Simon Stock were identified as one and the same person, in accounts written two hundred years after the supposed scapular vision. A fake papal letter recounting another vision of Our Lady to Pope John XXII promised that Mary would save anyone wearing the Carmelite habit from Purgatory on the first Saturday after they died (known from the Latin for Saturday as the *Sabbatine privilege*). All these stories became blended together with the Carmelites' existing devotion to Our Lady, and thus the brown scapular devotion was born.

It is up to the individual to decide whether or not Our Lady ever appeared to Saint Simon Stock. It cannot be disproved, but there is no reliable historical evidence for such a claim and plenty of evidence to show how such a legend may have arisen. Not believing in the scapular vision story does not prevent Carmelites from believing in the holiness of Saint Simon Stock, nor the symbolic value of the brown scapular.

Millions of people today wear the Carmelite brown scapular as a symbol of their consecration to Mary. What does it mean to be consecrated to Mary in the Carmelite Family? Hugh Clarke, O.Carm. (d. 2007), pointed out:

> Consecration in the strict sense can be made only to God and by God's initiative, since it is the total and exclusive offering of someone or something to God; it is an act of adoration which can be given only to God. Christopher O'Donnell, O.Carm., says: "When we speak of Marian consecration we must think first of Mary herself as the one most consecrated to God … she is above all the model and prototype

Chapter 12 ∎ Clothed with Carmel's Attitudes

Paintings of the reputed 'Scapular Vision'.

of consecration to which not only the Church but each Christian is invited to partake."

(*Mary and the Brown Scapular*)

The Carmelite Order in line with what the Church asks no longer preaches what used to be called the *Sabbatine privilege*, but we still advocate the scapular as a sign of trust in the love and mercy Jesus has for us, expressed through Mary's maternal care. The scapular is a *sacramental*; it is a symbol which teaches us something about the truths of our faith. The scapular signifies our salvation and liberation by Jesus Christ.

Stop and think: What does the scapular mean to you? How can it best be promoted today?

Oscar Romero (1917-80), the martyred Archbishop of San Salvador, preached about the Brown Scapular in a homily on the Feast of Our Lady of Mount Carmel (16th July 1977). He said:

> The scapular is a sign of salvation … If the Blessed Virgin were to give the scapular to Simon Stock today she would tell him: "This is the sign of protection, a sign of God's teaching, a sign of humanity's integral vocation, for the salvation of the whole person, now in this life. All who wear the scapular must be persons who live now in salvation on this earth and they must feel content to develop their human powers for the good of others".

Archbishop Oscar practiced what he preached. He preached the Good News of God's love for all, seeking peace in El Salvador when it was on the brink of civil war, and giving a voice to the weak and powerless in society. Echoing Mary's *Magnificat*, he stood up to those in power who oppressed the poor, which sealed his fate. He was wearing the Carmelite brown scapular when he was shot dead whilst celebrating Mass in the chapel of a cancer hospice run by the Carmelite sisters in San Salvador. Romero realised that the scapular is not so much a symbol of the next life, but of life lived now in the grace of the present. We are already a saved people, a gifted people, a loved people. All we have to do is accept Jesus' love and forgiveness and turn back to God the Father every day.

Archbishop Oscar Romero, who through the Brown Scapular was a member of the wider Carmelite Family

Did you know? The Carmelite sisters in San Salvador have kept Romero's blood-stained vestments as relics, but sunlight was causing them to disintegrate. The British Province of Carmelites paid for them to be placed in protective glass as a gesture of solidarity with the sisters and the poor they serve. Carmelites are among the millions of people around the world who look to Archbishop Romero as a patron-saint of justice and peace.

Wearing the scapular is a reminder of the fact that as Christians we must proclaim the *kerygma* and build-up the Kingdom of God, in which everybody is redeemed and loved, and therefore has a right to expect justice, equality, and dignity. Carmel's attitudes are those of the Kingdom – the Reign of God – which Jesus proclaimed and asks us to build for his return. Wearing the Brown Scapular therefore reminds us Carmelites of our prophetic role. We Carmelites are a 'company of prophets' whose prophetic inheritance comes from Elijah and Elisha, the Old Testament prophets of Carmel. In the Bible accounts of their lives, clothing is again symbolic.

Elijah: wrapped up in God

We might call Elijah the *Father of Carmelite attitudes*. He was a man of deep conviction and absolute faith in God. Overcoming fears and doubts, and in danger of his own life, Elijah spoke out against the false prophets of his time.

This is not to say that Elijah found it easy to live as God asked him to. When the battle for the true God was won on Mount Carmel (*1 Kings* 18) Elijah went on a journey of his own choosing, crumpled under the strain he had carried, and rested under a tree until the angel of the Lord brought him food and encouragement (*1 Kings* 19). The same is true for many of our modern-day prophets. Plenty of people today speak out against the false gods in our society: money, sex, drugs, status. Although they may seem tireless we don't see the strain they feel in private. When Elijah was weary, God's love and tenderness reached down and led him to healing. When living Carmel's attitudes makes a brother or sister of ours tired, our hearts can go out in compassion, not criticism, because we know our own weaknesses and failings, and those of even the prophets. There are times when we also need to rest, to retreat from our burdens. Elijah's story shows us we can trust that God will nourish us with bread from heaven.

Pulpit in Brussels from the former Carmelite church.

Did you know? This sculpted pulpit in Brussels used to stand in the city's Carmelite church. It depicts Elijah being brought bread by the angel. Why do you think this scene might have been chosen for a pulpit?

As Elijah ascended in the whirlwind and fiery chariot his cloak fell to Elisha.

'Elisha picked up the mantle of Elijah that had fallen from him, and went back and stood on the bank of the Jordan. He took the mantle ... and struck the water, saying "Where is the Lord, the God of Elijah?" When he had struck the water, the water was parted to the one side and to the other, and Elisha went over.' (2 Kings 2:13-14).

Elijah's cloak became Elisha's and ours

For Carmelites, Elijah's clothing is very symbolic, particularly his mantle or cloak. When Elijah heard the 'sound of sheer silence' on Mount Horeb (*1 Kings* 19:12) he 'wrapped his face in his mantle' as a sign of respect for God's presence.

God's commandment to Elijah on Horeb was for him to anoint Elisha as prophet in his place (*1 Kings* 19:16). Elijah made Elisha his disciple by wrapping his cloak around him (*1 Kings* 19:19). We later hear (*2 Kings* 2) that as Elijah ascended to heaven in a whirlwind he cast his cloak down to Elisha, a cloak which became the sign of Elijah's followers having authority and through which miracles were wrought.

This episode is discussed at length in the medieval masterpiece of Carmelite spirituality known as *The Ten Books on the Way of Life and Great Deeds of the Carmelites* (or *Book of the First Monks*). Whole chapters of this text (published in a complete English translation in 2005) are given over to discussing what clothes Carmelites should wear because of what they symbolise.

The cloak worn by the first Carmelite hermits on Mount Carmel was striped, but in the late thirteenth century the Order adopted a white cloak. The white cloak is the primary symbol of Carmelite identity, and for this reason it is worn in some provinces of the Order by not only the religious but also by members of the Third Order. In Europe and North America it is generally not the custom for Lay Carmelites to wear the white cloak, but whether they wear it or not they too have received the 'mantle' of Elijah spiritually, and seek to be clothed more and more with Carmel's attitudes. Wherever and however we follow the *Rule of Saint Albert*, Carmelites are called to pass on to those following us a clear and profound example of what it means to be a Carmelite. Are we worthy descendants of Elijah? Do we speak out about the reality of God, and God's love for humanity? Do we stand up for justice, and promote peace, or is our faith limited to false piety? Some Carmelites – particularly in the economically developing world – truly embody the spirit of Elijah in confronting gross injustices. Some have paid for this at the cost of their freedom or even their lives. But for most of us being a follower of Elijah in the Carmelite tradition is a matter of living out Carmel's attitudes in the ordinary circumstances in which we find ourselves day by day.

Chapter 12 ■ Clothed with Carmel's Attitudes

Many cultures, one company of prophets! Scenes from the 2006 International Congress of Lay Carmelites in Rome.

Rags to riches, or riches to rags?

Clothes can be expensive, but poverty is one of the attitudes which Carmelites adopt, particularly given our Order's mendicant tradition. Carmelites often speak of *the preferential option for the poor*. This means choosing to seek out and serve as a priority those in society who suffer from any form of poverty: financial, emotional, educational, spiritual, social.

Did you know? The Carmelites of the Province of Australia and Timor Leste have helped the people of Timor Leste (East Timor) with building, education, and healing. They have enabled the Timorese of Zumalai parish to establish water systems, farms, mobile health clinics and youth centres.

Members of the Carmelite Family in Timor Leste, where some Lay Carmelites wear a uniform.

Armour: clothing for defence, not attack

There is another sort of clothing that is very relevant to Carmelites: armour. As we have learned in previous chapters, the first Carmelites were hermits gathered on Mount Carmel, and some of them had probably been crusaders who had come to fight for control of the holy sites in the land where Christ had lived. However, they seem to have given up the armour of physical battle in order to take up the armour of spiritual battle, turning from outside enemies to focus on the battles raging within their own hearts.

Albert, Latin Patriarch of Jerusalem, acknowledged this when he wrote their *Way of Life*, now the Carmelite *Rule*. In the *Rule* Albert quoted from St. Paul's *Letter to the Ephesians* (6:10-17):

The early Carmelites rejected physical armour in favour of spiritual warfare.

> Because human life on earth is a trial, and all who wish to live devotedly in Christ must suffer persecution, and moreover since your adversary the devil prowls around like a roaring lion seeking whom he may devour, you shall use every care and diligence to put on the armour of God, so that you may be able to withstand the deceits of the enemy. The loins are to be girt with the cincture of chastity. Your breast is to be fortified with holy ponderings, for it is written: Holy ponderings will save you. The breastplate of justice is to be put on,

that you may love the Lord your God with all your heart and all your soul and all your strength, and your neighbour as yourself. In all things is to be taken up the shield of faith, with which you will be able to quench all the flaming arrows of the wicked one, for without faith it is impossible to please God. On your head is to be put the helmet of salvation, that you may hope for salvation from the only Saviour who saves his people from their sins. And the sword of the Spirit, which is the word of God, should dwell abundantly in your mouth and in your hearts. And whatever you have to do, let it all be done in the Word of the Lord. (*Rule of Saint Albert*, Chapters 18-19).

Albert tells us Carmelites to put on the *Armour of God* because of the power of the devil. It is unhealthy to be overly concerned with the devil, but we should also not doubt the existence of evil in the world, and the need to overcome our own selfishness with God's help. The Fathers and Mothers of the early Church, as well as the first Carmelites, were very aware of the power of the evil one, and the theme of *spiritual warfare* was very common in Patristic writings. Alone, in the silence of the desert, temptations of many sorts came to these men and women, and through silent meditation as well as life in community they had to face the realities about themselves, both good and bad.

It is in the silence and bleakness of the desert that we come face to face with our 'demons'. We do not have to literally enter a physical desert, but we need to make space in our lives for reflection. How we take distractions for granted! We might read something, watch something, talk to someone, or do some task … anything rather than face God and ourselves in the stark reality of silence. Putting on the armour of God is a means of defending ourselves from the distractions and deceptions surrounding us.

Stop and ponder: How do you understand the metaphor of spiritual armour? Does it apply to your life?

Casting off 'hand-me-down' clothing so Carmel's attitudes gradually enwrap us

Our 'inner clothing' speaks very much of our way of relating to God, to others, and to life itself. Many of our attitudes – our values and moral stances – come from our upbringing, family, peers, cultural norms of our generation and religious education. As we mature in faith we may need to examine these attitudes and ask ourselves if these 'clothes' still 'fit us'. Reading more widely, being with others on a spiritual journey, and most of all opening ourselves to the action of the Holy Spirit may cause us to reconsider the vital questions: Who am I? What is life all about? What sort of person am I? How should I live? For some, like Saint Paul, a dramatic conversion may happen; for others, being clothed with Carmel's attitudes is a slow process of transformation. We are gradually stripped of our old clothing, our outmoded ways of living, and instead clothe ourselves in Christ.

Some people are hesitant to approach Carmel or the Church in general because they feel that they are not worthy. What Jesus shows us is that God comes looking for us even in our weakness. We know God loves us and wants us to approach the Father because Jesus died for us *while we were still sinners* (*Romans* 5:8). We don't have to be perfect before making the journey. The journey itself can form us. We make the path by walking it. We don't have to know everything about Carmel and be perfect Carmelites before we put on the Brown Scapular. It does, however, require our openness to change and growth.

When we begin to live the Carmelite way many of us know very little about the 'clothes' that we have put on. We take one step at a time, reading, praying, listening and trying to live the life in as authentic a way as possible. We gradually learn where the habit of Carmel needs to be lengthened or shortened to fit us personally. We are called to wear the Carmelite habit in a way that's unique to each individual, but in a way that maintains the 'uniform' as recognisable. In this we can be inspired by those who have trod the journey ahead of us, especially those whom the Church has canonised as being worthy of example. We see what their attitudes say to us, then consider how to embody those attitudes in the circumstances God has placed us in. Let us look at the attitudes of some of our models in Carmel.

Teresa of Jesus

Saint Teresa of Jesus (of Avila) put on Carmel's attitudes. She was what we might call a *mulier fortis* or 'strong woman', and shows that Carmel's attitude of love is not to be confused with being weak or a pushover. Teresa was once asked why God did not choose a man for the work of reforming the Order and she replied that none were available

or willing! She had great faith, not from the beginning of her religious life but gradually through years of struggle and hard work until her 'second conversion' in her forties. Once she knew what God was asking of her she applied herself with fortitude and determination. She travelled widely in an age when this was not an easy option. She maintained a great sense of humour in the face of many difficulties. Once when her carriage sank in a stream she asked God why. 'That is how I treat my friends' was the reply. 'Then it's no wonder that you have so few of them!' was her retort. Underlying all else she had wonderful insights into Carmelite spirituality, particularly prayer, which guided her nuns, inspired John of the Cross to work with her, and which still inspire the Carmelite Family today. To Teresa prayer was 'intimate conversation with one we know loves us'. Reading the story of Teresa's life led to the conversion of Edith Stein and many others have been drawn to the contemplative life by Teresa.

This painting depicts Teresa of Jesus (left) and Mary Magdalene de'Pazzi (right) receiving a garment from Our Lady.

Thérèse's simple clothing

Being clothed with Carmel's attitudes is not a complicated business. In fact, Carmelites tend to choose simple ways of approaching relationships. Thérèse of Lisieux is the saint of *The Little Way of Spiritual Childhood*, which is a really simple means of coming to God like a child with complete trust and confidence. Thérèse manifested such total confidence in God, such complete surrender and love, and lived it out in the everyday life of an enclosed Carmelite monastery. She demonstrated the commitment of her faith, even through serious (and eventually terminal) illness and a lengthy period of spiritual darkness. Thérèse inspires us to see that we too can love God in the small acts of love, giving, sacrifice and penance that make up our lives. We may often doubt, feel fear or separation from God, but God's loving arms are still open and our 'feelings' do not have the last word. Thérèse's habitual disposition was towards faith and confidence, and in the end that won. She surrendered herself in death with the words: 'I love Him. My God, I love you.'

Thérèse enjoyed dressing up, as seen here in a play she wrote about St. Joan of Arc, performed in Lisieux Carmel in 1895.

'They have washed their robes white in the blood of the Lamb' (*Revelation* 7:14)

The Carmelite prophetic attitude, speaking out on behalf of the oppressed, was evident in the lives and deaths of three twentieth-century Carmelites, martyred by the National Socialists (Nazis) in the 1940s. Born into a Jewish family, Edith Stein was a philosopher who embraced Christianity as a young woman and became a Discalced Carmelite nun.

She refused to renounce her heritage as a Jew, and was gassed in Auschwitz concentration camp in 1942, just days after Carmelite friar Titus Brandsma was killed by lethal injection in Dachau. Dachau was also the place where four friars from the Carmelite friary in Krakow, Poland, were detained by the Gestapo. The prior, Hilary Januszewski, O.Carm. (1907-45), presented himself to be sent to Dachau in the place of an older sick friar. Together with Titus Brandsma he gave hope to the other inmates and ministered to the sick, before dying of typhus on 25 March 1945. In France a Discalced Carmelite friar, Lucien-Louis Bunel (1900-45), known by his religious name of Père Jacques, sheltered Jewish boys in his school, for which he was imprisoned by the Nazis. Though eventually liberated, he was left so weak that he died a month later. His heroism was made famous in the 1987 French film *Au revoir les enfants*.

Truly clothed in Carmel's attitudes (left-right): Hilary Januszewski (memorial in Poland); Edith Stein (sculpture by Geoff Lucas at Aylesford Priory); Lucien-Louis Bunel; Titus Brandsma.

Clothed with love

Inspired by our forebears, we Carmelites living today can daily re-invite the Holy Spirit to develop within us the dispositions and attitudes of Carmel. Let's take seriously the words of our teacher and model the Apostle Paul:

> As God's chosen people, holy and dearly loved, clothe yourselves with compassion, kindness, humility, gentleness and patience. Bear with each other and forgive whatever grievances you may have against another. Forgive as the Lord forgave you. And over all these virtues put on love which binds them together in perfect unity.
>
> (*Colossians* 3:12-14)

Conclusion: In this twelfth chapter we have seen how clothing can be a metaphor for our life as Christians and as Carmelites. The scapular and white cloak are symbols of the great heritage that has been handed down to us, and of the attitudes which we must learn to embody, not simply wear for outward show.

If you wish, conclude your time of study and reflection with a moment of prayer; perhaps simply read aloud Saint Paul's words about spiritual armour, either from the Bible or as they are quoted in the *Rule of Saint Albert*.

In the next chapter we will consider how our Carmelite attitudes are nourished by the Eucharist.

Ideas for Reflection, Discussion and Action

- Reflect on any passage in this chapter that has stood out as significant for you, either individually or as a community. If you had to summarise its main themes to explain to someone else, what would you highlight?

- If you attend meetings of a Carmelite community, take along a piece of clothing that has significance for you and explain to the group what it represents.

- Reread the Gospel and readings of the day. What is God saying to me about my attitudes?

- Recall the day you received the Brown Scapular and the promises you made. How have you lived that out? If you are preparing to receive the Brown Scapular, what attitudes are still developing within you?

- Where is my 'Armour of God' strong? Where are the 'chinks' in the armour?

- St. Teresa tells us: *Humility is truth*. She says we should know ourselves as well as knowing God. How well do I know myself?

- What do you think are the key 'attitudes' in the *Rule of Saint Albert* (the text is printed at the front of this book if you want to consult it)?

- What do you think is happening psychologically when children play at dressing-up?

- Do you think you can distinguish *Carmelite attitudes* from – say – Franciscan attitudes, Jesuit attitudes, or Benedictine attitudes?

- What 'attitudes' (good and bad) do you encounter in your Carmelite community?

- Read the commentary about Elisha inheriting the cloak of Elijah in Book 4 of *The Ten Books on the Way of Life and Great Deeds of the Carmelites*.

- Which model of Carmelite living most inspires you? Can you explain why? How has it changed your attitudes?

- Do you think that Lay Carmelites should wear the Third Order badge or Scapular visibly? Why do some Carmelite religious wear the habit on only certain occasions?

- If you wear or carry the Carmelite brown scapular, try to develop a habit of saying a prayer when putting it on each day; a popular and simple one is: 'Mary, use me in the service of your son Jesus today.'

Recommended Further Resources

Be careful when searching out resources on the Carmelite scapular; many are not written with a proper understanding of the scapular's history and symbolism. There are several books in print on the notion of 'spiritual armour'.

Benedict XVI, *Deus Caritas Est*, (Catholic Truth Society, 2006). Available online at: www.vatican.va

Carmelite Provincials (O.Carm. and O.C.D.) in North America, *The Scapular of Our Lady of Mount Carmel: Catechesis and Ritual*, (Washington, D.C.: I.C.S. Publications, 2000). This publication on the Scapular presents its history and symbolism in a very clear and pastoral way.

Joseph Chalmers, O.Carm., 'The Beginnings', in *Mary the Contemplative*, (Rome: Edizioni Carmelitane, 2001), pp. 6-18.

Hugh Clarke, O.Carm., *Mary and the Brown Scapular*, (Carmelite Charitable Trust, Second Edition 2002).

Richard Copsey, O.Carm., 'Simon Stock and the Scapular Vision', reprinted in his book *Carmel in Britain 3: The Hermits from Mount Carmel*, (Faversham & Rome: Saint Albert's Press & Edizioni Carmelitane, 2004), pp. 75-112.

Kilian J. Healy, O.Carm., *Methods of Prayer in the Directory of the Carmelite Reform of Touraine*, (1956, Reprinted Rome: Edizioni Carmelitane, 2005).

Jean Olwen Maynard, *Isidore Bakanja: Young Martyr of the Congo*, (London: Catholic Truth Society, 2001).

Patrick McMahon, O.Carm., 'Garment of Grace: A Historical Appreciation of the Carmelite Scapular', *Carmel in the World*, Volume XLIII Number 3, 2004, pp. 175-88.

Francis J. Murphy, *Père Jacques: Resplendent in Victory*, (Washington, D.C.: ICS Publications, 1998).

Maureen Pickman, T.O.C., 'Isidore Bakanja – Commemorating Blessed Isidore Bakanja's centenary of martyrdom', *Assumpta* Vol. 53 No. 3, April 2010, also available online on the Contemporary Authors page of the Spirituality section of www.carmelite.org

Felip Ribot, O.Carm., *The Ten Books on the Way of Life and Great Deeds of the Carmelites (including the Book of the First Monks)*, edited and translated by Richard Copsey, O.Carm., (Faversham: Saint Albert's Press, 2005, Second edition 2007).

Teresa of Jesus, *The Way of Perfection*, study edition by Kieran Kavanaugh (Washington, D.C.: ICS Publications, 2000).

Raphael Tijhuis, O.Carm., *Nothing Can Stop God from Reaching Us: A Dachau Diary by a Survivor*, (Rome: Edizioni Carmelitane, 2007).

Notes and reflections on Chapter 12

Carmel and the Eucharist

Summary: Set before us in this chapter is an inspiring meditation on different aspects of Carmel's devotion to the Eucharist. The Eucharist is the source and summit of Carmelite spirituality, as it is for the whole Church. Amongst other things we will consider: giving and receiving in the Eucharist; the Eucharist as an encounter with God; Eucharistic moments in the lives of Mary, Elijah, and the saints of Carmel; and Eucharist as expressed through our service and through our communities.

A celebration of the Eucharist at Aylesford Carmelite Priory in Kent, England, presided over by Fernando Millán Romeral, O.Carm., elected Prior General of the Order in 2007.

Get prepared: Before you sit down to read the chapter (which you might want to do in sections), gather any reading or writing materials that you might need. You might find it useful to have to hand a Bible and modern key texts of the Carmelite Order (such as the *Constitutions* of the friars and of the Third Order). Given that this chapter is about the Eucharist, which means thanksgiving, you might like to begin with some prayers of thanksgiving, or by counting the blessings God has given you in life.

Hungry for God

The false idols in our lives are never a satisfying substitute for God, who fills our hearts with love and purpose:

> Jesus said: "Those who eat my flesh and drink my blood have eternal life, and I will raise them up on the last day; for my flesh is true food and my blood is true drink. Those who eat my flesh and drink my blood abide in me, and I in them. Just as the living Father sent me, and I live because of the Father, so whoever eats me will live because of me. This is the bread that came down from heaven, not like that which your ancestors ate, and they died. But the one who eats this bread will live for ever." (*John* 6:54-58)

As we meditate on Jesus' own words in this Gospel text, we become aware of the greatness and enormity of the Eucharist: the power and splendour of God, the love, the intimate indwelling, the nourishment, and the promise of eternal life. When so many great writers have pondered the most holy Eucharist, where do we start?

Carmel is a Eucharistic community

The notion of Eucharist is of radical importance to all Christians. We Carmelites turn naturally to the *Rule of Saint Albert* (which you will find printed at the front of this book) to find out what role the Eucharist played in the lives of those first hermits on Carmel. The *Rule* places prayer – especially the Mass or Eucharist – literally at the heart of the Carmelite community:

In the Eucharist we offer ourselves to God, and God offers God's self to us.

An oratory should be built as conveniently as possible among the cells, where, if it can be done without difficulty, you are to gather each morning to hear Mass. (§14)

In the Middle Ages it would not have been usual to receive communion every day, but clearly the Latin Patriarch of Jerusalem, Saint Albert, wanted the hermits on Mount Carmel to celebrate the mystery of Jesus' complete self-giving as regularly as possible. Even before the Second Vatican Council encouraged everyone to receive communion frequently, it was common for many Carmelite communities to receive communion daily. Why? Because in the Eucharist we have a life-changing encounter with the Risen Christ.

Jesus gives himself to us completely

We've already learnt in previous chapters that we undertake the Carmelite journey as a response to God's initiative, to God's call, to God's love for us: 'God has made known to us his will for communion, calling men and women to share in his life' (2003 *Rule for the Third Order of Carmel* §1). The Mass recalls all the occasions when Christ gave himself to us: in sharing food with saints and sinners (especially the Last Supper), in his preaching and in his death on the cross. The Mass is therefore the Christian's highpoint for encountering Jesus in Word, Sacrament, and Community. As the *Rule for the Third Order of Carmel* reminds us, the Mass is as vital for today's Carmelite as for the first hermits:

> Sacramental life, centred on the Eucharist, is the source of the spiritual life. Carmelites are called to a deep sharing in the sacraments. Every day, if possible, they should approach the sacrifice of the altar and the banquet of life in which the Church finds all her richness, 'that is, Christ himself, our Pasch and the living bread' [cf. *Presbyterorum ordinis*, n. 5]. (§37)

The Eucharist – which is Greek for 'thanksgiving' – celebrates the *Paschal Mystery*, that is, Christ's dying and rising for humanity. It goes to the heart of the Christian story and the *kerygma*: God comes to tell us we are loved.

In the Eucharist God is not made any greater by our praise and worship; instead our veneration of God makes *us* grow in love and grace. As Preface IV of the Weekday Missal states: 'Father, you have no need of our praise, yet our desire to thank you is itself your gift. Our prayer of thanksgiving adds nothing to your greatness, but makes us grow in your grace, through Jesus Christ our Lord.'

The Church calls the Eucharist the *source and summit of the Christian life*. As Carmelites we are familiar with the image of the spiritual journey to the summit of Jesus 'the Mountain'. Jesus himself is our food for that journey, both the source and the summit.

The gift of self

As well as receiving Christ, in the Eucharist we give ourselves to him and become his body, the People of God. In the Middle Ages Carmelite friars joined the debate about what happened to the bread and wine at the consecration; today theologians are equally focussed on what happens to us when we celebrate together. During the

A painting in the Archives of the Carmelite Order in Rome of Blessed John Soreth holding a ciborium.

Eucharist the Holy Spirit is called down on the assembly that it too might become the body of Christ, the people of God. The Eucharist is a *sacrament*, that is, an outward sign of the mystery of God's love and power (grace) in our lives. Through the ordinary realities of bread and wine we perceive something of God. Taking part in the Eucharistic liturgy we become aware of God's great love and power, and share in God's life, fed from two sources: the Scriptures (as we read in Chapters 10 and 11) and the body and blood of Christ. It is a foretaste of the banquet in God's heavenly Kingdom.

Did you know? Carmelite saints are often renowned for their devotion to Christ in the Blessed Sacrament. Blessed Jean Soreth, the fifteenth-century prior general who formally incorporated nuns and lay people into the Carmelite Order, is usually depicted carrying a ciborium of consecrated hosts. This is because he rescued the Eucharist from the tabernacle during riots in Liège.

Did you know? The Eucharist unites all followers of Jesus in all time and space. We get a glimpse of this universality when the Eucharist is celebrated in Carmelite communities which have an international make up. Several houses of the Order – such as Whitefriars Hall in Washington D.C., Saint Albert's International Centre in Rome, and the Carmelite Friars in East Finchley, London (pictured opposite) – are study houses that welcome Carmelite religious and lay people from around the world.

The Eucharist is an encounter and the pledge of an eternal banquet

When we participate in the Eucharist, we encounter Jesus – the Alpha and the Omega and everything in between – to whom Carmelites give their allegiance (*Rule of Saint Albert*, Chapter 2). During the Eucharist the bread and wine become the body and blood of Jesus. We too will be transformed by God if we will let him. The Eucharist has such power to change our way of living that the Church teaches that 'the other sacraments and indeed all ecclesiastical ministries and the works of the apostolate are bound up with the Eucharist and oriented towards it.' (*Catechism of the Catholic Church* §1324:1).

One of the Fathers of the Church, Saint Augustine, said that when a Christian goes to communion, he or she must 'receive what you are, and become what you receive' (*Sermon on John* 26, 13). Centuries later Saint Thérèse of Lisieux wrote in her poem *The Sacristans of Carmel* that 'We are also communion hosts, which Jesus wants to change into himself'.

Carmelite Friars, East Finchley, in north London.

Saint Albert's International Centre (CISA) in Rome.

Thérèse truly understood that the Eucharist transforms us, stating in her autobiography, *Story of a Soul*: 'It is not to remain in a golden ciborium that God comes to us *each day* from heaven; it's to find another heaven, infinitely more dear to Him than the first: the heaven of our soul, made to His image, the living temple of the adorable Trinity!'

St. Thérèse (right) as sacristan in Lisieux Carmel, November 1896.

In the Blessed Sacrament we meet Jesus in an intimacy not of this world, and at the same time our eyes are opened to the world around us. Our lives are touched by Jesus in the Eucharist in such a way that:

(Lay) Carmelites are open to a transformation of mind and heart, of their vision and of their actions. Their whole person and existence awaken

to recognition of the caring and merciful action of God in the life of each one. (Lay) Carmelites discover that they are brothers and sisters, called to share a common path towards the fullness of holiness and to bring to all the news that we are children of the one God, brothers and sisters in Jesus. They become enthusiastic about the great works God performs and for which is required their commitment and contribution.
(2003 *Rule for the Third Order of Carmel* §32).

This intimacy and trust of Jesus giving himself to us in the Eucharist is truly awesome, in the proper meaning of that word. It is similar to the awe we might feel at the idea of Christ's Incarnation: heaven comes to earth and God comes to find us. Having found us, God entrusts to us his mission of love. God gives us the Eucharist as the nourishment we need to carry out his/her work.

Carmel: place of heavenly encounters

Elijah, the great Prophet of Carmel, knew how simultaneously comforting and disturbing it could be to enter into an intimate relationship with God. His service of the Lord exhausted Elijah physically and emotionally, but the Lord sent him sustenance on several occasions, all of which have Eucharistic echoes.

Firstly, at the outset of his prophetic ministry, Elijah was told to 'hide by the torrent of Cherith, east of the Jordan. You can drink from the stream, and I have ordered the ravens to bring you food there... the ravens brought him bread in the morning and meat in the evening, and he quenched his thirst at the stream.' (*1 Kings* 17:3-6).

When the stream dried up because of the drought Elijah had called down upon Israel, the prophet was sent by God to a widow in Zarephath (*1 Kings* 7-16). Despite having few resources at her disposal, the widow made them available to Elijah who, by God's power, was able to replenish her jar of meal and jug of oil.

A third occasion on which Elijah was sent food by God occurred after his triumph over the prophets of the false god Baal on Mount Carmel:

> Elijah went a day's journey into the wilderness, and came and sat down under a solitary broom tree. He asked that he might die: 'It is enough; now, O Lord, take away my

The prophet Elijah being fed by ravens depicted in a window by Frances Biggs at the Carmelite chapel at Terenure College, Dublin, Ireland.

A painting in the Carmelite Church at Transpontina in Rome of Elijah's encounter with the widow of Zarephath and her son.

life, for I am no better than my ancestors.' Then he lay down under the broom tree and fell asleep. Suddenly an angel touched him and said to him, 'Get up and eat.' He looked, and there at his head was a cake baked on hot stones, and a jar of water. He ate and drank, and lay down again. The angel of the Lord came a second time, touched him, and said, 'Get up and eat, otherwise the journey will be too much for you.' He got up, and ate and drank; then he went in the strength of that food for forty days and forty nights to Horeb the mount of God.

(*1 Kings* 19:4-8)

This Old Testament story is a 'type' or foreshadowing of the Christian Eucharist. It shows us that those who seek God gain their strength from God himself. The bread of life enables us to journey through the forty days (or life) to reach the mountain of God, and

A window depicting Elijah being comforted by an angel, created by Marc Chagall in the Stephanskirche in the German town of Mainz.

on this journey we will be filled like Elijah with 'a jealous zeal for the Lord God of hosts' to bring others to know his love through our service of them.

Mary: woman of the Eucharist

As with Elijah, Carmelites take inspiration from the Virgin Mary because in her *Fiat* declaration ('Yes, let it be so!') we see her accept the will of God regardless of the unforeseen consequences. In Luke's account of the Gospel we hear that Mary pondered the will of God in her heart, and as Mary's pregnancy progressed her love for Jesus grew. When she visited Elizabeth her cousin, Mary proclaimed her 'Eucharist' or thanksgiving in the *Magnificat*: 'My soul glorifies the Lord, and my spirit rejoices in God my Saviour' (*Luke* 1:46-55). Mary's hymn of praise is entirely focussed on God's work in her ('the Mighty One has done great things for me').

When we attend to the Gospel in Mass or in *Lectio Divina* we hear the words of Jesus. When we receive him in Holy Communion Jesus is silent, but we know from the story of Elijah on Mount Horeb (*1 Kings* 19) that God's presence can be powerfully encountered in silence and stillness. As we receive the Eucharist we become like Mary: the Word becomes flesh within us, he grows within us, we ponder the greatness of God, we are open to his marvellous works, and we sing a hymn of thanksgiving.

Carmelite laity and religious celebrating Mass at the medieval Marian shrine of Our Lady of the Crag in Knaresborough, Yorkshire, England.

Climbing the Mountain: The Carmelite Journey   317

Chapter 13 ■ Carmel and the Eucharist

The saints of Carmel and the Eucharist

We are so lucky to have in Carmel the example of wonderful saints who had great devotion to the Holy Eucharist. This was highlighted for us in 2005 (declared by the Church a special 'Year of the Eucharist') with the publication by the Irish Province of Carmelites of a book about the Eucharist in the Carmelite Tradition called *Hidden Riches*. In one chapter of that book Fr. Míceál O'Neill, O.Carm., describes the Eucharistic devotion of one of Carmel's great mystics, Saint Mary Magdalene de'Pazzi (1566-1607). Sister Mary Magdalene belonged to the community of Carmelite nuns in Florence which she had entered partly because the sisters were able to receive communion every day. She knew that communion was an encounter with the Triune God, saying: 'O sisters! If we would only comprehend the fact that while the Eucharistic species remains within us, Jesus is there working in us inseparably with the Father and the Holy Spirit and therefore the whole Holy Trinity is there.'

Saint Mary Magdalene de'Pazzi receiving Holy Communion, depicted in a window at the Carmelite convent in Boxmeer in The Netherlands.

Through the Eucharist Mary Magdalene de'Pazzi came to enjoy a powerful relationship with the Trinity, which gave her deep peace, captured well in a poem by Míceál O'Neill:

From all time and before the Father looked at the Son
he looked deeply and he loved what he saw.
The Spirit was in the looking and there was peace.

And the Son, the Word of God looked at the Father.
The Word looked deeply and he loved what he saw.
The Spirit was in the looking and there was peace.

In the beginning of time the Father and the Son looked into themselves.
They looked deeply and they loved what they saw,
and the Spirit was in the looking,
and the whole of creation came into being.
In God's own image and likeness it came into being,
and there was peace.

God looked into creation and found Mary.
God looked deeply and loved what he saw.
The Spirit was in the looking,
and the Word became flesh and the Word was peace.

Mary looked at the Word, the issue of her womb.
She looked deeply and she loved what she saw,
and the Spirit was in the looking,
and there was peace.

And Jesus looked at the world.
He looked deeply and he loved what he saw,
and he waits until the world looks back,
and looks deeply and loves what it sees,
and the Spirit is in the looking,
and there is peace.

Did you know? Saint Mary Magdalene de'Pazzi is the patron saint of the Carmelite Third Order. Although not a Lay Carmelite, she was canonised in 1669, a period when the Third Order was being formally organised for the first time.

Fed for service

Carmelites know the importance of living in God's presence (as we reflected in Chapter 9), of communicating with the one true God who makes his home in us. In the Mass God draws close to us in every physical and spiritual sense. It is in this deep intimacy and union with the real presence of the living God that we receive his special gift of healing, forgiveness, and peace. When Jesus comes to us – not hidden in the Holy Eucharist but revealed – we can be sure that his Father and the Holy Spirit are present also. The Trinity will be revealed in the loving actions of our lives as we are sent out from Mass 'to love and serve the Lord'. The Eucharist and service are inseparable.

The Mass gives us the strength to go out and be the body of Christ for others. Jesus' transforming action in our lives means we have a duty to bring the gift of his love to our sisters and brothers, to witness, and to evangelise. Receiving the Eucharist regularly means we are strengthened and able to take Jesus with us in the daily business of life, not so much by our words but by our example. In this way the Eucharist is not for us; it is for the world.

In Carmelite art Bartholomew Fanti is normally depicted in relation to the Eucharist.

Did you know? Blessed Bartholomew Fanti (d. 1495) was a Carmelite renowned for his devotion to the Eucharist. He was a great spiritual teacher and promoted popular devotion to Our Lady. He derived his strength for the active apostolate particularly from Christ in the Eucharist.

In modern society some people think it has become demeaning to 'serve' other people. Carmelites know that to serve others is a duty and an honour, shown to us by Jesus himself. The Holy Father is called to be 'the Servant of the Servants of God'. Saints are people of humility and service.

Did you know? Saint John is the only Evangelist not to include the 'Institution of the Eucharist' in his account of the Gospel; instead, he focuses on Jesus' washing of the disciples' feet at the Last Supper (*John* 13).

How one serves is unique to each individual, and Carmel does not promote one single apostolate but responds to the needs of the Church and the World by reading the signs of the times. As Carmelites, service is an indispensable part of our vocation, and prayer will help us discern how we can best be servants. Many (but not all) friars are called by God not only to the religious life but also to the ordained priesthood, and thus celebrate Mass as one expression of their service. Many Carmelite sisters and

The Carmelite Family: sharing Christ's presence in the Eucharist.

Lay Carmelites are called to Eucharistic ministry as one expression of their service. Anyone who has taken the Eucharistic Lord to the sick, especially if it has been *viaticum* ('food for the journey') will tell you what a humbling experience and an honour it is to bring Jesus to those who hunger and thirst for him.

Those Carmelites who are too old or too ill to undertake active service also have a part to play in the body of Christ. The Eucharist is intimately linked to Christ's sacrifice on the cross and his resurrection from the dead, and those who suffer physically or mentally can identify with Jesus in this way.

Did you know? Images of bread-breaking and Eucharist inspired the names of two Carmelite groups founded in Britain. The Corpus Christi Carmelite Sisters take their name from the Latin for 'the body of Christ'; they have a particular charism to honour the body of Christ by being a prayerful presence in the communities which they serve through various apostolates. The Leaven is a secular institute of single women who by living the Christian life in their own homes are like a leaven or yeast added to dough, unseen but giving life and growth to others.

The Corpus Christi Carmelite Sisters celebrating their centenary in Leicester, England, in 2008.

Community nourished by communion

'The Sacrament of Christ once dead and now risen, the Eucharist is here the sacrament of passing over from death to life, from this world to the Father' (*Catechism* §1524).

Going to Mass unites us with the community of Jesus' followers in every time and place, the living and the dead. For that reason we can feel a bond at every Mass with the first Christian community in Jerusalem that we read of in *The Acts of the Apostles* (2:46). One of the hallmarks of that community was the breaking of bread, and it was the Jerusalem community that Saint Albert had in mind when setting out in his *Rule* how the Carmelites were to live.

The early Christian communities and the letters addressed to them by the Apostles can be a great source of encouragement in our own day. In his 2003 encyclical *Ecclesia de Eucharistia* ('Church of the Eucharist'), Pope John Paul II reminded Christians of the words Saint Paul addressed to the community at Corinth:

> 'The bread which we break, is it not a communion in the body of Christ? Because there is one bread, we who are many are one body, for we all partake of the one bread' (*1 Corinthians* 10:16-17). Saint John Chrysostom's commentary on these words is profound and perceptive: 'For what is the bread? It is the body of Christ. And what do those who receive it become? The Body of Christ – not many bodies but one body. For as bread is completely one, though made up of many grains of wheat ... so too are we mutually joined to one another and together united with Christ.' (§23)

Carmelites have never regarded the Mass as a 'private affair'. Its correct name is the *Liturgy of the Eucharist* and 'liturgy' comes from the Greek word *leitourgia* sometimes translated as 'service' or 'work of the people'. The Mass – like the Divine Office which Carmelites pray – is part of the public and official prayer of the whole Church, gathering together laity and clergy alike. Individual prayer is vital for developing a personal relationship with Christ, but when we celebrate Mass we worship as part of a parish or other religious community.

There are times when we celebrate the Eucharist specifically as a Carmelite community. Carmelites of the Ancient Observance celebrated Mass according to the Rite of the Holy Sepulchre in Jerusalem until around the time of the Second Vatican Council, when it was decided that the Order should participate in the wider liturgical renewal of the Church. However, we still have our own missal and a *Carmelite Supplement to the Breviary* for Carmelite feasts and solemnities, as listed in the *Ordo* (calendar of feasts produced in most provinces).

For many Carmelite communities, particularly of Lay Carmelites, it is not possible to celebrate the Eucharist together as a community on a regular basis, and though desirable it is not essential to do so. Rather, many Lay Carmelites find other ways of being a Eucharistic community when together, as well as bringing the gifts of their Carmelite vocation to celebrations of the Eucharist in their own parish community.

Stop and think: If you are part of a Carmelite community that meets regularly, in what ways are your meetings 'Eucharistic'?

Eucharistic moments outside Mass

Carmelites know from the experience of retreats and community meetings the binding effect of the Divine Office and the Mass. Sharing space and prayer with others unites us. The thread or bond that binds us goes beyond words and thoughts, and it is this 'communion' that permeates all our being, that lives in us, that forms our community and links us all together.

Different branches of the Carmelite Family in Timor Leste (East Timor) sharing their faith in Christ.

It is not only during the Mass that we can share Eucharistic moments. Social time together is an essential element for any Carmelite community, lay or religious, because at such times we feed and nourish each other with friendship and solidarity. The Church is becoming increasingly aware of the importance of Christian fellowship growing together not only at Mass but through small communities. Speaking at a press conference in 2006 to launch a pastoral plan for the Archdiocese of Westminster in London, Cardinal Cormac Murphy-O'Connor remarked: 'It's going to be very difficult for any Christian to really be an active Christian without some kind of community. Not only the Eucharistic community on a Sunday but also some other form of community. That's why the small communities are, I think, essential to the life of the Church.' The Carmelite model of Eucharistic communities is thus a timely one for the body of Christ, the Church.

Carmelite friars and laity know that sharing food and fellowship at social occasions can be Eucharistic moments.

That great Carmelite of Avila, Saint Teresa of Jesus, had great Eucharistic insight, and in developing her monasteries of nuns sought to build intimate communities of friends. Teresa knew that her sisters would draw closer to Jesus as they drew closer to each other. An important word for her was 'companionship'. The word 'companion' literally means 'one with whom you share your bread'. Looked at in this way, there are many occasions when Carmelite companions share Eucharistic moments, not only in Mass but also when we gather for prayer, for discussion and for friendship.

Companions in Carmel: The nuns at Thicket Priory near York, England.

Saint Teresa and the Eucharist

It is worth considering in greater depth what Saint Teresa has to teach us about the Eucharist in the Carmelite tradition, which she helped to shape so powerfully. A Discalced Carmelite friar, Philip McParland, O.C.D., offers the following reflection:

Carmelite, Mystic, Writer, Doctor of the Church, Reformer, Founder, Teacher in the art of prayer – these are just some of the titles attributed to the woman known in her native Spain as *Le Madre* (Mother). When St. Teresa of Avila was discerning whether or not to found a new Carmelite monastery in a new location two criteria were foremost in her mind: would the sisters be able to have daily Mass, and would they have enough means to support themselves. This gives us an insight into the central place the Eucharist had in the life and spirituality of this sixteenth-century saint.

Today in the Church we speak about the four ways Christ is present to us when we celebrate the Eucharist. He is present in the community, in the person of the priest, in the Scriptures and in the bread and wine. While not neglecting the importance of the community, the priest and the Scriptures, St. Teresa's Eucharistic devotion focused mainly on Christ's presence in the bread and wine, which we call the *Blessed Sacrament* and which we believe to be the *Real Presence*. For Teresa the Blessed Sacrament was a wonderful gift, a gift that she personally experienced as a source of strength, a source of healing and a source of intimacy with Christ.

At the beginning of Chapter 34 of her book *The Way of Perfection* Teresa tells us that by the gift of the Blessed Sacrament Jesus remains with us to 'help, encourage and sustain us in doing God's will'. Then later in the same Chapter she says that Jesus has given us 'the manna and nourishment of his humanity that we might find him' and that 'He is teaching us to set our wills on heavenly things'. Teresa was motivated by the will of God; it was the driving force of her life. But she was aware of her own weakness. Left to herself, relying on her own strength, she knew that it was impossible for her to do the will of God, to live like Christ. It was in the bread of the Eucharist, the great source of spiritual nourishment, that she received the strength to be able to do the Lord's will in her daily life and so be conformed to Christ.

St. Teresa was in no doubt that the presence of Christ in the Blessed Sacrament is a powerful source of healing – spiritual healing, emotional healing, even physical healing. On this subject it is best to let her speak for herself:

Do you think this heavenly food fails to provide sustenance even for these bodies, that it is not a great medicine even for bodily ills? I know it is. I know a person with serious illness, who often experiences great pain, who through this bread had them taken away as though by a gesture of the hand and was made completely well. This is a common experience and the illnesses are very recognizable for I don't think they could be feigned ... Now, then, if when Christ went about in the world the mere touch of his robes cured the sick, why doubt, if we have faith, that miracles will be worked while

A sculpture of Saint Teresa in the Spanish town of Alba de Tormes.

he is within us and that he will give what we ask of him, since he is in our house? His Majesty is not accustomed to paying poorly for his lodging if the hospitality is good (*Way of Perfection*, Chapter 34, parts 6 & 8).

St. Teresa's conviction about the Eucharist as a source of healing is confirmed today in places like Lourdes where the daily Blessed Sacrament Procession brings healing in all sorts of ways to many who participate in it.

In Chapter 6 of St. John's Gospel Jesus says: 'Whoever eats my flesh and drinks my blood lives in me and I live in that person. As the living Father sent me and I draw life from the Father, so whoever eats me will draw life from me.' (*John* 6:56-57). This is the way it was for St. Teresa. Receiving Christ in the Eucharist was an experience of union with him. For Teresa the time after Communion was the time *par excellence* to be with her Lord, her friend, her beloved, to experience his presence, to abide in his love, to be intimate with him. St. Teresa had a deep longing to receive Communion; it was the longing of lovers. Because of her great desire to receive Christ in the Eucharist it is not surprising that many of her mystical experiences took place during the time after Communion. In one of these experiences Jesus showed her that the soul is filled with the Godhead, and she heard the words: 'Don't try to hold me within yourself, but try to hold yourself within me.' (*Spiritual Testimonies*, 14).

If the presence and love of Christ in the Blessed Sacrament could be such a powerful source of strength, healing and intimacy for St. Teresa of Ávila, surely it can be the same for us.

Carmel and Eucharistic Adoration

Saint Teresa had a great love for Jesus as she encountered him present in the Blessed Sacrament, and other holy women and men of Carmel have written about the importance of receiving Christ in the Eucharist, including John of the Cross, Thérèse of Lisieux, Edith Stein and Titus Brandsma (who in Dachau concentration camp kept the Blessed Sacrament hidden in his spectacles case). In this the saints of the Order were drawing on the richness of the Church's Eucharistic tradition.

As the theology of the Eucharist developed in the Middle Ages the practice grew of 'reserving' the consecrated host in a *tabernacle* ('tent of meeting') so that *viaticum* ('food for the journey') could be given to the dying. This led to people spending time before Jesus in the Blessed Sacrament, either reserved in the tabernacle or displayed in a *monstrance*. This practice of *Eucharistic Adoration* is common across the Western Church. Our Carmelite charism urges us to pray quietly, to focus our prayer on Jesus, and be open to the action of the Spirit.

For the Carmelite the focus of Eucharistic Adoration is perhaps more about Jesus looking at and speaking to us than it is about our attention to him. In Adoration we can just 'be' in the presence of the Lord. We gaze at Jesus, and Jesus gazes at us. And because Jesus loves us he wishes to answer those prayers we make which are in accordance with the will of his Father. Being in the presence of Jesus in the Eucharist can open our hearts to God's presence in the gift of contemplation, where words are not needed and peace flows. As Brian McKay, O.Carm., states in the book *Hidden Riches* 'the contemplative

A bust of the Servant of God Hermann Cohen in the friary he helped to found at Kensington, London.

is one who desires to rest in the Lord', and in Eucharistic Adoration we have the opportunity to simply 'be' in God's presence and to allow him to do with us what he wills. Sitting before the Blessed Sacrament we can 'ponder on the law of the Lord' as demanded by the Carmelite *Rule* (Chapter 10). In the Eucharist Jesus comes to dwell within the 'cell' of our hearts, if we create space for God (*vacare Deo*).

Did you know? Hermann Cohen (1820-71) converted to Christianity after a mystical experience whilst leading a choir singing at Benediction. He instituted the pious practice of nocturnal adoration of the Blessed Sacrament, and when he became a Discalced Carmelite friar took the name of Augustin-Marie of the Blessed Sacrament. He was instrumental in the foundation of the first Discalced Carmelite community in England, in the London borough of Kensington, in 1862.

For some branches of the Carmelite family, such as the Corpus Christi Carmelite Sisters, worship before the Blessed Sacrament is particularly important. In general, however, the Carmelite approach to the Eucharist is focussed more upon the liturgy, as the Carmelite historian Patrick Thomas McMahon, O.Carm., explains:

> In our Carmelite tradition the emphasis has always been on participating in the Eucharistic liturgy, that is, in the Mass. While Carmelites believe that Christ's presence continues in the Eucharist, reserved after Mass in the tabernacle, Eucharistic worship outside of Mass has never been a central part of Carmelite spirituality. We know that those hermits on Mount Carmel did not go to the chapel and pray to the Blessed Sacrament outside of Mass time. Their *Rule* explicitly commanded them to stay in their cells and to meditate there, in their cell, day and night on the law of the Lord. In Carmelite convents and monasteries in Europe before Vatican II, it was most often impossible for the friars or the cloistered nuns to even see the Blessed Sacrament on the altar of the Church because their choir was most often located

on the far side of a wall behind the altar. Among the Franciscans and the Dominicans the custom arose of communities dedicated to perpetual adoration. But this custom never arose in Carmel, primarily because the Carmelite has always prayed in the solitude of his or her cell and not in the oratory or chapel. Perhaps I should put the idea this way: the principal oratory of the Carmelite is his or her cell, not the community chapel. The Carmelite certainly can participate in all the rites and ceremonies of the Church including Perpetual Adoration. But this devotion is not of itself part of our Carmelite tradition. The Carmelite finds his or her Eucharistic centre to be the celebration of the Eucharistic Liturgy of the Mass. And if called by the Church, one wonderful ministry that the Lay Carmelite can offer his or her parish is to be willing to bring the Eucharist from the Mass to the housebound to enable them to receive the Lord more often. Bringing the Eucharist to the sick we also come to them with the word of God in Sacred Scripture which is another characteristic of our Carmelite life and spirituality.

(Patrick Thomas McMahon, 'Nine Themes in Carmelite Spirituality')

Carmelite friars distributing the Eucharist to pilgrims in Lourdes.

Poems of praise

In whatever way we encounter Jesus in the Eucharist, at the heart of the relationship is a dynamic of love. This love is captured well in a poem composed by Blessed Elizabeth of the Trinity (1880-1906), eighteen months before she entered Carmel:

> I love each day to come
> To hear you, to chat with you, to see you …
>
> I cannot tell all the delights
> Of these conversations alongside the Saviour …
>
> When I hear your voice
> O my spouse, my good Master,
> Who silences all my being,
> I understand and see nothing but you …

With such wonderful words from such noble saints, we are very well informed in Carmel of the transforming power of the Eucharist, which binds us together with God and all God's people.

Conclusion: In this thirteenth chapter we have considered the central place that the Eucharist plays in Carmelite life, primarily through the liturgical celebration of Mass, which brings the community together in prayer and nourishes us for service of others. We have understood the Eucharist as an encounter with Christ in a number of ways, and seen what an important part it has played in the lives of Carmel's saints.

Perhaps conclude your time of prayer and study with a prayer of thanksgiving to God.

In the next chapter we will reflect further on the ways that Carmelite brothers and sisters are brought together in community.

Ideas for Reflection, Discussion and Action

- Take any paragraph above that has captured your attention and reflect on what it means to you, individually and/or as a community. Perhaps discuss it with friends, or at your next community formation meeting. How would you summarise the main points in this chapter if describing it to someone else?

- How much, honestly, do I hunger for God?

- Do I recognise Jesus with the eyes of faith … in the Blessed Sacrament? in the Scriptures? in other people? in myself?

- Do I have a Eucharistic attitude, joyfully accepting God's freely given love?

- How has the Eucharist transformed me in my faith journey thus far?

- Do I feel part of the 'communion' of saints? Who are the 'companions' with whom I share bread?

- What challenges and opportunities does the Eucharistic table present as our Carmelite communities become more engaged in ecumenical dialogue?

- Why is yeast (leaven) added to dough? Reflect on what Jesus said about leaven in the Gospel: *Matthew* 13:33, 16:5-6; *Luke* 13:20-21; *Mark* 8:14-21.

- Try to obtain a copy of the 1987 Danish film *Babette's Feast*. Why do you think this is often called a 'Eucharistic film'?

- Reflecting on your prayer life, how often do you take time to thank God for his blessings to you? Do you take time to thank those who serve you in the community?

- Elijah was brought bread and meat by ravens (*1 Kings* 17:1-6). Read the reflection on the significance of this in Book 1 Chapter 8 of *The Ten Books on the Way of Life and Great Deeds of the Carmelites* (better known as *The Book of the First Monks*).

- If you belong to a Carmelite community, how much time is dedicated to socialising, and how much ought to be?

- How do I go out from Mass 'to love and serve the Lord'? What is the link between the Eucharist and service of others?

- Take time to thank God for his gifts by praying grace before and after meals.

- If you can, try to learn about the diverse liturgies of the Eucharist by attending a Byzantine celebration or other Rite.

Recommended Further Resources

There are many publications on the Eucharist, though only a limited number from a specifically Carmelite perspective.

Eltin Griffin, O.Carm., (ed.), *Hidden Riches: The Eucharist in the Carmelite Tradition*, (Columba Press, 2005).

Penny Hickey, O.C.D.S, *Bread of Heaven: A Treasury of Carmelite Prayers and Devotions on the Eucharist*, (Notre Dame, Indiana: Christian Classics, Ave Maria Press, 2006).

John Paul II, encyclical letters *Ecclesia de Eucharistia* (On the Eucharist & the Church) and *Mane Nobiscum Domine* (Abide with us Lord), available from the official publishers to the Holy See (such as Catholic Truth Society in Britain and Veritas in Ireland), and available online at: www.vatican.va

Patrick Thomas McMahon, O.Carm., 'Nine Themes in Carmelite Spirituality', published in multiple parts in 2009 in *Assumpta* and *Carmel in the World* magazines, and available online at www.carmelite.org

Mount Carmel magazine – Eucharist Issue – Volume 53/2, (April-June 2005).

Christopher O'Donnell, O.Carm., *Ecclesia: A Theological Encyclopedia of the Church*, (Liturgical Press, 1996).

E. Schillebeeckx, O.P., *The Eucharist*, (Sheed and Ward, 1968).

If these are not available in your local Carmelite community library, why not start collecting such resources and promoting their use?

Notes and reflections on Chapter 13

Notes and reflections on Chapter 13

CHAPTER 14

Community

Summary: The concept of community is not an optional aspect of the Carmelite way of life, but central to our charism. In this chapter we will reflect on how community-building has been at the centre of Carmel's rich tradition, look at its present reality, and ponder what role it might play in our future.

Carmelite Spirituality Groups in Britain bring together the Order's religious and laity with a wide variety of other people inspired by Carmel. These photos show the groups meeting with local bishops in York (above) and in London.

Get prepared: As well as gathering whatever resources you might need for study and reflection, such as stationery and Carmelite literature, before you sit down to read this chapter you might want to find out what Carmelite communities exist in your part of the world. There is much to ponder in each chapter, so don't feel you have to read the entire text in one sitting if you find it easier to read just a few pages at a time. If it helps you to remember what you've read, summarise each section of this chapter in your own words, or write down some thoughts and reactions on the blank page at the end. Why not begin this session by offering a prayer for the Carmelite Family:

> *Tender-hearted God,*
> > *renew the gift of the Holy Spirit within the Carmelite Family*
> > *as we seek to live following in the footsteps of Jesus Christ.*
> *Teach us, like Mary, to contemplate your wisdom.*
> *Fill us, like Elijah, with zeal for your glory.*
> *Inspire us, like Simon Stock, to ponder your will in times of change.*
> *Like Teresa, John, Thérèse and Titus,*
> > *may we live always in your presence,*
> > *and make us prophets of your Kingdom.*
> *May our lives of prayer, community, and service*
> > *be a sign to the world that God lives,*
> > *in whose presence we stand.*
> *This grace we ask in Jesus' name. Amen.*

Community is essential to Carmel

In earlier chapters we have seen that the notion of community has been central to the Carmelite way of life ever since the first hermits gathered together on Mount Carmel around the year 1200. The *Rule* which those hermits asked Saint Albert of Jerusalem to approve set out how the Carmelite brothers were to live together as solitaries brought into community.

In a much more recent document, the *Rule for the Third Order of Carmel* (*RTOC*) promulgated in 2003, we find at the very beginning the notion of Carmelites sharing their lives as friends of one another, and friends of God:

> In Jesus Christ, born of Mary, the invisible God speaks to all people as
> a friend and he dwells amongst them to bring them into communion
> with God and with one another with a view to the unity of the human
> race in the Kingdom. (§1)

God wants us to live in communion with one another, as this provides a foretaste of the heavenly Kingdom where we will all be united in the love of God. God's Kingdom is for everyone and not just for a few special people. The way God's Kingdom will be built up here on earth is through us living in communion with God and with one another. Living with a sense of community is *the* way to unite the whole of humanity.

Of course living in harmony with our sisters and brothers is not easy. It is a challenge that we always strive to respond to with love and commitment. To help us in our commitment, it is common in the Church and in the Order today to formulate a 'vision statement', that is, a shared declaration of how we seek to live as Carmelites.

Commitment to community

For example, the Third Order in the British Province of Carmelites formulated a vision statement in 2002 to help progress the reforms and renewals which it experienced in the 1990s. The document begins: 'We are a lay Carmelite community embracing all who have discerned a vocation to follow in the footsteps of Jesus Christ according to the Carmelite charism ... United with Mary and Elijah we are joined to one another as a spiritual family ... As family we offer experiences of prayer, community and service to people of all ages, all denominations and all walks of life'. In 2007 the Third Order in Britain renewed its vision statement, making the following statements about how it wanted to develop a sense of community within Lay Carmel:

> The Third Order and the Carmelite charism are not just for ourselves and our personal holiness. We are – through being 'love in the heart of the Church' – here for the world which God loves so much (cf. *RTOC* 28) ... We want to share with people an authentic experience of God. We will seek a deeper relationship with God, the friend who loves us, through prayer alone and with others ... We wish to become more inclusive, sharing life's journey with people of all walks of life. Our organisation must help us live the Carmelite charism; supporting structures must be ordered towards our mission to the world by building God's Kingdom. We need to remember the elderly, housebound, sick, and our 'distance' members. We seek to include those with (sometimes unseen) disabilities or specific needs, embracing the gifts they can bring to Carmel. The Order is international as well as local, regional and provincial; globalisation offers opportunities as well as challenges ... God wishes us to communicate. We seek to deepen the quality and effectiveness of communication between ourselves, as individuals, communities, and as a Province. Communication is a means of reaching out to the world.

Such bold resolutions make it very clear that the Carmelite Order offers to us a much deeper sense of community than any other Church organisation or group we might belong to, and in return demands from us a deep commitment to that community. Our Carmelite community stretches back over the centuries to the spiritual tradition of Elijah and Mary. It includes the great saints of Carmel: Simon Stock, Albert of Trapani, Nuno of Saint-Mary, John Soreth, Frances d'Amboise, Teresa of Jesus, John of the Cross, Mary Magdalene de'Pazzi, Angelo Paoli, Thérèse of Lisieux, Isidore Bakanja, Elizabeth of the Trinity, Titus Brandsma, Edith Stein, George Preca and all those who are living a Carmelite life today as friars, hermits, cloistered nuns, apostolic sisters, members of secular institutes, tertiaries, and through many other ways of living. In our own provinces and worldwide we form a *community of communities*.

Stop and think: Outside of any Carmelite community you might belong to, what other communities are you a member of? How is the Carmelite Family similar to them, and different?

Did you know? The Carmelite Family in Trapani, Sicily, is very much at the heart of the local community. The statue of Our Lady of Trapani is housed in the Carmelite church. In March 2006 she was declared patron of the local Diocese, and Saint Albert of Trapani – an early Carmelite saint – was made secondary patron.

La Madonna di Trapani (Our Lady of Trapani).

Holiness is not a personal possession but a gift for the community

As we read in Chapter 2 God's *call to holiness* is universal, for the whole of humanity. We often speak of holiness as a personal quality, but really it must be understood in the context of the wider community. As a Carmelite, my commitment to Carmel, my relationship with God in prayer, and my faithfulness in living the *Rule of Saint Albert* are not for myself alone, for my own personal sanctification. Saint Thérèse understood that a Carmelite vocation has a community dimension when she declared that her mission was to be *love in the heart of the Church*. To be a Carmelite is to be in communion with others – to *be* community.

Also Carmelites who live on their own as 'distance members' or as solitaries do not exist in isolation, but form an integral (if sometimes hidden) part of the wider community that is the Carmelite family. Actions that they undertake on their own have an effect in the wider Carmelite community. At times the community needs to act together, for example in the matter of formation. Formation in the Carmelite tradition is not a matter of individuals setting out on a private journey of conversion; growing in the Carmelite way of life requires a commitment from the wider community, a pilgrimage up Carmel towards God and with God, discovering God's loving presence both within myself and in others.

The Community of the Church

The Carmelite vision of community as a communion of united people mirrors the Second Vatican Council's vision of Church. The Church too is unlike any other organisation we may subscribe to, because *we are the Church*. The Council document on the nature of the Church, *Lumen Gentium* (Light of the Nations), published in 1964 reminds us that through baptism we are a special community, the people of God: 'The Church is in Christ like a sacrament or as a sign and instrument both of a very closely knit union with God and of the unity of the whole human race' (§1). This means that our life in God, in the Church, and in Carmel must be lived in communion with others. Whatever we do for God is for the community, and vice versa.

The community animated by Albert's *Rule*

Vatican II stressed that the Church is made up of all God's people, not only the senior levels of the hierarchy. This resonates with the democratic Carmelite model of community set out in the *Rule of Saint Albert* (printed at the front of this book). In this way of life document Saint Albert describes a community of hermit brothers who live, work and

All inspired by the *Rule of Saint Albert*: different members of the Carmelite Family gathered at Aylesford Priory for the Annual General Meeting of the British Province in 2006.

pray together as equals. They elect a prior (not an abbot) from among themselves, who is to consult the community and act in its name. In this sharing community all opinions are heard, responsibilities are shared, and the prior strives to work by consensus. As we read in Chapter 4: 'Carmelite communities are meant to be communities of friends who are friends with Jesus Christ. Distinctions which create divisions or hierarchies, whether secular or religious are to be vigorously shunned.' In this way those Carmelites who are ordained, or who are elected to positions of leadership, never stop being members of the community themselves.

Stop and reread: You might find it helpful – either now or later – to revisit what was said about the Carmelite notion of community in the *Rule of Saint Albert* as described in Chapter 7 of this book.

In Carmel we must learn to cooperate, collaborate, and consult one another. That doesn't mean that in order to build community we have to wait for someone else to act or to tell us what to do. At our baptism we were commissioned to build community as part of our mission as prophets, priests and kings. In our Profession as Carmelites we re-affirm this vocation. John Welch, O.Carm., tells us in his reflection *The Carmelite Tradition* that this is the supreme privilege of being loved by God. Knowing God's love brings with it an awesome responsibility to love and serve others in our communities, our families and the Church.

Did you know? As a *community of communities* the Carmelite Family and other religious orders are often in a good position to send aid quickly to parts of the world suffering from war or natural disaster. Having a presence in every continent on the planet means that usually the Carmelite Family is able to act in swift solidarity.

Walking in the footsteps of Jesus: the community of the disciples

As always Jesus of Nazareth is the foremost model of how Carmelites should live out their vocation. To understand what living in community meant for Jesus we need to read and listen to the Gospel accounts, pondering God's word as the Virgin Mary did.

Jesus was born into a community. Our impressions of life in the Holy Land in the first century A.D. are often influenced by beautiful Renaissance paintings, yet such images are often a far cry from the reality of what life must have been like. It is more than likely that the house of Mary and Joseph in Nazareth was similar to a *riyadh*, the type of dwelling used even today by many people in the Mediterranean region and North Africa. These are large houses with inner courtyards and balconies in which whole extended families share a communal life. Historians and Bible archaeologists have suggested that the stable in Bethlehem where Jesus was born might have been the outhouse of such a dwelling, and that the inn was probably a communal family home. Even today Bethlehem is a small town, and if Joseph was returning to the home of his ancestors to register he is likely to have been staying among his wider family rather than with total strangers.

Jesus spent the early years of his life on earth living in the communities of family, town, and synagogue. After his baptism and temptation in the desert Jesus' first action was to call together a community of disciples (followers) who would accompany him as he preached the Good News of God's Kingdom. We know from reading the Gospel accounts that the disciple community included more than the twelve Apostles who were named, and most certainly incorporated Jesus' mother Mary and other women. It was a diverse group of women and men from very different social backgrounds who in other circumstances would have been unlikely to meet, let alone live in community. Why did Jesus gather them together? So that they could support and challenge each other.

Carmelites gathered as a community around Mary. Many ancient Carmelite paintings such as this show Our Lady at the heart of Carmelite community life.

The challenges of community living

This first community of Christ-followers spent three years in Jesus' company, listening to his preaching and learning about who he was. But they sometimes failed to understand him, had doubts, asked questions and made mistakes. Living in a community is a challenge because it asks us to move beyond our own prejudices and our own needs, inviting us to respond generously to the needs of others, and to share one another's giftedness.

As we read the Gospel accounts we get hints of some of the difficulties, arguments and misunderstandings that must have occurred between the disciples, and we can try to imagine the efforts needed to reach an agreement. Even those gathered around Jesus found it hard to live in a community, so we should not be surprised when it poses a challenge to us.

As we read the four accounts of the Gospel it helps to remember that they were written with communities in mind. The Evangelists set down the Good News of Jesus so as to help the communities founded after Pentecost to recall and reflect on the life of Christ. Likewise many of the letters in the New Testament are addressed to communities, such as the churches in Rome, Corinth, and Ephesus. Many of the Scriptures were written to help struggling communities make sense of all that had happened to Jesus and his followers, and to address tensions within groups of people striving to follow *The Way*. Learning a little about these communities – especially in the writings of Matthew, Mark and Luke – can help to bring the Gospel to life for us and help us understand better the Good News.

According to ancient tradition, in her later years Our Lady lived with Saint John in this house near Ephesus (in modern-day Turkey).

Did you know? The Province of the Most Pure Heart of Mary (PCM) in America has created *virtual lay Carmelite communities* for prisoners. Inmates are kept in touch through newsletters and visits from Carmelite tertiaries. Saint John of the Cross spent time in a Carmelite prison.

The early Christian community

At the beginning of the *Acts of the Apostles*, Saint Luke describes the community of Jesus' followers waiting in an upper room in Jerusalem with Mary and the Apostles for the coming of the Holy Spirit at Pentecost. This community has always inspired the Carmelite notion of brotherhood and sisterhood, and is a model of prayer for us:

The apostles ... were constantly devoting themselves to prayer together with certain women, including Mary the mother of Jesus, as well as his brothers. (*Acts* 1:14)

These people had taken to heart what Jesus taught about praying in community:

Truly I tell you, if two of you agree on earth about anything you ask, it will be done for you by my Father in heaven. For where two or three are gathered in my name, I am there among them. (*Matthew* 18:19-20).

Since the first gathering of Jesus' followers in Jerusalem, Christian prayer has had both a communal and individual dimension. Likewise Carmelite prayer is both personal and public. As we learnt in the previous chapter, the Eucharist and Divine Office are at the

Pentecost depicted in the 'Reconstructed Carmelite Missal' now in the British Library, Ms. Additional 29704-5 folio 27v (detail).

heart of Carmelite life and are part of the liturgical prayer of the universal Church which gathers us into the body of Christ. As Carmelites we pray not only as individuals, but as a community.

In the *Acts* account we learn that after Mary, her relatives, and the Apostles received the Holy Spirit at Pentecost, many people were attracted to join the early Church. The description of the Jerusalem community has inspired Carmelites in every age:

> All who believed were together and had all things in common; they would sell their possessions and goods and distribute the proceeds to all, as any had need. Day by day, as they spent much time together in the temple, they broke bread at home and ate their food with glad and generous hearts, praising God and having the goodwill of all the people. And day by day the Lord added to their community ... (*Acts* 2:44-47).

Like these early Christians, Carmelites should strive to pray 'with one heart', united in person with our Carmelite sisters and brothers when we can, but always united in spirit with them even when we pray alone. Like the Jerusalem Christians we should also 'break bread' together, that is celebrate the Eucharist as the sacrament which unites us as a community and with the whole Church. And we should share what resources we have and contribute to the common good whenever we can, gladly and generously, praising God always.

When we compare the description of the community of the first Christians in the *Acts of the Apostles* with the ideal of community expressed by Saint Albert in his *Rule* (Chapters 10-15), we can see a number of similarities.

The first Christian community in *Acts of the Apostles*	The first Carmelite community in the *Rule of Saint Albert*
• Prayed regularly (*Acts* 2:42; 4:24)	• Personal prayer and vigilance (*Rule* 10)
• Went regularly to the Temple (*Acts* 2:46-47)	• Prayed the Liturgy in common (*Rule* 11)
• Held everything in common (*Acts* 2:42, 44; 4:32, 34-35)	• Put goods to common use (*Rule* 12 & 13)
• Broke the bread in their houses (*Acts* 2:42, 46)	• Celebrated Mass daily (*Rule* 14)
• Were united, heart and soul (*Acts* 4:32; 1:14)	• Reviewed the state of community (*Rule* 15)

The points that determined the communal life of the first Christians also formed the basis of community as it should be lived by the Carmelites.

Stop and ponder: How are these points of the Christian life in *The Acts of the Apostles* and the Carmelite life in *The Rule of Saint Albert* lived by Carmelite communities you know today?

The community of Mount Carmel

In Chapter 8 on the history of the Carmelite Family we learned how the first Carmelites lived on Mount Carmel as hermits following the tradition of the *Brotherhood* or *Company of the Prophets* (the community of Elijah's followers gathered around Elisha in *2 Kings* 2:7).

The hermits lived in both solitude and community, and recognised that there would be a creative tension in this way of life. The call to be in God's presence on one's own in the cell, but also to live in God's presence in community with other Carmelites, would prove to be a demanding challenge to which there were no easy answers. We experience this tension when we find it hard to live with others. Like those early Carmelites we have to work constantly, striving to achieve a unity that will be amazingly creative. This is the wonder and challenge of being truly Carmelite. It is the challenge of actually living the Gospel, of bringing about the Good News by the very way that I choose to live.

The connection between Mount Carmel and Elijah encourages us to reflect on the life of the Old Testament prophet whom we generally think of as a powerful yet solitary figure. Does Elijah

A window depicting Elisha (Eliseus) at Saint Albert's International Centre (CISA) in Rome.

have anything to say to us about community? Perhaps we might reflect on Elijah's encounter with the widow of Zarephath: the story of the miracle of flour and oil, and later the raising of the widow's son (*1 Kings* 17:8-24). Here was a very small community – just Elijah, the widow and her son – but prayer, faith, generosity, sharing and praise of God are all evident. Carmelite communities do not have to be big for God to work miracles in them.

At one point in his service of God Elijah felt that he was the last of the chosen people in all Israel, declaring '*I alone am left!*' (*1 Kings* 19:14). But God told Elijah that he had

This Carmelite painting depicts Elijah receiving his 'vision of Mary' in the little cloud rising from the sea. Behind him the community of his Carmelite 'descendants' are constructing the oratory on Mount Carmel in her honour.

preserved seven thousand Israelites who had remained faithful (*1 Kings* 19:18), and that Elijah should pass on his prophetic vocation to Elisha. At times we may feel alone in our Carmelite life, but God maintains our communities.

Trust in God's providential care was surely vital to the hermits on Mount Carmel who received their *Way of Life* from Albert, the Latin Patriarch in Jerusalem, sometime between 1206 and 1214. The hermits would no doubt have heard the stories of Elijah contained in the Scriptures and reflected on them. They believed themselves to be the successors of Elijah and Elisha's *company of prophets*. Living in the land of Jesus' ministry they modelled themselves on the early Christian Church and had a sense of responsibility for one another which Albert's *Way of Life* document developed further. In the *Way of Life* Albert tells the Carmelites about the importance of relationships, especially with their leader – the prior – whose ministry is of service to his brothers as a brother. The *Way of Life* document that became known as the *Rule of Saint Albert* reminds the Carmelites to celebrate Eucharist together each day when possible, to gather regularly so as to correct and encourage one another, to pray and to eat together, and to share what they have in common.

Refresh your memory: At some point you might like to go back to previous chapters and refresh your memory of the early hermits as discussed in Chapters 6 (Elijah), 7 (the Rule of Saint Albert) and 8 (Carmelite history).

Ceramic by Adam Kossowski depicting Saint Albert at Aylesford Priory in Kent, England.

Communities gathered around Mary

The first Carmelites on Mount Carmel were gathered – like the Church at Pentecost – in the presence of Mary, the *Lady of the Place*, and they dedicated their chapel to her. As first among her son's followers Mary lived her life in the community, and plays a unique role in the community of faith, the Church. To this day Mary is the maternal heart of the Order, gathering her brothers and sisters together into community. A medieval Carmelite legend illustrates this beautifully. It is said that in one of the Order's priories Our Lady would appear when the friars sung the *Salve Regina*. One day a novice entered the community with such a beautiful voice that the brothers agreed it would sound much nicer if he intoned the *Salve Regina* on his own. Much to the friars' consternation Our Lady stopped appearing during the *Salve*, and in their distress they prayed to her for an explanation. Our Lady duly appeared saying that she would always come when she heard her brothers at prayer together, but she had not been able to hear them singing; even if the sound was not as superficially 'beautiful' as the novice's solo voice, it was their singing together *as a community* that attracted her presence.

Communities 'in the midst of the people'

When the hermits became friars, from the mid-thirteenth century onwards, they located themselves in the heart of Europe's towns and cities. The Whitefriars felt called to be with God's people and formed communities within communities. Our Carmelite tradition speaks of the friars being 'in the midst of the people', but this is also true of apostolic women religious, and even (to some extent and in a distinct way) the enclosed nuns. It is certainly true of lay Carmelites, whose life 'lived in the world in the midst of the people, is dedicated to the cares and tasks of the world in the ordinary ups and downs of family and of society' (*RTOC* §28). Indeed, there are some places and communities that lay Carmelites have better access to than the Order's religious.

Lay members of the Carmelite Order are encouraged to live out their vocation not simply in imitation of religious communities, but truly 'in the midst of the people', in the world that God loves so much 'that he gave his only Son, so that everyone who believes in him may not perish but may have eternal life.' (*John* 3:16). The 2003 *Rule for the Third Order of Carmel* makes a strong case for lay Carmelites to build up community within the world around them.

> All Carmelites are in the world in some way, but the vocation of lay people is precisely to transform the secular world. So Tertiaries, in as much as they are committed lay people, have this secular characteristic by which they are called to treat the things of the world correctly and to order them according to God's will. Their life, lived in the world in the midst of the people, is dedicated to the cares and tasks of the world, in the ordinary ups and downs of family and of society. Tertiaries are invited by God to contribute to the holiness of the world: they are to have the spirit of the gospel in their work and to be guided by Carmelite spirituality. It is their calling to illuminate and order the world's activities so that these may be carried out according to Christ's intention and be a source of praise to the glory of the creator. (§28)

Today many Carmelite friars, sisters, and increasingly lay people, have a mission to build-up local communities through ministries in parishes and chaplaincies, bringing to those places something distinctly Carmelite: a hunger for knowledge and love of God, a contemplative attitude that seeks God's presence in all aspects of life.

Community presence in the mendicant tradition: University chaplaincy is an important and exciting ministry for many Carmelite provinces.

As the Order develops and adapts itself in every age, it responds to 'the signs of the times' whilst maintaining what is essential to the Carmelite tradition. Community is essential to Carmel in every age, but exactly how community is formed will adapt and

Paintings – of Our Lady of Mount Carmel and the Carmelite Family – at the Carmelite Centre in the parish of Calle Real, El Salvador.

develop according to present circumstances. Carmelite history shows us that there are times when one community or group moves in a particular direction which is resisted by other communities. Reform movements within the Order show that sometimes communities are willing to progress together, and on other occasions will splinter into differing groups. This is where the discernment of the community is so important, as Saint Albert highlighted at the very end of his *Rule*.

We can't be certain how Carmelite communities – religious and lay – will develop in the future. We can, though, be certain that by living in the presence of God – like the early Christians and the early Carmelites – we can confidently place the future in God's hands. The Apostles did not claim that the early Church grew because of their amazing preaching; they knew that it was the Lord who added to their numbers, because the Apostles cooperated with God. God has the future of the Church, of Carmel, and of our communities in his hands. We have no need to be anxious, only to give our open hands and hearts to God for him to use. Cultivating a spirit of *vacare Deo* (trust in and openness to God) will help our communities to flourish, according to God's will.

Did you know? Carmelites in Latin America are involved in pioneering new forms of community based on the Carmelite *Rule*. For example in the Brazilian city of Curitiba,

Community solidarity: Carmelite friars from the British Province visiting an orphanage in El Salvador in 2006.

the Order has formed a community for recovering drug-addicts who have been rejected by their families. This community follows the *Rule of Saint Albert*, and is dedicated to *Lectio Divina* as a way of inviting God to transform their lives. In the parish of Calle Real in El Salvador, Carmelite friars and lay people have built a community of prayer and social solidarity, supporting projects which develop farming, literacy, HIV-AIDS treatment and prevention, orphanages, and many other forms of outreach.

Who makes-up my community?

Carmelites undertake the journey to God not just as individuals but also as members of a community. We are not alone, whether we are lay Carmelites or religious. We may belong to a number of communities: a church parish, a workplace, a club, a family (the one we grew up in or the one we have helped to create through marriage or friendship), or a local community of the town or village where we live.

The religious of the Carmelite Order – the friars, the enclosed nuns, the apostolic sisters and the hermits – usually live in a very obvious form of community, namely a priory or monastery building. Some of these communities may be quite large; others consist of no more than two or three people. Generally their shared lives are given shape by common meals, common prayer times, and common recreation. For lay Carmelites the situation is normally quite different. Though some members of the Third Order Secular live in some form of community building, the vast majority live in their own homes, sometimes as single people or residing with others. Their lives may be full of 'community moments' at home, at work, at church, and so on. However, lay Carmelites are also called to share community *as Carmelites*.

Stop and think: How can lay Carmelites share a sense of community when most lay members of the Order live quite separate lives?

Probably the most important way in which lay Carmelites share community is by attending regular community meetings of Third Order Chapters, Carmelite Spirituality Groups, and so on. These meetings, usually monthly or more often, offer lay Carmelites a vital moment of contact with fellow Carmelites. These meetings consist of prayer (normally some form of liturgical prayer, silent meditation, and *Lectio Divina*), formation in the Carmelite tradition, and social time together. Such meetings may only last a few hours, but in that short time the Holy Spirit can be powerfully at work building communion. In addition to lay Carmelite community meetings, members of the Third Order (and similar groups such as Secular Institutes) can build up community at regional, national and international levels by participating in retreats and gatherings, study days and pilgrimages, social events and study courses.

Communities need communication

We are so fortunate that in today's globalised and technological world it is also possible to build community through various means of communication. Communication is a crucial part of building community. Being in contact with each other lets everyone know how and what we are thinking or doing. Communication might be anything from a smile and a nod, to a message sent using the latest technology.

The Vice Prior General of the Order, Christian Körner, O.Carm., launching in June 2009 the revised website of the British Province of Carmelites: www.carmelite.org

Even those of us who don't have the opportunity to attend regional, national or international gatherings of the Carmelite Family can still communicate with one another through our discussions, business meetings, telephone-calls, e-mails, and newsletters. Many provinces of the Order worldwide produce newsletters and magazines for friars and for members of the Third Order (such as *Assumpta* in Britain, *The Vine* in Australia, and *Carmel in the World* internationally). Websites, blogs and discussion groups can be great tools for sharing Carmelite spirituality and supporting one another in our vocations, as can news services such as CITOC (the Order's central news service).

As well as keeping in touch with one another we have a responsibility as Christians to share the Good News with others. Sometimes this evangelisation may be by personal contact with people we meet but we can also make use of other opportunities such as items in the media and on the internet to spread the message of Carmel.

Did you know? In 2006 an international gathering of lay Carmelites took place at Sassone near Rome. Its theme was *Formation and Communication at the Service of the Community*, and the various presentations and discussions were printed as a book by Edizioni Carmelitane (the Order's central publishing house) in 2007.

Membership of the Carmelite community from a distance
In many parts of the world members of the Third Order cannot actively take part in community meetings because of distance, illness or old age. These 'distance members' are still very much part of the Carmelite Family, and as a family we have a duty of care to maintain community with them through communication networks and prayer. If

Carmelite publications, particularly the official proceedings of conferences, are an excellent source of material for initial and ongoing formation.

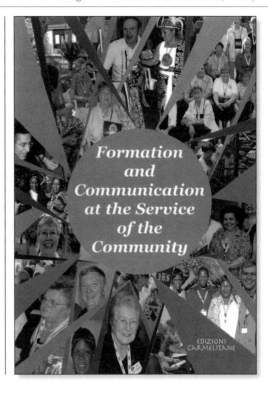

Formation and Communication at the Service of the Community

EDIZIONI CARMELITANE

people are received into the Third Order as distance members, it is especially important that ways are found to offer them some experience of Carmelite community. Without support and commitment it is very difficult for such people to receive authentic formation in the Carmelite way of life. It is also necessary for distance members to be in regular contact with the Order as a whole, since admission to the Order is not an individual's choice but is the decision of the community.

It is very important for Carmelites – both lay and religious – to support the common life of their community, contributing their time, energy, insights and experiences for the benefit of all. We all have a responsibility to be committed to our local Carmelite community. At the same time, however, it is crucial to remember that Carmelites belong primarily not to any one community but to the Order as a whole. When a Carmelite makes their profession, he or she makes a promise or vow not to an individual community but to the wider community of the Order.

Structures can help hold communities together

The *Rule of Saint Albert* is a vision for how Carmelites should live together in community, but it is the shortest of all religious rules and therefore needs elaboration in every age. All organisations – including the Church – need to have agreed ways of doing things otherwise we would have chaos; formal structures help hold our communities in place. Just imagine a river without banks or a body without a skeleton! Similarly, the Carmelites agree on *Constitutions* and *Statutes* that set out how the *Rule of Saint Albert* will be put into practice by communities today. Both religious and lay communities have *Constitutions* and *Statutes*. *Constitutions* teach us about the history and development of the Order, and articulate how Carmelite spirituality can be lived in the present day. We may not always be aware of the *Statutes* but they are referred to at times such as chapter elections to ensure that community-life and the law of the Church (Canon Law) are respected. Clear guidelines and structures established by the community allow us to get on with our Carmelite lives, which is the most important thing. An image sometimes used of such structures is a plant growing on a trellis or frame; the trellis is there to help the plant which would grow too large and collapse without support. The trellis therefore needs to be big enough to support the plant. However, if the trellis is too big then the plant will simply be dwarfed and we lose sight of the fact that it is the plant, not the trellis, that is important. Moderation and community discretion are key aspects in living the Carmelite life, as Saint Albert pointed out in the *Rule*.

Did you know? Medieval legal records inform us that forming Carmelite communities is not always easy! In the 1400s there were various cases of parents who said that their sons had been 'kidnapped' into becoming friars, and writs issued for friars who had run away from their communities!

Modern windows in the Karmeliterkloster (Carmelite friary) in the German city of Mainz depict medieval Whitefriars engaged in the tasks of daily community life.

Pioneering new forms of community

Discerning together the forms our communities should take is always a challenge facing the Order. Right from the origins of our family on Mount Carmel, it seems that we have pioneered new ways of bringing together the followers of Christ, always looking to the early Jerusalem Church as our model but developing fresh expressions. The first hermits on Carmel wanted to be rooted in the Church, but not follow the *Ways of Life* already existing within the Church. When the hermits became mendicants, the way of living together in community changed again. When Teresa of Jesus reformed the Order some centuries later, new models of community again emerged. Having lived in a very large community of *beatae* (consecrated women), Teresa wanted to form smaller and more intimate communities where 'all must be friends, all must be loved, all must be held dear, all must be helped.'

One model of community that we think of as modern but is in fact ancient is of Carmelite religious and laity living and working side-by-side. In the Middle Ages it was common for members of Carmelite confraternities – forerunners of the Third Order – to live close to communities of Whitefriars. We know that in Florence, for example, some lay people gave all their goods to the *Carmine* (the Carmelite friary) in exchange for being cared for the rest of their days and sharing with the community a life of prayer and service. In the twentieth century this model was revived when the *Carmine* stood almost empty, prompting lay Carmelites and friars to begin a project known as *La Famiglia* ('The

Family'). The friary is now home to many families – children, parents and grandparents – who live and pray with the friars, going out to ordinary jobs and schools. *La Famiglia* has brought new life to the cloisters of Carmel.

The famous Brancacci Chapel in the Florence *Carmine* contains some of the greatest frescos of Renaissance art, as well as a much-loved icon of 'La Madonna del Populo' (Our Lady of the People).

The idea of lay people living alongside Carmelite religious has also inspired a number of retirement and nursing homes across the world, such as *Carmelite Carefree Village* in the Illinois town of Darien in the United States.

The chapel at Carmelite Carefree Village in Darien, Illinois.

The most famous community in the British Province of Carmelites, Aylesford Priory, is also a place where different vocations within the Carmelite Family live together. At various times since its restoration in 1949, 'The Friars' has housed not only friars of the Order but also apostolic sisters, members of the *Donum Dei* Missionary Family, members of the Third Order, and Carmelite Solitaries.

Left: The Gatehouse at Aylesford has housed various different types of Carmelite over the years. Right: Outside the Gatehouse, Carmelite friars in conversation with a Carmelite Solitary.

Carmelites in the Dutch Province are also at the forefront of experimenting with new models of community. There are a number of women in The Netherlands who live as friars in community with men and who are in ministry alongside them. In Holland there is also a project known as *Karmelbeweging* (Carmelite Movement) which offers a community experience to those on the margins of the Church. *Karmelbeweging* was founded by lay Carmelites inspired by the *Rule of Saint Albert* and supported by the Dutch friars. In 1995 it was recognised as a new form of lay Carmelite organisation with its own articles of association. As one of its early members observed: 'Carmel in the Netherlands was growing, but not in a traditional or uniform way, but as one house with different rooms, as one tree with different growing branches, where people could grow in their own ways whilst nourished by the same source, namely the love of a God who invites us to live with a contemplative attitude in a secular context.'

It is this contemplative attitude lived in a largely secular society that informs the spirituality of new lay Carmelite groups in Ireland and Britain. In Dublin, the *Carmelite Explorers* group is pioneering a new form of community for lay people attracted to Carmel. In Britain *Carmelite Spirituality Groups* began to develop in the first decade of the twenty-first century as a way of offering an experience of 'Carmel' in a contemporary and inclusive way. These groups are convened by professed members of the Third Order and follow the Third Order's formation programme, but are open to anyone interested in the Carmelite way of life, not simply those seeking to make formal profession of promises. Carmelite Spirituality Groups are open to all enquirers, including different expressions of the Carmelite charism, and Christians of churches other than the Roman

Catholic Church who respect the Catholic ethos of the community. Many Carmelite Chapters of the Third Order in Britain are also open to enquirers from a wide variety of backgrounds, and are adopting the Spirituality Group meeting format, which puts a lot of emphasis upon formation, silent prayer and *Lectio Divina*, social time, and a varied and 'holistic' programme of events that address a wide range of life issues from a Carmelite perspective.

In 2009 the Carmelite Third Order Chapter in the northern English city of Leeds re-launched itself as a Carmelite Spirituality Group, finding a new way to form community.

Building community that is truly Carmelite

Whatever form a community takes, it is bound together by sharing a common story, a shared goal, and collective interests. Opinions and lifestyles will always vary within a group, but the more that its members subscribe to and share a common ideal the stronger the community will be. That is why the *Rule of Saint Albert* is so fundamental to all branches of the Carmelite Family, and why groupings within the Order compile common vision statements, and commit to shared projects and apostolates.

As the Order develops we need to ensure that a Carmelite group is not just *any* community but that it is authentically Carmelite in its life and vision. As it was put in Chapter 12, we need to put on *Carmel's attitudes*. There are many people who think they know what Carmelite spirituality is all about, but who actually promote a caricature of Carmel. They have perhaps read an inaccurate history of the Order, or read quotations from the saints of the Order out of context, or maybe they received a poor formation in Carmelite spirituality that was itself not truly rooted in the tradition. It is therefore imperative for the survival of the Carmelite Order that its members listen to authentic retellings of our 'family story', that they immerse themselves in the rich wisdom of

Carmel and reject superficial readings of our heritage. It is this concern for an *authentic* Carmelite spirituality that prompted the following observation of Patrick Thomas McMahon, O.Carm., a former Provincial Delegate to the Carmelite Tertiaries in one of the American Provinces of the Order:

> I am very concerned about the rapid growth of lay Carmel. Recently one of my Discalced Carmelite confreres said: 'The good news is that we are growing very fast and the bad news is that we are growing very fast'. We are growing faster perhaps than we can shape lay Carmel in harmony with the larger Order. We do not want ideas and practices that are not consistent with our 800 year-old tradition to worm their way into Carmel. We want to work together to keep that tradition pure so that Carmel can continue to offer the Church what it has always offered, a spirituality of following Jesus Christ in solitude and silence, in charity for our neighbour, and nourished by contemplative prayer and the support of our brothers and sisters. I know that this concern is shared by all the friars of both observances, the O.Carms and the Discalced. I have not only studied the traditions extensively, and not only do I teach the tradition to our students in formation as well as sabbatical students, but I spend a great amount of time working with the friars and nuns of the Discalced observance as we work together to preserve and propagate this tradition. Carmel is not 'make it up as you go along'. Carmel is a well defined spiritual tradition in the Church, and we must work to keep it pure and authentic. If it does not speak to you, do not try to change it, but leave it and find a group of Catholics who better reflect where the Holy Spirit is leading you. If this sounds blunt, know that it is the same advice I would give a vocation to the friars or the nuns who want to make Carmel over into something different than it has been for its eight centuries. We come to Carmel to be shaped by it, not to shape it into something of our own liking. Carmel has proved itself to be of great value to the Church through these eight centuries. We have provided three Doctors of the Church: Teresa, John of the Cross, and now, Thérèse of the Child Jesus. We have provided countless saints and blesseds. Pope John Paul II canonized and beatified many saints from our family: Blessed Titus Brandsma, Saint Edith Stein, Saint Raphael Kalinowski, Saint Teresa of the Andes, Blessed Elizabeth of the Trinity, the Martyrs of Compiègne, Blessed Isidore Bakanja, and others. Pope Benedict is continuing the flood of Carmelites being raised to the altars. I could go on and on and on. The Carmelite path is tried and true. Carmel is giving you the call, 'Come and follow Jesus Christ with us'. Turn to Teresa and John, Thérèse and Edith and Titus to learn what it means to be a disciple of Jesus Christ. You don't need to be a priest or a friar or a nun. You don't need to wear a habit or a veil. You don't need to live in a monastery. You don't need anything but to follow Jesus Christ

like those first hermits on Mount Carmel eight centuries ago, like
the great saints of the Order, like the thousands of men and women
around the world today who live a life of allegiance to Jesus Christ.
(*Nine Themes in Carmelite Spirituality*)

Carmelites acquire an authentic understanding of the Order's tradition and spirituality
through a process of formation. For an individual, the process of formation in the
Carmelite tradition is rarely easy, because it requires of us a willingness to change, an
openness to growth. The journey of formation is a journey of transformation, and it is a
journey with highs and lows. It is no wonder then that formation undertaken by a group,
by a community, is also a challenge. Like individuals, communities engaged in the process
of formation need hope and the courage to take risks, to do things differently, and to be
different. That is why Carmelite formation and discernment should normally happen in
the context of a community. To receive the tradition in a genuine manner enquirers need
experienced Carmelites to inform, guide and correct them. The collective wisdom of the
community can help to correct private errors. The community is there to help us discern
our vocation; we need to ask whether we feel 'at home' in the Carmelite community, and
whether others feel we have a place with them. We do not simply decide that we are
going to make profession as a Carmelite; we rely on the experience and recognition of
the community which has formed us.

Stop and reflect: Does Fr. McMahon's assessment of the rapid growth of lay Carmel
ring true for you? If you are a member of a Carmelite community, how conscious is that
community of being *authentically* Carmelite, in the true tradition of the Order? To what
extent do you feel 'at home' with your community? How have you been challenged by the
community, or challenged others?

The common goal of Carmelite communities: Contemplation

So what is the hallmark by which we judge whether our communities are authentically
Carmelite? Our goal as Carmelite communities is always to form true disciples of Jesus,
contemplatives who seek to know and love God, and to make God known and loved.
Our threefold charism of prayer, community-living and service holds in balance a tension
that finds its meaning in contemplation. Through prayer we discover God in our lives. At
first we may need the words of formal prayers to nurture our relationship with God, but
as this friendship deepens we become aware of a loving Presence in our lives that does
not require our words or religious structures. It is the recognition of this loving Presence
within myself which enables me to recognise it in others in the community and which
leads me to service or ministry as I seek to share that love with others. So the tension
between prayer, community and service actually creates an integrated whole; the three
aspects of Carmelite life become one. We will return to this idea shortly when we shall
reflect on the Trinity as a community of love.

As our Carmelite lives deepen through authentic formation, our communities will
begin to take on the characteristics that come from contemplation: we will be more
open and trusting, reflecting our confidence and trust in the presence and love of God in
good times and bad. As John Welch, O.Carm., reflected in the text of Chapter 4, prayer

that is open to God's gift of contemplation results in a renewed appreciation of those with whom we live and serve. We begin to see others through God's eyes and learn to appreciate and value what had previously gone unnoticed. We begin to see everyone as loved and equal. It is then that our relationships with others become true friendships, no longer self-centred but always wanting the best for the other.

Nurturing community: caring for God's garden

It is through the fruits of contemplation that authentic community is created. It is clearly God's work, not yours or mine, but that does not mean that we do not have responsibilities and work to do. Our task is to cooperate with God's grace, freely given. Teresa of Jesus and John of the Cross used analogies to help us understand grace, that is, God's work in us: images of water, castles and gardens. A garden is a very Carmelite metaphor. The Hebrew word כַּרְמֶל (Karmel) actually means *orchard*, *vineyard* or *garden*. Gardens – and communities – don't just grow; they require people to put in a lot of hard work preparing the ground, planting seeds, and tending them as they flourish. Like gardens our communities need to be cared for if they are to bear fruit, and we can all play a part. We each have different gifts, so while not everyone is called to be a community leader or councillor, each of us in our own way can share and give of ourselves by showing patience,

Pilgrims in God's garden of Carmel: participants at the 2006 International Lay Carmelite Congress in Sassone near Rome.

tolerance, and generosity. In her *Story of a Soul*, Saint Thérèse of Lisieux described herself as the smallest and least significant flower in God's garden, but loved and nurtured by God all the same. The *Little Flower* could only grow into a great saint because she was planted in the fertile soil of a community which constantly nurtured and challenged her, watered and pruned her. My Carmelite community, then, should be a place where I can grow as a person, which helps me on my spiritual journey to God and where I help others. It is a place where we should be able to journey together, supporting and helping one another, building an oasis in the desert.

The way we tend each other in the garden of Carmel affects how we grow. Listening to one another is especially important for Carmelites. We model ourselves on Mary who listened to and responded to the God who speaks (as we reflected in Chapter 10). Listening may not only apply to words spoken aloud; sometimes people find it difficult to express themselves and we must learn to 'listen' to other ways of communicating such as through body language. Building up a Carmelite community requires us to develop our relationship skills, and many Carmelite communities in recent years, lay and religious, have benefitted from professional workshops developing their awareness of group dynamics and faith-sharing in groups.

There are times too when Carmelite community life develops very easily; we can rest, feel at home, be playful, and enjoy God's garden. Rowan Williams (the Archbishop of Canterbury who is an expert on Teresa of Jesus) spoke about contemplative prayer as 'sunbathing in God's presence'. Poet Roy Campbell, paraphrasing John of the Cross' poem *The Dark Night*, expresses this beautifully: *From all endeavour ceasing, and all my cares releasing, threw them among the lilies there to fade.*

Communities that nurture humanity

Sadly Carmelite communities are sometimes thought of in the public imagination as overly ascetic places, lacking humour and humanity. Even if Teresa of Jesus had to teach the Discalced friars how to recreate together, such a caricature is not a true reflection of the Carmelite tradition, which basks in the joy of the Good News. The saints of Carmel have always grasped the importance of our communities having time to relax and enjoy each other's company in a human way, just as Jesus did. Sharing a meal, chatting over a drink, laughing together and being sociable are all parts of the human development that is so crucial to spiritual formation. If communities cannot enable their members to share together times of joy and laughter, then it is unlikely that they will be able to help individuals during their *dark nights* and the difficult times in life.

Building a sense of community among Carmelites is not an activity restricted to formal meetings of the community. We are invited to build the bonds of Carmel outside of the meeting room or chapel; in our homes, shopping centres, workplaces, art galleries, cinemas, gardens, wherever! For Carmelite religious most community-building is not done in the chapel or meeting room but in the ordinary trials and joys of living with other people, and this is an area where lay Carmelites have much to contribute to each other. They are encouraged by the words of the 2003 *Rule for the Third Order of Carmel*:

The communal life of lay Carmelites must shine with simplicity and authenticity. Every group must be a family in which everyone feels at home, welcomed, known, appreciated, encouraged on the path they are following and possibly even corrected with charity and kindness. Lay Carmelites commit themselves to co-operating with other members of the Carmelite family and with the whole Church so that it may realise its calling to be missionary in every circumstance and situation. (§43)

Valuing difference and diversity

One of the difficulties of community-life is that we are challenged by the people we meet. We may not always feel comfortable with the brothers and sisters around us. We may not share the same opinions. We may feel judged, or find ourselves judging others. We may suspect that it would feel more comfortable being in a community of like-minded people. We may even dislike people in our community. However, like the communities in the Gospel, we will most likely find that Carmelite groups have – and should have – a diverse membership in terms of gender, age, lifestyle, race, opinions, abilities and background. Diversity need not result in division. With diversity comes the potential for misunderstanding; we cannot assume that others think as we do. But with diversity also comes the potential for richness; an invitation to go out from ourselves to encounter others and to have a wider experience of God who is alive in all those present.

Teresa of Jesus reminds us that Carmelite communities are meant to be gatherings of friends who are friends with Jesus Christ. That does not mean that we will always agree with one another! It's sometimes said 'When you get two Carmelites there will be three opinions!' So long as I respect other people the best contribution I can make to my community is by my open and honest expression of my personality coupled with an openness to be changed. The strongest Carmelite communities are places where differences can be discussed honestly, and where people are willing to be transformed as well as to transform others. If agreement cannot be reached then at least a respectful understanding of the other's point of view can arise. In a world torn apart because fundamentalists of various religions would rather resort to violence than to dialogue, Carmelites have a real contribution to make. We can show that people can live together in mutual respect and love, despite our differences and failings. What matters is not being like-minded, but like-hearted.

Carmelite communities strive for 'unity in diversity'. A rainbow is made of many colours; each one is distinct, but all are united in the one rainbow. If the colours were simply merged we would be deprived of the rainbow's beauty. There is beauty to be found in difference.

In his book *What is the Point of Being a Christian?* the Dominican Timothy Radcliffe says that friendship can cope with anger and even grow through it. He quotes the poet William Blake:

> *I was angry with my friend;*
> *I told my wrath, my wrath did end.*
> *I was angry with my foe:*
> *I told it not, my wrath did grow.*

Radcliffe goes on to say: 'The Church is the community of those who have accepted Jesus' call to friendship, and so we ought to be able to face anger without fear. It is not a sign of disloyalty or the breaking of solidarity. Indeed, one of the roles of those who exercise leadership … should be to encourage those who are angry with them to dare to express it, confident that this will strengthen the communion of the Church. It should be a place where we learn to be angry not blindly but gently and with hope … There is a difference between hopeful anger – which believes that things need not be as they are and will struggle to ensure that they are not – and just moaning.'

Different moments in the life of Titus Brandsma.

Did you know? The Carmelite martyr Titus Brandsma formed and was formed by a variety of communities: family, parish, Carmelite Order, university colleagues and students, newspaper staff, and concentration camp.

Reaching out to the wider community

When Carmelites meet in community we pray together but we are not a 'prayer group' or pious sodality. Authentic Carmelite communities try to be of service to the Church and to society in a variety of ways, but we are not an apostolate like the Saint Vincent de Paul Society. Our vocation is different. We are called to prayer, to community, and to service; they are part of what we *are*, not what we *do*.

Carmelite communities, and not just individual Carmelites, are called to serve others. The Kingdom of God is for everyone, and we are asked to share with others the love that God has revealed to us in Jesus; we witness to this as a community, and not only as individuals. Often a community is better able to witness more powerfully to the binding love of God than one individual; it is remarkable how many of Carmel's martyrs have died as a community (such as the nuns of Compiègne, the martyrs of the Spanish civil war, and – according to ancient legend – some of the hermits on Mount Carmel).

It takes faith and courage to risk giving to others in service a share of the love we have received. What if we don't get it back? God is never outdone in generosity, and if we take God at his word and give generously – casting our bread upon the waters (*Ecclesiastes* 11:1) – we will receive a hundredfold in return. Parents of large families can assure us of this: rather than having to share a finite amount of love between their children so each receives an equal portion, something wonderful happens; there is a doubling or trebling of the love for each child, whose love for each other also grows. Jesus told us to be generous with love:

Give, and it will be given to you. A good measure, pressed down, shaken together, running over, will be put into your lap; for the measure you give will be the measure you get back.' (*Luke* 6:38).

The Trinity: a community of love

Blessed Elizabeth of the Trinity (1880-1906) pondered the mystery that God is in fact a community; three persons in one God united by love. She knew that the community of the Trinity finds its home within someone who has simplified life to the extent that they live only in the present moment of what is important: 'the soul thus simplified, unified, becomes the throne of the holy Trinity'. Sister Elizabeth sensed that she had to enter into the life of the Trinity, and she hungered for unification; all things coming together in God.

Comm-*unity* requires just that: *unity*. Unity reflects the action of God. As the Jesuit Gerald O'Mahony observes: 'Wherever unity is found the Trinity is found: in atoms, in electrons, in the movement of the stars, in animals, in families, in the unity which is a live human body, in the one world we live in' (*A Way in to the Trinity*, 2004). Thus, whenever we truly live in community we are, in some mysterious way, reflecting the life of the Trinity.

Elizabeth Catez (Bl. Elizabeth of the Trinity) aged 21, shortly before her entry into Carmel.

St. Andrei Rublev's beautiful icon (c.1410) of Abraham offering hospitality to angels at Mamre, is often interpreted as representing the Trinity.

You may know Andrei Rublev's icon of the three angels (*Hospitality at the Oak of Mamre*) which is often interpreted as representing the Trinity. The story (*Genesis* 18) tells how Abraham and Sarah gave hospitality to three strangers and later discovered that they had welcomed angels. As we gaze at the icon we become aware of the unity and perfection of the circle made up of the three figures representing the unity and perfection in love of the Trinity. We also see the space in front of the table with the figures pointing to where we are invited to sit.

It is the Trinity that transforms us and our communities. As a result our Carmelite communities can be blessings for the Church and the wider world. Wherever we go in our daily life we go as Carmelites, as part of an international community. We might well find that as Carmelites we are energised and able to contribute to other ministries in the Church or Society, but a particular ministry of the Carmelites is to share with the world our charism of prayer, community, and service. The world desperately needs to learn how to pray, and in this Carmelites can share their insights. The world desperately needs people willing to serve those on the margins of society, and in this Carmelites can share their presence. And the world desperately needs people who authentically build up community; in this, too, Carmelites can share their experience.

Conclusion: In this fourteenth chapter we have considered how and why Carmelites have formed communities over the centuries. The form of community life has varied in different times and places, but always before Carmelites is the vision of the *Rule of Saint Albert*, itself derived from the Christian community in Jerusalem.

If you wish to conclude your time of reflection and study with a moment of prayer, one suggestion might be to ponder the description of the Jerusalem Church in *Acts* and pray that Carmelite communities today be faithful to the Order's charism through prayer and service. You might also like to consider doing some small act of service that will build up your local community.

In the next chapter we will develop further the notion of community, looking at how Carmelites understand themselves as belonging to a family within the communion of saints.

Ideas for Reflection, Discussion and Action

- Take any paragraph or image that has captured your attention in this chapter and reflect on what it means to you, individually and/or as a community. Discussion with friends, or with a Carmelite community, might help you to appreciate matters more deeply.

- Who are my community? Think of the various communities you are part of.

- 'Who is my neighbour?' When a lawyer asked Jesus this question (*Luke* 10:29), Jesus responded by telling him the parable of the 'Good Samaritan'. What can this parable teach us about our communities and our identity as Carmelite Christians? Compare *Luke* 10:35 with the last chapter of the *Rule of Saint Albert*.

- Do we first encounter God in prayer, or does love of others first point us to God?

- What helps me feel part of my Carmelite community?

- What priority do I give to the Carmelite community I belong to?

- What gifts do others in the community have? How are these shared? Think of one thing you can do to nurture your community.

- Is there anything that makes me feel uncomfortable in my community? Can I speak about it? Why is that? What helps?

- Look back over earlier chapters (especially 4, 6, 7 & 8) and recall what they said about community.

- Think of one way in which you can communicate what it means to be Carmelite with another person inside or outside your community.

- Which Carmelite publications or news-services do you have access to? Is there anything that your community or other groups within the Order could provide to help you know more about the Carmelite Family?

- What should be the key features of a Carmelite community meeting?

- What sense do you have of being part of a 'community of communities'?

Recommended Further Resources

Since the Second Vatican Council the Carmelite Order has dedicated considerable energy to reflecting upon the role of community in the Carmelite charism. Most of the following resources are available in Carmelite libraries and bookshops.

Joseph Chalmers, O.Carm., 'A contemplative community in the midst of the people', in *In Allegiance to Jesus Christ*, (Rome: Edizioni Carmelitane, 1999), pp. 45-51.

Mark Davis, *Walking on the Shore: A Way of Sharing Faith in Groups*, (Matthew James Publishing, 2002). This is an excellent guide to how our communities can develop as places where people feel able and willing to share their faith experiences.

Keith J. Egan, T.O.C., 'The Solitude of Carmelite Prayer', in Keith J. Egan, T.O.C., *Carmelite Prayer: A Tradition for the 21ˢᵗ Century*, (New York: Paulist Press, 2003), pp. 38-62.

International Congress of Lay Carmelites, *Formation and Communication at the Service of the Community*, Proceedings of the Congress at Sassone, September 2006, (Rome: Edizioni Carmelitane, 2007).

John of the Cross, *The Poems of St. John of the Cross*, (trans.) Roy Campbell, (Harvill Press, 2000).

Patrick Thomas McMahon, O.Carm., 'Nine Themes in Carmelite Spirituality', published in multiple parts in 2009 in *Assumpta* and *Carmel in the World* magazines, and available online at www.carmelite.org

Gerald O'Mahoney, S.J., *A Way in to the Trinity*, (Leominster: Gracewing, 2004).

Timothy Radcliffe, O.P., *What is the Point of Being a Christian?* (Burns & Oates, 2005).

John Welch, O.Carm., 'The Carmelite Tradition' in *Journeying with Carmel: Extracts from the 1995 Constitutions*, (Melbourne: Carmelite Communications, 1997).

A practical contribution you might like to make to your Carmelite community is to purchase one of the resources above and to donate it to your group's library for all to use.

Notes and reflections on Chapter 14

Notes and reflections on Chapter 14

CHAPTER 15

The Carmelite Family and the Communion of Saints

Summary: In this chapter we continue looking at the notion of community in the wider context of how the Carmelite Family is part of the communion of saints. We will consider what – or who – makes a saint, their role within the Church, the ways by which the Church recognises holiness, and the characteristic spirituality of saints within the Carmelite Family. Within this context we shall reflect on the role of asceticism in the Carmelite way of life.

A painting of the holy women and men of Carmel at the Carmelite Centre in Calle Real, El Salvador.

Get prepared: This chapter ends with a blank page for you to write down your own thoughts, reactions or questions, so you might want some writing implements to hand. Your reading – which can be done in stages rather than all at once – might be supported by having reference books to hand, such as the Scriptures and the major documents of the Order. The phrase 'the Communion of Saints' is found in the Creed, so why not begin your time of study and reflection with a profession of faith, and/or the following prayer calling upon the intercession of Carmel's saints:

> *Holy men and women of Carmel,*
> *you found in the Carmelite Family a school of prayer,*
> *a community ready to serve others,*
> *and sure companions for your pilgrimage through life.*
> *From your place at the summit of Mount Carmel,*
> *Jesus Christ, help us to walk steadily in his footsteps,*
> *that our prayers and good works may further the mission of his Church. Amen.*

The Carmelite Family is part of the Communion of Saints

This chapter deals with the idea of saintliness and sainthood in the Carmelite Family. Before considering what a saint is, we need to define what we understand by *Carmelite Family*, a term that has come into widespread use in recent decades to cover all the different ways in which people are linked formally or informally to the Carmelite and Discalced Carmelite Orders.

To understand the term *Carmelite Family* it helps to know some of the older terminology that has been used to distinguish different vocations within Carmel. It was the Servite Order which originally categorised its members into various branches of *first*, *second* and *third* orders. The numbering of these branches is not meant to be hierarchical, but simply reflects the historical sequence in which each group was formalised.

Within a religious congregation the term *first order* refers to the male religious: hermits and friars, ordained or unordained, who have publically professed vows.

The *second order* refers to the enclosed nuns. It was commonly said that these women had 'left the world', though this language is now seen by many nuns as not entirely accurate because they are very much concerned with praying for the Church and Society at large. Although the sisters largely remain within the monastery enclosure, most communities of Carmelite nuns are in contact with 'the world' in various ways.

The *third order* in fact has two branches: the *third order regular*, which refers to active religious (such as sisters living the apostolic life out and about 'in the world'); and the *third order secular* which refers to formally professed members, mostly lay people, also living 'in the world'. The term *regular* comes from the Latin meaning 'following a rule of life', and the term *secular* derived from the Latin for 'world', means 'living in the world'. However, the terminology can be a little confusing because members of the Third Order Regular usually live active lives 'in the world', and members of the Third Order Secular follow a rule of life. The distinctions are not always precise! In some more modern religious congregations there are lay affiliates or associates but they are not normally full 'members' of the Order, unlike Tertiary/Secular Carmelites who are fully professed members of Carmel.

Laity and religious: all members of the one Carmelite Family.

Carmelites agree that whether people are in the first, second, or third orders, they are all fully members of the Order. All have received formation, and all make some form of profession, that is, a public statement of Carmelite identity and commitment.

Stop and think: Are these terms new to you? Do you find them helpful or not?

The wider Carmelite Family

Within the Carmelite Family there is also a wide range of lay people who are linked to the Order in some way less formally than in the Third Order. For instance, there are people who wear the Carmelite Brown Scapular, or who attend Carmelite parishes and feel some affinity with the Order, or who are attracted to one of Carmel's saints, but who do not profess promises or vows. These are less formal bonds with the Carmelite Order than profession, but they are bonds nevertheless, and such persons are usually referred to as the 'wider Carmelite Family'.

In the Ancient Observance of the Carmelite Order (O.Carm.), the term 'Lay Carmelites' usually refers to the members of the Third Order Secular (also referred to as *Secular Carmelites*, or *Tertiaries*) who have formally made profession. However, 'Lay Carmel' is also used by the Ancient Observance as a catchall term that incorporates the laity of the wider Carmelite Family, such as the Brown Scapular Confraternity and members of Secular Institutes (a formal belonging to the Order distinct from, but similar to, the Third Order). The term 'Lay Carmel' is also problematic when describing the

Different ways of life, but all Carmelites. A meeting in 2008 of students and tutors of the Carmelite Institute of Britain & Ireland (CIBI), a joint initiative of the Carmelite Family that offers distance-learning courses in Carmelite spirituality.

Secular/Third Orders because there are a number of ordained ministers (deacons, priests, and bishops) who are not lay people but who are professed members of the Secular/Third Orders. In the Teresian or Discalced Carmelite Order (O.C.D.), the term 'Lay Carmelite' is usually more restricted to only professed members of the 'Secular Order' (a term used by them in preference to 'Third Order'). In the Ancient Observance the abbreviation 'T.O.C.' refers to 'Third Order Carmelite'. In the Discalced tradition the abbreviation 'O.C.D.S.' refers to the 'Secular Order of Discalced Carmelites'.

All members of the one Carmelite Family

In 1983 the General Chapter of the Carmelite Order elected an American friar, John Malley, O.Carm., as Prior General. One of the values that he emphasised during his twelve years in office was the concept of being a *Carmelite Family*, with communication and cooperation between different branches of the Order at provincial and international level. The notion of Carmel as a family was an ancient one, but thanks to Fr. Malley's influence some of the barriers that had existed between laity and religious began to come down. The idea spread that whatever branch of the Order someone belonged to – 'Ancient' or 'Discalced', 'religious' or 'lay' – all were equally 'Carmelite' in their identity, rights and responsibilities. Members of the Third Order were invited to take a full part in commissions, projects and ministries of the Order. Instead of the laity simply 'learning Carmelite spirituality from the religious', it was acknowledged that friars, nuns and sisters could also grow in their appreciation of Carmel by meeting with and learning from lay Carmelites. The increased appreciation of the lay vocation was helped by the Second Vatican Council's teaching on the call to holiness all people receive.

Another important aspect of the growing sense of *Carmelite Family* was the increased contact between Carmelites of the Ancient Observance and those of the Teresian Discalced reform. Although there had always been contact between the O.Carm. friars and the O.C.D. friars over the centuries, the relationship had sometimes been strained,

Fr. John Malley, O.Carm., speaking at the 2006 International Lay Carmelite Congress in Rome.

and there was virtually no contact between members of the Third Order (T.O.C.) and the Secular Order (O.C.D.S.) at any official level. In the 1990s this began to change, with regular meetings taking place between John Malley and his Discalced counterpart Camilo Maccise. Under them the term *Carmelite Family* also came to incorporate new expressions of the Carmelite way of life, such as the Carmelites of Mary Immaculate (a distinct congregation, mostly based in India).

Stop for a moment: Has the information above clarified terminology for you? Are you more confused than before?! The important things to remember are that all professed Carmelites – lay and religious – are full members of the Order, and that there are other less formal ways of belonging to the wider 'family' of Carmel.

Having clarified what we mean by the *Carmelite Family*, let's consider how our family fits within the broader communion of saints.

What is a saint?

The word 'saint' comes from the Latin *sanctus* meaning 'holy'. As we learnt early in this programme of formation, all people are called to holiness. The *universal call to holiness* means we are each invited to take part in the life of God, and so when we speak of 'the saints' we mean not only those Christians before us who led exemplary lives of holiness but ourselves as well. Together all Christians living and dead make up the *communion of saints*, a phrase we use in the *Apostles' Creed*. As the 1992 *Catechism* states: 'The communion of saints is the Church' (§946), and Carmel is very much at the heart of the Church.

Saints of Carmel painted by Marelli Servino and hanging at the National Shrine of St. Thérèse at Darien, Illinois, U.S.A. (left-right): Albert of Sicily, Andrew Corsini, Thérèse, Mary Magdalene de'Pazzi, (Christ and Mary), Brocard, John of the Cross, Teresa of Jesus, Peter Thomas.

Saints are people transformed

In the Catholic and other Christian traditions saints are holy people whom we hold in esteem as people transformed by God. Saints are people who took to heart the words of our teacher and model Saint Paul:

> I appeal to you, brothers and sisters, by the mercies of God, to present your bodies as a living sacrifice, holy and acceptable to God, which is your spiritual worship. Do not be conformed to this world, but be transformed by the renewing of your minds, so that you may discern what is the will of God – what is good and acceptable and perfect. (*Romans* 12:1-2).

Saints are people who open their minds and hearts to God, practicing what Carmelites call *vacare Deo* or *space for God*. They are people who recognise that they have been created, redeemed and sanctified by God: Father, Son and Holy Spirit. Saints are not 'perfect' people, but people who try daily to reject false idols and deepen their relationship with God and with those around them. They are ordinary people who have made the extraordinary journey to discover that God lives deep inside them.

Saints are people reborn

Saints are people who live fully their baptismal calling. As John Dalrymple puts it in *Simple Prayer*, 'Baptism does not call us to a second-class, run-of-the-mill kind of Christianity with options later – should we feel like it – to turn into the first-class variety which we call holiness. Baptism calls us to the occupation of a saint.' As members of the Carmelite Order we have deepened our baptismal commitment by following a religious profession. According to the *Rule for the Third Order of Carmel* (*RTOC*): 'By means of profession the Tertiaries seek to strengthen their baptismal promises to love God more than anything else and to renounce Satan and all temptation' (§12).

Stop and think: How is your Carmelite identity linked to your calling as a baptised Christian?

Carmelites imitate the early Christian community

By profession we Carmelites undertake to live in the spirit of the early Christians, and that means loving each other and praying for each other. Saint Paul wrote to the Ephesians that they should pray all the time for the saints (*Ephesians* 6:18). Who are these saints? According to his *Letter to the Colossians*:

> You are God's chosen ones, his saints. He loves you and you should be clothed with compassion, kindness, humility, meekness, and patience. Bear with one another and, if anyone has a complaint against another, forgive each other; just as the Lord has forgiven you, so you also must forgive. Above all, clothe yourselves with love, which binds everything together in perfect harmony. (*Colossians* 3:12-14)

As Carmelites we wear the Brown Scapular which should be a daily reminder to us that we are God's saints, his chosen ones, who must clothe ourselves with love.

Carmel – receiving and giving grace

It is important to remember when discussing the community of saints that sanctification is God's work of transformation in us. Carmel's great insight is that God is the first-mover in all things. We are invited to cooperate with God by developing a contemplative attitude. The Carmelite recognises that our response to God, essential as this is, is not our own work but only possible because of God's grace at work within us. In proclaiming this we Carmelites can seem counter-cultural, even in the Church, since so many Christians seem to think that we can 'earn' our salvation by what we do rather than recognising God's free gift to us in Jesus. Here we can share Elijah's prophetic voice to tell the world that all are loved deeply and freely by God, who calls us into the desert-oasis of love.

Elijah's ascent to Paradise, depicted in a manuscript at the Carmelite friary in Straubing, Germany.

Stop and think: In what ways do you proclaim God's love to those around you? What methods of evangelisation are most effective?

Saints are united to God and to us

The person whose heart is open to God is gradually transformed over the course of their life to such as extent that they are 'filled with the utter fullness of God' (*Ephesians* 3:19). This process is sometimes called *divinisation* and through it we become united more and more closely to God. God grows in us and we grow in God to such an extent that a distinction is hard to make. As St. John put it:

> Beloved, we are God's children now; what we will be has not yet been revealed. What we do know is this: when he is revealed, we will be like him, for we will see him as he is. (*1 John* 3:2)

The place where St. Teresa was born is now a chapel within the church dedicated to her and cared for by the Discalced Carmelite friars in Avila, Spain.

Holy women and men begin to see God as God really is. They become absorbed into the life of God and their will conforms entirely with God's will. They also begin to see and love the world and those in it as God sees and loves: creatively. This is why Carmelites rarely speak these days of 'leaving the world'. All Carmelites are at the service of the world and love the world God loves. The great Carmelite reformers Teresa of Jesus (of Avila) and John of the Cross were great experts in the matter of *divinisation*, describing the process as like moving through a series of mansions to the heart of an *Interior Castle* where the Master

(Christ) lives. They realised that the union of the Christian pilgrim and God is never fully complete in this life, but that after death holy people become utterly united with God. In this life we can begin to 'practice the presence of God' (as discussed in Chapter 9) but after death we will know ourselves to be in God's presence for all time. Since people who have died are united with God, and since God himself – in Jesus – experienced new life after death, Christians believe that death does not entirely separate the living and the dead.

The idea of intercession
This is why Catholics and many other Christians ask for the prayers of those who have died. When

In Carmelite art (such as this window at the Ermitage in Lisieux) St. Thérèse is often shown giving a 'shower of roses' to depict the graces God bestows through her intercession.

we face a problem we may ask our friends, our family, or our church to remember us in their prayers. We ask them to *intercede* for us with God, to ask the Lord for whatever grace or blessing we may need. It is an ancient Christian belief that we can ask the dead to do the same, and we can also pray for them. Since we believe that after death holy men and women are united to God in a special way and are more fully alive than ever, we ask them to pray and intercede for us. We may do this through hymns, novenas (9 days of prayer), the rosary, or other forms of prayer. The Carmelite nun St. Thérèse of Lisieux famously said (in her *Last Conversations*) 'I want to spend my heaven in doing good on earth'.

Reflect for a moment: Have you experienced any instances of prayer being answered through the intercession of a saint? Do you intercede for other people in prayer?

The saints inspire us

The other great role of the saints in the Church is to inspire us, to give those of us still living on earth an example of how to lead a life that is open to God. As the *Eucharistic Preface for Holy Men and Women* has it: the saints inspire us by their heroic lives so that we can be the living sign of God's saving power. From reading their writings or by studying their lives we can learn how better to love God and our neighbours as ourselves. They are great witnesses to the Gospel – the Good News – of Jesus.

Stop and reflect: In your experience are the saints easy models of holiness for us to emulate? Are they people you can relate to and identify with?

Saints point us to Christ

The saints point us to the Good News of Jesus Christ and acclaim Jesus in his humanity and his divinity as the supreme revelation of God. The saints should never be a distraction from Jesus who is the supreme example of how to be holy, and any devotion to saints that is not ultimately *Christocentric* (leading to and focussed on Christ) should be avoided by the Carmelite. There is a difference between the worship

The oldest known icon of *Christ Pantocrator* dates from the 6th century and is venerated at Saint Catherine's Monastery in Sinai. The Greek term 'Pantocrator' is commonly translated as 'almighty', and depictions of Christ under this title show him as both a gentle human, and a divine judge.

and adoration given to God alone (known in theology as *latreia*) and the honour and worshipful reverence given to saints (*dulia*). No devotion, no saint's autobiography is ever more important than the Word of God as revealed in the Scriptures. Whilst asking the saints to intercede for us is an important part of the Christian life, seeking their prayers is never a substitute for developing our own personal relationship with Jesus Christ, the 'one mediator between God and humankind' (*1 Timothy* 2:5).

Mary - first of all the saints

Mary, Our Blessed Lady, is the greatest example of a saint who directs us to Christ. When people came seeking her advice at the wedding in Cana, she pointed to her son and spoke her last recorded words in John's account of the Gospel: 'Do whatever he tells you' (*John* 2:5). When she was asked to be the mother of Jesus, God accorded Miriam (the Hebrew for Mary) a special and unique honour among all the saints. Nevertheless, she is holy not simply because she gave life to Jesus, but because she 'heard the word of God and obeyed it' (*Luke* 11:28).

A fresco of the Annunciation at the ancient Carmelite church of San Felice del Benaco in northern Italy.

In Chapter 5 we read about why Mary is regarded as the first of all the saints. She was the woman of faith, hope, and love who gave herself entirely over to the will of God. In the Carmelite tradition we revere her as mother, sister, patron, queen, beauty of Carmel, and woman of pure heart (*puritas cordis*). At the end of Carmelite celebrations of the liturgy (such as the Eucharist and Divine Office) it is traditional to say or sing a hymn in honour of Mary. We are members of her Order, and strive to live with her *in allegiance to Jesus Christ* (*Rule of Saint Albert*, chapter 2).

In previous centuries devotion to Mary was sometimes promoted more than meditation of her son, which she would never wish. A popular nineteenth-century phrase was: *Through* Mary to Jesus. Today we are more conscious of her as a companion and guide, and so we travel *With* Mary to Jesus. In recent decades there has been a shift in theological understanding regarding saints. We still revere them, and speak of 'raising them to the altars'. However, we are much more aware now that holiness is not a hierarchy; we too are called to holiness, we too are invited to be saints here and now, praying for others and giving witness to the Gospel through our lives of prayer, community, and service. If we elevate the saints, it is not to keep them distant from us but to give us a height to aspire to on our journey up the mountain that is Christ.

Stop and think: Of all Mary's titles, particularly in the Carmelite tradition, which one appeals to you most and why?

The Coronation of Mary, first among the company of saints, depicted in the Carmelite Missal used in medieval London (British Library Ms. Additional 29704-5 folio 152v, detail).

Elijah – model for Carmelites

In Carmel we are blessed with other great saints who have 'ascended the mountain' before us, who have undertaken the journey of transformation, and whom we can imitate. Alongside Mary, Carmelites give special honour to Elijah (Elias) the prophet of Carmel, whose story we find in the Bible's *Books of the Kings*. As we read in Chapter 6 Elijah spoke in the name of the Lord to denounce the people's worship of false idols and to call them back to their God. Almost 3,000 years ago, in a materialistic and self-centred society, Elijah lived according to God's values. This is exactly what we are called to do. We can be glad that we have Elijah to guide us on our way in this world where false gods abound. The Carmelite Family is unique in the Western Church in venerating an Old Testament saint to such an extent. We bridge the Old and New Testaments and are a reminder that the communion of saints stretches across all time.

Ponder the word of God: When you have a moment for Bible reflection, read what is said about Elijah and Elisha in *Sirach/Ecclesiasticus* 48:1-16.

A statue of Elijah erected on Mount Carmel by the Discalced Carmelites. The inscription in Latin, Arabic and Hebrew reads: 'Then Elijah arose, a prophet like fire, and his word burned like a torch.' (Sirach/Ecclesiasticus 48:1)

Carmel – a family of saints

Carmelites have also traditionally had a great devotion to the saints associated with the family of Jesus: Mary his mother, her husband Joseph, her parents Anne and Joachim, and Jesus' cousin John the Baptist. Perhaps this is because we feel that we are 'brothers and sisters' of Mary, and also of Jesus. We revere Joseph as protector of Mary, and therefore he is hailed by her Order as 'Principal Protector of the Carmelite Order'. We uphold the example of John the Baptist, who possessed the spirit of Elijah in proclaiming the will of the Lord. We are invited to make the family of Jesus our own family and to live charitably as brothers and sisters. We are invited to be saints who are intimate with God.

Did you know? Some sections of the Carmelite Family have a particular devotion to Saint Jude. Jude was one of the Apostles, a relative of Jesus (*Matthew* 13:55), and the *Letter of Jude* in the Bible is attributed to him. He is renowned as the patron saint of difficult cases. The British Province of Carmelites established a shrine to Saint Jude in Faversham, Kent, in the 1950s. Christians – and Hindus – from around the world write to the Shrine with their petitions. The Shrine Office in Faversham distributes a newsletter to some 20,000 readers worldwide.

The National Shrine of Saint Jude, served by the Carmelite friars at Faversham in England, draws pilgrims and petitions from around the world.

Did you know? Medieval Carmelites believed that the Order had been founded by Elijah so they were not afraid to 'appropriate' early Christian saints as Carmelites. According to legend an early pope, Saint Telesphorus (c. 125), lived for a while as a recluse on Mount Carmel. He was therefore 'adopted' by the Order in the Middle Ages. Although no longer regarded officially as Carmelite, Saint Telesphorus is depicted in many Carmelite works of art dressed in the Order's habit. He is shown holding three Eucharistic hosts because of his declaration that clergy could celebrate three Masses at Christmas rather than the usual one.

A window depicting Telesphorus in Boxmeer Carmelite Priory in Holland.

Saints following a Rule

The *Rule of Saint Albert* (printed at the front of this book) is the document which inspires all Carmelites to 'put on holiness' (chapter 19). It emphasises the aspects of community life which help every Carmelite to grow in holiness: living as brothers and sisters full of charity, celebrating the Eucharist every day when possible, doing manual work, and sharing all property. The *Rule of Saint Albert* encourages us to see the presence of God in those around us. In some instances we recognise that presence so strongly that we are moved to proclaim someone as 'a saint' after their death. We will survey the lives of specific Carmelite saints and blesseds in Chapters 18 and 19; in this chapter let's consider the process by which such holy men and women are given official recognition within Carmel and the wider Church.

Recognising saints among us

Today the Church's formal declaration of someone as a saint is known as *canonisation*. In the early days of Christianity there was no formal process; instead someone's holiness was acknowledged by public acclaim. This is how some of the earliest holy men and women of Carmel came to be revered as 'saints' including Saint Brocard (the *Brother B* referred to in the *Rule of Saint Albert*), Saint Simon Stock, Saint Angelus, and Saint Albert of Trapani (these last two being known as 'the pillars' or 'fathers' of the Order).

Did you know? Religious orders are not above a little rivalry in describing the communion of saints! According to a medieval Carmelite legend, Saint Angelus met Saints Dominic and Francis – the two great founders of the mendicant movement – in the Lateran

The apocryphal encounter between Saints Angelus, Francis and Dominic, depicted in the Carmelite church of Santa Maria in Traspontina, Rome.

Basilica in Rome. He prophesied Francis' stigmata, and Dominic's promotion of the Rosary. They in turn held Angelus in yet higher honour, because he was able to teach them about the Bible. Again, there is a truth to this myth, namely that Carmelites ought to be recognised for their attentiveness to the Scriptures, meditating on the law of the Lord day and night.

As the Curia of the Holy See developed in Rome so the process of canonisation became formalised. The first step to 'official sainthood' in the Catholic Church is for a holy man or woman to be declared a *Servant of God*, normally not before five years have passed after their death. At this time a cause for sainthood is presented to the Vatican's Congregation for the Causes of Saints by the candidate's home diocese and – if they are a Carmelite – by the Order's *postulator*. The postulator's role is to compile a dossier (*proposito*) about the Servant of God, outlining their life story and their reputation for holiness. After the Congregation for the Causes of Saints has perused the dossier and decided that the candidate has led a life of 'heroic virtue', it may recommend to the Pope that he declares the candidate *Venerable* (worthy of veneration).

Stop and reflect: A previous postulator of the Carmelite Order was once asked why most of Carmel's saints came from 'Latin' cultures, notably Italy and Spain. His response was that 'North Europeans and North Americans don't have devotion to the saints, so they don't propose anyone for canonisation.' Do you think this view is accurate?

Did you know? Christians venerate the relics of saints as a reminder of their holy witness upon earth. Just as we might place a photo or keep-sake of a loved-one in pride of place in our homes, so we give special honour to the mortal remains or property of a blessed or saint. Since the 1990s the relics of Saint Thérèse of Lisieux have travelled the globe and been venerated by millions of people.

The Carmelite Family with Church leaders and the Dean and Chapter of York Minster gathered around the relics of St. Thérèse on 1st October 2009 during the visit of the relics to England and Wales. It was the first time the relics had been taken to a Protestant place of worship.

Once a candidate's heroic virtues have been officially recognised, the postulator promotes the life story of the *venerable* to the wider Church, encouraging people to imitate the holy person and to seek his/her intercession through prayer and perhaps the veneration of relics. If the Church can clearly attribute a miracle – an extraordinary act of God's grace – to the intercession of the *venerable*, then the candidate may be declared *Blessed* by the pope or his delegate at a service of *beatification* (a martyr may be declared blessed without evidence of a miracle because their death was itself a witness to God). There are many *blesseds* in the Carmelite Family: at the time of printing this includes Isidore Bakanja and Titus Brandsma (we say at time of printing because it is hoped that such figures will one day be formally recognised as saints).

After a sufficient period of time has passed (normally 25 years or more) and after another miracle has been canonically recognised, a *Blessed* can be declared a *Saint* in a canonisation ceremony which involves the reading of a papal *Bull of canonisation*.

Special roles for saints

Some holy women and men – because of their reputation – are attributed the role of *patron saint*. They may be the patron saint of a place, a people, or an activity. For example the Carmelite Thérèse of Lisieux is one of the patron saints of Church missionaries because in her autobiography *The Story of a Soul* she wrote of her great solidarity with them. The medieval Carmelite friar Albert of Trapani is a patron of the diocese in Sicily where he ministered. Saint Andrew Corsini (d. 1374) is patron saint of those involved

in riots because he was a noted peacemaker between quarrelling Italian houses! In 1999 Saint Teresa Benedicta of the Cross (Edith Stein) was declared one of the six patron saints of Europe which the Carmelite Family considers a great honour for 'one of our family'.

Another honour attributed to some saints – and even more rarely – is that of *Doctor of the Church*. Just as someone with a Ph.D. doctorate is considered to be an expert in his or her field of research, a *Doctor of the Church* is considered to have a particularly

This icon entitled the 'Sapientia Carmeli' – the Wisdom of Carmel – depicts the three Carmelite Doctors of the Church, and was written by the Carmelite School of Iconography in Trento in 1997.

important spiritual insight for the benefit of the whole people of God. There are only thirty-three *Doctors of the Church* of whom three are Carmelites: John of the Cross, Teresa of Jesus (of Avila), and Thérèse of the Child Jesus and the Holy Face (of Lisieux). The Church reveres them as having made a particularly significant impact through their lives and writings on the Church's understanding of God and the world. Other Carmelites are sometimes mentioned as possible candidates for this honour, including Edith Stein.

Holy men and women of the Carmelite Third Order Secular

Most of the venerables, blesseds, and saints revered in the Carmelite Family are 'religious' (hermits, friars, nuns, and sisters) though several of them were at one time lay Carmelites. The bias towards the canonisation of 'religious' is largely because historically the structures of the Carmelite and Discalced Carmelite Orders made it easier to recognise and to process their causes. However, since the Second Vatican Council put greater emphasis upon the holiness of the laity, the postulators of the two orders have been keen to hear

Venerable Lliberada Ferrarons i Vivés, T.O.C.

of lay Carmelites whose holiness is such an example to the Church and the World that they might be put forward for canonisation. At present the cause of Lliberada Ferrarons i Vivés (1803-42) – a Third Order Carmelite from Spain – is being promoted (a degree on her heroic virtues was promulgated in 2009), as well as half a dozen other Servants of God from within Lay Carmel. Some lay Carmelites whose sanctity has already been recognised by the Church include Blessed Joan of Toulouse (d. 1286), Blessed Josepha Naval Girbés, O.C.D.S. (1820-93), Blessed Isidore Bakanja (c.1887-1909), and Saint George Preca, T.O.C. (1880-1962). The lives of these holy men and women are related in books listed in the bibliography at the end of this chapter, especially the series *Profiles in Holiness*. It is the task of all Carmelites, lay and religious, to recognise and celebrate holiness in our midst; surely many of us know of Carmelite brothers and sisters whose holiness could be held up as an example to others.

Did you know? Attentiveness to the Word of God in the Bible is a hallmark of many Carmelite saints. The relationship between Carmel's saints and the Scriptures has been highlighted in two books by Fr. James McCaffrey, O.C.D., *The Carmelite Charism* and *Captive Flames*.

Saints are serious but not sombre

When we seek the presence of God in others, we should remember that there can be a difference between holiness and piety, between sanctity and being sanctimonious. The test of prayer is how we live when we are not at prayer. We seek to be people who do not 'say prayers' but rather are people of prayer. The benchmark of someone's holiness is not how often they say their prayers, how regularly they fast, how they wear their scapular, or how much they know about Carmel's saints. Rather, holiness is seen in those people who open themselves to God, who rely on God in the face of life's challenges, who live to the full the life which God has given them. As we grow in holiness we should not be seeking to separate 'spiritual life' from the other aspects of our life. There is only *LIFE*! The challenge is for us to recognise the presence of God in every part of our life, not only the 'spiritual' parts.

Saints of the Carmelite tradition depicted in stained glass at the National Shrine of St. Thérèse at Darien, Illinois, U.S.A.

Carmelite saints and asceticism

So, true saints do not spend all their time doing 'holy things'. Nor do true saints judge and criticise others, except when their prophetic role calls them to denounce injustice. Rather, true saints bring peace and joy to those around them: 'You will know them by their fruits' (*Matthew* 7:20). However, some people revere Carmelite saints because of their 'supernatural' fruits and are drawn to Carmel because of the mystical visions or superhuman fasting of some of its saints. This is a superficial aspect of the Christian life and Saint John of the Cross said that an interest in such things is for the spiritual beginner and must be swiftly put aside.

Asceticism – that is exercising denial and self-control over the body – is certainly an important part of a saintly life and of Carmelite spirituality. But asceticism is only valuable if it helps us reject the desires which distract us from God. True Carmelite living is no more ascetic than any other religious tradition, and when considering the saintly members of our family it is worth reflecting upon the role of asceticism in the Carmelite way of life. Simply put, asceticism means adopting certain disciplines so as to grow in holiness. Ascetic practices are not 'holy' in themselves, but all the world's major religions believe that self-mortification, self-denial, penance, and the renunciation of certain pleasures can help the believer to grow in virtue, overcome the sensual desires which distract them from God, and thus achieve a deeper relationship with God and other people freed from self-centredness. Ascetical practices deny the human appetites so that the appetite for God can flourish. However, unbalanced asceticism can lead to a completely self-centred focus.

Asceticism in the Gospel and early Church

As always we Carmelites turn first of all to the Bible and to Jesus to find examples of how we might live. In the Old Testament we find that the people of Israel did penance by giving alms to the poor, shaving their heads, and putting on sackcloth and ashes. In the Gospel it is clear that Jesus undertook ascetic practices, most notably fasting for forty days in the desert. John the Baptist also lived in the austerity of the desert.

Ponder the Law of the Lord: Have a look at *Mark* 2:18-22 to compare the feasting and the fasting of the followers of Jesus and John the Baptist. What does Jesus say on the matter?

Jesus did not follow ascetic practices simply from a sense of religious obligation or as a form of self-punishment. He criticised those who paraded their acts of penance before others (see *Matthew* Chapter 6), and realised the possible negative effects of asceticism: a feeling of self-importance and a readiness to judge others who are less 'observant'. Saint Paul realised that some people feast, whilst others fast, and that all have their place (*Romans* Chapter 14), and recommended discipline in the spiritual journey (see, for example, *1 Corinthians* 9:25).

After the time of Christ, and influenced by Greek philosophy, the Church approved various ascetic practices, conscious of their benefits when practiced temperately. In the fourth and fifth centuries ascetics emerged in the deserts of Egypt and Palestine, such as St. Anthony of Egypt (d. 373). From the desert ascetics emerged the first monastic communities. St. Benedict's *Rule* taught

St. Paul, painted by Tommaso Masaccio in 1426 for the Carmelite altarpiece in Pisa; now in the Museo Nazionale, Pisa, Italy.

that ascetic practices could be useful, but should be moderate. In this he was following St. Augustine's teaching that self-control could allow a greater flourishing of God's grace. The Church taught that a penitential attitude brings the Christian greater freedom in various areas of life, such as increased clarity of thought and the ability to resist potentially destructive temptations. In the early Church pilgrimage came to have an ascetic aspect, as pilgrims 'offered up' the difficulties of their journey in prayer.

Asceticism in the *Rule of Saint Albert* and the early life of Carmel

The first hermits on Mount Carmel were probably pilgrims to the Holy Land, and their way of life certainly seems to have had ascetical elements derived from the desert tradition. Those first Carmelites gave up the comforts of home and entered a valley between the sea and the desert to share a life of prayer and penance. However, the *Way of Life* given to the hermits by Saint Albert, which remains the foundation of the Carmelite way of life today, is not dominated by ascetical practices. Albert draws on the Bible and the traditions of the Church to suggest certain acts of self-discipline, including:

- the renunciation of personal property
- solitude
- obedience to a prior
- a timetable of regular prayer
- submitting to the correction of excesses and faults by the community
- fasting every day except Sundays from the feast of the Exultation of the Cross (September) until Easter Sunday
- abstaining from meat, unless the hermit is sick or frail
- work of some kind
- keeping silence at set times

Albert drew the ascetic elements in his *Way of Life* from the practices advocated in the Bible and in the monastic tradition. Although these are helpful in the spiritual journey, the *Rule of Saint Albert* is also tempered with appeals for common sense and humanity. Albert says that hermits can be excused from certain penitential practices if age or situation necessitate them, 'For necessity has no law' (16). In the final chapter he encourages people to strive for greater acts of holiness ('supererogation'), but does not demand them. Nor does Albert specify anywhere in his *Rule* any punishments to be imposed on brothers who do not live up to the ideal.

This image of 'Albert, Patriarch of the Church in Jerusalem', was painted by Jacqueline Geldart c.1955 for Saint Albert's Press, the printing house of the British Province of Carmelites.

Many people in today's world still find the moderate ascetical advice of the *Rule of Saint Albert* helpful in combating certain 'enslaving' lifestyles and the addictive effects of some substances: tobacco, drugs, alcohol, food and so on (for example, in the Brazilian city of Curitiba, Carmelite friars run a rehabilitation community for drug-addicts who find structure in life from the *Rule of Saint Albert*)

Medieval and Reformation approaches to asceticism

In the later Middle Ages various forms of ascetic devotions were encouraged, sometimes as penance for sin or to increase someone's religious faith. Mendicant orders began to stress the humanity of Jesus including his suffering and death, which prompted lay people to undertake penitential practices hitherto mostly practiced by monks and nuns.

The Protestant Reformation tended to reject asceticism because it could overemphasise the efforts of the individual Christian rather than the redeeming grace of God (the 'works vs. faith' argument). From before the Reformation Carmelites had recognised that human effort and God's grace go hand in hand. In the text known as *The Ten Books of the Way of Life and Great Deeds of the Carmelites* (better known as *The Book of the First Monks*), compiled c.1385 by the friar Felip Ribot, it is stated:

> The goal of this life is twofold. One part we acquire by our own effort and the exercise of the virtues, assisted by divine grace. This is to offer God a pure and holy heart, free from all stain of sin. … The other goal of this life is granted to us as the free gift of God, namely, to taste somewhat in the heart and to experience in the mind the power of the divine presence and the sweetness of heavenly glory, not only after death but already in this mortal life. (*The Ten Books*, Book 1, Chapter 2).

The purpose of asceticism is to offer God a pure heart (*puritas cordis*), so that God can fill us with his life and love. Ascetical practice helps us to develop a contemplative attitude, preparing the way for God to grant us the gift of contemplation, the gift of friendship and union with him.

Carmelites take up their crosses and follow Christ in this miniature in the Gradual of the Carmelite friars in Krakow, Poland (1644).

Asceticism and reform

Asceticism has always been an important factor in reforms of the Carmelite Family, as was evident in the 1430s in the 'Congregation of Mantua', and in the 1450s in the reforms of Blessed John Soreth (as we read about in Chapter 8). Saints Teresa of Jesus and John of the Cross admitted that the early stages of the Discalced Reform were marked by disproportionately ascetic piety, but this developed with experience into a moderate and balanced pursuit.

Thanks to Teresa, John of the Cross learnt to reject false asceticism. He realised that God wishes us to take pleasure in the beautiful things of creation that give us happiness, but to realise at the same time that these things are not, in themselves, God. Only God is God. John took quite some time to appreciate this truth. A biographer gives us this account of the young friar:

A woodcut depicting Teresa and John at the Carmelite foundation at Duruelo, Spain.

At twenty-two, Fray Juan saw that he could not escape his aloofness … If he came along when some of the brothers were speaking at a time they should have been silent, they would run away immediately. They knew if they stayed that he would give them a little sermon about the *Rule*. In fact, the other friars avoided him whenever possible … He still perceived spiritual life as 'spiritual' or otherworldly, and consequently he developed a severe, harsh attitude toward earthly life … He was one of the fervent types to be found in any novitiate – filled with a desire to be holy, but with an inhuman notion of holiness. However, this was simply too contrary to Juan's sensitive nature to last very long. He felt too strongly drawn by the fascination and beauty of the real world around him to deny its goodness. It gnawed at him. In an effort to end his yearning for it, he increased his ascetical practices as if they could free him of all this earthliness. He may have felt it necessary to get out of the world through disciplining his body, fasting, vigils, and long prayers, but unconsciously he was discovering how incarnate he was and how necessary this was to his becoming one with the God of Jesus.

(Richard P. Hardy, *John of the Cross: Man and Mystic*, pp. 21-22.)

John eventually learned to love Love, to find beauty in Beauty. He realised that he should not reject the world, nor cling to it. He came to see that he could not achieve holiness by ignoring the world around him, or gain sanctity by his own efforts, but only by opening his heart to the loving transformation of God, the *living flame of love*. It was this recognition that spiritual growth comes about through a collaboration between God and the soul that led John to stress that the truly beneficial penitential attitude is an asceticism of the heart. He taught that ascetic practices could liberate the heart from the attachments and false idols which keep the soul from questing for the one true God. John understood that asceticism, in the Carmelite tradition, is not simply about saying 'no' for the sake of it, but is geared towards being able to say 'yes' to God with full freedom. Carmelite asceticism does not aim at leaving our heart and our desires empty for the sake of it, but rather so that our heart can be filled by God. Discerning the benefits of ascetical practice will mean judging whether we have grown in love. As Jesus said, 'by their fruits will they be judged', which John of the Cross echoed by saying 'In the evening of life you will be examined on love'.

Stop and think: Do you think the person seeking God should go out looking for ascetical practices or self-discipline, or should he/she instead simply accept whatever suffering comes along?

The Reform of Touraine

In the late sixteenth century the Discalced observance developed into an independent religious order. The so-called 'Ancient Observance' continued, and though sometimes called 'unreformed' to distinguish it from the Discalced Reform, it did in fact undergo a process of spiritual renewal that has influenced Carmel (including the Teresian branch) right up to the present day. This spiritual renewal was the *Reform of Touraine*, a reform observance begun by the Carmelite friar Pierre Behourt who had joined the Order in 1582. Behourt began the reform in the Carmelite friary in the French city of Rennes, and the movement he initiated became known as the *Observance of Rennes*. Rennes was in the Carmelite Province of Touraine, and so the movement also became known as the *Reform of Touraine*. The Reform of Touraine called for a stricter observance of the *Rule of Saint Albert*, and introduced a programme of religious formation which emphasised the value of moderate asceticism. The spiritual master of the reform was Venerable John of Saint-Samson (1571-1636) whose teachings on asceticism and life in the Spirit caused a powerful breath of renewed spirituality to be felt across the whole Carmelite Family in seventeenth-century France. Another inspirational figure was Philip Thibault, elected Prior of the Carmelites at Rennes in 1608. He restored the liturgy in the house; the office was chanted, and soon the beauty of the services drew large numbers of the townspeople. Meditation twice daily was his chief innovation. He accomplished his most difficult task, restoring poverty, by emphasizing its spiritual advantages. Though he believed in the spiritual benefits of asceticism, he famously declared that he wanted 'less observance and more charity'.

Asceticism in Carmel today

Moderate asceticism continues to play a role in Carmelite life, and the life of the wider Church. Following the Second Vatican Council (1962-65) the Church has continued

Advocate of a balanced ascetical attitude: Venerable John of Saint-Samson, in a painting at Saint Albert's International Centre (CISA) in Rome.

to teach the value of moderate ascetic practices in the journey to holiness, though a growing understanding of psychology has prompted Christians to drop some penitential practices which are regarded as unhelpful. In 1966 Pope Paul VI wrote an Apostolic Constitution document called *Poenitemini* in which he set forth the correct principles of asceticism.

What do you think? Penitential attitudes have arguably diminished since the 1960s. Many have welcomed this as a healthy development, physically, psychologically, and spiritually. Others think that the modern world is too lax, and that more self-discipline is helpful, even vital, for a healthy society. What do you think? Can a balance be struck?

Encouraged by the Second Vatican Council's spirit of renewal, the Carmelite Family has approached the topic of asceticism afresh, and in recent years the major documents of all the main branches of the Carmelite Family have dealt with the topic, as the 2003 *Rule for the Third Order of Carmel* can illustrate:

> The desert experience which was so determining in the life of the Prophet [Elijah] becomes an obligatory phase for Carmelites who are called to be purified in the desert of life in order to meet the Lord authentically. Carmelites must travel along this road, in the desert of interior mortification. (§48)

Some people believe when reading the *Rule of Saint Albert* that the Carmelite way to holiness is primarily through rejecting the body and 'the world' in an attempt to focus on the divine. However, this is a false reading of true asceticism, and at odds with the Carmelite emphasis on approaching the divinity of Jesus through all that is truly human. In its practice of asceticism, Carmelite spirituality cannot be hijacked by political labels. It is neither 'conservative' nor 'liberal', neither 'traditional' nor 'progressive'. It is a *via media*, that is, a *middle way* lived between the tensions of life.

Carmel – an ancient path for today's pilgrim

Let's look again at the broader notion of holiness in the Carmelite Family, and the ways by which Carmel helps people to participate in the communion of saints.

All people are called to holiness and Carmel is not the only means by which people can lead good and holy lives. There are many journeys leading to God, though Carmel's path is a tried and tested route. In the Carmelite tradition our vocation or charism (our unique gift from God) stresses pondering God's word (especially as it comes to us in the Bible, in silence, and in other people), an openness to God (*vacare Deo*), a seeking of God's presence in both solitude and in community, as well as a blending of prayer with active service of those around us. Everyone called to Carmel shares something with other Carmelites, and at the same time brings something unique to Carmel.

Carmel is for everyone, though not everyone is for Carmel. Nevertheless, the saints of Carmel seem to have universal appeal in the Church; they are not the private domain of the Carmelite Family and provide intercession and an example for the wider communion of saints, the Church. There are millions of people around the world who revere our better-known saints (such as Simon Stock, Teresa, and Thérèse) without knowing anything of Carmel. Their partial knowledge of these saints can sometimes be an opportunity for us Carmelites to share something of our rich and ancient spirituality, but unless they have a vocation to Carmel we should not exploit their interest in our saints for 'recruitment'.

Prior General Fernando Millán Romeral praying alongside the relics of St. Thérèse during the visit to Aylesford Priory in October 2009. The devotion of many people to Carmel's saints offers Carmelites an opportunity to share with them something of our experience of relationship with God.

Carmelite saints are made in community

In the Carmelite tradition it is in the community that saints learn to grow in love. Even the early hermits on Mount Carmel came from the solitude of their cells to join together in prayer and discussion. It is usually in the joys and trials of a community that God gives us most opportunities for growth, be that a priory of friars, a monastery of nuns, a convent of sisters, a gathering of lay Carmelites, a family, or a parish. Building community is not always easy. Saint Thérèse frequently wished for the honour of martyrdom, but instead found that one of her greatest spiritual trials was having to endure one of her sisters in Carmel clicking her false teeth during prayers! Thérèse saw that she needed to love in a special way the sister who annoyed her, and she came to realise that her witness to the Good News of Jesus would not be 'heroic' in a dramatic way but rather lived out in small acts of love. Her vocation was to live a brief, enclosed, and somewhat ordinary life, yet she realised that every small action could be done with love and that through love the most ordinary people could become saints in God's eyes. Her *Little Way of Spiritual Childhood* is the means by which most of us grow as saints, trusting in God as a loving and merciful parent, and seeking to love him and others as ourselves through even the smallest acts of kindness.

As we experience God's presence in communities we are consoled and challenged.

Saints are heroic in little ways

Carmel is sometimes thought of as a complicated spirituality suitable only for those who are 'experts' in prayer, but the insight of Thérèse – *Doctor of the Church* – is that the way to God is really very simple. A former Prior General of the Order, Kilian Lynch, O.Carm., reiterated the teaching of St. Thérèse in a leaflet about Lay Carmel written in the 1950s: 'Sanctity is to be found in the commonplace, in the little things of the daily round; even the most insignificant of them is a sacrament or sign of God's will and a means of holiness'.

Carmelite saints go out to serve

The saints in our Carmelite Family thus not only nurtured their relationship with God through prayer and through community, but also through service of their brothers and sisters, in some cases striving to love those they found it difficult to live with. Many of those Carmelites who have been recognised as 'blesseds' or 'saints' in recent years are those who undertook some form of apostolic work in the community: founding schools, ministering in the workplace, labouring in hospitals and offices, and so on. They found opportunities to share God's love in every circumstance of life, and we are invited to do the same. Like them, we are asked to take on the attitudes of Carmel (as discussed in Chapter 12).

Wherever we find ourselves are the places we are called to be missionaries and evangelists.

Remembering our Carmelite Family in heaven

Those Carmelites who have been formally beatified or canonised are remembered each year on their *feast day*. This is usually the day on which they died and entered the new life of heaven, and it is marked by the celebration of a Mass or the Divine Office in their honour. The Carmelite and Discalced Carmelite Orders share a combined *Missal* (Mass texts), *Lectionary* (Mass readings) and *Proper of the Liturgy of the Hours* which give all the appropriate readings and prayers. On Carmelite feast days the texts

The 1993 Carmelite Proper of the Liturgy of the Hours

of the Divine Office (also known as the Breviary) are sometimes supplemented or replaced with readings from a book known as the *Carmelite Proper of the Liturgy of the Hours* (also known as the *Carmelite Supplement to the Breviary*). This presents reflections and texts either derived from, or appropriate to, each particular saint. Reading these texts can be a good way to learn more about the holy person, their particular response to God's grace, and their unique contribution to the Carmelite charism. In recent years the *Carmelite Proper* has been co-published by the Ancient and Discalced Observances of the Carmelite Family, and when beatifications or canonisations take place additional off-prints are produced.

The principal veneration of Carmelite saints is indeed through the liturgy of the Church, notably the Eucharist and the Divine Office. In the Roman rite a document called the *Calendarium Romanum* specifies which saints are to be venerated throughout the whole of the Church. The number of saints venerated across the universal Church is limited, and it is gratifying for the Carmelite Family that a proportionately high number of these are Carmelite.

Spot the Carmelites! As a challenge why not look in a weekday Missal or Church calendar and see which Carmelite saints and commemorations are observed across the Church.

As well as universally revered saints, the Church allows local communities – such as dioceses, nations, and religious orders – to celebrate some of their own saints proper to them. Whether or not a feast is celebrated varies according to the grade it is given:

Solemnities	A Solemnity is the highest ranking the Church can give to a feast, and is observed with particular emphasis.
Feast	A feast is the second highest ranking given by the Church to a saint or commemoration.
Memorial	A memorial listed in the Church calendar is an obligatory commemoration of a saint, though it is superseded by some liturgical celebrations (such as the Sundays of the year).
Optional Memorial	This is the lowest rank of feast, and it is up to the individual or community whether or not to observe it.

The way different branches of the Carmelite Family celebrate a feast depends upon local custom. For example, in many provinces optional memorias of Carmelite saints are not generally observed by communities, though individuals are at liberty to have private devotion to saints on their feast days. Liturgical ordos are calendars which set out which feasts are to be celebrated on which days. They take into account local traditions, and are read by Carmelites in conjunction with local diocesan ordos.

Remembering our Carmelite Family in heaven

A particularly important feast is that of *All Carmelite Saints* on 14th November, followed the next day by the *Commemoration of All Carmelite Souls*. This is the Carmelite Family's opportunity to celebrate the lives of all Carmelite saints – recognised and unrecognised, living and dead – who have sought to live *in allegiance to Jesus Christ*.

'It is a holy and wholesome thought to pray for the dead' (cf. 2 Maccabees 12:45). Carmelite friars visiting the cemetery of the British Province at Aylesford Priory.

Conclusion: In this fifteenth chapter we have considered how the Carmelite Family fits into the wider Communion of Saints. We have reflected on what sainthood is, and considered some of the ways recommended by the Carmelite tradition to nurture holiness, including prayer, community building, service of others, and moderate asceticism. We have understood the role of the saints in heaven as intercessors and models, and perhaps better appreciate our own role in bringing and being Good News for others.

Concluding your time of reflection and study with a moment of prayer would be very suitable.

Now that you are three quarters of the way through this journey of formation, reflect on how the experience has been thus far.

In the next chapter we will reflect on how the Carmelite Family is called to be of service to the wider World and Church.

Ideas for Reflection, Discussion and Action

- Take any paragraph, image or saint that has captured your attention in this chapter individually and/or as a community. What is the significance? What main themes have emerged for you? You might like to summarise your thoughts and feelings on the blank page at the end of the chapter.

- Emanuele Boaga, O.Carm., *Celebrating the Saints of Carmel*, (Rome: Edizioni Carmelitane, 2010).

- If someone says the word 'saint' to you what picture comes to mind?

- Do you think it is important for the Carmelite Family to put forward candidates for beatification and canonisation? What are the arguments for and against?

- Is your family, parish, or Carmelite community a place where 'saints' are welcome?

- Do you celebrate the feasts of the Carmelite Family? If so, how?

- Pray for the work of the Carmelite postulator's office.

- Which Carmelite saints do you find most inspiring and why? If you are a member of a Carmelite community, find a picture of a saint within the Order who inspires you, and tell your community something about his or her life.

- Should the Order make more effort to identify holy lay people as candidates for canonisation?

- Are you aware of being part of the *Communion of Saints* when you pray the Divine Office or the Eucharist?

- Pray *Lectio Divina* using *Colossians* 1:9-12.

- What part does asceticism have in your life as a Carmelite? How can we strike a healthy balance in our practice of self-denial?

- What act of service could you do to build up the Communion of Saints?

- Why not make a pilgrimage to a Carmelite shrine or place associated with one of the Order's saints?

Recommended Further Resources

Since holiness is the vocation we all receive from God, there are many publications and resources available to help us in our appreciation of being part of the communion of saints. There are an increasing number of books becoming available about Carmelite saints specifically.

Wendy Beckett, *Mystery of Love: Saints in Art Through the Centuries*, (Harper Collins, 1996).

Emanuele Boaga, O.Carm., *Celebrating the Saints of Carmel*, (Rome: Edizioni Carmelitane, 2010).

Gregory Burke, O.C.D., 'Charism and Conflict: Jerome Gracian and the Order's Self-Understanding' in *Mount Carmel*, Volume 54, Number 4 (October-December 2006), pp. 31-38 (p. 36).

Alban Butler, *Lives of the Saints*. Fr. Butler (1711-73) was an English Roman Catholic priest who compiled biographies of many saints. His compilation has been updated and printed in various editions of the centuries.

The Carmelite Missal (Carmelite Book Service, 1997).

Carmelite Postulator's Office: www.carmelites.info/postulator

Carmelite Proper of the Liturgy of the Hours (Institutum Carmelitanum, 1993).

Joseph Chalmers, O.Carm., 'Carmel in the World', in *In Allegiance to Jesus Christ*, (Rome: Edizioni Carmelitane, 1999), pp. 39-44.

John Dalrymple, *Simple Prayer*, (London: Darton, Longman & Todd, new edition 2010).

Hiliary Doran, O.C.D., *Asceticism in the Rule of St. Albert*, (2005, publisher unspecified).

Robert Ellsberg, *All Saints: Daily Reflections on Saints, Prophets, and Witnesses for Our Time*, (New York: The Crossroad Publishing Company, 1999).

Anne Gordon, *A Book of Saints: True stories of how they touch our lives*, (Harper Collins, 1994).

Richard P. Hardy, *John of the Cross: Man and Mystic*, (Pauline Books & Media, 2004).

John Malley, O.Carm., 'The Values and Fundamentals of living the Carmelite Way', in *Formation and Communication at the Service of the Community – Proceedings of the International Congress of Lay Carmelites, September 2006*, (Rome: Edizioni Carmelitane, 2007), pp. 19-34. This is a printed version of the presentation that Fr. Malley gave at the International Lay Carmelite Congress, in which he proposed ten fundamental values for Carmelites to live by that are well worth reflecting upon.

Patrick Thomas McMahon, O.Carm., *A Pattern for Life: The Rule of Saint Albert and the Carmelite Laity*, Carmel in the World Paperbacks 14, (Rome: Edizioni Carmelitane, 2007).

National Shrine of Saint Jude, Faversham, England: www.stjudeshrine.org.uk

Alacoque O'Reilly, O.C.D.S., 'Graced Experiences of Church: Priests and Laity Together', *Mount Carmel: A Review of the Spiritual Life*, Volume 58 Number 2, April-June 2010, pp. 16-21.

Steven Payne, O.C.D., *Saint Thérèse of Lisieux: Doctor of the Universal Church* (Alba House).

Vladimira Polišenská, T.O.C., 'The mission of the Lay Carmelite in today's world', in *In obsequio Jesu Christi: Praying and prophetic community in a changing world*, Proceedings of the 2007 General Chapter of the Carmelite Order, (Rome: Edizioni Carmelitane, 2007), pp. 117-119.

Redemptus M. Valabek, O.Carm., *Profiles in Holiness*, 3 volumes (Rome: Edizioni Carmelitane, 1996-2002).

Vatican Congregation for the Causes of Saints: www.vatican.va

Notes and reflections on Chapter 15

Carmel's Call to Service

Summary: In this chapter we reflect on service as an integral part of the Carmelite charism. Carmelites are not restricted to any one apostolate but respond to the needs of the Church and the World by reading the signs of the times. Our service is informed by our 'Carmelite attitudes', and together with prayer and community-building is part of our contemplative vocation, in fidelity to Christ's commands and example as revealed in Scripture.

Members of the Carmelite Family serving one another as pilgrims in Lourdes, and having their hands blessed for service.

Get prepared: This chapter is about a very practical subject, and thinking practically you might find it useful to make notes so have a pen to hand. Frequent reference is made in this text to the 2003 *Rule for the Third Order of Carmel (RTOC)* and the 1992 *Catechism of the Catholic Church*, so you may find it helpful to have a copy of these texts in front of you, in print or online. No doubt by now you are used to settling down to read these chapters with a Bible to follow up Scriptural references. All our service is underpinned by a spirit of prayer, so perhaps you might like to begin your reflection with these words of St. Ignatius, or any other text that helps you ponder the topic of service:

> *Teach us, good Lord, to serve you as you deserve;*
> *To give and not to count the cost;*
> *To fight and not to heed the wounds;*
> *To toil and not to seek for rest;*
> *To labour and not to seek reward,*
> *Save that of knowing we do your will.*
> *Through Jesus Christ our Lord. Amen.*

Service: a response to Love

Carmelites are ordinary people responding to an extraordinary love: the love of God. We learn how to serve first and foremost from God's example. In the Old Testament the

'If I, your Lord and Teacher, have washed your feet, you also ought to wash one another's feet.' (John 13:14).

Lord served and loved his people through the prophets. In the New Testament God's love for the human family was revealed in the Good News delivered in the preaching and person of Jesus of Nazareth, Son of God and Son of Man. Jesus said that he was sent by God 'to bring good news to the poor, to proclaim release to the captives and recovery of sight to the blind, to let the oppressed go free, to proclaim the year of the Lord's favour' (the *Lucan Manifesto* in *Luke* 4:16-20). Jesus came to us in a spirit not of mastery, but of service: 'The Son of Man came not to be served but to serve' (*Matthew* 20:28).

The love which Jesus showed for all people prompts us Christians as followers of *The Way* to try to love others as he did, to become *other Christs*. By living, as our *Rule of Saint Albert* puts it, 'in allegiance to Jesus Christ', we Carmelites must engage in the same sort of service our Master was: bringing good news, freedom to the poor, release to captives, the blind, and the oppressed. The inspiration for such service is love, and love comes from God. Service is God's love in action. When we serve our sisters and brothers we manifest God's love, putting into practice Christ's command to love God, and our neighbours as ourselves (*Mark* 12:28-34).

At our baptism we undertook to live out this double command to love God and our neighbour. Those of us who become Carmelite through Profession of promises or vows are not exempted from this command; rather, we commit ourselves to fulfil it more deeply. Being of service is as fundamental to our contemplative way of life as prayer and the building-up of community. As former Prior General, Joseph Chalmers, O.Carm., stated: 'all Carmelites are called to some form of service which is an integral part of the charism given to the Order by God' (quoted in the 2003 *Rule for the Third Order of Carmel* §46). The charism of the Order – that gift and mission which God has entrusted to our family – is not for our personal benefit alone but for the happiness and

'It is the task of deacons to assist the bishop and priests ... in the proclamation of the Gospel and preaching ... and in dedicating themselves to the various ministries of charity' (1992 *Catechism of the Catholic Church* §1570). The Carmelite Family contains ordained deacons not only among the friars but also among Lay Carmel.

holiness of the Church and the World. The charism is summarised very simply in the 1995 *Constitutions* of the friars: 'Carmelites live their life of allegiance to Christ through a commitment to seek the face of the living God (the contemplative dimension of life), through fraternity, and through service (diakonia) in the midst of the people' (§14). The Greek word διακονια (*diakonia*) means 'service'; it gives us the word *deacon*, meaning 'servant', and implies serving God through God's suffering people, especially the poorest and those most in need.

Why serve, and who?

We are called to serve because Jesus, to whom we Carmelites give our allegiance, has invited us into his service: 'Whoever serves me must follow me, and where I am, there will my servant be also. Whoever serves me, the Father will honour.' (*John* 12:26). The *Rule of Saint Albert* reminds us that we are called to serve Jesus before all else:

> In many and various ways the holy fathers have laid down how everyone, whatever their state of life or whatever kind of religious life they have chosen, should live in allegiance to Jesus Christ and <u>serve</u> him faithfully from a pure heart and a good conscience. (Chapter 2)

But how are we supposed to serve Jesus when he is not right in front of us? We find the answer from his own lips in Matthew's account of the Gospel:

> When the Son of Man comes in his glory … the king will say to those at his right hand, "Come, you that are blessed by my Father, inherit the kingdom prepared for you from the foundation of the world; for I was hungry and you gave me food, I was thirsty and you gave me something to drink, I was a stranger and you welcomed me, I was naked and you gave me clothing, I was sick and you took care of me, I was in prison and you visited me." Then the righteous will answer him, "Lord, when was it that we saw you hungry and gave you food, or thirsty and gave you something to drink? And when was it that we saw you a stranger and welcomed you, or naked and gave you clothing? And when was it that we saw you sick or in prison and visited you?" And the king will answer them, "Truly I tell you, just as you did it to one of the least of these who are members of my family, you did it to me." (*Matthew* 25:31-46)

If you know this Scriptural passage you will recall that those who do not care for the least of the Lord's family are separated from him. Jesus the Good Shepherd does not judge people on their religious practices, how often they say the rosary or how many prayer books they have. No, Jesus judges us on how much we have loved, which we demonstrate in concrete action for the neediest members of society.

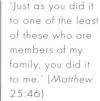

'Just as you did it to one of the least of these who are members of my family, you did it to me.' (*Matthew* 25:46)

Did you know? *Matthew* 25 and the *Book of Tobit* inspired the Church's ancient notion of the seven 'Corporal Works of Mercy' which tend to bodily needs: (1) feeding the hungry; (2) giving drink to the thirsty; (3) clothing the naked; (4) sheltering the homeless; (5) visiting the sick; (6) visiting the imprisoned; (7) burying the dead. There are likewise seven 'Spiritual Works of Mercy': (1) instructing the ignorant; (2) counselling the doubtful; (3) admonishing sinners; (4) bearing wrongs patiently; (5) forgiving offences willingly; (6) comforting the afflicted; (7) praying for the living and the dead.

Service is the fruit of our faith

In the light of the Gospel, one might say that the test of a true Carmelite vocation is not whether a Carmelite is overtly 'religious' or pious, but whether his or her faith motivates them to serve others out of love, as Jesus commands. As Carmelites we seek to be contemplatives, open to the presence of God encountered in prayer, community, and in our service of others, usually in the ordinariness of everyday life. This is put simply by Tony Lester, O.Carm. (Prior Provincial of the British Province of Carmelites between 2002 and 2008):

In essence the reality which we call Carmel has little or nothing to do with a particular way of doing things or of wearing religious clothes or of living in special houses. Neither is it the property of a particular group of people or organisation. Carmel stands for the intimate encounter which God brings about between the person and God in the midst of all that is most ordinary in life. So, if you are seeking visions and ecstatic experiences then you are in the wrong place. This is the mystery of the 'Word made flesh' who 'emptied himself to take the form of a slave... and then was humbler still...'

Jesus took the form of a slave, a servant (*Philippians* 2:7-9), and has given the Church – and the Carmelite Family within it – an awesome responsibility to continue his ministry of service. Jesus has asked us to continue building God's Kingdom here on earth, taking care of his 'little ones'. As the friars' *Ratio* puts it: 'As Carmelites we are in the Church and for the Church, and together with the Church we are at the service of the Kingdom' (§38). Carmel does not exist for our own benefit, but for the service of God and therefore all God's people. Not only fellow Christians but also non-Christians are included by God as his people.

A mural of Christ the Good Shepherd by Duncan Grant in the St. Blaise Chapel at Lincoln Cathedral, England.

Service is a Carmelite attitude

We sometime think of service as demeaning, but in truth it gives meaning and dignity to life. The Scriptures are full of examples of people who serve and are highly respected for it. If we are serious about our faith and sincere in our love for God it will inevitably show itself in the fruits of our actions and in our commitment to love and serve our neighbour. Service is not simply about *what we do* but about *who we are*. Perhaps we should speak not of *doing service* but rather of *being at the service of God's people*. Service is a manifestation of our love, and flows from our very being. It is one of the 'Carmelite attitudes' we discussed in Chapter 12.

We do good deeds of service not because we want to be saved or feel obligated but because the giving of ourselves is the natural response to the love God has given us as gift. Being redeemed and restored to a relationship with the Father is not dependent on our actions of service. Jesus has already saved us as a free gift, as the 1992 *Catechism of the Catholic Church* observes (§604): 'By giving up his own Son for our sins, God manifests that his plan for us is one of benevolent love, prior to any merit on our part: "In this is love, not that we loved God but that he loved us and sent his Son to be the expiation for our sins" (*1 John* 4:10, 19)'. Christianity is not essentially about what we do but about what God is doing in us:

> For by grace you have been saved through faith, and this is not your
> own doing; it is the gift of God – not the result of works, so that no
> one may boast. For we are what God has made us, created in Christ
> Jesus for good works, which God prepared beforehand to be our way
> of life.' (*Ephesians* 2:8-10).

Being of service is therefore about being open to God working in us in whatever way God sees fit: 'it is God who is at work in you, enabling you both to will and to work for his good pleasure' (*Philippians* 2:13). In response to God's love it is right for us to love in return. It is said *actions speak louder than words*, a sentiment which Saint James echoes: 'What good is it, my brothers and sisters, if you say you have faith but do not have works? … Show me your faith without works, and I by my works will show you my faith.' (*James* 2:14, 18).

Stop and think about your own experience: When you serve others, are you conscious of your motives? Do you serve out of duty, out of love, or both? Is your service inspired by God, or by your own motives? Do you allow others to be of service to you?

Being equipped for service

God never asks us to undertake an act of service which God won't equip us for, as we see in the example of Elijah who received from God what was needed to fulfil his enormously challenging missions. To enable us to be of service, God has given each person his or her own talents. Some people have more talents, others have less, and our abilities are to be used for the common good. There is no need to be unemployed in the Lord's vineyard! In our diverse Carmelite Family everyone has a place to be and a service that God has entrusted to them. As Cardinal John Henry Newman reflected:

God has created me to do him some definite service;
He has committed some work to me
      which he has committed to no other.
I have my mission…
I am a link in a chain, a bond of connection between persons.
He has not created me for naught.

There will be those among us who may feel their efforts to serve are restricted by age, infirmity, lack of resources, shortage of time, or other problems. For sure, we can experience real set-backs and restrictions in our service, we can worry that we aren't qualified or capable to serve effectively, but if we really open our hearts willingly to God in contemplation, God will show us that there are still works of service that are within our means.

It is true humility to acknowledge the gifts or talents God has given us, which are not for our own personal profit. The challenge from God, the invitation, is to try to develop our talents in the service of the Church and the World, building up the Kingdom of God in our own particular place and state of life that we are called to be in:

> The gifts Christ gave were that some would be apostles, some prophets, some evangelists, some pastors and teachers, to equip the saints for the work of ministry, for building up the body of Christ, until all of us come to the unity of the faith and of the knowledge of the Son of God, to maturity, to the measure of the full stature of Christ. (*Ephesians* 4:11-13).

Did you know? The founder of the *Legion of Mary*, Frank Duff (d. 1980) was a member of the Carmelite Third Order and inspired by Carmel's spirit of service. The *Legion*, established in Dublin in 1921, has millions of members worldwide making it one of the largest apostolic organisations of lay people in the Catholic Church, alongside groups such as the *Society of Saint Vincent de Paul*. The *Legion* encourages its members to care for the spiritual and social welfare of Catholics and non-Catholics alike. In a spirit of collaborative ministry with local clergy and parishes, the *Legion's* members visit families, the sick and the poor, in their homes, hospitals, and on the streets.

Servant of God
Frank Duff, T.O.C.

Quality not quantity

Not everyone in Carmel is able or asked to perform astonishingly heroic acts of service. The important thing with regard to our service is not the scale of what we do but the love with which we do it. The great Carmelite St. Thérèse of the Child Jesus and the Holy Face (of Lisieux) said that: 'Our Lord does not look so much at the greatness of our actions, nor even at their difficulty, but at the love with which we do them.' Thérèse didn't even say that the action had to be done particularly well or impressively; even an act of service that fails in human eyes is beautiful to God if done with love. Thérèse spoke of

There are so many ways for a Carmelite to offer others a helping hand.

'picking up a pin for the love of God', and such small acts of service, of love, are open to us daily: a kind word, a reassuring smile, recycling to care for the environment, solidarity with the homeless, telephoning a house-bound friend who is lonely, helping a neighbour with chores, patiently supporting a friend with mental-health problems, listening to someone bound by addiction, giving our widow's mite to charity. Each Carmelite has to work out for him/herself what form of service is possible, appropriate, and necessary. Any act of service that an individual Carmelite does is, in a mysterious but very real way, collaborating in the Order's ministry.

Whatever acts of service we are called to, small or large, if we try to live our vocation authentically, the charism and collective experience of Carmel can equip us for the service. As we learn to listen more attentively to the Word of God – especially in the Scriptures, in silent prayer, and in the community – we will better discern what service it is that God asks of us. As we become more contemplative in our gaze, we will learn to read in the world around us 'the signs of the times' (*Matthew* 16:3). It is important that we develop this sense of discernment, since there is no single form of 'Carmelite apostolate'. Unlike many religious orders, we were not founded with one particular ministry in mind, other than to develop a contemplative attitude within ourselves and others, summarised in the Latin phrase *contemplatione aliis tradere*, that is, to contemplate and to give to others the fruits of contemplation. The Order's charism gives us great flexibility in our range of apostolates, and therefore also a greater need to discern God's will.

Chapter 16 ▮ Carmel's Call to Service

Stop and think: How can we tell what service God is asking of us? Given that there is practically no place or situation where Carmelites cannot have a ministry, how do we decide where we must be? What does the final chapter of the *Rule of Saint Albert* have to say about collective discernment (the text of the *Rule* is printed at the front of this book)?

Ponder the words of Christ: Read what Jesus says about 'the signs of the times' in *Matthew* 16:1-4.

A praying community at the service of all God's people

Since the earliest days of Carmelite life, service has been an essential element. Even the hermits in their individual cells on Mount Carmel were to undertake some form of work, and to serve each other in community. The *Way of Life* they chose to follow was set out by Saint Albert of Jerusalem who deliberately modelled their fraternity on the early Christians as described in the *Acts of the Apostles* and the letters of St. Paul, in which we read that the community shared what they had in common, cared about each others' needs, and sought to outdo each other in love. Pilgrim accounts suggest that they offered the service of hospitality to visitors, and later ordained hermits served the pastoral needs of those in the surrounding area. The nuns and hermits in the Carmelite Family today likewise look for ways to serve those around them, within the possibilities of enclosure. By living in community in an intense way, enclosed Carmelites have daily opportunities to serve those they live with. As far as the wider world is concerned, their prayer for the Church and the World is also a form of service, hidden but life-giving, which can be shared by those lay Carmelites, friars and sisters who are too ill or elderly to undertake active apostolates. Those Carmelites who are retired from active ministry still have much to contribute.

'Lord, teach us to pray'. (*Luke* 11:1) Communities within Carmel, and in places such as Taizé in France, serve people by responding to the hunger many have to learn deeper forms of prayer and meditation.

Many Carmelites, ordained and unordained, religious and lay, offer their service for the common good within the Church, as ministers of the Word and the Eucharist, as welcomers, liturgists, altar servers, and so on. Our service within the Church is not self-serving but builds up the body of Christ.

Prayer is an essential service offered by the Carmelite Family. Society today is in desperate need of people of prayer who can give a word of encouragement and the benefit of their experience to those seeking meaning in life through a relationship with God. In a world facing the uncertainties of climate change, financial and political unrest, disease and terrorism, teaching people how to pray, meditate and nurture a calm stillness in their lives can be a tremendous act of service.

Stop and think: Do you reckon that sometimes Christians offer to pray for someone or a situation as a way of opting-out from doing something more practical? Does God answer prayer when there is something we could do ourselves to resolve a situation? Conversely, do Christians sometimes think that only practical action by their own efforts will solve problems, and neglect to present the issues to God in prayer?

A service of evangelisation

Part of the service the Carmelite must undertake is to communicate the reality of God to other people. Not everyone can be a missionary by travelling to new lands, but like St. Thérèse we can all support those engaged in mission abroad, and we all as baptised Christians have a mission at home to evangelise, that is, to spread the Good News that God exists and loves us. Jesus asked his followers to make this news known throughout the world, and we Carmelites can do this through our words and our actions. Indeed, actions can speak powerfully of God's love, prompting St. Francis to state: 'Preach the Gospel always, and if necessary use words'. In his 1975 Apostolic Exhortation *Evangelii Nuntiandi* Pope Paul VI recognised that people today 'listen more willingly to witnesses than to teachers, and if they do listen to teachers it is because they are witnesses.' Demonstrating our faith by our service can draw others to Carmel, and more importantly, to God: 'Carmelites, ready to witness to their faith by their works, receive the strength to draw people to God who may become the praise of God's glory. In times of loss and change, (Lay) Carmelites can give many people reliable direction.' (*RTOC* §47).

Service in the midst of the people

For most Carmelites their vocation is to live and serve *in the midst of the people*. The phrase *in the midst of the people* recurs frequently in the Carmelite tradition and is very important to the friars because it reminds them that they are mendicants, and therefore historically live, work and pray in the heart of society, not detached from it. Involvement in social outreach was essential to the survival of the Order after 1274 when the Second Council of Lyons demanded that Carmelites prove their usefulness to the Church or face suppression. It was the brothers' attentiveness to service of God and neighbour in medieval Europe that attracted lay people to their way of life, eventually giving birth to lay confraternities and the Third Order.

The notion of being *in the midst of the people* likewise applies to the Order's laypeople, apostolic (active) sisters, and even to some extent to the enclosed nuns. Immersion in the heart of society is particularly encouraged for lay Carmelites by the 2003 *Rule for the Third Order of Carmel*:

> Since it is the proper calling of lay people to live in the world and in the midst of secular affairs, they are called upon by God to carry out this mission of the Church so that there is a Christian yeast in the temporal activities which they are deeply engaged in. The faithful cannot renounce their participation in 'public life', in the many and various social, economic, legislative, administrative and cultural ventures which are meant to promote the common good institutionally (§46).

A Carmelite friar and lay person in conversation.

Did you know? The notion of being 'a Christian yeast' inspires *The Leaven* Secular Institute, known officially as *The Institute of Our Lady of Mount Carmel*. It was founded at Aylesford Priory in Britain in 1949 to offer a deep experience of Carmelite spirituality to its members, namely single women who live a consecrated life in their own homes and workplaces, and who profess the evangelical counsels of poverty, chastity and obedience. *The Leaven* was formally affiliated to the Carmelite Order in 1965.

Service in the home, workplace, and beyond

For many lay Carmelites the most common place of service will be the home and the workplace: 'Lay Carmelites understand and show in their lives that temporal activities and material work are themselves a sharing in the ever creative and transforming work of the Father. This is a real service offered to humanity and its authentic promotion.' (*RTOC* §49). One description of a tertiary is 'a Carmelite who works from home', and most homes offer plenty of opportunities to carry out responsibilities in a spirit of love and service. As the saying goes 'charity begins at home', but it doesn't end there.

Whether we serve at home or in the workplace, we are asked to see that service as part of our Carmelite vocation. After making Profession as a religious or lay Carmelite we are expected to offer service to the Carmelite Family, and on behalf of the Family. All professed Carmelites, religious or lay, represent the Order to the World. In the past there was a common feeling in some sections of the Third Order that Lay Carmel existed

Teresa of Jesus understood that 'God walks among the pots and pans'.

in order to promote the 'personal holiness' of its members, with little sense of looking outwards to the wider world. Yet true holiness always has an ecclesial and social element, participating in the mission and service of the Church. It is not only friars who undertake ministry on behalf of the Order, but all members of Carmel. Today there is a much broader sense that whatever service lay Carmelites undertake, they too are in ministry. That ministry may or may not be overtly 'religious', but by contributing to the wellbeing of humanity it contributes to the Order's service nonetheless. Lay Carmelites no longer depend entirely on the religious of Carmel to do service within the Church; instead all join together in what we call *collaborative ministry*, each branch of the Family undertaking whatever it is appropriate for them to do.

Did you know? A Carmelite very involved in the political service of his day was Saint Nuno Álvares Pereira (1360-1431). Nuno was a very successful military general whose service of the people of Portugal was decisive in their fight for independence from Castile (Spain). As a husband and father he was committed to the service of his family. After his wife's death Nuno became a Carmelite friar in Lisbon, specially dedicated to serving the poor that came to the friary for help. A hero in his native land, Nuno was canonised in 2009.

A painting of Saint Nuno in Saint Albert's International Centre (CISA) in Rome.

The teachings of the Second Vatican Council on service in the modern world

The growing appreciation of the laity's contribution to the ministry of the Church has been helped by the teachings of the Second Vatican Council. In particular the 1965 decree on the apostolate of the laity, *Apostolicam Actuositatem*, reminded the Church that it is legitimate for unordained Christians to immerse themselves in all kinds of works and apostolates that promote good things in life: 'the prosperity of the family, culture, economic matters, the arts and professions, the laws of the political community, international relations, and other matters' (§7). These are aspects of life made and blessed by God, who at the creation of the world 'saw all that he had made was very good' (*Genesis* 1:31). God is not only interested in what we might narrowly define as 'spiritual life', but in all aspects of life as it is meant to be lived, that is, in the Spirit. Sometimes in history temporal goods have been used and misused by men and women, but the activities and work of the world are intended for the common good, and so the role of the Christian – of the Carmelite – is to make sure that our work is done for the good of the Church and the World.

As Carmelites we are both immersed in our cultures, and counter-cultural; immersed in the world, but not belonging to the world. Like our teacher and model Saint Paul, we stand alongside our brothers and sisters in the marketplace and proclaim a message at which some will scoff whilst others will want to hear more (*Acts* 17:16-34). Like our brother Titus Brandsma we realise that 'those who want to win the world for Christ must have the courage to come into conflict with it'.

The other Vatican II document which should be read by all those serious about understanding why Carmelites must go into service of others is *Gaudium et Spes*, the Pastoral Constitution on the Church in the Modern World. *Gaudium et Spes* ('Joy and

Carmelites share the joys and hopes, griefs and anxieties of the people of this age.

Hope') opens with a beautiful summary of why Christians cannot remain isolated from the needs of others, both Christians and non-Christians:

> The joys and the hopes, the griefs and the anxieties of the people of this age, especially those who are poor or in any way afflicted, these are the joys and hopes, the griefs and anxieties of the followers of Christ. Indeed, nothing genuinely human fails to raise an echo in their hearts. For theirs is a community composed of men and women. United in Christ, they are led by the Holy Spirit in their journey to the Kingdom of their Father and they have welcomed the news of salvation which is meant for every man and woman. That is why this community [of the Church] realizes that it is truly linked with humankind and its history by the deepest of bonds.

For this reason our service doesn't only have to be overtly 'religious'; anything which contributes to the authentic building up of society is a holy work. We can serve God in any activity that is genuinely for the good of humanity because such service manifests the love of God for his people and is therefore holy. This is echoed in the *Rule for the Third Order of Carmel*:

> There should be no conflict between temporal well-being and the realisation of God's kingdom, given that the natural and spiritual orders both come from God (§29) … Witnesses in a world which neither fully appreciates, nor totally rejects that intimate and living relationship with God in daily life, lay Carmelites know and share with empathy the expectations and deepest aspirations of the world because they are called to be 'salt of the earth' and 'light of the world'. They proclaim the knowledge of salvation to the people. (§49)

For centuries the Church saw itself in opposition to 'the World', though such a division is contrary to the Gospel: 'For God so loved the world that he gave his only Son, so that everyone who believes in him may not perish but may have eternal life. Indeed, God did not send the Son into the world to condemn the world, but in order that the world might be saved through him' (*John* 3:16-17). Part of Carmel's mission is to overcome any false division between the Church and the World, the 'spiritual' and the 'material', which both come from God.

Stop and think: Earlier we listed the 'Spiritual' and the 'Corporal' Works of Mercy. Is the division between 'spiritual' and 'corporal' works a helpful or accurate one?

Future reflection: Carmelites seeking material for ongoing formation will find plenty of excellent material to ponder in *Gaudium et Spes*. The Church's centuries of teaching about the necessity of building up God's reign on earth through active ministries are also summarised in the 1992 *Catechism of the Catholic Church* and its companion volume, the 2005 *Compendium of the Social Teaching of the Catholic Church*.

Service of humanity is not a distraction from the divine

Some people fear that by engaging in the service of our fellow human beings we are somehow neglecting our relationship with God. Yet Carmelites – like all Christians – recognise in the incarnate person of Jesus of Nazareth that humanity is *the* way that we come to know God, and we should thus especially revere the human person. God our Father has chosen to reveal himself to us in the human form of Jesus. This is why Carmelite saints such as Teresa of Jesus rejected the idea that meditating on the humanity of Jesus was somehow an obstacle to appreciating his divinity. Carmelites look to how Jesus lived and related to people to discover what it truly means to be human, and thus know the way to God. As the 1992 *Catechism* puts it:

> Jesus the Son of God… worked with human hands; he thought with a human mind. He acted with a human will, and with a human heart he loved. Born of the Virgin Mary, he has truly been made one of us, like to us in all things except sin. (§2599)

Approaching the humanity of those around us – people made in the image and likeness of God – will help us to draw closer to the Creator who made them. In reaching out to the poor and marginalised, the weak, the vulnerable, and those without a voice or stake in society, it is not so much that we bring God's presence to them; rather, God's presence already in them is revealed to us, and we become informed and formed as a result. It is not possible to stand alongside the poor and marginalised without being changed by the encounter, because God is there.

Our service is not just of those in Carmel, or even those in the Church, but any and all of God's people, since all women and men are made in the image and likeness of God. All human beings – simply by virtue of being human – have the capacity for God (*capax Dei*). Our service is always to be for the good of others not for ourselves, however Scripture tells us and experience reminds us of what St. Francis of Assisi said: 'it is in giving that we receive'. Service must never be geared towards our own ends, or forcing ourselves and our will upon others. Service of this kind is not about sharing love but about wielding power. If our 'Carmelite service' is limited to making us feel safe and good then perhaps our Carmelite vocation is not being lived out as fully as it could be, and runs the risk of serving only ourselves and those we feel comfortable with.

Stop and think: Have you ever done an act of service which felt uncomfortable or difficult at the time, but which in hindsight was significant?

The fundamental option for the poor

Uncomfortable though it is, the truth is that our service is especially needed by the poor and marginalised of society: 'Through the gift of ourselves, we undertake to serve, in justice and charity, Jesus himself, who is present in all his brothers and sisters, especially in the little ones and those on the fringes of society' (*RTOC* §27). This means the materially and physically poor. It also means those who are spiritually and socially poor, perhaps excluded by Society, and sadly, even by the Church. Carmel exists – as St. Thérèse put it – to be 'love in the heart of the Church'. A heart pumps life to the rest of the body, to its very extremities, and so Carmel is given the vocation of spreading life to those on the very margins of Church and Society.

Stop and think: Who do you consider to be the poor and marginalised of today? Whom has Society excluded? Whom has the Church excluded? How can Carmel be of real service to them?

As Christians we are asked to make what the Church calls a *fundamental option for the poor*, since Jesus always addressed himself to the poor of his day before anyone else, often people excluded from social and religious circles. Carmelites are called to embrace poverty – one of the 'evangelical counsels' – as a way of living as Christ did amongst the poor, relying solely on God's providence, and seeing the world as the poor do with the eyes of faith. Evangelical poverty responds to 'the generous act of our Lord Jesus Christ, that though he was rich, yet for your sakes he became poor, so that by his poverty you might become rich' (*2 Corinthians* 8:9). Placing all our activities in God's hands, a spirit of poverty and poverty of spirit help us commit to the causes of justice, peace and the integrity of Creation at local, national, and international levels (which we shall consider in the next chapter). Realising our own poverty and sinfulness before God and grateful for his generous inclusion of us in his family, we learn to be inclusive of others.

Stop and think: It is often said that the poor are the most generous. Why do you think this might be?

Elijah and Mary: models of service

To assist and inspire us in our journey of service the Carmelite Family upholds two of God's great servants: Elijah and Mary.

As a prophet, Elijah the Tishbite disposed himself to God's service, speaking truth in the Lord's name. The spiritual father of our Order referred to himself in terms of service: 'As the Lord God lives, whom I serve' (*1 Kings* 18:15). He fearlessly proclaimed the justice and love of God in a world full of turmoil, condemning the injustice of the political rulers of the day and bringing words of comfort and tenderness to the oppressed people of Israel. He combined prayer and solitude with service of the poor and disenfranchised in the community. Elijah's relationship with the Widow of Zarephath (or Sarepta) was one of life-giving service: out of her poverty she provided him with food and drink at a time of drought, and he brought healing to her dying son (*1 Kings* 17:7-24). Elijah spoke out on behalf of the dispossessed in denouncing King Ahab and Queen Jezebel's theft of Naboth's vineyard (*1 Kings* 21). One of Elijah's final acts of service was to anoint Elisha as a prophet to succeed him, and Elisha became Elijah's servant (*1 Kings* 19:21). As spiritual descendents of the 'company of prophets' we Carmelites seek to serve God and his people by proclaiming, like Elijah and Elisha, the truth of the Lord's existence, by opposing tyrannical rule, and by bringing hope to the poor.

Carmelite devotion to Mary the mother of Jesus likewise inspires our service, and is always geared towards the woman we encounter in the Gospel, Miriam of Nazareth. There we find Mary is God's 'handmaid' or 'servant' (*Luke* 1:38), the 'first among the humble and poor of the Lord' (*RTOC* §34). Our Lady was totally open to whatever

Multi-narrative icons such as this depict different episodes in the life of Elijah.

service God asked of her because she possessed purity of heart (*puritas cordis*) and a spirit of openness to God (*vacare Deo*). The service she undertook was not of her choosing; rather, in her *Magnificat* song of praise to God we hear that she possessed a spirit of obedience that embraced God's will and enabled her to stand in solidarity with the poor.

Stop and ponder Mary's proclamation: Read the *Magnificat* (*Luke* 1:46-55).

Mary was Jesus' perfect disciple and therefore the most reliable model of all that Carmelites desire to be. Like Elijah, Mary served through her relationships, and for many Carmelites – notably lay Carmelites – a primary act of service is to care for their family members. In this Mary is again our inspiration; she was a tender wife to Joseph, a loving mother to Jesus, and a considerate cousin to Elizabeth.

Mary was at the service of her son, as mother and disciple. Mary is constantly at the service of her son's Church, always attentive to its needs. Just as she interceded with her son at the wedding in Cana – 'they have no more wine' (*John* 2:3) – so Mary asks Jesus for all the graces we need. Writing as Prior General to the 2001 International Lay Carmelite Congress, Joseph Chalmers, O.Carm., reminded Carmelites that 'devotion to Mary must involve the whole of life, including time for prayer and time for service of one's neighbour'. The best service we as Carmelites can render Mary, our mother and sister, is to imitate her life of care for others.

Mary was married, and the Church recognises in marriage a symbol of Christ's love for his Church. Through such commitment, many lay members of the Carmelite Family witness to the service of one another.

Use your imagination: If you had to identify two people who in our own times embody the spirit of service demonstrated by Elijah and by Mary, whom would you choose (remember, they needn't necessarily be 'religious' personalities)?

Contemplative service

One of the challenges facing the Order in its commitment to service today is overcoming the centuries-old dualistic attitude that perceives prayer and service in opposition to one another. The term 'contemplative' was – and often still is – used exclusively to describe a life of prayer and meditation, and many good Christians taught that such a vocation was superior to the 'active life' of service. The 'religious life' was upheld as 'contemplative' and therefore superior to the 'active life' of the laity. The Gospel story of Martha and Mary at Bethany was sometimes cited as illustrating the difference between 'contemplatives' and 'actives':

Now as they went on their way, Jesus entered a certain village where a woman named Martha welcomed him into her home. She had a sister named Mary, who sat at the Lord's feet and listened to what he was saying. But Martha was distracted by her many tasks; so she came to him and asked, 'Lord, do you not care that my sister has left me to do all the work by myself? Tell her then to help me.' But the Lord answered her, 'Martha, Martha, you are worried and distracted by many things; there is need of only one thing. Mary has chosen the better part, which will not be taken away from her.' (*Luke* 10:38-42)

A superficial reading of this episode might suggest that Jesus praised Mary 'the contemplative' over Martha 'the active'. However, another interpretation is not to see it as about 'contemplation vs. action' but 'contemplation vs. distraction'. Martha was someone whose service was not wholehearted: 'Martha, Martha, you are worried and distracted by many things'. Mary was not distracted; she focussed entirely on the presence of Jesus in her life, and thus had 'chosen the better part' (what mattered was not so much her paying 'attention' but rather giving Jesus her 'intention' of being with him). This does not mean that Mary would have spent all her time on her knees; rather her encounter with Jesus, her contemplation of God, meant that she was transformed and thus better able

to perceive the needs of those around her. No doubt Mary was willing to help her sister, but she knew that the important thing at that time was not to fret and fuss over many tasks but to offer Jesus true hospitality of the heart. Martha on the other hand was not fully motivated by love but was worried and distracted. Martha's apparent 'service' focussed on her own preoccupations. The result was not true hospitality but rather resentment of her

As well as from Mary, Jesus learned his spirit of service from Joseph, who is loved and revered as 'Joseph the Worker' on 1st May each year. In this statue above St. Joseph's monastery in Avila, St. Teresa's first foundation, the young Jesus holds his father's carpentry tools.

As Carmelites we seek to nurture hearts that offer hospitality to God and others.

sister Mary, whom she wouldn't even refer to by name, prompting Jesus to state Martha's name twice in gentle correction. Martha learned from the experience to open herself to Christ's presence with an undivided heart; so effective was this that later, following the death of her brother Lazarus, Martha was able to declare complete faith in Jesus (*John* 11:21-22).

There is something of both Martha and Mary in most of us. At Bethany Mary was truly contemplative in that her primary focus was friendship with Jesus. She knew that being in the Lord's presence was the 'one thing necessary', and from this flowed her service as well as her prayer. Contemplation is the inflowing of God into an open heart. It is God's free gift, given when and where he wishes to a soul willing to welcome and cooperate with him.

We Carmelites try to develop a 'contemplative attitude' of welcome to God, and this can come about not only through prayer but also through service, and through community interaction. That is why the *Ratios* (formation guidelines) of both the Carmelite friars and nuns state that: 'The contemplative dimension is not merely one of the elements of our charism (prayer, community and service): it is the dynamic element which unifies them all'. In the Carmelite understanding it is not properly possible to compare 'action vs. contemplation' as if they are opposites; contemplation is the dynamic which unites prayer, service and community, and it is both an active cooperation with God and a passive reception of his grace.

There are arguably certain forms of prayer and meditation that can better dispose us to a contemplative encounter with God, what is sometimes called *infused prayer*.

But the term *contemplative prayer* can be misleading if we don't set it alongside *contemplative service* and *contemplative community living*. Prayer is essential for us to receive God's gift of contemplation, but it is not the only means by which we become contemplative. As Thomas Merton put it: 'For a Carmelite, the apostolate in its own way encourages contemplation, just as contemplation is the source of a genuine apostolate.' Our service must flow from this understanding of contemplation, and an attitude of *being* at service.

Stop and think: Teresa of Jesus said that she knew contemplatives who practised vocal prayers, but that most seemed to progress through stages of meditation to a simple and silent resting in God's presence. If certain types of prayer do better dispose us to God's gift of contemplation, do you think that certain types of service better dispose us to contemplation too?

The Cistercian monk Thomas Merton (1915-68) is widely regarded as a modern mystic. As well as being a writer of theological prose he was a poet and social activist. Greatly inspired by Carmelite spirituality, he declared in his book *The Ascent to Truth*: 'There is no member of the Church who does not owe something to Carmel'.

Prayer and service inform one another

Carmelites believe that becoming contemplative – being open to the presence and action of God – is a gradual process of transformation. It enables us to grow in God's likeness, to see with the eyes of God and to love with the heart of God. The natural fruit of contemplation is therefore to go out in service of God's people, just as Jesus did; periods of prayer and reflection gave him strength to go into service of others. To serve people properly we must pray. Prayer inspires us to go out and serve, and service of others exposes our need for prayer. Without prayer – an intimate sharing with the God we know loves us – our service will be based on our own efforts and not the inspiration and grace of God. Without prayer the problems facing us may be insurmountable and we remain ineffective as servants. Without prayer our service can become, like Martha, detached from a true relationship with those we serve.

In her reform of Carmel, Teresa of Jesus (of Avila) wasn't seeking to marginalise the active apostolate, but to nourish it with prayer. She said that she became busiest when she was most deeply rooted in contemplation, and that prayer must show its fruits in good works. The link between prayer and service is captured well in the 2003 *Constitutions of the Secular Order of the Teresian Carmel* (O.C.D.S.):

Prayer and apostolate, when they are true, are inseparable. The observation of St. Teresa that the purpose of prayer is 'the birth of good works' reminds the Secular Order that graces received ought to have an effect on those who receive them. Individually or as a community, and above all as members of the Church, apostolic activity is the fruit of prayer. (§26)

A contemporary Carmelite likewise describes the link between prayer and service:

It is the contemplative dimension of Carmel which impels the community to pay special attention to the 'little ones' of the world, those left out of the world's attention and care. Contemplation leads one into an awareness of one's own poverty of spirit and the need to wait on God. From this self-knowledge it is possible to be in solidarity with and have concern for all who have to wait in hope for God's mercy and compassion. Contemplative prayer should be the deepest source of concern for the poor, the oppressed, and the marginalized of our world.

(John Welch, O.Carm., *The Carmelite Tradition*, printed in Chapter 4).

This painting depicts St. Teresa aged 7 setting out from Avila with her brother Rodrigo to preach the Gospel, until an uncle brought them home! She came to appreciate that her Christian vocation would have to be expressed in concrete care for others.

Quietism and activism

A false understanding of what contemplation is can lead to either a rejection of prayer, or a rejection of service. In the seventeenth century the notion of contemplation as God's gift to a willing soul was distorted by a philosophy known as *Quietism*. The Quietists placed great emphasis on intellectual stillness and interior passivity, believing that they could become perfect on earth purely by God's grace regardless of their own effort in collaborating with God; thus they did not feel the need to participate in the life and sacraments of the Church, or exercise any ministry of service. This idea was condemned as heresy by the Roman Catholic Church because although contemplation is indeed God's free gift and cannot be achieved solely by human actions, the effect of God's grace is for the Christian to cooperate with God, putting God's love into action through service and engaging fully in the life of the community.

The opposite danger of Quietism is Activism, that is, believing that action is the only worthwhile Christian practice, and that time spent in quiet reflection and prayer is wasted. As Carmelites we have to tread carefully between these two extremes, ensuring that all we do springs from a more authentic understanding of contemplation.

Stop and think for a moment: Do you reckon notions of Quietism and Activism persist in the Church today?

Contemplation, the reign of God, and the community

The contemplative attitude which the Carmelite tradition develops in us implies living with greater awareness, a wider consciousness of the world around us. Deepening our understanding of Carmelite spirituality does not remove us from the world; rather the opposite. Carmel throws us into the cut and thrust of life, into the world which Jesus immersed himself in. Jesus chose to become human and to take on the concerns of the human family. He is the supreme example of a contemplative whose heart was open to the Father, and thus also to his brothers and sisters. In this way Jesus announced the reign, the Kingdom, of God:

Carmelites live in the midst of fellow pilgrims on life's journey.

> To be contemplative is to live the Kingdom. It is the human response to the love that God lavishes upon us. As contemplatives we are called to have eyes that see and ears that hear. We are to be in relationship with the world and its peoples. Contemplation is not a withdrawal from the world's realities but a dialogue with them.
>
> (Damian Cassidy, O.Carm., *Contemplation and the Reign of God*)

Being open to those around us is a crucial aspect of Carmelite life, and the community dimension of our charism is indispensable if we are to be transformed in Christ. We are not transformed on our own but in and through our relationships with other people. Human beings need one another; that is the way we are made and it is through relationship with other human beings that we grow and develop emotionally. 'How we relate to people on a constant basis is the test of whether we are growing in the spiritual life or not' (Joseph Chalmers, O.Carm., *Mary the Contemplative*). The community is also the place where our service is inspired, tested, and – if need be – corrected.

Our Carmelite communities are places where we can be of service, even in the tiniest act of welcome, accompaniment and friendship. Forming communities is itself an act of service and a sign of hope. Those in leadership within Carmelite communities have a particular duty to foster a spirit of service, leading by example: the *Rule of Saint Albert* specifies that leaders must serve in the spirit of Christ, and St. Teresa of Jesus specifies in her nuns' *Constitutions* that the Prioress must be the first to sweep the floor.

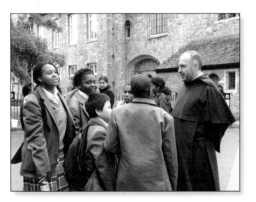

Carmelites welcome and accompany others.

Service as a community

Since service is an integral element of the Carmelite charism, apostolates can also be undertaken by communities as corporate activities, not solely by individuals within the community (exactly what form this will take depends on the circumstances). There are numerous benefits in a corporate approach to service. Firstly, it binds individual Carmelites together in a common purpose, helping erstwhile solitaries to become one body, as envisioned by Saint Paul. Secondly, it can render service more effective (the Bible is full of stories of people achieving more when they put their heads and hands together). Thirdly it helps Carmelite communities to be more outward-looking towards the world God loves. Linked to this is a fourth benefit, that of attracting new vocations to Carmel; communities that serve as communities tend to be happier, holier and thus more relevant and appealing groups, visible signs that God is at work in them. This applies not only at the level of individual communities, but also at the level of Delegations, Commissariats and Provinces within the Order. In recent times several Provinces – which are essentially a community of communities – have undertaken a collective mission or project, which often enables more to be done, and a more visible witness to be given. The increasing sense within Carmel of being part of a 'global village' offers many opportunities for real partnerships that span cultures.

Stop and think: Are you aware of any national or international project of service that your Province or region is involved in?

Through service in the community, and supported by the community, Carmelites come to *practice the presence of God* (see Chapter 9). By reading and listening each day to the Word of God, especially in *Lectio Divina*, and by receiving Jesus regularly in the Eucharist, God becomes a living reality in our lives. At the end of the Eucharist we are sent out 'to love and serve the Lord', having been given the nourishment necessary to do so.

Service as journey

When we are sent out to serve, we realise that service – like the Carmelite way of life – can be thought of as a journey. Think, for example, of Jesus' parable of the Good Samaritan and the journey he made in solidarity with a suffering stranger. As we advance on the Carmelites' pilgrim path, through the deserts and oases of life, we will encounter many challenges and opportunities to be of service to God in our neighbour. If we are to meet those challenges we will need to be continually growing in our relationship with God. As Carmelites our spirituality has to be authentically rooted in the Carmelite tradition, and through our ongoing formation we will develop a mature and fruitful Christianity.

Stop and read the last chapter of the *Rule of Saint Albert*: Some commentators have interpreted the phrase 'Our Lord at his second coming will reward anyone who does more than he is obliged to do' as an echo of the parable of the Good Samaritan, who says to the inn-keeper 'when I come back I will repay you whatever more you spend' (*Luke* 10:35). Why might Saint Albert have concluded our Carmelite *Way of Life* 'vision statement' with this phrase?

Conclusion: In this sixteenth chapter we have reflected on the vocation that Carmelites – like all Christians – receive to be of service to both the Church and the World out of love for God and neighbour. As ever we are inspired in our living out of the charism by the examples of Jesus Christ, Elijah, Mary, and the saints of Carmel. We also find inspirations to serve in the example of one another, and the teachings of the Church and the Order. We've reflected on how service is not opposed to contemplation but rather flows from and towards it. This chapter can only speak of service in rather theoretical terms; it is for each Carmelite individual as well as each community to work out exactly how they are to demonstrate a spirit of service in practice.

As well as concluding your time of reflection and study with prayer, why not think about doing some form of service for someone else?

In the next chapter we will see how Carmel's call to service is expressed partly in the Order's response to issues of justice, peace, and the integrity of Creation.

Ideas for Reflection, Discussion and Action

- Has anything in this chapter caught your attention, either individually or as a community. Apart from the text, has any image struck you? Can you recognise the significance of all the images to the topic of service?

- Try each morning, as you put on your scapular – which is essentially a form of the monastic apron and thus a sign of labour – to offer yourself in service, perhaps saying: 'Mary, use me in the service of your son Jesus today.'

- Is service something we are aware of as Carmelite individuals, as local communities, and as a Province? If not, what are the underlying reasons? Could the following be factors: fear; misunderstanding of our charism; age and illness; ignorance; being too busy; laziness; a lack of ideas and energy; failing to see our current service as part of Carmel's ministry?

- Would you agree with the statement 'Service is the biggest challenge, and richest opportunity, facing the Carmelite Family today'?

- If you belong to a Province or community that has a 'vision statement' or similar formulation of intentions, see what aspirations it articulates on the subject of service.

- A spirit of service is encouraged by sharing stories; do you have a project you could tell others about through Carmelite newsletters, websites or other forms of communication?

- What forms of service do you undertake already, at home, at work, at church? Are you known in those places as a Carmelite? Do you see this service as part of your Carmelite vocation?

- Do you agree that the distinction between 'contemplation' and 'action' is a false one? How can we develop a sense of *contemplative service* and *contemplative community living* as well as of *contemplative prayer*?

- How can those of us who are members of a Carmelite community be at the service of God's people *together*? How can those Carmelites who are not able to belong to a regular community contribute to a communal sense of service?

- How can Carmelites who are restricted in their capacities – because of age perhaps, or limited resources – nevertheless practice a spirit or attitude of service?

- Read about service in chapters 46-49 of the 2003 *Rule for the Third Order of Carmel*, and compare it with other modern legislation within the Carmelite Family.

- Are we concerned about what Society and even what the Church might think of us if we take the risk of serving certain groups of marginalised people?

- When did your Carmelite community last discuss how it could be of service to the local Church and wider Society? List the ways that you and/or your Carmelite community are at the service of the Church and the World; not as a means of praising yourself, but of realising to what extent you are open to God using you for the benefit of others. Does your community appreciate the Carmelite 'theory' or understanding of service, as well as the wide variety of possible apostolates?

- Could you give time or money to a charity or fund-raising event that benefits society at large? Are there people outside the church community who would appreciate a visit, perhaps someone in hospital, at home, or in prison? Could you get involved in a national or local interest group?

- How do I go out from Mass 'to love and serve the Lord'? What do I need to be properly equipped for service of others?

- In a spirit of *Lectio Divina* pray with one of the Gospel passages in this chapter.

- In what way is your prayer and meditation linked to the service of the Church and the World?

- Peter Slattery, O.Carm., describes Carmelites as 'Pilgrims, Poets and Prophets' (*Springs of Carmel*, p. 151). Does this resonate with you?

- If you are part of a Carmelite community, do you offer to visitors and enquirers an authentic experience of the Order's spirituality through some form of group service, as well as through prayer and community?

- Pray for the work of those in the Carmelite Family who do any form of active service, and ask God for an increased sense within Carmel of being at the service of the Church and the World.

Recommended Further Resources

There are plenty of resources available in most Christian community libraries and bookshops about the Church's teaching on service. Why not consider combining your further reading and researching with some form of practical service of others?

Apostolicam Actuositatem, Decree on the Apostolate of the Laity. Available in a variety of publications and editions, including those of the official publishers to the Holy See (such as the Catholic Truth Society in Britain or Veritas in Ireland) or online at www.vatican.va

Johan Bergström-Allen, T.O.C., 'At the Service of God's People', *Assumpta*, Vol. 52 Nos. 7 & 8, July/August 2009, pp. 44-58.

Damian Cassidy, O.Carm., 'Contemplation and the Reign of God', article in the spirituality section of the British Province of Carmelites: www.carmelite.org

Catholic Bishops' Conference of England and Wales, *The Common Good and the Catholic Church's Social Teaching*, 1996.

Joseph Chalmers, O.Carm., 'Planning for the future', in *In Allegiance to Jesus Christ*, (Rome: Edizioni Carmelitane, 1999), pp. 34-38.

Gaudium et Spes, The Pastoral Constitution on the Church in the Modern World. Available in a variety of publications and editions, including those of the official publishers to the Holy See (such as the Catholic Truth Society in Britain or Veritas in Ireland) or online at www.vatican.va

Michelle Jones, '*Imbuing All With Love*: The Apostolic Character of The Contemplative Life According to St. John of the Cross', *Carmelite Digest*, Volume 23 Number 4, Winter 2008, pp. 22-34.

Thomas Merton, O.C.S.O., 'Balancing Contemplation and Action' from the Epilogue of *Seven Storey Mountain*, available in various editions.

Pontifical Council for Justice and Peace, *Compendium of the Social Doctrine of the Catholic Church*, 2005.

Ratio of the Carmelite Friars (*Ratio Institutionis Vitæ Carmelitanæ*), Section E – Service among the people. Available in print (Rome: Curia of the Carmelite Order, 2000) or online at www.carmelite.org

Kevin Shanley, O.Carm., 'Frank Duff, T.O.Carm.: Founder of the Legion of Mary', *Carmel in the World*, Volume XLV Number 1, 2006, pp. 31-34.

Peter Slattery, O.Carm., 'Carmelite Spirituality Today', in *The Springs of Carmel: An Introduction to Carmelite Spirituality*, (New York: Alba House, 1991), pp. 135-152.

John Welch, O.Carm., *Seasons of the Heart – The Spiritual Dynamic of the Carmelite Life*, (Aylesford, Kent: Lay Carmel Central Office, 2002, Reprinted 2005).

Notes and reflections on Chapter 16

CHAPTER 17

Carmel and the Kingdom: Justice, Peace and the Integrity of Creation

Summary: By now we are used to speaking of the 'attitudes' that Carmelites seek to develop; ways of seeing the world, of relating to God and others, and living out our vocation of *allegiance to Jesus Christ* in fidelity to the Order's tradition. Though an ancient part of Christian teaching, in recent times the Church and the Order have become specially conscious of the essential 'attitude' of building peace, through justice, for the benefit of all Creation. In this chapter we will consider the beliefs underpinning 'justice, peace and the integrity of Creation', illustrated by some concrete examples of how this attitude is put into practice.

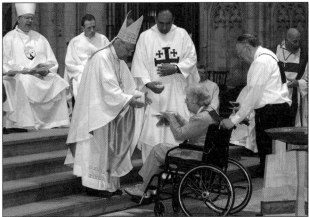

When the Carmelite Family celebrated the 8th centenary of the Carmelite Way of Life in 2007, the British Province of Carmelites marked the event with a Mass celebrated by St. Albert's successor as Latin Patriarch of Jerusalem, and a forum on building peace in the Holy Land.

Get prepared: There is much to ponder in this chapter, so perhaps approach it over a number of sittings. Don't forget that at the end is a blank page for you to record your thoughts and actions if you wish, so have writing implements to hand, as well as your Bible and reference materials. Consider beginning your time of reflection and study with a prayer, perhaps incorporating a symbol that speaks to you of peace, justice and the beauty of the earth: maybe a lamp that burns oil from the Holy Land; a plant or flowers; even a newspaper that reports on issues facing people of good will today. Many objects can serve as pointers to God's presence, but likewise you might find these a distraction; use whatever works best for you (or your group if you are with others). You might want to spend some time in silence before the discussion, or to offer a prayer or statement of hope, such as this one derived from Scripture that contains images so resonant for Carmelites:

> *In the days to come the mountain of the Lord's house*
> *shall be established as the highest of the mountains,*
> *and shall be raised above the hills; all the nations shall stream to it.*
> *Many peoples shall come and say,*
> *'Come, let us go up to the mountain of the Lord,*
> *to the house of the God of Jacob;*
> *that he may teach us his ways and that we may walk in his paths.'*
> *For out of Zion shall go forth instruction, and the word of the Lord from*
>   *Jerusalem.*
> *He shall judge between the nations, and shall arbitrate for many peoples;*
> *they shall beat their swords into ploughshares,*
> *and their spears into pruning-hooks;*
> *nation shall not lift up sword against nation,*
> *neither shall they learn war any more. (Isaiah 2:2–4)*

Carmelite values for living in the world

The Carmelite Family across the world seeks to preach Christ's Good News and build up God's Kingdom on earth by living in solidarity with the planet and its people. As we saw in the previous chapter on service, a vocation to Carmel is not for our personal piety but is God's gift to the Church and the World. A life geared towards contemplation awakens us to the world's concerns, and to issues of ethics and morality. We in Carmel seek to be God's servants, God's friends, and for this we need to nurture an awareness of and commitment to the issues of justice, peace, and the integrity of Creation (sometimes abbreviated to JPIC).

Justice and peace are certainly values we seek for those suffering extreme poverty or violence, but they are also attitudes we seek to live and incarnate in the ordinariness of everyday life in our own homes and communities. Just as service is an attitude of *being* that informs our *doing*, so concern for justice, peace and the integrity of Creation is about the way our concrete actions are motivated by our *being* Carmelite and living Carmel's attitudes (as discussed in Chapter 12). In this chapter we shall reflect on the ways in which we live these values holistically through every aspect our of lives, here and now.

Rooted in the Word

Carmelites are people rooted in the Word of God as expressed in the Bible, especially in the person of Jesus. Our inspiration for caring about JPIC issues has a deeply Scriptural basis. Pondering on the Bible as we continue our journey in Carmel (especially the practice of *Lectio Divina*) will deepen our understanding of justice and peace.

Fr. Carlos Mesters, O.Carm.

'God saw everything that he had made, and indeed, it was very good'.

Did you know? An important ministry of the Carmelite Family since the Second Vatican Council has been the promotion of *Lectio Divina* among what are sometimes called the Christian Base Communities, especially in economically developing countries. Christian Base Communities gather together the poor and sometimes illiterate into worshipping communities supported by the tutelage of a priest or lay member. For many people, particularly in rural areas, such communities are the primary way in which people have an experience of the Church. Their structure encourages discussion and solidarity, and a sense that the Holy Spirit primarily operates within the Church from the 'base' upwards. Through pondering the Bible together, even the very poorest in society have come to read their own lives within the light of the Good News of God's love. The Christian Base Communities were approved by the Conference of Latin American Bishops held in 1968 in the Colombian city of Medellín. One of the greatest Carmelite exponents of *Lectio Divina* amongst the Christian Base Communities in Brazil has been the Dutch-born friar Carlos Mesters, O.Carm. (b. 1931).

The Bible is the story of God's relationship with his people, and at its very beginning we find in the book of *Genesis* God the Creator making the world, finding it to be good, and entrusting it to the care of humanity, the greatest expression of his creativity: 'God blessed them [Adam and Eve], and God said to them, 'Be fruitful and multiply, and fill the earth and subdue it ... See, I have given you every plant yielding seed that is upon the face of all the earth, and every tree with seed in its fruit; you shall have them for food ... God saw everything that he had made, and indeed, it was very good' (*Genesis* 1:28-31).

We know that the relationship between God and his people was harmed through humanity's proud self-reliance, but throughout the Old Testament God called his people back to him, wishing them to live justly and in peace with one another in a landed wedded to him. God's heralds of justice and peace were the prophets, who declared: 'This is what YHWH asks of you, only this: to act justly, to love tenderly and to walk humbly with your God' (*Micah* 6:8).

Stop and ponder God's word: Read *Isaiah* 65 in which the elimination of misery and exploitation is a sign of God's Kingdom where people are happy and rejoice.

Justice, love and humility are the attitudes God seeks to nurture in us, and they are most perfectly preached and embodied in his son, Jesus of Nazareth. As Carmelites living *in allegiance to Jesus Christ* (*Rule of Saint Albert* Chapter 2) we turn to him as our primary model for living.

The Kingdom of God

Jesus came to bring the Good News of the Father's love for the human family, announcing the *Reign* or *Kingdom of God*. The Kingdom of God has been beautifully described as *God's dream for the world*. It is the new Eden, a place – and state of heart and mind – in which justice and peace have flourished, and God's will has been sought and obeyed. God's Kingdom is a place of faith, hope and love in which all people – including the poor and marginalised – are included. Jesus told us that the Kingdom of God is already here, and within us, yet he also told us to go on searching for it; it is 'already, but not yet'.

At the outset of his public ministry Jesus proclaimed in Nazareth synagogue his vision of the Kingdom, declaring that the Spirit had anointed him to bring good news to the poor,

At the Annunciation – depicted here by Adam Kossowski at Whitefriars, Faversham, England – the angel Gabriel declared of Jesus that 'of his Kingdom there will be no end' (Luke 1:33).

to proclaim release to captives, to give sight to the blind, to set the oppressed free, to decree a year of favour from the Lord (the 'Lucan manifesto' in *Luke* 4:16-19). If we are to be members of the Kingdom of God we too must bring good news to the poor, feed the hungry, clothe the naked, and visit those who are sick or in prison (cf. *Matthew* 25). Even if we are not in a position to do so literally, we can all strive to live in ways which contribute to making the world a better place, to building-up the Kingdom of God through a just and peaceful approach to all of Creation. The Gospel accounts are full of teaching about the Kingdom and it is in this context that we should look for what Jesus' meaning of God's Reign is. It is for all; no one is excluded from it, even the little ones and the powerless.

Stop and recall your pondering of God's word: Frequently Jesus says in the Gospel 'the Kingdom of God is like...', and then uses a metaphor or parable. Make a list of some of the ways Jesus describes the Kingdom. Then reflect on this passage of Scripture: 'Once Jesus was asked by the Pharisees when the kingdom of God was coming, and he answered, 'The kingdom of God is not coming with things that can be observed; nor will they say, 'Look, here it is!' or 'There it is!' For, in fact, the kingdom of God is among you.' (*Luke* 17:20-21).

Seeking God's Kingdom is the first priority for Carmelites

Making God's Kingdom a reality on earth is a task Jesus entrusted to his disciples: 'strive first for the Kingdom of God and his righteousness' (*Matthew* 6:33). Jesus sent his followers out to preach about the Kingdom and announce the Good News. That is the mission facing every Carmelite, indeed every Christian, to this day as we seek to know and love God, and to make God known and loved. We need to look for – and be – signs of the Kingdom in our own families, communities and neighbourhoods, doing what we can by God's grace to make his Reign more fully visible, pointing others in the direction of love.

The quest for God's Kingdom is both a journey beyond ourselves, and a journey within ourselves.

It is here and now in the places God has put us that we Carmelites need to strive for God's Kingdom. Pope John Paul II reminded Carmelites that we must constantly give God's Kingdom primary importance: 'In Carmel, humanity, taken up as it is with so many concerns, needs to be reminded that absolute priority must be given to the search 'for the Kingdom of God and his righteousness' (quoted in the 2003 *Rule for the Third Order of Carmel* §33). The search for the Reign of God is an <u>absolute priority</u>; this is how much Carmel values the Kingdom. Nothing is more important.

Stop and think: Do we need to be reminded to give priority to God's Kingdom? Have we really let our attention wander into other lesser concerns? Do we quibble over the meanings of words like 'righteousness' and 'justice', losing sight of the bigger vision Jesus offers us? Have we got used to hearing about the Kingdom and no longer really listen?

Ponder God's word: Jesus said, 'Let the little children come to me; do not stop them; for it is to such as these that the Kingdom of God belongs. In truth I tell you anyone who does not welcome the Kingdom of God like a little child will never enter it.' (*Mark* 10:14-15). What does it mean for us to be like a little child? Why is it necessary for us to enter the Kingdom like a child?

Jesus was formed by poverty

When Jesus spoke of the Kingdom of God, he did so not as an earthly king but as a poor man. The whole of Jesus' human life – from his birth in a barn to his violent death outside the city walls – took place among the poor. The Son of God knew what it was to be homeless, a refugee, hungry, betrayed and abused. It was through his poverty and his own experience of need that Jesus could meet people where they were, and come to better understand them. Occasionally the poor challenged him to be more inclusive (such as the Syrophoenician woman in *Mark* 7:25-30, paralleled in *Matthew* 15:21-28). In his poverty Jesus even needed to ask the Samaritan woman by the well for a drink of water (*John* 4:1-30).

Did you know? The encounter between the Samaritan woman and Jesus has inspired the name of a branch of the Carmelite Family. Jesus told the woman 'If you knew the gift of God and who it is that is saying to you, "Give me a drink", you would have asked him and he would have given you living water.' The Latin for 'gift of God' is *Donum Dei*. The *Donum Dei Missionary Workers* are a group of Lay Carmelites founded by French priest Marcel Roussel-Galle (1910-84). He gathered together a group of women in Paris in 1950, whose vocation consists in offering themselves to the merciful love of God as inspired by St. Thérèse. Their mission is to help humanity appreciate Jesus as God's gift, who offers living water. Shortly before his death Fr. Roussel sought to root the *Donum Dei* family in the Carmelite Order, and in 1987 they were incorporated as a branch of the Third Order Secular. Today there are some thirty communities spread across the five continents. By running houses of hospitality and restaurants (known as *L'Eau Vive* meaning *Living Water*) in various parts of the world, the *Donum Dei Workers* fund their apostolates among the poor, prostitutes, prisoners, as well as catechetical and chaplaincy work.

Members of the *Donum Dei Missionary Workers*.

The preferential option for the poor

Jesus was a poor man among the poor. It was his poverty which inspired the mendicant (begging) movement in medieval Europe, firstly amongst the followers of St. Francis and later adopted by the Carmelites. Carmelites are inspired by Christ's example and the mendicant tradition to make a *preferential option for the poor*, an ancient concept within the Church given particular focus since the time of Pope John XXIII (1881-1963). Christ came for all people, but he came first to the poor, and thus the *preferential option for the poor* means that the Church must put the poor first, in its use of resources, in its pastoral plans, in every aspect of its life. The *option for the poor* has often been misunderstood as a solely political notion, but the Gospel has political implications and the *option for the poor* is now clearly understood as God's option: God chooses the poor. It is not that poverty itself is good, but before any other section of human society God chooses to be amongst the poor who enjoy nothing but his presence, and on whose behalf he demands justice. God loves all his children – the rich as well as the poor – but when, in the Old Testament, the rich oppressed the weak, God spoke up for the poor of Israel. The prophets – especially our father Elijah – lived as poor men and preached that God was on the side of the poor, of the victims of injustice, of the persecuted and the weak. Jesus always chose to be on the side of those who were materially, spiritually and socially poor, wherever they were to be found. Carmelites are likewise invited to make this choice; just as we have received freely, so freely we give, as the American Carmelite John Welch, O.Carm., wrote in 1996:

> The foundation for the work of justice and peace is the unmerited love of God, given freely. The gratuitousness of this love is the overwhelming reality of our lives, more overwhelming than even the direst analysis of the poverty of our world. The well spring of our activity and ministry with the poor is not our sympathetic analysis but the realisation of the mercy of God, who forgives, heals, strengthens, and brings life … One proceeds to the work of justice not from a position of anger, nor from guilt, nor from a sense of fairness, nor from a sympathetic heart, and

not because the poor are better. We minister with the poor because God has chosen to live with us and wants us all to participate in the gifts of creation and be happy with God forever. Where people are not able to participate in these gifts, the presence of God is most clearly seen. God's will is most evident here, and in that way we can say that God resides with the poor. Our work of justice is a response to this love. It becomes God's work, God's way of inviting all to the banquet of life.

Whether we live among the poor, or whether (like St. Thérèse) our ministry amongst them if in the less direct form of prayer, we too must consider how we can make an *option for the poor* a reality in our lives.

Stop and think: In what aspects of your life are you poor? In your own particular circumstances, how can you live in solidarity with the poor? What does it mean to choose the *option for the poor*?

Did you know? The Carmelite friar Blessed Angelo Paoli (1642-1720) was nicknamed 'the father of the poor'. Though he distributed charity to the sick and poor of Rome, he said this was not enough; it was necessary to give something of oneself as well. He brought together rich and poor to better recognise each other as sisters and brothers.

A Kingdom of peace built on justice

Jesus came to proclaim God's Kingdom as a poor man and not as a king. Many of his contemporaries were expecting God's anointed one – the Messiah (Hebrew) or Christ (Greek) – to be a military leader who would drive the Roman occupiers out of Israel. Instead,

Jesus was a man of peace who renounced power based on violence, and who sought to reconcile people to God and one another. Though Jesus' concern for the poor could rouse his righteous anger against institutional injustice, he was never violent towards individual sinners. He told his followers to forgive, to turn the other cheek, and in his Resurrection appearances announced himself with words of peace.

In this, and many other ways, Jesus turned the prevailing expectations and attitudes of his day on their head; he was both of his culture, and counter-cultural. In his preaching of the *Beatitudes* (*Matthew* 5:1-12; *Luke* 6:20-23), Jesus proclaimed that the meek would inherit the earth, whilst the poor in spirit and those persecuted for the sake of righteousness would possess the Kingdom of heaven. The word *Beatitude* is derived from the Latin word for 'blessed' or 'happy', but in English it also sounds

Blessed Angelo Paoli, father of the poor, was beatified in 2010.

like *be-attitude*, that is, an attitude of how to be. The *Beatitudes* are vitally important to Christians for presenting a vision of how we should live; many Carmelites have written beautiful reflections on how they strike a chord with our Order's charism (for example, see in the reading list the articles by Deeney and FitzGerald).

In the *Beatitudes* Jesus proclaims to his listeners – both 2,000 years ago and to us – that those who hunger and thirst after justice will be satisfied and those who are peacemakers will be called sons and daughters of God. Justice and peace go together; without justice there can be no true peace. Later, towards the end of the Sermon on the Mount, Jesus said 'Set your hearts on God's Kingdom first and on God's saving justice, and all these other things will be given you as well' (*Matthew* 5:33). Justice and peace are primarily God's work not ours, but brought about through our collaboration.

Jesus' words echo the cry of the Old Testament prophets who announced a Kingdom of justice and peace. Isaiah said: 'The product of uprightness will be peace, the effect of uprightness being quiet and security for ever' (32:17), and in the *Grail* version of Psalm 85 we read:

> I will hear what the Lord has to say,
> a voice that speaks of peace,
> peace for his people and his friends
> and those who turn to him in their hearts.
> Mercy and faithfulness have met;
> justice and peace have embraced.
> Faithfulness shall spring from the earth
> and justice look down from heaven.

Peace will flow like a river when we learn to open ourselves to God's gift of contemplation.

In the Bible and in Christian art the dove is a symbol of peace and of the Holy Spirit.

Seeing with the eyes of the poor as God does

For Carmelites, standing in solidarity with the poor as Jesus did is a contemplative experience. Seeing with the perspective of the poor changes our hearts and makes us more open to the presence and vision of Christ who came to earth not only as saviour but also as liberator and bringer of justice. Those who resist such a tenderising of the heart label us as 'Christians who meddle in politics'. This inaccurate dismissal was well understood by Dom Hélder Câmara (1909-99), the Archbishop of Olinda and Recife in Brazil, who stated: 'When I give food to the poor, they call me a saint. When I ask why the poor have no food, they call me a Communist.'

A fellow religious leader in Latin America who wore the Carmelite brown scapular and was accused of interfering in politics by those whose corrupt power he undermined was Oscar Romero, Archbishop of San Salvador (1917-80). Monseñor Romero was a shy and rather bookish priest who was appointed as prelate in El Salvador at a time when the country's government was dominated by a military junta who oppressed the poor. When the priests, religious and laity spoke out on behalf of human rights, a significant number of them were killed. When his great friend Fr. Rutilio Grande, S.J., was assassinated with two parishioners in 1977, Romero realised that following the Good News of Jesus – building peace founded on justice – would bring him into direct conflict with those who wanted to hold on to power for their own ends. He became an uncompromising defender of the poor and of human rights, preaching powerfully of God's love for all. He strenuously defended the rights of the Church but had no illusions about what true faith consists of. He once said: 'Religion is not praying a great deal. It is the guarantee of having God near to me because I do good to my brothers and sisters. The proof of my prayers is not to say a great many words. The proof of my plea is easy to see: how do I act towards the poor? Because God is there.'

Romero was greatly inspired by Carmelite spirituality. Preaching on the scapular devotion he said:

> If the Virgin were to speak with Simon Stock today in 1977 and present him the scapular, she would say: this scapular is the sign of protection – a sign of the doctrine of God, a sign of the integral vocation of men and women, a sign of salvation for the whole person, a sign of salvation in this life. Those who carry this scapular have to be persons who live this salvation here on earth; they have to feel satisfied and capable of developing their human abilities for the good of others.

Like a true shepherd, Romero was deeply concerned with the good of others, particularly the poor. He did not seek to be a politician, holding back from civil war the extremists of both left and right, but Romero realised that the Gospel required him to take a stand alongside those being oppressed. It was a love to which he would witness as a martyr. On 23rd March 1980 he delivered a sermon calling upon Salvadorian soldiers, as Christians, to obey God's higher order and stop carrying out the government's repression, torture and violations of basic human rights. The following day, whilst celebrating Mass in the chapel of a cancer hospice run by the Carmelite Sisters in San Salvador, Oscar Romero was shot dead by a marksman's bullet.

Romero is far from alone in giving his blood for the Kingdom. It is reckoned by groups such as *Aid to the Church in Need* that more Christians were martyred in the twentieth century than any previous period. Part of our vocation as people of justice, peace and integrity is to stand in solidarity with the suffering Church, which is sometimes the

Many Carmelites in El Salvador and around the world await the beatification of Oscar Romero, seen by Christians of many denominations as the 'patron saint' of justice and peace.

only voice of conscience and restraint in places of conflict. We have a duty to protect freedom of speech, and freedom of religion. As people of faith we must insist on freedom of religion because we recognise that man (and woman) needs bread, but we cannot live by bread alone; we are all spiritual beings. Freedom of religion means not only the unhampered practice of Christianity, but also freedom of worship for those of other faiths, as well as freedom from religion for those who have no faith. All Christians are called by Christ to preach the Gospel, but respecting the rights of others to freedom of conscience means we must consider the appropriate methods by which we evangelise.

Pause for a moment: Hold before God in prayer places in today's world where human rights and freedom of religion and conscience are denied.

Theology of liberation

Oscar Romero, Hélder Câmara and other religious leaders in Latin America are associated with a movement known as *liberation theology*. Inspired by the calls of the Second Vatican Council and the Medellín Conference of Latin American Bishops for the Church to recommit itself to Christ's mission in the world among the poor, liberation theology informs the work of Christians in areas of social justice and human rights. Liberation theology approaches current issues from the viewpoint of the economically poor and oppressed, seeing in the teachings of Jesus a liberation from unjust political, economic and social conditions. Though influenced by modern social theory, this approach is as old as the Fathers and Mothers of the Church, as seen in the writings of St. John Chrysostom (c.347–407):

> What is the use of loading Christ's table with gold cups while he himself is starving? Feed the hungry and then if you have any money left over, spend it on the altar table. Will you make a cup of gold and

withhold a cup of water? What use is it to adorn the altar with cloth of gold hangings and deny Christ a coat for his back! What would that profit you? Tell me: if you saw someone starving and refused to give him any food but instead spent your money on adorning the altar with gold, would he thank you? Would he not rather be outraged?

In some sections of the Church, liberation theology was distorted in the 1970s and 80s by a Marxist political agenda, duly reprimanded by the Holy See, but for many it remains a vibrant and relevant movement within the Church because it is rooted in Christ's Gospel.

Justice and peace have embraced

One of the great contributions of liberation theology has been to highlight the fact that peace is not simply the absence of war but something to be worked towards. For peace to be built properly it must have a sure foundation in justice. This means that whilst the Church has a mission to feed the poor, it must also denounce the injustices that lead to poverty, since God's Kingdom and injustice are incompatible. The Peruvian Dominican theologian Gustavo Gutiérrez, sometimes hailed as the 'father of liberation theology', interprets the Christian tradition as having two responses to poverty: firstly, Christians embrace poverty as an act of love, standing in solidarity with the poor; secondly, Christians protest against poverty, wanting the poor to be liberated from suffering. Inspired as a Dominican by the mendicant tradition, Gutiérrez observes:

> Peace presupposes the establishment of justice … it presupposes the defence of the rights of the poor, punishment of the oppressors, a life free from the fear of being enslaved by others, the liberation of the oppressed. Peace, justice, love and freedom are not private realities: they are not only internal attitudes. They are social realities, implying a historical liberation.

Gutiérrez goes on to argue that we misunderstand our spirituality if we forget the human consequences of God's promises of judgement, and the teaching of the prophets, which imply that unjust social structures can and must be changed. The Church consistently teaches that structures in our world – social, political, religious, and economic – can have sinful aspects that must be transformed, and certain models of society must be promoted. Solidarity with the poor means that we do all we can to change sinful structures and promote the common good. We must ensure that we live justly in our families, our communities, our neighbourhoods; that we learn to hear the cry of the poor in our own society as well as the wider world and find peaceful ways to reduce tensions and resolve conflicts; that we are careful with the world's natural resources and learn to 'tread lightly on the earth'; that we pay workers a fair wage and trade ethically.

Stop and think: Who are the prophets in today's Church and wider World, speaking out for the poor?

The Common Good

Living justly and in peace are important if we are to have a rounded understanding of the human person and of the importance of solidarity. These are aspects of the concept of 'the common good', which the *Catechism* defines as 'the sum total of social conditions which allow people, either as groups or individuals, to reach their fulfilment more fully and more easily' (§1906). An appreciation of 'the common good' means that no one in society must be left out or deprived of what is essential. The notion of 'common good' reminds us that – without impinging on individual rights – all people are bound together as a human family.

In their 2010 document *Choosing the Common Good*, the Catholic Bishops of England and Wales observed that:

> The common good is about how to live well together. It is the whole network of social conditions which enable human individuals and groups to flourish and live a full, genuinely human life. At the heart of the common good, solidarity acknowledges that all are responsible for all, not only as individuals but collectively at every level. The principle of the common good expands our understanding of who we are and opens up new sources of motivation. The fulfilment which the common good seeks to serve is the flourishing of humanity, expressed in the phrase 'integral human development'. Such development requires that people are rescued from every form of poverty, from hunger to illiteracy; it requires the opportunities for education, creating a vision of true partnership and solidarity between peoples; it calls for active participation in economic and political processes and it recognises that every human person is a spiritual being with instincts for love and truth and aspirations for happiness. Development must always include this spiritual growth, with openness to God.

The bishops – reflecting in particular the teaching of Pope Benedict XVI in his 2009 encyclical *Caritas in Veritate* – go on to identify some key social teachings of the Church that can help to revitalise political life and society in general, promoting good citizenship and genuine neighbourliness. The first issue they identify is the need to restore trust between individuals, between the citizen and the state, and in institutions. A second factor is the practice of virtue, since virtuous action springs from a sense of one's own dignity and that of others, and from self-respect as a citizen. Among the virtues highlighted by the bishops are those of prudence (right reason in action), courage (readiness to stand by what we believe), temperance (learning to desire well), and justice, which they define as: 'the virtue by which we strive to give what is due to others by respecting their rights and fulfilling our duties towards them. Justice expands our notion of 'self' by strengthening the ties between us all. Justice towards God is the 'virtue of religion' which frees us from the tyranny of false gods who would claim our worship.' The core principles of the common good, integral human development and the pursuit of virtue are not presented by the bishops or the wider Church as a detailed political programme, but they help to illuminate aspects of political debate on particular issues. They offer principles by

Engaging in the political process so as to build God's Kingdom is a moral duty for Christians.

which we can act in the political sphere. It is important for Carmelites to engage in legitimate political processes, whilst remembering that we all have a personal responsibility to act in love and there are limits to what any government can achieve.

Choose life
(*Deuteronomy* 30:19)

A sense of justice, peace, the common good, integral human development and virtue inform our attitude as Christians towards human life, from conception to natural death. The Church insists on the dignity of every human life as a gift from God. Abortion and euthanasia are the most obvious 'life issues', but the bishops of England and Wales teach in *Choosing the Common Good* that these must be linked to a broader appreciation of life issues: 'Opposition to abortion requires a commitment to the alleviation of child poverty and high infant mortality; opposition to euthanasia demands concerted effort to remedy the social and economic conditions which lead to neglect, isolation, ill-health, and in poorer parts of the world low life expectancy among the elderly... There are strong links between life ethics and social ethics.'

Stop and think: Is care of the elderly an issue in your Carmelite community? How can this matter be pondered in the light of the pursuit for peace and justice?

The Church teaches that closely connected with the right to life is the right to employment, and the right of workers to be protected and to unionise. When speaking of 'rights' it is important to balance this with 'responsibilities', and to realise that some human rights are more fundamental than others. All people, for instance, have a right to security and peace. Many societies argue that to secure this it is necessary to have the military infrastructure of an army. However, if a government – in the name of the people – spends more money on the army in the name of defending the right to security than it spends on aid thus defending the right of all for food, then there is a moral imbalance. Military might must only be used as a last resort in ways that are legal and ethical.

Stop and think: Do you believe in pacifism, or accept the theory of 'just war'? What role do military forces have in peace-keeping? How closely should the Church be aligned to the military?

Ethics and the economy

In the realm of economics the Church condemns any protectionism that hurts the weak. The Church regards money itself as morally neutral; how we use it is the ethical question, and St. Paul warns that 'the love of money is a root of all kinds of evil' (*1 Timothy* 6:10). Since all the world's resources are meant to be shared by God's children, massive differences in lifestyle between rich and poor prompt us to ask difficult questions. Seeing the appalling level of need in our world can at times make us feel overwhelmed at our inability to change the situation. Yet, even in small ways, we can be generous in giving – even if it is a 'widow's mite' – to charitable organisations that help the poor; financial support as well as our prayers are vital in maintaining such work. Generosity is truly a sign of the Kingdom.

Generous financial support of Christian development organisations such as *CAFOD*, *Caritas International*, and *Christian Aid* is a real contribution to building up God's Kingdom. Our donations enable them to work in situations where they have experience, skills and understanding that we might not have. Members of the Carmelite Family are directly involved in the work of post-war reconstruction in parts of the world which have suffered conflict in recent times, including Timor Leste (East Timor), Zimbabwe, Liberia, Iraq and Latin America.

In the west African state of Liberia, riven by civil wars in the 1990s, the Corpus Christi Carmelite Sisters provide education, employment and health-care.

Financial aid and relieving poverty through debt cancellation are a basic necessity to sustain life, but development is not simply a matter of hand-outs; it demands trade justice, giving the poor an opportunity to participate in their own future and access to markets. In a world where multinational companies often have more money than nations, the way we act as consumers of products and services has huge moral implications.

Did you know? The Fair Trade movement was begun by religious groups and charitable organisations shortly after the Second World War and has developed into a major force for promoting social and economic change for the good. Fair Trade advocates the payment of a higher price to producers in economically developing countries, thus promoting financial sustainability and higher environmental standards. To date most Fair Trade commodities have been exports from developing economies that produce handicrafts, tea, coffee, cocoa, sugar, cotton, fruit, wine, and so on. Carmelite communities in economically more developed countries often choose to purchase Fair Trade products, and in so doing can be recognised as part of Fair Trade parishes and towns by the national bodies that regulate Fair Trade standards.

Fair Trade marks of various styles around the globe are a guarantee that the producers of the product will be paid a decent wage that will help them out of poverty.

Justice has various faces and is a matter of right relationships

Many contemporary Carmelites are involved in the work for peace built on justice. An Irish friar who spent several years ministering in Latin America, Míceál O'Neill, O.Carm., has spoken of the various faces of justice. There is *retributive justice* that demands a person who does good is rewarded whilst a wrongdoer is punished. There is *distributive justice* which is about society's responsibility for ensuring that every person has what is necessary for a dignified human existence. Justice can also be a quality of the human person, associated with goodness and moral rectitude; we might think perhaps of Saint Joseph who is described in the Gospel as a 'just' or 'righteous' man.

Fr. Míceál O'Neill, O.Carm.

Justice is also a question of right relationships between people, between people and Creation, and between people and God. Míceál O'Neill argues that 'the search for justice is to build constructive and liberating relationships … Right relationships are those in which the participants grow as persons.' An example of this is the *restorative justice* which underpinned the *Truth and Reconciliation Commissions* in South Africa in recent memory, enabling victims and perpetrators of violence to face one another with the truth spoken in love. Through truth and love, justice speaks, relationships are restored, and lives begin to be healed.

Did you know? Restorative justice has been introduced into a number of prisons. In England and Wales the *Prison Fellowship* operates a programme called *Sycamore Tree*. Inspired by Zacchaeus who climbed a sycamore in order to see Jesus, and who as a result of his encounter restored what he had extorted (*Luke* 19:1-10), *Sycamore Tree* brings together offender and victim in the hope of reconciliation and restoration.

God's ways are above our ways

Peace is built on justice, and as we read the Gospel and ponder on Jesus' teaching through parables we begin to see that his meaning of God's justice is rather different from that of the people around him and from some of our ideas too. Jesus uses the language of the Old Testament – the Torah and the Law – but he teaches that the Law is to be lived and understood in the light of God's revelation to Moses on Mount Sinai: 'YHWH, YHWH, God of tenderness and compassion, slow to anger, rich in faithful love and constancy, maintaining his faithful love to thousands, forgiving fault, crime and sin …' (*Exodus* 34:6, 7). The God whom Jesus came to reveal to us is the God of forgiveness and unconditional love, and if we are to be committed to JPIC issues we have to make this true image of God known and spread Christ's message of reconciliation. If we read the Old Testament prayerfully we can see God's forgiveness, mercy and love are threads running throughout: for example in *Jeremiah* (31:3, 29: 11-14); in *Isaiah* where God's love is beautifully likened to maternal love (42:14, 49:14-16, 66:12-13), and in *Hosea* (11:1-9) where God's love proves to be stronger than his vengeance. Saint Thérèse came to appreciate that God is indeed just, because God takes into account our human weakness and has mercy upon us.

Did you know? Saint Thérèse showed a deep concern for reconciliation. She prayed for a convicted murderer, Henri Pranzini, who repented on the execution scaffold and of whose salvation Thérèse had her characteristic bold confidence. The Church has gradually come to its current position that the death penalty is always immoral.

The Prodigal Son or The Forgiving Father?

Part of becoming contemplative means learning to see God's relationship with humanity through God's eyes, not our own. Therefore perhaps we need to approach the Gospel parables afresh. Think for a moment of the story we know as *The Prodigal Son* (*Luke* 15:11-32). It is as much the story of the merciful father as of the wayward son, and we might call it instead *The Forgiving Father*. Here Jesus challenges us to a new understanding of the God he came to reveal. Think, too, of the *Labourers in the Vineyard* (*Matthew* 20:1-16) or *The Unmerciful Servant* (*Matthew* 18:21-35). If we change the emphasis and use the alternative – but equally valid – titles of *The Good Employer* or *The Merciful Master*, we find images of a God whose ways are beyond our ways, who is compassionate and who goes far beyond our human understanding of law and justice. God's behaviour might seem to human eyes unreasonable, foolish, reckless, because his motive is love alone. For us to follow in Christ's footsteps means going beyond our limited vision and allowing God's compassion into the world as we share what we have with others.

Liberation from religious oppression

Another way in which Jesus revealed the Father's unconditional love for humanity was through his challenging of the religious structures of his day. Jesus was truly immersed in God's Law and defended authentic faith, but he was highly critical of religious rigmarole if it unjustly separates people from their relationships with God and with one another. The 'Golden Rule' Jesus taught was that our love of God must be reflected in how we treat our brothers and sisters: 'In everything do to others as you would have them do to you; for this is the law and the prophets' (*Matthew* 7:12). Jesus taught his followers that their faith in God cannot be divorced from a relationship with others, prompting Saint John to write: 'Those who say, 'I love God', and hate their brothers or sisters, are liars; for those who do not love a brother or sister whom they have seen, cannot love God whom they have not seen. The commandment we have from him is this: those who love God must love their brothers and sisters also.' (*1 John* 4:20-21)

Jesus thus called people to have integrity in the practice of their faith, replacing sacrifices made to God with a spirit of obedience and self-giving (cf. *Hebrews* 10). In particular Jesus had little time for the Jewish purity laws with their hundreds of rules about every tiny aspect of life which prevented people – especially the poor who could not afford the things required for full observance – from enjoying a relationship with God. Frequently Jesus became 'ritually unclean' in the eyes of his critics, breaking religious taboos in order to reach out to the marginalised. He also was highly critical of religious hypocrites and faith leaders who made life more difficult for others by their rules of human origin.

Stop, read and think: Ponder the words of Christ in *Matthew* 23:1-13. How can we be on guard against religious institutionalism in Carmel?

Our attitude to the marginalised

The Hebrew term *anawim* refers to 'the least' or 'God's little ones'. The *anawim* of today might include the uneducated, those with disabilities, the disadvantaged, the marginalised, minority groups, and those we find it hard to love. Recognising their giftedness in God's eyes keeps us humble, enables us to listen to them, to learn from them, and avoids any tendency to be patronising or condescending; these are attitudes which destroy any good God might otherwise work through us. As well as respecting the marginalised in others, we too need to embrace the elements of our own lives that we push to the margins. We are all *anawim* to an extent, little ones in need of love. Jesus told us to love our neighbours as ourselves, and therefore we must learn to love ourselves for we cannot give to others what we do not have. Responding to JPIC issues therefore calls for a holistic

A late 19th-century Mexican retablo of Our Lady of Mount Carmel.

approach to life, and a sense of peace and justice towards ourselves. As the psychologist Carl Jung put it, it is easy to accept our duty to love others, 'But what if I should discover that the least of all brethren, the poorest of all beggars, the most insolent of all offenders, yes even the very enemy himself – that these live within me, that I myself stand in need of the alms of my own kindness.' Jung stated that the problems in the world stem precisely from the fact that we love others as we love ourselves, that is to say, not enough.

Stop and think: What can be done if we have a poor sense of love for ourselves?

Reflect further: At some point you might like to reflect on what is said about proper love of self in *The Ten Books on the Way of Life and Great Deeds of the Carmelites* (better known as *The Book of the First Monks*), Book 1, Chapter 6.

Mary's song for the poor

Mary – Miriam of Nazareth – was one of the *anawim*, who recognised the loving action of God in her life. Mary, as we encounter her in the Gospel, belonged to the poor of Israel, and it was because she was poor and humble that God chose her. The words of her canticle the *Magnificat* (*Luke* 1:46-55) are very familiar to us Carmelites who pray the text daily in the Evening Prayer of the Church. In the *Magnificat*, Mary, true to the tradition of her Jewish faith, sings in praise of God and his protection of the lowly and poor through the ages, who now will know the Messiah. The theologian Elizabeth Johnson interprets Mary's song thus:

> Through God's action, the social hierarchy of wealth and poverty, poverty and subjugation, is to be turned upside down. Jubilation breaks out as the proud are scattered and the mighty are pulled from their thrones while the lowly are exalted and mercy in the form of food fills the bellies of the hungry. All will be well, and all manner of thing will be well, because God's mercy, pledged in covenant love, is faithful through every generation … God protects the poor, noticing their tears, while challenging the comfortable and the proud to conversion.

Carmelites revere Mary as their patron, mother and sister. She provides in the Church a life-giving female presence, and as Carmelites we learn from our relationship with Mary to have a deep and profound respect for the role and dignity of women, who all too often in history have been amongst the poor and marginalised. Cultivating an awareness of gender, sex and sexuality issues is important if we are to grow in understanding of humanity in its diversity. Likewise Carmelites – if we are to be just people – must inform ourselves about minority issues, the needs of the 'minores' (little ones) in society, in terms of race, culture, and so on.

Did you know? In many Carmelite shrines Mary has been honoured as 'Woman of the People'. In the famous Brancacci Chapel in the Carmine (Carmelite friary) in Florence there is a thirteenth-century icon revered as *Our Lady of the People* (*Madonna del Popolo*), displayed overleaf. It shows Mary as a tender mother and sister.

Elijah and Elisha are prophetic models

Mary was herself formed as a just and peaceful person by the Jewish heritage. Foremost in upholding this heritage were the prophets, and for Carmelites the prophet Elijah has particular significance as an inspiration in the work of justice and peace. He was not afraid, even when his life was in danger, to speak out against the actions of powerful but corrupt people, and Elijah inspires Carmelites today to act as prophets who proclaim the truth. 'In the prophet Elijah, we see a man who translated his contemplative experience into prophetic action.' (Joseph Chalmers, O.Carm., 2004).

Refresh your memory: We read in the previous chapter about Elijah's proclamation of God's love and justice, his care for the poor in the person of the Widow of Zarephath, and his denunciation of corruption in the case of Naboth's vineyard. Read the material again if it helps to refresh your memory, and then reflect on how Carmelites today can truly be descendents of the 'company of prophets'.

La Madonna del Popolo (Our Lady of the People) at the Carmelite friary in Florence.

Elijah was a man very much in touch with the natural world around him, so much so in fact that at his command no rain fell in Israel for three years (*1 Kings* 17:1). This prophetic action was done to prompt King Ahab to reject the worship of false gods and return to the one true God; the whole nation suffered because its leader acted unjustly. The immediate upshot of the drought was that Elijah had to live as a poor man entirely dependent upon God for his sustenance. Elijah was fed by ravens at the brook Cherith (*1 Kings* 17) and later, through the generosity of the Widow of Zarephath and her son, God continued to provide food for Elijah. Access to food is one of the fundamental rights of every human being, and those with plenty have a moral duty to ensure in justice that no one starves. The story of Elijah and the Widow shows how far a little charitable sharing will go. That willingness to share the essentials of life prompted Jesus to feed five thousand people with only five loaves and two fish (*John* 6:1-15). This miracle was foreshadowed by Elijah's successor Elisha, who fed one hundred people with only a few loaves (*2 Kings* 4:42-44). Also like Jesus, Elisha healed lepers (*2 Kings* 5:1-27) and brought people back to life. Elisha's name

A medieval stained-glass window depicting Elisha in St. Mary the Virgin Church, Shrewsbury, England.

means 'God is salvation'; the name Jesus means 'God saves'. Elisha is another inspiration for Carmelites in their work for justice, peace, and the integrity of Creation, bringing healing and wholeness to others.

Carmelite friar Patrick Thomas McMahon, O.Carm., makes the following link between Elijah and the Carmelites' pursuit of justice and peace:

> Elijah was a fearless prophet who stood strong and tall against the injustice of his day. He defended the farmer and the peasant against the mighty kings and lords. And that is why the Order of Carmel today has stood with the Church in making the preferential option for the poor. Carmel chooses to stand up for the cause of the poor. We stand with the teachings of Popes John XXIII, Paul VI, John Paul II, and now Pope Benedict XVI, and with their teaching about the rights of immigrants and the rights of workers and the rights of women and the rights of all human persons for housing, health care, and education. Carmel stands for nothing more than what the popes have stood for in their brilliant encyclical letters when they call for rights of the poor to be protected … The Carmelite, like Elijah stands up for the poor, for the victims of injustice, for those who have no voice of their own with which to cry out to heaven.
>
> *(Nine Themes in Carmelite Spirituality)*

JPIC is the tradition of the Church

From all our pondering of Scripture in this chapter it is very clear that *justice and peace* is a biblical notion, and in every age the Church has lived out its divine mission of building-up God's Kingdom by 'reading the signs of the times' and committing to JPIC issues accordingly. In the modern period one of the ground-breaking documents of the Church was Pope Leo XIII's 1891 encyclical letter *Rerum Novarum* (Of New Things), which discussed the rights of workers and the responsibilities of governments. In the decades since *Rerum Novarum* the Magisterium of the Church has developed a considerable body of 'Social Teaching', sometimes damningly called 'the best-kept secret of the Catholic Church'. A number of papal encyclicals have addressed JPIC issues, including John XXIII's *Pacem in Terris* (Peace on Earth, 1963), Paul VI's *Populorum Progressio* (on the development of peoples, 1967) and Benedict XVI's *Caritas in Veritate* (on integral human development in charity and truth, 2009). Love (charity) is the heart of the Church's social teaching, which is summarised in the 1992 *Catechism of the Catholic Church*, and amplified in its companion volume the 2005 *Compendium of the Social Doctrine of the Church*.

Stop and think: Have you ever read these important Church teachings?

Through such teachings the Church urges Christians to have a concern for the integrity of Creation, for the environment of planet Earth, as for the first time in human history we have the power to destroy life by misuse of nuclear power and by environmental

God's beautiful Creation has been entrusted to our care; God will ask us to account for our stewardship.

degradation. The *Catechism* points out that concern for our neighbour, including the generations to come, 'requires a religious respect for the integrity of creation' (§2415).

Did you know? Carmelites care for Creation in a variety of ways. Many Carmelite community and parish buildings are now built with environment concerns foremost, harnessing renewable energy and reducing the consumption of finite resources. Some communities have planted woodland, peace gardens, and habitats for wildlife. Many communities and individuals try to use energy-efficient household appliances and lighting, and conserve their use of water. Recycling, reusing and composting have become second-nature for many. Carmelite religious and laity have lobbied governments on the issue of Climate Change (or Climate Justice). In short, Carmelites try to *live simply, that others may simply live.*

Justice and peace: a way of life for all Christians

In 1967 Pope Paul VI chose the term *justice and peace* (from Psalm 85) for a Pontifical Commission which met shortly after the Second Vatican Council (and was inspired by its spirit expressed in documents such as *Gaudium et Spes*) to consider how Christians could engage with issues facing the world. The expression *justice and peace* symbolises God's intention to transform suffering humanity by a new Creation. Justice and peace

Carmelites were among thousands of Christians and other people of good will who marched in the 'Wave for Climate Justice' in London ahead of the United Nations summit on Climate Change in December 2009.

are the pillars of the new heavens and the new earth 'where the Lord will wipe away the tears from every eye and death will be no more' (1992 *Catechism of the Catholic Church* §1043-44). The bishops who took part in the 1971 *Synod on Justice in the World* placed justice at the very heart of the Church's mission, declaring that 'the pursuit of justice is a constitutive dimension of the preaching of the gospel'. Since the 1960s Justice and Peace commissions, task forces and groups have been set up worldwide in dioceses and religious orders, including the Carmelites at local, provincial and international levels.

Get informed: Find out if your Carmelite province or region has a JPIC group. See if there are ways you could support its projects, since JPIC is the responsibility of all.

Communications and technology

A concern for justice, peace and the integrity of Creation must be nurtured within each individual, but also at the communal and social level. With the advent of global travel and 24-hour communications, Society and the Church have become much more conscious of the interconnected nature of our lives, and we are much better informed about JPIC issues. The media has an important role to play in informing us about social and ethical issues at home and abroad. We need to be formed and informed. Awareness of current issues and a critical reading of the news are important if we are to read the signs of the times. We must also learn to analyse print and electronic news with a critical mind and loving heart, seeing where objective facts are distorted by private interests and prejudice, and pondering God's will in our response.

The media is just one area of life that has been revolutionised by science and technology. Other examples include medical science and agricultural production. Such advances have great benefits for society, but they come with risks too, and Carmelites need to be discerning of whether what is labelled 'progress' actually contributes to integral human development.

JPIC in the first Carmelite community

Commitment to JPIC has been articulated in a particular way since the 1960s, but the concept – perhaps expressed in different ways – has always been essential to Christianity

In the icon of Saint Albert written by Sister Petra Clare in 2007 for the Carmelites in Faversham, England, the hermits are shown living in harmony with the landscape of Mount Carmel.

and our Carmelite heritage. The first Carmelite community – the hermit brothers living on Mount Carmel – sought to live in solidarity with one another like the first Christian community in Jerusalem, and in harmony with their environment, caring for the land as responsible stewards. They reared some animals and probably farmed on a small scale, but did not selfishly exploit the land. Having perhaps been Crusading warriors, they turned their 'swords into ploughshares' and sought peace within themselves and with their neighbours. They were solitaries who came together to form a community, overcoming as they did so the poverty of isolation and alienation. The 1995 *Constitutions* of the Carmelite friars points out the hermits' shared sense of justice and peace as set out in the *Way of Life* given to them by the Latin Patriarch of Jerusalem:

> The *Rule of Saint Albert* speaks of a community whose members are open to the indwelling of the Spirit and formed by the Spirit's values: chastity, holy thoughts, justice, love, faith, the expectation of salvation, work accomplished in peace, silence which, as the Prophet tells us, is the cult of justice and brings wisdom to word and action; and discernment, 'the guide and moderator of all virtues'. (§16)

Did you know? Conflict in the land made holy by Christ's presence is an enduring source of sorrow for the Carmelite family, and all people of good will. The Discalced Carmelite priory of *Stella Maris* on Mount Carmel is home to a dozen friars who pray for peace in the Middle East. Most Christian holy sites in the land where Jesus walked are in the care of the Franciscans. The Pope and bishops frequently call on Christians worldwide to show their solidarity with the people of the Holy Land.

Various Carmelite communities have lamps bearing the word 'Peace' in different languages. The lamps and the oil they burn are produced by Christians in the Palestinian village of Taybeh. The Taybeh Peace Lamps Initiative provides much needed employment and aspires to unite hundreds of thousands of churches in praying for peace in the Holy Land.

Carmelites and Creation

Living in harmony with the land on Mount Carmel, the hermits were following the example of Jesus who understood the wonder of the natural world and people's dependency on it. Jesus taught using images of sheep, birds, flowers in the fields, seeds, and particularly bread, wine and water. Many of Carmel's saints – including Teresa of Jesus, John of the Cross, Lawrence of the Resurrection, Thérèse of Lisieux and Titus Brandsma – have used images from the natural world to describe the presence and action of God. Carmelites today appreciate that the whole of Creation reflects God's glory, and many shrines of the Order are places of physical beauty. Even those of us who live in dense urban areas can often tend a small plot of earth or a simple plant as a reminder of our dependence upon the planet.

Many Carmelite priories – such as those in Malta (left, Valletta; right, Sliema) – reflect God's beauty in Creation through the beauty of their architecture.

JPIC in the Carmelite tradition today

Recent documents of the Carmelite Order make it apparent that we cannot 'opt out' of concern for peace built on justice, and the right stewardship of God's Creation. Our active service must be rooted in a prayerful relationship with God, and that prayer must naturally express itself in works of charity, as we saw in the previous chapter, where we also read how the notion of being *in the midst of the people* is integral to the identity of Carmelite religious and laity. According to the 1995 *Constitutions* of the friars:

> This way of being *in the midst of the people* is a sign and a prophetic witness of new relationships, of fraternity and friendship among men and women everywhere. It is a prophetic message of justice and peace in society and among peoples. As an integral part of the Good News, this prophecy must be fulfilled through active commitment to the transformation of sinful systems and structures into grace-filled systems and structures. It is also an expression of the choice to share in the lives of 'the little ones' (*minores*) of history, so that we may speak

a word of hope and of salvation from their midst – more by our life than by our words. This option flows naturally from our profession of poverty in a mendicant fraternity, and is in keeping with our allegiance to Christ Jesus, lived out also through allegiance to the poor and to those in whom the face of our Lord is reflected in a preferential way. (§24)

The Constitutions of the Third/Secular Order, the 2003 *Rule for the Third Order of Carmel*, likewise addresses the Carmelite vocation to care for God's planet and one another in love, so as to build up the Kingdom that is 'already and not yet' here:

> Through belonging to Christ, Lord and King of the Universe, tertiaries share in his royal office through which they are called to the service of God's Kingdom and to its spread throughout history. Christ's kingship implies, above all, a spiritual combat to defeat the tyranny of sin in ourselves. Through the gift of ourselves we undertake to serve, in justice and charity, Jesus himself who is present in all his brothers and sisters, especially in the little ones and those on the fringes of society. This means restoring creation to its original goodness. In ordering creation for the true good of humanity, an activity which is supported by grace, tertiaries share in the exercise of that power by which the Risen Christ draws all things to himself. (§27)

Reflect again: In the previous chapter you were invited to reflect upon who is marginalised in today's World and Church. Reflect once more; has your thinking developed at all?

Encouragement from the Prior General

In recent times the Prior General, the most senior brother within the Order, has sought to nurture a deep commitment to JPIC by addressing letters on the topic to the Carmelite Family, the first entitled *The God of Our Contemplation* (2004), and the second *The Lord Hears the Cry of the Poor* (2006). In recent years the Priors General and their Councils have called for a renewal of the Carmelite Family's commitment to upholding justice, peace and the integrity of Creation, and as members of that family we must think how we might respond. Living and perhaps also working in places where we have opportunities for acting and being more just and peaceful, we Carmelites can be part of the transformation of society that the Priors General – and the Church – are calling for.

The Carmelite NGO

At the start of the third millennium the Carmelite Order (O.Carm.) established a NGO (non-governmental organisation) presence at the United Nations (UN). The United Nations, though in need of continual reform like any large institution, is the only worldwide forum for the discussion of transnational issues, bringing about understanding and reducing injustice so that the family of nations can live in peace. Having a Carmelite NGO presence at the UN means that the Order can proclaim Christian values at the highest levels of international discussion, prioritise the voice of the poor, collaborate with people of good will (including other religious orders who have consultative status), and better inform the Carmelite Family about issues facing a globalised society.

The Carmelite NGO crest.

The Carmelite NGO encourages informed prayer and prayerful action, disseminating information through its website and its newsletter *CarmeNGO*. The Carmelite NGO organises two Days of Prayer each year – on 5th June (World Environment Day) and 10th December (World Human Rights Day) – to inform Carmelites on issues of global significance and inspire them to reflection and appropriate action. Issues it has highlighted include human trafficking, climate change, and socio-political unrest in Zimbabwe.

In 2008 Pope Benedict XVI addressed the United Nations at its headquarters in New York. The following year he spoke at the UN's World Summit on Food Security, urging better access to trading markets for farmers in poor countries.

Did you know? Just as at the United Nations, at provincial and local levels the Carmelite Order works with organisations experienced in specific area of JPIC work. To give one example, members of the Carmelite Family in Britain support groups that promote JPIC issues including *CAFOD* and *SCIAF* (members of *Caritas International*), *Fairtrade*, *Trade Justice*, *Christian Aid*, *Pax Christi*, *Christian Ecology Link*, *Operation Noah*, *Make Poverty History* and animal welfare organisations, among many others, all of which have a great deal to contribute to making the world a more just and peaceful place. NGOs and charities are constantly on the watch against bureaucracy, since to spend more on administration and internal affairs than on the issues they are highlighting would be unjust.

Tolerance, welcome, harmony and hospitality

As Carmelites we are part of an international family, as well as members of humanity's 'global village'. Globalisation presents challenges but it also offers opportunities for us to become more tolerant people who embrace diversity. Carmelites cultivate listening hearts which can help us be peace-makers and reconcilers. Some of us will live in areas where there are immigrants whose way of life is perhaps very different from our own. Here is a real opportunity to search for the Kingdom as we strive to not only passively tolerate and understand but actively welcome and celebrate different lifestyles, races and faiths. Listening helps understanding, which in turn helps us to be more welcoming.

Stop and think: Many Carmelite communities are in contact with people affected in some way by issues of migration and asylum. How aware are you of the economic and political factors that influence the movement of peoples?

Carmel's prophetic stand against the sins of racial and religious prejudice was embodied in the mid-twentieth century by two great Carmelites, the nun Edith Stein (Teresa Benedicta of the Cross) and the friar Titus Brandsma. They gave everything – even their very lives – to follow Christ by standing up to the appalling injustice and hatred of Nazi ideology.

Carmel and Interfaith dialogue

The Roman Catholic Church today strongly encourages encounter and dialogue between people of different faiths. In 1965 the Second Vatican Council published a declaration on the relation of the Church with Non-Christian Religions entitled *Nostra Aetate* ('In our Age'), which has laid the ground for much fruitful dialogue, including the 1986 meeting in Assisi of leaders of different religions.

As Carmelites we are committed to building peace through interfaith encounter and dialogue, which has never been so necessary in our world. In an age where extremists motivated by religious convictions kill because of their certainty about who God is and what God wants, we Carmelites have a prophetic role to declare 'Let God be God', and not allow zealots to distort the true face of God who is love.

Stop and think: How can we best respond to those critics who say that most conflicts in the world have a basis in religious difference? How can Carmel challenge those who use religion as an excuse for terrorism? Read what is said about Carmel and inter-religious dialogue in the 1995 *Constitutions of the Carmelite Friars* §96.

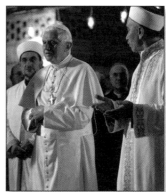

During his visit to Istanbul in 2006 Pope Benedict XVI met with the Orthodox Ecumenical Patriarch Bartholomew I and visited the Blue Mosque.

Food for the journey

If we are to commit ourselves seriously to issues of justice, peace, and the integrity of Creation, that is, if we are going to undertake the journey of transformation that our Carmelite vocation is asking of us, we need God's nourishment. The food for our journey is the Eucharist, which provides all the strength we – the Body of Christ – need for the work God asks us to cooperate in, healing relationships, promoting justice and peace, and proclaiming the Good News. As God told Saint Paul 'My grace is enough for you' (*2 Corinthians* 12:9).

When we celebrate the Eucharist and Divine Office we pray the *Our Father*, asking for the coming of God's Kingdom, a Kingdom of justice and peace 'on earth as it is in heaven'. We gather together as one people of diverse ages, genders, abilities and cultural backgrounds, all invited to participate actively in the liturgy. There are the moments in the Mass when we speak of reconciliation: at the Penitential Rite when we acknowledge our failings which affect the good of the community; at the *Our Father* when we pray not only to be forgiven but also to be forgiving; and at the Sign of Peace when we pray for the peace and unity of God's Kingdom. In the intercessions we may pray for those in our own communities or in the wider world who suffer injustice or who are in need of peace and harmony. A collection may be taken for those in need; as the former superior general of the Jesuits, Pedro Arrupe, said, 'We cannot properly receive the Bread of Life unless at the same time we give bread for life to those in need, wherever, whoever they may be' (*Hunger for Bread and Evangelization*, 1974). Finally, we are dismissed from Mass with the words 'Go in peace to love and serve the Lord'.

Carmelites need to care about justice, peace and the integrity of Creation

Perhaps you are already committed to God and his Kingdom through awareness and action inspired by JPIC issues. Perhaps the Church's social teaching has been till now a 'secret' you were unaware of or indifferent to, or perhaps you have heard the words *justice and peace* so often that you question what they have to do with you. By opening the Gospel book, pondering therein the words of Jesus and meditating on his human life and relations, we will gradually appreciate that what the Church and the Order is teaching us is an integral part of being Christian, and therefore a necessary part of our Carmelite journey of formation. By making space for God (*vacare Deo*) through our lives of prayer and service lived out in the community and beyond, we develop by God's grace a contemplative attitude, gradually seeing the world as God sees it, loving as God loves, and understanding justice and peace as God understands them.

We conclude this chapter as we began, with an extract from Scripture:

> *O God, give your judgment to the king,*
> *to a king's son your justice,*
> *that he may judge your people in justice*
> *and your poor in right judgment.*
> *May the mountains bring forth peace for the people*
> *and the hills, justice.*
> *May he defend the poor of the people*

*and save the children of the needy
and crush the oppressor.
He shall endure like the sun and the moon
from age to age.
He shall descend like rain on the meadow,
like raindrops on the earth.
In his days justice shall flourish
and peace till the moon fails ...* (Psalm 71/72)

Conclusion: In this seventeenth chapter we have seen how we Christians are called into this broken world to witness to and work for the coming of God's Kingdom. Our compassionate service is rooted in prayer, and prayer sends us into service. As Carmelites, seeking to live *in allegiance to Jesus Christ*, a concern for justice, peace and the planet cannot be optional extras that we may or may not find personally interesting or appealing; they are essential and integral to our vocation, to our search for God's Kingdom, and to our commitment to love.

You might like to conclude your time of study and reflection with a prayer of your own choosing, or with the following text:

*Tender-hearted God,
    you created the world and saw that it is good,
    you gathered the outcast children of Israel,
    you sent your Son to reconcile all peoples to yourself.
Touch our minds and our hearts
    that we may be peacemakers,
    just stewards of Creation,
    and advocates for the outcasts of society.
May your Spirit prompt us
    to share with the poor what is theirs,
    to speak out for those who are oppressed,
    to turn away from prejudice,
    and to preach the Gospel by our actions.
This we ask in Jesus' name. Amen.*

In the next chapter we will see how the thirst for justice, the pursuit of peace, and care for God's Creation was manifest in the lives of the early saints of the Carmelite Order.

Ideas for Reflection, Discussion and Action

- Has anything caught your attention in this chapter, either individually or as a community? Have you learned something new, or was the material familiar to you already? How would you summarise the key points?

- It is sometimes said that a mature Christian faith is seen in someone who is politically and socially aware, committed to upholding justice, peace, and the integrity of Creation. Would you agree with this?

- What does 'The Kingdom of God' mean to you?

- What ministries in your parish have a Carmelite presence already? Make a list. Are there opportunities for Carmelites to be involved in any others?

- Does your parish or diocese have a Justice and Peace Group? Have they ever been invited to your Carmelite community meeting? Do they know about Carmel? Have members of your community attended any of their events? Do such groups encourage awareness of JPIC issues, or do they result in people feeling they can opt out and leave the issues to others?

- What or who are the most reliable sources of information on matters of justice, peace and the integrity of Creation? The media? NGOs? Governments? Faith leaders?

- How do you welcome visitors in your parish? How does your Carmelite community greet newcomers? How do you personally welcome people?

- Read the letters of the Carmelite Prior General on justice, peace and the integrity of Creation, published in 2004 and 2006 (listed in the resources below).

- Undertake an environmental audit of your community and its meetings; are there ways you can reduce your 'footprint' in terms of consuming carbon, energy, water, etc.

- Are there underlying or unspoken conflicts in your community? Has anyone taken steps to resolve the difficulties and restore peace?

- If you go away on holiday, are you aware of the principles of ethical tourism?

- Subscribe to the Carmelite NGO newsletter.

- Does your Carmelite community know about the concept of Fairtrade, and why it is important? Do you use Fairtrade and environmentally-sound products?

- What is the link between JPIC issues and ecumenical dialogue?

- According to the document *Choosing the Common Good*, 'the future of society passes by way of the family', and 'families, for better or worse, are the first school of life and love where the capacity to relate to others is founded'. How can communities of the 'Carmelite Family' learn to be more welcoming places from the model of the family?

- Would you agree that access for the sick and disabled to public buildings (including those of the Church and the Order) is a matter of justice?

- As a Carmelite community sponsor a charitable project, raising not only funds but also awareness about a particular JPIC issue.

- Make a visit as an individual and/or as a Carmelite community to a non-Christian place of worship to build up inter-faith understanding.

- Does your parish or Carmelite community have members from other countries? Which ones? What languages do they speak? Have they ever been invited to share an aspect of their culture at your community meeting?

- Do you have access to a garden? Who cares for it? Do you know the names of the plants and trees in it? How much of your household waste is recycled?

- Do you thank God and those who have provided for you by praying grace at meals?

- What could you and/or your community do to support peace in the Holy Land?

- Jesus said 'You have the poor with you always' (*Mark* 4:7; *Matthew* 26:11). If God has a special love for the poor, is it a bad thing to have the poor with us always?

- To better inform yourself on JPIC issues use some of the resources – especially those online – listed overleaf.

Recommended Further Resources

With the growth of awareness, resources on justice, peace and the integrity of Creation are becoming more available. Since many JPIC issues are ongoing, one of the best ways to keep informed is through the internet, and several useful websites are listed below.

Francis Cardinal Arinze, *Religions for Peace: A Call for Solidarity to the Religions of the World*, (London: Darton, Longman and Todd, 2002).

Benedict XVI, *Caritas in Veritate – Integral Human Development in Truth and Love*, Encyclical Letter, 2009. Printed by the various publishers to the Holy See, and available on the Vatican website www.vatican.va

Johan Bergström-Allen, T.O.C., 'Justice, Peace, and the Integrity of Creation', *Assumpta*, June 2004.

Hélder Câmara, *Sister Earth: Ecology & the Spirit*, (London: New City, 1990).

Joseph Chalmers, O.Carm., *The God of Our Contemplation* (2004) and *The Lord Hears the Cry of the Poor* (2006). Available from Edizioni Carmelitane and its distributors (such as Saint Albert's Press in Britain and Carmelite Media in North America) and online at www.carmelite.org

Joseph Chalmers, O.Carm., 'The prophetic element of the Carmelite charism', in *In Allegiance to Jesus Christ*, (Rome: Edizioni Carmelitane, 1999), pp. 52-58.

Catholic Bishops' Conference of England and Wales, *Choosing the Common Good*, (2010).

Catholic Bishops' Conference of England and Wales, *The Common Good and the Catholic Church's Social Teaching*, (1996).

Aloysius Deeney, O.C.D., 'The Beatitudes and Your Vocation to Carmel' in *Welcome to the Secular Order of Discalced Carmelites*, (Washington, D.C.: ICS Publications, 2009), pp. 63-77.

Donal Dorr, *Integral Spirituality: Resources for Community, Justice, Peace and the Earth*, (Orbis, 1990).

Edward P. Echlin, *The Cosmic Circle: Jesus & Ecology*, (Dublin: The Columba Press, 2004).

Charles Elliott, *Praying the Kingdom: Towards a Political Spirituality*, (London: Darton, Longman and Todd, 1986).

Robert Ellsberg, *Blessed Among All Women: Women saints, prophets and witnesses for our time*, (London: Darton, Longman and Todd, 2006).

Julian Filochowski & Peter Stanford (eds.), *Opening Up: Speaking Out in the Church*, (Darton, Longman and Todd, 2005).

Constance FitzGerald, O.C.D., *Carmelite Beatitudes*, published in *Assumpta* magazine of the Carmelite Third Order in Britain, February 2009, and available online at www.carmelite.org in the Carmelite Spirituality section.

Michael L. Fitzgerald & John Borelli, *Interfaith Dialogue: A Catholic View*, (Maryknoll, New York: Orbis Books, 2006).

John Fuellenbach, *The Kingdom of God: Message of Jesus Today*, (Orbis, 1996).

Gaudium et Spes, The Pastoral Constitution on the Church in the Modern World. Available in a variety of publications and editions, including those of the official publishers to the Holy See (such as the Catholic Truth Society in Britain or Veritas in Ireland) or online at www.vatican.va

Vigen Guroian, *The Fragrance of God: Reflections on Finding God through the Beauty and Glory of the Natural World*, (London: Darton, Longman and Todd, 2007).

Paul Haffner, *Towards a Theology of the Environment*, (Leominster: Gracewing, 2008).

Bernard Haring, *The Healing Power of Peace and Nonviolence*, (St. Paul's Publications, 1986).

Elizabeth A. Johnson, *Truly Our Sister: A Theology of Mary in the Communion of Saints*, (Continuum, 2003).

Fransiscus Kosasih, O.Carm., *The Prophetic Dimension of the Carmelite Charism: New Developments since the Second Vatican Council in the light of Biblical, Theological and Historical Foundations*, (Rome: Edizioni Carmelitane, 2001).

Robert Lentz & Edwina Gateley, *Christ in the Margins*, (Maryknoll, New York: Orbis Books, 2003).

Sylvia Lucas, T.O.C., 'Already but not yet', *Assumpta*, December 2004.

Sylvia Lucas, T.O.C., 'Carmel and Interfaith Dialogue', published in parts across various editions of *Assumpta*, the magazine of Lay Carmelites in Britain, in 2009.

Sylvia Lucas, T.O.C., 'Saint Joseph the just man', *Assumpta*, March 2005.

Hilary Marlow, *Biblical Prophets and Contemporary Environmental Ethics*, (Oxford: Oxford University Press, 2009).

Sean McDonagh, S.S.C., numerous titles including *The Greening of the Church* (1990) and *Dying for Water* (2003).

Wilfrid McGreal, O.Carm., *Mendicant Friars – Justice and Peace*, available online www.carmelite.org

Patrick Thomas McMahon, O.Carm., *Nine Themes in Carmelite Spirituality*, printed in 2009 in *Carmel in the World* and *Assumpta* magazines, and available online at www.carmelite.org

Oliver McTernan, *Violence in God's Name* (Darton, Longman and Todd, 2003).

Nostra Aetate, Declaration of the Second Vatican Council on the relation of the Church with Non-Christian Religions. Available in a variety of publications and editions, including those of the official publishers to the Holy See (such as the Catholic Truth Society in Britain or Veritas in Ireland) or online at www.vatican.va

Míceál O'Neill, O.Carm., *Spirituality and Justice*, available online at www.carmelites.ie and www.carmelite.org

Pontifical Council for Justice and Peace, *Compendium of the Social Doctrine of the Church*, 2005.

Fran Porter, *It Will Not Be Taken Away From Her: A feminist engagement with women's Christian experience*, (London: Darton, Longman and Todd, 2004).

The Poverty and Justice Bible – Contemporary English Version, (Swindon: Bible Society, 2008). This edition of the Bible highlights over 2,000 Scripture verses that touch on issues of poverty and justice. Additional resources can be found online at www.povertyandjusticebible.org

Ratio of the Carmelite Friars (*Ratio Institutionis Vitæ Carmelitanæ*), section E – Service among the people. Available in print (Curia of the Carmelite Order, 2000) or online at www.carmelite.org

Timothy Radcliffe, O.P., 'A praying and prophetic community', in *In obsequio Jesu Christi: Praying and prophetic community in a changing world*, Proceedings of the 2007 General Chapter of the Carmelite Order, (Rome: Edizioni Carmelitane, 2007), pp. 37-46.

Anthony G. Reddie, *Acting in Solidarity: Reflections in Critical Christianity*, (London: Darton, Longman and Todd, 2005).

Angela Tilby, *Let There Be Light: Praying with Genesis*, (London: Darton, Longman and Todd, 1989, revised edition 2006).

John Welch, O.Carm., 'Contemplation and Compassion: The Tradition as Resource for Justice and Peace', in *The Carmelite Way: An Ancient Path for Today's Pilgrim*, (Leominster: Gracewing, 2006), pp. 141-159.

John Welch, O.Carm., 'Men, Women, and Contemplation: Gender Issues in the Spiritual Life', in *The Carmelite Way: An Ancient Path for Today's Pilgrim*, (Leominster: Gracewing, 2006), pp. 102-121.

John Welch, O.Carm., *Seasons of the Heart – The Spiritual Dynamic of the Carmelite Life*, (Aylesford, Kent: Lay Carmel Central Office, 2002, Reprinted 2005), also available online at www.carmelite.org

Barbara Wood, *The Gifts of Peace*, (Pax Christi, 1989).

Websites of some JPIC organisations in Britain and beyond

Two notes of caution are necessary here: firstly, the organisations listed below are widely regarded by people of faith as making a good contribution in JPIC issues, but it is up to each individual to inform themselves of their work and decide on their respective merits; secondly, website addresses often change, so it may be necessary to locate these sites through a search engine.

Amnesty International: www.amnesty.org.uk
Archbishop Romero Trust: www.romerotrust.org.uk
Caritas Internationalis: www.caritas.org
Caritas Social Action Network: www.caritas-socialaction.org.uk
Carmelite NGO at the United Nations: www.carmelitengo.org
CAFOD (Catholic Agency for Overseas Development): www.cafod.org.uk
Catholic Coalition on Climate Change: www.catholicsandclimatechange.org
Christian Ecology Link: www.christian-ecology.org.uk
Conference of Religious of England and Wales: www.corew.org
Fairtrade Foundation: www.fairtrade.org.uk
Friends of the Holy Land: www.friendsoftheholyland.org.uk
Interfaith Network for the UK: www.interfaith.org.uk
Medaille Trust: www.medaille.co.uk
National Justice & Peace Network: www.justice-and-peace.org.uk
Network of Christian Peace Organisations: www.ncpo.org.uk
Operation Noah: *www.operationnoah.org*
Pax Christi (UK): www.paxchristi.org.uk
Poverty and Justice Bible: www.povertyandjusticebible.org
Progressio: www.progressio.org.uk
Prison Fellowship International: www.pfi.org
Red Cross: www.redcross.org.uk
Sciaf (Scottish Catholic International Aid Fund): www.sciaf.org.uk
Sister Helen Prejean: www.prejean.org
Trócaire: www.trocaire.org
United Nations Economic & Social Council (ECOSOC): www.un.org/en/ecosoc

Notes and Reflections on Chapter 17

Notes and Reflections on Chapter 17

CHAPTER 18

Holy Men and Women of Carmel: Part 1 – Early Saints

Summary: All God's people are called to holiness, and the Carmelite way of life has proved itself to be a sure route on the pilgrimage through life, as witnessed by the remarkable men and women of our Order. They are members of our family who intercede for us and inspire us, so it is right that we should know something of their lives.

Though art frequently depicts the saints of Carmel in scenes of heavenly grandeur and glory, their holiness was often expressed on earth in the most ordinary events of everyday life, and in this we can all identify with them.

Get prepared: If you have any books about Carmelite saints you might like to have them to hand for reference or further reading, likewise a Bible and modern documents of the Order, but all the information you will need is contained within the text of this chapter. Certainly having writing implements to hand would be helpful if you intend to take notes or highlight anything in the text, and remember, you don't have to read all the material in one go. If you are going to discuss this material with a community, perhaps you might come to the meeting with a picture of a favourite Carmelite saint, or an extract from their writings that inspires you. It is good to commit our time of formation to God, so you might like to offer this prayer composed by Saint Mary Magdalen de'Pazzi:

> *How truly wonderful you are, O Word of God, in the Holy Spirit; you cause*
> *him to infuse the soul with you, that it may join itself to God, conceive God,*
> *savour God, taste nothing but God … Come, Holy Spirit. May the union*
> *of the Father and the will of the Son come to us. You, Spirit of truth, are*
> *the reward of the saints, the refreshment of souls, light in darkness, the*
> *riches of the poor, the treasure of lovers, the satisfaction of the hungry, the*
> *consolation of the pilgrim Church; you are he in whom all treasures are*
> *contained.*
>
> From *On Revelation and On Temptation*, printed in the
> *Carmelite Proper of the Liturgy of the Hours* (Rome, 1993),
> pp. 110-111.

Why study Carmelite saints in particular?

Most people are, to a certain extent, fascinated by saints: the spiritual heroes to whom we look for inspiration and intercession. Chapter 15 addressed the relationship between the Carmelite Family and the wider communion of saints. In this chapter and the next we'll meet specific individuals who trod Carmel's pathway to God. As part of our formation as Carmelites it is important that we know about and come to love as family the earlier saints in our Order; without their foundations Carmel would not be alive today. They are perfect examples of the flowering of God's grace within the Carmelite tradition and have contributed significantly to the Order's contemplative charism of prayer, community and service. We shall begin by looking briefly at saints who predated the existence of the Carmelite Order, but who have inspired our religious family.

Elijah and Elisha

Carmel is Elijan, that is to say, we look to the prophet Elijah – who lived over 800 years before Christ – and find great inspiration in him. Carmelites regard Elijah not as founder of our Order but as our earliest inspiration. In our tradition he is revered as *Pater et Dux Carmelitarum* (Father and Leader of Carmelites).

Did you know? A popular legend among medieval Carmelites was the *Dream of Sobac*. According to patristic (early Christian) writings, Elijah's father was called Sobac (or Sabacha), and whilst Elijah was still in his mother's womb Sobac dreamt that men dressed in white were greeting the new-born baby. Medieval Carmelites interpreted this as a vision of angels whose white robes prefigured the white cloaks of Elijah's followers.

Sobac's dream has been depicted in a number of paintings, including this one by Gaspard Dughet in the Carmelite church of San Martino ai Monti in Rome.

Stop and think: In many respects Elijah was a restless figure, filled with energy for God, anxious to spend that energy on God's Kingdom, and always searching to know God's will. In what ways is Elijah what Saint James called him, 'a man like us'?

All Carmelites need to know the Elijah stories that we find in the Bible at the end of the *First Book of Kings* and at the beginning of the *Second Book of Kings*, but since Elijah has been considered throughout our formation journey (especially Chapter 6) we shall briefly consider here just one episode: Elijah's calling of Elisha, son of Shaphat, as his disciple (*1 Kings* 19:19-21).

At Abel-meholah, east of the River Jordan, at God's command Elijah cast his mantle over Elisha as the young man passed by with his oxen. No words were uttered, only the symbolic invitation to be clothed in the same garment as the prophet, to share his charism, his gifts, his lot. As Mary would do centuries later, Elisha accepted the call to do God's will. We might be surprised that God called a young farmer to take on the role of prophet, but Elisha exemplifies the sort of people for whom God seeks: individuals who respond enthusiastically to God's call. Elisha killed his oxen and made a feast for the people; the community was nourished by Elisha's response showing that a vocation is a gift not only for the one called but for the benefit of all. For the next ten years Elisha was

Sculpture of Elijah and Elisha at the Cathedral of St. John the Divine in New York.

like a son to Elijah, even though the two men were quite different: Elisha, in spite of his youth, was bald; unlike Elijah who was at home in the desert and on the remote heights of Carmel, Elisha frequented towns and even had a home of his own in Samaria. Nevertheless Elijah and Elisha shared the same spirit. When the time came for Elijah to be taken up to heaven in a whirlwind accompanied by a chariot of fire, Elisha's vocation matured and he found the courage to ask his teacher for what he really wanted: a double portion of Elijah's spirit (*2 Kings* 2:9). There is a lot to be said for brave honesty and confidence in prayer, rather than politely asking for less (one is reminded of Thérèse of Lisieux: 'I choose all!'). Elisha's ministry lasted for half a century and spanned the reigns of four Kings of Israel, each of whom sought his counsel. Though Elisha took an active part in political affairs, and healed the leprosy of Naaman the King of Damascus' general (*2 Kings* 5), his main mission was to relieve the ordinary needs of those whose lives he shared, for example by feeding the hungry (*2 Kings* 4), and sweetening the water of Jericho that had become polluted (*2 Kings* 2:19-22).

Elisha depicted in stained glass by Richard Joseph King at Whitefriars, Faversham, England.

Mary

Alongside Elijah and Elisha, Carmelites give special reverence to Mary, Our Lady. Like Elijah, she was never a 'member' of the Order but as the Carmelite community on Mount Carmel developed in the thirteenth century it looked to Mary as patron and sister (as we considered in Chapter 5). In particular, Carmelites have tried to imitate Mary's purity of heart (*puritas cordis*) by doing away with all that does not lead to Jesus.

Our relationship with Mary is rightly considered foundational to the Carmelite way of life. The foundations of a building are not usually seen but are sunk deep, securing the stability on which the structure can be built. Carmelite devotion to Mary is likewise not always on show, but Our Lady's model of how to follow Jesus is what underpins the whole edifice of Carmel. Mary is the supreme example of the wise person who built their house on rock by hearing the words of Jesus and acting upon them (*Matthew* 7:24). The way Mary pondered the Word of the Lord is what inspires the Carmelites' distinctive approach to her, as is well put by Discalced Carmelite friar Aloysius Deeney:

A painting of Our Lady of Mount Carmel revered at San Martino ai Monti Church in Rome.

> There are many Catholics who wear the scapular for all the correct reasons and with sincere dedication to Mary who are not called to be Carmelites. Not only that, but there are some people who come to the Order precisely because of devotion to Mary, the scapular, and the rosary who do not have a vocation to be members of the Order. The particular aspect of the Blessed Virgin Mary that must be present in any person called to Carmel is that of an inclination to 'meditate in the heart', the phrase that Saint Luke's Gospel uses twice to describe Mary's attitude vis-à-vis her Son. Yes, all the other aspects of Marian life and devotion can be present: devotion to the scapular, the rosary, and other things. They are, however, secondary to this aspect of Marian devotion. Mary is our model of prayer and meditation. This interest in learning to meditate or inclination to meditation is a fundamental characteristic of any Carmelite. It is perhaps the most basic.
> (Aloysius Deeney, O.C.D., *Welcome to the Secular Order*, pp. 11-12.)

Did you know? The Carmelites in Darien near Chicago in the United States of America have a huge display of statues of Our Lady of Mount Carmel from around the world.

The diversity of images of Our Lady of Mount Carmel on display in Darien show how the Carmelite 'approach' to Mary has been embraced and adapted by every culture around the globe.

Saint Joseph

In Carmelite tradition Mary's spouse, Saint Joseph, also has a place of special affection Jesus, conceived by the Holy Spirit, was born into Joseph's household and it is through him that Jesus became 'Son of David'. The Bible makes it clear that Jesus related to Joseph as his father, and it was from Joseph that Jesus learned how to be a man. The Gospel references to Joseph are sparse, describing him simply as a 'just' or 'righteous' man (*Matthew* 1:19).

Devotion to St. Joseph is promoted by Carmelites in Dublin, Ireland. Left: A stained glass window by Frances Biggs at Terenure College depicts St. Joseph's dream. Centre: A stained glass window of St. Joseph at Gort Muire Carmelite community. Right: A chapel dedicated to St. Joseph at Whitefriar Street Carmelite Church.

During the first thousand years of Christianity Joseph was obscured behind a wealth of colourful legends originating from the second-century apocryphal text the *Protevangelium* (First Gospel) *of James*. During the Middle Ages certain saints such as Bernard of Clairvaux and Bernadine of Siena began to explore the role of Saint Joseph in the Gospel, using the loving intuition of their hearts rather than searching for non-existent facts.

The medieval Carmelites believed that if the Virgin Mary was patron of their Order, then Saint Joseph – who was Mary's protector – must by extension also be protector of the Order which was founded in Mary's honour. Saint Joseph is today revered by the Carmelites of the Ancient Observance (O.Carm.) as 'Principal

A wooden sculpture of St. Joseph by Philip Lindsey Clark at the Carmelite friary in York, England.

St. Joseph 'the Gossip' in the Incarnation Monastery in Avila.

This sculpture of St. Joseph at The Friars, Aylesford, England, shows Carmelites at the feet of their protector.

Protector of the Carmelite Order', whose feast day on 19th March is observed as a Solemnity (ranking the feast alongside the Order's other two solemnities, those of Our Lady of Mount Carmel and Saint Elijah).

It was the Carmelite Teresa of Jesus (of Avila) who nurtured our Order's devotion to Saint Joseph by 'adopting' him as father. She dedicated her first reformed convent to the saint, and referring to Joseph in her autobiography she wrote: 'he gave me greater blessings than I could ask' (*Life*, Chapter 6). Teresa seems to have understood that Joseph was protector of the Holy Family and, by extension, of the Church.

Did you know? In Saint Teresa's monastery of the Incarnation in Avila, there is a statue known as *Saint Joseph the Gossip*! Teresa used to say that the statue told her what her sisters had been doing whilst she was away on her travels!

When discerning where to go in our lives, pondering the life of Saint Joseph is a grea[t] source of help. He was detached from his own desires, allowing himself to be guide[d] by God's will, even when this involved enormous inconvenience (such as the flight int[o] Egypt).

A statue of Joseph and the infant Jesus in the grounds of the Whitehouse Carmelite friary at Darien, Illinois, in the United States of America.

Stop and think: What place, if any, has devotion to Saint Joseph had in your life thus far?

Holy Family

As well as revering Mary and Joseph, devotion to the other members of the Holy Family is common in many Carmelite communities. Carmelites have traditionally had a great devotion to the saints who were the blood family of Jesus, perhaps because since the Middle Ages Carmelites have had a sense of being the spiritual 'brothers and sisters' of Mary, and thereby related also to Jesus, who is the firstborn within a large family (cf. *Romans* 8:29; *Hebrews* 2:10). Scripture speaks of us being brothers and sisters of Christ, the adopted children and heirs of God the Father, and therefore Carmelites have found it natural to regard the family of Jesus as their own family and to live charitably as brothers and sisters.

Saints Anne and Joachim

Since the late Middle Ages Carmelites have promoted reverence of Saints Anne and Joachim. Although they are not mentioned in the Bible, Anne and Joachim were named as the parents of the Virgin Mary in the early Christian text known as the *Protoevangelium of James*. According to this apocryphal *First Gospel of James*, Anne and her husband Joachim were blessed with a daughter, Mary, after years of childlessness, and they dedicated the child to God's service in the Temple at Jerusalem.

A Carmelite altar piece in Vienna (c.1437) depicts the life of the Virgin Mary, including the meeting of her parents, Anne and Joachim, at the Golden Gate in Jerusalem.

Devotion to Anne and (to a lesser extent) Joachim developed in the Eastern Church as early as the sixth century and came to the Western Church prior to the late twelfth century. Anne is often depicted in western iconography holding a book, teaching the infant Mary to read the Scriptures. Some statutes – known by the German phrase *Anna Selbdritt* – show Anne holding both the infant Mary and the infant Jesus, emphasising her place in Christ's ancestry. The feast day of Saints Anne and Joachim in the West is 26th July.

A late medieval Flemish statue of Saint Anne holding both Mary and Jesus as infants is a popular image of popular devotion at Aylesford Carmelite Priory in Kent, England.

The Saint Anne Chapel at Aylesford Priory, which depicts the early life of Our Lady in beautiful ceramics and sgraffito work, is dedicated to prayer for families.

As devotion to Saint Anne developed within Western Christianity, the Carmelite Order took a particular interest in it. For example, German Carmelites developed confraternities of Saint Anne, and the friars' church in Frankfurt possessed what it claimed was a relic of her. In the fifteenth century an anonymous Dutch Carmelite compiled a *Life of Saint Anne* which helped spread devotion to her, as well as the idea that she married three times, conceiving a daughter with each husband: the Virgin Mary, Mary of Clopas, and Mary Salomae. This notion gave rise to the *Feast of the Three Marys* in the medieval Carmelite Order, and the Carmelites also developed an Office of Saint Anne. As the medieval Carmelites argued for the Virgin Mary's Immaculate Conception, the place of Saint Anne in salvation history came to be highlighted.

Although we now know that the Carmelite Order did not exist before the early 1200s, the medieval Carmelites thought that they were derived from a hermit community – the 'company of prophets' – founded by the prophet Elijah 800 years before Christ, and legends grew up within the Order that the pre-Christian Carmelites on Mount Carmel had been advisors to Christ's ancestors. According to legend, Saint Anne's mother, Saint Emerenciana, was said to have taken her daughter to meet the

In this painting from St. Teresa's Church in Avila, Joachim is taking Mary to present her for service at the Temple in Jerusalem. The child is dressed in a Carmelite habit!

In Whitefriar Street Carmelite Church in Dublin, Saint Anne is depicted teaching Mary to read the Bible. The inscription on the altar frontal makes the holy matriarch's role clear: "Saint Anne, care for us too".

hermits on Mount Carmel, and in turn Anne and Joachim were said to have brought the Virgin Mary to visit the community. The legends claimed that Mary decided to imitate the hermits' way of life, especially their vow of chastity.

Carmelites declared Saints Anne and Joachim to be secondary protectors of the Carmelite Order, after Our Lady and Saint Joseph. Just as Carmelites revered Mary's husband because she protected Our Lady, and by extension her Order, so they revered Our Lady's parents who provided for her in her childhood.

This depiction of Mary flanked by Anne and Joachim is in the 'Carmelite Carefree Village', a retirement community run by the Carmelite friars in Darien, Illinois, U.S.A. Devotion to Saint Anne is especially significant for retired people, who may well be grandparents like her. She is also invoked by people seeking children, and partners.

Stop and think: Why do you think Saint Anne is often depicted teaching Mary to read? What message does that teach Carmelites?

John the Baptist

As stated before, Carmelites have honoured the relatives of Christ because of our desire to be close to the Messiah. We call ourselves the *Brothers* (and sisters) *of the Blessed Virgin Mary of Mount Carmel*, and so we Carmelites have a strong sense of belonging to Our Lady's family. Carmelites have long nurtured devotion to Jesus' cousin John the Baptist.

In 2001 the Vatican's Congregation for Divine Worship issued a *Directory on Popular Piety and the Liturgy*. Other than Our Lady and Saint Joseph, the only saint to merit a detailed discussion in this document is John the Baptist:

In western art Saint John the Baptist is often depicted in animal skins, holding a cross, and pointing towards heaven or Christ, such as in this statue atop St. Peter's Basilica in Rome.

St. John the Baptist, the son of Zachary and Elizabeth, straddles both the Old and New Testaments. His parents were reckoned as 'just before God' (*Luke* 1:6). John the Baptist is a major figure in the history of salvation. While in his mother's womb, he recognised the Saviour, as he was borne in his mother's womb (cf. *Luke* 1:39-45); his birth was accompanied by great signs (cf. *Luke* 1:57-66); he retired to the desert where he led a life of austerity and penance (cf. *Luke* 1:80; *Matthew* 3:4); 'Prophet of the Most High' (*Luke* 1:76), the word of God descended on him (*Luke* 3:2); he went through the whole of the Jordan district proclaiming a baptism of repentance for the forgiveness of sins (*Luke* 3:3); like the new Elijah, humble and strong, he prepared his people to receive the Lord (cf. *Luke* 1:17); in accordance with God's saving plan, he baptized the Saviour of the World in the waters of the Jordan (cf. *Matthew* 3:13-16); to his disciples, he showed that Jesus was 'the Lamb of God' (*John* 1:29), 'the Son of God' (*John* 1:34),

The 'Reconstructed Carmelite Missal' belonging to the Order in medieval London includes a depiction of the decollation (beheading) of John the Baptist, with a friar praying alongside (bottom right). British Library Ms. Additional 29704-5 fol. 136v detail.

the Bridegroom of the new messianic community (cf. *John* 3:28-30); he was imprisoned and decapitated by Herod for his heroic witness to the truth (cf. *Mark* 6:14-29), thereby becoming the Precursor of the Lord's own violent death, as he had been in his prodigious birth and prophetic preaching. Jesus praised him by attributing to him the glorious phrase 'of all children born to women, there is no one greater than John' (*Luke* 7:28).

The cult of St. John the Baptist has been present in the Christian Church since ancient time. From a very early date, it acquired popular forms and connotations. In addition to the celebration of his death (29th August), of all the Saints he is the only one whose birth is also celebrated (24th June) – as with Christ and the Blessed Virgin Mary.

Directory on Popular Piety and the Liturgy §224-225

Since Christ himself praised his cousin, it is proper for the Christian community to celebrate him. His birth and prophetic role are also recalled by Carmelites and the wider Church each day during Morning Prayer when we pray the *Canticle of Zachary* (the *Benedictus*).

Within the Carmelite Family, John the Baptist also has a special role as a desert prophet. In the New Testament several people likened John to Elijah, the prophet of Carmel, which must have been significant to the first hermits who lived on that mountain. John the Baptist apparently possessed 'the spirit and power of Elijah' in proclaiming the will of

In this medieval Carmelite altarpiece in Italy, John the Baptist is depicted (second right) between Elijah and the Madonna and Child.

the Lord (*Luke* 1:17). John the Baptist was regarded by early Christians as a prototype of hermits and monks (as was Elijah), and as a desert figure appealed to the Carmelite sense of self identity. As the Carmelite Order grew in medieval Europe, it began to link itself to early Christian saints as a way of asserting its antiquity. John the Baptist was an obvious choice, and several statues of him dressed as a Carmelite are known to have existed in England before the Reformation.

In the medieval document known as *The Ten Books on the Way of Life and Great Deeds of the Carmelites* (better known as *The Book of the First Monks*), John the Baptist is described in Book Five as 'the first to baptise the members of the Carmelite Order, and he not only prophesied to them of the coming of Christ but revealed his presence and predicted that they would be baptised with the baptism of Christ.'

John the Baptist depicted in mosaic by Fr. Marko Ivan Rupnik at the Rosary Basilica in Lourdes, France.

What do you reckon? It is clear that the Carmelite Family used to have strong devotion to Saint John the Baptist, and it is clear that the Church today encourages that he be held in high esteem by the faithful generally. Should Carmelites seek new ways in which to promote devotion towards this cousin of Christ?

Jude the Apostle

Saint Jude can be considered within the family of Christ because the Bible suggests that 'Jude of James' or 'Thaddeus' was a kinsman of Jesus, and Apostle (*Luke* 6:16, *Matthew* 10:3, *Acts* 1:13). He was the author of a letter preserved in the New Testament. Because of confusion with Judas Iscariot, devotion to Saint Jude Thaddeus developed late in the Church. He is now the object of wide-spread popular piety, being revered as 'patron saint of desperate cases'.

Given the Carmelites' interest in promoting devotion to saints who were related to Christ, it would seem natural that the Order should have given him prominence early in its history. However, devotion to Saint Jude does not seem to have been widespread in the Carmelite Family until the twentieth century. This came about largely because of the popularity of the British National Shrine to Saint Jude, established in the town of Faversham in the county of Kent, not very far from Aylesford Priory. The devotion arose by an accident of history, or perhaps by divine providence! The Carmelite friars of the Ancient Observance came to Faversham in the 1920s. To support their work and

The statue and relic of Saint Jude at his national shrine in Faversham, England.

ministry they developed the Carmelite Press which produced prayer cards and small booklets on popular piety. The friars were asked to produce a card of Saint Jude which was distributed around Britain. People started sending in petitions and donations to the Shrine of Saint Jude in Faversham, which did not at that time exist. The friars, under the leadership of the prior Fr. Elias Lynch, O.Carm., perceived the need for such a shrine as a way of supporting their growing ministry and as a focus for popular piety towards the patron saint of desperate cases. In 1955 the Shrine of Saint Jude was dedicated, containing a statue of the saint and a relic of him.

Today hundreds of pilgrims come to Faversham over the weekends nearest to the feast of Saint Jude on 28th October, and throughout the year. The Carmelites maintain a newsletter for the shrine which corresponds with some 20,000 people all around the world. Through its newsletter and website, the Shrine of Saint Jude receives many requests for prayer, and testimonies from those who thank Saint Jude for prayers answered through his intercession. Many of these supporters of the shrine send donations which help to finance the work of the British Province of Carmelites, and so – like Christ's other relatives – Jude has become renowned as a patron and protector of Carmelites. From Britain devotion to Saint Jude has spread to other parts of the Carmelite Family throughout the world.

Devotion to Saint Jude is spreading across the world as Carmelites respond to the piety of the people. Images of Jude are now revered at (left-right): Whitefriar Street Carmelite Church in Dublin, Ireland; the Carmelite shrine at Darien, Illinois, U.S.A.; the lower Carmelite Church in Salamanca, Spain, where Saint John of the Cross studied.

Stop and think: According to Scripture, Jesus Christ is 'the first of many brothers and sisters'. How do you relate to Christ's earthly family?

Early Christian saints

Since the emergence of the Order in the thirteenth century, Carmelites have been devoted to other saints from Christianity's early days. This may be

This icon was written in 2008 by Br. Claude Lane, O.S.B., for the California-Arizona Province of Discalced Carmelite Friars. It depicts Mount Carmel, at whose summit (Christ) stand Saints Elijah and Paul, both holding a flaming sword representing the Word of God. Mary is represented by a lily on the mountain slope, and at the bottom Saint Albert hands the Carmelite Way of Life to Saint Brocard, behind whom stands Saint Teresa of Jesus.

because we originally claimed to derive from before the time of Christ and thus sought to associate ourselves with the earliest saints. Although we now accept that the Order began in the Middle Ages, Carmelites have always felt a special affinity with the first community of believers in Jerusalem, as described in the *Acts of the Apostles*, whose pattern of life is mirrored in our *Rule of Saint Albert*. Medieval texts such as *The Ten Books* (*Book of the First Monks*) described how Carmelites helped the Apostles to spread the Good News across the globe. The Christian faith is built on the Good News handed to us from the first followers of Jesus, and therefore it is appropriate that we look to these saints for inspiration when we seek to live 'in allegiance to Jesus Christ'. The *Rule of Saint Albert* reminds us that Carmelites should have a particular regard for the Apostle Saint Paul, whom we are to take as our teacher and model (Chapter 20).

Among the early saints to whom Carmelites have turned, particular mention should be made to the early 'Fathers and Mothers' of the Church (sometimes known from the Latin for 'father' as the *Patristic* writers). In the first few centuries of the early Church figures such as Justin Martyr (c.100-c.165), Irenaeus of Lyons (c.130-c.200), Origen (c.185-c.254), Basil of Caesarea (c.330-379) and Cyril of Alexandria (d. 444) helped to develop key Christian doctrines, established the canon of the New Testament, and saw Christianity develop from a persecuted religion to one embraced by the State.

Did you know? Since 1299 the Carmelites have been responsible for the church of San Martino ai Monti (Saint Martin on the Hill) in Rome. The basilica stands on what many scholars think is an ancient Christian site known as a *titulus*, one of the first churches of Rome. It was founded in the 3rd or 4th century as a 'house-church' in a private home, and gradually developed as a parish. Carmelites can feel a link with the early Christians when they consider that in San Martino the Eucharist has been celebrated for centuries.

Beneath the high altar in San Martino is an older altar, and beneath that are the 'scavi' or excavations which give a glimpse back to ancient Rome. Christians have prayed here for centuries, venerating an unusual mosaic of Our Lady blessing a Pope.

Among the early saints, particularly important for the development of the Carmelite way of life were the hermits, ascetics and monks known collectively as the 'desert fathers'. Inspired by the experiences of Christ and John the Baptist in the desert, they fled the cities in order to devote themselves to God through solitude, labour, poverty, fasting, charity and prayer. Gradually individual hermits came together in communities

A painting of the hermits gathered around the Well of Elijah on Mount Carmel, created in 1329 by Pietro Lorenzetti for a Carmelite altarpiece in Siena, Italy, now in the city's Pinacoteca Nazionale.

for mutual support. Saint Anthony the Great (of Egypt, c.251-356) is usually regarded as the father of monasticism, and taught the value of a desert existence for purifying the desires of the heart in order to come to union with the Divine. From small communities in the deserts of north Africa and the Middle East, eremitic monasticism (solitary hermits) developed into coenobitic monasticism (communities following a shared way of life).

The holy hermits of Mount Carmel

We know from historical sources that the Carmelite Order emerged early in the thirteenth century from a

Saint Brocard depicted in stained glass by Richard Joseph King at Whitefriars, Faversham, England.

community of Christian hermits living on Mount Carmel. We know very little about these men, but we assume that they lived holy lives and because of their great legacy it is common for Carmelites to revere the early hermits of Mount Carmel as saints. The *Brother B.* to whom the Carmelite *Rule* is addressed is often known as Saint Brocard. Another name connected with the early hermits is Saint Berthold, but there is some confusion about who he was (if he existed at all); *The Ten Books* refers to Berthold as the first formal prior on Carmel, and a medieval catalogue of Carmelite saints lists him as the second prior of Carmel and Brocard's successor.

Refresh your memory: The saints and blesseds of the Order are venerated by the Carmelite Family in a particular way on their feast day when the texts of the Divine Office are sometimes supplemented or replaced with readings from a book known as the *Carmelite Proper of the Liturgy of the Hours* (also known as the *Carmelite Supplement to the Breviary*). Reread what is said about this text towards the end of Chapter 15.

Albert of Jerusalem

A much better documented saint associated with the Mount Carmel hermits is Albert, Latin Patriarch of Jerusalem (d. 1214). A canon-regular, lawyer, theologian, and peace-maker, Albert Avogadro was born in Italy in a period of social and religious turmoil, but it was also an epoch of cultural rebirth and religious reform. Little is known of Albert's early life, but his considerable talents must have been recognised because he was made bishop of the north Italian town of Bobbio in 1184, gaining a reputation as a peacemaker in political disputes.

Perhaps because of these skills he was made Latin Patriarch of Jerusalem in 1205, a difficult job which inevitably involved negotiation with Muslims. He established his See at Acre because Jerusalem was in the hands of the Saracens. At some point in the ensuing years he was approached by the hermits living near the Well of Elijah on Mount Carmel and asked to write or at least approve a *Way of Life* (*formula vitae*) for them (as discussed

in Chapter 7), just as he had done for other religious communities. This text later came to be known as *The Rule of Saint Albert*.

In what way is Albert a Carmelite saint, when he was not himself a 'member' of the hermit community on Carmel? Albert is called 'lawgiver of Carmel', not its founder, since Albert was not so much founding a religious order as recognizing a

Saint Albert depicted in stained glass by Giuliani (1999) at the Domus Carmelitana (the Order's hotel next to Saint Albert's International Centre in Rome).

community that already existed. The Carmelite charism is rooted in the experience and vision of the community, not restricted by reference to one founding figure. Looking briefly at Albert's *Rule* (printed at the front of this book) one is immediately struck by the riches it contains. Albert begins by blessing the hermits; as successor to the Apostles his blessing incorporated the fledgling community into the wider body of the Church. Albert emphasises prayer, especially rooted in the Bible (Chapter 10); the *Rule* is so entwined with Scripture that the author must have been wholly steeped in the Word of God. Liturgical prayer is also important, notably the Eucharist (Chapter 14) and the Divine Office (Chapter 11). Albert underlines the necessity of service, both in the ordinary tasks of daily life (Chapter 20) and in the spiritual battle for the Lord God of Hosts, for which we must put on the armour of God (Chapter 18). Looking at the *Rule* we encounter Albert as a man of God; prayerful and full of common sense.

The hermits migrated from Mount Carmel from the 1230s onwards, bringing the Carmelite way of life to Europe. Some of the foundational saints of the Order emerged at this time.

Albert and Angelus: 'Fathers of the Order'

During the thirteenth century a young Carmelite called Albert (not to be confused with Albert of Jerusalem or the Dominican Albert the Great) became distinguished for his preaching, his role as a thaumaturge (miracle worker), and his desire for prayer. He had been born in the Sicilian town of Trapani and he died in Messina, probably in 1307. He was the first saint whose cult spread throughout the Order. As a result Albert of Trapani (also known as Albert of Sicily) is considered another patron and protector, or 'Father of the Order', a title he shared with another Carmelite saint of his time, Angelus, who was reputedly a hermit who had migrated from Mount Carmel to Sicily where he was martyred. You may recall the legend, recounted in Chapter 15, of Angelus teaching Saints Francis and Dominic about the Bible.

In 1524 the Carmelite friars agreed that on the seal of their General Chapter would be placed images of Saint Albert of Trapani and Saint John the Baptist alongside the image of Our Lady. In the same century it was also decided that every Carmelite church should have an altar dedicated to Saint Albert of Trapani. Saints Teresa of Jesus and Mary Magdalene de'Pazzi both had great devotion to him.

This very old fresco in the Carmelite friary at San Felice del Benaco in Italy shows Saint Albert of Trapani trampling the devil and surrounded by early Carmelite saints.

A seventeenth-century seal of the General Chapter of the Carmelite Order depicting at the top (left-right) Albert of Trapani, Our Lady with the infant Jesus, and John the Baptist.

St. Albert's Well in Whitefriar Street Carmelite Church, Dublin, Ireland.

Did you know? At the Whitefriar Street Carmelite Church in Dublin there is a popular shrine of Albert of Trapani by a well; drinking *Saint Albert's water* is reputed to bring healing.

Simon Stock

Perhaps the most famous – but most obscure – early Carmelite saint is Simon Stock, also known as Simon the Englishman. The first recognisable account of the 'Simon Stock legend' was written sometime between 1413-26 (that is well after his death, thought to have occurred in 1265). This account describes Simon as an Englishman, the sixth prior general of the Carmelites, who prayed to the Virgin Mary for assistance for his Order, and who in return received a vision of Our Lady holding the Carmelite scapular as a pledge of salvation. Since the word 'stock' is a Middle English term for a tree trunk, some traditions claimed that he lived as a hermit inside one; a more likely explanation of his name is that Simon came from the village of Stockbury in Kent, not far from Aylesford, the 'Second Carmel', which became such an important place in the Order's history when it hosted the first General Chapter in 1247.

Very few facts are known about Simon Stock. He was probably elected prior general in the 1250s or 60s (not in 1247 at Aylesford as often suggested), and so he was responsible for the Order at a time of great expansion and development, when the brothers were making the transition from hermits to friars. Simon is thus often invoked by Carmelites in moments of change. The Carmelite hymn *Flos Carmeli* (*Flower of Carmel*) is sometimes attributed to him. Simon's family perhaps had trading links with the English colony in Bordeaux, France, where he died and was buried. Since a cult developed around his tomb – which still exists in Bordeaux Cathedral – he certainly had a reputation for holiness.

An early modern carving, probably from the Low Countries, of Our Lady of Mount Carmel and Saint Simon Stock at Aylesford Priory in Kent, a place strongly linked with legends about his life.

Saint Andrew's Cathedral in Bordeaux continues to draw pilgrims to the tomb of Simon Stock. From here relics of Saint Simon have been sent to the Carmelites at Aylesford Priory, to the Carmelites in New York, and elsewhere.

As we observed earlier, unlike most religious orders the Carmelites had no individual founder. The Carmelite Order derives from a place, and a community. What trauma it must have been then for the hermits to abandon Mount Carmel. According to the scapular legend Simon inspired courage that enabled the early Carmelites to establish themselves afresh in Europe. Although there is no reliable historical evidence for the 'scapular vision' we would be foolish to dismiss the message behind it. As we reflected in Chapter 12, the scapular is part of the spiritual mythology and symbolism of Carmel: when Mary clothes us with her habit – a symbol of our belonging to Carmel – we put on the yoke of Christ, and commit ourselves to service of the Church and the World. Like Simon Stock we Carmelites are consecrated to Jesus in the Order of his mother.

Stop and reflect: For you, what is the most significant aspect of Simon Stock's life?

Simon Stock is one of the most frequently depicted Carmelite saints around the world, as seen in these images (top-bottom, left-right): the Lady Chapel of Westminster Cathedral in London; Carmelite Spiritual Center in Darien, Illinois; the shrine of Our Lady at Knock, Ireland; Aylesford Priory, England; the Carmelite Curia, Rome.

Peter Thomas

About forty years after the death of Simon Stock in France, Saint Peter Thomas was born in the same country. He entered the Carmelite Order aged twenty-one and was chosen to be its procurator general (the person who liaises between the Order and the Holy See) at the Papal Court in Avignon in 1345. In 1354 he was ordained bishop, and as a diplomat and peace-maker he was entrusted with papal missions to promote unity with the Eastern Churches. In 1363 he was appointed Archbishop of Crete and the following year Latin Patriarch of Constantinople. It is said that he learned the local languages of the places he was sent, so that he could properly dialogue with the people. He died on Cyprus in 1366, and has been hailed by Carmelites ever since as an apostle of ecumenism.

Peter Thomas's secretary, Philip de Mézières, wrote a biography of his master and recorded his holy death in terms full of Carmelite symbolism:

St. Peter Thomas depicted in artwork at (left) Aylesford Priory in Kent, England, and (right) Whitefriar Street Church in Dublin, Ireland.

He was affected by the cold and caught an infection in the throat, for he was weakened by fasting and vigils and wore only light clothing, following the example of the holy fathers of the desert ... he began to recite the penitential psalms in a loud clear voice suggestive of a man in full health "Lord, rebuke me not in your anger." With those around him making the responses he continued till about half way through the seven psalms. At last, however, his strength gave out, though his mind remained clear, and he signalled to his vicar-bishop to join in and support him, and thus the whole seven psalms were completed. As the vicar anointed him with the holy oil he managed to make all the responses of the ritual, striving to keep from the eyes of others the threadbare tunic and scapular he always wore. When the anointing was finished, my father devoutly recited the *Confiteor* and received absolution from the bishop. He humbly asked forgiveness of him, his household and all the assisting clergy if he had in any way offended them in the exercise of his office; and at the same time he requested them to ask on his behalf the pardon of all the inhabitants of Cyprus and elsewhere. Finally, he gave up his soul to the God who made him.

(*Carmelite Proper of the Liturgy of the Hours*, pp. 50-51)

Stop and reflect: Peter Thomas inspires Carmelites to engage in dialogue with others, particularly Christians of different denominations. What part does ecumenism play in your Carmelite vocation?

Carmelite saints from Tuscany

The feast of Saint Peter Thomas occurs on 8th January, and the following day Carmelites revere another brother and bishop from the same historical period who obtained sanctity by God's grace. Saint Andrew Corsini (d. 1374) entered the Carmelite Order in the Italian city of Florence and became bishop of nearby Fiesole in 1350. He was renowned for his simplicity of life, care of the poor, and zeal in preaching. He is the patron-saint of those caught up in riots, because he sought to build peace between people. In his *Life of Saint Andrew*, Bishop Francesco Venturi recalled: 'The holy bishop dedicated much time to settling quarrels among the citizens of Florence. Privately he eliminated hatred by means of friendly conversations; publicly he preached Christian charity and civic harmony.' Saint Andrew is buried in the *Carmine* (Carmelite friary) in Florence, where he is still revered.

Left: The tomb of Saint Andrew in the Corsini Chapel at the Carmine in Florence.
Right: Saint Andrew depicted in ceramic by Adam Kossowski at Aylesford Priory, England.

A further Carmelite born in or near Florence, sometime before 1386, was Blessed Angelus Augustine Mazzinghi. He was a prior of various houses and the first member of a reform observance within the Order dedicated to Our Lady of the Wood. He was noted for his work in preaching the Word of God, and he died in 1438.

Saint Avertanus was a French *conversus* (lay brother attached to the Carmelite Order). He was famous for making pilgrimages, and died sometime before 1284 whilst in the Tuscan town of Lucca where he is buried. He is often revered with his supposed travelling companion, Blessed Romeo of Limoges, though there is no evidence that Romeo was Carmelite.

Disclaimer!

Romeo is just one of several holy people that the Carmelite Order once claimed as its own. In older Carmelite books and works of art you will encounter saints who have subsequently been disclaimed by the Order, either because they were not really associated with our family or because there is not sufficient evidence that they existed. Amongst these are Saint Telesphorus (an early pope), and Saint Cyril (an alleged early prior general).

Holy laypeople in Carmel

At various points in the Middle Ages the Order tried to claim a number of prominent laypeople as Carmelites, including Saint Louis (King of France), Saint Edward (King of England), and Saint Henry (first Duke of Lancaster). It is unlikely that any of these died in the Carmelite habit; rather, some friars were seeking to promote the developing Order by aligning it with powerful political and religious figures.

According to medieval Carmelite legend, Saint Louis, King of France, was facing shipwreck as he sailed away from the Holy Land. Hearing a monastery bell sound over the waves, and learning that it was the community on Mount Carmel, he promised Our Lady that he would pray there if he survived the storm. He duly did so, and was so impressed with the brethren that he took some of them back to Paris from where they spread throughout France and Germany. The episode is depicted in stained glass at Boxmeer Carmelite priory in Holland.

In fact, the earliest laypeople to become Carmelite saints (if you discount the hermits on Mount Carmel who were mostly unordained) were not usually powerful people in the earthly sense. They were women and men who simply wanted to draw on the rich spirituality of the friars. In the absence of formal legislation, lay affiliation to the Order took a variety of forms. Some lay people set-up hermitages and anchorholds alongside Carmelite communities and followed the spirit of the *Rule of Saint Albert*. Others made vows and wore a religious habit but lived in their own homes. Some were aggregated to the Order by 'letters of confraternity', whilst *confratres* lived in the world but regularly met in Carmelite churches for direction from the friars.

Joan, Franco and Louis

One of the earliest such lay Carmelites was Blessed Joan (or Jane) of Toulouse. She lived near the friary in that city, working with the sick and the poor, and praying the whole Psalter daily. She frequently conversed with the young friars, giving them instruction. During her life and after her death sometime in the late 1200s many miracles were attributed to her intercession, and she was beatified in 1895. There is now some doubt about her exact relationship with the Order, but she continues to inspire lay people who collaborate in ministry with the Order's religious.

Joan of Toulouse depicted in Whitefriar Street Carmelite Church, Dublin, Ireland.

Blessed Franco of Siena (also known as Francis Lippi of Grotti, d. 1291) was another lay person attracted to the Carmelite perspective on the Christian story. According to the most reliable hagiography he was a riotous youth but was converted by a preacher and the experience of being miraculously cured of blindness during a pilgrimage. Franco became a lay brother attached to the chapel of Our Lady in Siena, where he may also have been a member of the Carmelite confraternity. It is said that he received frequent apparitions of Christ, his Mother, and angels, and had the spirit of prophecy, though precise details about his life have become confused because there is a Servite 'blessed' of the same name.

A portrait of Blessed Francis of Siena in the Librarian's Office at Saint Albert's International Centre in Rome.

Did you know? The Maltese priest Saint George Preca (1880-1962) took the name of

'Franco' at his profession in the Carmelite Third Order, after Blessed Franco of Siena. He did so because – like Blessed Franco – George believed that he had come to Carmel after having been a great sinner. George studied and imitated the life of Blessed Franco, and several times in his writings he used his tertiary name rather than his baptismal name.

Blessed Louis Morbioli (d. 1485) was similar to Blessed Franco in that he was notorious for his dissipated lifestyle until he converted following a serious illness. He was distinguished as a teacher of Christian doctrine and as a beggar on behalf of the poor. Because of his simple habit it was thought that he was a member of the Carmelite Third Order, and although it is now known that he was not, Louis is still revered by some Carmelites in his native Bologna.

Saint Nuno

A Carmelite who spent most of his life as a lay person was Nuno Álvares Pereira. He lived in the fourteenth century, a time of great expansion for the Carmelite Family in Europe, but also a very difficult period socially and spiritually. The plague – known as the Black Death – killed almost 20 million people across the continent and wars took yet more lives. However, adverse conditions can give birth to great sanctity, as was seen in the life of Nuno Álvares Pereira. Nuno was born in 1360 near Lisbon in Portugal. A gifted soldier, he was made commander of Portugal's armies when he was only 23. Impetuous, resourceful and courageous, Nuno would kneel and pray on battlefields, and refused to share in the spoils of war.

A statue in Batalha, Portugal, of Saint Nuno, the country's 'Holy Constable'

Between the years 1383-85 there was a crisis in Portuguese politics concerning independence from Castile (Spain). Nuno led an outnumbered army to a heroic victory which brought him honours and wealth that he spent on building churches. He showed a practical love for the poor, particularly orphaned children to whom he frequently became godfather. In 1423, following the death of his wife, he became a Carmelite brother in the Lisbon convent taking the religious name Nuno of Saint-Mary. Here he acted as porter at the community gatehouse, giving food, shelter and friendship to the poor.

The ruins of the 'Carmo', the Carmelite friary in Lisbon, which Nuno had helped to found; it was destroyed by an earthquake in 1755.

As his epitaph declares: 'His worldly honours were countless, but he turned his back on them. He was a great Prince, but he made himself a humble monk.' Still revered as a hero in Portugal, he was a man of deep prayer and compassion for the poor and outcast. In Nuno Carmelites can find a great model of someone who read the signs of the times

The clothing of Saint Nuno as a Carmelite, painted in 1913 by Giuseppe Gonella.

in the light of the Gospel, and who showed practical interest in the issues and needs of his day. Centuries after his death, Nuno was canonised in 2009.

Saint Nuno appeals to our sense of romance! He was husband, widower, father, friar. He was literally a knight in shining armour who influenced the history of his nation. He was a great soldier who hated war; a man of position who was sufficiently detached to renounce wealth in favour of a life of poverty and penance. Like Elijah, Nuno was truly a contemplative in the Carmelite model: a man of service as well as of prayer, who helped to build community. Saint Nuno was a person who seized history in his hands and breathed the breath of God into it.

Did you know? The Carmelite Order has a retreat and conference centre at the Portuguese shrine of Fátima named in honour of Nuno. Following his canonisation in 2009, the Casa Beato Nuno (Blessed Nuno House) has been renamed Casa São Nuno (Saint Nuno House).

Reforming Saints

The fifteenth century brought great change to Church, society, and to Carmel. In 1453 the Hundred Years War ended just as the first printing press came into operation. This period of revolution in communication and technological growth is not unlike our own times.

There was an explosion of new ideas as the Renaissance got into full swing, and ideas of reform spread across the Church which some perceived as being slack. Within the Carmelite Order too, some felt that the original purity and inspiration of Carmel had declined.

During this period Carmel nurtured a number of saints who can be classified as reformers. One of the first major reforms within the Order was begun in the Italian city of Mantua by friars who wanted to live the *Rule of Saint Albert* more rigorously whilst remaining a full part of the Order. Houses that took part in the reform were known collectively as the *Congregation of Mantua*. A great saint of this reform movement, Blessed Bartholomew Fanti, was born in Mantua and by 1452 had become a priest of the Congregation. For thirty-five years he was rector of one of the earliest formal organisations within Lay Carmel, the *Confraternity of the Blessed Virgin Mary*, for which he composed a rule and statutes. He died in 1495 and is especially remembered for his love of the Eucharist.

This painting in Saint Albert's International Centre (CISA) in Rome depicts Bl. Bartholomew Fanti preaching about the Eucharist before Bl. Baptist of Mantua and fellow friars.

A window depicting Saint Nuno at Whitefriar Street Carmelite Church in Dublin.

Another holy Carmelite born in Mantua was Blessed Baptist Spagnoli (1447-1516). As a youth he joined the Congregation of Mantua, becoming its vicar general, and eventually Prior General of the whole Order in 1513. Baptist of Mantua was a renowned scholar and poet, and drew many people to a better Christian life by his writings. Like all Carmelites he regarded the Bible as the most important writing of all, as he stated in a treatise *On Patience*:

> You will find that the reading of sacred scripture is a great and powerful remedy against bodily suffering and depression of mind. In my opinion, there is no other writing, no matter how eloquent and stylish it may be, that can bring such peace to our minds and so thoroughly dissolve our cares as sacred scripture can.

This painting of Blessed Baptist Spagnoli of Mantua in the Domus Carmelitana in Rome depicts the Carmelite wearing the laurels of a poet.

As we have read in previous chapters, women played an important part in the ongoing reform and renewal of the Carmelite Family, and the first communities of women religious were incorporated into the Order after the papal bull *Cum Nulla* in 1452. Blessed Joanna (or Jane) Scopelli (1428-91) was a Carmelite woman involved in the Mantuan reform, introducing its good effects into the convent in Regio Emilia. In the Carmel of Parma Blessed Archangela Girlani (1460-95) spread the same desire for a fulfilling relationship with God, and she bore a special devotion to the Holy Trinity.

Jane Scopelli is usually shown with the Christ child, as in this painting in Saint Albert's International Centre (CISA) in Rome.

John Soreth

The formal incorporation of women into Carmel – and later lay people in general – was thanks to the efforts of the greatest reformer of this period, Blessed John Soreth. As we read in Chapter 8, John was from Normandy and became Prior General of the Carmelite Order in 1451, a post he held until his death (as was usual in those days) twenty years later. The first focus of John's interest was the holiness of his friars, based on faithfully observing the *Rule of Saint Albert* on which he wrote a beautiful *Commentary*. In each province John visited he established reformed houses to act as magnets for attracting brothers who were serious in their vocation. These friaries radiated prayer and service into the community. Instead of forcing reform, John had the gift of appealing to people's idealism, making them *want* to be better. Thanks to John's securing of the papal bull *Cum Nulla* in 1452, communities of Carmelite women quickly sprang up in various parts of Europe. John published the first *Rule for the Third Order* in March 1455, making use of the new printing technology. When we reflect on more recent developments within the Carmelite Family it is profoundly humbling to remember our debt to this great prior general.

John's work of reform was greatly assisted by Blessed Frances d'Amboise (1427-85). She was the widow of the Duke of Brittany, and under the direction of John Soreth she

Blesseds John Soreth and Frances d'Amboise depicted in ceramic by Adam Kossowski at Aylesford Priory in Kent, England.

took the Carmelite habit in a monastery she had previously established. She is considered the founder of the Carmelite nuns in France.

The poor helping the poor

A contemporary of Frances d'Amboise was another holy Carmelite to hail from near Trapani, Blessed Aloysius (or Louis) Rabatà. He was born about the middle of the fifteenth century and after joining the Carmelites eventually became prior of his community. In 1490 he died from a head wound, but forgave his attacker and refused to reveal his identity. A witness during his beatification process said of him: 'Brother Aloysius shared in every task, even the humblest, being willing to go from door to door begging bread to support the community and to help others in need. While he was on his begging rounds other poor people would in turn asks alms from him, knowing they would never be refused.'

Blessed Aloysius Rabatà.

Teresa de Cepeda y Ahumada

It would be fair to say that Teresa of Jesus (1515-82), the saint from the central Spanish town of Avila, was the greatest of all Carmelite reformers, and of course her efforts gave rise to the *Discalced* (or *Teresian*) branch of the Carmelite Family. Although the great number of the Order's saints who precede Teresa show that it is possible to be fully Carmelite without reference to her, she has made an indelible impression upon Carmel and should be studied and revered by all branches of the Carmelite Family. It is impossible to do justice to Teresa's life and character in so short a space as this chapter, but you might like to look back at the information given about her in Chapter 8, and to consult some of the recommended resources listed at the end.

Stop and think: What are your existing impressions of Teresa of Jesus? Is she someone you think you would get along well with?

Teresa was born (significantly of Jewish ancestry) in the province of Avila in central Spain in 1515. A pious and romantic child, she entered The Encarnación (*Incarnation*) in Avila, which was a beaterìa, that is, a house of women (numbering over 100) with varying degrees of commitment within the Carmelite Order. In the cloister Teresa suffered greatly from illness, but found consolation and guidance in a wide variety of spiritual texts that taught her the principles of prayer and meditation. She had a number of mystical

A statue of Teresa outside the church named after her in Avila, Spain.

Teresa (right) and Thérèse sculpted in wood at Aylesford Carmelite Priory in Kent, England.

experiences and visions, but was equally remarkable for her grounded approach to life, humour and common sense. The Church at the time was undergoing a period of renewal following the Reformation, and Teresa was inspired by new ecclesiastical movements such as the Jesuits and the Discalced Franciscans. Despite initial protests from civil and religious authorities, in 1562 Teresa (now in her late forties) established a new monastery in Avila, St. Joseph's, dedicated to a simpler and more profound observance of the *Rule of Saint Albert*. The Prior General of the Carmelite Order encouraged her to establish further houses, prompting Teresa to travel through nearly all the provinces of Spain, and earning her the title of *La Madre* (Mother). She enlisted the help of Carmelite brothers, notably Anthony of Jesus and John of the Cross, who established the first convent of Discalced Carmelite friars at Duruello in 1568. The Discalced reform was not without its critics, especially among the friars of the Order, and Teresa herself came under the scrutiny of the Inquisition. The Discalced reform could not develop further until the intervention of King Philip II of Spain. After twenty years of reforming activity, Teresa died in 1582 at Alba de Tormes. After her death reform and renewal continued, with the Discalced Carmelites eventually requesting to become a distinct religious order. Teresa was canonised forty years after her death in 1622, and declared a Doctor of the Church in 1970.

Teresa was a warm, energetic woman, a complex character with many gifts. We learn much about her from her writings, including her *Life*, *The Interior Castle*, *The Way of Perfection*, *The Book of Foundations*, and her many letters.

SE LE HA DADO LA
GLORIA DEL LÍBANO
Y LA HERMOSURA DEL
CARMELO

An icon of Teresa with the Virgin Mary and Christ written by the nuns of the Carmel of the Theotokos and Unity at Harissa, Lebanon.

It is for Teresa's wonderfully accessible teaching on prayer that she is most esteemed. Her writing provides almost limitless insights on the subject, but let us look at just one of her images of the process of prayer, from her *Life*, Chapter 14 onwards. Carmel means 'garden', 'orchard' or 'vineyard' and Teresa imagines the soul as a garden in which we labour as tenants on behalf of the Master Gardener who is the Lord. Our concern is to water the garden so that the flowers (virtues) will flourish. Normally, in the beginning especially, our work of watering is very hard. We have to lug a heavy bucket to and from the well, hoping all the time that there will actually be any water in it. The water here is best described as 'an interior feeling of devotion'. This represents the 'donkey work' of prayer: the seemingly endless task of persevering whether we feel inspired or not, year-in and year-out, often for little obvious reward. Yet if we do persevere, the Master Gardener takes pity on us and makes our task easier with a pump, enabling us to draw more water from the well with greater ease. We still need to make an effort – we must operate the pump and still resort to the bucket at times – but the whole process is simpler and smoother. Recollection is easier to achieve and one gets the overwhelming feeling that there is more prayer for less effort.

Prayer that flowers

Teresa emphasises that whether we notice much water or not the acid test of our prayer is the quality of the flowers, that is, the virtues. If our lives are increasingly marked by the virtues of loving God and neighbour, there isn't much wrong with our prayer. If, on the other hand, our prayer seems exciting and wonderful but no love is growing in the garden, then we have got something wrong.

There are more phases in Teresa's watering metaphor, more mysterious because they describe the work of God in prayer. One of these is the emergence of a stream, bubbling-up unbidden from an underground spring, from which water can run along channels into the garden. Suddenly we seem to have water provided for us and our only task is to direct it to the flowers, making sure that the irrigation ditches don't get clogged-up. Even this water is not only for our delight; it is for the plants to flourish. A further phase brings cloudbursts of rain which saturate the garden. Teresa writes: 'we can see how much rest the gardener would be able to have if the Lord never ceased to send rain whenever it was necessary ... But during this life, that is impossible, and when one kind of water fails, we must always be thinking about obtaining another.'

For Teresa, the most important thing about prayer is that it makes us more open to doing the will of God. She was not worried about personal holiness simply for the sake of her own salvation; rather she wanted herself and her sisters to grow in holiness so that they would better be able to discern what God was asking of them.

Stop and think: What is the purpose of prayer in your life?

Juan de Yepes y Alvarez

Like Teresa of Jesus, Saint John of the Cross (1542-91) is a Doctor of the Church. He is renowned for his teaching on the union of the soul with Christ, for his fruitful friendship with Teresa and help in the Discalced reform of the friars, for his teaching on spiritual growth, and for his beautiful poetry.

John's father was disinherited because of his marriage to Catalina. She was left a widow with John being the youngest of three children.

This window by Frances Biggs at Terenure College in Dublin depicts Teresa's spiritual doctrine. Teresa is shown seated, the posture of a teacher. The fountain of water represents her teaching on prayer (water enabling the flowers to grow as prayer enables virtues to grow). The butterfly signifies the transformation of the soul through prayer.

John's adolescence was spent in poverty, although Catalina generated great warmth and love in the family, giving her children an early and vital experience of community. As a young man John served in a hospital nursing those suffering from syphilis. He joined the Carmelites, but being dissatisfied he was ready to leave and enter the Carthusians, until he was persuaded otherwise by Teresa. She enlisted his help in her reform, a partnership of mutual benefit. In his role as spiritual director John was able to develop and exercise his astonishing gifts.

A key experience of John's life was being imprisoned for nine months by his fellow friars (who distrusted his reform) in a tiny cell in the priory at Toledo. John was cut-off from all his friends who didn't know what had become of him; it was the darkest of experiences, yet during this time in prison John wrote much of his poetry which is a sublime expression not of desolation but of God's secret work in his soul.

Did you know? Christian mystics usually feel compelled to write down their spiritual insights, but because the journey into God can never been adequately expressed in words they often express frustration about writing. John of the Cross felt that his poetry better expressed what he wanted to say about the love of God than his prose commentaries, which fellow Carmelites asked him to write to explain his verse.

A statue of John of the Cross in Alba de Tormes, Spain.

Trying to de-mystify John (for those who are mystified!)

Many of us find John of the Cross difficult. He is too … everything! Too passionate, too obscure, too remote from everyday life. We can sense the beauty and grandeur of his insights but maybe feel that his teaching is not relevant for us. Yet in a nutshell what John of the Cross says is an echo of Jesus in the Gospel:

> They who have my commandments and keep them are those who love me; and those who love me will be loved by my Father, and I will love them and reveal myself to them … Those who love me will keep my word, and my Father will love them, and we will come to them and make our home with them. (*John* 14: 21, 23)

Our part in the spiritual journey is realising that God's initiative comes first, to which we respond by loving God and keeping his word so that God will make a home in us. Many obstacles prevent us from doing this: our sins, our fears and even our more innocent attachments to people, places and objects that can actually become false idols that we worship in place of the one true God. As we gradually try and free ourselves from these false gods we become increasingly open to the Lord's loving in-flow. For John a key theme is the need to develop detachment from desires that ensnare us, for only God is enough to satisfy our deepest longings.

An icon of John of the Cross
at Whitefriars Carmelite
community in York, England.

Much of John's imagery is derived from the Bible's *Song of Songs*, and he sees the
relationship between God and the human soul as a lover's quest for his beloved. John also
describes the work of God's divine love in the human soul as like a *living flame*. This work
of God in his children (or as John would say God's lovers) can take a lifetime or it can be
accomplished very quickly. But happen it must before we can be fully united with God.

God speaks in the night

For the most part this secret work of God's love occurs in 'darkness', in the obscurity of
faith:

> How well I know the living spring that flows, though it is night!
> That ever-living spring is hidden fast,
> and yet I found its dwelling place at last, although by night.
> *Song of the soul that rejoices to know God by faith*, v.1-2

John understands 'night' as the period or process of transformation during which God hollows out our heart to make space to dwell within. The dark night plays a part in creating what the Carmelite tradition calls *vacare Deo* or 'space for God'. The dark night experience may feel like a time when God has abandoned us, but in fact it is a period of 'sheer grace' when God is removing all the obstacles – even religion – which prevent our hearts from fully loving God.

Refresh your memory: You might like to re-read the section on the dark night in Chapter 9.

The 'dark night' is sometimes confused with depression or suffering. There is much pain in the world and all people suffer to some extent. Yet not all of these are experiences of the 'dark night'. In order for an experience of suffering or sorrow to become 'sheer grace' it must be accepted with trust. John is a reminder that saints are not simply people who always experience joy and religious fervour; rather they are people who trust God in difficult times as well as good.

Some of Teresa's other followers

Given the brilliance of Teresa and John it is sometimes easy to overlook the saints who were their contemporaries or who followed immediately after them.

One of the first followers of Teresa was Blessed Anne of Saint-Bartholomew (1549-1626). She made her profession in the hands of Teresa at the convent of St. Joseph's in Avila. She was the *Madre*'s companion and nurse, and brought the Teresian spirit to France and Belgium.

Also of note among Teresa's disciples is Blessed Barbe (Barbara) Avrillot (1566-1618),

Anne of Saint-Bartholomew was said to have received a vision of the prophet Elijah extending his cloak over the Carmelite chapter at Valladolid. The event is depicted in a woodcut in the *Speculum Carmelitanum* of 1680.

better known by her married name of Barbe Acarie, or her religious name Mary (Marie) of the Incarnation (and not to be confused with an Ursuline blessed of the same name). She was a busy housewife who was inspired by Teresa's writings to introduce the Discalced Carmelite nuns into France. After her husband's death she became a nun herself and was distinguished by her spirit of prayer and zeal for propagating the Catholic faith. Other followers of Teresa worthy of memory are Anne of Jesus (1545-1621), Anne of Saint-Augustine (1555-1624), and Madeleine of Saint-Joseph (1578-1637). Amongst the male Teresian Carmelites, Venerable Dominic of Jesus and Mary (1559-1630) is notable for his humility and charity.

Blessed Marie of the Incarnation.

The Ancient Observance (O.Carm. branch) of the Carmelite Family can also speak proudly of several Carmelites from the sixteenth century. Of particular note is Juan Sanz of Valencia (1557-1608), a friar noted for his prayer life and humility. His story is told in the *Profiles in Holiness* series of books, as is that of Venerable Miguel de la Fuente (1573-1625), another Spanish friar, noted for his work with the Third Order and for showing that contemplation living can include active service.

Maria Maddalena de'Pazzi

Again because of Teresa's great legacy it is sometimes forgotten that there were women religious in Carmel before her reform, and after her life there continued to be nuns in the Ancient as well as Discalced Observance. The greatest of these was Saint Mary Magdalene de'Pazzi (1566-1607).

Venerable Miguel de la Fuente.

Born in Florence to a noble family, she was baptised Caterina. She was an unusually prayerful child with a very strong devotion to Our Lord in the Eucharist. She made her first communion at the then early age of 10 and soon after vowed her virginity to God. Despite some parental opposition she felt she had a vocation to the religious life and chose the Carmelite monastery in Florence, known for its fidelity to the *Rule of Saint Albert* and for the fact that the nuns received daily communion (a rare privilege at the time).

A window of St. Mary Magdalene de'Pazzi in the chapel of the Carmelite Curia in Rome.

A statue of Mary Magdelene de'Pazzi in the Incarnation monastery in Avila.

As a nun Sr. Mary Magdalene's life was marked by many mystical phenomena, daily raptures, and ecstasies at the time of Holy Communion. Among her many extraordinary gifts was the ability to read hearts ('cardiognosis'). More important though was her wisdom and strong common sense which made her an invaluable novice mistress. She was also artistically gifted, expressing her spirituality through drama, painting and embroidery. Despite being enclosed she appears to have had a deep awareness of the outside world and of the redemptive use of suffering offered up for her fellow human-beings.

After Sr. Mary Magdalene's death in 1607, many miracles were attributed to her intercession, and her body was found to be incorrupt. She was canonised in 1669, and her feast on 25th May inserted into the General Roman Calendar.

In 2007, the fourth centenary of St. Mary Magdalene de'Pazzi's death, Pope Benedict XVI wrote to Cardinal Ennio Antonelli, Archbishop of Florence: 'This great saint has for everyone the gift of being a spiritual teacher... Whilst she was alive, grasping the monastery bells, she urged her sisters with the cry "Come and love Love!" ... [May the Carmelites who] draw their inspiration from her still make her voice heard in all the Church, spreading to every human creature the proclamation to love God.'

Standing as she does at the threshold of the modern age, Mary Magdelene de'Pazzi is a beacon for much that we value in the Carmelite charism. Although the spiritual life is not a matter of receiving spectacular favours, and Carmelites are naturally suspicious of mystical phenomena, Mary Magdalene was grateful for all the graces God gave her, weaving both unusual and more pedestrian gifts into the seamless whole of a life lived for

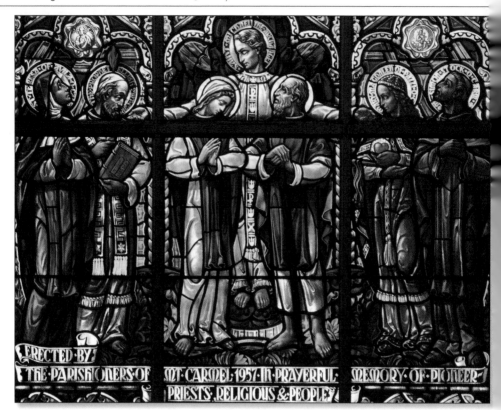

Saints of Carmel depicted in glass at Our Lady of Mount Carmel Church in Waterloo, Australia. Left-right: Teresa of Jesus, Elijah, Saint Michael flanked by male and female Carmelites, Mary Magdalene de'Pazzi, Simon Stock.

God. She faced both outwards and inwards, her heart constantly seeking God in prayer, in service, and in community.

Saints then and now

In some cases we know very few facts about the many holy men and women who walked the path of Carmel before us in the early centuries of the Order, but they still stand out as torch-bearers, prepared to pass on the truth of God's love and the insights of Carmelite spirituality. The mission we Carmelites face today is remarkably similar to that which faced them: spreading a vision of God and of life which is a challenge not only to ourselves but to the society in which we live.

Sometimes it is easy to forget that holiness is not what an individual does but is the result of what God does in, through, and with that person. The lives of Carmelite saints, lay and religious, witness that sainthood can follow whenever an individual soul gives space for God (*vacare Deo*).

Conclusion: In this eighteenth chapter we have seen how the Carmelite way of prayer, community and service has been a sure and proven path of holiness well trodden by many of the Order's saints, great and small alike over many centuries, who serve as reliable models of holiness for us to imitate.

Perhaps conclude your time of reflection and study with a moment of prayer, asking the saints of Carmel to intercede for you and the whole Carmelite Family.

In the next chapter we will continue our reflection on the holy men and women of Carmel by learning about the later saints in our family's history.

Ideas for Reflection, Discussion and Action

- Has anything or any particular saint caught your attention as you have studied this chapter either on your own or with others? Is there anything more you would have said about a particular saint? What do you understand to be the key themes running throughout the chapter? Perhaps jot your thoughts down on the blank page at the end.

- What do you think it is about Carmelite spirituality that has encouraged so many people on the path to sainthood?

- The succession of reforms in the Carmelite Family show us that even holy people do not always agree on how to live a life pleasing to God. How can we account for these differences of opinion?

- Baptist Spagnoli of Mantua and John of the Cross were both poets. Do you think that poetry is a good way of speaking about the experience of God?

- Pray for the work of Carmelite shrines throughout the world that keep alive the memory of our saints.

- The first hermits on Mount Carmel were probably crusading soldiers. Blessed Franco and Saint Nuno were both soldiers. Why do you imagine they turned from physical warfare to spiritual battle?

- Do you find it easy to think of Mary and Elijah as 'Carmelite'?

- How do you feel about God being your 'lover', as John of the Cross describes the relationship?

- How important is it for us to know historical facts about the holy men and women of Carmel?

- Like Saint Peter Thomas, try to find out more about our brethren in the Eastern Churches.

- What act of service performed by a Carmelite saint do you find most inspiring?

- Is it more important to read about the lives and teachings of Carmel's saints, or to show devotion to them through acts of piety such as pilgrimages to their shrines or veneration of their relics?

- The *Rule of Saint Albert* places special emphasis upon Saint Paul as model and teacher of Carmelites. How do you relate to the Apostle?

- Is devotion to and study of the saints of Carmel an essential aspect of Carmelite spirituality?

Recommended Further Resources

There are many resources (books, films, recordings) associated with Carmel's better known saints, widely available in not only Carmelite bookstores but more general Christian shops. However, it is not so easy finding good and accurate resources about the less well known Carmelite saints, particularly from the Order's medieval period.

Emanuele Boaga, O.Carm., *Celebrating the Saints of Carmel*, (Rome: Edizioni Carmelitane, 2010).

Emanuele Boaga, O.Carm., 'St. Mary Magdelene de'Pazzi: Protector of the Third Order of Carmel', *Carmel in the World*, Volume XLV Number 2, 2006, pp. 109-114.

Sanny Bruijns, O.Carm., *A Journey With Mary: How God Touches Our Lives*, (Institute of Spirituality in Asia, 2005). This book includes information about the apocryphal stories of Mary's birth, as well as information on Marian pilgrimage and devotional practices. This book can be found in major Carmelite libraries.

Congregation for Divine Worship and the Discipline of the Sacraments, *Directory on Popular Piety and the Liturgy – Principles and Guidelines*, (Rome, 2001). It is published in English by the various official publishers to the Holy See worldwide such as Veritas in Ireland, and the Catholic Truth Society (CTS) in Britain. It is also available online at the Vatican website: www.vatican.va

Kevin Culligan, O.C.D., 'The Dark Night and Depression', in Keith J. Egan, T.O.C., *Carmelite Prayer: A Tradition for the 21st Century*, (New York: Paulist Press, 2003), pp. 119-138.

Kevin Culligan, O.C.D., 'From Imprisonment to Transformation: John of the Cross in Toledo', in Kevin Culligan, O.C.D., & Regis Jordan, O.C.D., (eds.), *Carmel and Contemplation: Transforming Human Consciousness*, Carmelite Studies 8, (Washington, D.C.: I.C.S. Publications, 2000), pp. 209-239.

Aloysius Deeney, O.C.D., *Welcome to the Secular Order of Discalced Carmelites*, (Washington, D.C.: ICS Publications, 2009).

Andrew Doze, *Discovering Saint Joseph*, (London & Maynooth: St. Pauls, 1991).

Thomas Dubay, *Fire Within: Teresa of Avila, John of the Cross and the Gospel – On Prayer*, (Ignatius Press, 1989).

Keith Egan, T.O.C., *From the Wadi to San Jose: Teresa's Renewal of Contemplative Prayer*, CD audio recording of a presentation, (Washington, D.C.: CC Communications).

Thomas H. Green, S.J., *When the Well Runs Dry* (Ave Maria Press, 1998).

Michael D. Griffin, O.C.D., 'Saint Teresa and the Vocation to a Life of Prayer', in *Welcome to Carmel: A Handbook for Aspirants to the Discalced Carmelite Secular Order*, Growth in Carmel Series, (Hubertus, Wisconsin: Teresian Charism Press, 2006), pp. 35-45.

Giovanni Grosso, O.Carm., 'Albert of Trapani: A Saint of Yesterday for Today', *Carmel in the World*, Volume XLVI Number 2, 2007, pp. 94-112.

John of the Cross, *The Collected Works of St. John of the Cross*, translated by Kieran Kavanaugh, O.C.D., and Otilio Rodriguez, O.C.D., (Washington, D.C.: I.C.S. Publications, 1991).

John of the Cross, DVD of the movie directed by Leonardo Defilippis, (Saint Luke Productions and Ignatius Press, 1997).

James W. Kinn, *The Practice of Contemplation According to John of the Cross*, (Washington, D.C.: I.C.S. Publications, 2009).

Francis Kemsley, O.Carm., *The Church of Our Lady of Mount Carmel and the Shrine of St. Jude, Whitefriars, Faversham, Kent*, (Faversham: Saint Albert's Press, 2004).

Camilo Maccise, O.C.D, 'A Mirror of Contemplation: St. Joseph in the Carmelite Tradition', *Mount Carmel* magazine, Volume 54, Number 2, April-June 2006.

Armando Maggi, *Maria Maddalena de'Pazzi: Selected Revelations*, Classics of Western Spirituality, (New Jersey: Paulist Press, 2000).

Iain Matthew, O.C.D., *The Impact of God: Soundings from St. John of the Cross*, (London: Hodder and Stoughton, 1995). This is one of the most influential English publications about John of the Cross in recent years.

James McCaffrey, O.C.D., 'Rediscovering Saint Joseph: A Gospel Portrait', in *The Carmelite Charism: Exploring the Biblical Roots*, (Dublin: Veritas, 2004).

Wilfrid McGreal, O.Carm., *Friar Beyond the Pale: A biography of Carmelite friar Fr. Elias Lynch (1897-1967)*, (Faversham: Saint Albert's Press, 2007). This is a biography of the friar who established the National Shrine of St. Jude at Faversham, England.

National Shrine of St. Jude in Britain: www.stjudeshrine.org.uk

Virginia Nixon, *Mary's Mother: Saint Anne in Late Medieval Europe*, (Penn State University Press, 2004). This academic book is available in most university libraries.

Agnes Orpen, O.C.D., 'Introducing St. Teresa: A Great Teacher of Prayer and Love', *Mount Carmel: A Review of the Spiritual Life*, Volume 57 Number 1, January-March 2009, pp. 16-21.

Pius Sammut, O.C.D., *God is a Feast: A New Look at Saint John of the Cross*, (Luton: New Life Publishing, 1992).

Peter Slattery, O.Carm., 'St. Teresa of Avila, her Life and Spirit', and 'St. John of the Cross, the Poet', in *The Springs of Carmel: An Introduction to Carmelite Spirituality*, (New York: Alba House, 1991).

Teresa of Avila, *The Collected Works of St. Teresa of Avila*, 3 volumes, translated by Kieran Kavanaugh, O.C.D., & Otilio Rodriguez, O.C.D., (Washington, D.C.: I.C.S. Publications, 1976-85). This is the standard edition of Teresa's writings and should be in every Carmelite library. I.C.S. Publications have also produced editions of Teresa's letters, as well as stand-alone printings and study-editions of her major works.

Redemptus M. Valabek, O.Carm., *Profiles in Holiness*, 3 volumes (Rome: Edizioni Carmelitane, 1996-2002).

Rowan Williams, *Teresa of Avila*, (London: Continuum, 1991). This book by the Archbishop of Canterbury is one of the most highly regarded modern expositions of Teresa's life and teachings.

As well as these resources, the lives and teachings of Carmel's saints are included in distance-learning Carmelite Studies programmes offered by Carmelite Institutes and study centres around the world, including the Carmelite Institute of Britain & Ireland (www.cibi.ie).

Notes and reflections on Chapter 18

Notes and reflections on Chapter 18

Holy Men and Women of Carmel: Part 2 – Later Saints

Summary: In the second half of its 800-year history the Carmelite Order has continued to nurture women and men of outstanding holiness, who remember us before the face of the living God and from whom we can take inspiration as we seek God's face. In this chapter we shall learn something of their lives and teachings, which point us to Christ.

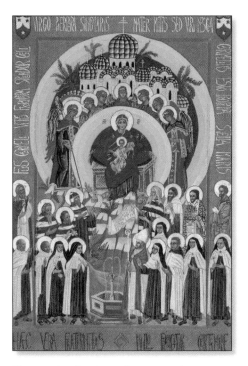

This icon by the Carmelite nuns in Ravenna shows that the saints of Carmel – like all true saints – are centred entirely on Christ, and point us to him.

Get prepared: As with the previous chapter, perhaps you would find it helpful to keep at hand any resources you might have on the saints of Carmel, as well as a Bible and modern documentation of the Carmelite Family for reference. Just as important though are your own notes, so have a pen and paper to hand, or use the blank page at the end of the chapter to record your thoughts, feelings, questions and ideas. Again, if you are going to discuss this material with a community, perhaps you might come to the meeting with a picture of a favourite Carmelite saint, or an extract from their writings that inspires you. We are nearing the end of our journey of initial formation in the Carmelite tradition, and whilst study and reflection are important, it is more important that we let God lead us through life's pilgrimage, as this prayer attributed to St. Edith Stein acknowledges:

> *Lord, let me walk blindly on the path you have traced out for me.*
> *I do not seek to understand your way:*
> *I am your child.*
> *Wisdom's font and Father,*
> *You are my Father too.*
> *Your road may lead through darkness,*
> *but it will lead to you.*

Carmel: It's all about people and God

The Carmelite story is all about God, about people, and the relationship between God and God's people. All human beings are called to be saints, that is, people who love the Lord and one another in the Kingdom of God, both here on earth and later in heaven. Jesus himself revealed how we could inhabit the Kingdom: 'I am the way, and the truth and the life … no one can come to the Father except through me' (*John* 14:6). So the way to sainthood is to follow Christ closely. Saints shouldn't distract us from Jesus: rather they lead towards him, giving us an example to follow.

In the Carmelite tradition saints are people who have taken to heart the words of the first Psalm, which is echoed in our *Rule of Saint Albert*:

> Happy are those who do not follow the advice of the wicked,
> or take the path that sinners tread, or sit in the seat of scoffers;
> but their delight is in the law of the Lord,
> and on his law they meditate day and night.
>
> *Psalm* 1:1-2

The legacy of reform

In the previous chapter we looked at Carmelite saints until around 1600, culminating in a range of reforming saints. We begin this chapter on Carmelite saints up to the present day by looking at holy people who emerged from another reform movement, the Reform of Touraine, which has had a long-lasting effect on the Carmelite Family. This seventeenth-century reform took place in Rennes, France, in the Carmelite Province of Touraine, principally under the leadership of two friars called Jean Behourt and Philippe Thibault (1572-1638). These men sought to live a fuller observance of religious life, and

A bronze sculpture of John of Saint-Samson at the Carmelite priory in Straubing, Germany.

show that the Carmelite and Discalced Carmelite Orders (which had split by this time) did not have opposing values but rather shared a desire for living as fully for God as possible.

The spirit of the Touraine Reform was expressed in the writings of a great musical mystic, Venerable John of Saint-Samson (1571-1636). John was blind from the age of three, but despite many difficulties in early life made his way to Paris where he encountered the Carmelites. In the various communities he joined the friars were impressed with his wisdom. Settling finally in Rennes where he was novice master, John had a particular compassion for the sick. John has been called the 'John of the Cross of the Ancient Observance' because of his insights about prayer, and his appeal for the brothers to live a simple lifestyle. Both Johns believed that the Carmelite way of life is not about living in ecstasies but seeking union with the God who is a living flame within us. To prepare ourselves for union with God John of Saint-Samson advised Carmelites to develop a type of prayer known as *aspiration* which basically means that in our desire for God we must open ourselves to 'breathe' God.

Did you know? The Revolution of 1789 forced the closure of 153 houses of the Carmelite Order in France. In the 1980s the Ancient Observance of the Order decided to re-establish a French presence. The main friary, in Nantes, has a shrine to John of Saint-Samson.

Contemporary with John of Saint-Samson was a French Discalced Carmelite friar called Denis of the Nativity (Pierre Berthelot, b. 1600). He was a cartographer and naval commander before joining the Discalced Carmelites in Goa in 1635. It was also at Goa that a Portuguese lay brother, Thomas Rodriguez de Cunha (b. 1598) made his profession as a Discalced friar in 1615, taking the name Redemptus of the Cross. Denis and Redemptus were sent as missionaries to the island of Sumatra, where they were martyred in 1638. Living *in allegiance to Jesus Christ* as expected by the Carmelite *Rule*, they took seriously his command 'Go, make disciples of all the nations' (*Matthew* 28:19).

Blessed Denis of the Nativity depicted in a window in the church of Genneville in Calvados.

They are reminders to us that Carmelites are called to be missionaries; to spread the Good News of God's love to all peoples in whatever circumstances we find ourselves. Like them we are called to witness to God by our lives and possibly even by our deaths.

Among the holy men and women of Carmel in the sixteenth century we can also mention Francis of the Cross, O.Carm. (1585-1647). Francis was a lay brother and he reminds us that holiness is not dependent upon academic ability. He found reading and writing a real effort, but had a profound relationship with God. He made a three-year long pilgrimage from his native Spain to Jerusalem and back, carrying a wooden cross on his shoulders.

Reformers and martyrs

At the time of the reforms in the Carmelite Order, the Discalced Reform continued in Spain and beyond. Notable holy Carmelites from this period include Blessed Mary of Jesus (María López Rivas, 1560-1640), a Discalced nun known as a great contemplative who often drew inspiration from the liturgy. Like Teresa, who admired her, Blessed Mary regarded prayer as conversation with a friend, a growing relationship with Christ who drew her to himself to the point where his interests became hers and she could exclaim with Saint Paul that 'it is no longer I that live, but Christ lives in me' (*Galatians* 2:20).

Both the ancient and Teresian branches of the Carmelite Family produced saintly nuns at this period, including Venerable Serafina of God (1621-99), Chiara Maria della Passione (1610-75), and the stigmatic and visionary Venerable Rosemary Serio (1647-1726). In the previous chapter we learned about Blessed Barbe Acarie who helped establish the Discalced nuns in France. She also introduced Carmelite spirituality to her daughter, who became a nun taking the name Marguerite of the Blessed Sacrament (1590-1660). Another nun of the same religious name, born Marguerite Parigot (1619-48) is regarded as 'Venerable'. She entered the Carmel of Beaune in France at the age of just twelve, so perhaps it is not surprising that she identified closely with the Infant Christ and began a confraternity known as 'the family of the Child Jesus'.

From this time Carmel also remembers with gratitude holy women such as Venerable Anne of Jesus and her followers who founded monasteries of nuns on the Continent. These attracted a number of vocations from Britain because Catholics in England, Wales and Scotland were still at that time forbidden to practice the faith in their homeland.

The Carmelite Family in Britain still honours the remarkable witness given by saintly Carmelite friars who gave their lives for the Catholic faith. Following the Reformation in England the last surviving Whitefriar, George Rayner, was imprisoned and died for the faith in York Castle in the early 1600s. The Servant of God George Halley (1622-43), born into a noble family in Herefordshire, became a Discalced Carmelite friar in Dublin taking the name Angelus of Saint-Joseph. Like fellow friars Thomas Aquinas of Saint-Teresa and Peter of the Mother-of-God, Angelus was put to death in Ireland for being a Roman Catholic religious. We do not remember these martyrs in a sectarian way;

Venerable Jerome Terzo helped establish the Shrine of Mary, Stairway of Heaven.

rather in today's climate of violence in the name of religion they are witnesses to the need for toleration, dialogue, and freedom of conscience.

Stop and think: What is the best way to honour the memory of martyrs?

The martyrs' took to heart the words of Saint John that we cannot love God whom we cannot see if we do not love our neighbour whom we do see (*1 John* 4:20). This teaching also inspired Venerable Girolamo (Jerome) Terzo (1683-1758), a Carmelite lay brother in the Sicilian Province. As a young man Jerome was a shoemaker, before spending most of his life as a hermit. He only became a friar late in life and never felt called to priesthood. Nevertheless he was active in pastoral outreach. He founded a place of pilgrimage, the Sanctuary of Mary – Stairway of Heaven. He was a great catechist and preacher, and did missionary work among the Muslims of Malta.

A witness to the presence of God

A much-loved Carmelite of the seventeenth century, Brother Lawrence of the Resurrection, (Nicolas Herman, d. 1691) is not a saint in the formal sense, but his spiritual insights mean that he is regarded with special affection by the Carmelite Family. Lawrence was a brother in the Discalced friary in Paris where among his everyday tasks as a cook and cobbler he enjoyed a continual sense of God's presence and love. Lawrence maintained a regular correspondence and received many people seeking his advice, realising that since Jesus became human and 'dwelt among us' (*John* 1:14) he too had to be where the people are, with and for those needing help. After Lawrence's death his letters and spiritual maxims were published, and the resulting book *The Practice of the Presence of God* is an international bestseller among both Catholics and Protestants (it was highly recommended by the Methodist John Wesley).

Carmel's Marian mystics

Two contemporaries of Lawrence have become revered for their teachings on the life of Mary, Our Lady, and how we can imitate it. The friar Venerable Michael of Saint-Augustine (1621-84) and the tertiary Venerable Mary of Saint-Teresa Petijt (Maria Petyt 1623-77) were Carmelites from the Lowlands who saw that Mary lived the beatitude 'blessed are the pure in heart'. They perceived that Carmelites must become 'other Marys', imitating her purity of heart (*puritas cordis*). For members of Our Lady's Order it is not enough for Mary to be something external; instead our lives should be just like hers and lived with her.

Venerable Michael of Saint-Augustine, O.Carm., and Venerable Maria Petyt, T.O.C.

Stop and reflect: In what ways do you consider yourself to be 'another Mary'?

Servants of the Poor

Someone whose devotion to Our Lady inspired him to join the Carmelites was Blessed Angelo Paoli (1642-1720). Angelo was born into a modest farming family in Tuscany and as a youth he sought out the solitude of the local hills for prayer. As a friar he became bursar of the San Martino ai Monti community in Rome and this brought him into regular contact with the poor and hungry who came to the friary door. Eventually Angelo – nicknamed 'the father of the poor' – was feeding 300 people daily, a ministry which his community continues to this day.

Paintings of Blessed Angelo Paoli in Saint Albert's International Centre (CISA) in Rome.

Angelo's simple cell has been preserved at San Martino ai Monti friary.

Like a true saint Angelo wasn't selfish or possessive about his apostolate; he involved as many people as he could, inspiring scores of the most illustrious people in Rome to spend time getting to know the poor of the city. Angelo also organized the first hospital for convalescents in Rome. His pastoral work flowed from his deep life of prayer, and shows how contemplation in the Carmelite understanding is a blending of prayer, active service of others, and the building up of community. Angelo – who was beatified in April 2010 – is still much loved by the people of the Eternal City who pray at his tomb in San Martino.

Stop and think: Blessed Angelo not only dispensed charity, but also arranged for rich and poor to meet each other. Why do you think this was significant to his ministry?

A contemporary particularly known for his love of the poor was Venerable Giovanni Domenico Lucchesi (1652-1714). He was a friar of the reform movement known as the Congregation of Mantua, and sought out by many as a sound spiritual guide.

A fellow Italian, Venerable Maria Angela Virgili (1662-1734), was a member of the Carmelite Third Order Secular. Raised by poor but prayerful parents, after their death she dedicated herself to God as a lay Carmelite, and committed to loving those around her. In particular she cared for both the physical and spiritual needs of the sick. She was not afraid, like Christ, to reach out to those despised by much of society, particularly prostitutes. Her cause for beatification is being examined by Vatican theologians at the Congregation for the Causes of Saints.

Venerable Maria Angela Virgili, T.O.C.

Carmelite saints in Italy

The Servant of God Maria Maddalena Mazzoni (1683-1749) is another Italian whose introduction to Carmel was through the Third Order. Born in Bologna and baptized

Caterina, she wanted to become a religious but out of obedience to her parents she was married at the age of nineteen. After twelve years of married life her husband died (as had three of their six children). Her grief left Caterina disoriented and on the verge of death herself. She recovered, and under the guidance of a Carmelite priest she made profession in the Third Order in 1721, changing her name to Maria Maddalena (after Saint Mary Magdalene de'Pazzi). As a tertiary Maria Maddalena wanted to develop a deep interior life inspired by the Carmelite tradition while still living with her family. She gave herself more and more to works of mercy, especially teaching Christian doctrine to young and old, and visiting prisoners. A few years after joining Lay Carmel Maria Maddalena, together with 5 or 6 companions, started a community called the 'Small Carmel' or 'Tiny Carmel of Mary'. The community's aim was to educate needy young girls, and it grew into a religious congregation known today as the *Carmelite Sisters of the Graces*. For her being a Carmelite meant being available to God (practicing *vacare Deo*) and being on call to help those around her. She was a mother, a Carmelite, and a saintly woman who discerned an extraordinary vocation in an ordinary life.

Another Italian Carmelite who found God in the everyday was Blessed Mary of the Angels (1661-1717), a Discalced nun in Turin who was ardent in her love of God despite continual spiritual trials. True to the Carmelite spirit she was devoted to Saint Joseph, in whose honour Sr. Mary helped to found a convent.

Italy seems to have provided fertile soil for holy Carmelite women in the eighteenth century. In Florence Anna Maria Redi (Saint Teresa Margaret Redi, 1747-70) entered the Discalced Carmel and took the name Sr. Teresa Margaret of the Sacred Heart. As well as having great devotion to Christ's Sacred Heart she had a profound sense of the meaning of Eucharist which went beyond the liturgical celebration of Mass. One of her responsibilities in the monastery was the care of the sick sisters; when some of her community expressed concern that Teresa Margaret's infirmary duties prevented her from having time to 'prepare' for Holy Communion she replied 'Can there be any better preparation than the performance of duties given one by obedience, particularly when it is also serving the sick?' Before her death at the age of just twenty-three, Teresa Margaret was given a special contemplative experience concerning the words of Saint John that 'God is love'.

Such Carmelites remind us that it's important to speak about the contemplative life without romanticising or over-spiritualising it; they were open to God's presence and transforming action in their lives as experienced through community, through service, and through prayer.

Carmelite saints in France

France was also fruitful in producing Carmelite saints in the eighteenth century, though the circumstances were different from Italy. In the 1700s new ideas and Enlightenment philosophies began to spread. The extreme contrast between the lives of the rich and the poor bred resentment which turned into the violence of the French Revolution. The revolutionaries targeted those they believed had been repressing the people, namely the aristocracy and the Church. There was certainly some truth in this accusation, but it was equally the case that some Christians gave up positions of wealth and power in solidarity with the poor. For example, Venerable Mother Teresa of Saint-Augustine (1737-87), daughter of King Louis XV, gave up royal privileges in favour of entering one of the poorest Carmels, Saint-Denis near Paris. She is not to be confused with another French Carmelite of the same religious name, Blessed Teresa of Saint-Augustine (Madeleine-Claudine Ledoin, b. 1752) superior of the Monastery of the Incarnation in Compiègne north of Paris. Together with her sisters and community servants she was arrested by citizens angry at the Church. The women – beginning with the novice and concluding with Mother Teresa – were put to death in Paris on 17ᵗʰ July 1794. It is ironic that the revolutionaries – who sought the wonderful values of 'liberty, equality, fraternity' – targeted a community that embodied those values. Convicted of 'crimes against the state', the Carmelite martyrs of Compiègne offered their lives as a sacrifice to God, hoping that their martyrdom would bring peace to the nation and the Church.

Did you know? The martyrdom of the Compiègne nuns inspired French composer Francis Poulenc to write a famous opera called *Dialogues des Carmélites* (*Dialogue of the Carmelites*).

The lives of Carmel's saints have inspired a number of artists, filmmakers and musicians, including Francis Poulenc in his opera 'Dialogue of the Carmelites'.

Another Carmelite witness to Christ during the French Revolution was Blessed Jacques Retouret, O.Carm. (1746-94). Like the majority of other clergy he refused to accept the civil law introduced by the revolutionaries which decreed that the hierarchy and pope were subject to decisions made by the state. After enduring terrible conditions on board a prison ship, Jacques died at the age of forty-eight. He was beatified in 1995 as part of a group of sixty-four martyrs which included the Discalced friars Jean-Baptiste Duverneuil (1737-94), Michel-Louis

The Carmelite martyrs of the French Revolution witnessed to Christ with their lives.

Brulard (1758-94) and Jacques Gagnot (1753-94). Lay Carmel also has its own martyr from the French Revolution, the Servant of God Anna Rosa Bernard. She and her friend Thérèse Thiac were found guilty of sheltering a Carmelite friar who had refused to accept the state's restrictions on the Church, Fr. Martinien Pannetier (who was a great supporter of Lay Carmel). Together the three of them were executed during the octave of Our Lady of Mount Carmel 1794.

Carmelites in Catalonia and Spain

Ill will towards the Catholic Church spread from Paris to other cities, including Barcelona where Saint Joachina de Vedruna de Mas (1783-1854) lived. She bore her husband nine children, but ten years after his death she was prompted by the Spirit to found the *Congregation of Carmelite Sisters of Charity*, establishing houses for the care of the sick and the education of children, especially the poor.

In the 1800s two other young women from Spain stand out in our family story: Venerable Liberata Ferrarons y Vivés (1803-42) and Blessed Josepha Naval Girbés (1820-93). Josepha was a member of the Discalced Carmelite Secular Order (O.C.D.S.). She dedicated herself to works of mercy in her parish community, opening a school in her own home. Before her beatification in 1988 her life was studied by a Theological Commission, and at the conclusion the General Promoter of the Faith declared: 'Josepha Naval Girbés is an exceptional mistress of secular holiness; a model of Christian life in her heroic simplicity … Without extraordinary gifts and without dazzling events in her life, the Servant of God was an exceptional woman in her genuine simplicity as a daughter of the people. She carried out her duties faithfully, in intense union with God, in the midst of the ordinary circumstances of her working day.' Likewise Liberata Ferrarons, a young worker in a textile factory and member of the Carmelite Third Order (T.O.C.) shows us the true meaning of 'heroic sanctity'; not performing superhuman feats, but rather loving and living Christ in the joys and boredoms of daily life. Like the Lord on Horeb, Liberata was *a still small voice* who brought others to know the presence of God in gentleness and quiet.

Venerable Liberata
Ferrarons y Vivés, T.O.C.

Stop and think: How would you define 'heroic sanctity'? Have you ever witnessed it?

Icons of Christ

Saints are essentially people who respond to the call of God that we hear about in sacred Scripture:

> We know that by turning everything to their good God co-operates with all those who love him, with all those that he has called according to his purpose. They are the ones he chose specially long ago and intended to become true images of his Son, so that his Son might be the eldest within a large family. (*Romans* 8:28-29)

Among the Carmelites of the nineteenth century who became 'true images of Jesus' one of the most gifted was the Servant of God Hermann Cohen (1821-71). Hermann was born into a Jewish family in Hamburg, Germany. He lived a very worldly life but as a composer produced beautiful music, and it was music that drew him to Christianity. One day he was asked to substitute as a choir director for a church music festival, and during Benediction he became aware of the presence of God: 'I felt something deep within me as if I had found myself. It was like the prodigal son facing himself.' After his conversion Hermann became a Discalced Carmelite friar, taking the name Augustin-Marie of the Blessed Sacrament. He was so devoted to the Eucharist that he began the *Nocturnal Adoration Society*. He continued to write music, and founded several convents before dying of smallpox.

New branches on the vine of Carmel

Thousands of miles away, in Kerala, India, Blessed Kuriakose Elias Chavara (1805-

Blessed Kuriakose Elias Chavara depicted in an icon created in 2008 by Sister Petra Clare for the Carmelite-served Shrine of St. Jude at Faversham, England.

71) was to have a massive influence on the future direction of the Carmelite Family. He was ordained priest in 1829, and two years later he co-founded the *Carmelites of Mary Immaculate* (the C.M.I. brothers), taking his religious name from the prophet Elijah (Elias). This religious congregation combined the spirituality of Carmel with the rites and heritage of the Syro-Malabar Church, one of the twenty or so 'Eastern' churches in communion with Rome, which had existed in India since the days of the apostle Thomas.

Blessed Elias became vicar general for the Syro-Malabar Church, defending its unity with Rome, and through the CMIs he made great strides in the spiritual renovation of the Church of Malabar. The CMI brothers dedicated themselves to the renewal of the Church by building seminaries, a publishing house, schools, and a house for the dying and destitute. In 1866 Elias co-founded, with the support of a Discalced friar, another Carmelite congregation, the Sisters of the Mother of Carmel. If holiness can be judged by the fruits a Christian produces (*Matthew* 7:20) then Elias is indeed a great saint. The congregation he founded has dedicated itself to serving the people of God, and at the start of the twenty-first century it numbered 7 bishops, 2100 priests, 55 brothers, 482 seminarians, and 208 novices. The CMIs are now spreading beyond India to undertake missions in Europe and America. Elias was beatified in 1986.

A Carmelite with an experience not unlike Blessed Elias was Mariam Baouardy, better known as Blessed Mary of Jesus Crucified or by her nicknames of 'The Little Arab' and 'Al Qiddisa' (the holy one). She was born near Nazareth in 1846 as a Catholic of the Greek Melchite Rite. After suffering a very difficult childhood, in 1867 she entered the Discalced Carmelites at Pau in France and in 1870 was sent to India where she was part of a group that founded the Carmel of Mangalore. In 1875 she returned to the Holy Land where she built a monastery in Bethlehem. Her life in Carmel was marked by various supernatural phenomena including levitations, knowledge of hearts, and the stigmata of her crucified Saviour whom she loved with great passion. Blending the traditions of East and West, in Carmel Mariam was also able to integrate the Old and New Testaments. In the convent she was known to dance in front of the altar, declaring 'David danced before the Ark, and I dance before the tabernacle'. She had an intense devotion to the Holy Spirit, praying: 'Holy Spirit, inspire me. Love of God consume me. Along the true road, lead me. Mary, my good mother, look down upon me. With Jesus, bless me. From all evil, all illusion, all danger, preserve me.' Blessed Mary died aged 33, the reputed age when Christ was crucified.

Blessed Francis Palau y Quer (1811-72) was a Discalced Carmelite friar who lived much of his life in exile from his native mainland Spain because of civil turmoil and opposition to the school he established. In the 1860s he founded the *Congregations of Carmelite Brothers and Carmelite Sisters*, and preached popular missions, spreading love of Our Lady wherever he went. He was beatified in 1980. Another Discalced

Blessed Mary of Jesus Crucified (Mariam Baouardy).

Thérèse aged 13.

friar renowned for holiness is Saint Raphael Kalinowski (1835-1907). He was a Polish Teresian Carmelite who contributed greatly to restoring his Order in Poland, and his life was distinguished by zeal for Church unity and his unflagging dedication as confessor and spiritual director. A third Discalced friar from this period, Antonio Augusto Intreccialagli (1852-1924) was also noted for his loving service to the Church as Archbishop of Monreale in Sicily. He was declared 'Venerable' by the Pope in 1991.

'The greatest saint of modern times'

Saint Thérèse of the Child Jesus and the Holy Face (1873-97) needs little introduction; the 'Little Flower' is probably the best-known and most-loved saint that Carmel has produced, with millions of devotees worldwide.

Thérèse Martin was born in the French town of Alençon in 1873 into a bourgeois family. Her parents both suffered from severe illness: her mother Zélie Guérin died of breast cancer whilst Thérèse was still an infant, and her father Louis Martin suffered from mental illness in his final years. Yet the Martin family was bound together by love and deep faith in God. All the surviving children entered religious life, and in 2008 Louis and Zélie were beatified by the Church.

Losing her mother at the age of four had a profoundly debilitating impact on the young Thérèse. She became withdrawn and self-centred, and by her own admission was very much the baby of the family. Following what she described as her 'conversion' one Christmas at the age of fourteen, Thérèse began to mature and nurture adult relationships, not only with her father and sisters but also with Jesus Christ. As Thérèse grew up she felt a strong vocation to enter the Carmelite monastery in

Blesseds Zélie Guérin and Louis Martin.

Lisieux, which she did at the age of 15 in 1888. Seven years later at the request of the Mother Prioress Sister Agnes (her blood sister Pauline), Thérèse began writing her autobiography, *Story of a Soul*, stating that she would use the opportunity to 'sing of the mercies of the Lord'. After Thérèse's death of tuberculosis in 1897 aged just twenty-four, this text was circulated to other Carmelite monasteries. The book was full of such spiritual wisdom put so simply yet profoundly that it became an instant success. Within a quarter-century of Thérèse's death the story of this young French girl who had spent all her adult life within monastic enclosure had spread across the globe. Hailed by Pope Pius X as 'the greatest saint of modern times', Thérèse was canonised in 1925.

Stop and think: What aspect of Thérèse's life or teaching is most significant for you?

It is sometimes possible for the real Thérèse to be lost behind the pious and sentimental images of her. We should not be deceived by her nickname 'The Little Flower' into thinking that Thérèse was somehow a shrinking violet. In her autobiography Thérèse describes periods of great darkness, doubt, and depression that have helped many people through similar experiences. In an age of religious conservatism Thérèse expressed radical ideas, such as her desire to be a priest, and her bold confidence in a loving and merciful God. She believed that the love and mercy of God was more powerful than any sin: 'I was absolutely confident in the mercy of Jesus.' Thérèse was so certain of God's love – not because of her greatness but because of God's – that she declared: 'Even if I had on my conscience all the sins that can be committed, I would go, my heart broken with repentance, to throw myself into the arms of Jesus … If I had committed all the crimes it

is possible to commit, I would still have the same confidence, I would feel that this multitude of offences would be like a drop of water thrown into a raging blaze.'

Thérèse's core insight is referred to as 'the Little Way of Spiritual Childhood', which she believed was a 'short cut' to God for ordinary people. There are two parts to this teaching. Firstly, Thérèse realised that it is possible to reach union with God, to be contemplative, to be a saint, through little acts of love and by remaining little in spirit. Inspired by Jesus' instruction that the Kingdom of God is open to those who become like little children, Thérèse realised that great and heroic deeds were beyond her she had only to remain small and humble, loving God and others through even the

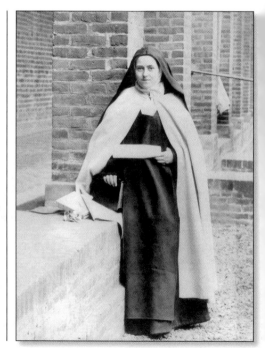

St. Thérèse in the cloister courtyard at Lisieux Carmel in 1896.

iniest acts of kindness. She understood that God does not judge our actions on their greatness, or even their success, but on their motivation by love. The second aspect of the 'Little Way' is the notion of 'Spiritual Childhood', that is, relating to God as a child relates to a loving parent with complete confidence and abandonment. Thérèse came to entrust herself more and more to the love of God, whom she came to appreciate by pondering Scripture 'is as tender as a mother'. Thérèse came to understand that by living with simplicity and openness, we can trust that God will carry us towards heaven like a parent picking up a child. The smaller the child, the easier it is for it to trust absolutely. Thérèse therefore did not seek to become a 'giant' saint but rather found opportunities in the ordinary activities of everyday to renounce selfish desires and express thanks to God. As she put it in a letter to another of her sisters, Céline: 'when I am *feeling* nothing, when I am incapable of praying, of practising virtue, then is the moment for seeking opportunities, *nothings*, which please Jesus more than mastery of the world or even martyrdom suffered with generosity. For example, a smile, a friendly word when I would want to say nothing, or put on a look of annoyance.' (*Letter* 143).

In a culture that emphasised the importance of heroic deeds, and humanity's sinfulness arousing God's anger, Thérèse's rediscovery of the Good News that God loves us and asks us to love in return was a breath of fresh air. Thérèse and her 'Little Way' have been credited with bringing holiness within the reach of ordinary people, and in some senses prefigured the teaching of the Second Vatican Council.

Thérèse had a deep hunger for the word of God in Scripture, and it was through reading St. Paul's letters that she came to understand that her vocation was to be love in the heart of the Church. Anticipating the revival of *Lectio Divina* by some decades, Thérèse wrote: 'In my helplessness, Holy Scripture comes to my aid. In the Bible I discover a very *pure* nourishment. But it is especially the *Gospels* which sustain me during my hours of prayer, for in them I find what is necessary for my poor little soul. I am constantly discovering in them new lights, hidden and mysterious meanings.'

Did you know? Thérèse is one of the patron saints of missionary activity. To help support Carmelite missions worldwide, the General Curia of the Order runs a charity called *The Society of the Little Flower* in honour of Thérèse.

Members of the Carmelite Family were among the hundreds of thousands of pilgrims who welcomed the relics of Saint Thérèse to England and Wales in the autumn of 2009.

Thérèse's teachings have been judged so universally important for all Christians that in 1997 she was declared a Doctor of the Church. Before her death Thérèse promised that she would spend her heaven 'doing good on earth', asking God to bestow graces like a shower of roses. Many people testify to the powerful inspiration and intercession of Thérèse. Since the 1990s more people have come to know Thérèse and her message of hope through the visits around the world of her relics. In Thérèse the prophesy of Daniel has come true: 'Those who are wise shall shine like the brightness of the sky, and those who lead many to righteousness like the stars for ever and ever' (*Daniel* 12:3).

Monastic and apostolic Carmelite women

A contemporary and compatriot of Thérèse was Élisabeth Catez (1880-1906) known in Carmel as Sister Elizabeth of the Trinity. Like Thérèse, Elizabeth lost a parent (her father) when she was young, and could be a wilful child. As she grew she developed a deep understanding of the world and its creator, in particular a profound love of the Trinity (her best known text is the prayer *Holy Trinity whom I adore*). Most of her life was spent as a lay woman; she was gregarious and a talented musician. Declining several offers of marriage, Elizabeth entered the Discalced Carmelite monastery in Dijon in 1901. Her life in Carmel was a mixture of high and low points, in which she always detected God's presence: 'I find Him everywhere, while doing the washing as well as

Blessed Elizabeth of the Trinity.

while praying.' Particularly significant for Elizabeth was her name, which means 'house of God'; Elizabeth came to realise that God dwelt within her, and she let God have possession of her heart. Elizabeth recorded her experiences in various writings, in which she sometimes gave advice to friends seeking to deepen their prayer life, drawing strongly on the Carmelite tradition of silence and stillness in God's presence: 'Always love prayer; but when I say prayer I do not mean reciting a vast quantity of vocal prayers every day. I mean the elevation of the soul to God through all things, which places us in a kind of continual communion with the Holy Trinity so that everything we do is done under God's watchful gaze' (*Letter* 191). Suffering from Addison's disease, Elizabeth felt – like Thérèse – that God was calling her to heaven to draw souls to him, and she died in 1906 aged 26. She was beatified in 1984.

Stop and think: Most of Carmel's saints who died young lived as lay people for longer than they did as religious. How important was their life outside the monastery for their formation in holiness?

Like Elizabeth and Thérèse, Blessed Elisha of Saint-Clement (Theodora Fracasso, 1901-27) was a Discalced Carmelite nun who died very young, but having made a great impression on her sisters in the Italian town of Bari. Elsewhere in Italy one of Elisha's sisters in the Teresian Carmel was Blessed Mother Maria Candida of the Eucharist (Maria Barba, 1884-1949). She appreciated the enormous love that existed between Jesus and his mother, writing: 'I would like to be like Mary, to be Mary for Jesus, to take the place of his Mamma. I have Mary also present in my communions. I want to receive Jesus from her hands. She must help me to become only one thing with him … Hail, O Body born of Mary! Hail Mary, dawn of the Eucharist!' Maria Candida was beatified in 2004.

Some might question the value of these women living an enclosed life. Carmelite monasteries of nuns can be compared to the rainforests. It wasn't until the rainforests were cleared for 'useful' purposes that we came to realise how vital they are for maintaining a healthy planet climate. The rainforests make a vital contribution not by doing anything visible but simply by being there. Carmelite nuns are like lungs in the Church. They breathe in the needs, the loneliness, the poverty, the empty wealth, the hopes and fears of the people of the world, and breathe out love and faith. In Carmel, the 'vineyard of the Lord', they fertilise the Church with their constant praise of God.

The vocation to enclosed life in a Carmelite monastery is only for those truly called to it, and some saints in our family tried it before discerning that God was calling them elsewhere. One such was Blessed Maria Teresa Scrilli (1825-89) who was beatified in 2006 in her native Italian diocese of Fiesole. Maria Teresa entered the monastery of Saint Mary Magdalene de'Pazzi in Florence in 1846, but she wrote in her *Autobiography* that whilst she loved the cloister she felt called by God to bring people outside its walls to know the love of God. This became clearer when back in her home village friends began entrusting their children to her. Maria Teresa eventually went on to found *The Institute of Our Lady of Mount Carmel*, which had as its particular apostolate the education of youth, especially the poorest. Maria Teresa believed that the goal of education is growth in holiness, and for this reason she required her sisters to add a fourth vow to the three customary ones of poverty, chastity and obedience, namely to 'give oneself to the service of one's neighbour by means of Christian and civil moral instruction'. Maria Teresa's Institute was born in a period of political insurrection in the unification of Italy and for this reason her venture was crushed almost as soon as it had begun. This, combined with the untimely deaths of several sisters, meant that when Mother Maria herself died in 1889 the community numbered only two sisters, one novice and one postulant. Today the Institute numbers about 250 sisters worldwide, and this success is a reminder that we do not always see the fruits of good works in our own lifetimes, but like the parable of the mustard seed (*Luke* 13:19) great things can come from small beginnings.

Solidarity with the poor

Blessed Maria Teresa's Institute is part of the Carmelite Third Order Regular, that is, the branch of the Carmelite Family consisting of religious sisters in active apostolates. The first of Carmel's congregations of active sisters was founded by Mary Magdalene Mazzoni Sangiorgi (1683-1749) who was

Blessed Maria Teresa Scrilli.

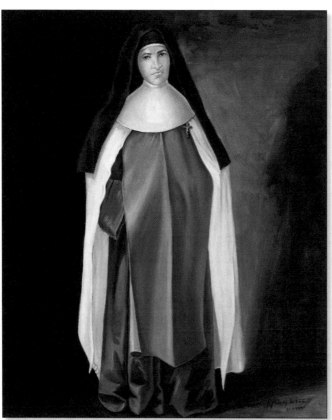

an outstanding example of holiness. Thanks to her pioneering form of Carmelite life other institutes quickly developed. For example, the *Carmelite Sisters of Mother Candelaria* are named after their founder, Blessed Candelaria of Saint-Joseph (Susanna Paz Castillo Ramírez, 1863-1940). Her beatification in 2008 brought the South American nation of Venezuela its first native saint, who was a servant to the poorest of the poor.

Blessed Candelaria of Saint-Joseph.

Servant of God Mother Angeline
Teresa McCrory, O.Carm.

The nineteenth century explosion of religious institutes which affiliated to the Carmelite Order has given us other inspiring examples, such as Mother Elisea Maria Oliver Molina (1869-1931), founder of the *Carmelite Sisters of Orihuela*, Arcángela Badosa (1878-1918) of the same institute, and Mother Angeline Teresa (born Bridget McCrory, 1893-1984), founder of the *Carmelite Sisters for the Aged and Infirm*. Bridget was born in Northern Ireland and moved to Scotland aged eight. In 1912 she joined the *Little Sisters of the Poor*, a French community in which she learned reverence and respect for the aging and dying, and in 1915 they sent her to work in New York. There her encounters with the elderly inspired her to look for new ways to care for the aged in a manner that was more respectful of their independence and lifestyle. This led her and her community to break from the Little Sisters and look instead to the Carmelite Order for affiliation. At the start of the twenty-first century the *Carmelite Sisters for the Aged and Infirm* were caring for some five thousand people in residential homes. Their mission statement, formulated by Mother Angeline states: 'Our apostolate is not only to staff and operate up-to-date homes for the aged, but as religious it is to bring Christ to every person under our care. Bringing Christ means giving them His compassion, His interest, His loving care, His warmth morning, noon and night. It means inspiring the lay people who work with us to give the same type of loving care.' Mother Angeline's cause for beatification is being considered by the Vatican.

The United States of America became home to another institute in the 1920s, the *Carmelite Sisters of the Most Sacred Heart of Los Angeles*. Their founder, Mother Maria Luisa Josefa of the Most Blessed Sacrament (1866-1937) was declared Venerable by the Holy Father in the year 2000. As a young woman Luisa had married and with her husband, a doctor, had constructed a hospital for the poor. When she was widowed she entered the Carmel of Guadalajara in Mexico, and split her time between the cloister and working in the hospital. Through this ministry many staff and patients were drawn to Carmelite life. In 1927 when Mexican revolutionaries put a bounty on the heads of religious, she fled to Los Angeles where her institute flourished despite a massive lack of resources. Like the hermits who had fled Mount Carmel, Mother Maria Luisa found that God bestowed great blessings during her exile.

One of the wonderful things about the Carmelite Family is that we are very embracing in who we count amongst 'our own', and many people draw inspiration from our spirituality. It is therefore appropriate to give mention to Saint Henry de Osso y Cervello (1840-96). A Spanish priest, he was an apostle to young people. He was fascinated by Saint Teresa of Jesus (of Avila), and inspired by her teaching he founded the *Company of Saint Teresa* (Teresian Missionary Sisters), dedicated to educating women in the school of the Gospel. Through printing and preaching he spread the Good News and the insights of Teresa. Another person inspired by Saint Teresa was Blessed Teresa Mary Manetti of the Cross (b. 1846). She founded the *Congregation of Carmelite Sisters of Saint Teresa* in Florence. There and in the Holy Land her sisters reached out with maternal care to children and to the poor. She died in 1910 and was beatified in 1986. She learnt to live without continual diversion and gratification, finding instead contentment with a simple lifestyle and steady rhythm that enabled her to explore her own inner depths where God sought to make a home.

Such a lifestyle was also lived by Saint Juanita Fernandez Solar, known in religion as Teresa of Jesus (1900-20). She was born in Santiago, Chile, and entered the Discalced Carmelite monastery in Los Andes. Like several other nuns of the period Saint Teresa 'of the Andes' seems to have grown greatly in wisdom and holiness before a premature death (this was a time when many died young, especially amongst the poor, whose lot the sisters shared). Juanita understood the fear that prevents some people from believing that God will fill their emptiness with meaning and satisfy the human yearning to be loved. She wrote:

> Are you perhaps afraid that the abyss of the greatness of God and that of your nothingness cannot be united? There is love in him. His passionate love made him take flesh in order that by seeing a Man-God, we would not be afraid to draw near him. This passionate love made him become bread in order to assimilate our nothingness and make it disappear into his infinite being. This passionate love made him give his life by dying on the cross. Are you perhaps afraid to draw near him? Look at him surrounded by little children … Look at him at the tomb of Lazarus. And listen to what he says of the Magdalene … What do you discover in these flashes from the Gospel except a heart that is good, gentle, tender, compassionate; in other words, the heart of a God?

Juanita was canonised in 1993, the first Chilean to be so honoured.

Like Juanita, Venerable Maria Teresa (Teresita) González-Quevedo (1930-50) died at just twenty years old. In that short time Teresita lived an intense life. She went to Our Lady of Mount Carmel Academy and on a school retreat at the age of eleven she wrote a resolution in her notebook: 'I have decided to become a saint'. Teresita was a popular, pretty girl with a flair for tennis and driving her father's car too fast, but she decided to dedicate her vivacity to God. In 1947 she was admitted to the *Carmelites of Charity* but her novitiate was cut short by the diagnosis of tubercular meningitis. Shortly before her death, in the Holy Year of 1950, she made her final profession. Her sisters and friends perceived in Teresita someone who truly wished to live *in allegiance to Jesus Christ*. Teresita grew up during the terrible religious persecution of the Spanish Civil War, in which three of her uncles were killed.

Martyrs of the Spanish Civil War

More martyrs gave their lives for Christ in the twentieth century than any other. A large number of Christians were killed during the Spanish Civil War (1936-39); as during the French Revolution, some saw the Church as part of a conservative establishment and deliberately targeted priests, religious and laity. Among the first to be formally recognised by the Church were three Discalced Carmelite nuns known as the Martyrs of Guadalajara (Blesseds Maria Pilar, Teresa, and Maria Angeles), killed in 1936 having offered their lives for Christ's body the Church. They were beatified in 1987. Ten years later Pope John Paul II approved the decree establishing the martyrdom of another Spanish nun, Blessed Maria Sagrario of Saint-Aloysius Gonzaga (born Elvira Moragas Cantarero in 1881). A

A statue of St. Teresa de los Andes outside her Sanctuary in Chile.

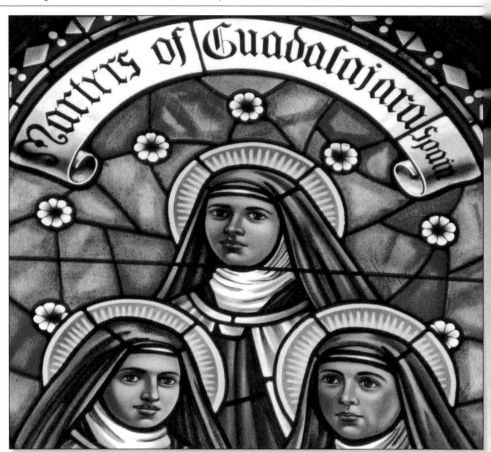

The Blessed Martyrs of Guadalajara, Spain.

talented student, she was one of the first women in Spain to obtain a degree in pharmacy. However she knew her vocation was to put her skills to use in a religious community, and in 1915 she entered the Teresian Carmel of St. Anne and St. Joseph in Madrid where she eventually became prioress. As leader of her community she was noted for her service of the sisters, and she ensured their safety when the convent was attacked by a violent crowd shortly after the outbreak of the civil war. She was arrested and shot. Her fate was shared by yet another Discalced nun, Blessed Maria Mercedes Prat, who was shot in 1936 because she was a religious. A nun from the O.Carm. branch of the Carmelite Family, Maria Badia (1903-36) was likewise killed.

In October 2007, in the largest ever ceremony of beatification, Pope Benedict XVI declared blessed 498 Christians killed during the religious persecutions. Among these were Carmelites of the Ancient Observance from the Province of Cataluña (Catalonia), including Fr. Ángel María Prat Hostench, O.Carm. (1896-1936) who was beatified along with 15 companion friars (including students of the Order) and a nun. Another group who witnessed to Christ were the martyrs of Segorbe diocese where the bishop,

Miguel Serra y Sucarrats, and 213 companions – including 50 Carmelite and Discalced Carmelite friars, 3 nuns, and a lay Carmelite – were killed. Also vibrant in Carmelite memory are the deaths of Fr. Carmelo Moyano Linares, O.Carm., Provincial of Andalusia (now Baetica) and his nine companions, known as the martyrs of Córdoba or of Baetica, and Alberto María Marco Alemán, O.Carm., superior of the main Carmelite house in Madrid who died with eight companions known as the martyrs of Castile.

Stop and think: Many people get caught up in the crossfire of war. What is distinctive about Carmelites that they are considered martyrs and not merely victims of circumstance?

Martyrs of World War II

The atrocities – committed by both sides – of the Spanish Civil War, were reflected in some of the dreadful violence of the Second World War which followed shortly afterwards (1939-45). But at such times, Carmelites have spoken out with a prophetic voice in defence of love. In the mid-twentieth century two great Carmelites, the nun Edith Stein (Teresa Benedicta of the Cross) and the friar Titus Brandsma, gave everything to follow

Christ by standing up to the appalling injustice of National Socialism. The Nazis sought to wipe out whole sections of society that they deemed not fully human or damaging to society, including Jews, gypsies, homosexuals, and the mentally or physically disabled. Those Christians and people of good will who spoke out against such evil were likewise incarcerated. On 20th July 1942 the Dutch Bishops' Conference had a pastoral letter read in all the churches of Holland condemning Nazi racism. In a retaliatory response the Nazis arrested all Jews who had embraced Christianity, who had previously been spared. Among these was Edith Stein (1891-1942). Edith was born a Jew in Germany, and even after her conversion to Christianity and her becoming a Discalced Carmelite nun Edith retained a profound sense of her Jewish inheritance. As a young woman her constant search for truth led her to study philosophy. However, she declared that she found a greater truth in reading the autobiography of Saint Teresa of Jesus, and decided to enter the Carmel in Cologne, Germany.

Titus Brandsma and Edith Stein depicted in stained glass at the National Shrine of St. Thérèse at Darien, Illinois, U.S.A.

Transferred for her safety with her blood sister Anna to the Carmel in Echt, Holland Edith refused to abandon Anna or renounce her Jewish identity. Together they were arrested and transported to the concentration camp at Auschwitz where they were gassed on 9th August. Since her canonisation in 1998, Edith has been proclaimed one of the six patron saints of Europe.

Another martyr of World War II is Blessed Titus Brandsma, O.Carm. (1881-1942). Titus was a Carmelite friar from the Netherlands. A professor of theology at Nijmegen University, he was an expert in Carmelite spirituality. He was also a journalist, and spiritual advisor to the Catholic press in Holland. In 1942 he was arrested by the Nazis for stating that no Catholic publication could justify printing fascist propaganda because it fundamentally contradicted the values of the Kingdom of God. For this he was imprisoned in concentration camps where he brought humanity to people degraded by the Nazi regime, including his captors. Titus was killed by lethal injection at Dachau on 26th July 1942. Like all true Carmelites Titus looked to Mary, Our Lady, as the perfect example of someone who followed Jesus, who could help us in times of suffering. Titus wrote: 'Mary, who kept all God's words in her heart, in the fullness of grace granted her, understood the great value of suffering. While the apostles fled, she went out to meet the Saviour on the way to Calvary and stood beneath the cross, in order to share his grief and shame to the end. And she carried him to the grave, firmly trusting that he would rise.' (Introduction to *Het lijden vergoddelijkt*). Titus was beatified as a martyr in 1985, and his canonisation is eagerly anticipated by Carmelites and other Christians around the world.

Blessed Titus Brandsma.

Did you know? Titus Brandsma preferred public transport to driving. It is therefore appropriate that in 2006 a Dutch train was named in his honour. Several public buildings, churches, study institutes, as well as an award for journalistic integrity also bear his name.

In Dachau Titus was joined by other Carmelites, including Blessed Hilary Januszewski (1907-45). Again like Titus, this friar was a scholar, having been professor at the institute of the Polish Province in Krakow, where he was also prior. On 18th September 1940 the Gestapo arrested four friars from the Krakow community; Father Hilary decided to present himself in exchange for an older and sick friar. The 2003 *Rule for the Third Order of Carmel* (§13) says that holiness lies in fulfilling Jesus' double command to love God and to love our neighbour. That's what Hilary did in Dachau by joining a group of priests who helped the sick, but his apostolate was cut short by his death from Typhus. He was beatified by fellow countryman John Paul II in 1999, alongside many other martyrs including the Discalced friar Blessed Alphonsus Mary Mazurek (1891-1944).

Did you know? The prophetic witness of the Polish martyrs is continued today in the work of the *Volunteers of the Prophet Elijah*. Since 2002 a team of 100 young people associated with the Carmelites in Krakow has been visiting needy people in hospitals and orphanages.

Servant of God Jacques de Jesus Bunel, O.C.D. (1900-45) was another friar who suffered at the hands of fascism. He was headmaster of the *Petite College* in Avon, France. His teaching style was revolutionary for its time, and he was much loved by his pupils. During the war Père Jacques harboured Jewish boys in his Catholic school to protect them from Nazi persecution. He was exposed and interned in three different prison camps. After liberation in 1945 he would not leave the camp until those he had been nursing had left, and the harsh conditions had so weakened him that he died shortly afterwards. His story was made famous by the 1987 film *Au Revoir Les Enfants*.

In contrast to the atrocities of the Nazi regime, holiness flourished in Germany in the person of Brother Alois Ehrlich, O.Carm. (1868-1945). Like his saviour, Alois was a carpenter. He travelled the Carmelite Province of Upper Germany and beyond using his skill for the glory of God and the benefit of his community. He had a great love of Scripture which helped him to be a wise and prayerful brother.

Stop and think: Would you agree that the most terrible conditions of suffering also expose the most remarkable examples of holiness?

Carmelites bringing new life

The British Province of Carmelites remembers with pride a Carmelite who took a mission from England to many parts of the world. As a young girl Clare Perrins (later known as Mother Mary Ellerker, 1875-1949) converted to Catholicism. She began a small religious community which spread from the Midlands of England to the Caribbean, becoming affiliated to the Carmelite Order as the *Corpus Christi Carmelite Sisters*.

Two years after the birth of Mary Ellerker, Maria Carolina Scampone was born. Maria also died two years after Mary, in 1951, in a hospice for the aged poor, having been received into the Third Order some days before. This Italian lay Carmelite led a varied life as mother, housewife, widow, and even prisoner during World War II. Throughout these experiences she was known as a woman of prayer. Her reputation for sanctity does not lie in extraordinary feats of holiness but rather in kind acts which although small have led her to be acclaimed as a saint by the people who knew and remembered her. Sometimes even saints are not well remembered with the passage of time. One such lay Carmelite is María Concetta Todaro (1858-1923) from Palermo, the capital of Sicily. During her lifetime, however, María Concetta was sought out as a spiritual guide and intercessor. People came to her asking for prayers and reassurance, particularly during the difficult years of the First World War. She joined the Third Order in 1887 at a time when the friars had been suppressed in her native city, and not for the first time it was lay people such as María Concetta who preserved the Carmelite spirit during the absence of religious. To mark her profession María Concetta made clothes to distribute to the poor: as she took on the habit of Carmel this simple gesture showed solidarity with those in need and a real understanding of her vocation.

A contemporary was Wilhelmina Ronconi (1864-1936), a prominent member of the Carmelite Third Order in Italy. She was one of the most sought-after woman speakers of her time who used her powers of rhetoric to highlight social problems and champion justice. She understood that the Church's concern with matters of faith must necessarily impinge on civic and economic issues. She had contact with every social class from the aristocracy to slum-dwellers, improving the lot of all through her educational projects.

Someone equally interested in the social issues of Italy at the time was Wiera Francia (1898-1928), though unlike Wilhelmina she was a shy young woman. Reluctantly she held positions of responsibility in several Catholic organisations because her colleagues recognised her God-given talents. For Wiera the Carmelite Third Order was a support for her activities in the world. In a talk she delivered to a congress of Carmelite tertiaries Wiera said: 'We are listless and degenerate Christians. Enter, then, the Third Order, to shake us up with the abundance of its graces, with the wisdom of its rules and the eloquence of its examples. Come, let it teach us how every day to live even the noisiest of lives, or the most humble and ordinary lives, and at the same time be more closely united to the Lord.'

Sainthood: a sign of unity?

An equally dynamic though very different character was Saint Maria Maravillas of Jesus (1891-1974). She entered Carmel as a nun in El Escorial near Madrid, but soon felt that the Discalced Carmelites had lost the spirit of Teresa and John of the Cross as she perceived it. Maravillas (which means 'marvels') protested that she did not wish to found a new order or 'branch off' from the Discalced Order, but felt called by God to make a new foundation, the first of what she called *Teresian Carmelite Monasteries* because they rigorously followed what was then thought to be the original *Constitutions* of Saint Teresa rather than contemporary guidelines. After the difficult years of the Spanish Civil War Mother Maravillas went on to found eleven monasteries of nuns in Spain and India, and sent nuns to several of the oldest Discalced communities.

Saint Maravillas of Jesus.

Saints inspire strong and sometimes conflicting emotions, and it must be said that Maravillas is one of Carmel's more controversial saints. This should not dismay us: Teresa was examined by the Inquisition and is now a Doctor of the Church! Why is Maravillas controversial? Speaking at her canonisation in 2003 Pope John Paul II said that she 'lived inspired by a heroic faith, made concrete in the response of an austere vocation'. Carmelites have been divided about Maravillas's austere interpretation of religious life. After the Second Vatican Council her reforms seemed to many to be a step backwards rather than forwards. Just as with the Teresian Reform centuries earlier, there was influence from outside the Order by Spanish politicians and the Vatican. Following her death there was divided opinion among the Discalced Carmelites about the way their Order should progress, which resulted in two different sets of *Constitutions* being issued for the nuns in the 1990s: one for those who followed the teachings of Maravillas (about

.5% of monasteries worldwide), and another for those who did not. Those who followed Maravillas' vision split away from the governance of the Discalced Superior General. Sister Constance FitzGerald, O.C.D., has summarised the splintering:

> The renewal of religious life mandated by Vatican II has given rise to two major interpretations of Carmelite life. One focuses on the ministry of contemplative prayer and the retrieval of mysticism, particularly Teresa of Avila, John of the Cross, Thérèse of Lisieux, etc. This reading of the charism … is willing to experiment with various ways how the life of contemplative prayer/liturgy can be lived and shared with the people. It values solitary prayer and shared life in a community of equals. The other highlights separation from the world and a literal fidelity to the life as it has been lived in the past. It values preservation, therefore, and sees enclosure as the essential manifestation of contemplative Carmelite Life. Although these two readings seem to be a contemporary expression of the order's age-old tension between solitary prayer and community, the hermit emphasis and the mendicant effort, communities are diverse and complex, spread along a continuum between these two poles.

The question always facing religious families such as ours is whether we should focus on preserving traditions intact or reinterpreting them. Are we called to be faithful to the lifestyle of the first hermits or of Saint Teresa, or are we called to adapt their vision for our own time and place? Both attitudes deserve respect: both are trying to be faithful to the Carmelite tradition, and the Carmelite Family can accommodate a variety of vocations. Saint Maravillas was undoubtedly a holy woman, whatever the legacy of her reform, which is itself a reminder to us of the teaching of Saint Paul that there are many different ways to come to God, and that people with different attitudes can all be seen as saints:

> Those who eat must not despise those who abstain, and those who abstain must not pass judgement on those who eat; for God has welcomed them. Who are you to pass judgement on servants of another? It is before their own lord that they stand or fall. And they will be upheld, for the Lord is able to make them stand. Some judge one day to be better than another, while others judge all days to be alike. Let all be fully convinced in their own minds. Those who observe the day, observe it in honour of the Lord. Also those who eat, eat in honour of the Lord, since they give thanks to God; while those who abstain, abstain in honour of the Lord and give thanks to God. (*Romans* 14:3-6).

Stop and think: Do you think Carmelites today are called to be faithful to the lifestyle of the first hermits, or of Blessed John Soreth, or of Saint Teresa, or are we called to adapt their vision for our own time and place?

Saintly members of Lay Carmel

Someone who gave honour to God in every circumstance of his life and also in death was Blessed Isidore Bakanja (d. 1909), a labourer in the Belgian Congo. He converted to Christianity aged eighteen and sought to bring others to the faith. He was devoted to Our Lady by praying the Rosary and wearing the Brown Scapular, the miniature Carmelite habit, and as such he was a member of the extended Carmelite Family. Isidore worked for Belgian colonists, many of whom were atheists who hated Christians because they insisted on justice and rights for the native people. This hatred was turned on Isidore who was teaching people how to pray on the rubber plantation where he worked. The supervisor told

A painting of Blessed Isidore Bakanja by Christopher Oluoch.

Isidore to stop preaching the Gospel and discard his scapular and when he wouldn't Isidore was flogged and chained. His torn skin became infected and Isidore was close to death. When an inspector came to visit the plantation the supervisor sought to hide Isidore but he was seen and taken to the inspector's house to heal. His wounds were too great, however, and Isidore told the inspector 'tell them that I am dying because I am a Christian.' Missionaries in the area visited Isidore and urged him to forgive the supervisor. He assured them that he already had, declaring 'When I am in heaven, I shall pray for him very much.' Isidore was beatified in 1994, and has become a powerful figure of reconciliation between people of different cultures and races. He was not an 'expert' in Carmelite spirituality. His faith was simple. But the life and death of this young man are a brilliant witness to the life and death of Jesus and we are proud to number Isidore among the martyrs of Carmel.

Another young lay Carmelite whose sanctity is worth remembering is Santos Franco Sánchez (1942-54). He went to a Carmelite school where he was known as a peacemaker for mediating in the quarrels of his peers. He was not without typical childish faults but he earnestly desired to do the will of God. Because of a misdiagnosis he died of meningitis aged just eleven. During two months of suffering he showed remarkable patience, saying to his mother 'Don't be sad Mama. I want to do only the will of God and I am offering all to Him for sinners, for the missions, and for whatever God wants.' Santos told his family that his own experience of intense headaches and fevers helped him to understand the love Jesus demonstrated in wearing a crown of thorns. His final words were 'Whatever the will of God desires.'

Santos Franco Sánchez.

Carmel has a further young candidate for beatification, Ramón Montero Navarro (1931-45). He was from the Spanish region of La Mancha, and proves once again the words of Christ that the deepest mysteries would be revealed to little children. Like Santos, Ramón suffered from illness, Pott's disease, and confined to bed he would read the *Little Office of Our Lady* according to the Carmelite Rite. He became known in the locale as a prayerful boy, and when visitors came to see him on his sick bed they asked him to pray for their intentions. One day he was asked to pray – in the aftermath of the Spanish Civil War – for a good school run by religious in his home town of Tomelloso. Shortly after, the Carmelite friars came to the town becoming close friends with Ramón and his family, and eventually the child was received into the Third Order (the only male tertiary in Tomelloso!) and given the Order's habit in which the teenager was buried.

Stop and think: Can you put an age restriction on holiness, or can even small children be considered saints?

The Office of the Carmelite Postulator General has about a hundred cases under consideration by the Vatican, including many lay Carmelites, and others may be proposed. We cannot possibly review them all, but Carmen de Sojo (1856-90), a Carmelite tertiary from Barcelona, is an interesting example of holiness. She was only fifteen when she married, and much of Carmen's life centred around her family with husband Jorge and five children. She believed that her vocation was to attain holiness through her married status and her tender relationship with her husband was where she learned the joys and trials of love. Her rapport with her mother was difficult, and as a member of the Carmelite Third Order Carmen seems to have found Mary, Our Lady, to be a comforting mother and sister. Some aspects of Carmen's life may be hard for us to understand: her poor health was not helped by her elaborate self-mortifications, and she seems to have compensated for her mother's lack of attention towards her by being somewhat strict with her own children. But in the life of Carmen de Sojo we see someone trying to do her best, and seeking to live out the will of God in the confusions of life; not a perfect woman, but a woman who found that Carmel helped make sense of her spiritual journey. By reflection and self-examination she was able to become aware of her motives and desires and sought to bring them into line with Gospel values.

Stop and think: Do you think saintliness consists in being 'perfect', or in asking God to help overcome imperfections?

Anicka (Annie) Zelikova (1924-41) was an outstanding member of the Carmelite Third Order. In the series of books on Carmelite saints, *Profiles in Holiness*, she is considered as another Saint Thérèse, and like the Little Flower she died at a tender age, just seventeen.

Annie was born in Moravia, the eastern province of what is now the Czech Republic, the daughter of a farmer. A vivacious girl, she brought happiness to others right up to her death from tuberculosis. Even when she was too weak for anything else, she practiced her 'apostleship of smiling', declaring 'I must smile to my last breath. Ah, all I can give God now are my heartbeats and my smile. Nothing is left to me except love and trust.' Annie was like Saint Thérèse in recognising that holiness can come through little acts of love. In 1940 she wrote 'true beauty is hidden in faithfulness in little things. I always desired to do great and heroic deeds of love, but when I saw that I was unable, I was grieved by it. Now I find great heroism precisely in little things, so that now I haven't the slightest regret whether I can do something or not.' Like the Little Flower Annie had a great desire to enter Carmel as a nun, but her poor health prevented it. In fact Annie was so ill that she was given special permission to make profession as a member of the Carmelite Third Order Secular. Seven months later she died, smiling to the end. Her final statement was 'I trust', and the last audible word she could speak was 'Carmel'. She was buried with the *Rule for the Third Order* over her heart.

 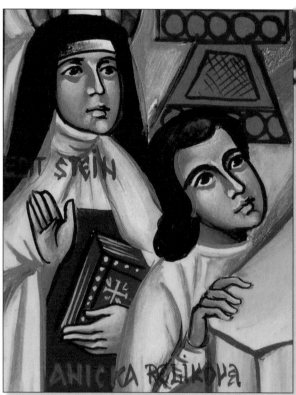

A Romanian icon depicting Our Lady as the 'Theotokos of Carmel' shows representatives of the Carmelite Family sheltering under Mary's mantle: Titus Brandsma for the friars, Isidore Bakanja for the scapular confraternity, Edith Stein for the nuns, and Anicka Zelikova for the Third Order.

The lay vocation in Carmel was also close to the heart of Fr. Marie-Eugène of the Child Jesus, O.C.D., (Henri Grialou, 1894-1967), founder of the *Institute of Notre-Dame de Vie*, and to Amata Cerretelli, TOC (1907-63), founder of the Carmelite movement *La Famiglia* (The Family). Rooted in the Carmelite house in Castellina near Florence, *La Famiglia* consists of several branches: the Third Order, St. Raphael's group for engaged couples, the 'Swallows' club for young people, the Samaritans who look after the sick, the 'Elders of the Family', artists' groups, sports teams, prayer groups for vocations, and so on. The idea of the movement's founder was that it should help ordinary people to find and share holiness in every sphere of life, inspired by the Carmelite vision.

It is not only lay people who are able to join the Third Order. Diocesan clergy are allowed to enter the Carmelite Family in this way too, and Saint George Preca (1880-1962), a priest from the Diocese of Malta and Gozo, found his Third Order community a crucial support on his road to holiness. He founded the Society of Christian Doctrine, a group of lay catechists, and he is popularly referred to as the 'Second Apostle of Malta' after Saint Paul. He was canonized in 2007.

Saint George Preca, T.O.C.

Blessed Maria Crocifissa Curcio (1877-1957) is another religious whose journey in Carmel took her through the Third Order, making profession as a teenager. She was the seventh of ten children born into an Italian family. Her father disapproved of her desire to study, but nevertheless she came upon a book about Saint Teresa of Jesus that changed her life. She was also greatly influenced by the 'Little Way' of Saint Thérèse and went on to found a religious community, the *Carmelite Missionaries of Saint Thérèse of Lisieux*. She was beatified in 2005.

Blessed Maria Crocifissa Curcio.

Carmel: Love in the heart of the Church and of Society

Though we're proud as Carmelites to belong to a distinct and distinguished family, we are not aloof from the Church. Quite the opposite! We are immersed in her heart at every level. This was proved in the life of two Carmelites who contributed to the Second Vatican Council. The Servant of God Fr. Bartolomé F. M. Xiberta, O.Carm. (1897-1967) was born in Girona in Spain, and was noted for living his Carmelite vocation in a very profound way with great devotion to Mary. He was elected an Assistant General of the Order and distinguished himself as a theologian, researcher, historian and teacher, which led to his being a Consulter at the Second Vatican Council.

Servant of God Bartolomé Xiberta, O.Carm.

Another figure at the Council was Bishop Donal R. Lamont, O.Carm. (1911-2003). Donal was born in Ireland and educated by the Carmelites at Terenure College in Dublin. He made profession as a friar in 1930 and was appointed superior of the Carmelite mission in Rhodesia (now Zimbabwe) in 1946. In 1957 Donal was made Bishop of Umtali (now Mutare) Diocese. Two years later he founded a diocesan congregation of sisters, the *Handmaids of Our Lady of Mount Carmel*. As a bishop he made an intervention at the Second Vatican Council which paved the way for the decree on the missions *Ad Gentes*. At the Council he was elected to the newly formed Secretariat for Christian Unity and his passion for ecumenical work continued when he retired to Ireland, particularly in the north. His most outstanding work, however, was as a leading opponent of the Rhodesian government's oppression of the black population. His first pastoral letter, *A Purchased People*, became a classic statement on racial injustice and human rights. The regime sentenced Donal to ten years in prison with hard labour (commuted on appeal to deportation in 1977). During his exile he was nominated for a Nobel Peace Prize, and the government of Kenya issued a postage stamp to honour his contribution to the people of Africa. He returned to Zimbabwe after independence where he served as bishop for a further two years. The Carmelites who lived with Bishop Donal would remind us that he was not a perfect saint: he had faults and foibles like the rest of us. But he read the signs of the times (*Matthew* 16:3), and opened the eyes of the world to injustice. Surely bishop Donal would have agreed with the homily at his funeral: 'How do we sum up his life? We don't – the final judgement must be left to God. In the end all human achievement except love is as straw in God's eyes; we all must come in the end to rely not on what we have done, but solely on God's mercy.'

Ireland was home to another Carmelite who – like Bishop Lamont – received a round of applause from the bishops at Vatican II. Frank Duff (1889-1980) founded the *Legion of Mary* in 1921 as a means of supporting the lay apostolate in the Church. The Legion's Marian spirituality was heavily dependent upon Frank's own membership of the Carmelite Third Order. In July 1996 the cause for his beatification was introduced by the Archbishop of Dublin.

Appreciating the saints around us

The communion of saints incorporates the faithful on earth, in purgatory, and in heaven. We saints – God's holy people on earth – can celebrate the memory of the Carmelites in heaven whether or not their holiness has been formally recognized by the Church. It is good for us to model our lives on those who have been transformed by an encounter with Christ, as Saint Paul advised: 'Join in following my example, brothers and sisters; keep an eye on those who are behaving like us, whom you have as your model.' (*Philippians* 3:17).

A painting of the saints of Carmel by Ariel Agemian.

Conclusion: In this nineteenth chapter we have seen how diverse are the ways in which Carmelites have responded to God's invitation to holiness, and how the recent history of the Carmelite Family has been anything but short of saintly models of inspiration for our contemplative lives of prayer, community and service.

Perhaps conclude your time of reflection and study with a moment of prayer, asking the saints of Carmel to intercede for you and the whole Carmelite Family.

In the next and final chapter we will reflect on what it means to commit oneself to the service of God within the Carmelite Family.

Ideas for Reflection, Discussion and Action

- Has anything or any particular saint caught your attention as you have studied this chapter either on your own or with others? Is there anything more you would have said about a particular saint? What do you understand to be the key themes running throughout the chapter? Perhaps jot your thoughts down on the blank page at the end.

- Does it come as a shock to you to see how many Carmelites have been martyred in recent times?

- One of the objections sometimes made against the beatification of Carmelites killed during wars is that 'They weren't true martyrs; they just got in the way'. What do you think?

- Many of the Carmelite saints of the last two hundred years were educators. Why do you think the Order's charism has encouraged this ministry?

- Pray for the work of Carmelite journalists, inspired by the witness of Titus Brandsma to the freedom of the press and freedom of conscience.

- What role should the memory and example of the saints play in discussions about the future of the Carmelite Order?

- Physical illness and suffering seems to have been a common feature in the lives of the saints. Why do you think that is, and is it essential to holiness?

- The majority of Carmelite saints seem to have come from France, Italy, or Spain. Do you think the reasons for this are cultural or spiritual?

- Are you surprised how young many of Carmel's saints were when they died?

- Can you identify with the saints of the Order as members of your own religious family, or are they distant figures separated by too much time and space?

- Can you recognise holiness in Carmelites living today? By what criteria would you judge this?

Recommended Further Resources

As noted in the previous chapter, there are many resources (books, films, audio recordings) associated with Carmel's better known saints, widely available in not only Carmelite bookstores but more general Christian shops. Lesser-known saints are sometimes discussed in series such as *Profiles in Holiness*.

Josse Alzin, *A Dangerous Little Friar: Father Titus Brandsma*, (Burns & Oates, 1957).

Hans Urs Von Balthasar, *Two Sisters in the Spirit – Thérèse of Lisieux and Elizabeth of the Trinity*, (San Francisco: Ignatius Press, 1992).

Johan Bergström-Allen, T.O.C., & Wilfrid McGreal, O.Carm., (eds.), *The Gospel Sustains Me: The Word of God in the Life and Love of Saint Thérèse of Lisieux*, (Faversham: Saint Albert's Press, 2009).

Emanuele Boaga, O.Carm., *Celebrating the Saints of Carmel*, (Rome: Edizioni Carmelitane, 2010).

Raymond Boisvert, FIC, & James Conlon, AA, *Bakanja*, (Nairobi: Paulines Publications Africa, 1996).

British Province of Carmelites website section on saints: www.carmelite.org

Gregory Burke, O.C.D., 'Fire in the Heart: Francisco Palau, a Carmelite Saint in the Secular World', *Mount Carmel: A Review of the Spiritual Life*, Volume 57 Number 4, October-December 2009, pp. 14-21.

William Bush, *To Quell the Terror: The Mystery of the Vocation of the Sixteen Carmelites of Compiègne*, (Washington, D.C.: ICS Publications, 1999).

Joseph Chalmers, O.Carm., *Blessed Maria Teresa Scrilli: From the school of life to the school of holiness*, (Rome: Edizioni Carmelitane, 2006). Also available online via the website of the Carmelite Curia: www.ocarm.org

Elizabeth of the Trinity, *Always Believe in Love*, edited by Marian T. Murphy, O.C.D., (Hyde Park, New York: New City Press, 2009).

Constance FitzGerald, O.C.D., 'Passion in the Carmelite Tradition: Edith Stein', in Keith J. Egan, T.O.C., *Carmelite Prayer: A Tradition for the 21st Century*, (New York: Paulist Press, 2003), pp. 174-201.

Guy Gaucher, O.C.D., *John and Thérèse – Flames of Love: The Influence of St. John of the Cross in the Life and Writings of St. Thérèse of Lisieux*, (New York: Alba House, 2000).

Guy Gaucher, O.C.D., *The Story of a Life: St. Thérèse of Lisieux*, (London: HarperCollins, 1987). Bishop Gaucher served as Auxiliary Bishop of Bayeux and Lisieux, and is a world authority on St. Thérèse.

Alfred Isacsson, O.Carm., 'Brother John of Saint Samon – Love for One Another', *Carmel in the World*, Volume XLV, No. 1, 2006.

Ernest Larkin, O.Carm., 'Aspiratory Prayer in the Carmelite Tradition', *Carmel in the World*, Volume XLVII Number 2, 2008, pp. 142-55.

James McCaffrey, O.C.D., *The Fire of Love: Praying with Thérèse of Lisieux*, (Norwich: Canterbury Press, 1998).

Conrad de Meester, O.C.D., *With Empty Hands: The Message of Thérèse of Lisieux*, (London: Burns and Oates, 1987). This is a very important study of Thérèse by one of the foremost scholars of her life.

Fernando Millán Romeral, O.Carm., *Serving Him Through the Poor: Letter from the Prior General to the Carmelite Family on the occasion of the beatification of Mother Candelaria of Saint-Joseph*, (Rome: Edizioni Carmelitane, 2008).

Jennifer Moorcroft, T.O.C., *God is All Joy: The Life of St. Teresa of the Andes*, (Washington, D.C.: I.C.S. Publications, 2009).

Gordon Mursell, (ed.), *The Story of Christian Spirituality: Two thousand years, from East to West*, (Lion Publishing, 2001).

Thomas R. Nevin, *Thérèse of Lisieux – God's Gentle Warrior*, (Oxford: Oxford University Press, 2006).

Elizabeth Ruth Obbard, *Saints of Carmel*, (Darlington Carmel).

Christopher O'Donnell, O.Carm., *Love in the heart of the Church – The Mission of Thérèse of Lisieux*, (Dublin: Veritas, 1997).

Christopher O'Donnell, O.Carm., *Prayer: Insights from Thérèse of Lisieux*, (Dublin: Veritas, 2001).

Vincent O'Hara, O.C.D., 'Introducing the Life of St. Thérèse, 'The Greatest Saint of Modern Times', *Mount Carmel: A Review of the Spiritual Life*, Volume 57 Number 3, July-September 2009, pp. 15-23.

Robert Opala, O.C.D., *Raphael Kalinowski*, CD audio recording of a presentation, (Glasgow: Glasgow Carmel, 2008).

Eulogio Pacho, *Father Francisco Palau y Quer: A Passion for the Church*, translated by David Joseph Centner, (Rome: Carmelite Missionaries, Second Edition 1997).

Salvatore Sciurba, O.C.D., *Carmel and the French Revolution: The Martyrs of Compiègne*, CD audio recording of a presentation, (Washington, D.C.: CC Communications).

Kevin Shanley, O.Carm., 'Frank Duff, T.O.Carm.: Founder of the Legion of Mary', *Carmel in the World*, Volume XLV Number 1, 2006, pp. 31-34.

Peter Slattery, O.Carm., 'Titus Brandsma, Martyr', and 'Edith Stein, Carmelite and Feminist', in *The Springs of Carmel: An Introduction to Carmelite Spirituality*, (New York: Alba House, 1991).

Edith Stein, *Potency and Act*, translated by Walter Redmond, The Collected Works of Edith Stein XI, (Washington, D.C.: I.C.S. Publications, 2009).

Climbing the Mountain: The Carmelite Journey   565

Chapter 19 ■ Holy Men and Women of Carmel: Part 2 – Later Saints

Thérèse of Lisieux, *Story of a Soul*, trans. John Clarke, O.C.D., (Washington, D.C.: I.C.S. Publications, third edition 1996, and study edition prepared by Marc Foley 2005). This is the best edition of Thérèse's autobiography, especially as some older editions don't print the whole text as Thérèse wrote it because it was adapted by her sisters in Carmel. I.C.S. Publications have also produced editions of Thérèse's letters, plays, poems and prayers, as well as her *Last Conversations*.

Thérèse of Lisieux Internet Gateway: www.thereseoflisieux.org

Paulinus Redmon, *Louis and Zélie Martin: The Seed and the Root of the Little Flower*, (London: Quiller Press, 1995).

Society of the Little Flower: www.littleflower.org & www.littleflower.eu

Joachim Smet, O.Carm., 'Carmelites and the Spanish Civil War, 1936-1939', *Carmel in the World*, Volume XLVII Number 2, 2008, pp. 116-29.

Redemptus Valabek, O.Carm., 'Malta's Modern Apostle: Don George Preca', *Carmel in the World*, Volume XXXIX Number 1, 2000, pp. 41-54.

Redemptus Valabek, O.Carm., *Profiles in Holiness*, 3 volumes, (Edizioni Carmelitane, 1996-2002).

John Welch, O.Carm., 'Thérèse and the Eternal Shore', in Keith J. Egan, T.O.C., *Carmelite Prayer: A Tradition for the 21st Century*, (New York: Paulist Press, 2003), pp. 162-173.

Remember that as well as these resources, the lives and teachings of Carmel's saints are included in distance-learning programmes offered by Carmelite Institutes and study centres around the world, including the Carmelite Institute of Britain & Ireland (www.cibi.ie).

Notes and reflections on Chapter 19

Notes and reflections on Chapter 19

CHAPTER 20

Commitment in Carmel

Summary: The journey to Christ 'the Mountain' is a life-long pilgrimage, and Carmel offers a reliable map and companions on the way. The initial part of our journey in following the Carmelite tradition is reaching an end, so now is the time to consider what role Carmel and its spirituality will have in your future. This chapter is about discerning God's call, and what it might mean for someone to make a commitment within the Carmelite Family through public profession of promises or vows. The chapter recaps many of the key themes that have recurred throughout this book.

Profession is the deepest form of commitment within Carmel for religious and laity.

Get prepared: All the information you will need is contained within the text of this chapter, but it would be useful to have other reference books to hand, especially a copy of the 2003 *Rule for the Third Order of Carmel (RTOC)* and other modern documents of the Carmelite Family. Having writing implements would also be helpful if you intend to take notes or highlight anything in the text, and pondering the text reflectively in small sections is arguably more profitable than reading it all in one sitting. As with all the previous chapters, it is good to commit your time of study and reflection to God in prayer. A sense of God's commitment to us even when our commitment is distracted is conveyed in the simple words attributed to Sir Jacob Astley before the Battle of Edgehill in 1642:

> *O Lord, thou knowest how busy I must be this day;*
> *if I forget thee, do not thou forget me. Amen.*

A highpoint on our journey – but not the summit

This is the final chapter in our programme of initial formation which has been undertaken by people wishing to deepen their awareness of Carmelite spirituality. Some people reading this text are already committed to Carmel as lay or religious members of the Order. Other readers will now be discerning whether or not they feel called by God to commit themselves to make profession within a particular branch of the Carmelite Family. This chapter may help you to reflect on your own journey thus far, your own vocation, and to consider questions such as: Does the Carmelite story feel like *my* story? Am I called to devote myself more deeply to this community and contribute to its ongoing tradition? Should I be looking to continue my spiritual journey elsewhere? What can I give to Carmel, and what can it give to me?

Each person's journey in Carmel is individual and this chapter won't be able to address everyone's story or the questions they may have, but it might help you to think about how you have come to this point on the journey. Perhaps you have not 'found' Carmel so much as it has found you and seems to be offering you a home. Perhaps the story of your journey is a mystery that cannot be fully understood or told simply in words.

Elijah and Elisha are depicted on the bronze doors of the Basilica of Saint Paul Outside the Walls in Rome.

Stop and reflect: Jesus said that Elijah and Elisha had been committed a task by God to take God's message to foreigners, not just to their own people (*Luke* 4:16-30). As Carmelites who take inspiration from Elijah and Elisha, how can we share their mission of taking God's word to the foreigner and outsider? What commitment do we need to make?

God commits to us first

Before we speak about making a commitment within the Church it's important to remember that God is always the first mover and our ultimate goal. Before we were born God called each one of us to enter into a relationship with him (the 'universal call to holiness' discussed in Chapter 2). Thus making a commitment in Carmel is first and foremost a statement not of our fidelity to God but of God's fidelity to his people. It is our response to God's invitation to holiness, a statement that we believe in God's commitment to us as individuals and to the whole human family.

Our first formal response to God's call was through baptism, by which all Christians are called to spread the Good News of God's love to the world. As Christians we have to not only preach the Good News, we also have to *be* Good News, proclaiming the Kingdom of God. That is the commitment that we (or our godparents on our behalf) made at our baptism, and it is the dedication we renew each time we profess the Creed.

Did you know? The Carmelite mission to take the Good News throughout the world continues. Among the most challenging areas for the Order are parts of Asia and Africa where some governments strictly monitor religious activity.

Commitment to follow Jesus

As Carmelites we embrace the Christian mission at a particularly deep level, understanding our commitment within the Order as a deepening of our baptismal vocation. A commitment within Carmel shows our desire to live in the presence of God (as discussed in Chapter 9), a public echo of Elijah's statement that 'the Lord God lives in whose presence I stand' (*1 Kings* 17:1).

Whatever our role within the Carmelite Family, the commitment we make as Carmelites is to live *in allegiance to Jesus Christ, serving the Master unswervingly, pure in heart and stout in conscience*, as it is put in Chapter 2 of our foundational *Rule of Saint Albert*. Like the first hermits on Mount Carmel we strive to follow in the footsteps of Jesus, Son and image of the Father. We strive to imitate him, to follow his teachings, to live in the spirit of his Good News.

Carmelite life is entirely centred on Jesus Christ, our Master and Brother, depicted here in ceramic by Adam Kossowski at Whitefriars in Faversham, England.

Commitment in Carmel means committing first and foremost to a relationship wit
Jesus. As the 2003 *Rule for the Third Order of Carmel* puts it:

> Gradually Jesus must become the most important person in the (lay)
> Carmelites' existence. This means having a personal, warm, affectionate
> and constant relationship with Jesus. This bond is nourished by the
> Eucharist, the liturgy in general, by Holy Scripture and by various
> forms of prayer. All these encourage the tertiaries to recognise Jesus
> in their neighbour and in daily events; it propels them to give witness
> along the highways and byways of the world to the decisive nature of
> his presence. (*RTOC* §19).

Called to Christ in different but complimentary ways: Timothy Radcliffe, O.P. (former Master
General of the Dominicans, left), with Joseph Chalmers, O.Carm. (former Prior General of the
Carmelites) at the Carmelite General Chapter in 2007.

Of course, it is not necessary to be a Carmelite in order to have a relationship with Jesus
Christ and commit to his Gospel. There are other ways, rich traditions and venerable
spiritual families within the Church which can help nurture friendship with God.
Commitment to Jesus is not unique to Carmel, and not everyone is called to Carmelite
life. As Albert acknowledges at the start of his *Rule*, 'Many and varied are the ways in
which our saintly forebears laid down how everyone, whatever their station or the kind of
religious observance they have chosen, should live a life in allegiance to Jesus'.

o why Carmel?

ince we've already committed to following Jesus through baptism, and since there are so ιany paths to follow him within the Church, why make a further commitment within ιe community of Carmel specifically?

A dedication to follow Christ in Carmel is a promise to *live in allegiance to Jesus Christ* y embracing as our own the insights and experience of the Carmelite way of life, as ιanded down to us by the saints of Carmel, a tradition continuously being rediscovered nd reinterpreted for the present day. In joining the Order today no one is committing ɔ live as the hermits on Mount Carmel did 800 years ago, but rather undertaking to ontinue the Carmelite heritage in a way that is appropriate to the candidate and the ιeeds of Church and Society (cf. *RTOC* §30). It is a commitment to make the Carmelite tory our own story, and to become part of that story told to others.

In Carmel we can cooperate with God and receive his gift of contemplation through prayer, service and community-building.

What is distinctive about the Carmelite way of life is our understanding of *contemplation*. Contemplation – being open to the presence and friendship of God – is gift that God wants to share with all. The three main elements of the Carmelite charism are prayer, community, and service, and contemplation is not limited to one of these but the dynamic that unites them all. Those who are called to commit to Jesus as Carmelite are led on the path of contemplation. The friars' *Ratio* speaks of contemplation as 'a inner journey which takes us from the dispersive fringes of life to the inner core of ou being, where God dwells and where he unites us with himself' (§24). Contemplatio means seeking union with God in the depths of our heart, and sharing the fruits of tha experience with others; we seek to know and love God, and to make God known an loved.

If we have indeed encountered Jesus and embraced his Good News, and made th radical decision – literally from the root up – to grow in our friendship with him, the the question facing all of us is: Does Jesus want me to develop our relationship by m being immersed in Carmel?

Discerning the call

To answer this question we need to practice *discernment*, seeking to know God's will Following the Carmelite way of life is a *vocation*, a calling from God. The dynamic wover throughout the Carmelite story – from Elijah on Mount Horeb, to Mary in Nazareth to the *Rule* of Saint Albert, to our own day – has been people listening attentively for an

Among the friars, discerning the future of the Order as a whole is done through the collective wisdom of a General Chapter, held every six years.

oproaching God with a heart that is open to doing God's will. Sometimes discernment omes quickly; usually though we have to be patient and not rush the process since God peaks in God's own time. Discernment is not simply about emotional feelings, choosing o do what seems nicest, easiest or most comfortable. Rather we listen to God with an pen heart, and then we strive to do God's will. Saint Teresa of Jesus (of Avila) said that he whole purpose of life is to seek and to do the will of God.

The process of discernment can be done in a number of ways. Most of us cannot expect God's will to be revealed to us in a bolt of lightning or a voice from heaven. Instead we eed first of all to open ourselves to God in prayer – especially, in our tradition, silent rayer and *Lectio Divina* meditation on the Bible – and allow God to reveal God's will in he inner depths of our hearts. By nurturing a spirit of *vacare Deo* (space for God), we will ot hear audible words but God will speak direct to the core of our being in love beyond vords. Discernment can also involve the mind: it requires the use of our God-given gift of reason to *think* about what kind of life God

might be calling us to, given what we know about ourselves, our interests, our experiences, our weaknesses and our strengths. For this elf-knowledge and honesty is vital.

Discernment is both a private and community affair

Discernment is not a solitary process but is done with the help of other people, particularly – as the *Rule of Saint Albert* puts it – the wiser and more mature members of our communities. Sometimes we cannot see clearly what God is asking of us – even if we think we do! – so we have to rely on the advice and direction of people we trust to act as a mirror for us. The Holy Spirit speaks through the body of Christ, the Church, so no Christian should dismiss the guidance God gives through the collective wisdom of their brothers and sisters. That is why before making religious profession a candidate must have the approval of the wider Church. Making a commitment within a community means that our enthusiasm can be curbed or encouraged, depending on our need: coals burning together will stay alight and spread warmth.

No one commits to Carmel in a formal way outside of a community context. Even 'distance members' of the Third Order Secular or Carmelite religious living outside of community maintain regular contact with the

Before any individual makes a commitment within Carmel, whether religious or lay, the community must discern God's will with them.

Mary is the great model of one who discerned God's will. This statue of Our Lady of Mount Carmel is from the parish church of Los Boliches in Fuengirola near Málaga, Spain.

Order of which they are a part. The community is there to help guide and nurture a Carmelite vocation, perhaps showing a candidate that they have a calling they didn't previously know existed, but unless the community recognises a vocation as true a commitment within Carmel is not possible. Before profession within the Order as either a lay person or religious there is a vote by the community (or sometimes its council) to determine whether someone is recognised as a Carmelite. Recognising that vocation also commits the community to embrace and support the new member. It is a two-way pledge of love.

Difficult decisions

Discernment sometimes requires us to make tough decisions if we are truly to follow the will of God and not our own desires. It is unlikely that everyone who began reading this book of formation topics will have discerned a call to make a commitment within Carmel. It is possible that in some sections of the Order some people who joined Carmel without a proper programme of formation may discern that their initial call was misguided. There is no shame in leaving Carmel after a period of enquiry; rather, it shows attentiveness to God calling elsewhere. For others, reading this formation programme and sharing an experience of Carmel with others will have strengthened their sense of vocation, enabling them to say: *Yes, this is where I belong, this is my story, this is who I am.* The important thing in any situation is that we say to God, like Mary: 'Your will be done'.

Stop and think: Do you reckon that some people enter a faith community without sufficient formation, discernment, and community guidance? Why might that be?

When speaking of discerning a Carmelite vocation, we must bear in mind that it is impossible to 'make a Carmelite'; rather, the process of formation and discernment gradually reveals whether or not the Carmelite spirit already exists within someone. Discerning a vocation to Carmel is a process that requires wise and impartial guidance from a variety of sources, including friends, family, spiritual directors, and the community.

Further reflection: A number of Carmelite provinces around the world produce guidelines for people discerning a vocation to the Order, which you might find helpful. Advice from an experienced Carmelite or spiritual director can also provide good guidance.

Commitment can bring us happiness

If a true vocation is discerned and followed it will bring us joy; not all the time, but it will give us a deep sense of 'belonging'. There will be times when the journey in Carmel is smooth and pleasant, and other times when it will feel like we're carrying our crosses after Jesus. We may not always feel contented in Carmel, we may feel challenged, we may not get on with every other Carmelite, but ultimately we will feel 'at home' and learn to value and recognise others as fellow Carmelites even when we don't see eye to eye. Carmel is 'a source of energy and a school for life' (*RTOC* §4) and ultimately a true vocation will be a source of blessing for us, despite our worries and inevitable disappointments. Carmel can be an attractive community and way of life to commit to; it can make us feel safe and give us a sense of belonging. This can be a wonderful gift, but also a danger, if Carmel itself becomes a replacement for God.

Did you know? Some lay people dedicate themselves to God in Carmel at a young age, whilst others do so late in life. As we read in the previous chapter, Maria Carolina Scampone died in 1951 in a hospice for the aged poor, having been received into the Third Order only days before. Though her formal entry into Carmel came at the end of her life, it was in fact an acknowledgement that she had been Carmelite throughout her life.

The different callings within Carmel today

The process of discerning a Carmelite vocation should not be rushed. That is why there are several stages between reception/clothing in the Order and final/solemn profession; no one makes a commitment within Carmel without plenty of time for reflection, and opportunities for withdrawal. Part of being informed about what we're getting into is being sure that we are committing ourselves to Carmel in the branch of the Carmelite Family that's right for us: not necessarily where we feel comfortable, but where we can grow. The Carmelite charism is lived out in many different but equally valid ways. As we saw in Chapter 15, since the Middle Ages the Carmelites and other religious orders have copied the Servites in classifying membership of the Order into branches:

- The first order: friars (brothers, some of whom are ordained) or male hermits
- The second order: enclosed nuns or female hermits
- The third order regular: apostolic sisters who are not enclosed
- The third order secular: lay people and diocesan clergy who live 'in the world'

This is not a hierarchy of importance, simply a reflection of the order in which the different groups gained formal recognition. All these groups, whether religious or lay, make profession and are considered fully Carmelite. The vocation of Third Order

Enrolment in the Carmelite brown scapular is ideal for those people who have devotion to Our Lady of Mount Carmel but who do not feel called to commit themselves to the formation, prayer, ministry and community-life of those in the first, second and third orders.

Carmelites (also known as tertiaries or lay Carmelites) is taken as seriously by the Order today as that of the religious. Tertiaries are not 'affiliated' to the Carmelite Order but are all members of it. Profession in the Third Order is for lay people and diocesan clergy 'the fullest form of belonging' to the Carmelite Family (*RTOC* §30). Like members of Carmelite Secular Institutes (such as *The Leaven*) and Carmelite Solitaries, Tertiaries make a formal profession of promises which gives them a legal status within the Order and the Church. It is therefore a serious commitment soberly made.

In addition to the first, second, and third orders, there are many people who are linked to the Carmelite Family less formally, such as by being members of the Brown Scapular Confraternity or enquirers who are interested in Carmel's spirituality. Usually such people do not make any formal act of commitment within the Order.

Did you know? During the years of Communist rule, it was thought that the Carmelite Family had largely died out in central Europe, religious orders being banned from receiving new members. However, Carmelite friars and nuns continued to be professed in secret, each living in their own homes. When religious groups could operate freely after the Velvet Revolution of 1989, it transpired that there were dozens of friars of whom the wider Order had no knowledge. Today the Carmelites in the region known as 'Bohemia and Moravia' are engaged in many ministries, and are the largest printers of Christian literature in the Czech Republic (including this book).

The Church of St. Gall in the centre of the Czech capital Prague became a Carmelite priory in 1627, and though the Order was expelled from the property it still contains Carmelite works of art, and is served at times by Carmelites.

A distinct and dignified place in the life of the Order

Although the lay Carmelite's commitment is as serious as that of a religious, tertiaries should be careful not to think of themselves as quasi-religious or 'pretend friars and nuns'. Lay Carmelites have a unique and dignified calling within the Carmelite Order and a distinctive contribution to make to it. Just as lay Carmelites look to friars, nuns and apostolic sisters for guidance and inspiration, the Order's religious look to lay Carmelites in the same manner.

Since the overall governance of the Order is entrusted to the friars, all other branches of the Carmelite Family can legitimately look to the brothers for direction and support; they are distinct from the friars, though not independent of them. However, that doesn't mean that members of the second or third orders abdicate responsibility for their own self-governance. The *Rule for the Third Order of Carmel* stresses the autonomy of lay Carmelites in taking initiatives and electing their own leaders (§11). Lay Carmelites and women religious do not rely on the friars to be Carmelites in the world: all share that mission, and collaborate in ministry. By committing to Carmel tertiaries take on 'a fully co-responsible share in the task of evangelisation and in the ministry specific to Carmel' (*RTOC* §15). In Carmel we are united by deep bonds, but in a family every person has their place and we are not all meant to be the same; there are ways of being and doing that are perhaps more appropriate for a lay Carmelite, just as there are things that only a friar is called to do and be. There will always be great variety across our Carmelite Family in terms of routines, ministries, and demands on our time and resources. For most lay Carmelites the family, workplace, parish and wider society are the places where God has called them to live out their Carmelite identity 'in the midst of the people'.

Stop and think: How do you understand the relationship between the friars and other branches of the Carmelite Family? Is it one of dependency, collaboration, or both?

Faithful to the charism of prayer, community, and service

Since the Second Vatican Council the Church has grown in her understanding of the lay vocation and the fact that all people are called to holiness. In old manuals of the Third Order this was encouraged through a series of daily practices, such as praying the rosary and texts specific to Lay Carmel, devotions which remain a valuable contribution to the life of the Order. Yet we have grown in our understanding that commitment within Carmel for the lay person (or indeed for the religious) isn't committing to *do* something as such. Carmelites aren't bound to a specific set of prayers, meetings, or activities; rather, they aspire to *be* something beautiful for God. Committing to the Order is not so much about doing specific actions but rather giving ourselves over freely to live the charism of the Order: prayer, community, and service. Particular prayers and practices can help us to grow and be transformed, and they may be the natural fruit of our commitment, but they are not the goal in themselves. We commit to deepen our relationship with God in prayer, since, as Blessed Titus Brandsma said, 'prayer is life, not an oasis in the desert of life' (quoted in *RTOC* §36), but there is not one single way in which Carmelites should pray. Today all Carmelites including tertiaries are returning to the types of prayer most in keeping with the Carmelite spirit as set out by Saint Albert: liturgical prayer (especially the Eucharist and Divine Office), Bible meditation 'day and night' through *Lectio Divina*, and sharing an experience of Carmel in a community context. The *Rule for he Third Order of Carmel* calls lay Carmelites to dedicate themselves daily, when possible, o the Eucharist, Divine Office, and the Scriptures (*RTOC* §19, 37 & 58). A set time for meditation, ideally in silence, is also recommended by the Carmelite tradition.

When it comes to the community dimension of our commitment, we are not dedicating ourselves to a particular way of *doing* things at a meeting but to a way of *being* community. The way that lay and religious communities and chapters have met has changed over the centuries, and we are not restricted to always doing the same thing in the same place at the same time.

At profession Carmelites do not commit to any particular apostolate either, but we do commit to serve others, even when we find it hard to do so. Service is not an optional part of our commitment; as we saw in Chapter 16, service is integral to who we are as Carmelites. Even if we are too old or too ill to be physically active in our service we can still adopt an attitude of caring for our neighbours in other ways, including through our prayer. The scapular is a sign of our service, not a badge of honour. For Carmelites, both lay and religious, the scapular is a sign of our membership of and commitment to a religious family. It is a reminder that (in the words of Chapter 12) we are to be clothed in Carmel's attitudes, and that our commitment must go deeper than mere outward appearance.

Did you know? In some branches of our Family, Carmelites do commit to a specific apostolate. In the *Institute of Our Lady of Mount Carmel*, founded by Blessed Maria Teresa Scrilli, the sisters vow not only poverty, chastity and obedience but also make a fourth vow 'to give oneself to the service of one's neighbour by means of Christian and civil moral instruction'.

Balancing our commitments

For lay Carmelites in particular, as 'Carmelites who work from home', there is usually no hard and fast rule for how their commitment to Carmel should be lived out, other than growing in the spirit of the Gospel, especially the Beatitudes, and the spirit of the Order's charism, namely to be contemplatives committed to prayer, community and service. Whatever our vocation, lay or religious, the place of Carmel in our lives needs to be organic and holistic, woven into the very fabric of our hearts. We do not seek to live a 'spiritual life' as if somehow life and the spirit are separated, but instead we strive to live 'life in the spirit'. Contemplation is not about hiding from the world but rather embracing the virtues of the Beatitudes (the 'be-attitudes'). In the case of a Carmelite tertiary, each needs to integrate her or his vocation with all their other commitments and undertakings so as 'to overcome in themselves the division between the Gospel and life' (*RTOC* §10). The lay Carmelite cannot use Carmel as an excuse not to carry out their responsibilities to their family, to friends, to an employer, to a local church, or indeed to his or her own wellbeing. Likewise, these responsibilities do not release the lay Carmelite from playing a part in the life of the Order, and it may be necessary for the tertiary to reduce the number of her or his other commitments which might come into conflict with the fundamental importance due to Carmel.

Stop and consider: What priority does Carmel currently have in your life? What priority would you – and more importantly God – like it to have?

Love in the heart of the Church

Committing to Carmel is, for both a religious and a lay person, a deepening of one's baptismal commitment, not a replacement for it. It is not possible to say 'I've committed myself to Carmel and that's enough.' Carmelite commitment calls for a redoubling of our involvement in our own parish, diocese, and civil society because Carmel is in the Church and in the World and exists for the service of both. Joining Carmel is not usually about 'taking on more tasks', but about learning to approach our existing commitments from a Carmelite perspective. Carmelites need to live their vocation in the ordinary circumstances of life, building up the Kingdom. Like Elijah we are told to get up, not to retreat from the world and our fears, and to awaken people to God's presence, not through stormy winds and earthquakes but in the stillness and ordinariness of everyday life. Jesus saved the world not from the outside but by immersing himself in it, in its cultures and its people. We are asked to contribute to his work of salvation. Profession is not simply for our own holiness, for our own benefit, but rather so that we may further collaborate in realising God's Kingdom for the good of all.

There is no doubt that being a member of the Carmelite Family costs us some resources: we must give time, share our talents, and make our financial contribution. In many parts of the Order there is a decline in vocations to religious life but a surge of vocations to Lay Carmel: it will thus increasingly fall to lay Carmelites to fund the costs of Lay Carmel. Carmelite religious also contribute to the finances of their communities through their various apostolates, as well as relying on the generosity of donors. The more we give the more we receive: God is never outdone in generosity.

Since 1980 the Carmelite friars in Britain have served in the south London parish of Walworth. This is in one of the capital's financially poorer suburbs but enjoys a rich mixture of cultures and has a thriving community of committed Church-goers. The view from the top of the friary looks out over Europe's largest housing estates towards the financial hub of the City; a visual reminder of the need for Carmelites to take the reality of God's love into a busy world.

The formal recognition of Carmelite identity: profession

The layperson or religious who has discerned, together with their community, a vocation to the Carmelite Order, makes a public 'profession' of their desire to live as a committed and consecrated Carmelite. This is normally done in the context of the Carmelite or wider Church community, so is not a private affair but is rather an ecclesial act of witness. Though the processes and rituals for making profession have changed slightly over the centuries, and vary in small ways from place to place, essentially it remains a public act of self-giving to God.

To emphasise the serious and long-term commitment of the Carmelite tertiary, the 2003 *Rule for the Third Order of Carmel* has stipulated that profession is now (as it has been for the religious of the Order) a two-part process of making 'first' and then 'final promises'.

As described in Chapter 12, the first stage of admission to the Order for a lay person is 'Reception'; for a religious it is normally called 'Clothing'. This leads to a period of initial formation, sometimes called the Novitiate. The *Rule for the Third Order of Carmel* (§81) specifies that this must last a minimum of one year; in many provinces it is in fact at least two. After this time, and with the approval of the community, the tertiary can make First Profession (known as Simple Profession for religious). For both religious and laity this period of first profession or simple vows lasts for a minimum of three years, during which time the candidate seeks to deepen his or her Carmelite identity. After this period, and with the blessing and witness of the Church, the candidate can apply to make Final Profession (known as Solemn Profession for the religious of the ancient orders, such as Carmel).

Final profession brings with it all the rights and responsibilities of a commitment to Carmel. A fully professed member has the possibility, within the regulations of the Order, of exercising a vote in community affairs and of taking on a leadership role (such as prior/prioress/leader or councillor); they become, in effect, part of the *wiser and more mature* part of the community that Saint Albert spoke of in Chapters 4 and 6 of his *Rule*.

Promises and vows

At the times of first and final profession, Carmelite religious take vows whilst Carmelite laity make promises. Essentially the commitment is much the same, and in the mind and law of the Church both are serious and binding undertakings to live in a particular way. The distinction is essentially that whereas promises can be dispensed by the Prior Provincial, vows require dispensation from Rome. The 2003 *Rule for the Third Order of Carmel* (§12 & 14) recognises that over the centuries different types of profession and commitment within Lay Carmel have developed, and although it is usual practice for a tertiary to make profession of promises, there is in fact a long tradition of lay Carmelites making profession of vows, a practice which has been revived in some parts of the Order. Some tertiaries who have been finally professed, normally for five years or more, who have demonstrated a commitment to Carmel and ongoing formation and who feel especially called, may dedicate themselves to God by vows of obedience and chastity according to their state in life. Making vows in addition to promises is not the norm and if someone feels specially called to make this step there needs to be discernment amongst the wider community. These vows, which oblige in conscience, are private vows and as such are distinguished from the public vows taken by Carmelite religious; they add no rights, responsibilities, or privileges to the lay Carmelite.

The 'Evangelical Counsels'

Whether we make profession of promises or vows, and whether we are religious or laity, Carmelites are expected to live in the spirit of the three *evangelical counsels* of poverty, chastity, and obedience. They are called the 'evangelical' counsels because we find them lived and therefore recommended (counselled) by Jesus in the four accounts of the Gospel (*evangelium* in Latin). Jesus Christ was poor in spirit, chaste in heart, and obedient in love to the will of his Father. The evangelical counsels are a useful support in our pursuit of living *in allegiance to Jesus Christ*. All Christians are called to live as Christ lived and Carmelites profess to do this publicly through the evangelical counsels.

The evangelical counsels are closely linked to the way of life of religious communities, because although people have been living the evangelical counsels since the time of Jesus it was not until the development of monastic and mendicant communities that these virtues were professed publicly with the swearing of a vow or promise. Vows of poverty, chastity and obedience are now taken in some form by all formal congregations and orders of religious in the Roman Catholic Church, and the counsels are regarded as the foundation of their conduct and way of life.

A universal invitation

However, the invitation to live poor, chaste and obedient is not restricted to religious and clergy. All Jesus' followers are invited to adopt these principles in whatever way is appropriate to them. The evangelical counsels are recommended for all the baptised. Both the 1983 *Code of Canon Law* (§207 # 2) and the 1992 *Catechism of the Catholic Church* (§873) remind us that within both the clergy and the laity 'there exist Christian faithful who are consecrated to God in their own special manner and serve the salvific mission of the Church through the profession of the evangelical counsels.' The *Catechism* states

The evangelical counsels of poverty, chastity and obedience are for all Christians, not only religious and clergy.

hat those who profess the evangelical counsels publicly within a permanent state of ife recognised by the Church live a consecrated life. So it can be said that, even though hey are not religious, in making the profession proper to the Carmelite Third Order, lay Carmelites consecrate their lives to God as a deepening of their baptismal commitment.

The 2003 *Rule for the Third Order of Carmel* also reminds lay Carmelites that they are nvited in a special way to adopt poverty, chastity and obedience as part of their way of ife:

> The spirit of the evangelical counsels, common to all Christians, becomes for the Tertiaries a plan for life which touches the areas of power, of sensuality and of material goods. The vows are an ever greater demand not to serve false idols, but to attain that freedom of loving God and neighbour which is above all forms of egoism. Holiness lies in the fulfilment of this double command to love. (§13)

Poverty, chastity, and obedience are not ends in themselves; they are virtues we practice so as to conform more closely to Jesus Christ. By professing these counsels as a free choice, Carmelites become prophets in the heart of the Church, reminding all people by our dedication to Christ that God alone can set us free to be fully human and alive.

Before reading further: Think for a moment of what you understand as the principal benefits of poverty, of chastity, and of obedience. You might like to jot your answers down, and then compare them with the following reflection.

Poverty

The long-standing tradition within the Carmelite Third/Secular Order (T.O.C.) is to make promises of obedience and chastity (*RTOC* §12-13), but not the promise of poverty because of lay Carmelites' personal responsibilities to support themselves, their families and friends. However, members of the Discalced Carmelite Secular Order (O.C.D.S.) do include poverty in the promises they make. Whether or not we profess to live in material poverty we are nevertheless asked to be poor in spirit and to follow the vision of Saint Albert's *Rule* in sharing our resources.

The virtues associated with poverty resonate with the core of the Carmelite charism. Poverty is closely linked to the Carmelite notion of *vacare Deo*; leaving space for God to act in our lives and trusting in God's providence. Having a spirit of poverty allows us to make space for God and do away with false idols, since 'you cannot serve both God and wealth' (*Luke* 16:13). Ultimately only God, not things, will satisfy and save us. Material goods are tools given to us by God and are not bad in themselves, but possessions can come to possess us and enslave our hearts. Carmelites strive to live more simply, being not excessively concerned with material things.

Through poverty God gradually releases our hearts to love not only him, but also in solidarity those who have less than ourselves, physically and spiritually. By practising poverty we come to respect the created world of which we are stewards, and to be grateful for God's bounty which is for all people. Embracing voluntary poverty condemns

There are many forms of poverty in today's world; some can be a gateway to God's riches, and others demand justice. Are we ready to embrace poverty as a way of life?

possession of the poor and the idolatry of wealth, and impels us to seek justice and peace (as discussed in Chapter 17).

Did you know? On 3rd June 2007 the Maltese priest and Third Order Carmelite George Preca was declared a saint. It has been said that George lived deeply the virtue of poverty, owning only the shoes he stood-up in.

Chastity

Chastity is often confused with the vocation of celibacy, but chastity is concerned not only with bodily purity but more importantly with purity of mind and heart, what the Carmelite traditions calls *puritas cordis*. In the Carmelite tradition Albert's *Rule* speaks of the 'cincture of chastity' (Chapter 19) and Mary, Our Lady, is hailed as the woman who kept a heart pure for God so that God could pour into her whatever grace he willed.

At profession Carmelite religious undertake a vow of chastity, and lay Carmelites promise chastity according to their state in life. This does not mean cutting off relationships because of Carmel; quite the opposite. We are asked to deepen our relationships, to make our actions selfless rather than selfish, and to be an experience of God for other people. In our relationships we are invited by the virtue of chastity to encounter the spirit of God dwelling in other people, and so not be demeaning or abusive. Chastity is not about a prudish rejection of physical love, but a statement that God alone can fully and finally satisfy the longing of our hearts. Chastity is a way of living open to everyone, whether we are single or in a relationship, clerical or lay.

Professing to live in chastity is described as follows in the 2003 *Constitutions* of the Discalced Carmelite Secular Order:

> The promise of chastity reinforces the commitment to love God above all else, and to love others with the love God has for them. In this promise the Secular Carmelite seeks the freedom to love God and neighbour unselfishly giving witness to the divine intimacy promised by the beatitude 'blessed are the pure of heart for they shall see God' (*Matthew* 5:8). The promise of chastity is a commitment to Christian love in its personal and social dimensions in order to create authentic community in the world. By this promise the Secular Carmelite also expresses the conscious desire to respect each person as required by God's law and one's state of life, as a single person or married or widowed. This promise does not prevent a change in state of life. (§13)

Some people within the Carmelite Family – mostly the religious – take the further step of committing to live not only chaste but also celibate, that is, forsaking sexual relations so as to be available freely to serve all people and thus build up the Kingdom of God. However, celibacy is a vocation and gift in its own right and is not given to the majority of lay Carmelites, who through their commitment to their families and loved-ones (sometimes though not always in sexual relationships) also contribute to the building up of God's Kingdom.

Obedience

The term *obedience* comes from the Latin *ob-audire*, 'to listen to'. It is not simply about ordering people to do our bidding because we have power over them, nor is it about blindly doing the will of others against our conscience or reason. Obedience in the proper sense is not an exercise of power but rather about listening, discerning together the will of God, and respecting legitimate authority even when we cannot understand from our

During the rite of profession for religious a vow of obedience is made to the superior and his/her successors.

limited perspective why something is being asked of us. When we commit ourselves in Carmel, we commit everything to God. We hand over control and learn to cooperate with God, so that the Spirit can work in and through us.

According to an ancient formula the traditional promise made by a Carmelite, lay or religious, is obedience to God, to the Blessed Virgin Mary, and to the Prior General. The Prior General is the visible sign of unity in the Order, 'a spiritual father, head and bond of unity' (*RTOC* §11), and he is committed to all members of the Carmelite Family just as we are committed to him (*RTOC* §53). Although it is unlikely that the Prior General will ever ask anything directly of most Carmelites, it is possible, and this needs to be considered seriously when pledging oneself in the service of the Order. More likely we may be asked to do something by the people to whom the Prior General delegates his authority, normally a Prior Provincial or his representatives. Again, particularly for lay Carmelites, such a request will be rare, but it is possible. At a local level when we commit to Carmel we subscribe to be obedient to the people chosen by the community to lead us. Leaders are also asked to be obedient to the will of God as expressed through the community. That may include taking up responsibilities within Carmel even when we do not want to because we have been asked by our brothers and sisters. In the Carmelite tradition it is very significant that those in leadership are always chosen by the consent of the community.

The *Rule of Saint Albert* arguably has more to say about obedience than it does about either poverty or chastity, addressed as it is to 'Brother B. and the other hermits living *'n obedience to him'*. It was not until Pope Innocent IV approved Albert's *Way of Life* text as a formal *Rule* for religious in 1247 that vows of poverty and chastity were explicitly incorporated into the text in Chapter 4. As Carmelites we therefore need to reflect very seriously on the virtue of obedience, which according to our *Rule of Saint Albert* will help us merit the reward of eternal life (Chapter 23). The *Rule* also reminds us that we should revere those who serve us in leadership roles, our minds set not on the individual but on Christ who has placed him over you' (Chapter 23). The leader of the Carmelite community is also reminded by the *Rule* to 'put into practice what our Lord said in the Gospel: Whoever has a mind to become a leader among you must make yourself servant to the rest' (Chapter 22).

Stop and reflect: What model of obedience does the *Rule of Saint Albert* propose to the Carmelite Family? To your knowledge, is it distinctive from other groups within the Church?

Through baptism we undertake to listen to the wisdom and authority of the Church. By entering Carmel we also submit to the authority of the 'elder and wiser part' of the Order (*Rule* Chapter 4). We are asked to be faithful to what is authentically Carmelite, and at times submit our minds to the teachings of the tradition and of the Church, though an informed conscience is always the ultimate authority. Being obedient does not mean we stop thinking for ourselves, but it does mean that we need to have minds that are open to having our ways of thinking challenged.

Stop and think: Have you found your ways of thinking changed by your membership of the Carmelite Family? Have you had to exercise 'obedience' to accept ideas proposed by the Order or the Church?

When we commit to Carmel we do not give up the unique gifts that we bring to the Family. The proper exercising of authority in our tradition is to help the gifts and experience of individuals to flourish in the community. It used to be said that obedience was about driving out our individuality and making us conform to one standard 'ideal' of Carmelite life. Today we understand that we need to find a balance between expressing our own God-given identity and individuality, whilst allowing God and those around us to transform those parts of us that still need to change.

The statutes of the lay Carmelites in one of the provinces in North America describe the vow of obedience this way:

> The Lay Carmelite professes obedience according to the Carmelite Way of Life and the documents proper to the Lay Carmelite toward his/her superiors in the Church … this means obedience and respect for the Superiors of the Order and their delegates as well as a spirit of cooperation with one's local community and its officers. In matters pertaining to our life as Catholic Christians, this requires the Lay Carmelite to show obedience and respect to the Pope as Universal Shepherd, and to the local Bishop and his assistant bishops as shepherds

of the local Church. One is also to show a cooperative spirit and courteous behaviour towards one's priest and various non-ordained staff members of the local parish. Of course, as Christians Lay Carmelites would extend this respect to all.

Lay Carmelites in a Third Order chapter erected on the Caribbean island of Aruba.

Through promising obedience Carmelites undertake a serious commitment, but rather than demanding commitment from us the Order invites us to give of ourselves freely. However, having made that commitment through profession we are at the call of the Order, and asked to be obedient to it. By entering Carmel a candidate is committing to something more than a club, a prayer group or pious sodality; henceforth he or she belongs to a religious order, and the Order does not belong to him or her. Membership of Carmel does bring responsibilities and obligations, as well as rights. Embracing a vocation within the Order should be a free acceptance of our obligations within the Carmelite Family, not a burden thrust on us or accepted half-heartedly that we come to resent.

Practice makes perfect

The evangelical counsels offer us a challenge to be as perfect as we can be – or better put – to be as loving as we can be. The counsels are a way for us to cooperate with God. We can choose whether or not to take up the challenge; neither God nor the Carmelite Order will ever force us to be obedient, poor, or chaste, but we are invited by Jesus to adopt these values as a way of living so that we grow in true love and thus build up the Kingdom of God.

The evangelical counsels are ideals to live up to, and it is likely that at times we will fail to do so. We do not have to be perfect in our living of the evangelical counsels to make the step of trying to live them day by day, publicly or privately. All we are asked to do is to have an open heart to try and live them as best we can, and God will do the rest. This idea is captured in the friars' document on formation, the *Ratio* issued in 2000:

> When they are embraced with the generous commitment which flows from love, the evangelical counsels contribute to purification of the heart and to spiritual freedom. By means of the evangelical counsels the Holy Spirit gradually transforms us and conforms us to Christ. We become a living memorial of Jesus' way of living and acting. (§9)

It is the Holy Spirit that is working in us through the evangelical counsels. What if we were to imagine the Holy Spirit as an eagle, as well as a dove?

What if the commitment is too much for me?

Carmel, like the wider Church, is a Family not a club; people are not immediately dismissed for breaking 'the rules'. However, as with any family, there are boundaries, expectations, and guidelines for our conduct.

Although correction and discipline is part of Carmelite life (see the *Rule of Saint Albert* Chapter 15) it is not in keeping with the Carmelite spirit or indeed the Gospel to criticise people who do not seem as committed as ourselves. Rather, Saint Albert concludes his *Rule* by saying that: 'Here are a few points I have written down to provide you with a standard of conduct to live up to; but our Lord, at his second coming, will reward anyone who does more than he is obliged to do' (Chapter 24). The same is true of Carmel today: we have a basic standard to live up to, and if we can do more that is wonderful, but it is not demanded.

There will inevitably be times when we fail to live up to our commitment in Carmel. This should not stop us from getting back on the journey and starting each new day afresh. The more we become open to the will of God and conformed to his image, the more we Carmelites will be imitating Elijah and Mary, and become 'enthusiastic about the great works God performs and for which is required our commitment and contribution' (*RTOC* §36).

Carmelites learn from our father Elijah how to commit ourselves to God with zeal.

What *Rule* do we follow?

When we make profession we promise to follow the Carmelite way of life. In recent years there has been some debate within the Carmelite Order about the most appropriate way for lay people to do this. As was stated in Chapter 7, most members of the Carmelite Family now accept that there is only one *Rule*, that is, the text written by Saint Albert 800 years ago which is for all Carmelites, lay or religious. That text was originally written for hermits who were mostly laymen, and although it does not apply to most of us in a literal way the *Rule of Saint Albert* captures the spirit to which all in Carmel are called.

When the hermits became friars they developed *Constitutions* or guidelines to interpret the *Rule* for everyday living. When lay people were again formally admitted to the Order in 1452, the prior general Blessed John Soreth wrote a *Rule* specifically for tertiaries, which was revised in the seventeenth century and subsequently. The tradition of having a separate *Rule for the Third Order* has continued to this day, with the latest edition promulgated in 2003 (also known as *Living the Carmelite Way*). However, that text was printed alongside the *Rule of Saint Albert*, and is widely regarded as being effectively a set of *Constitutions* for the Third Order (as per the Prior General's accompanying letter of promulgation).

The *Rule for the Third Order of Carmel* has two parts: the first deals with the spirituality of Carmel for lay people; the second deals with general statutes regarding the government of the Third Order that applies worldwide. Because these statutes have an international jurisdiction they are kept simple, and each Province of the Order is required to issue local statutes which deal with matters more specifically, appropriate to the local culture.

To summarise: when tertiaries make profession in the Carmelite Third Order they are committing to live in the spirit of the *Rule of Saint Albert*, interpreted by the *Rule for the Third Order* (Constitutions) and the *Statutes* of their province. Before making profession a candidate should have studied all three documents so that he or she knows the letter – but more importantly the spirit – of the law we follow in Carmel. The purpose of these regulations is never to be legalistic; they are there to give us structures and practices that help us grow.

Did you know? An increasing number of Christians from non-Roman Catholic Churches are expressing an interest in Carmelite spirituality. In several provinces of the Order, these have been admitted as 'associate members' by making some form of commitment based on the *Rule of Saint Albert*.

Ongoing formation

Making a commitment within Carmel, such as profession, is not the end of a journey. Rather, it is an important stage on the life-long ascent up the mountain whose summit is Jesus (as he is described in Carmelite liturgy). It is not always an easy journey to make; sometimes we need to rest, but we should never give up. It's a journey many people have trodden before us, and their experience can help us.

When we join a family or a group of friends, it is expected that we will get to know them more and more as we go along. This is why formation within the Carmelite tradition is an ongoing process, and a process not just a programme. Facts and good information are an important part of formation, but formation is not only about learning. Formation is primarily about relationships and encounters: the candidate learning about themselves, about other people, and ultimately about God. Committing to Carmel means committing to ongoing formation, undertaking continual growth as a whole person, in whatever way is appropriate to the candidate and their community, in consultation with the authorities of the Order.

Lay Carmelites of the St. Elias (New York) Province gather annually for a 'Building Strong Communities Workshop', as part of their ongoing formation and development.

A commitment to be faithful and generous

There are pressing challenges that face the Order in our age; indeed they have been challenges in every period of our 800-year-old history. First of all, we need to be faithful to what is *authentically* Carmelite. That means Carmelite individuals and communities need to nurture what is truly part of the Order's tradition, and not confuse Carmelite values and practices with distracting trends in Church and Society. The second challenge is the counterbalance; we need to share the treasure of Carmel with other people and not be possessive of it. Religious orders can be in danger of becoming inward-looking, and by preserving their spirituality for themselves they may promote ways of living that are too individualistic and self-absorbed. Our task is to share the great insights of Carmel – what it has to say about God and our life in God – with a world hungry for meaning and fulfilment. This is something we all have to commit to. Carmel does not exist for our personal benefit. It is a gift of God for all the people of the world, and is therefore a gift we have to give away. It has been committed to us, and we have to find other people to commit it to. All the time we have to be faithful to the tradition in doing this, but we need to find new ways of sharing Carmel. We need to communicate the 'true voice' and wisdom of our Family in a language that can be understood today. By formally joining the Carmelite Family we commit to a present, and we commit to a future, which is going to be rooted in but different from the past.

Stop and reflect: In many parts of the world the Order is experiencing growth and new life, particularly in Lay Carmel. What are the opportunities and challenges of this? Would you agree that the future of Carmel is likely to become more and more the responsibility of lay Carmelites?

In July 2010 some 200 young lay people associated with the Order across Europe came to Rome for a 'Pilgrimage of Hope'. Such initiatives are planting the seeds for Carmel in the future.

Ponder the words of Christ: 'Be perfect, therefore, as your heavenly Father is perfect.' (*Matthew* 5:48). How might commitment within Carmel help us to follow Christ's invitation?

Trusting in God's commitment to us

By calling us to commit to Carmel, God is in fact inviting us to seek the perfection that can only be found in God. Making profession is not dependent upon us having reached 'perfection', and it will not turn us instantly into perfect saints. Our ascent of the mountain is an ongoing journey of gradual transformation, and God will supply what we need if we are open to God's gifts. When we make promises at our profession, God also romises to support us. We can trust in God's commitment to us, and commit to God ur faith, our doubts, our sufferings, and our joys.

At a Carmelite profession the Church – the body of Christ on earth – asks what the andidate seeks. This is an echo of Jesus' question to Bartimaeus: 'What do you want ne to do for you?' (*Mark* 10:51) A prospective member of Carmel could do worse than nake their own Bartimaeus's bold reply made literally in 'blind faith': 'Teacher, let me ee again'.

Let us conclude with the Epilogue of the *Rule for the Third Order of Carmel* which peautifully describes our journey to the summit of Mount Carmel which is Christ:

> The members of the Third Order of Carmel commit themselves to incarnate the Carmelite vocation set out in this Rule. Let them undertake this one brief voyage of earthly life as a colony of citizens whose homeland is heaven. Let them strive, with the help of the saints, to understand all the dimensions of the love of Christ which surpasses all knowledge, hurrying with a fervent and true desire to reach that place that the Lord as he was leaving this earth, promised to prepare for us. Rooted and grounded in charity, always alert and holding lanterns alight they are aware that 'in the evening of life they will be examined on love.' Let them multiply their talents so that at the hour of their death they will deserve to hear the Lord's invitation to enter into his joy.

Conclusion: In this twentieth and final chapter we have reflected on the wide range of vocations within the Carmelite Family. A call to live in Carmel as either a religious or lay person requires commitment, from God, from the individual, and from the community. An individual's commitment can only be made after sufficient formation and discernment, as a free response to the commitment God has made to us. The call to Carmel requires a response from us, a serious undertaking to tread Carmel's ancient path with all the joys and pains that that might bring.

Perhaps conclude your time of reflection and study – and indeed your reading of this book – with a moment of prayer.

The journey of formation continues ...

Ideas for Reflection, Discussion and Action

- In reading this chapter alone or with others has any idea or phrase particularly caught your attention? How would you summarise it for another person? Perhaps jot your thoughts down on the blank page at the end.

- Looking back over your reading of this book on formation, does the Carmelite story feel like your story? Do the images and themes of Carmelite spirituality resonate with you?

- How much of your Carmelite journey has been clear to you and how much has been a mystery?

- In your opinion is the lay Carmelite vocation as serious as the calling of a friar, nun sister or married person?

- Are you committed to Carmel in your acts of service, as well as in your prayer, and in the building up of community? What is your ministry within Carmel?

- Do you think a candidate needs to consult his or her family before making profession in the Carmelite Order?

- Pray for vocations to every branch of the Carmelite Family.

- What resources does Lay Carmel need at local, provincial and international levels?

- How are you going to pass Carmel on to another person?

- If you are part of a Carmelite community, what is your commitment to that community?

- Pray for those Carmelites working in regimes where religious freedom is curtailed.

- Read and reflect on the sections of the *Catechism of the Catholic Church* which deal with 'The Consecrated Life' (§914 onwards).

- What does it mean to be poor in today's society?

- How do you practice a spirit of poverty?

- What is your 'state in life' in terms of relationships with other people?

- What do you think is the benefit of chastity?

- What are the obstacles to people being obedient?

- Does your Carmelite community have a regular collection to share the financial resources and responsibilities of the group? Does the community ever support others in need of material goods?

- Pray for local Carmelite leaders that they may be obedient to the will of God and respectful of those who have chosen them to have authority. Pray for the Prior General of the Carmelite Order, and the Superior General of the Discalced Carmelite Order.

- The public sign of commitment within Carmel is to profess promises (or vows) of chastity according to our state in life, obedience to the Prior General and his delegates, and – for religious – poverty. What exactly does it mean to make these promises? Why is our vocation as Carmelites linked to what the Church calls the *evangelical counsels*?

- When a candidate commits to Carmel, the Order also commits to him/her. What level of care and concern should an individual Carmelite, lay or religious, expect to receive from – and give to – Carmel?

- Should there be an age limit on admission to Carmel as either a lay person or religious?

- Do you consider Carmelite spirituality to be 'something you do' or 'something you are'?

- What form(s) should ongoing formation take? What are the best ways to support and encourage ongoing formation?

Recommended Further Resources

Several publications have been produced in recent years to help prospective members of the Carmelite Family to discern their vocation, and are available from Carmelite book sellers around the globe. Resources on the evangelical counsels from a more general Christian perspective are widely available in print and online.

Carmelite Curia, *Authority at the Service of the Charism: Proceedings of the XV Council of Provinces, Fatima 2003*, (Rome: Edizioni Carmelitane, 2003).

Joseph Chalmers, O.Carm., 'Freedom under authority', in *In Allegiance to Jesus Christ* (Rome: Edizioni Carmelitane, 1999), pp. 24-28.

Teresa Clements, D.M.J., *Carmelite Spirituality*, available online via the Contemporary Authors page of the Carmelite Spirituality section of the website of the British Province of Carmelites: www.carmelite.org

Quinn Connors, O.Carm., 'The Vows: A Call to Transformation', chapter 17 of *Horizons: Carmelite Spiritual Directory Project*, (Melbourne: Carmelite Communications, 1999).

Constitutions of the Discalced Carmelite Secular Order (2003), available online at: www. carmelite.org.uk and www.ocd.pcn.net

Aloysius Deeney, O.C.D., *Welcome to the Secular Order of Discalced Carmelites*, (Washington, D.C.: ICS Publications, 2009).

Avery Dulles, *Authority and Conscience*, available online at: www.vatican2voice.org

Michael D. Griffin, O.C.D., 'The Christian Decision-Making Process', in *Welcome to Carmel: A Handbook for Aspirants to the Discalced Carmelite Secular Order*, Growth in Carmel Series, (Hubertus, Wisconsin: Teresian Charism Press, 2006), pp. 57-68.

Francis Kemsley, O.Carm., *Carmel: Expressing Our Baptismal Call*, available online via the Contemporary Authors page of the Carmelite Spirituality section of the website of the British Province of Carmelites: www.carmelite.org

Ernest Larkin, O.Carm., 'Spiritual Poverty: The Message of John of the Cross', *Carmel in the World*, Volume XLVIII Number 2, 2009, pp. 107-117.

Living the Carmelite Way: Rule for the Third Order of Carmel, (Edizioni Carmelitane, 2003), available online at: www.ocarm.org

Patrick Thomas McMahon, O.Carm., *A Pattern for Life: The Rule of Saint Albert and the Carmelite Laity*, Carmel in the World Paperbacks 14, (Rome: Edizioni Carmelitane, 2007).

Renée Prieur, T.M., 'Lay Carmelites and the New Evangelisation', *Carmel in the World*, Volume XXXVIII Number 1, 2000, pp. 2-21.

Barbara Smethurst, O.C.D.S., 'A Priestly People: A Challenge to Lay People Today', *Mount Carmel: A Review of the Spiritual Life*, Volume 58 Number 2, April-June 2010, pp. 60-66.

Miguel Norbert Ubarri, T.O.C., 'A model for the Carmelite laity of the 21st century', in *In obsequio Jesu Christi: Praying and prophetic community in a changing world*, Proceedings of the 2007 General Chapter of the Carmelite Order, (Rome: Edizioni Carmelitane, 2007), pp. 109-111.

Thomas Zeitvogel, T.O.C., *Challenges Facing the Third Order*, available online via the Contemporary Authors page of the Carmelite Spirituality section of the website of the British Province of Carmelites: www.carmelite.org

Remember that as well as these resources, it is possible to learn a lot about Carmelite spirituality from participation in the Order's retreats and days of reflection, as well as from the distance-learning programmes in Carmelite Studies offered by Carmelite Institutes and study centres around the world, including the Carmelite Institute of Britain & Ireland (www.cibi.ie) and the Carmelite Institute in Washington, D.C.

Notes and reflections on Chapter 20

The Carmelite Family in Britain

The Carmelite Order is one of the ancient religious orders of the Roman Catholic Church. Known officially as the *Brothers (and Sisters) of the Blessed Virgin Mary of Mount Carmel*, the Order developed from a group of hermits in thirteenth-century Israel-Palestine; priests and lay people living a contemplative life modelled on the prophet Elijah and the Virgin Mary. By the year 1214 the Carmelites had received a *Way of Life* from Saint Albert, the Latin Patriarch of Jerusalem.

Carmelites first came to Britain in 1242. The hermits became an order of mendicant friars following a General Chapter held in Aylesford, Kent, in 1247. Nuns, and lay men and women have always played a major part in the life of the Order, and have had formal participation since 1452. Over centuries of development and reform, the Carmelites have continued their distinctive mission of living 'in allegiance to Jesus Christ', by forming praying communities at the service of all God's people. The heart of the Carmelite vocation is contemplation, that is, openness to and friendship with God, pondering God's will in our lives.

Like the spirituality of all the major religious orders (Benedictines, Franciscans, Jesuits, etc.), Carmelite spirituality is a distinct preaching of the one Christian message, the Good News of Jesus Christ. Carmelites blend a life of deep prayer with active service of those around them, and their apostolates take many different forms depending on the time and the place Carmelites find themselves in.

Over the centuries 'Carmel' has produced some of the greatest Christian thinkers, mystics, and philosophers, such as Teresa of Jesus (of Avila), John of the Cross, and Thérèse of Lisieux (three Carmelite 'Doctors of the Church'). In the twentieth century, the Carmelite Family bore witness to the Gospel in the martyrdoms of Titus Brandsma, Edith Stein, and Isidore Bakanja.

England boasted the largest Carmelite Province in the Order until its suppression at the Reformation. The British Province was re-established under the patronage of Our Lady of the Assumption in the twentieth century. There are communities of friars, sisters and lay Carmelites across England, Scotland, and Wales. Similar communities exist in Ireland, and throughout the world. The international Order of Discalced (Teresian) Carmelite friars, nuns, and laity is also present in Britain and Ireland. Members of the Carmelite and Discalced Carmelite Orders work, live, and pray together to make up the wider 'Carmelite Family', which seeks the face of the Living God in parishes, retreat centres, prisons, university and hospital chaplaincies, workplaces, schools, publishing, research, justice and peace work, counselling, and through many other forms of ministry and presence.

Further sources of information
on Carmelite spirituality include:

John Welch, O.Carm.
The Carmelite Way: An Ancient Path for Today's Pilgrim
(Leominster: Gracewing, 1996).

Wilfrid McGreal, O.Carm.
At the Fountain of Elijah: The Carmelite Tradition
(London: Darton, Longman and Todd, 1999).

Website of the British Province of Carmelites
www.carmelite.org

Carmel on the web

a selection of English-language Carmelite websites

The British Province of Carmelites
www.carmelite.org

Lay Carmel in Britain
www.laycarmel.org

Aylesford Priory, Kent
www.thefriars.org.uk

National Shrine of Saint Jude, Faversham
www.stjudeshrine.org.uk

Corpus Christi Carmelite Sisters
www.corpuschristicarmelites.org

Discalced Carmelite Family in England, Scotland & Wales
www.carmelite.org.uk

Irish Province of Carmelites
www.carmelites.ie

Anglo-Irish Province of Discalced Carmelites
www.ocd.ie

Association of Discalced Carmelite Nuns in Great Britain
www.carmelnuns.org.uk

Association of Discalced Carmelite Nuns in Ireland
www.carmelitesisters.ie

Carmelite Forum of Britain and Ireland
www.carmeliteforum.org

Carmelite Institute of Britain and Ireland
www.cibi.ie

International Carmelite Index
www.carmelites.info

The General Curia of the Carmelite Order
www.ocarm.org

CITOC – Carmelite Communications Office
www.carmelites.info/citoc

Carmelite N.G.O. at the United Nations
www.carmelitengo.org

Edizioni Carmelitane
www.carmelites.info/edizioni

Domus Carmelitana, Rome
www.domuscarmelitana.com

American Province of the Most Pure Heart of Mary
www.carmelnet.org

American Province of St. Elias
www.carmelites.com

Australian Province of Carmelites
www.carmelites.org.au

The O.Carm. – O.C.D web portal
www.ocarm-ocd.org

Supplementary information

Excellent resources for ongoing formation
are the distance-learning courses in Carmelite spirituality, history and culture
offered by Carmelite study institutes around the world, including
The Carmelite Institute of Britain & Ireland (CIBI).

CIBI was established in 2005 by the British Province of Carmelites,
the Irish Province of Carmelites, and the Anglo-Irish Province
of Discalced Carmelites.

The purpose of the Institute is to diffuse the charism,
heritage and spirituality of 'Carmel' through part-time distance-learning courses
in Carmelite Studies at introductory and more advanced levels.

The Institute's scholarly but accessible programmes are open to members
of the Carmelite Family and anyone interested in the field of Carmelite Studies.
Through its interdisciplinary courses and activities the Institute offers
an opportunity to learn about Carmelite life in its many forms,
as well as a means to grow intellectually, spiritually and professionally.

CIBI's programmes – ranging from an *Adult Education Diploma*
to postgraduates courses in Carmelite Studies – are accredited by ecclesiastical
and secular institutions of Higher Education, giving professional qualifications
to those students who opt to submit assessments.

Thanks to the founders and sponsors of the Institute,
programmes are made available to students at very reasonable rates,
with a certain number of bursaries awarded to deserving individuals.

Though based in Britain and Ireland, CIBI enjoys close links
with study institutes, libraries and heritage projects around the world,
and welcomes student applications from any country.

For further information and a prospectus, please contact:

The Carmelite Institute of Britain & Ireland
Gort Muire Carmelite Centre, Ballinteer, Dublin 16, Ireland

☎ +353 (0)1 298 7706   Fax +353 (0)1 298 7714
E-mail: admin@cibi.ie
Website: www.cibi.ie

Suppliers of Carmelite resources

The Friars Bookshop The Friars Aylesford Kent ME20 7BX United Kingdom ☎ + 44 (0)1622 715770 E-mail: bookshop@thefriars.org.uk Web: www.thefriars.org.uk	Saint Albert's Press Book Distribution Carmelite Friars P.O. Box 140 ME20 7SJ United Kingdom ☎ + 44 (0)1795 537038 E-mail: saintalbertspress@carmelites.org.uk Web: www.carmelite.org/sap	Edizioni Carmelitane Via Sforza Pallavicini, 10 00193 Roma Italy E-mail: edizioni@ocarm.org Web: www.carmelites.info/edizioni
Carmelite Book Service Discalced Carmelite Priory Boars Hill Oxford OX1 5HB United Kingdom ☎ +44 (0)1865 730183 E-mail: info@carmelitebooks.com Web: www.carmelite.org.uk	Carmelite Gift & Book Store National Shrine of St. Thérèse 8501 Bailey Road Darien, IL. 60561 USA ☎ +1 630 969 0001 E-mail: bookstore@carmelnet.org Web: www.carmelitegifts.com	Carmelite Gift Store National Shrine of Our Lady of Mount Carmel P.O. Box 2163 70 Carmelite Drive Middletown, NY 10940-0879 USA ☎ +1 845 344 2226 E-mail: carmelitegiftstore@yahoo.com Web: www.carmelitegiftstore.com
Mount Carmel Gift Shop Mount Carmel Spiritual Centre 7021 Stanley Avenue – Niagara Falls, Ontario, L2G 7B7 Canada ☎ +1 905 356 0047 E-mail: mtcarmelgiftshop@carmelniagara.com Web: www.carmelniagara.com	Carmelite Communications 75 Wright Street Middle Park Victoria 3206 Australia ☎ +61 (03) 9699 1922 Email: ocarmprov@ie.net.au Web: www.carmelites.org.au	Carmelite Media – Publications 1540 Glenn Street Tucson, AZ 85719 ☎ +1 520 325 1537 ext. 25 Email: publications@carmelnet.org Web: www.carmelnet.org

A selection of other titles available from Saint Albert's Press

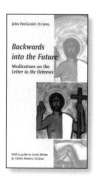

John FitzGerald, O.Carm.
*Backwards into the Future: Meditations
on the Letter to the Hebrews*

Joseph Chalmers, O.Carm.
*The Sound of Silence: Listening to the Word of God
with Elijah the Prophet*

Johan Bergström-Allen, T.O.C. & Wilfrid McGreal,
O.Carm. (eds.)
*The Gospel Sustains Me: The Word of God in the life
and love of Saint Thérèse of Lisieux*

Francis Kemsley, O.Carm.
*The Church of Our Lady of Mount Carmel
and the Shrine of St. Jude, Faversham*

Felip Ribot, O.Carm.
*The Ten Books on the Way of Life and Great Deeds of the
Carmelites*, translated by Richard Copsey, O.Carm.

Richard Copsey, O.Carm.
Carmel in Britain 3: The Hermits from Mount Carmel

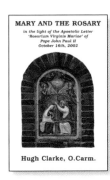

Hugh Clarke, O.Carm.
Mary and the Rosary

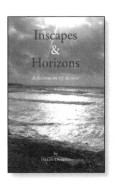

Helen Overell
Inscapes & Horizons: Reflections on life in verse

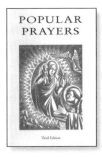

Johan Bergström-Allen, T.O.C. (ed.)
Popular Prayers (Third Edition)

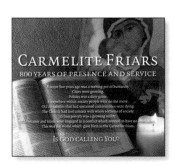

British Province of Carmelites
Carmelite Friars: 800 Years of Presence and Service

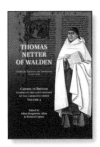

Johan Bergström-Allen, T.O.C., & Richard Copsey,
O.Carm., (eds.),
*Thomas Netter of Walden: Carmelite,
Diplomat and Theologian (c.1372-1430)*

Wilfrid McGreal, O.Carm.
*Friar Beyond the Pale: A biography of Carmelite friar
Fr. Elias Lunch (1897-1967)*

We shall not cease from exploration
And the end of all our exploring
Will be to arrive where we started
And know the place for the first time.

T. S. Eliot
Four Quartets – Little Gidding

LAUS DEO SEMPER ET MARIAE